PHILIP'S

ROAD ATLAS

Britain

G000292809

About Philip's maps

This atlas contains maps at different scales to get you to your destination as easily and as quickly as possible.

Route planning maps show the whole country at a glance, so you can choose the most direct route, whether on motorways or A-roads. Road numbers, junction numbers, motorway services and dual carriageways are all clearly marked.

Road maps at 3 miles to 1 inch (Scottish Highlands and Islands at 4 miles to 1 inch) show the road network in detail and mark hundreds of places of interest. The roads are colour coded according to importance. Scenic routes are highlighted and in country areas lanes over 4 metres wide are coloured yellow.

Approach maps at 1⅓ miles to 1 inch guide you through the suburbs of major cities, and give road names as well as numbers.

Town plans show the streets in the central area and mark one ways, car parks, stations and important buildings.

Philip's road maps were voted the clearest and most detailed in an independent consumer survey with 442 respondents.

Contents

Our Top 10 Tips
to avoid
speeding penalties

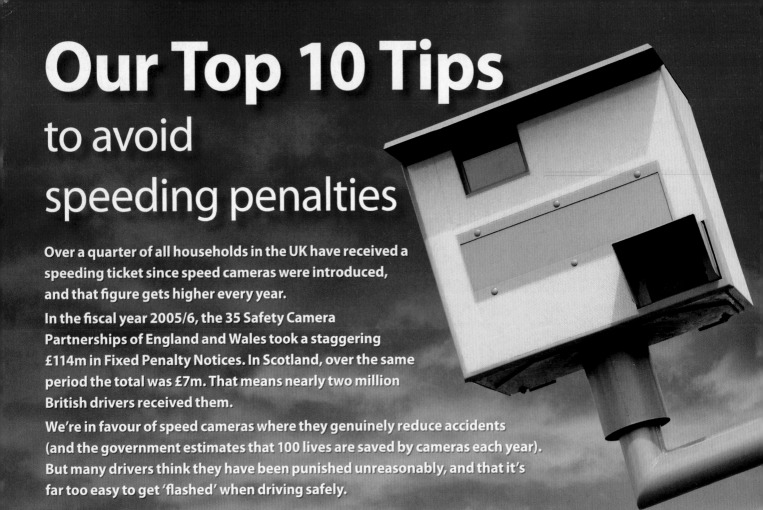

Over a quarter of all households in the UK have received a speeding ticket since speed cameras were introduced, and that figure gets higher every year.

In the fiscal year 2005/6, the 35 Safety Camera Partnerships of England and Wales took a staggering £114m in Fixed Penalty Notices. In Scotland, over the same period the total was £7m. That means nearly two million British drivers received them.

We're in favour of speed cameras where they genuinely reduce accidents (and the government estimates that 100 lives are saved by cameras each year). But many drivers think they have been punished unreasonably, and that it's far too easy to get 'flashed' when driving safely.

We asked Stephen Mesquita, our speed camera expert, to explain how the system works, and to give his Top 10 Tips about what you can and can't do to keep penalty points off your licence.

First, some facts: There are now over 3,300 fixed camera sites in the UK and about 3,400 'located' mobile sites listed on the official websites. So the total's climbing towards 7,000 (far more than the 4,500 some websites quote).

If you are caught speeding, you can agree to pay a fixed £60 fine and get 3 points on your licence. The points normally stay on your licence for 4 years (11 if the conviction was drink- or drug-related, or you failed to provide a specimen for analysis). In some cases, breaking a temporary speed limit where there are roadworks will only trigger the fine, not the endorsement. If you get 12 points on your licence within a three year period – or just 6 in your first two years as a driver – you will be banned from driving.

If you go over the speed limit by too much, you'll get an automatic summons – then, at the discretion of the court, the fines will be higher and the points could go up to 6 or even a ban. You can challenge the penalty in court. But if you lose, it's likely to prove expensive.

1 Beware camera-infested areas

Yes, I know. It's not a very practical suggestion but there is a serious point behind it. The Safety Camera Partnerships stress that there are strict criteria for the siting of cameras – but nonetheless it seems that some areas have a concentration of cameras even if they aren't the busiest or most dangerous to drive in.

England and Wales

So, if the number of fixed cameras is anything to go by, here are the Top 10 partnership areas to avoid in England and Wales (in order of fixed camera numbers):

1	London	6	Mid and South Wales
2	Staffordshire	7	West Yorkshire
3	Lancashire	8	Derbyshire
4	West Midlands	9	Hertfordshire
5	Thames Valley	10	Devon and Cornwall

Some of those you'd expect to be in the list. Others are a surprise. There are some quite busy areas, like Hampshire and Surrey, that have less than a third of the fixed cameras of any of those in our list.

But more to the point, which partnership areas raised the most revenue – and were they the ones with the most fixed cameras? Here are the top 10 income generators from Fixed Penalty Notices in 2005-6 Financial Year in England and Wales:

1	London	6	Thames Valley
2	Mid and South Wales	7	Essex
3	West Yorkshire	8	Northumberland
4	Avon and Somerset	9	Greater Manchester
5	Lancashire	10	Hertfordshire

You'd expect London to be top. But productivity in Northumbria, whose website lists only around 120 fixed and mobile sites, is remarkable.

We haven't produced a similar table for 'located' mobile sites, because it is impossible to find a consistent measure. Some safety camera partnerships only publicise the sites they are likely to monitor that week. Others give no mobile site information at all. Some define a mobile site with pinpoint accuracy, while others, like Fife in Scotland, simply highlight a stretch of road that could be 10 miles long. And how on earth did the inhabitants of Carmarthenshire earn a quarter of all the mobile locations in Wales? Confused by all this? So are we.

Scotland

Don't think you can escape in Scotland. There are fewer fixed cameras in the whole of Scotland than in any of the Top 5 English partnership areas, but not surprisingly, Strathclyde and Lothian and Borders are the most camera-infested regions, with few or no fixed cameras in Highland, Fife or Dumfries and Galloway. Mobile camera sites are more evenly spread through the regions.

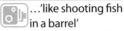 ...'like shooting fish in a barrel'

Ireland

In the North, there are only 4 fixed cameras and 71 mobile sites. In the Republic, there are just 3 cameras working in 20 boxes at any one time. But beware: a government report has recommended privatising speed cameras and allowing 600 of them to be operated by private operators – and not just at accident black spots. Not surprisingly, this has caused an outcry among the motoring organizations ('like shooting fish in a barrel' said one) – so watch this space.

2 Beware 30 and 40mph limits

What are the speed limits for the majority of camera locations?

If your vision of the most common speeding ticket is the event we all see by the side of the motorway (a car stopped by the police car doing well over 70) then you're in for a surprise. The majority of speeding cameras – over 70% of both fixed and 'located' mobile cameras – are in zones where the limit is 30 to 40mph.

Of course, mobile cameras can be anywhere. But our tip No 2 is – be especially careful of 30 and 40 mile an hour limits. Other than in London, the least guarded speed limit is 50mph.

3 Stick to the B-roads and motorways

Fact: over 60% of the fixed camera sites and over 50% of the 'located' mobile sites are on A-roads. Most of the rest are on unclassified roads – generally in towns and villages. B-roads and motorways are relatively unsurveyed – although the motorways may have a lot of 'unlocated' sites.

4 Drive like a woman (it's safer)

More than 80% of all speeding penalties are given to men.

There are two types of speeder – the deliberate speeder and the accidental speeder.

If you are interested in the camera locations in this atlas so that you can break the speed limit between them, you're a deliberate speeder, and almost certainly a man. Read on. Our Top 10 Tips might make you more conscious of the chances – and consequences – of being caught.

Who are the accidental speeders? Almost everyone at some time. We've all done it. You're in an area that you're not familiar with. It's dark. You're quite alert but you're caught up in the rush hour and the traffic is moving fast. You've gone from a 40 zone to a 30 but you haven't seen the sign. Flash!

The truth is – most of us speed both deliberately and accidentally at some stage in our driving careers. The message is – cameras are widespread and they're not very forgiving.

So if you don't want the fine or the endorsement, you need to concentrate as much on your speed as you concentrate on not having an accident.

If you are a conscientious driver who feels the need to develop your skills of concentration in particular and defensive driving in general, then I'd recommend The Institute of Advanced Motorists (IAM) tel: 020 8996 9600.

5 Know your speed limit rules

Street lights = 30mph, unless it says otherwise. It's a horrible rule. Lots of people who should know about it don't. Lots of people who do know about it would like to see it changed.

Speed limits (mph)	Built-up area	Single carriageway	Dual carriageway	Motorway
Cars and motorcycles	30	60	70	70
Cars towing caravans and trailers	30	50	60	60
Buses and Coaches	30	50	60	60
Goods vehicles under 7.5 tonnes	30	50	60	70 (60 if articulated or towing)

Add to that the apparently arbitrary definition of 30mph and 40mph limits, and the frequency with which they change, and you have a recipe for confusion. Again, lots of inconsistencies to baffle the motorist.

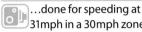 ...done for speeding at 31mph in a 30mph zone

The round white sign with a black diagonal flash through it means 60mph max, except on dual carriageways and motorways.

How much leeway do you have? Is it zero tolerance? Is it the ACPO guidelines of +10%+2mph (that's the Association of Chief Police Officers, by the way)? Or is it somewhere in between? Well, the law is this – you can be done for speeding at 31mph in a 30mph zone. As to the complicated equation, the police stress that guidelines are just that and they do not alter the law. But they probably would admit that they would be inundated if they stopped every motorist who is driving a couple of mph over the limit.

You are probably getting a bit of help from your speedometer. It's the clever idea of the car makers to set our speedometers 2–3mph faster than we are actually going. Now that so many of us have GPS in the car, this is getting more widely known. Now you know, it might be wiser to use the extra mph as air between you and a ticket.

6 Learn to tell your Gatso from your Digital Specs

Here's a concise guide to cameras. There are loads of different species, so we're only going to describe the main families.

Gatso – the most common ones. Generally in yellow boxes, they flash you from the back and store your number plate on film. As the film only has 400 exposures, don't assume, if you see the flash in your rear-view mirror, that you've been done. In fact it's reckoned that you have a three in four chance that the one you've just passed is not working.

Truvelo – pink-eyes. The pink eye gives you an infrared flash from the front, after sensors in the road have registered your speed. Unlike the GATSO, which can't identify the driver (worth remembering if you want to argue) the TRUVELO gets a mug-shot.

Digital Specs – pairs of video cameras set some distance apart to create a no-speeding zone between them. If your average speed over the distance exceeds the limit, you are snapped with an infrared flash. So they are much more testing for the driver. It's one thing slowing down when you see a camera, it's another thing maintaining an average speed over a distance of several miles. Still relatively rare.

DS2s – strips in the road detect your speed and pass the information to an innocent-looking post at the side of the road. Look out for the detector van nearby, because that's what does the business.

Red light cameras – the UK total is creeping up towards 1,000. If you drive through a traffic light when it's at red, sensors in the road tell the camera to flash you.

All of the above can be detected using GPS devices for fixed cameras but not these -

Lasers – most mobile cameras are Lasers. You normally see a tripod in a van with the backdoors open and facing you; or on a motorway bridge or handheld by the side of the road. They work – although rumour has it not in very bad weather – and they can't be detected by any of the GPS devices. If you happen to see a local villager touting a laser gun, you may get a letter asking you to drive more carefully but not a fine or penalty points.

7 Know where the cameras are

If you are serious about not getting caught speeding, there are some obvious precautions you can take before setting out.

- Check in this atlas whether there are fixed cameras on the route you are planning to take. They are marked on the map by the 40 symbol, with the figures inside the red circle indicating the speed limit in mph (see the key to map symbols for further details).
- Check in the listings whether there are 'located' mobile sites on your route.
- Use a camera detector, such as those marketed by Road Angel, Road Pilot or Cyclops. These are perfectly legal, if expensive; they just tell you where the cameras are. Devices that detect and jam police laser detectors are about to be banned.
- Use the websites for up-to-date information, including guidelines (but only guidelines) about where the police are locating their mobile vans each week. Each Safety Camera Partnership has a website (search for the county name followed by Safety Camera Partnership). Don't use the Department for Transport listings, which were 18 months out of date at the time we went to press.

8 If you do get a ticket, check it carefully

Even if there is film in the camera, you may not get a ticket.

...tractor caught speeding at 85mph in Wales

A close study of the accounts of each of the Safety Camera Partnerships of England and Wales reveals varying success in actually sending out the tickets and collecting the money. Some areas are collecting 100% of their fines. Others, particularly in the major urban areas, collect only just over 50%. The official reason is that tickets are not issued to owners of unregistered cars, foreign-registered cars and emergency vehicles caught on camera(!). As an example, one coastal area with a lot of ferry traffic collected at 77% in 2004/5.

There's always a chance you may not get your ticket – but if you do, check it carefully. Make sure it is your car, and that you were driving at the time and place recorded. The cameras aren't perfect, and mistakes have been made. My favourite is the tractor caught speeding at 85mph in Wales. It turned out there was a 'confusion about the number plate' – the tractor had never been to Wales and could only do a max of 26mph.

9 Don't challenge a penalty without good reason

If you are caught speeding, you've got two choices. Pay the £60 and accept the 3 points. It's humiliating and irritating but then that's the idea. Or contest it.

From the 2004/05 Partnership accounts, about 10% of people challenge and don't pay the fixed penalty fines. Rumour is that the percentage is rising. You may get off, but if you contest a penalty and lose, you could pay a stiffer penalty.

If you do decide to fight, do as much research and get as much information about the circumstances as you can; and get as much case-study information as you can about the camera involved. The more witnesses and information you have, the more a good lawyer can build a case on your behalf.

Again, www.speed-trap.co.uk has some interesting case studies.

But don't expect success with a fabricated defence. The safety camera partnerships know the scams to look out for and lies can turn a simple speeding fine into something much more serious. In fact, you can be prosecuted for trying to pervert the course of justice. A criminal record can cost you much more than the £60 fixed penalty.

10 Avoid the points by going back to school

In a few areas, the police are giving drivers who are caught speeding another option. They can go on a Speed Awareness Scheme. These normally last half a day, you have to pay for them (probably more than £60) but you don't get the penalty points. So, if you like the sound of this as an option, it's worth considering.

Your alternative is to ask for your case to go forward for prosecution (see Top Tip No. 9)

And finally...

If you've got this far, you're obviously a bit of an aficionado on the subject of speeding, so I'm going to allow myself just one bit of preaching.

The 'Speed Kills' slogan has become much used. But here are three pieces of information that certainly make me think twice about letting the needle stray over the prescribed limit:

1 Every year we kill over 3,000 of our fellow-citizens on our roads and we seriously injure 35,000. If you happen to live in a reasonable-sized town, just work that out as a percentage of the population of where you live. Road deaths have not fallen substantially since the proliferation of speed cameras – but the evidence seems to be reasonably conclusive that speed cameras reduce the number of deaths and serious injuries at the sites themselves.

2 The argument rages about whether speed is the cause of accidents or not. But that's all rather academic (isn't it?). A car that's not moving is not likely to injure someone. If the accident happens when the car is in motion, speed is at least part of the cause.

But here's the point. This is the 'if I hit a pedestrian, will I kill them?' chart ➤

So if you hit a pedestrian in a 30mph area and you're doing just 35mph (just on the 10%+2mph leeway) you're more than twice as likely to kill them. Not a nice thought. Maybe I should have called that the 'if I am hit by a car while on foot, will I be killed by it?' chart.

3 Every death costs us, as taxpayers, £1.5m and every serious injury £100,000. And that's doesn't take into account the human cost.

So, at the end of all this, my 11th Top 10 Tip is

11 Don't press the pedal to the metal

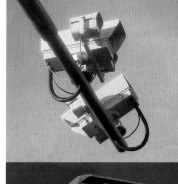

Top Gantry-mounted SPECS cameras in Cornwall
Above Truvelo camera

What's new with road pricing?
Though 1.8m drivers signed a petition against road pricing in spring 2007, the government continues to push forward with local schemes and a national scheme is expected to be in place by 2015.

Under the latest proposals, Britain will be divided into zones, and drivers will be charged at a fixed rate for every mile covered within each zone, regardless of whether they are on a main road, a country lane or a residential street.

Zones with the highest congestion will have the highest per mile prices – rates as high as £1.00 per mile have been suggested.

The Government says it may reduce fuel duty and road tax to compensate for road pricing, and says that road pricing will not add to the overall tax on drivers in the year it is introduced. But it has not ruled out increases in road taxes in the years before road pricing begins.

There are currently 33 million vehicles in Britain,

Websites for further information
Official
Safety Camera Partnerships (use Google and put in Safety Camera Partnership plus the area you want)
- www.safetycamera.org.uk • www.dvla.gov.uk
- www.thinkroadsafety.gov.uk • www.dft.gov.uk
- www.road-safe.org

Safety pressure groups
- www.rospa.com • www.transport2000.com
- www.roadpeace.org • www.brake.org.uk

Anti-camera pressure groups and websites
- www.speed-trap.co.uk • ukgatsos.com
- www.ukspeedcameras.co.uk
- www.abd.org.uk • www.ukspeedtraps.co.uk
- www.speedcam.co.uk
- www.speedcamerasuk.com

Below The probability that a pedestrian will be killed when struck by a vehicle travelling between 20mph and 40mph

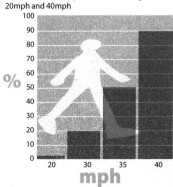

Mobile speed camera sites

The vast majority of speed cameras used on Britain's roads are operated by safety camera partnerships. This table lists the sites where each safety camera partnership may enforce speed limits through the use of mobile cameras or detectors. These are usually set up on the roadside or a bridge spanning the road and operated by a police or civilian enforcement officer. The speed limit at each site (if available) is shown in red type, followed by the approximate location in black type.

England

Avon and Somerset

Bath and North East Somerset, Bristol, North Somerset, Somerset, South Gloucestershire

M32
- 60 Bristol Stadium

A4
- 30 Bath, Newbridge Rd
- 30 Bristol, Anchor Rd
- 30 Bristol, Totterdown Bridge
- 50 Nr Keynsham, Keynsham Bypass jct A4175 Durley Hill
- 50 Portway
- 30 Portway, nr A4176 Bridge Valley Rd

A4/B4054
- 30 Bristol, Avonmouth Rd

A30
- 50 Cricket St Thomas
- 30 East Chinnock
- 40 Roundham
- 40 Yeovil, Hospital Rdbt
- 30 Yeovil, Sherborne Rd

A37
- 30 Bristol, Wells Rd (nr jct Airport Rd)
- 30 Bristol, Wells Rd (nr St Johns La)
- 60 Chilthorne Domer (east)
- 50 Emborough
- 30 Gurney Slade (north)
- 60 Lydford to Bristol
- 40 Lydford to Yeovil
- 60 Fosse Way, north of Podimore Rdbt
- 30 Shepton Mallet

A38
- 40 Aztec West, nr Bradley Stoke Way
- 30 Bathpool
- 40 Bedminster Down, Bridgwater Rd
- 40 Bristol, Bedminster Down Rd nr Bishopsworth Rd
- 30 Bristol, Bedminster Down Rd/West St
- 30 Bristol, Cheltenham Rd/Gloucester Rd, nr Cranbrook Rd
- 30 Bristol, Gloucester Rd nr B4052 Ashley Down Rd
- 30 Bristol, Stokes Croft nr Bond St
- 40 Churchill – Langford
- 40 Cross
- 30 East Reach/Toneway
- 40 Filton, Gloucester Rd (north) nr B4057 Gypsy Patch Lane
- 50 Heatherton Grange
- 40,30 North Petherton
- 40 Patchway, Gloucester Rd nr Highwood Rd
- 50 Pawlett (south)
- 50 Redhill
- 30 Rooks Bridge (east)
- 30 Taunton – Bridgwater
- 30 Taunton, Wellington Rd (inbound)
- 30 Taunton, Wellington Rd (outbound)
- 30 West Huntspill (north)

A39
- 30 Ashcott
- 30 Bilbrook
- 30 Bridgwater, Bath Rd
- 30 Bridgwater, North Broadway nr A38 Taunton Rd
- 30 Bridgwater, North Broadway/Broadway/Monmouth St
- 30 Chewton Mendip
- 40 Coxley nr Wells
- 50 Green Ore (south)
- 40 Horsey, Bath Rd
- 30 Quantock Rd
- 30 Walton

A46
- 60 Bath to Wickwar Rd
- 40 Dunkirk

A303
- 50 Buckland St Mary
- 50 Downhead nr Ilchester

A303/A3088
- 70 Cartgate Rdbt

A303/A358
- 60 Southfields Rdbt

A357
- 30 Templecombe

A358
- 60 Ashill
- 30 Donyatt
- 30 Henlade, nr M5 jct 25
- 40 Hornsbury Mill
- 40 Pen Elm (south)
- 30 Staplegrove Rd
- 30 Taunton Deane, Priorswood Rd
- 30 Taunton, Greenway Rd

A359
- 30 Mudford (north)

A361
- 30 Doulting
- 40 Durston
- 60 Frome Bypass
- 30 Othery
- 30 Pilton
- 30 West Pennard

A362
- 40 Terry Hill

A367
- 30 Bath, Green Park Rd
- 30 Bath, Bear Flat
- 30 Radstock, Wells Rd

A369
- 40 Abbots Leigh
- 60 Easton-in-Gordano, Martcombe Rd nr M5 jct 19

A370
- 30 Cleeve Village
- 30 Congresbury, Station Rd, Bristol Rd
- 30 Flax Bourton nr B3130
- 40 Long Ashton Bypass, Bristol End
- 50 West Wick, Somerset Avenue, west of M5 jct 21
- 30 Weston-super-Mare, Beach Rd
- 50 Weston-super-Mare, Herluin Way nr Winterstoke Rd
- 50 Weston-super-Mare, Somerset Avenue (central reservation)
- 50 Weston-super-Mare, Somerset Avenue, jct Moor Lane
- 30 Weston-super-Mare, Winterstoke Rd

A371
- 30 Draycott
- 40 Priestleigh (south)
- 30 Winscombe, Sidcot Lane nr jct A38,

A372
- 30 Aller

A378
- 30 Curry Rivel
- 40 Wrantage

A403
- 40 Avonmouth Docks

A420
- 30 Bristol, Lawrence Hill
- 30 Kingswood, Two Mile Hill Rd, Regent St
- 30 Old Market, nr Temple Way/Bond St
- 30 Redfield, Church Rd
- 30 St George, Clouds Hill Rd/Bell Hill Rd
- 30 Warmley, High St London Rd nr A4175 Bath Rd
- 60 Wick, Tog Hill

A432
- 30 Bristol, Fishponds Rd nr B4048 Lodge Causeway
- 30 Bristol, Fishponds Rd nr B4469 Royate Hill
- 30 Bristol, Fishponds Rd with B4469 Muller Rd
- 30 Bristol, Stapleton Rd nr jct A4320 Easton Way
- 40 Hambrook, Badminton Rd nr A4174 Avon Ring Rd
- 40 Kendleshire
- 30 Yate, Station Rd/B4059 Stover Rd

A3027
- 30 North St/East St

A3029
- 40 Bristol, Avon Bridge

A3039
- 30 Devonshire Rd

A3088
- 30 Yeovil, Lysander Rd

A3259
- 30 Monkton Heathfield

A4018
- 30 Bristol, Black Boy Hill/Whiteladies Rd
- 30 Bristol, Cribbs Causeway jct 17 M5
- 30 Bristol, Westbury Rd nr B4054 North View
- 30 Bristol, Whiteladies Rd into Queens Rd
- 30 Westbury on Trym, Falcondale Rd

A4044
- 30 Bristol, Temple Way/Redcliffe Way

A4081
- 40 Catbrain

A4162
- 30 Bristol, Sylvan Way/Dingle Rd/Canford Lane

A4174
- 50 Avon Ring Rd nr jct 1 M32
- 30 Bristol, Hartcliffe Way
- 40 Bristol, Hengrove Way/Airport Rd nr Creswicke Rd
- 50 Bromley Heath
- 50 Filton, Filton Rd/Avon Ring Rd nr Coldharbour Lane
- 40 Filton, Station Rd, nr Great Stoke Way

A4320
- 30 Bristol, at A4 Bath Rd nr Sandy Park Rd

B3124
- 30 Clevedon, Walton Rd

B3130
- 30 Nailsea, Stockway (north)/Chapel Avenue
- 30,40 Wraxall

B3133
- 30 Clevedon, Central Way

B3139
- 30,40 Mark Causeway
- 30 Chilcompton

B3140
- 30 Berrow, Coast Rd

B3141
- 30 East Huntspill

B3151
- 30 Compton Dundon
- 30 Ilchester
- 30 St, Somerton Rd

B3153
- 30 Keinton Mandeville (east Somerton)

B3170
- 30 Shoreditch Rd

B3440
- 30 Weston-super-Mare, Locking Rd/Regent St/Alexandra Parade

B4051
- 30 Bristol, Park Row/Perry Rd

B4054
- 30 Sea Mills, Shirehampton Rd

B4056
- 30 Bristol, Northumbria Drive/Linden Rd/Westbury Park
- 30 Bristol, Southmead Rd nr Pen Park Rd
- 30 Bristol, Southmead Rd nr Wellington Hill

B4057
- 30 Bristol, Crow Lane nr A4018 Passage Rd
- 30 Gypsy Patch Lane nr Hatchet Rd
- 50 Winterbourne Rd nr B4427 Gloucester Rd

B4058
- 30 Bristol, Frenchay Park Rd
- 30 Winterbourne, Winterbourne Hill/High St

B4059
- 30 Yate, Goose Green Way

B4060
- 30 Yate, Station Rd/Bowling Hill/Rounceval St

B4061
- 30 Thornbury, Bristol Rd

B4465
- 30 Mangotsfield, Broad St
- 30 Staple Hill, Staple Hill Rd/High St nr Forest Rd

Unclassified
- 30 Bristol, Bishopsworth, Whitchurch/Hareclive Rd
- 30 Bristol, Bishport Avenue
- 30 Knowle Bristol, Broadwalk
- 30 Bristol, Hengrove, Hawkfield Rd nr A4174 Hartcliffe Way
- 30 Bristol, Kingsway
- 30 Bristol, Long Cross, Lawrence Weston
- 30 Bristol, Stoke Hill/Stoke Rd nr Saville Rd, Clifton
- 30 Bristol, Sturminster Rd
- 30 Bristol, Whitchurch Lane nr Dundry Rd
- 30 Little Stoke, Little Stoke Lane
- 30 Taunton, Cheddon Rd
- 30 Taunton, Chestnut Drive
- 30 Taunton, Lisieux Way
- 30 Taunton, Trull Rd
- 50 Watergore, Harp Rd
- 30 Yeovil, Combe St

Bedfordshire and Luton

A5
- 60 Battlesden
- 50 Dunstable
- 40 Hockcliffe
- 60 Kensworth

A6
- 30 Clapham, High St
- 60 Gravenhurst, Barton Rd
- 30 Kempston, Ampthill Rd
- 30 Luton, New Bedford Rd
- 60 Pulloxhill, Barton Rd
- 60 Silsoe

A421
- 50 Brogborough
- 60 Link Rd
- 60 Wootton, south of Fields Rd

A428
- 30 Bedford, Bromham Rd
- 30 Bedford, Goldington Rd

A505
- 30 Dunstable, Luton Rd
- 60 Leighton to Linslade Bypass
- 30 Luton, Dunstable Rd
- 30 Luton, Park Viaduct

A507
- 30 Ridgemont (East)
- 30 Ridgemont (West)
- 60 Shefford, nr New Rd

A603
- 30 Bedford, Cardington Rd
- 30 Bedford, Lovell Rd
- 40 Willington

A1081
- 30,40,70 Luton, Capability Green, Airport Way
- 30,60 Luton, Gipsy Lane, Airport Way

A4146
- 40 Leighton Buzzard, Billington Rd

A5120
- 40 Houghton Regis, Bedford Rd
- 40 Toddington, nr Jct 12 M1

A5134
- 30 Kempston, High St

B530
- 60 Houghton Conquest

B1040
- 30 Biggleswade, Potton Rd

Unclassified
- 30 Bedford, Cardington Rd
- 30 Bedford, Park Avenue
- 30 Bedford, Roff Avenue
- 30 Bedford, Wentworth Drive
- 30 Biggleswade, Potton Rd
- 30 Bromham, Stagsden Rd
- 30 Bromham, Village Rd
- 30 Clapham, Highbury Grange
- 30 Cranfield, High St
- 30 Eaton Bray, Bower Lane
- 30 Flitwick, Ampthill Rd
- 30 Flitwick, Dunstable Rd
- 30 Harlington, Goswell End Rd
- 30 Heath and Reach, Woburn Rd
- 30 Houghton Regis, Parkside Drive
- 30 Kempston, Bedford Rd
- 30 Kempston, High Street
- 30 Leighton Buzzard, Heath Rd
- 30 Luton, Crawley Green Rd
- 30 Luton, Grange Avenue
- 30 Luton, Leagrave High St
- 30 Luton, Marsh Rd
- 30 Luton, New Bedford Rd
- 30 Luton, Park Viaduct
- 30 Luton, Waller Avenue
- 30 Luton, Whitehorse Vale
- 30 Slip End, Markyate Rd
- 30 Upper Caldecote, Hitchin Rd

Berkshire

see Thames Valley

Buckinghamshire

see Thames Valley

Cambridgeshire

A10
- Littleport

A14
- East/Westbound

A15
- New Fletton, London Rd

A141
- Clews Corner
- Warboys
- Wimblington/Doddington Bypass

A142
- Soham Bypass
- Witchford Bypass

A505
- Whittlesford

A605
- Elton, Bullock Rd
- Kings Dyke

A1073
- Eye Green, Peterborough Rd

A1123
- Bluntisham, Needingworth Bypass
- St Ives, Houghton Hill
- Wiburton Village

A1134
- Cambridge

A1303
- Cambridge

A1307
- Bartlow crossroads
- Hills Rd
- Linton Bypass

Cheshire

A50
- 30 Grappenhall, Knutsford Rd
- 30 Knutsford, Manchester/Toft Rd
- 30 Warrington, Long Lane

A54
- 60&70 Ashton, Kelsall Rd

A56
- 40 Lymm, Camsley Lane

A57
- 40 Paddington, New Manchester Rd

A523
- 30 Poynton, London Rd

A532
- 30 Crewe, West St

A533
- 40 Middlewich, Booth Lane

A537
- 50 Macclesfield, Buxton Rd nr Wildboarclough

A5019
- 30 Crewe, Mill St

A5032
- 30 Whitby, Chester Rd

A5034
- 60 Mere, Mereside Rd

A5104
- 30 Chester, Hough Green

B5071
- 30 Crewe, Gresty Rd

B5078
- 30 Alsager, Sandbach Rd North

B5082
- 30 Northwich, Middlewich Rd

B5132
- 30 Ellesmere Port, Overpool Rd

B5153
- 30 Mill Lane/Hollow Lane (speed indicator sign)

B5463
- 30 Little Sutton, Station Rd

B5470
- 30 Macclesfield, Rainow Rd

Unclassified
- 30 Burtonwood, Lumber Lane
- 30 Ellesmere Port, Overpool Rd
- 30 Fearnhead, Harpers Rd
- 30 Hough Green, Prescot Rd
- 30 Howley, Battersby Lane
- 40 Runcorn, Astmoor Rd
- 30 Runcorn, Boston Avenue
- 30 Runcorn, Clifton Rd
- 30 Runcorn, Halton Rd
- 30 Runcorn, Heath Rd
- 30 Runcorn, Northwich Rd
- 30 Runcorn, Warrington Rd
- 30 Vale Royal, Woodford Lane (St John's Drive)
- 30 Whitecross, Lovely Lane
- 30 Widnes, Birchfield Rd
- 30 Widnes, Hough Green Rd
- 30 Wilmslow, Hough Lane
- 40 Winsford, Bradford Rd

Cleveland

Darlington, Hartlepool, Middlesbrough, Redcar and Cleveland

A171
- 50 Redcar, Charltons

A172
- 40 Middlesbrough, Morton Rd from crossroads to St Lukes
- 30 Middlesbrough, Morton Rd from Longlands to St Lukes
- 40 Middlesbrough, Stokesley – from Guisborough Rd jct to Captain Cooks Crescent

A177
- 50,60 Stockton, Durham Rd

A178
- 30 Seaton Carew, The Front

A179
- 30,40,50 Hartlepool, Easington Rd/Powlett Rd

A689
- 50 to 40 Hartlepool, from Sappers Corner

B1380
- 40 Middlesbrough, Ladgate Lane
- 30 Redcar, Eston

Unclassified
- 30 Hartlepool, Catcote Rd
- 40,30 Hartlepool, Coronation Drive
- 30 Hartlepool, Elwick Rd
- 30 Hartlepool, King Oswy Drive
- 30 Hartlepool, Owton Manor Lane and Wynyard Rd
- 30 Hartlepool, Oxford Rd
- 30 Hartlepool, Raby Rd
- 30 Hartlepool, Seaton Lane
- 30 Hartlepool, Station Lane
- 30 Hartlepool, Throston Grange Lane
- 30 Hartlepool, Winterbottom Avenue
- 30 Middlesbrough, Acklam Rd
- 40 Middlesbrough, Acklam Rd from Blue Bell to the Crematorium
- 30 Middlesbrough, Mandale Rd
- 30 Middlesbrough, Ormesby, Normanby Rd
- 30 Middlesbrough, Ormesby Rd
- 30 Middlesbrough, Trimdon Avenue
- 30 Redcar, Bankfields Rd
- 30 Redcar, Carlin How
- 30 Redcar, Church Lane
- 30 Redcar, Dormanstow, Broadway
- 30 Redcar, Flatts Lane
- 30 Redcar, Greenstones Rd
- 30,40 Redcar, Kirkleatham Lane
- 30 Redcar, Marske High St
- 30 Redcar, Normanby Rd
- 30 Redcar, Ormesby Bank
- 30 Redcar, Redcar Lane
- 30 Redcar, Redcar Rd
- 30 Redcar, Stanghow Rd
- 30 Redcar, West Dyke Rd
- 30 Stockton, Thornaby, Acklam Rd
- 40 Stockton, Bishopton Avenue
- 30 Stockton, Bishopton Rd West
- 30 Stockton, Thornaby, Cunningham Drive
- 30 Stockton, Darlington Lane
- 30 Stockton, Harrogate Lane
- 30 Stockton, Junction Rd
- 30 Stockton, Thames Rd
- 30 Stockton, Thornaby Rd
- 30 Stockton, Whitehouse Rd
- 30 Stockton, Eaglescliffe, Yarm Rd

Cumbria

M6
- 70 Brunthwaite
- 70 Capplerigg
- 70 Cowperthwaite
- 70 Tebay

A6
- 60 Garnett Bridge/Hollowgate
- 30 Kendal, Milnthorpe Rd
- 30 Kendal, Shap Rd
- 30 London Rd
- 30 Penrith, Scotland Rd
- 60 Thiefside

A7
- 60 Westlinton Crossroads

A65
- 30 Kendal, Burton Rd
- 40 Kirby Lonsdale, Devils Bridge
- 60 Kirkby Lonsdale, Hollin Hall to Hornsbarrow

A66
- 60 Brigham/Broughton to Chapel Brow
- 60 Crackenthorpe
- 60 Dubwath/Bass Lake
- 60 Sandford Rd Ends
- 60 Troutbeck/Mungrisdale
- 60 Warcop, Brough Hill

A69
- 60 Aglionby
- 60 Scarrow Hill

A74
- 70 Kendal, Floriston

A590
- 60 Bouth Rd Ends
- 60 Haverthwaite/Backbarrow
- 70 Heaves/Levens/Gilpin
- 60 Newlands

A592
- 30,40 Rayrigg Rd

A595
- 60 Broughton, Wreaks End
- 30 Carlisle, Wigton Rd
- 60 Red Dial, Greenhill Hotel
- 60 West Woodside/Curthwaite Jct
- 40 Whitehaven, Loop Rd

A596
- 60 Micklethwaite

A683
- 60 Middleton to Cautley

A685
- 30 Kendal, Appleby Rd

A686
- 60 Edenhall to Meathaw Hill

A5087
- 30 Ulverston

B5277
- 30 Grange, Lindale Rd

B5299
- 40 Carlisle, Dalston Rd

Unclassified
- 30 Carlisle, Durdar Rd/Blackwell Rd
- 30 Barrow in Furness, Abbey Rd
- 30 Barrow in Furness, Michelson Rd

Derbyshire

A6
- 30 Allestree
- Alvaston
- Alvaston to Raynesway
- Ashford in the Water
- 30 Bakewell
- 30 Belper
- Belper to Ambergate
- Buxton to Dove Holes
- Cromford
- Darley Dale
- 30 Derby, London Rd
- Dove Holes
- Dove Holes to Chapel
- Duffield
- Furness Vale to Newtown
- Homesford Cottage to Cromford
- Matlock
- Matlock Bath
- Milford to Belper
- Northwood
- Rowsley to Bakewell
- Shardlow to Derby
- 50 Taddington to Buxton

A52
- 30 Derby, Ashbourne Rd
- East of Brailsford
- 40 Mackworth
- Shirley Hollow

A57
- Snake Rd

A511
- Swadlincote, Ashby Rd East

A514
- Hartshorne
- 30 Swadlincote
- 40 Swadlincote to Hartshorne
- 30 Ticknall

A515
- Alsop-en-le-Dale
- Sudbury

A516
- Derby, Uttoxeter New Rd
- Derby, Uttoxeter Rd

A601
- 30 Derby, Abbey St

A608
- 30 Heanor, Heanor Rd
- 30 Smalley

A609
- 30 Ilkeston, Nottingham Rd
- 30 Kilburn to Horsley Woodhouse
- Stanley Common

A610
- 40 Codnor Gate

A615
- Tansley to Wessington

A616
- 30 Clowne
- 30 Creswell

A617
- 40 Bramley Vale
- 40 Glapwell to Pleasley

A619
- Eastmoor

A623
- Peak to Barmoor Clough
- Peak Forest
- 30 Stoney Middleton

A624
- 50 Chunal to Little Hayfield
- Glossop
- Hayfield to Chinley

A628
- Tintwistle to Boundary

A632
- 30 Bolsover
- Hady to Calow
- 30 Matlock

A5250
- 30 Derby, Burton Rd
- 30 Littleover, Burton Rd

A6005
- 30 Draycott to Breaston
- Long Eaton, Derby Rd
- Spondon, Derby Rd
- Spondon, Nottingham Rd

A6007
- 30 Codnor to Heanor

A6096
- 30 Kirk Hallam, Ladywood Rd

A6175
- 30 Holmewood
- 30 North Wingfield

B600
- Somercotes

B5010
- Sandiacre, Derby Rd

B5353
- 30 Newhall, Park Rd

B6019
- South Normanton

B6051
- 30 Chesterfield, Newbold Rd
- 30 Newbold, Newbold Rd

B6052
- 30 Whittington

B6057
- Chesterfield, Sheffield Rd

B6062
- 30 Chinley

B6179
- Denby
- 30 Little Eaton
- 40 Lower Kilburn
- 50 Lower Kilburn to Little Eaton
- 30 Ripley to Marehay

B6540
- 30 Long Eaton, Tamworth Rd

Unclassified
- Bolsover, Shuttlewood Rd
- 30 Charlesworth, Long Lane
- 30 Chesterfield, Boythorpe Rd
- 30 Derby, Blagreaves Lane
- 30 Derby, Kedleston Rd
- 30 Derby, Stenson Rd
- Mickleover, Station Rd
- 30 Shardlow, London Rd
- 40 Stenson Fields, Stenson Rd
- 30 Swadlincote, Hearthcote Rd

Devon and Cornwall

A30
- 60 Chiverton Cross
- 70 Highgate (Eastbound)
- 70 Highgate Hill
- 40 Exeter, Sowton
- 60 Temple

A38
- 70 Bittaford Straight, Wrangaton
- 70 Deep Lane
- 70 Lee Mill, Lee Mill On-slip
- 70 Lower Clicker Tor
- 70 Overbridge, Smithaleigh
- 70 Smithaleigh, Smithaleigh Overbridge
- 70 Wrangaton, Bittaford Straight

A39
- 60 Barras Moor
- 30 Camelford, Valley Truckle
- 40 Perranarworthal, nr Truro

A361
- 50 Barnstaple, Ashford
- 30 Barnstaple, Eastern Avenue
- 40 Braunton, Knowle
- 30 Braunton, Knowle (Westerland)
- 30 Wrafton

A374
- 40 Plymouth, Plymouth Rd (Inbound)
- 40 Plymouth, Plymouth Rd (Outbound)
- 30 Torpoint, Anthony Rd

A376
- 30 Ebford
- 30 Exmouth, Exeter Rd

A377
- 30 Copplestone
- 30 Crediton, Western Rd
- 30 Exeter, Alphington Rd

A379
- 30 Brixton Village
- 30 Paignton, Dartmouth Rd
- 30 Starcross
- 30 Starcross, The Strand
- 30 Teignmouth, Teignmouth Rd
- 30 Torquay, Babbacombe Rd
- 30 Yealmpton

A380
- 40 Kingskerswell, Newton Rd

A381
- 30 Newton Abbott, East St

A385
- 30 Paignton, Collaton St Mary, Totnes Rd
- 30 Totnes, Ashburton Rd

A386
- 60 Chubb Tor
- 30 Plymouth, Outland Rd
- 60 Plymouth, Roborough Down
- 40 Plymouth, Tavistock Rd

A388
- 30,40 Callington, Kelly Bray

A390
- 60 Penstraze
- 60 Sticker Bypass

A394
- 40 Kenneggy Downs

A396
- 30 Rewe
- 30 Stoke Canon, Exeter Rd

A3015
- 30 Exeter, Topsham Rd

A3047
- 30 St Ives, Carbis Bay
- 30 Camborne, Pool, Trevenson Rd
- 30 Camborne, Tuckingmill

A3058
- 30 St Austell, Trewoon

A3064
- 30 Plymouth, St Budeaux Bypass

A3075
- 60 Newquay, Rosecliston

B3165
- 30 Raymonds Hill, Crewkerne Rd

B3174
- 30 Ottery St Mary, Barrack Rd

B3183
- 30 Exeter, Heavitree Rd
- 30 Exeter, New North Rd

B3212
- 30 Exeter, Dunsford Rd
- 30 Exeter, Pinhoe Rd

B3213
- 30 Wrangaton Village, nr South Brent

B3233
- 30 Barnstaple, Bickington Rd

B3250
- 30 Plymouth, North Hill

B3284
60 Liskey
30 Perranporth, Liskey
30 Chudleigh, Station Hill

B3396
30 Plymouth, Milehouse Rd

Unclassified
30 Avonwick Village
30 Buddle Lane, Exwick Rd
30 Elburton, Haye Rd
30 Exeter, Exwick Lane
30 Fraddon Village, nr Indian Queens
60 Goss Moor, Castle an Dinas
30 Honicknowle, Shakespeare Rd
30 Ivybridge, Exeter Rd
40 Monkton Village
30 Paignton, Colley End Rd
30 Paignton, Preston Down Rd
30 Plymouth, Beacon Park Rd
30 Plymouth, Church Hill
30 Plymouth, Devonport Rd
30 Plymouth, Eggbuckland Rd
30 Plymouth, Glen Rd
30 Plymouth, Honicknowle Lane
30 Plymouth, Honicknowle Lane (North)
30 Plymouth, Lipson Rd
30 Plymouth, Mannamead Rd
30 Plymouth, Molesworth Rd
30 Plymouth, North Prospect Rd
40 Plymouth, Novorrossiysk Rd
30 Plymouth, Pomphlett Rd
30 Plymouth, St Levan Rd
30 Plymouth, Southway Drive
30 Plymouth, Tamerton Foliot Rd
30 Plymouth, Union St
30 Plymouth, Weston Park Rd
30 Plymouth, Wolseley Rd (Both Directions)
30 Plympton, Glen Rd
30 St Judes, Grenville Rd
30 Saltash, Callington Rd

Dorset

A30
70 Babylon Hill
40 Shaftesbury, Long Cross

A31
40 Winterbourne Zelston

A35
60 Bridport, Cross Dykes nr Whiteway Cross
60 btwn Morden Mill & Slepe
70 Christchurch Bypass
60 Dorchester, Friary Press
60 Kingston Russell
60 Lyndhurst Rd
50 Lytchett Minster, Bakers Arms
30 Poole, Upton Rd
40 Sea Rd South
60 Vinney Cross

A37
60 Holywell Cross
60 Long Ash Lane
60 Staggs Folly

A338
50 Cooper Dean, Wessex Way
70 Spur Rd

A348
40 Bear Cross, Ringwood Rd

A349
40 Poole, Gravell Hill

A350
50 Holes Bay Rd to Sterte Rd
60 Poole Rd
70 Poole, Upton Country Park
30 Stourplane, Shashton Rd

A352
30 Wool, Dorchester Rd

A354
30 Dorchester Rd Manor Rdbt
40 Redlands, Dorchester Rd
60 Ridgeway Hill, Dorchester Rd
30 Upwey, Dorchester Rd
30 Weymouth, Buxton Rd
30 Whitechurch, Winterbourne

B3065
30 Poole, Pinecliff Rd
30 Poole, The Avenue

B3073
40 West Parley, Christchurch Rd
30 Wimborne, Oakley Hill

B3074
30 Poole, Higher Blandford Rd

B3081
30 Ebblake, Ringwood Rd

B3082
60 Bradbury Rings, Blandford Rd

B3092
n/a Gillingham, Colesbrook

B3157
30 Lanehouse Rocks Rd
50 Limekiln Hill
30 Portesham

B3369
30 Poole, Sandbanks Rd
30 Poole, Shore Rd

Unclassified
30 Blandford, Salisbury Rd
30 Bournemouth, Branksome Wood Rd
30 Bournemouth, Crabery Avenue
30 Bournemouth, Littledown Avenue
30 Bournemouth, Southbourne Overcliff Drive
30 Poole, Old Wareham Rd
30 Portland, Weston Rd
40 Staplehill, Wimbourne Rd
30 Upton, Poole Rd
30 Weymouth, Chickerell Rd

Essex

A12
Braintree, Overbridge nr Kelvedon Interchange

A13
30 Castle Point, High St (Hadleigh twds London)
30 Leigh on Sea, London Rd
Southend, Bournes Green Chase
Southend, North Shoebury
Southend, Southchurch Boulevard

A113
30 Epping, High Rd

A120
Little Bentley, Pellens Corner

A121
30 Epping, High Rd
30 Loughton, Goldings Hill (j/w Monkchester Close)
Loughton, High Rd
Waltham Abbey, Farm Hill Rd
Waltham Abbey, Sewardstine Rd

A126
30 Grays, London Rd
30 Tilbury, Montreal Rd

A128
Chipping Ongar, High St
30 Ingrave/Herongate, Brentwood Rd

A129
30 Basildon, Crays Hill
Billericay, Southend Rd
Rayleigh, London Rd
30 Wickford, London Rd
Wickford, Southend Rd

A130
30 Canvey Island, Long Rd
South Benfleet, Canvey Way

A133
30 Elmstead Market, Clacton Rd
Little Bentley, Colchester Rd

A134
40 Great Horkesley, Nayland Rd

A137
30 Lawford, Wignall St

A1016
30 Chelmsford, Waterhouse Lane

A1017
30 Sible Hedingham, Swan St

A1023
30 Brentwood, Chelmsford Rd
30 Brentwood, London Rd
30 Brentwood, Shenfield Rd

A1025
40 Harlow, Third Avenue

A1060
Little Hallingbury, Lower Rd

A1090
30 Purfleet, London Rd
30 Purfleet, Tank Hill Rd

A1124
30 Colchester, Lexden Rd

A1158
30 Westcliff on Sea, Southbourne Grove

A1168
30 Loughton, Rectors Lane

A1169
40 Harlow, Southern Way

A1205
40 Harlow, Second Avenue

B170
Loughton, Roding Lane
Chigwell, Chigwell Rise

B172
Theydon Bois, Coppice Row

B173
Chigwell, Lambourne Rd

B184
40 Great Easton, Snow Hill

B186
30 South Ockendon, South Rd

B1002
30 Ingatestone, High St

B1007
30 Billericay, Laindon Rd
30 Billericay, Stock Rd
40 Chelmsford, Stock Rd

B1008
30 Chelmsford, Broomfield Rd

B1013
30 Hawkwell, High Rd
30 Hawkwell, Main Rd
30 Hockley/Hawkwell, Southend Rd
Rayleigh, High Rd
30 Rayleigh, Hockley Rd

B1014
30 South Benfleet, Benfleet Rd

B1018
30 Latchingdon, The St
30 Maldon, The Causeway

B1019
30 Hatfield Peveral, Maldon Rd

B1021
Burnham on Crouch, Church Rd

B1022
30 Colchester, Maldon Rd
30 Heckfordbridge, Maldon Rd
30 Maldon, Colchester Rd
30 Tiptree Heath, Maldon Rd

B1027
30 Clacton-on-Sea, Valley Rd/Old Rd
30 St Osyth, Pump Hill
40 Wivenhoe, Brightlingsea Rd

B1028
30 Wivenhoe, Colchester Rd
30 Wivenhoe, The Avenue

B1033
30 Kirby Cross, Frinton Rd

B1335
40 South Ockendon, Stifford Rd

B1352
Harwich, Main Rd

B1383
30 Newport, London Rd
Stansted Mountfitchet, Cambridge Rd

B1389
30 Witham, Colchester Rd
30 Witham, Hatfield Rd

B1393
30 Epping, Palmers Hill

B1441
30 Clacton-on-Sea, London Rd

B1442
30 Clacton-on-Sea, Thorpe Rd

B1464
30 Bowers Gifford, London Rd

Unclassified
40 Alresford, St Osyth Rd
30 Aveley, Purfleet Rd
Aveley, Romford Rd
30 Barstable, Sandon Rd
30 Basildon, Ashlyns
40 Basildon, Cranes Farm Rd (j/w Honywood Rd)
Basildon, Crayhill Rd
30 Basildon, Felmores
Basildon, London Rd, Wickford
30 Basildon, Vange Hill Drive
30 Basildon, Whitmore Way
30 Basildon, Wickford Avenue
30 Billericay, Mountnessing Rd
30 Bowers Gifford, London Rd
30 Braintree, Coldnailhurst Avenue
30 Brentwood, Eagle Way (nr j/w Clive Rd twds Warley Rd)
30 Buckhurst Hill, Buckhurst Way/Albert Rd
30 Canvey Island, Dovervelt Rd
30 Canvey Island, Link Rd
30 Canvey Island, Thorney Bay Rd
Chadwell St Mary, Brentwood Rd
30 Chadwell St Mary, Linford Rd
30 Chadwell St Mary, Riverview
30 Chelmsford, Baddow Rd
30 Chelmsford, Chignall Rd
30 Chelmsford, Copperfield Rd
Chelmsford, Galleywood Rd
30 Chelmsford, Longstomps Avenue
30 Clacton-on-Sea, St Johns Rd
30 Clacton, Kings Parade
30 Clacton, Marine Parade East
30 Colchester, Abbots Rd
30 Colchester, Avon Way
30 Colchester, Bromley Rd
Colchester, Ipswich Rd
30 Colchester, Old Heath Rd
30 Colchester, Shrub End Rd
30 Corringham, Southend Rd
30 Corringham, Springhouse Rd
Danbury, Maldon Rd
30 Daws Heath, Daws Heath Rd
30 Eastwood, Green Lane j/w Kendal Way
30 Eastwood, Western Approaches j/w Rockall
30 Grays, Blackshots Lane
30 Grays, Lodge Lane
Grays, London Rd (nr Angel Rd)
Grays, London Rd (nr Bransons Way)
40 Harlow, Abercrombie Way, twds Southern Way
40 Harlow, Howard Way
30 Hullbridge, Coventry Hill
30 Laindon, Durham Rd
30 Laindon, Nightingales
30 Laindon, Wash Rd
Langdon Hills, High Rd
30 Leigh on Sea, Belton Way East
30 Leigh on Sea, Belton Way West
30 Leigh on Sea, Blenhelm Chase
30 Leigh on Sea, Grand Parade/ Cliff Parade
30 Leigh on Sea, Hadleigh Rd
30 Leigh on Sea, Highlands Boulevard
30 Leigh on Sea, Manchester Drive
30 Leigh on Sea, Mountdale Gardens
30 Leigh on Sea, Western Rd
30 Loughton, Alderton Hill
30 Loughton, Loughton Way
Loughton, Valley Hill
30 Maldon, Fambridge Rd
30 Maldon, Holloway Rd
30 Maldon, Mundon Rd
30 Pitsea, Rectory Rd
30 Prittlewell, Kenilworth Gardens
30 Prittlewell, Prittlewell Chase
30 Rayleigh, Bull Lane
Rayleigh, Downhall Rd
30 Rayleigh, Trinity Rd, nr Church Rd
30 Rochford, Ashingdon Rd
30 Rochford, Rectory Rd
Rush Green, St Osyth Rd
30 Shoeburyness, Ness Rd
30 South Woodham Ferrers, Hullbridge Rd
30 South Woodham Ferrers, Inchbonnie Rd
30 Southend on Sea, Lifstan Way
Southend, Bournemouth Park Rd
30 Southend, Hamstel Rd
Southend, Western Esplanade/Westcliff on Sea
30 Southend, Woodgrange Drive j/w Sandringham Rd
30 Springfield, New Bowers Way
30 Stanford le Hope, London Rd
30 Tendring, Burrs Rd, Clacton
Tendring, Harwich Rd, Wix Arch Cottages to Cansey Lane
Theydon Bois, Piercing Hill
30 Thorpe Bay, Barnstaple Rd
30 Thorpe Bay, Thorpe Hall Avenue
Waltham Abbey, Paternoster Hill
Weeley Heath, Clacton Rd
30 West Thurrock, London Rd
30 Westcliff on Sea, Chalkwell Avenue
30 Westcliff on Sea, Kings Rd
30 Wickford, Radwinter Avenue
30 Witham, Powers Hall End
30 Witham, Rickstones Rd

Gloucestershire

A38
40 Twigworth

A40
60 Andoversford
50 Churcham
60 Farmington
40 Gloucester Rd
60 Hampnett
60 Hazleton
60 Northleach
60 The Barringtons
60 Whittington Area

A46
30 Ashchurch
40 North of Nailsworth

A48
60 Stroat

A417
70 Burford Jct
40 Corse, Gloucester Rd
70 Dartley Bottom
40 Lechlade
30 Maisemore
40 North of Hartpury

A419
40 Oldends Lane to Stonehouse Court

A429
60 Nr Bourton-on-the-Water
40 Fossebridge

A430
40 Hempsted Bypass

A435
60 Colesbourne

A436
60 Jct with B4068

A4013
30 Gloucester, Princess Elizabeth Way
30 Gloucester, Princess Elizabeth Way (Arle)

A4019
50 Uckington

A4136
40 Brierley
40 Coleford, Lower Lane
40 Harrow Hill
40 Little London

A4151
40 Steam Mills

A4173
30 nr St Peters School

B4008
40 Hardwicke, Bristol Rd south of Tesco rdbt
30 Olympus Park Area, Bristol Rd
30 Stonehouse, Gloucester Rd

B4060
30 Katharine Lady Berkeley's School

B4215
50 South east of Rudford
50 South of Newent Bypass

B4221
30 Picklenash School
40 Kilcot Village

B4226
60 Speech House

B4228
30 Coleford, Old Station Way
40 Perrygrove

B4231
30 Bream, Coleford Rd

B4633
30 Cheltenham, Gloucester Rd

Unclassified
30 Gloucester, Abbeymead Avenue
30 Gloucester, Barrow Hill
30 Gloucester, Chesterton Lane
30 Gloucester, Parkend Fancy Rd
30 Gloucester, St Georges Rd
30 Gloucester, Swindon Lane
30 Gloucester, Wymans Lane
30 Lydney, Highfield Rd
40 Minchinhampton Common
30 Siddington
40 Tewkesbury, Gloucester Rd

Greater Manchester

A6
Manchester, Stockport Rd
Salford, Manchester Rd

A34
Manchester, Birchfield Road

A49
Marus Bridge, Warrington Rd

A56
Bury, Bury New Rd
Bury, Walmersley Rd
Bury, Whalley Rd

A57
Manchester, Hyde Rd
Salford, Liverpool Rd
Tameside, Manchester Rd

A58
Bury, Bury & Bolton Rd
Bury, Rochdale Rd

A62
Manchester, Oldham Rd
Oldham, Oldham Rd
Oldham, Oldham Way

A575
Salford, Walkden Rd

A580
Salford, East Lancashire Rd

A627
Oldham, Chadderton Way
Oldham, Ashton Rd

A662
Manchester, Ashton New Rd

A663
Oldham, Broadway

A664
Manchester, Rochdale Rd

A665
Bury, New Rd
Bury, Radcliffe New Rd

A666
Bolton, Blackburn Rd
Bolton, St Peter's Way
Salford, Manchester Rd

A667
Bury, Ringley Rd West

A5103
Manchester, Princess Parkway/Road

A6010
Manchester, Alan Turing Way

A6044
Prestwich, Sheepfoot Lane
Prestwich, Hilton Lane

A6053
Radcliffe, Dumers Lane

A6104
Blackley, Victoria Avenue

B6196
Ainsworth, Church Street
Ainsworth, Cockey Moor Rd

B6213
Tottington, Turton Rd

B6214
Greenmount, Brandlesholme Rd
Holcombe, Helmshore Rd
Holcombe Brook, Longsight Rd

B6226
Horwich, Chorley Old Rd

Unclassified
Ashton on Mersey, Ashton Lane
Bolton, Chorley Old Rd
Bolton, Hardy Mill Rd
Bolton, Hulton Lane
Bolton, Lever Park Avenue
Bolton, Plodder Lane
Bolton, Stitch Mi Lane
Bredbury, Ashton Rd
Bury, Croft Lane
Bury, Higher Lane
Bury, Stand Lane
Bury, Walshaw Rd
Manchester, Blackley New Rd
Manchester, Kingsway
Manchester, Mancunian Way
Oldham, Abbey Hills Rd
Oldham, Manchester Rd
Rochdale, Bagslate Moor Rd
Rochdale, Broad Lane
Rochdale, Bury Old Rd
Rochdale, Caldershaw Rd
Rochdale, Edenfield Rd
Rochdale, Halifax Rd
Rochdale, Heywood Old Rd
Rochdale, Hollin Lane
Rochdale, Manchester Rd
Rochdale, Queens Park Rd
Rochdale, Shawclough Rd
Rochdale, Smithybridge Rd
Rochdale, Todmorden Rd
Rochdale, Wildhouse Lane
Salford, Belvedere Rd
Salford, Langley Rd
Stockport, Birdhall Lane
Stockport, Bridge Lane
Stockport, Buxton Rd
Stockport, Chester Rd
Stockport, Councillor Lane
Stockport, Dialstone Lane
Stockport, Harrytown
Stockport, Jacksons Lane
Stockport, Kingsway
Stockport, Longhurst Lane
Stockport, Marple Rd
Stockport, Sandy Lane
Stockport, Schools Hill
Stockport, Strines Rd
Stockport, Styal Rd
Stockport, Wellington Rd North
Tameside, Mossley Rd
Tameside, Mottram Old Rd
Tameside, Mottram Rd
Tameside, Stamford Rd
Tameside, Stamford Street
Trafford, Church Rd
Trafford, Edge Lane
Trafford, Glebelands Rd
Trafford, Hope Rd
Trafford, Mosley Rd
Trafford, Norris Rd
Trafford, Park Rd
Trafford, Seymour Grove
Trafford, Warburton Lane
Trafford, Westinghouse Rd
Wigan, Almond Brook Rd
Wigan, Bickershaw Lane
Wigan, Bolton Rd
Wigan, Chaddock Lane
Wigan, Chorley Rd
Wigan, Crow Orchard Rd
Wigan, Lily Lane
Wigan, Newton Rd
Wigan, Pemberton Rd
Wigan, Scot Lane
Wigan, Victoria Street
Wigan, Wigan Rd

Hampshire and Isle of Wight

A3
70 Liphook
30 Petersfield

A27
40 Fareham (east and west bound)
30 Fareham, Portchester Rd (eastbound)
30 Fareham, Portchester Rd (westbound)
30 Fareham, The Avenue

A30
30 Blackwater
30 Hook, London Rd

A32
30 West Meon

A33
50 Basingstoke
50 Chandlers Green
50 Sherfield on Loddon
50 Southampton, Millbrook Rd (western end of Flyover to Regents Park Rd)
30 West Quay Rd

A35
50 Totton

A325
40 East Hampshire (south)
70 Farnborough, Farnborough Rd
40 Rushmoor (north)

A334/B2177
40 Wickham

A335
30 Eastleigh

A337
30 New Forest (east)
40 New Forest (west)

A338
40 New Forest (south and north bound)

A339
60 Lasham

A340
30 Basingstoke
30 Tadley

A343
30 Hurstbourne Tarrant

A3020
40 Blackwater Rd

A3024
40 Bursledon Rd
30 Northam Rd to southern river bank

A3054
30 Newport, Fairlee Rd
30 Wootton / Lushington Hill, High St

B3037/A335
30,40 Eastleigh

B3055
40 New Forest

B3395
30 Sandown, Culver Parade

Unclassified
30 Apse Heath
30 Binstead Hill
30 Brading, High St New Rd
30 East Cowes, Victoria Grove/ Adelaide Grove
30 East Cowes, York Avenue
40 Fareham, Western Way
30 Fleet, Reading Rd South
30 Newport, Staplers Rd/Long Lane
30 Portsmouth, Northern Rd (north and south bound)
40 Southampton, The Avenue (north and south bound)
30 Swanick, Swanick Lane
50 Totton / Redbridge, Redbridge Flyover

Herefordshire

see West Mercia

Hertfordshire

A119
30 Hertford, North Rd

A409
30 Bushey, Heathbourne Rd

A411
30 Bushey, London Rd
30 Elstree, Barnet Lane
30 Watford, Hempstead Rd

A414
40 Hemel Hempstead, St Albans Rd
40 Hertford, Hertingfordbury Rd

A505
30 Hitchin, Cambridge Rd

A600
30 Hitchin, Bedford Rd

A602
40 Hitchin, Stevenage Rd
40 Stevenage, Broadhall Way
40 Stevenage, Monkswood Way

A1000
40 Potters Bar, Barnet Rd

A1057
40 Hatfield, St Albans Rd West
30 St Albans, Hatfield Rd

A1170
30 Turnford, High Rd

A4125
40 South Oxhey, Sandy Lane
30 Watford, Eastbury Rd

A4145
30 Watford, Tolpits Lane

A4147
30 Hemel Hempstead, Leverstock Green Rd

A4251
30 Bourne End, London Rd

A5183
30 St Albans, Frogmore Rd

A6141
60 Letchworth, Letchworth Gate

B156
30 Cheshunt, Goffs Lane

B176
30 Cheshunt, High Street

B197
30 Baldock, London Rd
30 Stevenage, North Rd

B462
30 Bushey, Aldenham Rd

B487
30 Harpenden, Hatching Green, Redbourn Lane
40 Hemel Hempstead, Queensway

B488
40 Tring, Icknield Way

B556
30 Potters Bar, Mutton Lane

B1004
30 Bishops Stortford, Windhill

B1197
30 Hertford, London Rd

B1502
30 Hertford, Stansted Rd

B4505
30 Bovingdon, Chesham Rd

B4630
30 St Albans, Watford Rd

B5378
30 Elstree, Borehamwood, Allum Lane
40 London Colney, Shenleybury

B6426
30 Hatfield, Cavendish Way

Unclassified
30 Cheshunt, Hammond St Rd
30 Hemel Hempstead, Bennetts End Rd
30 Hemel Hempstead, High Street Green
30 Hemel Hempstead, Long Chaulden
30 Hoddesdon, Essex Rd
30 Letchworth, Pixmore Way
30 Royston, Old North Rd
30 South Oxhey, Hayling Rd
30 St Albans, Sandpit Lane
30 Stevenage, Clovelly Way
30 Stevenage, Grace Way
40 Stevenage, Gresley Way
30 Watford, Radlett Rd
30 Watford, Whippendell Rd
30 Welwyn Garden City, Heronswood Rd
30 Welwyn Garden City, Howlands

Humberside

East Riding of Yorkshire, Hull, North East Lincolnshire, North Lincolnshire

M180
NSL North Lincolnshire, West of River Trent

A18
NSL North East Lincolnshire, Barton St Central
NSL North East Lincolnshire, Barton St North
NSL North East Lincolnshire, Barton St South
30 North Lincolnshire, Wrawby

A63
50 East Riding, Melton
40 Hull, Castle St
40 Hull, Daltry St Flyover

A161
30 Belton

A163
30 Holme on Spalding Moor

A164
30 Leconfield

A165
30 Beeford
40 East Riding, Coniston
30 Freetown Way
40 Holderness Rd
30 Skirlaugh

A180
NSL Great Coates Jct

A614
40 Holme on Spalding Moor
30 Middleton on the Wolds
NSL Shiptonthorpe, north of rdbt
NSL Shiptonthorpe, south of rdbt

A1033
40 Thomas Clarkson Way
30 Thorngumbald, Main St
30 Withernsea

A1077
30 Barton

A1079
50 Barmby Moor
30 Bishop Burton
30 Hull, Beverley Rd (Desmond Ave to Riverdale Rd)
40 Hull, Beverley Rd (Sutton Rd to Mizzen Rd)

A1084
30 Brigg, Bigby High Rd

A1174
30 Dunswell
30 Woodmansey

B1206
30 Barrow, Wold Rd

B1230
40 Gilberdyke
40 Newport

B1398
40 Greetwell

Unclassified
30 Ashby, Grange Lane South
30 Ashby, Messingham Rd
30 Belton, Westgate Rd
30 Beverley, Hull Bridge Rd
30 Bilton, Main Rd
30 Bridlington, Kingsgate
30 Bridlington, Quay Rd/St John's St
30 Broughton, High St
30 Cleethorpes, Clee Rd
30 East Halton, College Rd
30 Goole, Airmyn Rd
30 Grimsby, Cromwell Rd
30 Grimsby, Great Coates Rd
30 Grimsby, Laceby Rd
30 Grimsby, Louth Rd
30 Grimsby, Waltham Rd
30 Grimsby, Weelsby Rd
30 Hessle, Beverley Rd
30 Hornsea, Rolston Rd
30 Howden, Thorpe Rd
30 Hull, Anlaby Rd
40 Hull, Boothferry Rd
30 Hull, Bricknell Avenue
30 Hull, Greenwood Avenue
30 Hull, Hall Rd
30 Hull, John Newton Way/Bude Rd
30 Hull, Leads Rd
30 Hull, Marfleet Lane
30 Hull, Marfleet Lane/Marfleet Avenue
30 Hull, Priory Rd
30 Hull, Saltshouse Rd
40 Hull, Spring Bank West
30 Hull, Wawne Rd
30 Humberston, Tetney Rd
30 Immingham, Pelham Rd
NSL Laceby Bypass
30 Preston, Station Rd
30 Scunthorpe, Ashby Rd
30 Scunthorpe, Cambridge Avenue
30 Scunthorpe, Cottage Beck Rd
40 Scunthorpe, Doncaster Rd
30 Scunthorpe, Luneburg Way
40 Scunthorpe, Queensway
30 Scunthorpe, Rowland Rd
30 South Killingholme, Top Rd
30 Yaddlethorpe, Moorwell Rd

Kent and Medway

A2
70 Canterbury
60 Dover, Guston
70 Dover, Lydden
40 Medway, London Rd

A20
70,40 Dover, Dover Rd/Archcliffe
40,50 Tonbridge and Malling, London Rd

A21
70 Sevenoaks Bypass
60 Tonbridge and Malling, Castle Hill
60 Tunbridge Wells, Key's Green

A25
30 Sevenoaks, Seal Rd

A26
40 Tonbridge and Malling, Maidstone Rd

A28
40 Ashford, Ashford Rd

A224
30 Sevenoaks, Tubs Hill

A225
30 Sevenoaks, Sevenoaks Rd

A226
50 Gravesham, Rochester Rd/Gravesend Rd through Chalk
50 Gravesham, Rochester Rd/Gravesend Rd through Shorne
40 Gravesham, Rochester Rd/Gravesend Rd through Higham

A227
30 Gravesham, through Culverstone Green
40 Gravesham, through Istead Rise
30 Gravesham, through Meopham Green

A228
40 Medway, Ratcliffe Highway

A229
50 Maidstone, Bluebell Hill
40,30 Maidstone, Linton Rd/Loose Rd
30 Medway, City Way
40 Tunbridge Wells, Angley Rd (Hartley Rd)

A249
70 Maidstone, Chalky Rd/Rumstead Lane, South St
70 Swale, Chestnut St

A253
30 Thanet, Canterbury Rd West

A256
70 Dover
30 Dover, London Rd
40 Thanet, Haine Rd

A258
50 Dover, Dover Rd

A259
40 Shepway
60 Shepway, Guldeford Lane
30 Shepway, High St

A262
30 Ashford, High St

A268
30 Tunbridge Wells, Queen St

A289
50 Medway, Medway Tunnel
70 Medway, Wainscott Bypass

A290
30 Canterbury, Blean

A291
30 Canterbury, Canterbury Rd

A292
30 Ashford, Mace Lane

A2033
30 Shepway, Dover Rd

A2990
60 Canterbury, Old Thanet Way

B258
30 Dartford, Barn End Lane

B2015
40 Nettlestead Green, Maidstone Rd

B2017
30 Tunbridge Wells, Badsell Rd

B2067
60 Ashford, Ashford Rd
30 Ashford, Woodchurch Rd

B2071
30 Shepway, Littlestone Rd

B2097
30 Rochester, Maidstone Rd

B2205
30 Swale, Mill Way

Unclassified
30 Canterbury, Mickleburgh Hill
30 Canterbury, Rough Common Rd
30 Dartford, Ash Rd/Hartley Rd
30 Gravesham, Sole St
30 Medway, Beechings Way
30 Medway, Esplanade
30 Medway, Maidstone Rd
30 Medway, St End Rd
30 Medway, Walderslade Rd
30 Sevenoaks, Ash Rd/Hartley Rd
30 Swale, Lower Rd
30 Thanet, Shottendane Rd

Lancashire

A6
40 Broughton, Garstang Rd (north of M55)
30 Chorley, Bolton Rd
30 Fulwood, Garstang Rd (south of M55)
30 Fulwood, Garstang Rd, north of Blackpool Rd
30 Lancaster, Greaves Rd
50 Lancaster, Scotforth Rd nr Burrow Lane Bailrigg
30 Preston, North Rd
30 Preston, Ringway

A56
30 Colne, Albert Rd
30 Colne, Burnley Rd
30 Nelson, Leeds Rd

A59
60 Gisburn, Gisburn Rd
50 Hutton, Liverpool Rd
30 Preston, New Hall Lane

A65
40 Lancaster, Cowan Bridge

A570
40 Scarisbrick, Southport Rd, Brook House Farm

A581
40 Ulnes Walton, Southport Rd

A583+A5073
30 Blackpool, Whitegate Drive/Waterloo Rd

A583+B5266
30 Blackpool, Church St/Newton Drive

A584
30 Blackpool, Promenade
30 Lytham, West/Central Beach
30 Warton, Lytham Rd

A584+A587
30 Blackpool, Promenade/Fleetwood Rd

A587
30 Blackpool, East/North Park Drive
30 Cleveleys, Rossall Rd/Crescent East

A588
60 Pilling, Head Dyke Lane
60 Wyre, Lancaster Rd, Cockerham at Gulf Lane

A666
30 Darwen, Blackburn Rd
30 Darwen, Bolton Rd nr Cross St
30 Darwen, Duckworth St

A671
30 Read, Whalley Rd

A674
30 Cherry Tree, Preston Old Rd

A675
50 Belmont, Belmont Rd (south of village)
50 Darwen, Belmont Rd, north of Belmont Village
60 Withnell, Bolton Rd (Dole Lane to Calf Hey Bridge)

A680
40 Edenfield, Rochdalee Rd

A682
60 Barrowford, Gisburn Rd nr Moorcock Inn
30 Brierfield, Colne Rd
40 Crawshawbooth, Burnley Rd
60 Gisburn, Gisburn Rd
60 Gisburn, Long Preston Rd

A683
30 Lancaster, Morecambe Rd

A5073
30 Blackpool, Waterloo Rd

A5085
30 Lane Ends, Blackpool Rd

A5209
30 Newburgh, Course Lane/Ash Brow

A6068
50 Barrowford, Barrowford Rd

A6114
30 Burnley, Casterton Avenue

A6177
50 Haslingden, Grane Rd West of Holcombe Rd
50 Hyndburn, Haslingden Rd/Elton Rd

B5192
30 Kirkham, Preston St

B5251
30 Chorley, Pall Mall

B5254
30 Lostock Hall, Leyland Rd/Watkin Lane
30 South Ribble, Leyland Rd

B5256
30 Leyland, Turpin Green Lane

B5269
40 Goosnargh, Whittingham Lane

B6231
30 Oswaldtwistle, Union Rd

Unclassified
60 Belmont, Egerton Rd
30 Blackburn, East Park Rd
30 Blackburn, Whalley Old Rd, west of Railway Bridge
30 Blackpool, Dickson Rd, Queens St to Pleasant St
30 Briercliffe, Burnley Rd
30 Darwen, Lower Eccleshill Rd
60 Galgate, Bay Horse Rd
30 Nelson, Netherfield Rd
30 Preston, Lytham Rd
30 Preston, St Georges Rd
30 St Anne's, Church Rd to Albany Rd, nr High School

Leicestershire and Rutland

A1
70 Empingham, Great North Rd
70 Stretton, Great North Rd

A5
60 Hinckley, Watling St (B578 to M69)
50 Hinckley, Watling St (M69 to A47)
70 Sharnford, Watling St (Highcross to B4114)

A6
40 Birstall, Loughborough Rd
40 Leicester, Abbey Lane
30 Leicester, London Rd (Knighton Drive)
30 Loughborough, Derby Rd
40 Oadby, Glen Rd/Harborough Rd

A47
60 Barrowden, Peterborough Rd
60 Bisbrooke, Uppingham Rd
30 Earl Shilton, Hinckley Rd
40 Houghton on the Hill, Uppingham Rd
30 Leicester, Hinckley Rd
30 Leicester, Humberstone Rd
30 Morcott, Glaston Rd
50 Skeffington, Uppingham Rd
50 Tugby, Uppingham Rd

A50
70 Hemmington to Lockington
40 Leicester/Glenfield, Groby Rd/Leicester Rd
30 Woodgate

A426
30 Dunchurch, Rugby Rd
50 Dunton Bassett, Lutterworth Rd
40 Glen Parva, Leicester Rd
60 Lutterworth, Leicester Rd
60 Whetstone, Lutterworth Rd

A444
40 Fenny Drayton, Atherstone Rd
30 Twycross Village, Main St
30 Twycross, Norton Juxta

A447
60 Cadeby, Hinckley Rd
40 Ravenstone, Wash Lane

A512
30 Loughborough, Ashby Rd
40 Shepshed, Ashby Rd Central

A563
30 Leicester, Attlee Way
30 Leicester, Colchester Rd/Hungarton Boulevard
30 Leicester, Glenhills Way
40 Leicester, Krefield Way
30 Leicester, New Parks Way

A594
30 Leicester, St Georges Way

A606
60 Barnsdale, Stamford Rd
60 Leicester, Broughton/Old Dalby
60 Tinwell, Stamford Rd

A607
30 Leicester, Melton Rd
30 Melton, Norman Way
70 Thurmaston, Newark Rd
60 Waltham on the Wolds, Melton Rd
60 Waltham/Croxton Kerrial, Melton Rd

A4304
40 Market Harborough, Lubbenham Hill

A5199
30 Leicester, Welford Rd
30 Wigston, Bull Head St
30 Wigston, Leicester Rd

A5460
40 Leicester, Narborough Rd

A6004
30 Loughborough, Alan Moss Rd

A6030
30 Leicester, Wakerley Rd/Broad Avenue

A6121
30 Ketton, Stamford Rd

B568
30 Leicester, Victoria Park Rd

B581
30 Broughton Astley, Broughton Way

B582
30 Blaby, Little Glen Rd

B590
30 Hinckley, Rugby Rd

B591
60 Charley, Loughborough Rd

B676
60 Freeby, Saxby Rd

B4114
40 Enderby/Narborough, Leicester Rd/King Edward Avenue
30 Leicester, Sharnford

B4616
30 Leicester, East Park Rd

B4666
30 Hinckley, Coventry Rd

B5003
40 Norris Hill, Ashby Rd

B5350
30 Loughborough, Foreset Rd
30 Loughborough, Nanpantan Rd

B5366
30 Leicester, Saffron Lane

Unclassified
30 Barrow upon Soar, Sileby Rd
30 Blaby, Lutterworth Rd
30 Ibstock, Leicester Rd
30 Leicester, Fosse Rd South
30 Shepshed, Leicester Rd

Lincolnshire

A15
60 Ashby Lodge
60 Aswarby

A15-B1191
60 Dunsby Hollow

A16
60 Boston, Boston Tytton Lane
40 Burwell
60 Deeping Bypass
60 Grainsby to Holton-le-Clay
60 North Thoresby

A17
60 Fleet Hargate
60 Hoffleet Stow
60 Moulton Common

A50
60 Thulston, London/Shardlow Rd

A52
60 Bridge End
60 Horbling and Swaton
60 Ropsley

A153
40 Billinghay
50 Tattershall

A158
50 Scremby to Candlesby

A631
60 Hemswell
60 West Rasen, Dale Bridge

A6005
40 Breaston to Long Eaton

B1188
30 Branston
60 Canwick, Highfield House
60 Potterhanworth

London

M11
Chadwell

M25
Egham
Elmbridge, Byfleet
Hillingdon
Hillingdon, Colnbrook
Runneymeade
Spelthorne
Wraysbury

A3
Kingston Bypass
Wandsworth, Kingston Rd

A4
Hounslow, Brentford, Great West Rd
Hounslow, Great West Rd

A5
Barnet, Hendon Broadway
Brent, Edgware Rd

A10
Enfield, Great Cambridge Rd
Hackney, Stamford Hill

A13
Barking and Dagenham, Alfreds Way
Barking and Dagenham, Ripple Rd
Dagenham, Ripple Rd
Newham, Alfreds Way

A20
Bexley, Sidcup Rd
Bromley, Sidcup Bypass
Greenwick, Sidcup Rd

A21
Lewisham, Bromley Rd

A22
Croydon, Godstone Rd

A40
City of Westminster, Westway
Ealing, Perivale
Ealing, Western Avenue
Hammersmith and Fulham, Westway
Hillingdon, Ruislip, Western Avenue

A110
Enfield, Enfield Rd

A124
Newham, Barking Rd

A205
Richmond upon Thames
Richmond upon Thames, Upper Richmond Rd West

A213
Bromley, Croydon Rd

A214
Wandsworth, Trinity Rd

A215
Croydon, Beulah Hill

A217
Croydon, Garratt Lane

A219
Hammersmith and Fulham, Scrubs Lane

A222
Bromley, Bromley Rd

A232
Sutton, Cheam Rd

A298
West Barnes, Bushey Rd

A312
Hillingdon

A315
Hounslow, High St

A406
Barking and Dagenham, Barking Relief Rd
Barnet, North Circular Rd
Redbridge, Southend Rd

A501
Camden, Euston Rd

A503
Haringey, Seven Sisters Rd

A3220
Wandsworth, Latchmere Rd

A4006
Brent, Kenton Rd

B178
Barking and Dagenham, Ballards Rd

B272
Sutton, Foresters Rd

B278
Sutton, Green Lane

B279
Sutton, Tudor Drive

Unclassified
Barnet, Oakleigh Rd South
Bexley, Abbey Rd
Bexley, Bellegrove Rd
Bexley, Erith Rd
Bexley, Farady Avenue
Bexley, King Harolds Way
Bexley, Lower Rd
Bexley, Penhill Rd
Bexley, Pickford Lane
Bexley, Well Hall Rd
Bexley, Woolwich Rd
Brent, Crest Rd
Brent, Hillside
Brent, Kingsbury Rd
Brent, Kingsbury, Fryent Way
Brent, Sudbury, Watford Rd
Brent, Wembley, Watford Rd
Brent, Woodcock Hill
Bromley, Beckenham Rd
Bromley, Burnt Ash Lane
Bromley, Crystal Palace Park Rd
Bromley, Elmers End Rd
Bromley, Main Rd
Bromley, Sevenoaks Way
Bromley, Wickham Way
City of Westminster, Great Western Rd
City of Westminster, Millbank
City of Westminster, Vauxhall Bridge Rd
Croydon, Addiscombe, Long Lane
Croydon, Brigstock Rd
Croydon, Coulsdon, Coulsdon Rd
Croydon, Coulsdon, Portnalls Rd
Croydon, Thornton Rd
Ealing, Greenford, Greenford Rd
Ealing, Horn Lane
Ealing, Lady Margaret Rd
Ealing, Ruislip Rd
Ealing, Southall, Greenford Rd
Ealing, Uxbridge Rd
Eastcote, Field End Rd
Enfield, Fore St
Forest Hill, Stanstead Rd
Forest Hill, Stanstead Rd
Greenwick, Beresford St
Greenwick, Court Rd
Greenwick, Creek Rd
Greenwick, Glenesk Rd
Greenwick, Rochester Way
Greenwick, Rochester Way
Greenwick, Woolwich Church St
Hackney, Clapton Common
Hackney, Seven Sisters Rd
Hackney, Upper Clapton Rd
Hammersmith and Fulham, Fulham Palace Rd
Hammersmith and Fulham, Uxbridge Rd
Hammersmith and Fulham, Westway
Haringey, Belmont Rd
Haringey, Bounds Green Rd
Haringey, Seven Sisters Rd
Haringey, White Hart Lane
Harrow, Alexandra Avenue
Harrow, Harrow View
Harrow, Harrow Weald, Uxbridge Rd
Harrow, Honeypot Lane
Harrow, Porlock Avenue
Harrow, Watford Rd
Havering, Chase Cross Rd
Havering, Eastern Avenue
Havering, Eastern Avenue East
Havering, Hall Lane
Havering, Hornchurch, Parkstone Avenue
Havering, Ockenden Rd
Havering, Romford, Brentwood Rd
Havering, Wingletye Lane
Hillingdon, Cowley, Cowley Rd
Hillingdon, Cowley, High Rd
Hillingdon, Harefield, Church Hill
Hillingdon, Hayes, Kingshill Avenue
Hillingdon, Hayes, Uxbridge Rd
Hillingdon, Northwood Hills, Joel St
Hillingdon, Park Rd
Hillingdon, Stockley Rd
Hillingdon, Uxbridge, Cowley Rd
Hounslow, Bedfont, Hatton Rd
Hounslow, Great West Rd
Hounslow, Hanworth, Castle Way
Hounslow, Harlington Rd West
Islington, Holloway Rd
Islington, Seven Sisters Rd
Islington, Upper St
Kensington and Chelsea, Barlby Rd
Kensington and Chelsea, Chelsea Embankment
Kensington and Chelsea, Chesterton Rd
Kensington and Chelsea, Holand Park Avenue
Kensington and Chelsea, Holland Villas Rd
Kensington and Chelsea, Kensington Park Rd
Kensington and Chelsea, Kensington Rd
Kensington and Chelsea, Ladbroke Grove
Kensington and Chelsea, Latimer Rd
Kensington and Chelsea, Royal Hospital Rd
Kensington and Chelsea, Sloane St
Kensington and Chelsea, St Helens Gardens
Kingston upon Thames, Kingston Rd
Kingston upon Thames, Manor Drive North
Kingston upon Thames, Richmond Rd
Lambeth, Atkins Rd
Lambeth, Brixton Hill
Lambeth, Brixton Rd
Lambeth, Clapham Rd
Lambeth, Herne Hill Rd
Lambeth, Kennington Park Rd
Lambeth, Kings Avenue
Lambeth, Streatham High Rd
Lewisham, Brockley Rd
Lewisham, Brownhill Rd
Lewisham, Burnt Ash Hill
Lewisham, Lee High Rd
Lewisham, Lewisham Way
Lewisham, Westwood Hill
Merton, Central Rd
Merton, Colliers Wood, High St
Merton, Hillcross Avenue
Merton, London Rd
Merton, Martin Way
Merton, Ridgway Place
Merton, West Barnes Lane
Newham, Barking Rd
Newham, Romford Rd
Newham, Royal Albert Dock, Spine Rd
Newham, Royal Docks Rd
North Dagenham, Rainham Rd
Redbridge, Hainault, Manford Way
Redbridge, Woodford Avenue
Redbridge, Woodford Rd
Richmond upon Thames, Kew Rd
Richmond upon Thames, Sixth Cross Rd
Richmond upon Thames, Uxbridge Rd
Southwark, Albany Rd
Southwark, Alleyn Park
Southwark, Brenchley Gardens
Southwark, Camberwell New Rd
Southwark, Denmark Hill
Southwark, Kennington Park Rd
Southwark, Linden Grove
Southwark, Old Kent Rd
Southwark, Peckham Rye
Southwark, Salter Rd
Southwark, Sunray Avenue
Streatham, Streatham High Rd
Sutton, Beddington Lane
Sutton, Cheam Common Rd
Sutton, Maiden Rd
Sutton, Middleton Rd
Tower Hamlets, Bow Rd
Tower Hamlets, Cambridge Heath Rd
Tower Hamlets, Homerton High Rd
Tower Hamlets, Manchester Rd
Tower Hamlets, Mile End Rd
Tower Hamlets, Upper Clapton Rd
Tower Hamlets, Westferry Rd
Waltham Forest, Chingford Rd
Waltham Forest, Hoe St
Waltham Forest, Larksall Rd
Wandsworth, Battersea Park Rd
Wandsworth, Garratt Lane
Wandsworth, Upper Richmond Rd
Woolwich, Woolwich Church St

Merseyside

A57
Liverpool, East Prescot Rd

A58
St Helens, Prescot Rd

A506
Liverpool, Longmoor Lane

A551
Wirral, Leasowe Rd

A553
Wirral, Laird Street

A561
Liverpool, Speke Rd/Speke Boulevard

A562
Liverpool, Parliament Street/Upper Parliament Street

A572
St Helens, Common Rd

A580
Liverpool, Townsend Avenue
St Helens, East Lancashire Rd

A5038
Sefton, Southport Rd/Liverpool Boundary to Oxford Rd
Sefton, Southport Rd/Oxford Rd to Northfield Rd

A5080
Liverpool, Bowring Park Rd/Roby Rd

A5098
Liverpool, Hornby Rd

Unclassified
Liverpool, Great Homer Street
Liverpool, Green Lane
Liverpool, Lower House Lane/Dwerry House Lane
Liverpool, Muirhead Avenue
Liverpool, Netherfield Rd North
Liverpool, Utting Avevnue East
Sefton, Park Lane
Wirral, New Chester Rd

Norfolk

A10
Stow Bardolph
Tottenhill/Watlington

A11
Attleborough Bypass
Ketteringham
Roundham
Snetterton
Wymondham/Bestthorpe

A47
East Winch
Emneth
Honington/Easton
Lingwood/Acle
Mautby/Halvergate
Narborough
Postwick
Pullover Rdbt
Scarning
Swaffham/Sporle
Terrington St John
Tuddenham
Wendling/Framsham

A140
Aylsham
Dickleburgh Moor
Erpingham
Long Stratton/Tivetshall St Mary
Newton Flotman
Newton Flotman/Saxlingham Thorpe
Norwich, Harford Bridge
Roughton village
Scole Bypass
St. Faiths

A143
Billingford/Brockdish

A148
Bodham
Fakenham Bypass
King's Lynn, Grimston Rd
Pretty Corner
Thursford

A149
Caister Bypass
Catfield
Catfield/Potter Heigham
Hunstanton
Kings Lynn/Nth Runcton
Knights Hill
Little Snoring
Roughton (N and S Repps)
Sandringham
Wayford Bridge East
Wayford Bridge West/Smallburgh

Northamptonshire

A5
60 DIRFT to County Boundary
60 Norton/Whilton Crossroads
30/40 Towcester Racecourse to A43

A6
60 Burton Latimer Bypass

A14
70 Kelmarsh
70 Kelmarsh Junctions 7-10

A43
60 Laxton Turn to A47 Duddington
60 Mawsley to A14 Junc 8 (inc Mawsley Spur)
70 Towcester to M1 Junc 15a

A45
60 M1 June 16 to Weedon
60 Stanwick to Raunds

A361
60 Byfield to Chipping Warden

A422
60 Brackley West to A43

A428
60 East Haddon
30/60 Great Houghton to Yardley Hastings

A508
30 Northampton, Plough Gyratory
30 Northampton, St Georges Avenue to Holly Lodge Rd
30 Northampton, St Peters Way to St Georges Avenue
30/60 Stoke Bruerne to A5
70 Wootton Flyover to M1 Junc 15

A509
60 Wellingborough to Isham

A605
40/60 Thrapston to Warmington

A4256
30 Daventry, Eastern Way

A4500
40/60 Great Billing to Earls Barton
30 Northampton, Abington Park to York Rd
30 Northampton, Park Avenue to Booth Lane South
30 Northampton, Weedon Rd to Duston Rd

A5076
40 Mere Way
40 Northampton, Great Billing Way South

A5193
30/40 Wellingborough, London Rd

A6003
50/60 Kettering to Corby

A6014
40/60 Corby, Oakley Rd

B569
50 Irchester to Rushden

B576
60 Desborough to Rothwell

B4038
30/60 Kilsby, Rugby Rd

B4525
40/60 Welsh Lane

B5385
60 Watford to West Haddon

Unclassified
30 Brackmills Industrial Estate
30 Northampton, Grange Rd

Northumbria

Gateshead, Newcastle-upon-Tyne, North Tyneside, Northumberland, South Tyneside, Sunderland

A1
60 Berwick Bypass, Dunns Jct (N)

A68
60 Colt Crag

A69
60 Haltwhistle Bypass
70 Hexham, Two Mile Cottage

A167
30 Newcastle, Stamfordham Rd

A182
30 Sunderland, Houghton Rd

A183
30 Broadway, Chester Rd

A186
40 Denton Burn, West Rd
30 Newcastle, City Rd at Beamish House
40 Newcastle, West Rd at Turret Rd
30 Newcastle, Westgate Rd at Elwick Row

A189
70 Cramlington, High Pitt
70 Cramlington, Spine Rd
30 South Gosforth, Haddricks Mill Rd

A191
30 Benton, Whitley Rd
30 Fenham, Springfield Rd

A193
30 Wallsend, Church Bank

A194
40 Simonside, Newcastle Rd
A196
30 Blackclose Bank
A690
30 Sunderland, Durham Rd
50 Sunderland, Stoneygate, Houghton, Durham Rd
A692
30 Gateshead, Church Street
A694
30 Gateshead, Rowlands Gill, Station Rd
40 Gateshead, Winlaton Mill (Spa Well Rd)
A695
60 Gateshead, Crawcrook Bypass
40 Prudhoe Jct B6395

30 Belsay Village
60 Blaxter Cottages
60 Kirkwhelpiington
60 Otterburn Monkridge
A697
60 Morpeth, Heighley Gate
60 Wooperton
A1018
30 Sunderland, Ryhope Rd, Irene Avenue
A1058
30 Newcastle, Jesmond Rd at Akenside Terrace
A1068
30 Amble Ind Est
A1147
30 Stakeford, Gordon Terrace
A1171
30 Cramlington, Dudley Lane
A1290
30 Sunderland, Southwick, Keir Hardie Way
A1300
30 South Tyneside, Nook, Prince Edward Rd
A6085
40 Newcastle, Lemington Rd
A6127
30 Gateshead, Barley Mow, Durham Rd
B1286
30 Sunderland, Burdon Rd
30 Sunderland, Tunstall Bank
B1288
40 Gateshead, Leam Lane/A195
B1296
30 Gateshead, Sheriffs Highway, QE Hospital
30 Gateshead, Sheriffs Highway, Split Crow Rd
B1297
30 South Tyneside, Blackett Street
B1298
30 South Tyneside, Boldon Colliery, New Rd
B1301
30 South Tyneside, Dean Rd (John Clay St)
30 South Tyneside, Laygate, Eglesfield Rd
B1316
30 North Shields, Lynn Rd
B1318
30 North Tyneside, Seaton Burn, Bridge St
B1404
30 Sunderland, Seaham Rd
B1426
30 Gateshead, Felling, Sunderland Rd
B1505
30 North Tyneside, West Moor, Great Lime Rd
B6315
30 Gateshead, High Spen, Hookergate Lane
B6317
30 Gateshead, Ryton, Main Rd
30 Gateshead, Whickham Highway
B6318
60 Whitchester, Military Rd
60 Whittington Fell, Military Rd
B6324
40 Newcastle, Stamfordham Rd southeast of Walbottle Rd
B6918
30 Newcastle, Woolsington Village
Unclassified
30 Ashington, Barrington Rd
30 Ashington, Station Rd
30 Benton, Coach Lane
30 Gateshead, Askew Rd West
30 Gateshead, Blaydon, Shibdon Bank
30 Gateshead, Chopwell, Mill Rd
30 Gateshead, Crawcrook, Greenside Rd
30 Gateshead, Felling, Watermill Lane
30 Gateshead, Whickham, Fellside Rd
30 Hebburn, Campbell Park Rd
70 Nafferton
60 Newcastle, Dinnington Rd North Brunton Lane
40 Newcastle, West Denton Way east of Hawksley
30 North Shields, Norham Rd
30 South Tyneside, Harton Lane
40 South Tyneside, Hedworth Lane, Abingdon Way
30 Sunderland, Allendale Rd
30 Sunderland, Burdon Lane
40 Sunderland, Farringdon, North Moor Lane
40 Sunderland, North Hylton Rd, Castletown Way
30 Sunderland, Parkway at Barrington Drive
30 Sunderland, St Aidens Terrace at the Vicarage
30 Sunderland, Silksworth Rd, Rutland Avenue
30 Sunderland, Springwell Rd
30 Sunderland, Warwick Terrace
30 Wallsend, Battle Hill Drive
30 Whiteleas, Nevinson Avenue

Nottinghamshire

A1
70 East Markham (Northbound)
A52
40 Clifton Boulevard
A60
30 Carlton in Lindrick
30 Mansfield, Nottingham Rd
60 Market Warsop/Cuckney
30 Nottingham, Bellar Gate to Woodthorpe Drive
30 Nottingham, London Rd
50 Ravenshead
30 South, Nottingham
A609
30 Nottingham, Ilkeston Rd/Wollaton Rd/Russell Drive
A610
30 Nottingham, Bobbers Mill
A611
30 Annelsey, Derby Rd
30 Nottingham, Hucknall Rd
A612
30 Southwell, Nottingham Rd
A614
60 Arnold, Burnt Stump
A617
40 Mansfield, Chesterfield Rd South
A620
40 Retford, Welham Rd
A631
50 Beckingham Bypass
50 Beckingham, Flood Plain Rd
50 Beckingham, nr Wood Lane
60 Gringley to Beckingham, nr Mutton Lane
50 West of Beckingham
A6005
30 Nottingham, Castle Boulevard/Abbey Bridge/Beeston Rd
A6008
30 Nottingham, Canal St
A6130
30 Nottingham, Gregory Boulevard
30 Nottingham, Radford and Lenton Boulevards
A6200/A52
30 Nottingham, Derby Rd
A679
30 West Bridgford, Wilford Lane
B682
30 Nottingham, Sherwood Rise/Nottingham Rd/Vernon Rd
B6004
40 Arnold, Oxclose Lane
B6010
30 Giltbrook, Nottingham Rd
B6011
30 Hucknall, Annesley Rd/Nottingham Rd/Portland Rd
B6020
30 Rainworth, Kirklington Rd
B6040
30 Worksop, Retford Rd
B6166
30 Newark on Trent, Lincoln Rd/Northgate
B6326
40 Newark on Trent, London Rd
Unclassified
30 Newark, Balderton, Hawton Lane
30 Nottingham, Beechdale Rd/Wigman Rd
30 Nottingham, Bestwood Park Drive
Nottingham, Radford Boulevard/Lenton Boulevard
30 Nottingham, Ridge Way/Top Valley Drive

Oxfordshire

see Thames Valley

Shropshire

see West Mercia

Somerset

see Avon and Somerset

South Yorkshire

A18
60 Doncaster, Slay Pits to Tudworth, Epworth Rd
40 Doncaster, Carr House Rd/Leger Way
A57
40,60 Anston, Sheffield Rd/Worksop Rd
60 Rotherham, Worksop Rd
60 Sheffield, Mosborough Parkway
A60
60 Tickhill, Doncaster Rd
30,60 Tickhill, Worksop Rd
A61
30 Cutting Edge, Park Rd
30,40 Sheffield, Chesterfield Rd/Chesterfield Rd South
30,40 Sheffield, Halifax Rd
30 Sheffield, Penistone Rd
A614
60 Thorne, Selby Rd
A618
40 Wales Bar, Mansfield Rd
A628
30,40 Barnsley, Cundy Cross to Shafton Two Gates
40,60 Barnsley, Dodworth
40 Penistone, Barnsley Rd
A629
60 Barnsley, Wortley
30 Burncross, Hallwood Rd/Burncross Rd
40 Rotherham, New Wortley Rd
30,40 Rotherham, Wortley Rd/Upper Wortley Rd
A630
30,40,60 Dalton/Thrybergh, Doncaster Rd
30,40,60 Doncaster, Balby Flyover to Hill Top
40 Doncaster, Wheatley Hall Rd
40,50 Rotherham, Centenary Way
A631
40 Brinsworth, Bawtry Rd
30,40 Hellaby/Maltby, Bawtry Rd/Rotherham Rd
50 Rotherham, West Bawtry Rd
40 Wickersley/Brecks, Bawtry Rd
A633
30 Athersley South, Rotherham Rd
40 Monk Bretton, Rotherham Rd
30 Wath upon Dearne, Sandygate
30,40 Wombwell, Barnsley Rd
A635
30,40,60 Barnsley, Doncaster Rd/Saltersbrook Rd
A638
40 Doncaster, Bawtry Rd
40,50 Doncaster, Great North Rd/York Rd
A6022
30 Rotherham, Swinton
A6101
40 Sheffield, Rivelin Valley Rd
A6102
30,40 Hillsborough/Deepcar, Manchester Rd/Langsett Rd
A6109
40 Rotherham, Meadow Bank Rd
A6123
40 Rotherham, Herringthorpe Valley Rd
A6135
40 Sheffield, Ecclesfield Rd/Chapeltown Rd
B6059
30,40 Rotherham, Kiveton/Wales
B6089
40 Thorn Hill/Greasbrough, Greasbrough Rd/Greasbrough St
B6096
30 Barnsley, Wombwell to Snape Hill
B6097
30,60 Wath upon Dearne, Doncaster Rd
B6100
30 Barnsley, Ardsley Rd/Hunningley Lane
B6411
30 Thurnscoe, Houghton Rd
B6463
60 Tickhill, Stripe Rd
Unclassified
30 Armthorpe, Hatfield Lane/Mill St
30 Armthorpe, Nutwell Lane
30 Barnsley, Pogmoor Rd
30 Bolton upon Dearne, Dearne Rd
30 Doncaster, Melton Rd/Sprotbrough Rd
30 Doncaster, Urban Rd
30,60 Edlington/Warmsworth, Broomhouse Lane/Springwell Lane
40,60 Finningley, Hurst Lane
30 Grimethorpe, Brierley Rd
30,60 Rotherham, Fenton Rd
30,40 Rotherham, Haugh Rd
30 Rotherham, Kilnhurst Rd
30 Stainforth, Station Rd
40 Wath upon Dearne, Barnsley Rd
30 Wheatley, Thorne Rd

Staffordshire

A5
60 A5127 to A38 – Wall Island to Weeford Island
60,70,60,30 btwn A34 Churchbridge and The Turf Pub Island (B4154)
50,40 from A38 to Hints Lane
70 from A461 to A5127 (Muckley Corner Island to Wall Island Lichfield/Tamworth)
60,70,60 Hanney Hay/Barracks Lane Island to Muckley Corner Island
50 M6 jct 12 to A460/A4601 Island
50,30 South Cannock, A460/A4601 to A34 Longford Island to A34 Bridgetown
A34
30 Cannock North, North of Holly Lane jct to A34/B5012 rdbt
30,50,30 Cannock South to County Boundary
30 Cannock South, A34 from south of jct of A5 Walstall Rd to north of jct with Jones Lane
40 Newcastle North, from Wolstanton Rd/Dimsdale Parade west Island to Milehouse Lane/B5367
30,40 Newcastle Rd btwn Hanford Island to London Rd Bowling Club
40 Newcastle South, Barracks Rd to Stoke City Boundary
70,40 Newcastle under Lyme to Talke, btwn Wolstanton Rd/Dimsdale Parade West Island to Jct of A500
30,40 Stafford South, from A449 jct to Acton Hill Lane Jct
40,30 Stone Rd from jct of Longton Rd/A5035 to Handford Island/A500
40,30 Stone Rd Redhill (A513/A34) island to Lloyds Island, Eccleshall Rd
Talke, Jct A500 (Peacock Hay Rd) to Jct A5011
A50
30 Kidsgrove, btwn City Boundary and Oldcott Drive
A51
30,40,60 Lichfield, from A5127 Birmingham Rd to Heath Rd
50 Pasturefields, A51 from south of jct with Amerton Lane to south of Hoomill Lane
40,30 Rugeley North, from A51 jct with Bower Lane to island of A460 Sandy Lane and B5013 Elmore Lane
30,40 Rugeley South, from south of island of A460/Sandy Lane and B5013 Elmore Lane to Brereton Island
30 Tamworth, A51 Tamworth Rd/Dosthill Rd from south of jct with Peelers Way to jct with A51 Ascot Drive
60,40,50 Weston, btwn New Rd and 500m past Sandy Lane (going north)
A52
30 Stoke on Trent, Werrington Rd – btwn jct of B5040 to half mile east of Brookhouse Lane (Ashbank)
30,40 Stoke, Werrington Rd, btwn Brookhouse Lane and Kingsley Rd
A53
Blackshaw Moor btwn Thorncliffe Rd and Hazel Barrow Lane
40,30,40,60 Endon, from A53 Leek New Rd from jct with Nursery Avenue to jct with Dunwood Lane
60,40,30 Longsden, from A53 jct with Dunwood Lane to A53 jct with Wallbridge Drive
A444
30 Stanton Rd – St Peters Bridge to Derbyshire boundary
A449
70,40 Coven, btwn Station Drive by Four Ashes to just before M54 island
60,70 Gailey, btwn Rodbaston Drive and Station Drive
40 Penkridge, Lynehill Lane to 0.5mile north of Goodstation Lane
30 Stafford, Lichfield Rd to Gravel Lane
Stourton btwn Ashwood Lower Lane and Dunsley Lane
A454
50 Trescott, Bridgenorth Rd btwn Brantley Lane and Shop Lane
A460
30 Rugeley, A460 from A51/A460 jct of Sandy Lane/Hednesford Rd to south of jct A460 Stile Cop Rd
A511
40,30 Burton North, btwn Anslow Lane to island of A5121
30 Burton South, island of A5121 to Brizlincote Lane (by Derbyshire boundary)
A518
30 Stafford, btwn M6 and Bridge St
30,40 Stafford, Riverway to Blackheath Lane
A519
40 Newcastle, Clayton Rd – from south of A519 Clayton Rd/Friars Wood and Brook Lane to rdbt on A519
A520
30 Sandon Rd btwn Grange Rd and A50
30 Weston Rd – from north of the A50 to City boundary (Park Hall) through Meir and Weston Coyney
A4601
30 Cannock, btwn A34 Walsall Rd jct to Longford Island A5
30 Old Hednesford Rd btwn jct with A5190 Lichfield Rd and jct with A460 Eastern Way
30,40 Wedges Mill, Longford Island twd jct 11 to just before Saredon Rd
A5005
Stoke on Trent, Lightwood Rd btwn A520 and A50
A5035
30 Trentham, Longton Rd btwn Trentham Rdbt A34 and A50 jct at Longton
A5121
50,40,30 Burton, from Island Junction with B5108 Branston to Borough Rd
30,40 Burton, from jct with Byrkley St, Horninglow to jct with Hillfield Lane
A5127
30 Lichfield, from jct with Upper St John St towards Streethay (incs change in speed limit over railway bridge)
A5189
30,40 Burton, btwn Wellington Rd jct along St Peters Bridge to Stapenhill Rd rdbt
A5190
30 Burntwood, Cannock Rd from Attwood Rd to Stockhay Lane Jct
30,40,60 Cannock, from Five Ways Island to Hednesford Rd
B5044
30 Silverdale, btwn Sneyd Terrace and the jct of the B5368 (Church Lane/Cemetery Rd)
B5051
30 btwn Sneyd Hill Rd and Brown Edge
B5080
30,40 Tamworth, Pennine Way btwn B5000 and Pennymoor Rd
B5404
40,30 Tamworth, from Sutton Rd to jct of A4091 (Coleshill Rd/Fazeley Rd)
30 Tamworth, Watling St btwn jct with A51 and A5
Unclassified
30 Burton, Rosliston Rd btwn A5189 St Peters Bridge and County Boundary by Railway Bridge
30 Cannock, Pye Green Rd
30 Cedar Rd btwn Crackley Bank and B5500 Audley Rd
30,40 Leek New Rd – btwn B5049 Hanley Rd and B5051 jct with A53 at Endon
30 Oxford Rd/Chell Heath Rd btwn A527 and B5051
30 Stoke on Trent, Dividy Rd – btwn B5039 and A52

Suffolk

A11
50 Barton Mills
Elveden
40 Elveden Cross Rds
Elveden, Chalk Hall
A12
40 Blythburgh
Kelsale
30 Little Glemham
Lound
40 Melton
Saxmundham
A14
Exning
Rougham
A134
40 Barnham
Long Melford
40 Nowton
A137
30 Brantham
A140
50 Thwaite
A143
30 Bury St Edmunds
30 Chedburgh
40 Stanton Bypass
40 Stradishall, Highpoint Prison
A144
30 Ilketshall St Lawrence
A146
50 Barnby Bends
A1065
40 Eriswell
Mildenhall
North of RAF Lakenheath
A1071
40 Boxford
Hadleigh, Lady Lane
A1092
30 Cavendish
30 Clare
40 Glemsford, Skates Hill
A1101
30 Flempton
A1117
30 Lowestoft, Saltwater Way
A1120
30 Stonham Aspal
A1156
30 Ipswich, Norwich Rd
A1302
30 Bury St Edmunds
A1304
Newmarket, Golf Club
B1078
30 Barking
30 Needham Market
B1106
30 Fornham
B1113
40 Bramford
B1115
40 Chilton
B1384
30 Carlton Colville
B1438
30 Melton Hill
B1506
40 Kentford
Moulton
Unclassified
30 Felixstowe, Grange Farm Avenue
30 Ipswich, Foxhall Rd
30 Ipswich, Nacton Rd
30 Kesgrave, Ropes Drive

Surrey

A3
Grayshott to Cobham
A23
Salfords, Brighton Rd
A24
Mickleham
A25
Westcott to West Clandon
A30
Staines
A31
Hogs Back (Central and Eastern sections)
A217
Lower Kingswood to Banstead
A242
Reigate to Merstham
A243
Hook
A246
Guildford
A248
Chilworth
A307
Esher
A308
Staines
A320
Guildford to Staines
A3016
Hale
A3100
Guildford to Godalming
B367
Ripley
B375
Chertsey
B380
Mayford
B385
Woodham
B386
Windlesham
B389
Virginia Water
B2030
Caterham to Old Coulsdon
B2031
Caterham to Chaldon
B2126
Holmbury St Mary
B2127
Ewhurst
B2130
Godalming
B3411
Ash Vale
Unclassified
Effingham, Effingham Common Rd
Epsom, Longdown Lane South
Frith Hill, Charterhouse Rd
Hurtmore, Hurtmore Rd
Leigh, Apners Rd
Lightwater, Macdonald Rd
Staines, Kingston Rd

Thames Valley

Bracknell Forest, Buckinghamshire, Milton Keynes, Oxfordshire, Reading, Slough, West Berkshire, Windsor and Maidenhead, Wokingham

A5
70 Wolverton
70 Bletchley
A30
30 Sunningdale, London Rd
A34
70 Radley
70 Kennington
A40
60 Cassington
70 Forest Hills
A41
70 Buckland
A44
50 Kiddington with Asterleigh
A338
50 Hungerford
A361
30 Chipping Norton, Burford Rd
60 Little Faringdon
A404
70 Little Marlow, Marlow Bypass
A413
60 Swanbourne
60 Weedon
60 Hardwick
60 Wendover Bypass
A421
70 Tingewick Bypass
60 Wavendon
A422
50 Radclive cum Chackmore
A509
70 Newport Pagnell
60 Emberton Bypass
A4074
60 Dorchester
50 Nuneham Courteney
A4095
40 Freeland, Witney Rd
A4130
60 Nuffield
40 Remenham Hill
A4155
30 Shipiake
A4260
50 Shipton on Cherwell, Banbury Rd
60 Rousham, Banbury Rd
30 Steeple Aston
B4009
50 Ewelme
B4011
60 Piddington
B4494
60 Leckhampstead
Unclassified
30 Abingdon, Drayton Rd
30 Abingdon, Oxford Rd
30 Aylesbury, Buckingham Rd
30 Aylesbury, Gatehouse Rd
30 Aylesbury, Oakfield Rd
30 Aylesbury, Tring Rd
30 Aylesbury, Walton St
30 Aylesbury, Wendover Rd
30 Barkham, Barkham Rd
60 Beenham, Bath Rd
30 Blackbird Leys, Watlington Rd
30 Bletchley, Buckingham Rd
40 Bracknell, Bagshot Rd
50 Bracknell, Nine Mile Ride
30 Bracknell, Opladen Way
30 Buckingham, Stratford Rd
50 Burnham, Bath Rd
30 Chalfont St Peter, Gravel Hill
40 Chipping Norton, London Rd
40 Curbridge, Bampton Rd
40 Denham, North Orbital Rd
30 Denham, Oxford Rd
40 Earley, London Rd
30 Great Missenden, Rignall Rd
60 Hardmead, Newport Rd
30 Hazelmere, Sawpit Hill
30 High Wycombe, Holmers Farm Way
30 High Wycombe, Marlow Hill
30 High Wycombe, New Rd
30 High Wycombe, West Wycombe Rd
60 Hungerford, Bath Rd
30 Kidlington, Oxford Rd
60 Kintbury, Bath Rd
30 Long Crendon, Bicester Rd
40 Maidenhead, Braywick Rd
70 Milton Keynes, Woughton on the Green, Standing Way
30 Milton Keynes, Avebury Boulevard
30 Milton Keynes, Midsummer Boulevard
30 Milton Keynes, Silbury Boulevard
30 Monks Risborough, Aylesbury Rd
30 Oxford, Church Cowley Rd
30 Oxford, Headington Rd
30 Oxford, London Rd
30 Oxford, Windmill Rd
30 Reading, Berkeley Avenue
30 Reading, Castle Hill
30 Reading, Kings Rd
30 Reading, Park Lane
30 Reading, Vastern Rd
30 Reading, Wokingham Rd
30 Slough, Buckingham Rd
30 Slough, Cippenham Lane
40 Slough, London Rd
30 Slough, Parlaunt Rd
30 Slough, Sussex Place
60 Speen, Bath Rd
30 Stanford in the Vale, Faringdon Rd
40 Sunninghill, Brockenhurst Rd
30 Tiddington, Oxford Rd
40 Tilehurst, Bath Rd
30 Wantage, Charlton Rd
70 Winkfield, Bagshot Rd
30 Witney, Corn St
30 Wokingham, London Rd
60 Wroxton, Stratford Rd

Warwickshire

A5
50 Grendon to Atherstone, Watling Street
60 Rugby, Churchover, Watling Street
A44
60 Little Compton, London Rd
A46
60 Stratford Northern Bypass, nr Snitterfield
70 Warwick, Stoneleigh, Kenilworth Bypass
A47
40 Nuneaton and Bedworth, The Longshoot
A422
30 Pillerton Priors, Banbury Rd
30 Stratford, Alcester Rd
A423
60 Farnborough, Southam Rd
60 Fenny Compton, Banbury Rd
60 Rugby, nr Marton, Oxford Rd
30 Rugby, Marton, Coventry Rd
60 south of Southam, Southam Rd
A425
30 Warwick, Radford Semele, Radford Rd
A426
30 Rugby, Dunchurch Rd
60 Stockton, Rugby Rd
A428
30 Rugby, Binley Woods, Rugby Rd
60 Rugby, Church Lawford, Coventry Rd
40 Rugby, Long Lawford, Coventry Rd
A429
60 Stretton on Fosse
30 Warwick, Coventry Rd
60 Wellesbourne, Ettington Rd
A435
40 Mappleborough Green
A439
50 Stratford, nr Fisherman's car park
50 Warwick Rd nr Hatton Rock
A445
40 Leamington Spa, Leicester Lane
A446
60 Allen End, London Rd
60 Bassetts Pole, London Rd
A452
60 Warwick, Greys Mallory, Banbury Rd
60 Warwick, Heathcote, Europa Way
A3400
30 Alderminster, Shipston Rd
40 Henley in Arden, Stratford Rd
60 Little Wolford, London Rd
30 Long Compton, Main Street
30 Newbold on Stour, Stratford Rd
50 Pathlow, Birmingham Rd
50 Wootton Wawen, Stratford Rd
A4189
60 Lower Norton, Henley Rd
B439
60 Cranhill, Evesham Rd
B4035
30 Upper Brailes, Main Rd
B4065
30 Ansty, Main Rd
B4087
30 Wellesbourne, Newbold Rd
B4089
30 Stratford, Alcester, Arden Rd
B4098
40 Corley, Tamworth Rd
B4100
60 Bishop's Tachbrook, north of Harwood's House
60 south of Gaydon, Banbury Rd

B4101
40 Tamworth in Arden, Broad Lane

B4102
30 Nuneaton, Arbury Rd

B4109
40 Bulkington, Coventry Rd

B4111
30 Nuneaton, Mancetter Rd

B4112
40 Nuneaton, Ansley Rd

B4113
30 Nuneaton, Coventry Rd

B4114
30 Ansley Common, Coleshill Rd
60 Church End, Coleshill Rd
60 Rugby, Burton Hastings, Lutterworth Rd

B4429
40 Rugby, Ashlawn Rd

B4455
60 Rugby, Fosse Way south of Princethorpe

Unclassified
30 Ash Green, Royal Oak Lane
30 Ash Green, St Giles Rd
30 Ash Green, Vicarage Lane
30 Butlers Marston, Kineton Rd
30 Coleshill, Station Rd
30 Exhall, School Lane
30 Lighthorne, Chesterton Rd
60 Monks Kirby, Coalpit Lane
30 Nuneaton, Donnithorne Avenue
30 Rugby, Vicarage Hill, Clifton Rd
40 Salford Priors, Station Rd
40 Sambourne, Middletown Lane
30 Warwick, Woodloes Park, Primrose Hill

West Mercia

Herefordshire, Shropshire, Telford and Wrekin, Worcestershire

A5
NSL Aston
NSL Gobowen, Moreton Bridge
60 Montford Bridge
NSL West Felton

A40
50 Pencraig

A41
40,NSL Albrighton Bypass
NSL Chetwynd nr Newport
40 Tern Hill
NSL Whitchurch Bypass

A44
40 Wickhamford
30 Worcester, Bromyard Rd

A46
50 Beckford
NSL Evesham Bypass

A49
NSL Ashton
30 Dorrington
40 Herefordshire, Harewood End

A417
40 Ledbury, Parkway

A438
60 Staunton-on-Wye

A442
40 Crudgington

A448
30 Bromsgrove, Kidderminster Rd

A456
30 Blakedown
30 Newnham Bridge

A458
40 Morville
30 Much Wenlock

A465
NSL Allensmore

A491
50 Bromsgrove, Stourbridge Rd
NSL Hagley, Sandy Lane

A528
30 Shrewsbury, Ellesmere Rd

A4103
NSL Hereford, Lumber Lane/Lugg Bridge
40 Newtown Cross
50 Stiffords Bridge/Storridge

A4104
30 Welland, Drake St
30 Welland, Marlbank Rd

A4110
30 Hereford, Three Elms Rd

A5064
30 Shrewsbury, London Rd

B4084
40 Cropthorne

B4096
30 Bromsgrove, Old Birmingham Rd

B4208
30 Welland

B4211
30 Malvern, Barnards Green Rd

B4368
40 Hungerford

B4373
40 Telford, Castlefields Way
40 Telford, Wrockwardine Wood Way

B4638
30 Worcester, Woodgreen Drive

B5060
40 Telford, Castle Farm Way

B5062
60 Newport, Edgmond Rd
30 Shrewsbury, Sundorne Rd

Unclassified
30 Hadley, Britannia Way
30 Hereford, Yazor Rd
30 Kidderminster, Habberley Lane
30 Newport, Wellington Rd
30 Redditch, Bromsgrove Rd
40 Redditch, Coldfield Drive
30 Shrewsbury, Monkmoor Rd
30 Shropshire, Longden Rd (Rural)
30 Telford, Britannia Way

West Midlands

Birmingham, Coventry, Dudley, Sandwell, Solihull, Walsall, Wolverhampton

A5
60 Brownhills, Watling St
50 Cannock, Watling St
60 Wall, Watling St

A41
40 Albrighton Bypass towards Wolverhampton
40,60 Albrighton, Albrighton Bypass towards Newport
30 Silhill, Warwick Rd

A46
70 Stoneleigh, Kenilworth Bypass

A51
30 Lichfield, Tamworth Rd
60 Weeford, Watling St

A446
60 Allens End, London Rd
60 Bassetts Pole, London Rd

A449
40 Coven, Wolverhampton Rd
60 Gailey, Wolverhampton Rd

A452
50 Smith's Wood, Collector Rd

A4034
30 Langley, Oldbury Rd

A4036
40 Netherton Woodside and St Andrew's, Pedmore Rd

A4040
30 Hodge Hill, Bromford Lane

A4123
40 Castle and Priory, Birmingham New Rd

A4177
60 Hasley Knob, Honiley Rd

A5127
30 Lichfield, Trent Valley Rd

A4600
40 Wyken, Ansty Rd

B425
30 Elmdon, Lode Lane

B4065
30 Ansty, Main Rd

B4098
40 Fillongley, Coventry Rd
60 Fillongley, Tamworth Rd

B4101
40 Tanworth, Broad Lane

B4103
30 Kenilworth, Castle Rd
30 Kenilworth, Clinton Lane

B4109
40 Bulkington, Coventry Rd

B4114
30 Hodge Hill, Washwood Heath Rd

B4121
40 Bartley Green, Barnes Hill
40 Weoley, Shenley Lane

B4135
30 Soho and Victoria, Heath Street

Unclassified
30 Ash Green, Royal Oak Lane
30 Ash Green, St Giles Rd
30 Ash Green, Vicarage Lane
30 Coleshill, Station Rd
30 Oxley, The Droveway
30 St Alphege, Widney Manor Rd

West Yorkshire

M606
50 Mill Carr Hill Bridge

A58
40 Leeds, Easterly Rd

A61
40 Leeds, Alwoodley, Harrogate Rd
40 Leeds, Scott Hall Rd
40,60 Rothwell, Wakefield Rd

A62
30 Huddersfield, Manchester Rd
30 Kirklees, Birstall, Gelderd Rd
30 Slaithwaite, Manchester Rd

A64
40 Leeds, York Rd

A65
30 Guiseley, Otley Rd
40 Ilkley, Ilkley Rd

A616
40 Huddersfield, Woodhead Rd

A629
30 Cullingworth, Halifax Rd
50 Elland, Calderdale Way southbound
50 Halifax, Keighley Rd
30 Halifax, Ovenden Rd
30 Halifax, Skircoat Rd
30 Keighley, Halifax Rd
40 Shelley, Pennistone Rd

A635
30 Kirklees, Holmfirth, Holmfirth Rd

A636
30 Wakefield, Denby Dale Rd

A638
50 Ossett Bypass
30 Wakefield, Dewsbury Rd

A640
30 Huddersfield, Westbourne Rd

A642
30 Wakefield, Horbury, Northfield Lane

A644
30 Brighouse, Denholme Rd
30 Kirklees, Dewsbury, Huddersfield Rd
30 Mirfield, Huddersfield Rd

A645
30 Wakefield, Featherstone, Pontefract Rd
30 Wakefield, Featherstone, Wakefield Rd

A646
30 Calderdale, Cornholme, Burnley Rd
30 Calderdale, Luddenden Foot, Burnley Rd
30 Calderdale, Todmorden, Halifax Rd
30 Portsmouth, Burnley Rd jct Durn St
30 Todmorden, Halifax Rd jct Hallroyd Rd

A647
30 Bradford, Great Horton Rd
30 Clayton Heights, Highgate Rd
40 Pudsey, Bradford Rd

A650
30 Frizinghall, Bradford Rd

A651
30 Birkenshaw, Bradford Rd

A652
30 Batley, Bradford Rd
40 Birstall, Bradford Rd

A653
40 Leeds, Shaw Cross, Leeds Rd

A657
30 Shipley, Leeds Rd
30 Thackley, Leeds Rd

A6025
50 Elland, Elland Rd

A6036
30 Calderdale, Northowram, Bradford Rd

A6037/A650
40 Bradford, Shipley Airedale Rd

A6038
40 Baildon, Otley Rd
40 Esholt, Otley Rd

A6120
30 Leeds, Cross Gates, Station Rd

A6177
30 Bradford, Ingleby Rd
40 Bradford, Rooley Lane

A6186
30 Wakefield, Durkar, Asdale Rd

B6124
30 Wakefield, Batley Rd

B6144
30 Bradford, Haworth Rd Daisy Hill
30 Bradford, Toller Lane

B6145
30 Bradford, Thornton Rd

B6265
30 Stockbridge, Bradford Rd

B6269
40 Shipley, Cottingley Cliffe Rd

B6273
30 Wakefield, Kinsley, Wakefield Rd

B6380
30 Bradford, Beacon Rd

Unclassified
30 Bradford, Cutler Heights Lane
30 Bradford, Dick Lane
30 Bradford, Gain Lane
30 Bradford, Moore Avenue
30 Calderdale, Crag Lane
30 Huddersfield, Dalton, Long Lane
30 Leeds, Burley, Willow Rd/Cardigan Rd
30 Leeds, Horsforth, Low Lane
30 Leeds, Lawnswood, Otley Old Rd
30 Leeds, Sandford, Broad Lane
30 South Elmsall, Minsthorpe Lane
30 South Kirby, Minsthorpe
60 Walton, Wetherby Rd

Wiltshire and Swindon

M4
70 east and west of jct 15
70 east and west of jct 16
70 east and west of jct 17

A4
40 Froxfield
60 West Overton

A30
40 Fovant
60 The Pheasant

A36
60 Brickworth
60 Hanging Langford
50 Knook
30 Salisbury, Wilton Rd
60 south of Whaddon
60 Stapleford to East Clyffe

A303
50 Chicklade
60 Parsonage Down
60 Willoughby Hedge

A338
40 Bosscombe
30 nr Little Woodbury
60 nr Southgrove Copse

A342
60 Chirton to Charlton
30 Ludgershall, Andover Rd
50 Lydeway

A346
60 Chiseldon Firs
60 Whitefield

A350
60 Heywood
70 Pretty Chimneys

A354
40 Coombe Bissett

A360/A344
60 Airmans Corner

A361
60 Inglesham
60 nr Blackland Turning
70 nr jct with B3101
60 nr Shepherds Shore
30 Southwick
30 Trowbridge, Frome Rd
60 west of Beckhampton

A363
30 Bradford on Avon, Trowbridge Rd
30 North Bradley, Woodmarsh
40 Trowle Common

A419
70 Cricklade
70 nr Covingham
70 Widhill

A420
60 Giddeahall to Ford

A3026
40 Ludgershall, Tidworth Rd

A3028
40 Durrington, Larkhill Rd

A3102
30 Calme, Oxford Rd
30 Lyneham
30 Melksham, Sandridge Rd
30 Wootten Bassett

A4259
50 nr Coate
40 Swindon, Queens Drive

A4361
60 Broad Hinton
60 Uffcott Xrd
30 Wroughton, Swindon Rd

B390
60 Maddington Farm

B3105
30 Hilperton, Hill St/Marsh St

B4006
40 Swindon, Marlborough Rd

B3098
30 Bratton

B3106
30 Hilperton, Hammond Way

B3107
30 Bradford on Avon, Holt Rd

B4006
30 Stratton St Margaret, Swindon Rd
30 Swindon, Whitworth Rd

B4040
50 Leigh

B4041
30 Wootten Bassett, Station Rd

B4143
30 Swindon, Bridge End Rd

B4192
50 Liddington

B4289
40 Great Western Way nr Bruce St Bridges

B4553
40 Swindon, Tewkesbury Way

B4587
30 Swindon, Akers Way

Unclassified
30 Corsham, Park Lane
30 Swindon, Ermin St
30 Swindon, Merlin Way
30 Swindon, Moredon Rd
30 Trowbridge, Wiltshire Drive

Worcestershire

see West Mercia

Wales

Mid and South Wales

Blaenau Gwent, Bridgend, Caerphilly, Cardiff, Carmarthenshire, Merthyr Tydfil, Monmouthshire, Neath Port Talbot, Newport, Pembrokeshire, Rhondda Cynon Taff, Swansea, Torfaen, Vale of Glamorgan

M4
70 2km east of Jct35
30 east of Jct36, nr Sarn
40 1.5km west of Jct37, nr Pyle
30 Llanmartin Overbridge
30 Toll Plaza

A40
40 Bancyfelin Bypass
30 Buckland Hall, Brecon to Abergavenny
30 Johnstown, Carmarthen to St Clears
30 Llanhamlach, Brecon to Abergavenny
50 Llansantffried Jct
30 Monmouth, Llangattock Lodge
30 Rhosmaen
30 Scethrog, Brecon to Abergavenny
30 Trecastle
40 Whitemill

A44
30 Forest Bends
30 Gwystre
30 Llanbadarn Fawr
30 Llanfihangel, Nant Melan
30 Rhydgaled, Sweet Lamb

A48
30 Baglan, Dinas Baglan
30 Berryhill
40 Bonvilston
40 Castleton
50 Cowbridge, Cowbridge Bypass
30 Foelgastell
70 Langstone, Chepstow Rd
30 Llanddarog
30 Morriston, Clasemont Rd
30 Nantycaws
30 Parkwall, Parkwall Hill
30 north of Pont Abraham
30 Pontarddulais, Bolgoed Rd
30 Pontardulais, Carmarthen Rd
60 Pontardulais, Fforest Rd
30 Port Talbot, Margam Rd
30 Wenvoe, St Nicholas

A410
30 Porthcawl, The Porthway

A422
40 Cowbridge, Aberthin Rd

A438
30 Bronllys
60 Three Cocks

A449
30 north of Coldra
60 Llandenny
30 Llantrissent nr Usk

A458
60 Cefn Bridge
30 Llanfair Caereinion (Neuadd Bridge)
40 Trewern

A465
30 btwn Aberbaden and Llanfoist
40 Abergavenny, llanfoist
30 Abergavenny, Triley Mill
30 Glynneath Bank
30 Pandy
30 Resolven north
60 Rheola

A466
60 Llandogo
30 Monmouth, High Beech Rdbt to Old Hospital
30 Monmouth, Redbrook Rd
70 Monmouth, Whitecross Street
30 St Arvans to Livox Ends
40 Tintern

A467
30 Aberbeeg, Aberbeeg Rd
60 Abertillery, Aberbeeg Rd
40 Blaina, Abertillery Rd
70 Danycraig, Risca

A468
30 Machen Village
30 Rhiwderin, Caerphilly Rd

A469
30 Llanbradach, Lower Rhymney Valley Relief Rd
30 Tir-Y-Birth, New Rd

A470
30 Aberduhonw, south of Builth
30 Aberfan
30 Abernant, south of Builth
30 Beacons Reservoir
30 Cilfynydd
30 Erwood
30 Erwood South
30 Llandinam to Caersws Jct
30 Llanidloes to Llandinam
30 Llwyn y Celyn, Brecon to Merthyr
60 Llyswen
30 Newbridge to Rhayader, Argoed Mill
30 Newbridge on Wye
70 Rhydyfelin
30 nr Taffs Well
30 Ysgiog, south of Builth

A472
60 Hafodrynys, Hafod yr ynys Rd
30 Maes y cwmmer, Main Rd
30 Monkswood, Little Mill
30 Usk Bridge to Old Saw Mill
30 Ystrad Mynach to Nelson

A473
30 Bridgend, Bryntirion Hill
40 Bridgend, Coychurch Bypass
30 Bryncae, New Rd
30 Pencoed, Penybont Rd
30 Upper Boat, Main Rd

A474
60 Alltwen, Graig Rd
30 Briton Ferry, Briton Ferry Rd
40 Garnant, Glanffrwd Est Jct
40 Heol-y-Gors
60 Neath, Penywern Rd
30 Pontamman to Glanaman
60 Rhyd y Fro, Commercial St

A475
30 Lampeter, Pentrebach, County Rd
30 Llanwnen

A476
30 Carmel, Stag and Pheasant
30 Carmel to NSL at Temple Bar
30 Ffairfach, 30 mph to the Square
30 Gorslas, The Gate
40 Llannon, Erw Non Jct to Clos Rebecca Jct
30 Swiss Valley, Thomas Arms
30 Upper Tumble, Llannon Rd and Bethania Rd

A477
30 Llanddowror

A478
30 Clunderwen
30 Llandissilio, Nr school
30 Pentlepoir

A482 & A475
30 Lampeter

A482
30 Aberaeron, Lampeter Rd
30 Cwmann, North
30 Cwmann, South
30 Llanwrda

A483
30 Abbey Cwm Hir Jct
30 Ammanford, Penybanc Rd
30 north of Crossgates
30 south of Cwmgwili, Pontarddulais Rd
30 Ffairfach to Llandeilo Bridge
30 Garthmyl, Refail Garage
60 Garthmyl, Welshpool
30 Llandeilo, Rhosmaen St
30 Llandrindod, Midway Bends
30 Swansea, Fabian Way

A484
30 Bronwydd Village
30 Cenarth
50 Cwmffrwd
30 Cynwyl Elfed
30 Idole, from 200m s.w. of B4309 Jct south to NSL
30 Llanelli, Sandy Rd
60 Llanelli, Trostre Rdbt to Berwick Rdbt
30 Newcastle Emlyn
60 Pembrey
40 Pembrey, Lando Rd
60 Pentrecagel
30 Rhos
60 Saron

A485
40 Alltwalis
30 Cwmann, from the A482 Jct N
30 Llanllwwni
30 Llanybydder
50 Peniel

A486
30 Llandysul, Well Street
30 New Quay

A487 & A4120
30 Aberystwyth, Southgate

A487
30 Aberaeron, Greenland Terrace
30 Bow Street
30 Eglwyswrw
30 Furnace
30 Llanarth, Alma Street
30 Llanfarian
70 Llanrhystud
30 Newgale
40 Newport
30 Penparc
30 Rhydyfelin
30 Rhydypennau
30 Talybont
30 Waunfawr, Penglais Hill

A489
30 Caersws Jct to Penstrowed
30 Kerry, County Rd, Glanmule Garage
30 Newtown, west of Hafren coll
30 Penstrowed to Newtown

A490
40 Llanffyllin

A4042
30 Llanover
50 Mamhilad

A4043
40 Abersychan, Cwmavon Rd

A4046
30 Ebbw Vale (nr Tesco's)
70 Ebbw Vale, College Rd
40 Waunllwyd, Station Rd

A4047
30 Brynmawr, Beaufort Hill and High St

A4048
30 Argoed
30 Blackwood (Sunnybank)
30 Cwmfelinfach Village
30 Hollybush
30 Pontllanfraith, Blackwood Rd

A4050
40 Barry, Jenner Rd

A4054
30 Cilfynydd, Cilfynydd Rd
30 Edwardsville, Nantddu
30 Merthyr Vale, Cardiff Rd
30 Mountain Ash, New Rd
40 Pontypridd, Pentrebach Rd
70 Upper Boat, Cardiff Rd

A4055
30 Barry, Gladstone Rd

A4058
30 Pontypridd, Broadway

A4061
40 Ogmore Vale, Cemetery Rd

A4063
30 Llangynwyd, Bridgend Rd
30 Penyfai, Bridgend Rd
30 Sarn Bypass

A4066
60 Broadway
30 Pendine, Llanmiloe
40 Pendine, Marsh Rd

A4067
30 Abercraf By-pass
30 Crai
40 Mumbles Rd

A4068
30 Cwmtwrch, Bethel Rd
30 Cwmtwrch, Heol Gleien

A4069
40 Brynamman, Brynamman Rd
30 Llandovery, Broad St
30 Llangadog, Station Rd

A4075
40 Pembroke

A4076
30 Hubberston, St Lawrence Hill
30 Johnston, Milford Rd
30 Johnston, Vine Rd
40 Steynton, Steynton Rd

A4078
30 Carew

A4093
40 Blackmill
70 Glynogwr
40 Hendreforgan, Gilfach Rd

A4102
30 Gellideg, Swansea Rd

A4106
30 Porthcawl, Bridgend Rd
30 Porthcawl, Newton Nottage Rd

A4107
70 Abergwynfi, High St

A4109
70 Aberdulias, Main Rd
30 Crynant, Main Rd
40 Glynneath
40 Seven Sisters, Dulais Rd

A4118
30 Fairwood Common

A4119
30 Cardiff, Llantrisant Rd
30 Groesfaen
30 Llantrisant, Mwyndy Cross

A4139
30 Pembroke, Orange Way
30 Pembroke Dock, Bush Street
30 Tenby, Marsh Rd

A4216
30 Cockett, Cockett Rd

A4222
30 Brynsadler, Cowbridge Rd
30 Cowbridge, Cardiff Rd
30 Maendy, Maendy Rd

A4226
30 Rhoose, Waycock Rd

A4232
30 Cardiff, Ely Link

A4233
30 Ferndale, The Parade

B4181
30 Bridgend, Coity Rd

B4223
30 Gelli, Gelli Rd
30 Ton Pentre, Maindy Rd
30 Ton Pentre, Pentwyn Rd

B4235
30 Gwernesney nr Usk

B4236
30 Llanfrechfa, Caerleon Rd

B4237
30 Maesglas, Cardiff Rd
30 Newport, opp Power Station, Risca Rd

B4239
30 Newport, Lighthouse Rd

B4245
30 Langstone, Magor Rd
30 Leechpool, Cartref to Uplands
30 Penpedairheol, Pengam Rd
40 Rogiet, Caldicot Rd
60 Rogiet, Green Farm

B4246
40 Abersychan, Varteg
60 Garndiffaith, New Rd

B4248
70 Blaenavon, Garn Rd

B4251
30 Abergavenny, Hereford Rd
40 Caerphilly, Kendon Hill

B4265
40 Llantwit Major, Llantwit Major Bypass
30 St Brides Major, Ewenny Rd
30 St Brides Major, St Brides Rd

B4275
30 Abercynon, Abercynon Rd

B4278
30 Dinas, Dinas Rd
30 Tonyrefail, Penrhiwfer Rd

B4281
30 Cefn Cribwr, Cefn Rd
30 Kenfig Hill, High St

B4282
30 Bryn, Measteg Rd
30 Maesteg, Bridgend Rd and Castle St

B4283
30 North Cornelly, Heol Fach

B4290
30 Jersey Marine, New Rd
30 Skewen, Burrows Rd
30 Skewen, Pen-yr-Heol and Crymlyn Rd

B4293
70 Trellech Village
40 Trellech, Monmouth Road

B4295
30 Crofty, New Rd
30 btwn Gowerton and Penclawdd
30 btwn Penclawdd and Llanrhidian

B4296
40 Waungren, Pentre Rd

B4297
30 Bynea, Lougher Bridge Rdbt to Station Rd Jct
30 Capel Hendre
60 Fforest
40 Llanedi
30 Llangennech, Cleviston Park Jct to Park Lane Jct
30 Llangennech, Pontarddulais Rd
30 Llwynhendy, from Capel Soar to the Police Station

B4301
30 Bronwydd Village

B4302
30 Talley

B4303
30 Llanelli, Dafen Rdbt to Felinfoel Rdbt

B4304
40 Llanelli, Copperworks Rdbt to Morfa Rdbt
30 Llanelli, Lower Trostre Rd Rdbt to Trostre Rd Rdbt
60 Llanelli, New Dock Rd

B4306
40 Bancffosfelen, Heol Y Banc
50 Crwbin
40 Hendy, Heol Y Banc
30 Llangendeirn
30 Pontyberem, Llanon Rd

B4308
30 Penmynnydd

B4309
30 Cynheidre
60 Five Roads

B4310
30 Drefach, Heol Caegwyn

B4312
30 Llangain

B4314
30 Moorfield Road, Nr school
30 Pendine

B4317
30 Carway, East
30 Carway, West
70 Ponthenri, Myrtle Hill
30 Pontyberem, Heol Capel Ifan
30 Pontyberem, Station Rd

B4320
30 Hundleton

B4322
40 Pembroke Dock, Pembroke Rd

B4325
30 Llanstadwell, Honeyborough Rd
60 Neyland, High Street
60 Neyland, The Promenade

B4328
30 Whitland, Trevaughan

B4333
30 Cynwyl Elfed (North)
30 Hermon
30 Newcastle Emlyn, Aber-arad

B4336
60 Llandysul, Pont-tyweli
30 Llanfihangel Ar Arth

B4337
30 Llanybydder
30 Talsarn

B4347
30 Newcastle Village

B4350
60 Glasbury, Llwyn au bach

B4436
30 Bishopton, Northway
30 Killay, Goetre Fawr Rd
40 Kittle, Pennard Rd

B4459
30 Pencader

B4471
30 Llanhilleth, Oak Leaf Terrace, Commercial Rd

B4478
30 Beaufort, Letchworth Rd

B4486
30 Ebbw Vale, Steelworks Rd

B4524
30 Corntown, Corntown Rd

B4538
30 Cardigan

B4556
70 Blaenau, Penygroes Rd
70 Caerbryn
70 Pengroes, Norton Rd

B4560
40 Beaufort, Ebbw Vale, Llangynidr Rd

B4591
30 Highcross, Risca Rd
30 Pontymister, Risca Rd
30 Risca, opp Power Station, Risca Rd

B4598
30 Abergavenny, Horse and Jockey
30 Llancayo

B4599
30 Ystradgynlais

B4603
40 Clydach, Pontardawe Rd
30 Ynystawe, Clydach Rd

B4622
30 Bridgend, Broadlands Link Rd

B4623
40 Caerphilly, Mountain Rd

Unclassified
40 Aberbargoed, Bedwellty and Coedymoeth Rd Jct
30 Abercwmboi, Park View Terrace
30 Abergwili, Ambulance Station to the Bypass Rdbt
60 Abersychan, Foundry Rd
60 Abertillery, Gwern Berthi
60 Abertillery, Roseheyworth Rd
30 Aberystwyth Town, Park Avenue
60 Ammanford, Dyffryn Rd
70 Ammanford, New Rd and Pantyffynnon Rd
30 Ammanford, layby outside Saron Church, Saron Rd
30 Barry, Buttrills Rd
30 Barry, Holton Rd
30 Barry, Winston Rd
40 Beddau, Bryniteg Hill
30 Beddau, Gwaunmiskin Rd
70 Betws, Betws Rd
30 Betws, Maesquarre Rd
30 Birchgrove, Birchgrove Rd
30 Blaenavon, Upper Coedcae Rd
30 Blaina, Bourneville Rd
30 Blaina, Farm Rd
30 Blaina, Surgery Rd
30 Brackla, Brackla Way
30 Bridgend, Pen-Y-Cae Lane
30 Bridgend Ind Est, Kingsway
30 Bridgend Ind Est, North Rd
30 Bridgend Ind Est, South Rd
30 Bridgend Ind Est, Western Avenue
30 Britton Ferry, Old Rd
40 Brynna, Brynna Rd
40 Caerleon, Ponthir Rd
30 Caerphilly, Lansbury Park Ring Rd
30 Caldicot, Chepstow Rd
30 Cardiff, Cherry Orchard Rd, M4 bridge site
30 Cardiff, Cyncoed Rd
30 Cardiff, Excalibur Drive
30 Cardiff, Heath, Maescoed Rd
30 Cardiff, Heol Isaf
30 Cardiff, Leckwith Rd
30 Cardiff, Newport Rd
30 Cardiff, Pencisely Rd
30 Cardiff, Penylan, Colchester Avenue
30 Cardiff, Rhiwbina Hill
30 Cardiff, Roath, Lake Rd East/West
30 Cardiff, St Fagans Rd
30 Cardiff, Westloog Avenue
30 Cardiff, Willowbrook Drive
30 Carmarthen, Lime Grove Avenue and Fountain Head Tce
30 Cefn Glas, Merlin Crescent
30 Cefncoed, High St
30 Cefncoed, Vaynor Rd
30 Cefneithin
30 Chepstow, Mathern Rd
30 Church Village, Station Rd
40 Clydach, Vadre Rd
30 Coity, Heol Spencer
60 Coldharbour, Usk to Raglan Rd
30 Crumlin, Hafodyrynys Hill
40 Cwm Govilon, Bryn Awelon Rd
30 Cwmavon, Cwmavon Rd
30 Cwmbran, Greenforge Way
30 Cwmbran, Henllys Way
30 Cwmbran, Hollybush Way
30 Cwmbran, Llanfrechfa Way
30 Cwmbran, Maendy Way
70 Cwmbran, Pontnewydd, Chapel Street
30 Cwmbran, Thornhill Rd
30 Cwmbran, Ty Canol Way
30 Cwmbran, Ty Gwyn Way and Greenmeadow Way
30 Cwmbran, Upper Cwmbran Rd
30 Cwmgwili
70 Cwmgwili, Thornhill Rd
60 Deri, New Rd
30 Derwen Fawr, Rhy-Y-Defaid Drive
30 Dinas Powys, Pen-y-turnpike Rd
30 Dowlais, High St
50 Drefach, Heol Blawnhirwaun
30 Ebbw Vale, Newchurch Rd
30 Felinfoel, Llethri Rd
30 Fforest Fach, Carmarthen Rd
60 Fochrie, Olgivie Terrace
30 Forden
50 Gelli, Gelli Ind Est
30 Gelligaer, Church Rd
30 Gilwern, Cae Meldon (aka Ty Mawr Lane)
30 Glyncorrwg, Heol y Glyn
30 Gorseinon, Frampton Rd
70 Gorslas, Pengroes Rd
30 Grovesend
30 Haverfordwest, New Rd/Uzmaston Rd
30 Heol-Tai-Mawr
30 Hopkinstown, Hopkinstown Rd
30 Johnstown, St Clears Rd
50 Llanbradach, Coed y Brain Rd to Glyn Bedw
30 Llanelli, Denham Avenue
30 Llanelli, Heol Goffa
30 Llanfihangel Ar Arth (South)
30 Llangan
30 Llangyfelach, Swansea Rd
30 Llanharan, Brynna Rd
30 Llanhenock, Caerleon to Usk Rd – Apple tree farm
30 Llantwit Major, Llanmaes Rd
30 Maesteg, Heol-Ty-Gwyn
30 Maesteg, Heol Ty-Wyth
30 Malpas, Rowan Way
30 Merthyr Vale, Nixonvale
30 Merthyr Tydfil, Brecon Rd
30 Merthyr Tydfil, Goatmill Rd
30 Merthyr Tydfil, Gumos Rd
30 Merthyr Tydfil, Heolgerrig Rd
30 Merthyr Tydfil, Plymouth St
30 Merthyr Tydfil, Rocky Rd
30 Merthyr Tydfil, The Walk
30 Milford Haven, Priory Rd
40 Milford Haven, Thornton Rd
30 Monmouth, Devauden Village
60 Monmouth, Dixton Rd
30 Monmouth, Llangybi
70 Monmouth, Magor (West)
30 Morriston, Caemawr Rd
30 Mount Pleasant, Cardiff Rd
30 Mountain Ash, Llanwonno Rd
30 Mountain Ash, Miskin Rd
30 Nantgarw, Oxford St
30 Nantycaws Hill
30 Nash Village, West Nash Rd
60 New Tredegar, White Roase Way
30 Newbridge, Park Rd
30 Newport, Allt-Yr-Yn Avenue
30 Newport, Corporation Rd
40 Newport, Marshfield Rd
30 North Connelly, Fairfield Rd
30 Pant, Pant Rd
60 Pembroke Rd
30 Pencoed, Felindre Rd
30 Pendine
60 Pentrecagel
30 Penydarren, High Street
30 Pontardawe, Ynys-Meudwy Rd
40 Ponthir, Caerleon Rd
30 Pontllanfraith, Bryn Rd
60 Pontlottyn, Southend Terrace
30 Pontnewynydd, Plas Y Coed Rd
40 Pontyclun, Cowbridge Rd
60 Pontypool, Little Mill
40 Porthcawl, Fulmar Rd
30 Portskewett, Caldicot Rd
30 Rassau, Reservoir Rd
30 Rhymney, Llys Joseph Parry (nr Farmers Arms)
30 Rhymney, Wellington Way
30 Risca, Cromwell Rd
40 Risca, Holly Rd
30 Rogerstone, Pontymason Lane
30 Rogerstone, Tregwillym Rd
30 St Athan, Cowbridge Rd
50 Sandfields, Village Rd
30 Saron
30 Seven Sisters, Golwg-y-Bryn
30 Sully, Hayes Rd
30 Sully, South Rd
30 Swansea, Mynydd Newydd Rd, Caemawr Rd, Parry Rd, Vicarage Rd
30 Swansea, Pentregethin Rd
30 Tiers Cross
30 Tonteg, Church Rd
30 Tonyrefail, Gilfach Rd
30 Trebanos, Swansea Rd
30 Treboeth, Llangyfelach Rd
30 Tredegar, Merthyr Rd
30 Tredegar, Vale Terrace
30 Trehafod, Gyfeillion Rd
30 Trelewis, Gelligaer Rd
30 Usk, Maryport St
30 Usk, Porthycarne St
30 Whitland
30 Whitland, Market St
40 Whitland (East), Spring Gardens
30 Willowtow, Gwaun Helyg Rd
30 Ynysawdre, Heol-Yr-Ysgol
40 Ynysybwl, New Rd
30 Ystrad Mynah, Pengram Rd

North Wales

Ceredigion, Conwy, Denbighshire, Flintshire, Gwynedd, Isle of Anglesey, Powys, Wrexham

A5
30 Holyhead

A5/A5025
50 Holyhead to Llanfachraeth

A470
30,60 Conwy Valley
40,60 Dolgellau
40,60 (30 at rdbts) Llandudno to the A55
30,40,60 Tal-y-waenydd to Congl-y-wal (Blaenau)

A483/A5
60 Ruabon to Chirk

A487
30,40,50,60 Caernarfon to Dolbenmaen
30,40,60 Penmorfa to Gellilydan

A494
40,60 Bala to Glanrafon
30 Llyn Tegid, Bala
40,60 Ruthin to Llanferres

A496
30,40,60 Harlech to Llanbedr

A499
30,40,60 Pwllheli

A525
40,60 Denbigh to Ruthin
30,40,60 Llanfair Dyffryn Clwyd to Llandegla
30,60 Wrexham to Minera
30,40,60 Wrexham to Redbrook Maelor

A534
30 Holt Rd

A539
30,60 Llangollen, Mill St
30,40,60 Trevor to Erbistock

A541
30 Mold Rd
30,40,60,70 Mold to Caergwrle
30,40,60,70 Wrexham to Cefn-y-bedd

A541/525
30,40,60 St Asaph to Bodfari

A545
30,40 Menai Bridge to Beaumaris

A547
30,40,50 Colwyn Bay
30,40,60 Prestatyn to Rhuddlan
30 Rhyl, Vale Rd/Rhuddlan Rd

A548
30,40 Abergele to Kinmel Bay
30 Abergele, Dundonald Avenue
30,40,50,60,70 Gronant to Flint (Oakenholt)
30,40 Rhyl to Prestatyn

A549
30,60 Mynydd Isa to Buckley

A550/B5125
30 Hawarden

A4086
30,40,60 Cwm-y-glo to Llanrug

A4212
60 Graig Las/Tryweryn to Trawsfynydd

A4244
60 Ty Mawr to Cym-y-glo

A5025
30,40,50,60 Amlwch, Menai Bridge

A5104
30 Coed-Talon to Leeswood

A5112
30,40 Llandygai to Bangor

A5119
30,50,60 Mold to Flint

A5152
30,60 Bala
30 Chester Rd
30,40 Rhostyllen

B4545
30,40 Kingsland to Valley

B5108
30,60 Benllech

B5109
30 Llangefni

B5113
30 Colwyn Bay, Kings Rd/Kings Drive

B5115
30 Llandrillo, Llandudno Rd
30,40 Llandudno Promenade to Rhos Point

B5118
30 Rhyl Promenade

B5120
30 Prestatyn, Pendyffryn Rd

B5129
30,60 Kelsterton to Saltney Ferry

B5420
30 Menai Bridge

B5425
30,60 Llay, New Rd

B5443
30 Rossett

Unclassified
30,40,60 Johnstown
30,60 Kinmel Bay, St Asaph Avenue
30,40,60 Menai Bridge to Gwalchmai

Scotland

Dumfries and Galloway

A74(M)
70 Cogries

A7
60 Langholm

A76
Auldgirth
60 Closeburn
30 Dumfries, Glasgow Rd
Gateside

A77
60 Balyett
60 Cairnryan
60 Whiteleys

A701
30 Moffat
60 Mollinburn/St Anns

A709
60 Burnside

A711
50 Beeswing
30 Kirkcudbright

A716
60 Stoneykirk

A718
60 Craichmore

B721
30 Eastriggs

Fife

A91
Deer Centre to Stratheden Jct
Guardbridge to St Andrews
Melville Lodges to St Andrews

A92
Cadham to New Inn
Cardenden Overbridge to Chapel
Cowdenbeath to Lochgelly
Crossgates to New Inn
Melville Lodges to Lindifferon
New Inn to Tay Bridge
Rathillet (south) to Easter Kinnear

A823
Dunfermline, Queensferryroad
Dunfermline, St Margaret Drive

A907
Dunfermline, Halbeath Rd

A911
Glenrothes to Leslie
Glenrothes to Milton

A914
Edenwood to Cupar
Forgan to St Michaels
Kettlebridge
New Inn to Cupar
Pitlessie to Clushford Toll

A915
Checkbar Jct to Percival Jcts

A921
Kirkcaldy, Esplanade
Kirkcaldy, High St/Path
Kirkcaldy, Rosslyn St
Kirkcaldy, St Clair St

A977
Kincardine, Fere Gait

A985
Culross (west) to C38 Valleyfield
Kincardine to Rosyth
Rosyth, Admiralty Rd
Waukmill to Brankholm

B914
Redcraigs to Greenknowes

B942
East of Collinsburgh

B980
Rosyth, Castlandhill Rd

B981
Cowdenbeath, Broad St
Gosshill to Ballingry
Kirkcaldy, Dunnikier Way

B9157
Bankhead of Pitheadle to Kirkcaldy
Orrock to East Balbairdie
Sheriff Rdbt to Kirkcaldy
White Lodge Jct to Croftgary

Unclassified
Buckhaven, Methilhaven Rd
Dunfermline, Townhill Rd
Glenrothes, Formonthills Rd
Glenrothes, Woodside Rd
Glenrothes, Woodside Way
Kirkcaldy, Hendry Rd
Leven, Glenlyon Rd
Methil, Methilhaven Rd

Lothian and Borders

East Lothian, Edinburgh, Midlothian, Scottish Borders, West Lothian

A7
60 Crookston
NSL Galashiels, Buckholmside to Bowland
30 Hawick Sandbed to Galalaw
30 Stow to Bowland

A8
40 Edinburgh, at Ratho station

A68
30 Jedburgh
NSL Soutra Hill

A70
30 Edinburgh, Balerno between Bridge Rd and Stewart Rd

A71
30 Breich
30 Polbeth

A72
NSL Borders, Holylee nr Walkerburn
NSL Castlecraig nr Blyth bridge
30 Peebles, Innerleithen Rd

A90
40 Edinburgh, Southbound from Burnshot flyover to Cammo Rd

A697
30 Greenlaw and south approach
NSL Orange Lane
NSL Ploughlands to Hatchednize

A697/8
30 Coldstream

A698
NSL Ashybank
NSL Crailinghall

A699
40 Maxton Village

A701
NSL Blyth Bridge to Cowdenburn
30 Rachan Mill, Broughton to A72

A702
NSL Dolphinton to Medwyn Mains

A703
30 Eddleston and approaches
NSL Leadburn to Shiplaw
30 Peebles to Milkieston
30 Peebles, Edinburgh Rd

A705
30 between Whitburn and East Whitburn

A706
30 Whitburn, Carnie Place

A720
50 Edinburgh, City Bypass, east of Gogar Rdbt

A899
50 btwn Lizzie Bryce Rdbt and Almond Interchange
50 South of Deer Park Rdbt

A6091
NSL Melrose bypass

A6105
30 Gordon and approaches

B6374
30 Galashiels, Station Bridge to Lowood Bridge

Unclassified
30 Edinburgh, Bruntsfield place btwn Thorneybauk and Merchiston place
40 Edinburgh, Comiston Rd btwn Oxgangs Rd and Buckstone Dr
40,60 Edinburgh, Frogston Rd west btwn Mountholy loan and Mortonhall gate
30 Edinburgh, Lower Granton Rd btwn Granton Square and Trinity Rd
30 Edinburgh, Muirhouse Parkway
40 Edinburgh, West Approach Rd btwn Morrison St Link and Dundee St
30 Edinburgh, West Granton Rd
30 Whitburn, West Main St

North East Scotland

Aberdeen, Aberdeenshire, Moray

A90
40 Aberdeen, Midstocket Rd to Whitestripes Avenue Rdbt
60 btwn bend at South of Leys and Bogbrae
60 btwn Bogbrae and north of Bridgend
70 btwn Candy and Upper Criggie
60 btwn Jct with B9032 and A98 at Fraserburgh
70 btwn Laurencekirk and north of Fourdon
70 btwn Mill of Barnes and Laurencekirk
60 btwn St Fergus and access Rd to Bilbo
70 Dundee to Aberdeen Rd at Jct with B9120 Laurencekirk
70 north of Newtonhill Jct to South of Schoolhill Rd
60 Peterhead and St Fergus, btwn A982 North Rd
60 Peterhead, btwn north of Bridgend and Blackhills
70 Portlethen to South Damhead (southbound), south of Schoolhill Rd
70 south of Schoolhill Rd, Portlethen to South Damhead (northbound)

A92
60 btwn Johnshaven and Inverbervie
60 btwn rdside of Kinneff and Mill of Uras

A93
30 Aboyne
40 at Banchory eastbound from Caravan Site
30 at Banchory westbound from Church
60 btwn Cambus O'May and Dinnet
60 btwn Dinnet to Aboyne
60 btwn Kincardine O'Neil and Haugh of Sluie

A95
30 Cornhill
60 btwn 30mph at Keith and Davoch of Grange

A96
60 btwn East Mill of Carden at B9002 Jct and north of Pitmachie
60 btwn Forgie and A98 Jct at Fochabers
60 btwn north of Pitmachie and Jct with A920 at Kirton of Culsalmond
30 Haudigain rdbt to Chapel of Stoneywood
60 Mosstodloch to Lhanbryde (East)
40 South Damhead to Midstocket Rd

A98
30 Banff
60 btwn Carnoch Farm Rd, Buckie and 30mph at Cullen
60 btwn Fochabers 30mph and Mill of Tynet
60 Buckle, btwn Mill of Tynet and Barhill Rd Jct

A941
60 btwn 30mph at Lossiemouth and 40mph at Elgin
60 btwn Clackmarras Rd and South Netherglen
60 btwn Glassgreen and Clackmarras Rd
60 from South Netherglen and Rothes

A947
60 btwn Mains of Tulloch Jct and Fyvie
60 btwn Newmachar and Whiterashes

A948
60 btwn Ellon to Auchnagatt

A952
60 btwn New Leeds and Jct with A90 at Cortes

B9040
60 btwn Silver Sands Caravan Park to Jct with B9012

B9089
60 from Kinloss and crossroads at Roseisle Maltings

Unclassified
30 Aberdeen, Beach Boulevard to Links Rd
30 Aberdeen, Beach Boulevard to Wales St
30 Aberdeen, Great Northern Rd
30 Aberdeen, Great Southern Rd
30 Aberdeen, King St
30 Aberdeen, Springhill Rd
30 Aberdeen, St Machar Drive
40 Aberdeen, Wellington Rd
40 Aberdeen, West Tullos Rd

Northern Scotland

Highland, Orkney, Shetland, Western Isles

A9
Altnasleanach by Inverness
Caulmaillie, Golspie, Sutherland
Cuaich by Dalwhinnie
Daviot, by Inverness
Fearn, by Tain
North Kessock jct (both directions)
North of Dalwhinnie junction nr Dalwhinnie
South of the Mound, by Golspie

A82
Altsigh Youth Hostel, by Inverness
Drumnadrochit, Temple Pier
Invergarry Power Station
Kingshouse Hotel, Glencoe
White Corries, Rannoch Moor, Lochaber

A87
West of Bunloyne jct

A95
by Grantown on Spey, Congash
Drumuillie by Boat of Garten
North of Cromdale

A96
East Auldearn jct, by Nairn
Gollanfield, by Nairn
Nairn, West Auldern Jct
West of Allanfearn jct, by Inverness

A99
Hempriggs, south of Wick

A834
Dingwall, nr Foddarty Bridge
Dingwall, Strathpeffer Rd

A835
Inverlael straight nr Ullapool

A939
Ferness to Grantown, Spey Rd

B9006
Sunnyside, Culloden, Inverness

Strathclyde

Argyll & Bute, East Ayrshire, East Dunbartonshire, East Renfrewshire, Glasgow, Inverclyde, North Ayrshire, North Lanarkshire, Renfrewshire, South Ayrshire, South Lanarkshire, West Dunbartonshire

M74
Abington, Jct 13 (northbound)

A70
East Tarelgin

A73
Airdrie, Carlisle Rd

A76
New Cumnock, nr Lime Rd

A78
Fairlie, Main Rd

A82
Bridge of Orchy
Milton, Dunbarton Rd

A85
west of Tyndrum

A89
Airdrie, Forrest St

A706
South of Forth

A730
Rutherglen, Blairbeth Rd

A737
Dairy, New St/Kilwinning Rd

A749
East Kilbride Rd btwn Cathkin Rd and Cairnmuir Rd

A807
Bardowie, Balmore Rd

A814
Dunbarton, Cardross Rd

A815
nr Ardkinglass

B768
Rutherglen, Burnhill St

B803
Airdrie to Glenmavis, Coatbridge Rd

B814
Duntocher Rd

B8048
Kirkintilloch, Waterside Rd

Unclassified
Bargeddie, Glasgow Rd
Barrhead, Aurs Rd
Bishopbriggs, Woodhill Rd
Clydebank, Glasgow Rd
Coatbridge, Townhead Rd
Drymen Rd/Duntocher Rd
East Kilbride, Maxwelton Rd
at Kirkoswald (South)
Johnstone, Beith Rd
Neilston, Kingston Rd
Newton Mearns, Mearns Rd
Paisley, Glasgow Rd nr Newtyle Rd
Rutherglen, Glasgow Rd
Rutherglen, Mill St
Troon, Craigend Rd

Tayside

Angus, Dundee, Perth & Kinross

A9
60 Inverness to Perth road, nr Balnansteuartach
70 Perth to Inverness road, nr Inveralmond Industrial Estate
70 Stirling to Perth road, btwn Broom of Dalreoch and Upper Cairnie
70 Stirling to Perth road, Tibbermore jct

A90
40 Dundee nr Fountainbleau Drive, Forfar Rd
70 Dundee to Perth road, Walnut Grove to Inchyra
70 Dundee to Perth road, west of Longforgan village
50 Dundee, Kingsway
50 Dundee, Swallow rdbt to Strathmartine Rd rdbt

A91
60 Milnathort to Devon Bridge

A92
60 Arbroath to Montrose
30 Dundee btwn Arbroath Rd and Craigie Avenue, Greendykes Rd
40 Dundee, East Dock St

A93
60 Guildtown to Blairgowrie
60 Old Scone to Guildtown

A94
60 Scone to Coupar Angus

A822
60 Crieff to Braco

A923
60 Blairgowrie to Tullybaccart

A933
60 Colliston to Redford

A935
60 Brechin to Montrose

A972
40 Dundee, Kingsway East to Pitairlie Rd

A977
60 Kinross to Crook of Devon

B961
30 Dundee, Drumgeith Rd

B996
60 Kinross to Kelty

Unclassified
30 Dundee, Broughty Ferry Rd
30 Dundee, Charleston Drive
30 Dundee, Laird St
30 Dundee, Old Glamis Rd
30 Dundee, Perth Rd
30 Dundee, Strathmartine Rd

Abbreviations

adj	adjacent
btwn	between
j/w	junction with
nr	near
NSL	National Speed Limit
o/s	outside
rdbts	roundabouts
twds	towards

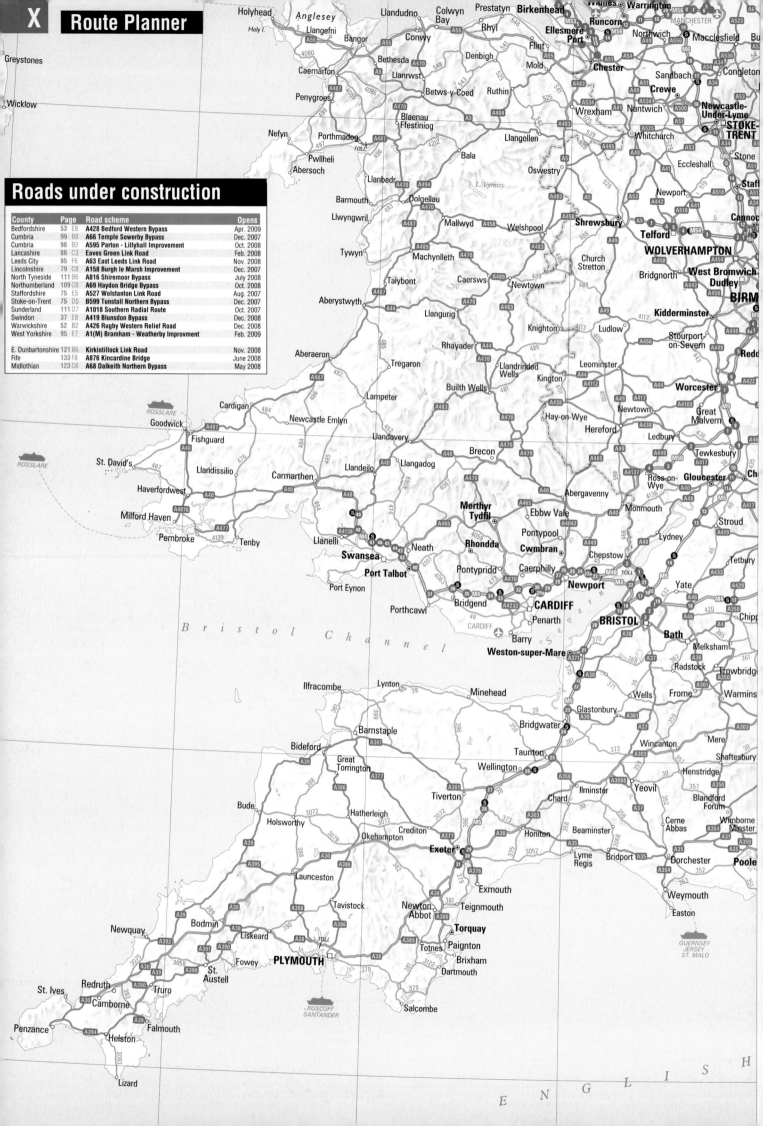

Roads under construction

County	Page		Road scheme	Opens
Bedfordshire	53	E8	A428 Bedford Western Bypass	Apr. 2009
Cumbria	99	B8	A66 Temple Sowerby Bypass	Dec. 2007
Cumbria	98	B2	A595 Parton - Lillyhall Improvement	Oct. 2008
Lancashire	86	C3	Eaves Green Link Road	Feb. 2008
Leeds City	95	F6	A63 East Leeds Link Road	Nov. 2008
Lincolnshire	79	C8	A158 Burgh le Marsh Improvement	Dec. 2007
North Tyneside	111	B6	A816 Shiremoor Bypass	July 2008
Northumberland	109	C8	A69 Haydon Bridge Bypass	Oct. 2008
Staffordshire	75	E5	A527 Wolstanton Link Road	Aug. 2007
Stoke-on-Trent	75	D5	B599 Tunstall Northern Bypass	Dec. 2007
Sunderland	111	D7	A1018 Southern Radial Route	Oct. 2007
Swindon	37	E8	A419 Blunsdon Bypass	Dec. 2008
Warwickshire	52	B2	A426 Rugby Western Relief Road	Dec. 2008
West Yorkshire	95	E7	A1(M) Bramham - Weatherby Improvment	Feb. 2009
E. Dunbartonshire	121	B6	Kirkintilloch Link Road	Nov. 2008
Fife	133	F8	A876 Kincardine Bridge	June 2008
Midlothian	123	C6	A68 Dalkeith Northern Bypass	May 2008

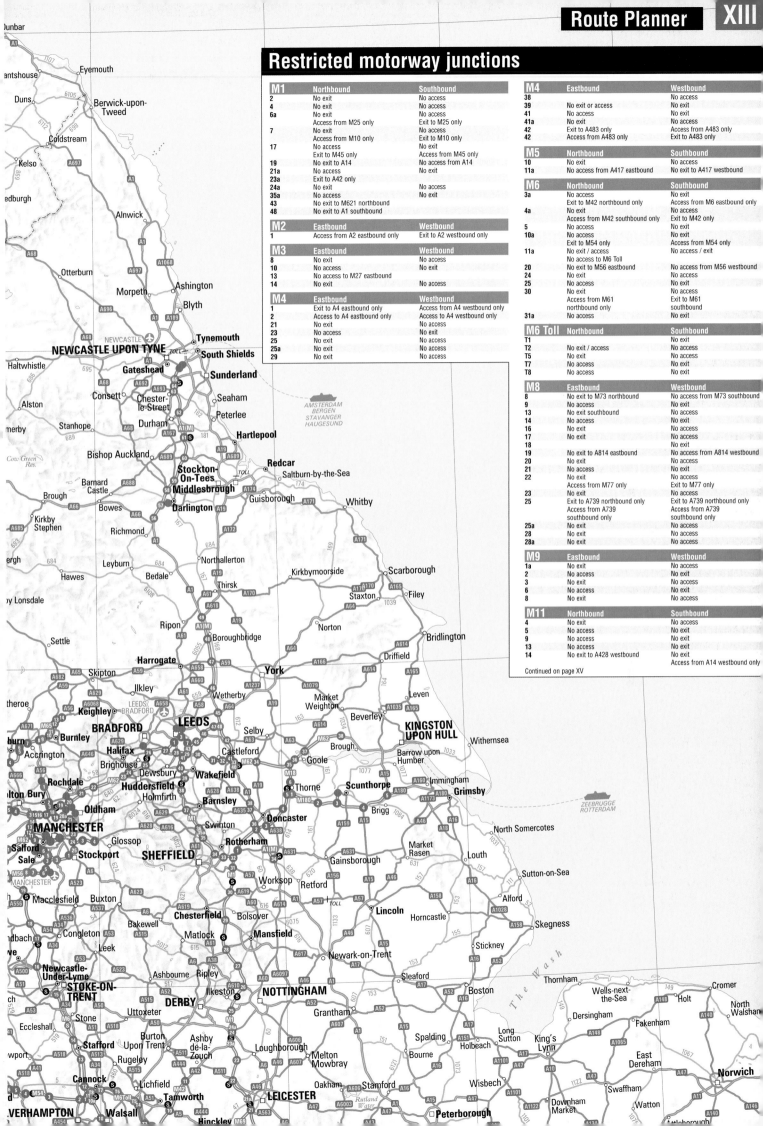

Restricted motorway junctions

M1	Northbound	Southbound
2	No exit	No access
4	No exit	No access
6a	No exit	No access
	Access from M25 only	Exit to M25 only
7	No exit	No access
	Access from M10 only	Exit to M10 only
17	No access	No exit
	Exit to M45 only	Access from M45 only
19	No exit to A14	No access from A14
21a	No access	No exit
23a	Exit to A42 only	
24a	No exit	No access
35a	No access	No exit
43	No exit to M621 northbound	
48	No exit to A1 southbound	

M2	Eastbound	Westbound
1	Access from A2 eastbound only	Exit to A2 westbound only

M3	Eastbound	Westbound
8	No exit	No access
10	No access	No exit
13	No access to M27 eastbound	
14	No exit	No access

M4	Eastbound	Westbound
1	Exit to A4 eastbound only	Access from A4 westbound only
2	Access to A4 eastbound only	Access to A4 westbound only
21	No exit	No access
23	No access	No exit
25	No exit	No access
25a	No exit	No access
29	No exit	No access

M4	Eastbound	Westbound
38		No access
39	No exit or access	No exit
41	No access	No exit
41a	No exit	No access
42	Exit to A483 only	Access from A483 only
42	Access from A483 only	Exit to A483 only

M5	Northbound	Southbound
10	No exit	No access
11a	No access from A417 eastbound	No exit to A417 westbound

M6	Northbound	Southbound
3a	No access	No exit
	Exit to M42 northbound only	Access from M6 eastbound only
4a	No exit	Access from M42 southbound only	Exit to M42 only
5	No access	No exit
10a	No access	No exit
	Exit to M54 only	Access from M54 only
11a	No exit / access	No access / exit
	No access to M6 Toll	
20	No exit to M56 eastbound	No access from M56 westbound
24	No exit	No access
25	No access	No exit
30	No exit	No access
	Access from M61 northbound only	Exit to M61 southbound
31a	No access	No exit

M6 Toll	Northbound	Southbound
T1		No exit
T2	No exit / access	No access
T5	No exit	No access
T7	No access	No access
T8	No access	No exit

M8	Eastbound	Westbound
8	No exit to M73 northbound	No access from M73 southbound
9	No access	No exit
13	No exit southbound	No access
14	No access	No exit
16	No exit	No access
17	No exit	No access
18		No exit
19	No exit to A814 eastbound	No access from A814 westbound
20	No exit	No access
21	No access	No exit
22	No exit	No access
	Access from M77 only	Exit to M77 only
23	No exit	No access
25	Exit to A739 northbound only	Exit to A739 northbound only
	Access from A739 southbound only	Access from A739 southbound only
25a	No exit	No access
28	No access	No access
28a	No exit	No access

M9	Eastbound	Westbound
1a	No exit	No access
2	No access	No exit
3	No exit	No access
6	No access	No exit
8	No exit	No access

M11	Northbound	Southbound
4	No exit	No access
5	No access	No exit
9	No access	No exit
13	No access	No exit
14	No exit to A428 westbound	No exit
		Access from A14 westbound only

Continued on page XV

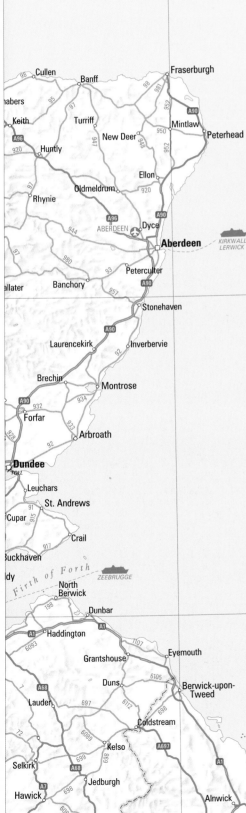

Restricted motorway junctions

Continuation from page XIII

M20
	Eastbound	Westbound
2	No access	No exit
3	No exit	No access
	Access from M26 eastbound only	Exit to M26 westbound only
11a	No access	No exit

M23
	Northbound	Southbound
7	No exit to A23 southbound	No access from A23 northbound
10a	No exit	No access

M25
	Clockwise	Anticlockwise
5	No exit to M26 eastbound	No access from M26 westbound
19	No access	No exit
21	No exit to M1 southbound	No exit to M1 southbound
	Access from M1 southbound only	Access from M1 southbound only
31	No exit	No access

M27
	Eastbound	Westbound
10	No exit	No access
12	No access	No exit

M40
	Eastbound	Westbound
3	No exit	No access
7	No exit	No access
8	No exit	No access
13	No exit	No access
14	No access	No exit
16	No access	No exit

M42
	Northbound	Southbound
1	No exit	No access
7	No access	No exit
	Exit to M6 northbound only	Access from M6 northbound only
7a	No access	No exit
	Exit to M6 only	Access from M6 northbound only
8	No exit	Exit to M6 northbound
	Access from M6 southbound only	Access from M6 southbound only

M45
	Eastbound	Westbound
M1 junc 17	Access to M1 southbound only	No access from M1 southbound
With A45 (Dunchurch)		No exit

M48
	Eastbound	Westbound
M4 junc 21	No exit to M4 westbound	No access from M4 eastbound
M4 junc 23	No access from M4 westbound	No exit to M4 eastbound

M49
	Southbound
18a	No exit to M5 northbound

M53
	Northbound	Southbound
11	Exit to M56 eastbound only	Exit to M56 eastbound only
	Access from M56 westbound only	Access from M56 westbound only

M56
	Eastbound	Westbound
2	No exit	No access
3	No access	No exit
4	No exit	No access
7		No access
8	No exit or access	No exit
9	No access from M6 northbound	No access to M6 southbound
15	No exit to M53	No access from M53 northbound

M57
	Northbound	Southbound
3	No exit	No access
5	No exit	No access

M58
	Eastbound	Westbound
1	No exit	No access

M60
	Clockwise	Anticlockwise
2	No exit	No access
3	No exit to A34 northbound	No exit to A34 northbound
4	No access to M56	No exit to M56
5	No exit to A5103 southbound	No exit to A5103 northbound
14	No exit to A580	No access from A580
16	No exit	No access
20	No access	No exit
22		No access
25	No access	
26		No exit or access
27	No exit	No access

M61
	Northbound	Southbound
2	No access from A580 eastbound	No exit to A580 westbound
3	No access from A580 eastbound	No exit to A580 westbound
	No access from A666 southbound	
M6 junc 30	No exit to M6 southbound	No access from M6 northbound

M62
	Eastbound	Westbound
23	No access	No exit

M65
	Eastbound	Westbound
9	No access	No exit
11	No exit	No access

M66
	Northbound	Southbound
1	No access	No exit

M67
	Eastbound	Westbound
1a	No access	No exit
2	No exit	No access

M69
	Northbound	Southbound
2	No exit	No access

M73
	Northbound	Southbound
2	No access from M8 or A89 eastbound	No exit to M8 or A89 westbound
	No exit to A89	No access from A89
3	Exit to A80 northbound only	Access from A80 southbound only

M74
	Northbound	Southbound
2	No access	No exit
3	No exit	No access
7	No exit	No access
9	No exit or access	No access
10		No exit
11	No exit	No access
12	No access	No exit

M77
	Northbound	Southbound
4	No exit	No access
6	No exit	No access
7	No exit or access	
8	No access	No access
M8 junc 22	Exit to M8 eastbound only	Access from M8 westbound only

M80
	Northbound	Southbound
3	No access	No exit
5	No access from M876	No exit to M876

M90
	Northbound	Southbound
2a	No access	No exit
7	No exit	No access
8	No access	No exit
10	No access from A912	No exit to A912

M180
	Northbound	Southbound
1	No access	No exit

M621
	Eastbound	Westbound
2a	No exit	No access
4	No exit or access	
5	No exit	No access
6	No access	No exit

M876
	Northbound	Southbound
2	No access	No exit

A1(M)
	Northbound	Southbound
2	No access	No exit
3		No access
5	No exit	No access
40	No access	No exit
44	No exit, access from M1 only	Exit to M1 only
57	No access	No exit
65	No access	No exit

A3(M)
	Northbound	Southbound
1		No access
4	No access	No exit

A38(M)
	Northbound	Southbound
With Victoria Road (Park Circus) Birmingham	No exit	No access

A48(M)
	Northbound	Southbound
M4 Junc 29	Exit to M4 eastbound only	Access from M4 westbound only
29a	Access from A48 eastbound only	Exit to A48 westbound only

A57(M)
	Eastbound	Westbound
With A5103	No access	No exit
With A34	No access	No exit

A58(M)
	Southbound
With Park Lane and Westgate, Leeds	No access

A64(M)
	Eastbound	Westbound
With A58 Clay Pit Lane, Leeds	No access	No exit
With Regent Street, Leeds	No access	No access

A74(M)
	Northbound	Southbound
18	No access	No exit
22	No access	No exit

A167(M)
	Northbound	Southbound
With Camden St, Newcastle	No exit	No exit or access

A194(M)
	Northbound	Southbound
A1(M) junc 65 Gateshead Western Bypass	Access from A1(M) northbound only	Exit to A1(M) southbound only

Distance table

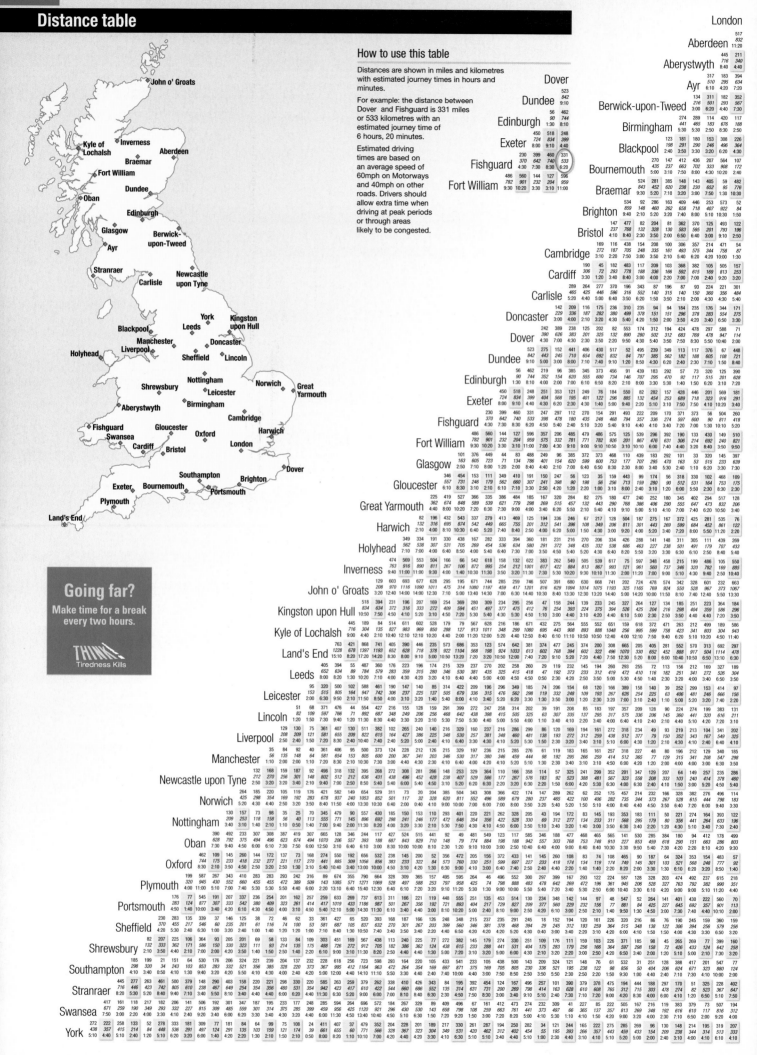

How to use this table

Distances are shown in miles and kilometres with estimated journey times in hours and minutes.

For example: the distance between Dover and Fishguard is 331 miles or 533 kilometres with an estimated journey time of 6 hours, 20 minutes.

Estimated driving times are based on an average speed of 60mph on Motorways and 40mph on other roads. Drivers should allow extra time when driving at peak periods or through areas likely to be congested.

Going far?
Make time for a break every two hours.

THINK!
Tiredness Kills

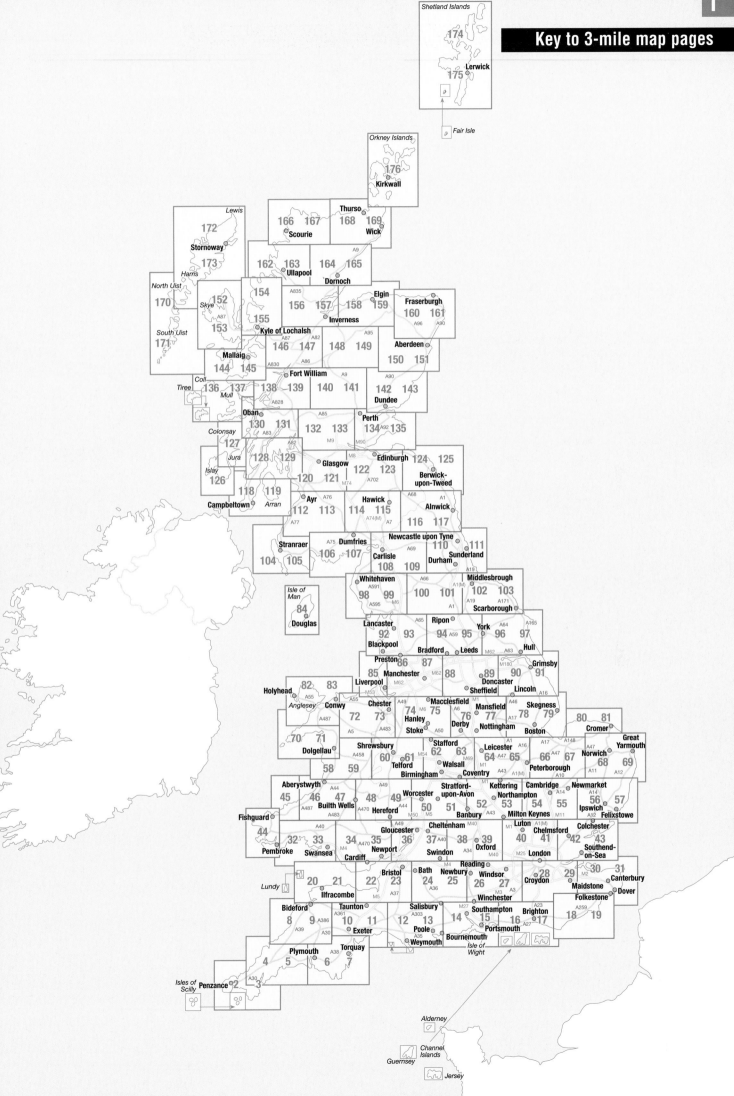

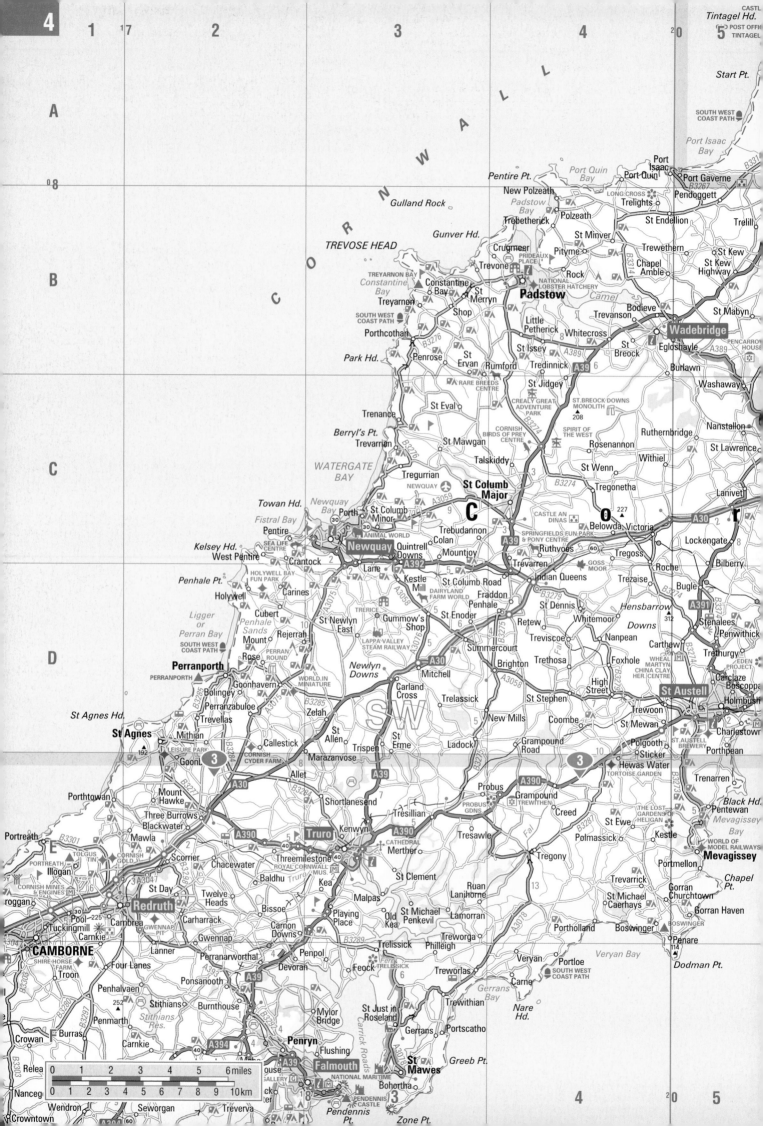

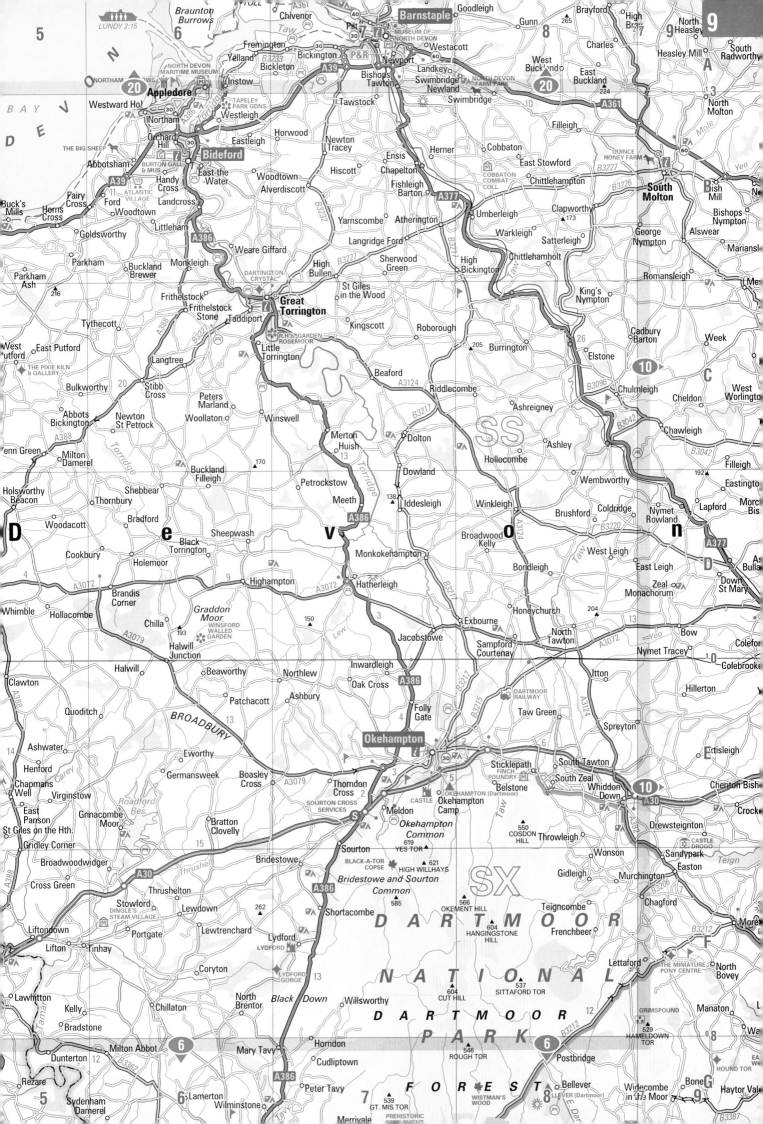

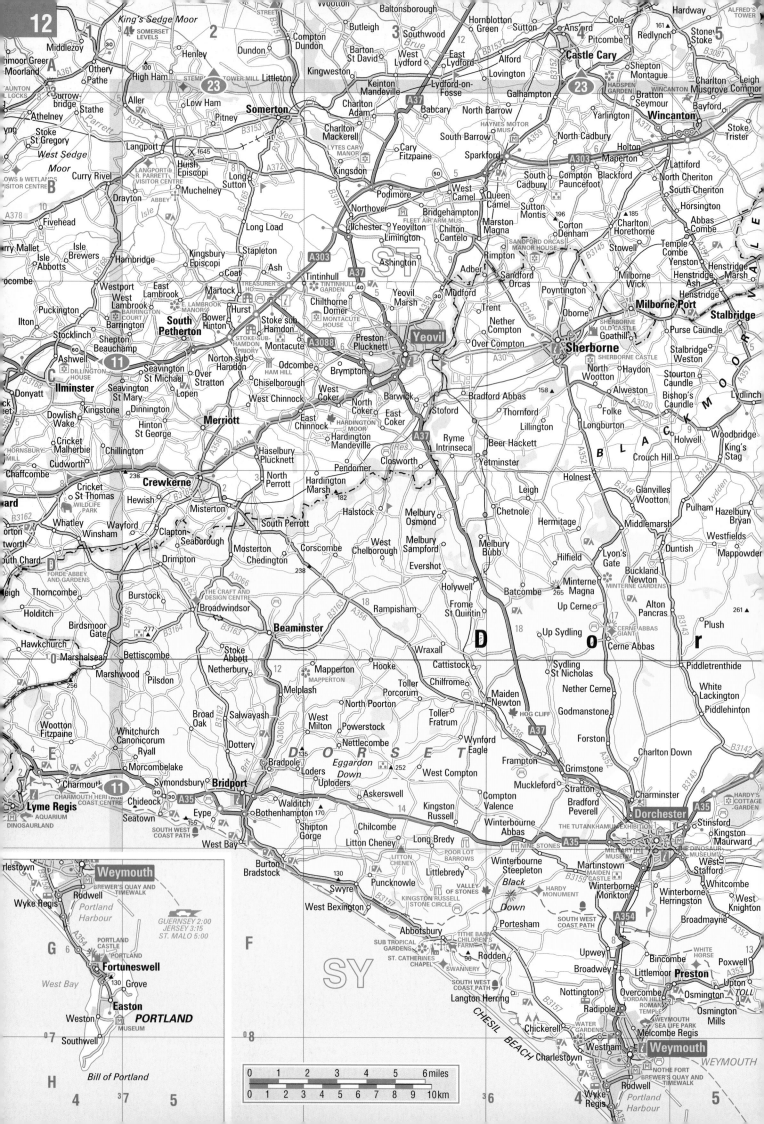

1   2 3   2   3   4   5

A

¹8

B

¹5

²2

North West Point   *North East Point*

LUNDY

LUNDY MARINE NATURE RESERVE

14▲²▲

ILFRACOMBE 2:15
BIDEFORD 2:15

C

South West Point   *Surf Point*

²1

²3

¹4

D

SS

N
O
R
T
H

D
E
V
O
N

LUNDY 2:15

OLD CORN MILL

Rillage Pt.   Combe Martin Bay

Ilfracombe   ILFRACOMBE MUSEUM   WATERMOUTH CASTLE   *Girt Down*   Trentishoe

Hele   10   Heale   349▲

Bull Pt.   Berrynarbor   **Combe Martin**

Rockham Bay   Lee   Whitestone   Slade   206   Sterridge   WILDLIFE & DINOSAUR PARK

Morte Point   Mortehoe   ONCE UPON A TIME   Trimstone   Cheglinch   269▲   *Berry Down*   Berry Down Cross   Patchole   Kentisbury

E

Woolacombe   *Berry Down*   East Down   Kentisbury Ford

MORTE BAY   210▲   Dean   West Down   Bittadon   Churchill

Woolacombe Sand   SOUTH WEST COAST PATH   North Buckland   Milltown   Arlington   ARLINGTON COURT

Pickwell   Nethercott   Muddiford   Loxhore

Putsborough   Halsinger   11

Baggy Pt.   Georgeham   Darracott   Knowle   Marwood   Guineaford   198▲   Shirwell   Bratton Fleming

Croyde Bay   Croyde   158   Lobb   Pippacott   MARWOOD HILL GARDENS   Kingsheanton   Prixford   Shirwell Cross   Stoke Rivers

Saunton   14   Heanton Punchardon   Ashford   Burridge   Goodleigh

F

Saunton Sands   Wrafton   TOLL   Chivenor   40   **Barnstaple**   Gunn

ELLIOT GALLERY   *Braunton Burrows*   40   MUSEUM OF NORTH DEVON

LUNDY 2:15   Pilton   30   Westacott

Taw   Newport   60

Fremington   30   Bishops Tawton   North Devon Farm Park

Yelland   30   Bickington   Landkey   Swimbridge Newland

BIDEFORD BAY   NORTH DEVON MARITIME MUSEUM   Instow   A39   7   Swimbridge   10

NORTHAM BURROWS   TAPELEY PARK GDNS   Horwood   Newton Tracey   Herner   Cobbaton   East Stowford

¹3   **Appledore**   COBBATON COMBAT-COLL.

Westward Ho!   **Bideford**   Eastleigh   Ensis   Chapelton

Northam   30   Orchard Hill   Newton Tracey

Titchl   THE BIG SHEEP   Woodtown   Hiscott   Chittlehampton

9   Abbotsham   BURTON GALL. & MUS.   East-the-Water   Handy

CLOVELLY VILLAGE

0 1 2 3 4 5 6 miles
0 1 2 3 4 5 6 7 8 9 10km

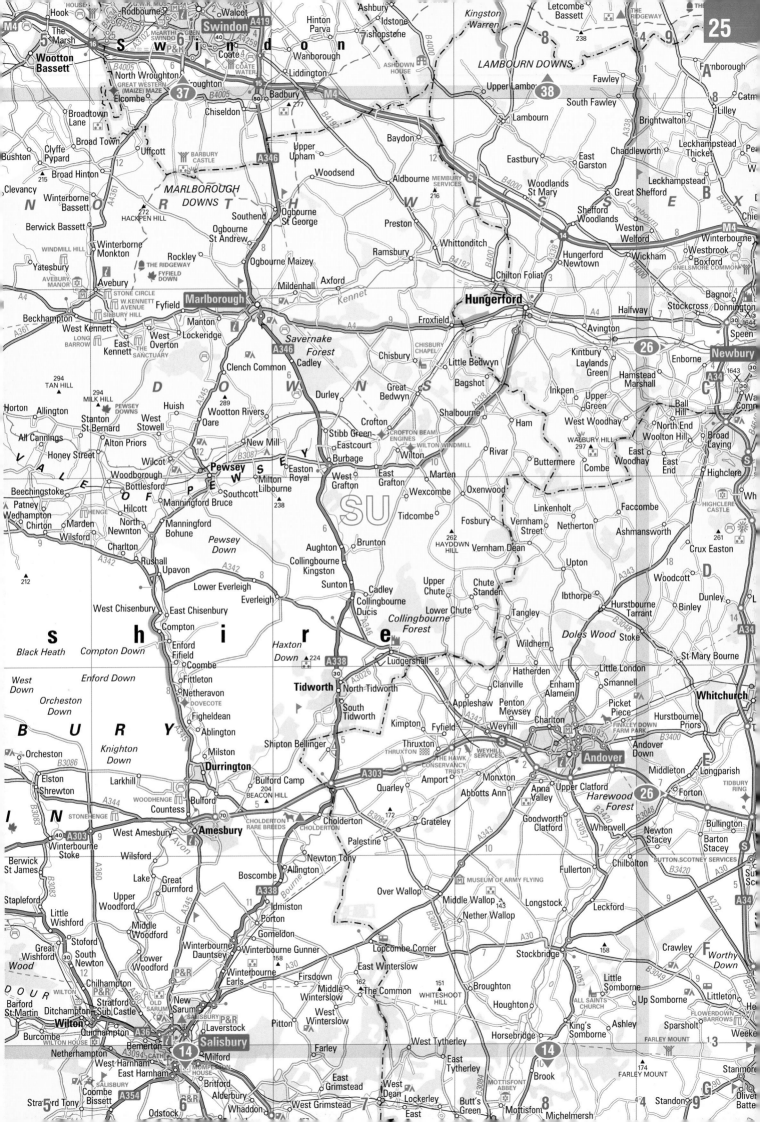

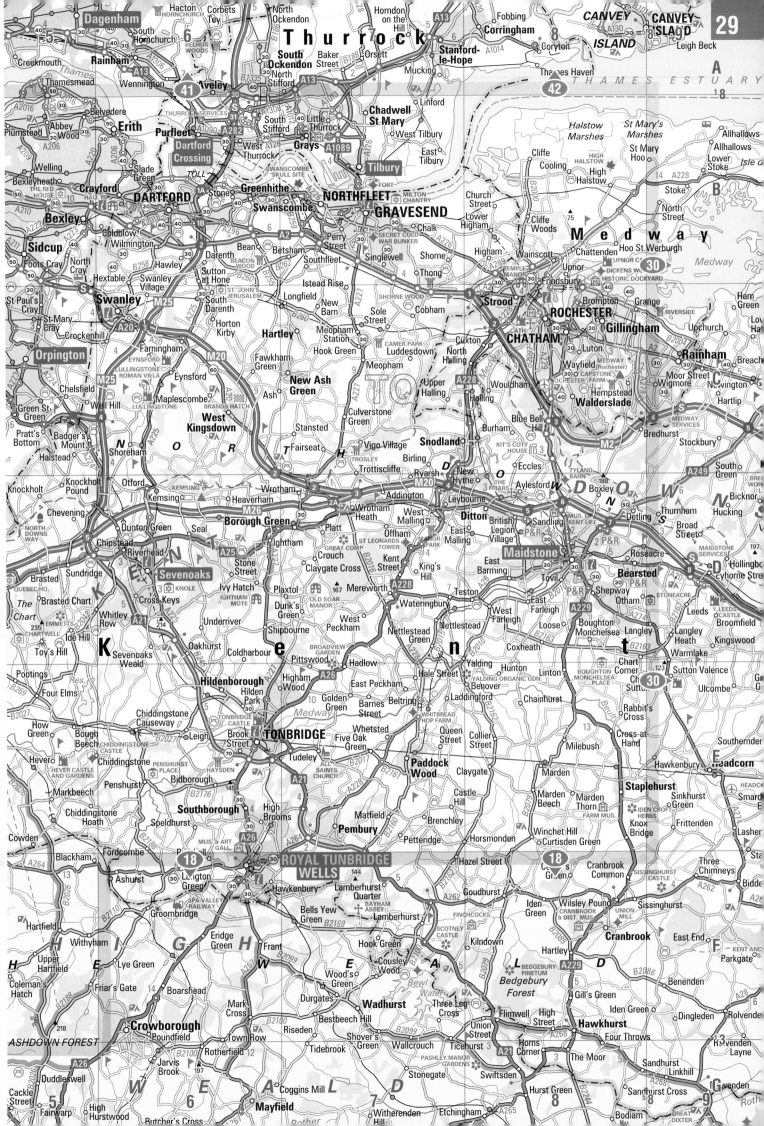

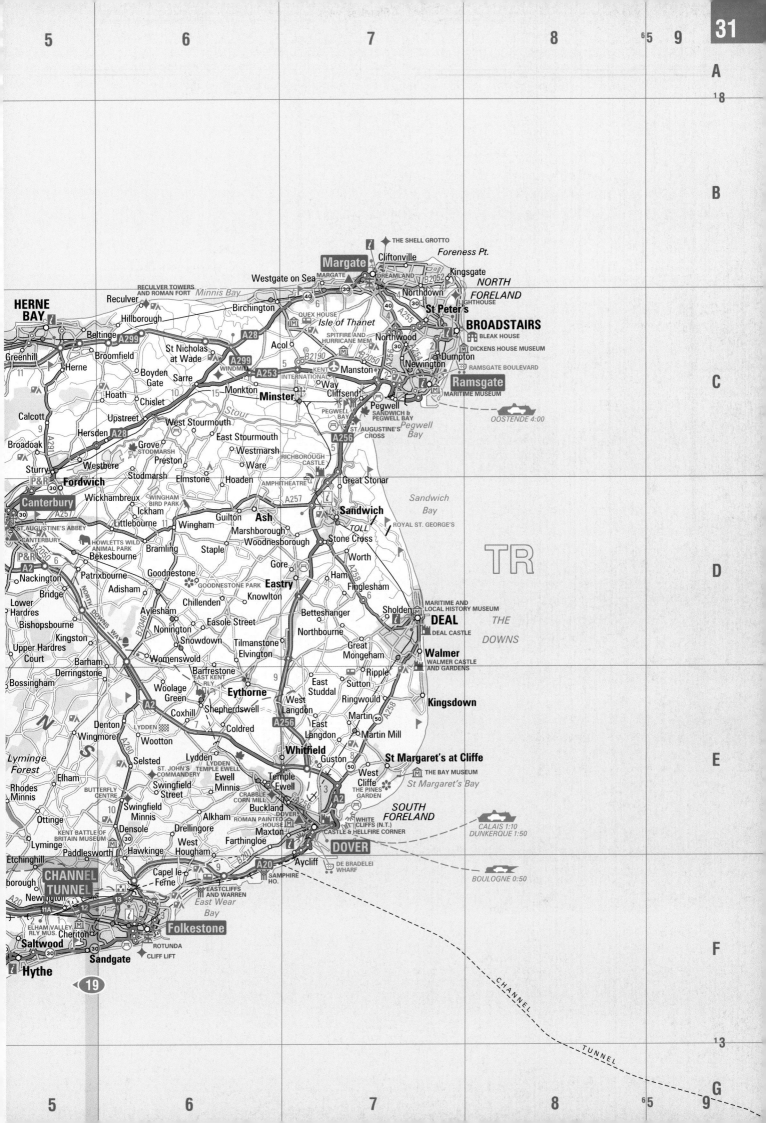

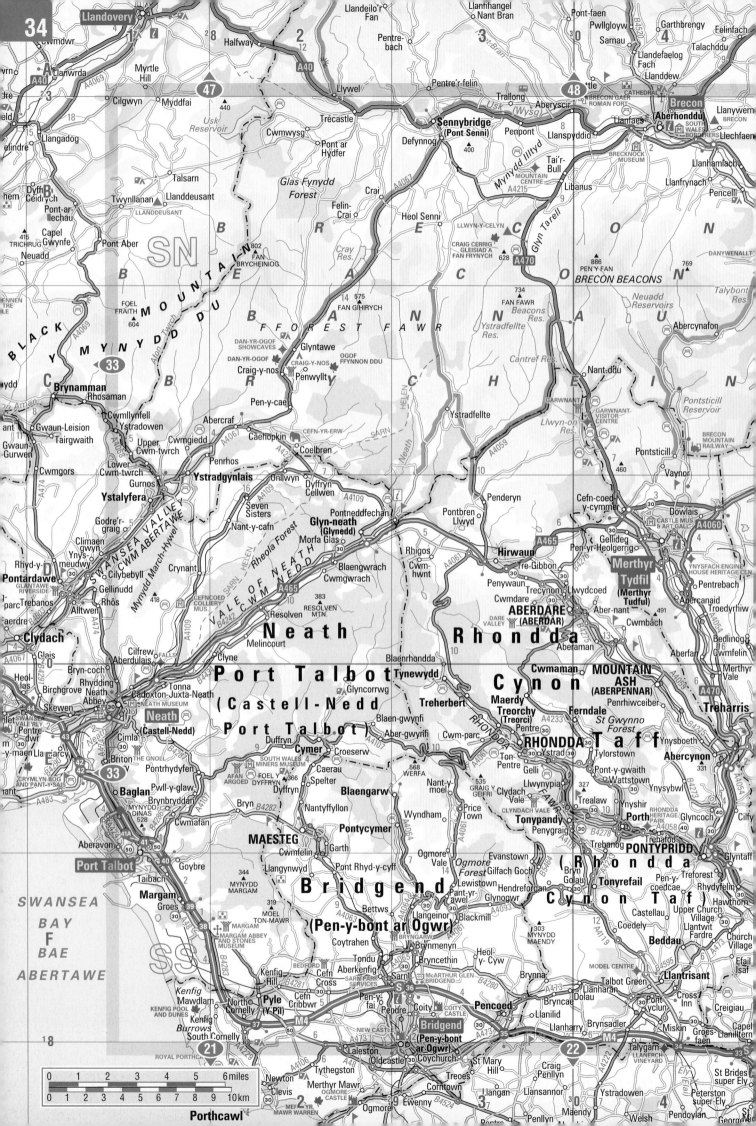

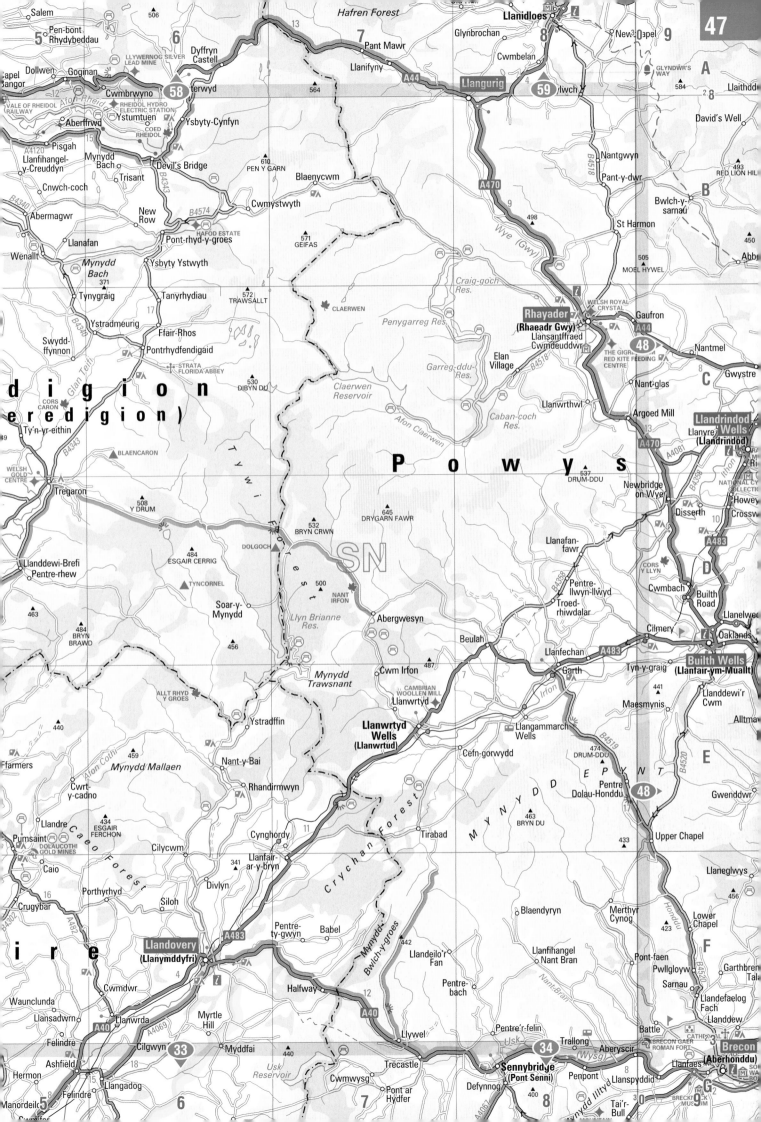

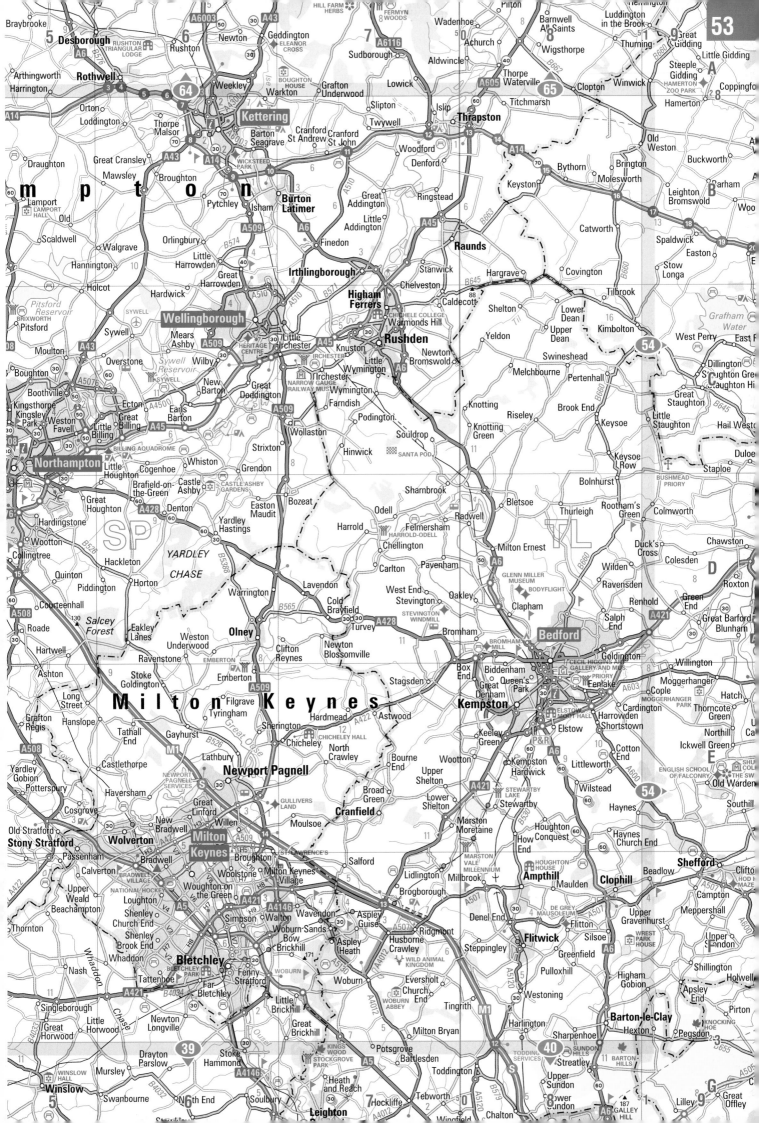

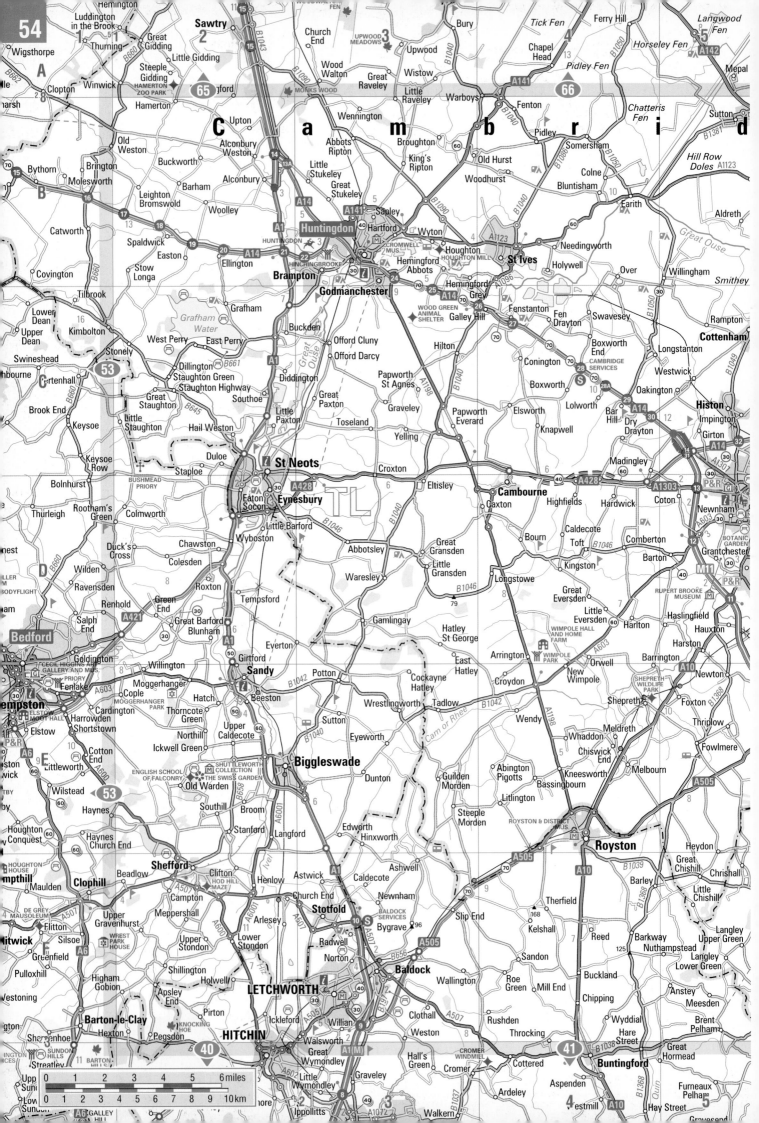

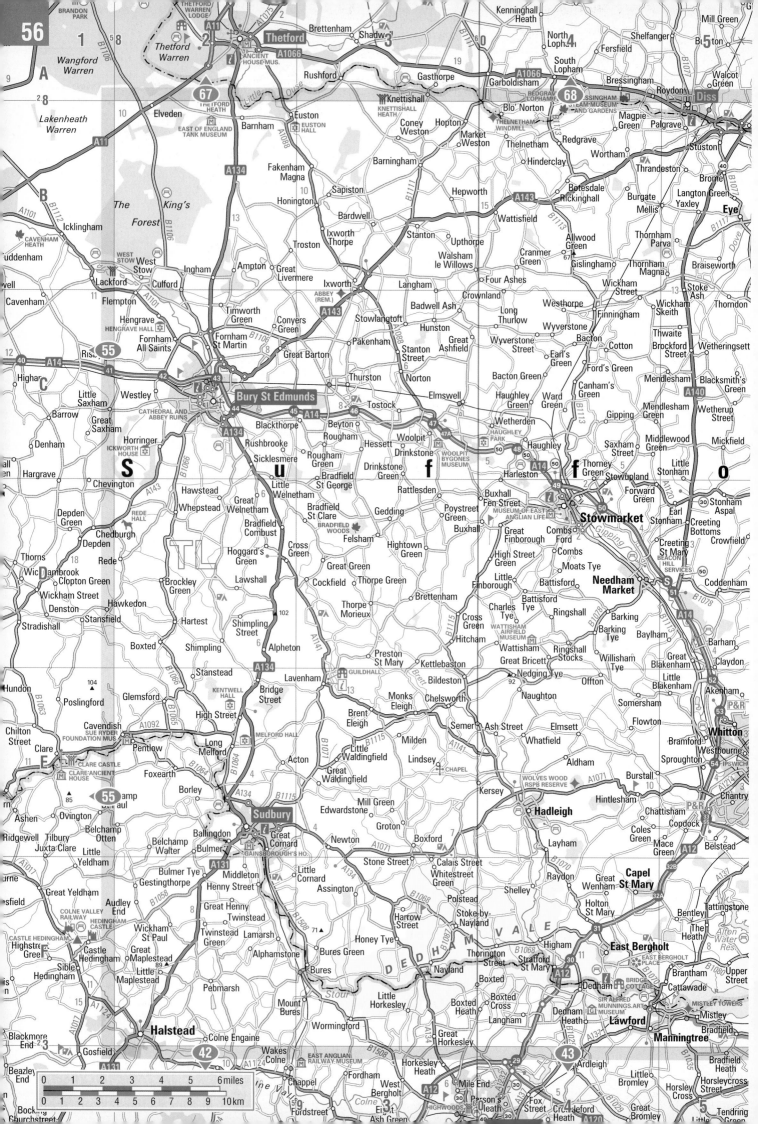

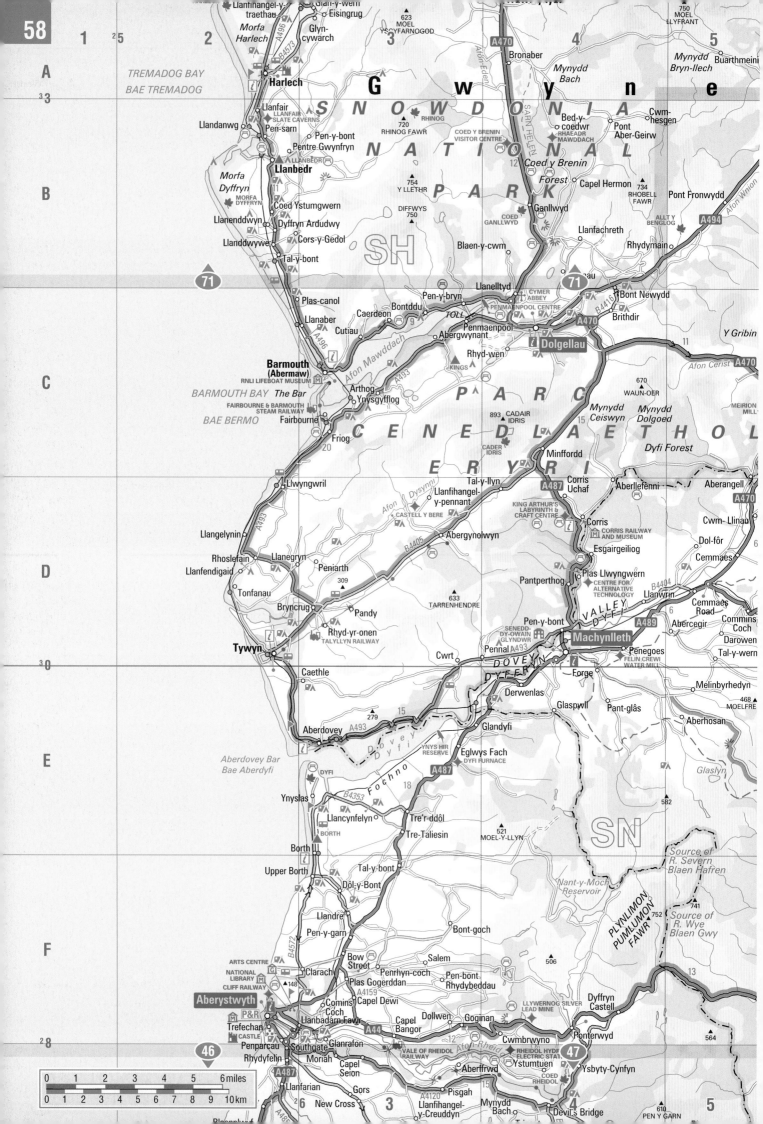

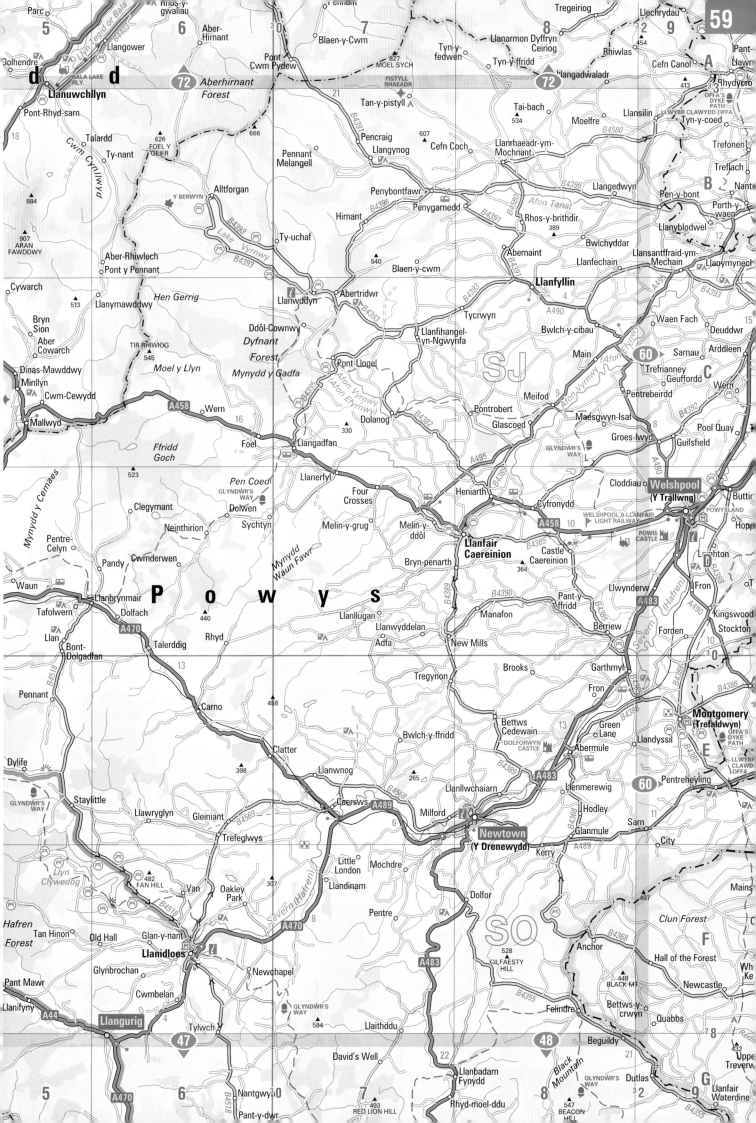

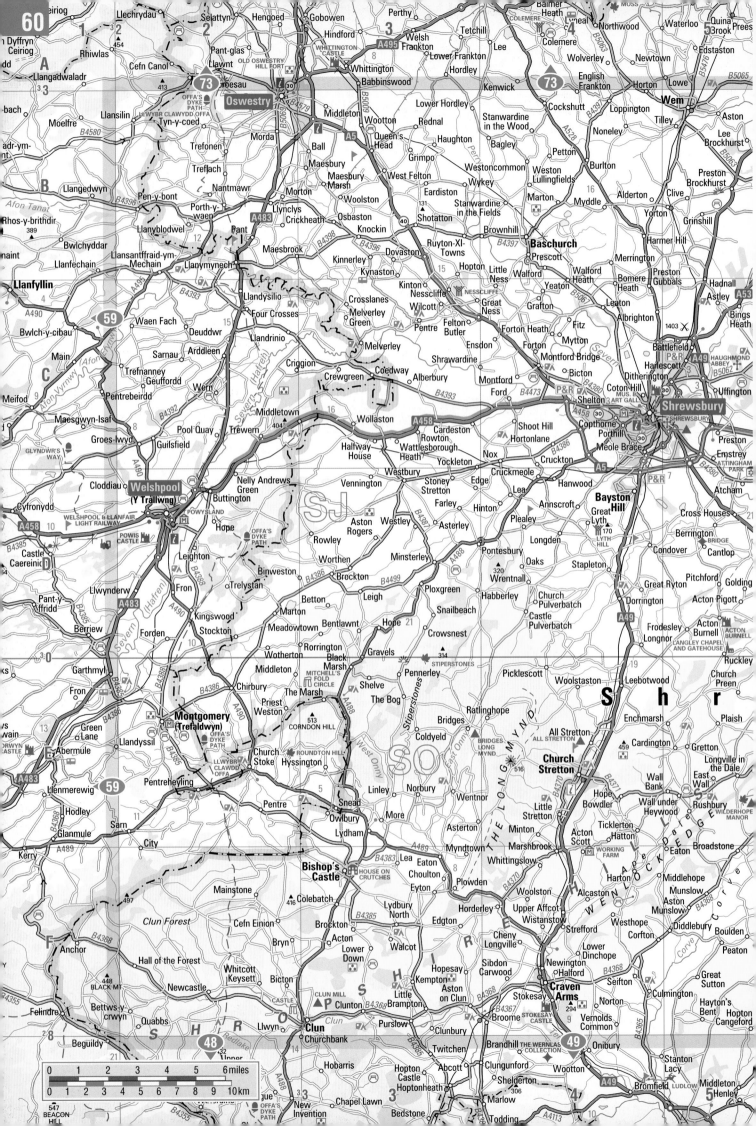

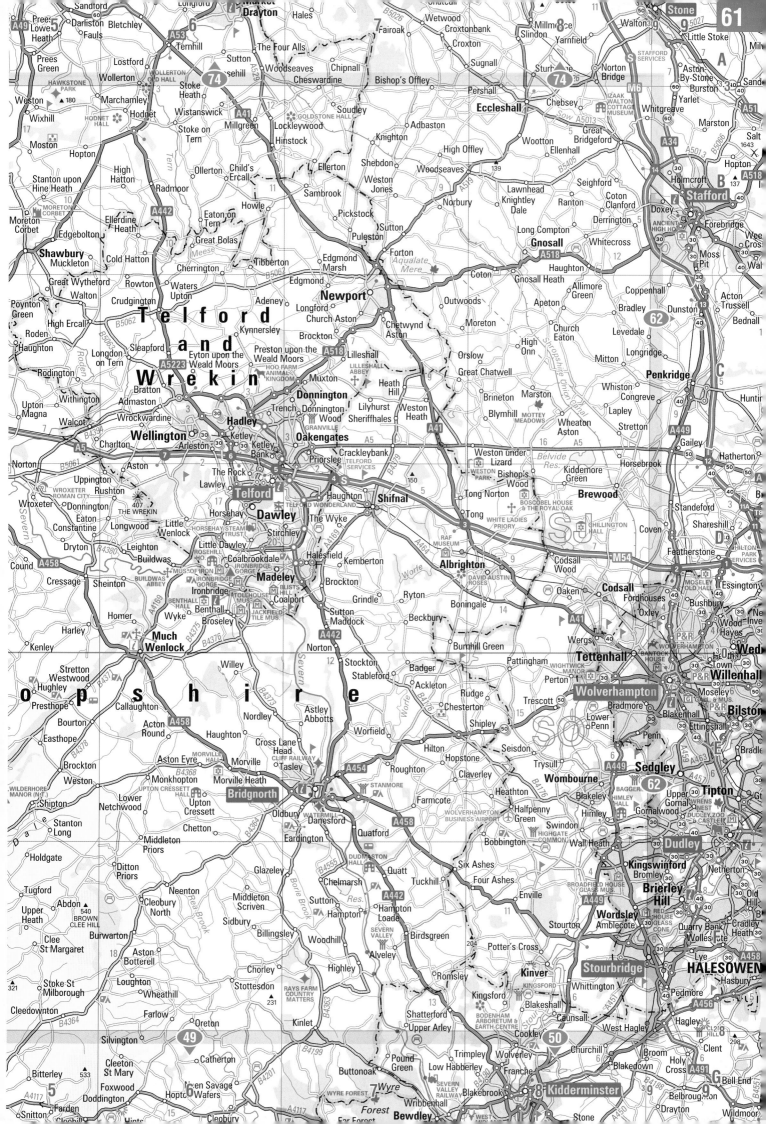

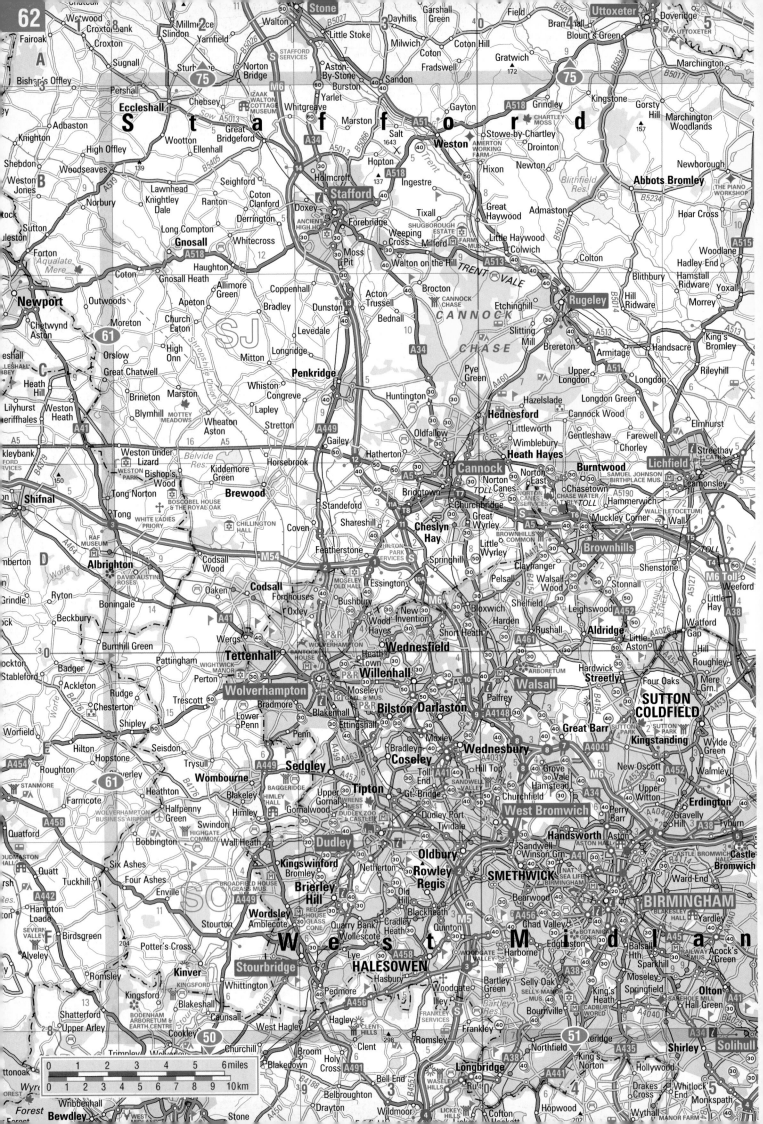

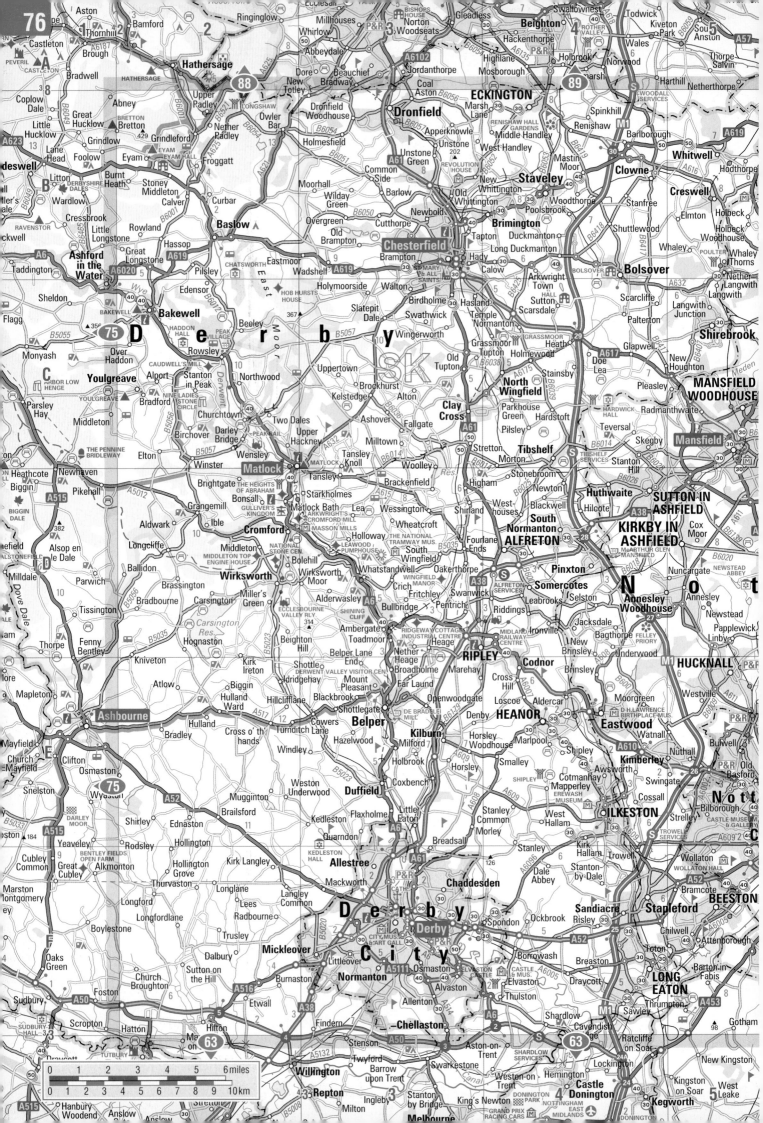

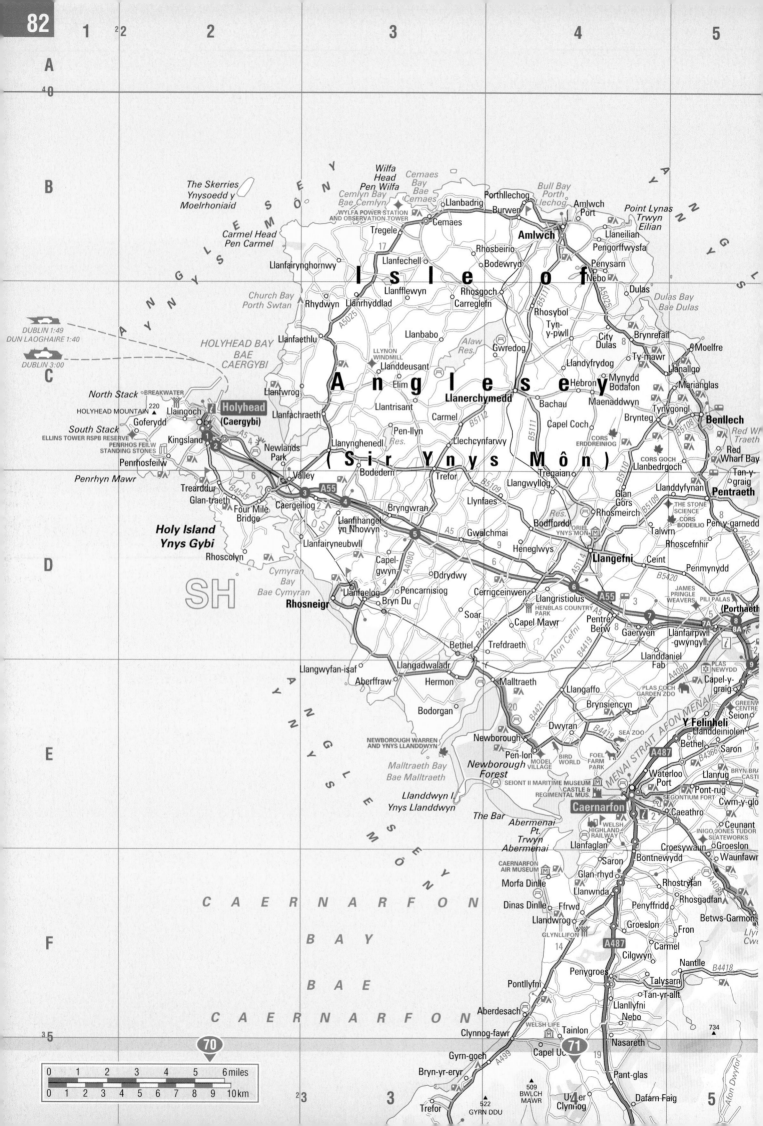

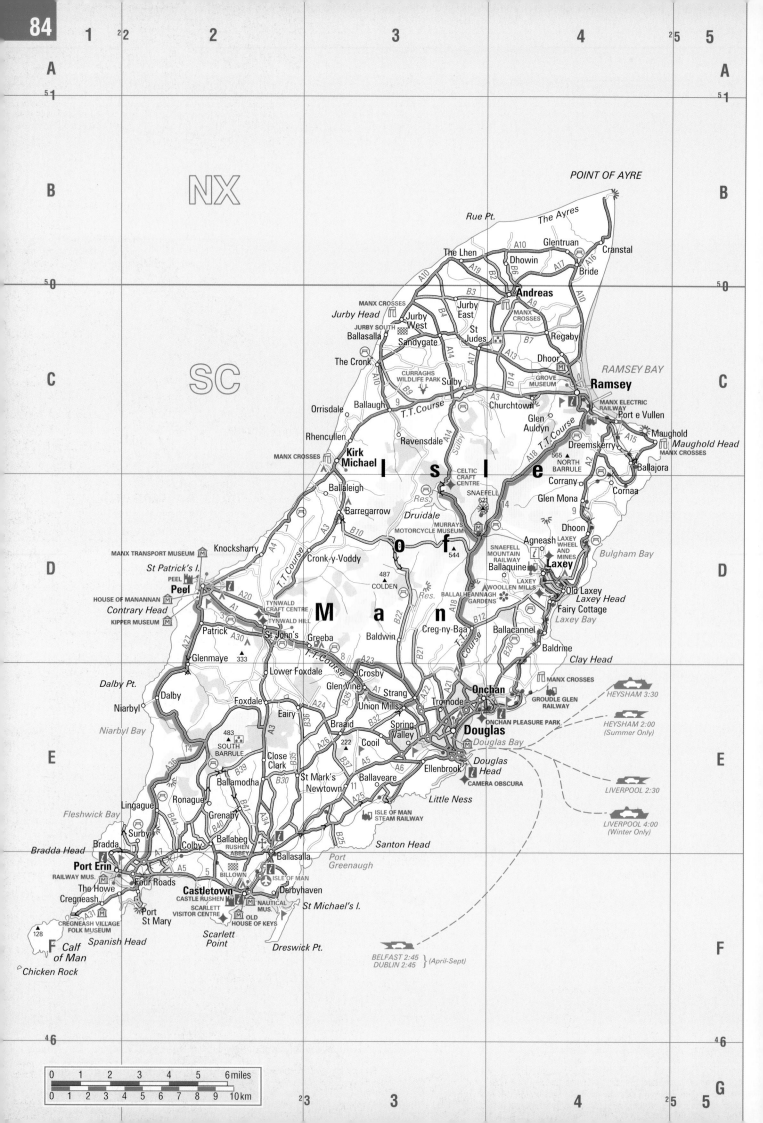

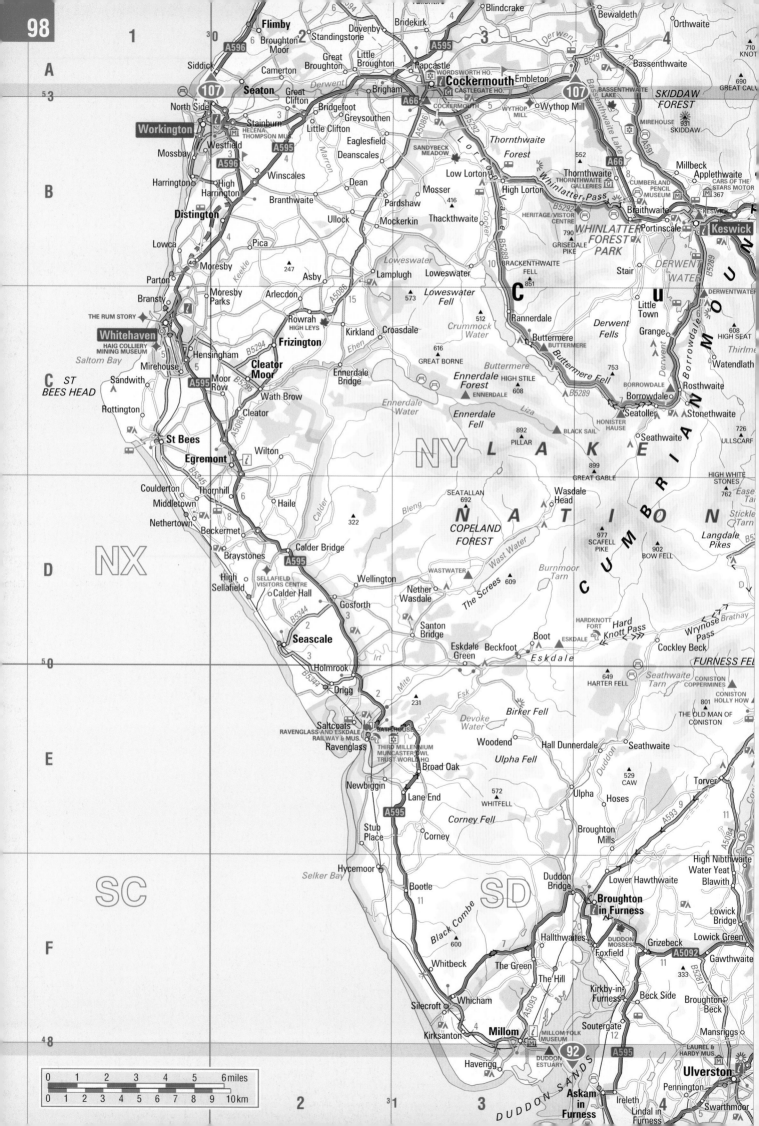

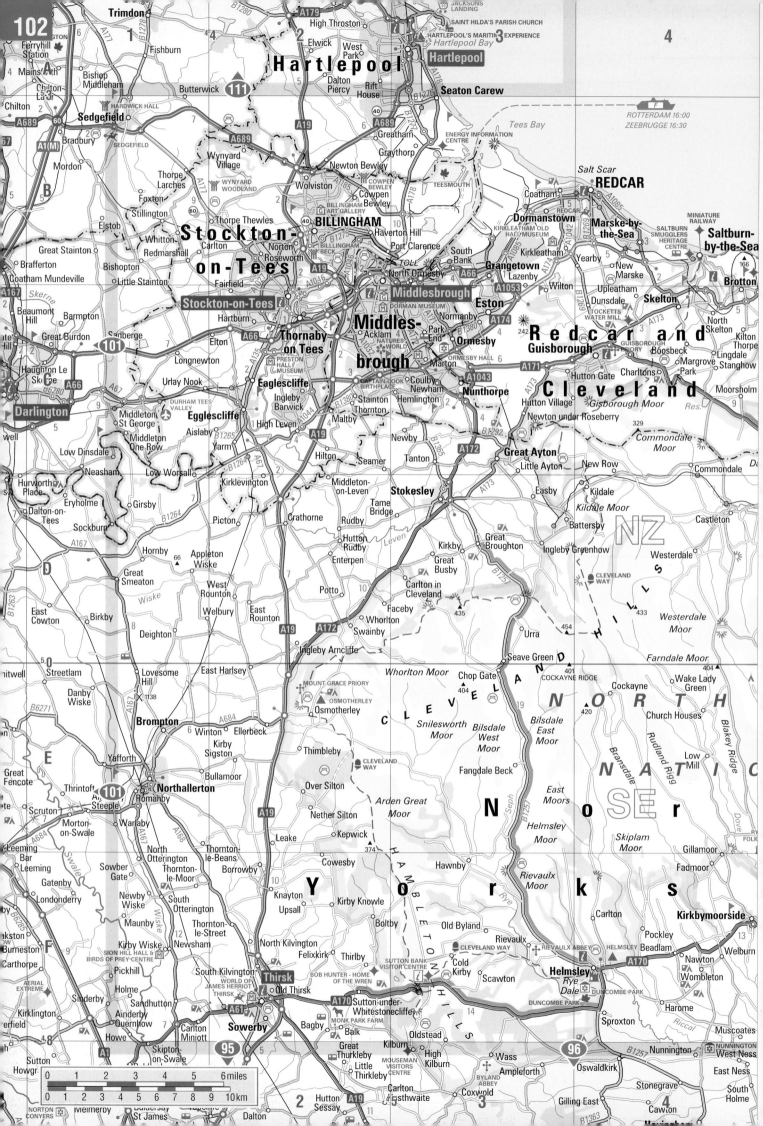

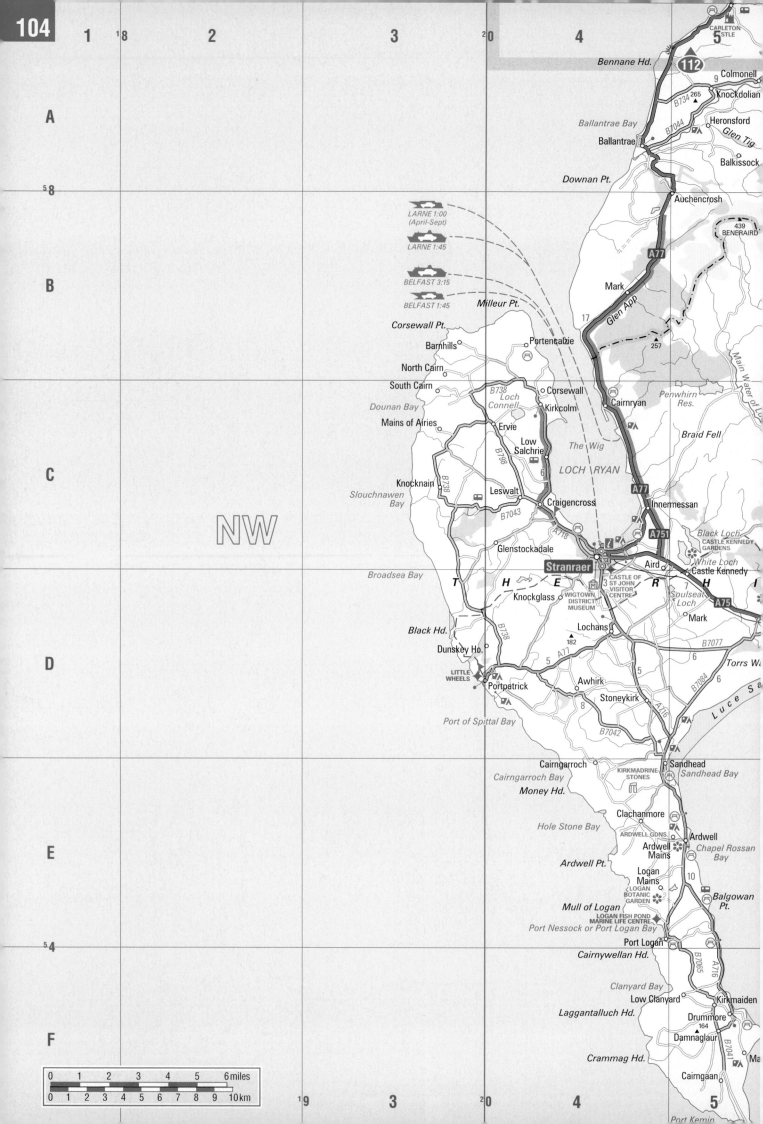

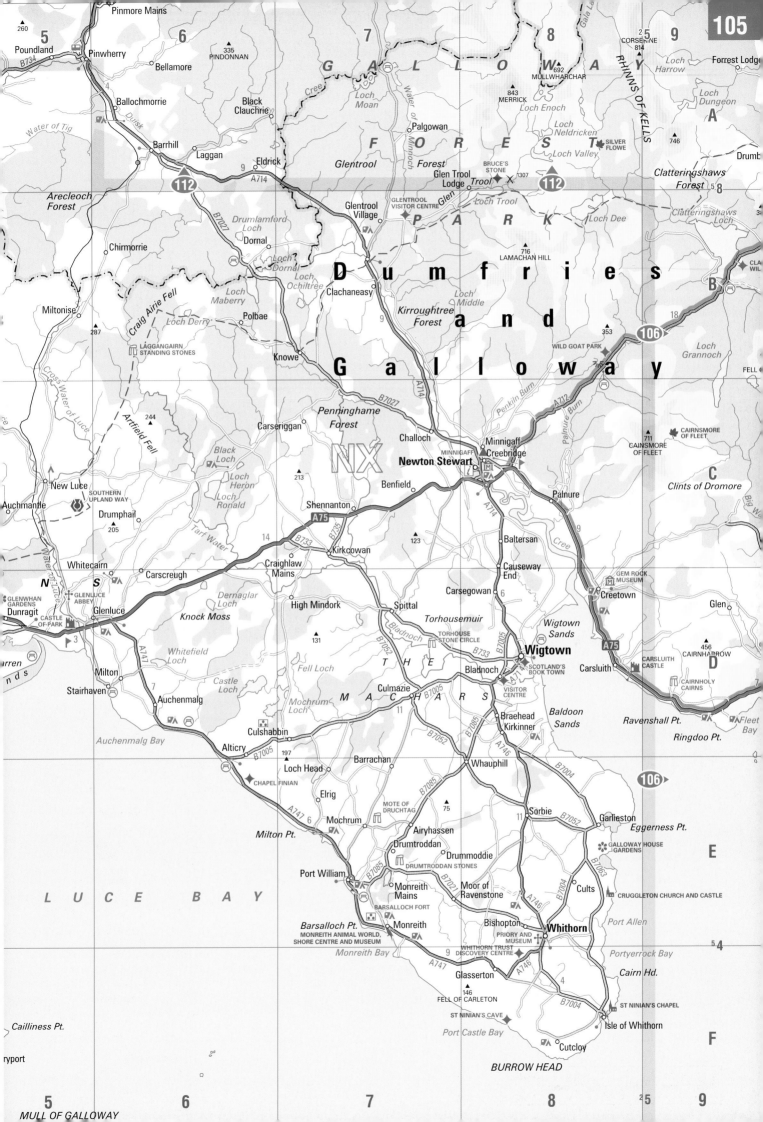

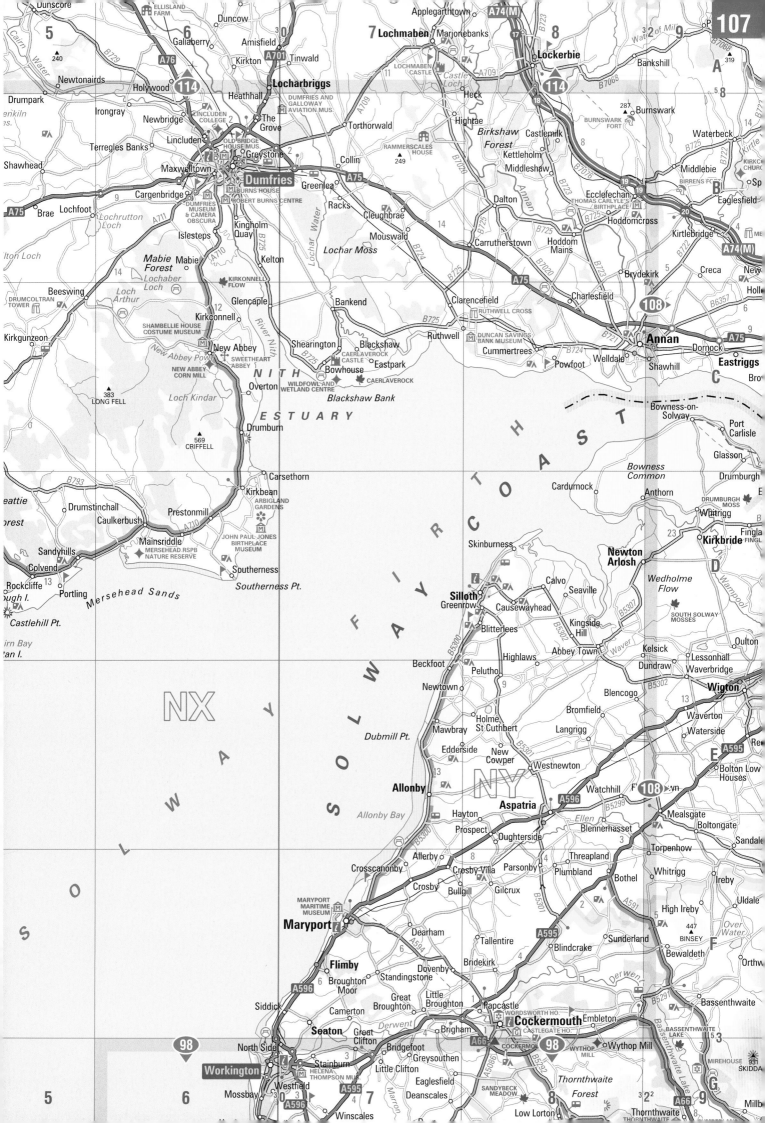

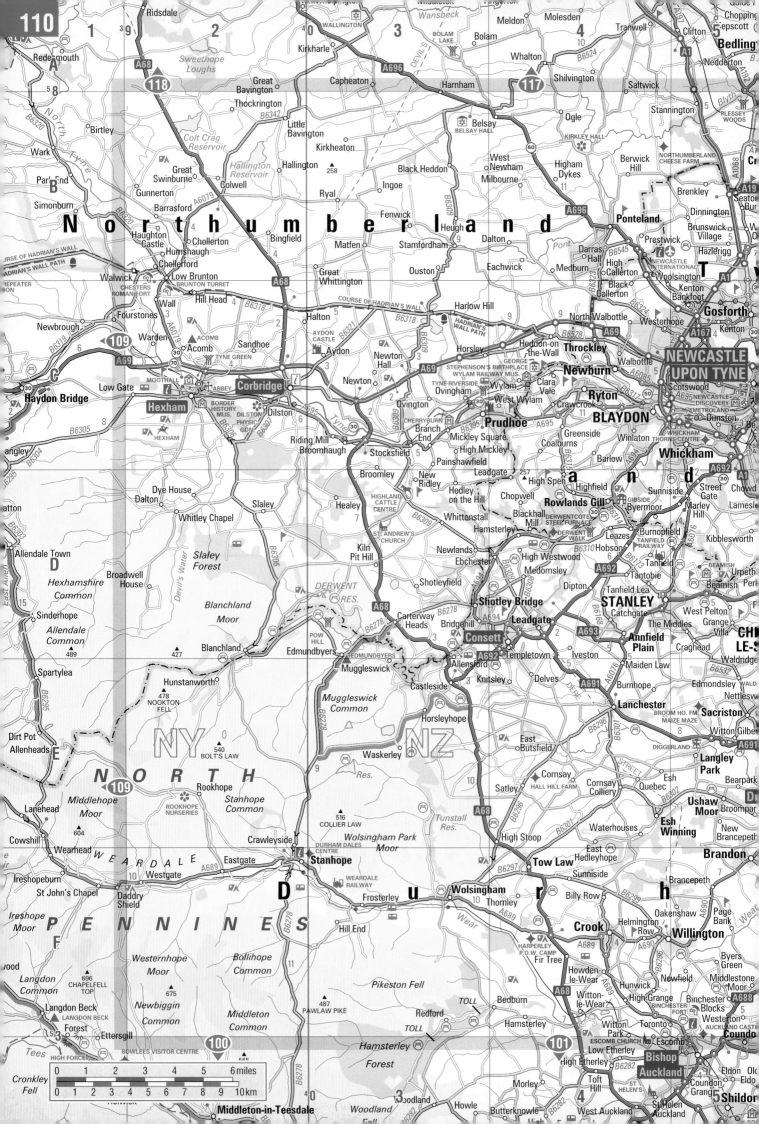

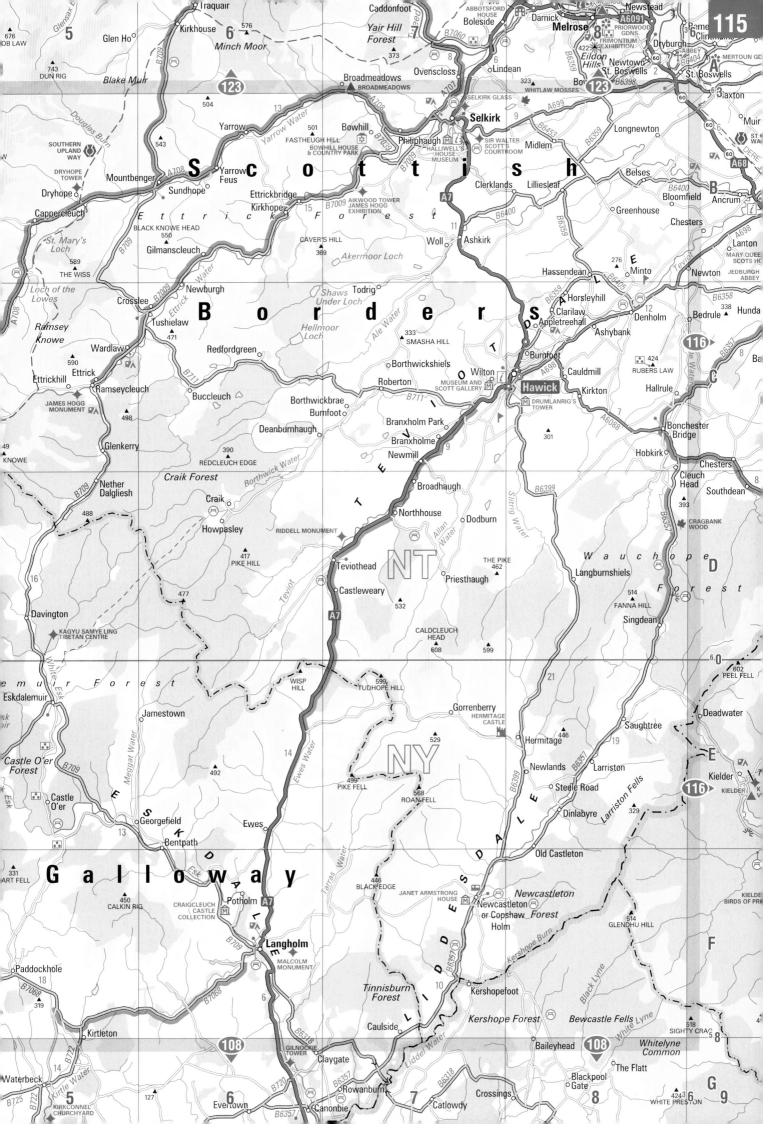

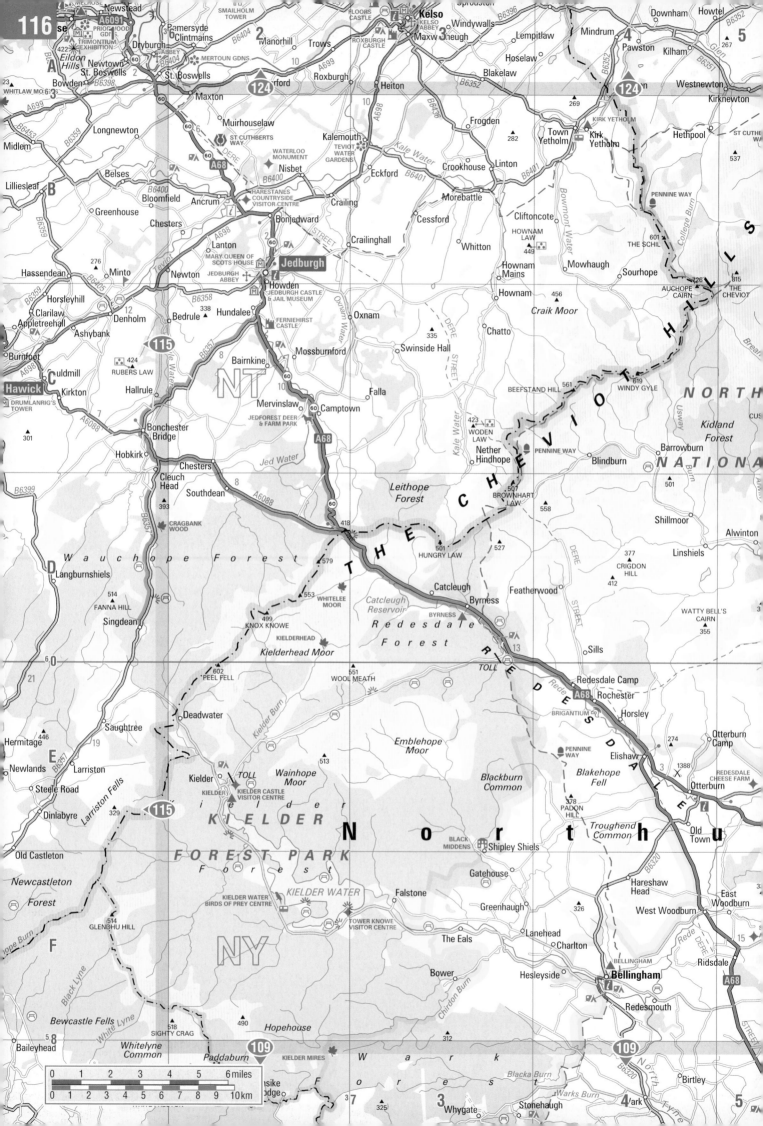

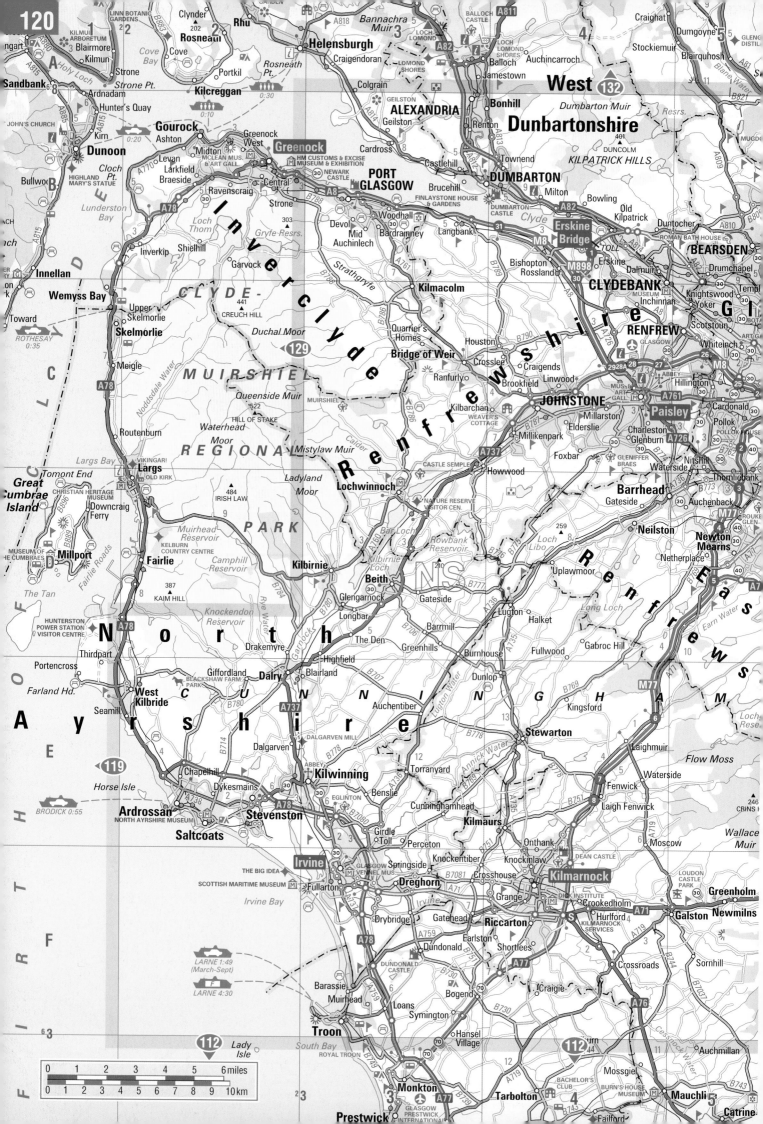

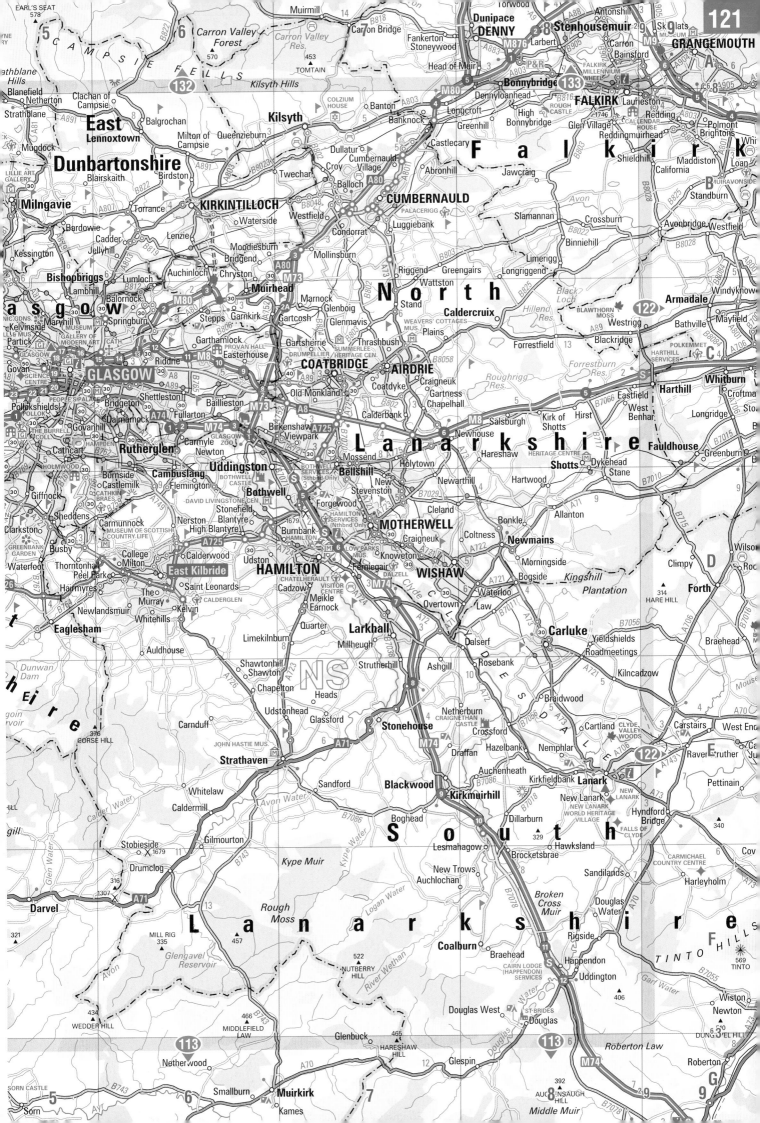

A

B

C

D

E

F

G

5   40   6   7   8   43   9

6   8

6   3

43   9

EYEMOUTH MUSEUM

Burnmouth

Lamberton Beach

Lamberton

1333

Highfields

Berwick-upon-Tweed

BARRACKS MUSEUM & RAMPARTS

East Ord

Tweedmouth

TOWER HOUSE POTTERY

Spittal

Prior Park

Redshin Cove

108

Murton

Thornton

Scremerston

West Allerdean

Shoresdean

Cheswick

Goswick

Ancroft

North Low

Haggerston

Berrington

South Low

Beal

Bowsden

Barmoor Castle

Barmoor Lane End

West Kyloe

Fenwick

Lowick

Kyloe Hills

East Kyloe

Buckton

ST CUTHBERTS WAY

Holburn

Detchant

Middleton

Elwick

Ross

Kimmerston

Fenton Town

Nesbit

North Hazelrigg

Hetton Steads

211

Belford

Easington

Waren Mill

Budle Bay

BAMBURGH CASTLE

FARNE ISLANDS

Inner Sound

Bamburgh

Farne Islands

Staple Sound

Budle

Spindlestone

Glororum

Burton

Doddington

200

157

South Hazelrigg

West Horton

East Horton

Mousen

Bradford

Bellshill

Elford

North Sunderland

Seahouses

Newtown

Akeld

1402

Weetwood Hall

10

Warenton

Adderstone

Lucker

Humbleton

Wooler

WOOLER

Chatton

Greendikes

Warenford

Newham Hall

Swinhoe

Benthall

Bea

Beadnell Bay

Earle

166

Haugh Head

CHILLINGHAM CASTLE

Chillingham

CHILLINGHAM WILD CATTLE

Rosebrough

Newstead

Chathill

Newham

Fleetham

Ellingham

High Newton-by-the-Sea

HUT SMITHY WOOD WORKSHOP

THERSLAW MILL

LADY WATERFORD HALL

NU

NORTH SEA

NORTHUMBERLAND COAST

LINDISFARNE

Emmanuel Hd.

Holy Island (Lindisfarne)

LINDISFARNE CASTLE

Holy Island

Castle Pt.

Causeway

Holy Island Sands

Fenham

Guile Pt.

HERITAGE CENTRE

LINDISFARNE PRIORY

Middleton Hall

A697

A698

A1

117

117

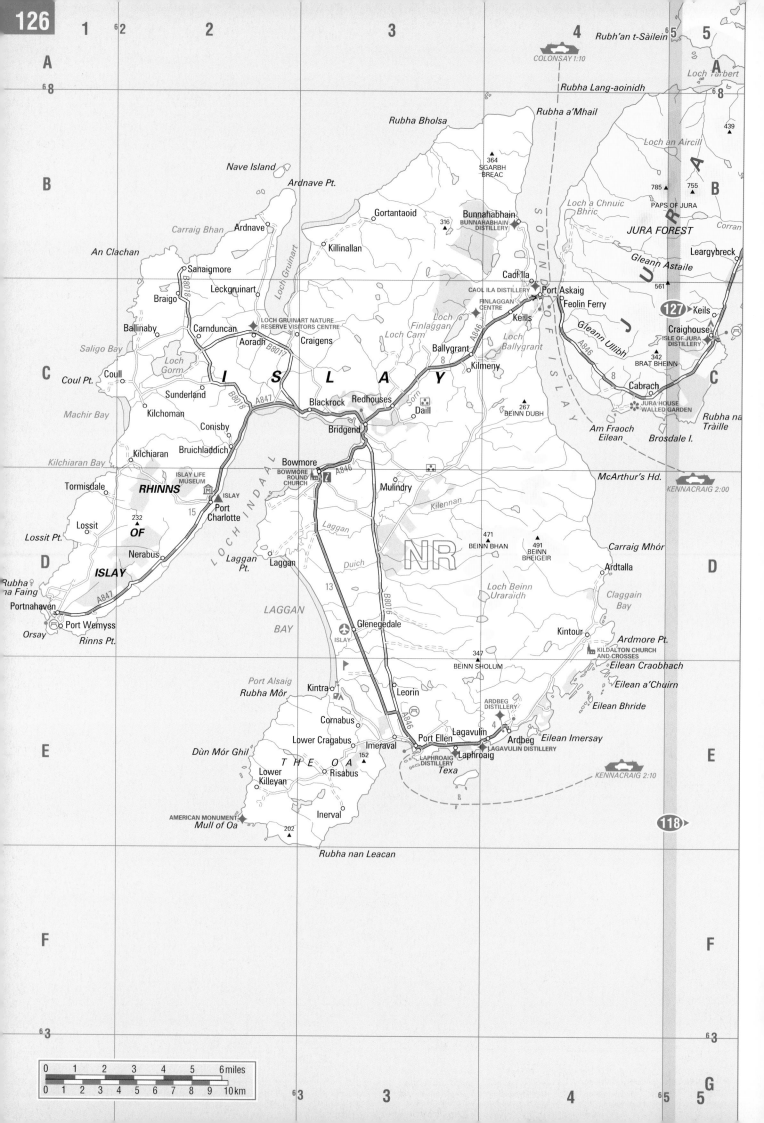

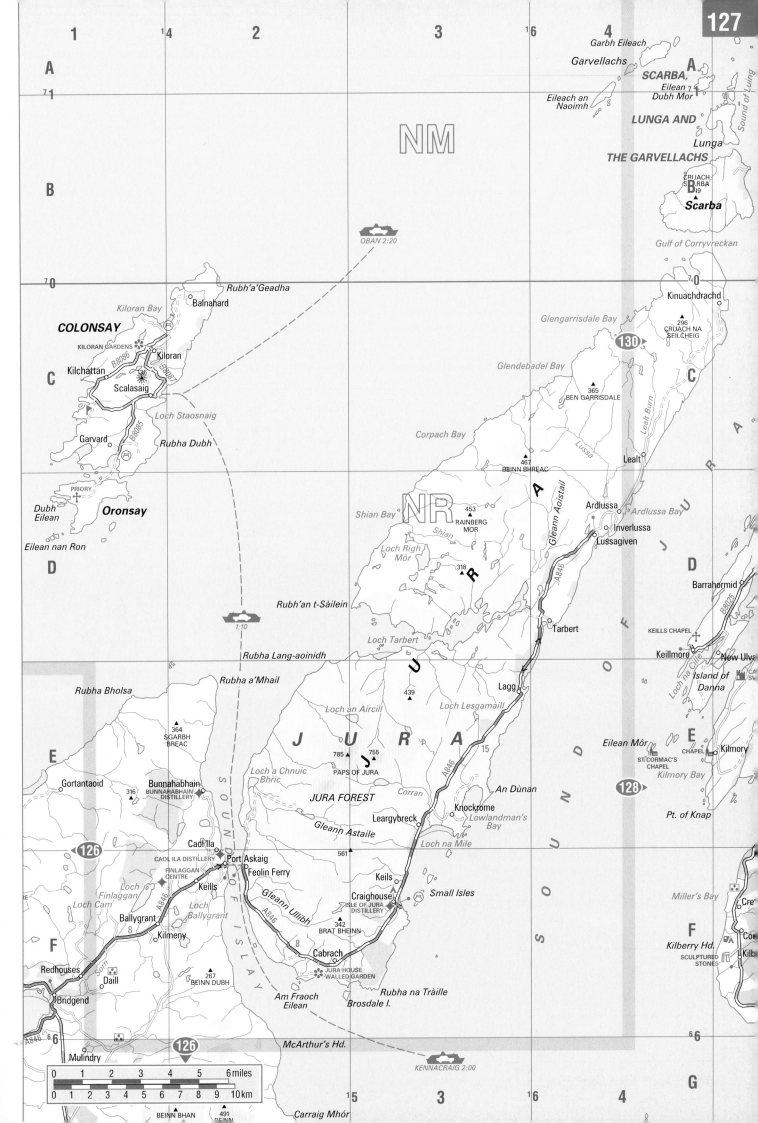

A 1 B 2 C 3 D 4 E F G

Garbh Eileach
Garvellachs
SCARBA,
Eileach an
Naoimh
Eilean
Dubh Mor
LUNGA AND
Lunga
THE GARVELLACHS
CRUACH
SCARBA
449
Scarba

Sound of Luing

Gulf of Corryvreckan

NM

OBAN 2:20

Rubh'a'Geadha
Balnahard
Kinuachdrachd
Kiloran Bay
COLONSAY
Glengarrisdale Bay
130
296
CRUACH NA
SEILCHEIG
KILORAN GARDENS
Kiloran
Glendebadel Bay
Kilchattan
36
Scalasaig
365
BEN GARRISDALE
B8086
B8087
Loch Staosnaig
Corpach Bay
Garvard
B8085
Rubha Dubh
467
BEINN BHREAC
Lealt Burn
Lealt

PRIORY
NR
453
RAINBERG
MOR
Shian Bay
Ardlussa
Ardlussa Bay
Dubh
Eilean
Oronsay
Shian
Inverlussa
Lussagiven
Eilean nan Ron
Loch Righ
Mòr
318
R
Gleann Aoistail

Rubh'an t-Sàilein
1:10
A846
Barrahormid
B8025
KEILLS CHAPEL
Loch Tarbert
Tarbert
Rubha Lang-aoinidh
Keillmore
Keills na Cille
New Ulva
Rubha a'Mhail
U
Island of
Danna
Rubha Bholsa
Lagg
Loch Lesgamaill
Loch an Aircill
364
SGARBH
BREAC
439
Eilean Mòr
CHAPEL
Kilmory
St CORMAC'S
CHAPEL
128
Kilmory Bay
Gortantaoid
J U R A
Loch a Chnuic
Bhric
785 755
PAPS OF JURA
Corran
An Dùnan
Pt. of Knap
Bunnahabhain
316
BUNNAHABHAIN
DISTILLERY
JURA FOREST
15
A846
Knockrome
Lowlandman's
Bay
Miller's Bay
Leargybreck
Gleann Astaile
Loch na Mile
Caol Ila
CAOL ILA DISTILLERY
561
Keils
Cre
FINLAGGAN
CENTRE
Port Askaig
Feolin Ferry
Small Isles
126
Keills
Gleann Ullibh
Craighouse
ISLE OF JURA
DISTILLERY
Loch
Finlaggan
Loch
Ballygrant
A846
Ballygrant
8
342
BRAT BHEINN
Loch Cam
Kilmeny
8
Cabrach
Kilberry Hd.
Co
SCULPTURED
STONES
Redhouses
Daill
267
BEINN DUBH
JURA HOUSE
WALLED GARDEN
Kilb
Bridgend
Am Fraoch
Eilean
Rubha na Tràille
A846
6
Brosdale I.
Mulindry
126
McArthur's Hd.

0 1 2 3 4 5 6 miles
0 1 2 3 4 5 6 7 8 9 10km

KENNACRAIG 2:00

BEINN BHAN
491
BEINN
Carraig Mhòr

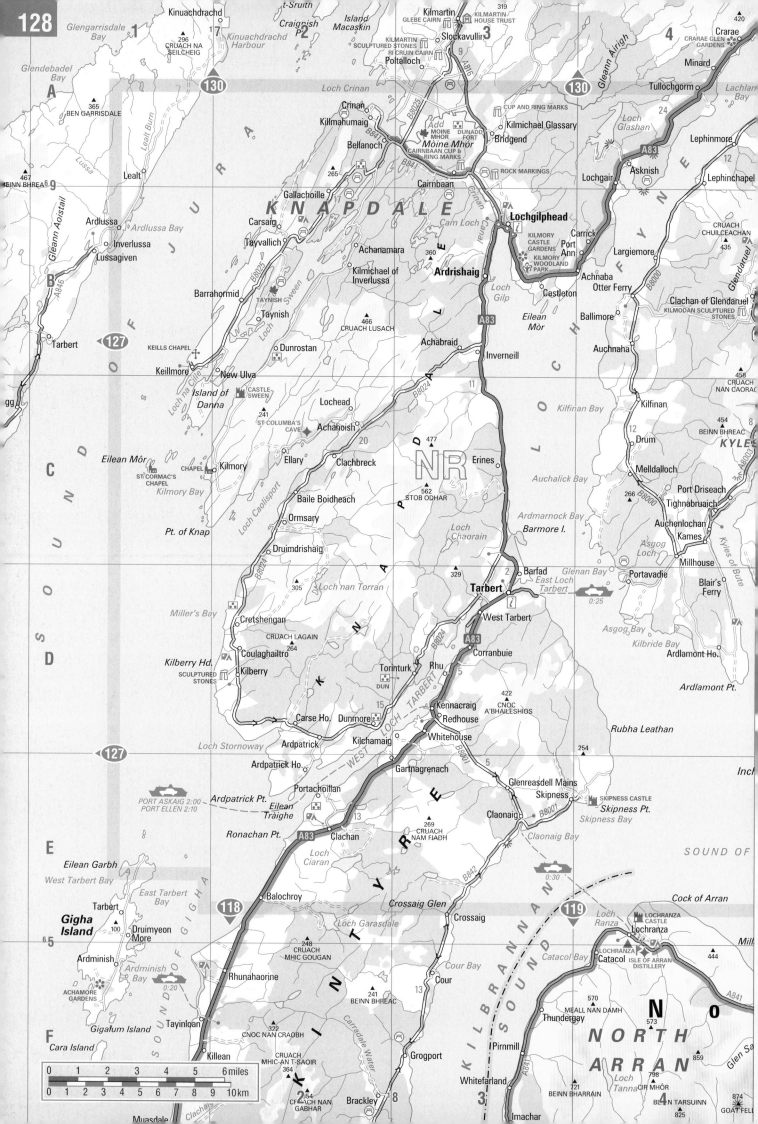

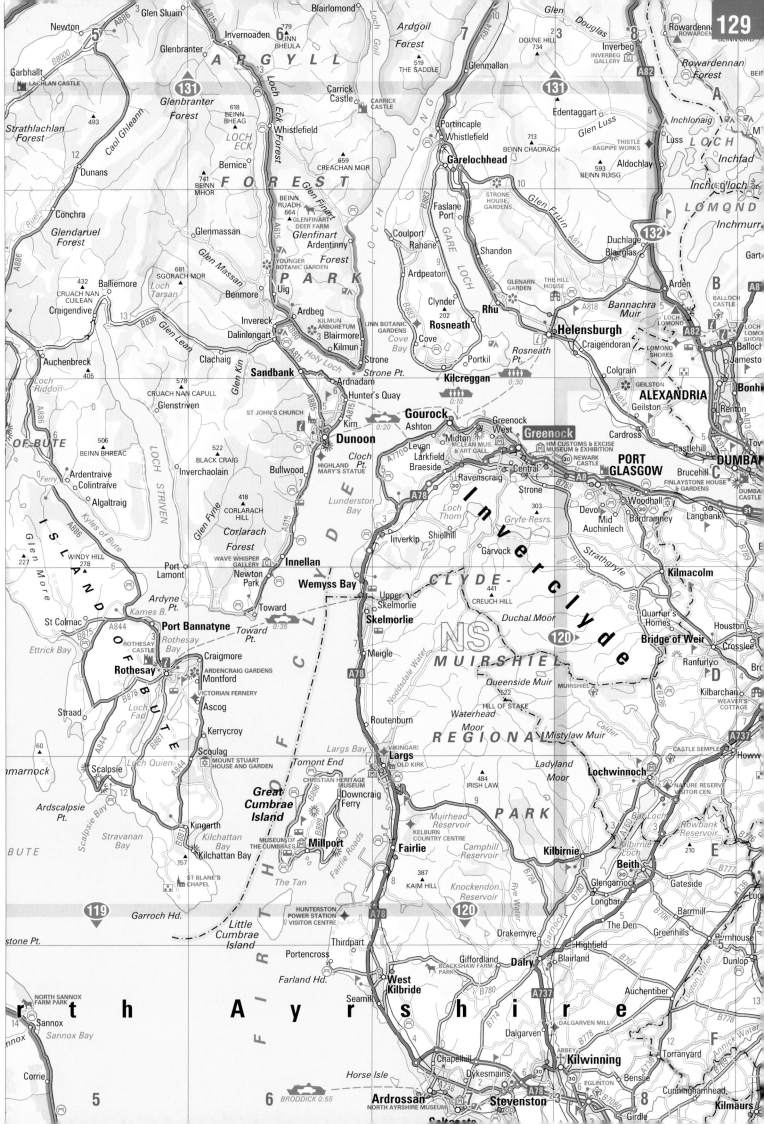

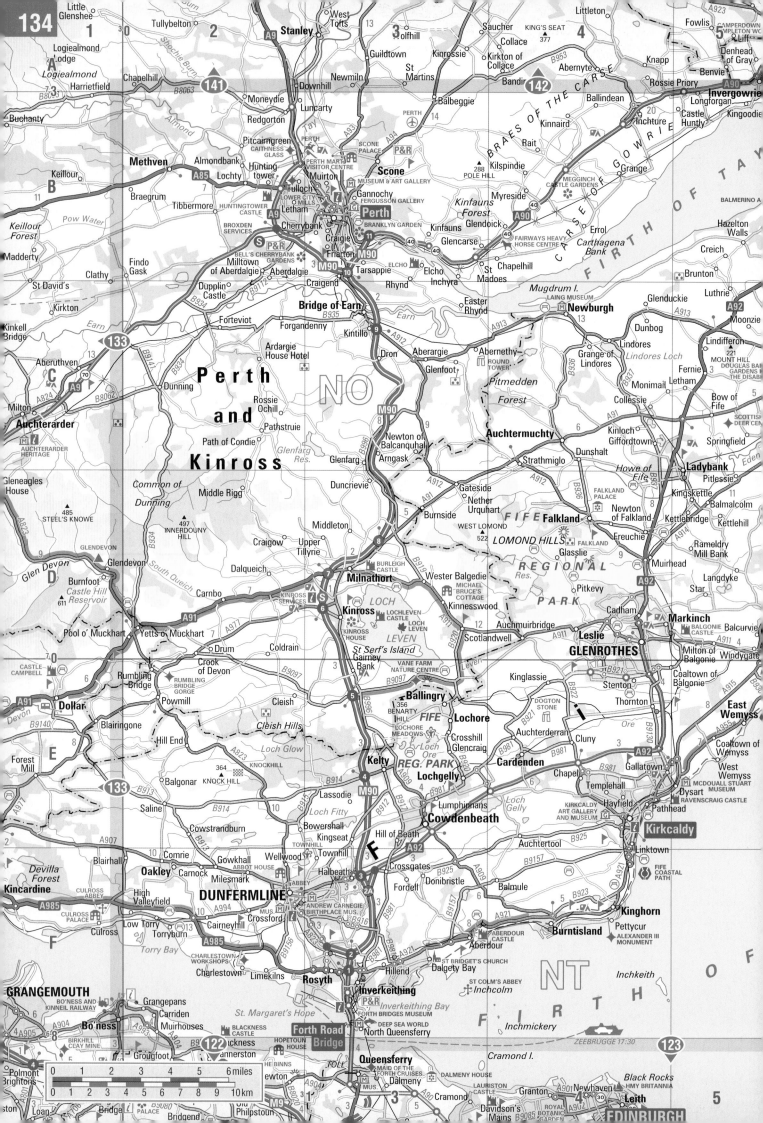

A

B

7

144

Po
Ardnam
ARDNAMURCHAN LI

Cairns of Coll

Rubha Mor   *Eilean Mor*

Sorisdale

Bousd

Cliad Bay
Arnabost   Gallanach
Grishipoll   B8072

COLL   OBAN 2:40

Ballyhaugh   Loch
                   Cliad   73
▲104   B8071

Hogh Bay   Quinish

Totronald   B8070   *Rubha
                                                        an Aird*
C   *Feall* Arileod   Acha   Arinagour   Caliach Pt.   Sunipol

     Bay   *Eilean   M o r n i s h*
                                    Ornsay*
     Calgary Pt. Breachacha   Loch
                    Castle Friesland Eatharna   Calgary

Gunna   Loch   *Calgary Bay*

     Crossapol *Soa* Breachacha   Ensay
      Bay   *Treshnish Pt.*
                                                          Haunn   B8073
T I R E E   *Vaul*   CARN
Balephetrish Bay Salum Caolas   *Rubh a'Chaoil*   Kilninian
Bay   Vaul   *Rubha Dubh*   Burg
         B8069 Ruaig
D Kenovay *Gott Bay* *Soa*   *Treshnish Isles*   *Fladda*
   B8068   0:55
   TIREE Scarinish   NM   *Eilean Dioghlum*   *L O C H*
   B8065 Heanish   *Lunga*
Crossapol *Rubha Traigh*   *Gometra*   *Bearnus*
Hynish Bay *an Duin*
Balemartine   *U*
Mannal
                                               Bac Mor

E
                                                              *Little
                                                               Colonsay*

                                                    Staffa ♣ STAFFA
     0   1   2   3   4   5   6 miles   ◆ FINGAL'S CAVE
     0 1 2 3 4 5 6 7 8 9 10km
                                              A r g y l l

                                                         Erisgeir
                                               2

                                                  (April-Oct)
                                                   0:45

NL   T I R E E   *Vaul*
                    Bay
Hough   Balevullin *Balephetrish* Salum Caolas
Skerries   *Bay*   Vaul
                              B8069
R. Chraiginis   Ruaig
F Kilkenneth Kenovay   *Gott Bay*   *Eilean
   Moss   B8068   Annraidh*   *Rubha nan Cearc*
Middleton Heylipol TIREE Scarinish   MACLEAN'S CROSS
Port Mor B8065   COLL 0:55   IONA ABBEY AND
   Barrapol Crossapol Heanish   CATHEDRAL   Kintra
   B8067 Balemartine *Rubha Traigh*   IONA HERITAGE CENTRE
Loch   *an Duin*   ST COLUMBA EXHIBITION
a'Phuill Balephuil   *Hynish Bay*   & WELCOME CENTRE
Rinn   ▲141 Mannal   Iona   Baile Mor Aridhglas   Eorabus
Thorbhais Balephuil   NM   *Stac an*   A849
4   B8068   *Aoineidh* Fionnphort
        Hynish   Fidden   Tiraghoil   Bunessa
Balephuil *Port Snoig*   *Loch
  Bay   *Erraid*   ▲   Assapol*
G   *Eilean a'Chalmain* R O S S O F
   1   10   2   3   *Soa I.*   Ardalanish Uiskeo
9   125 Ardchiavai
                                                    4
                                              Rubh Ardalanish

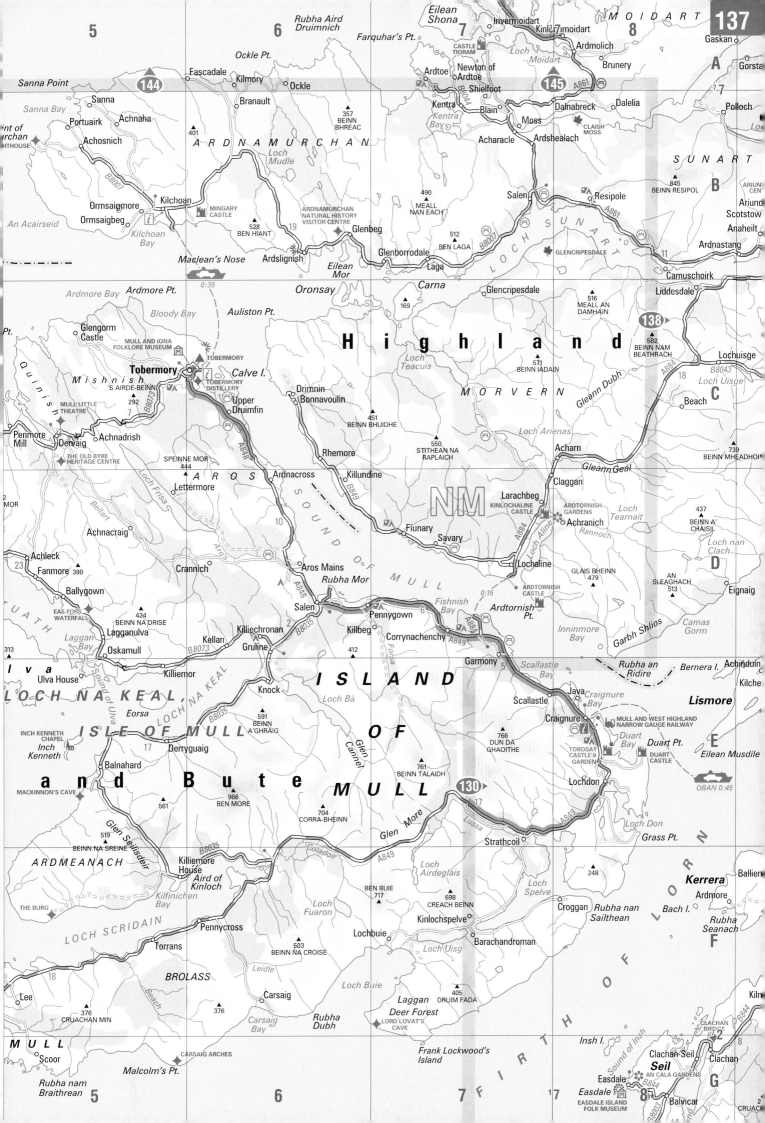

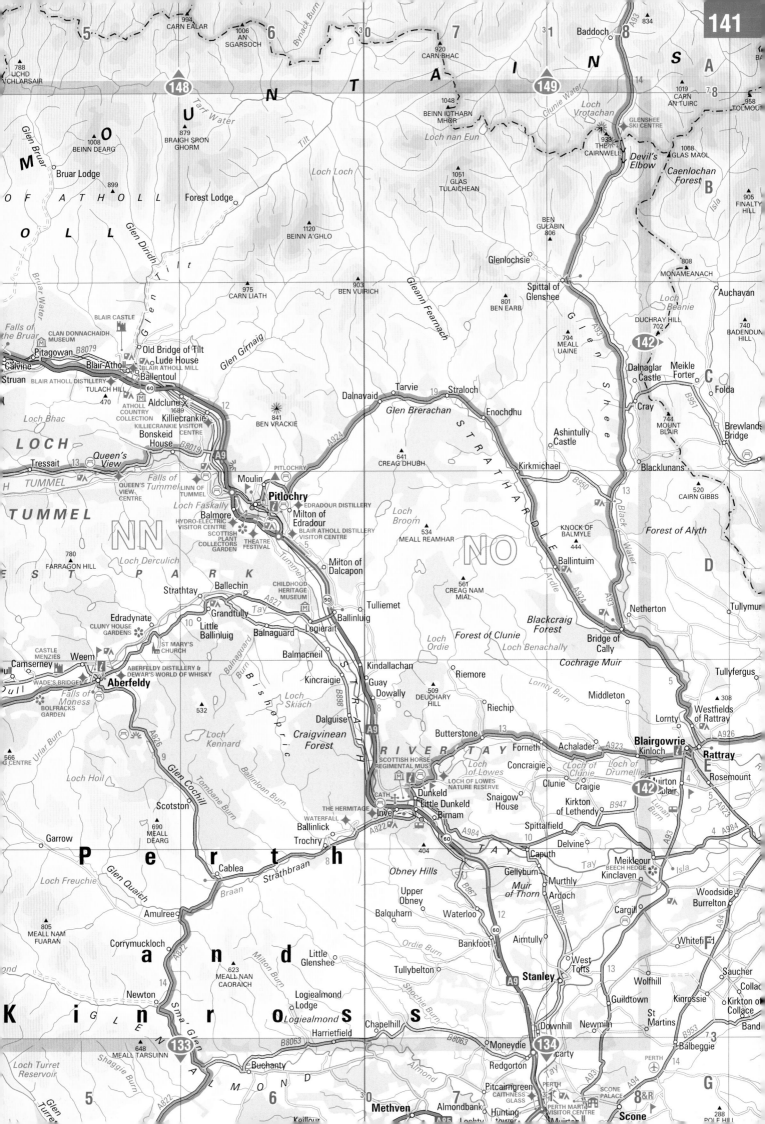

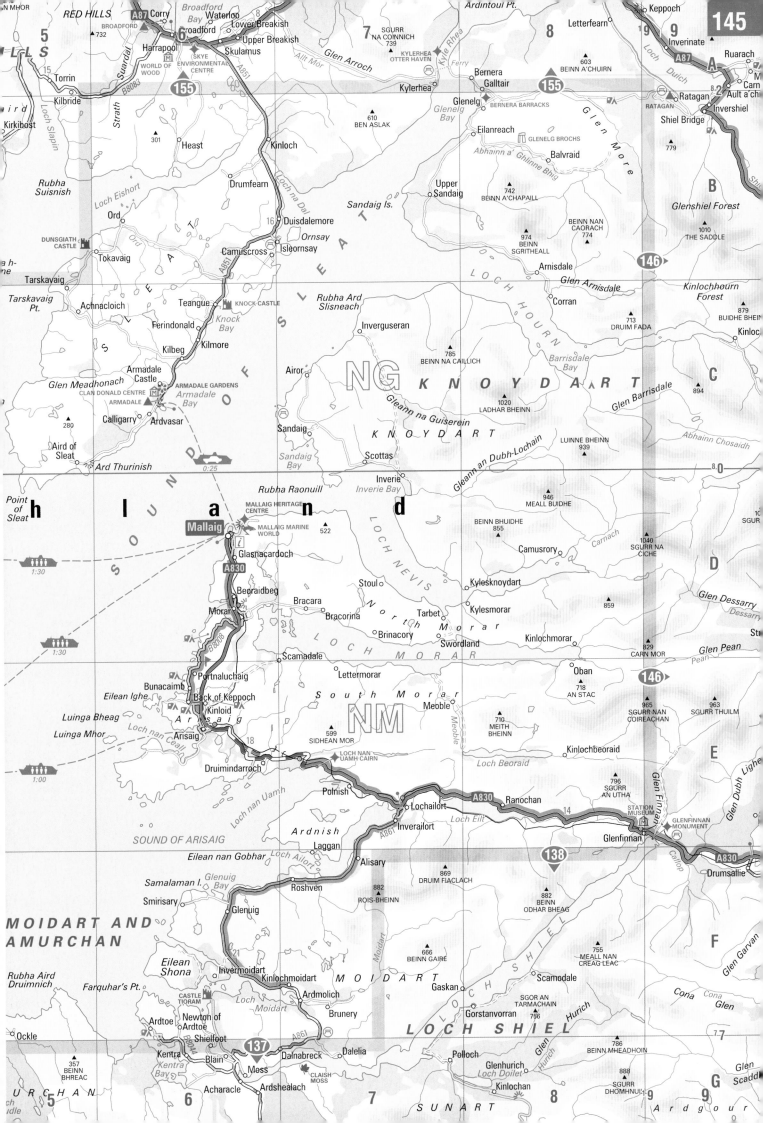

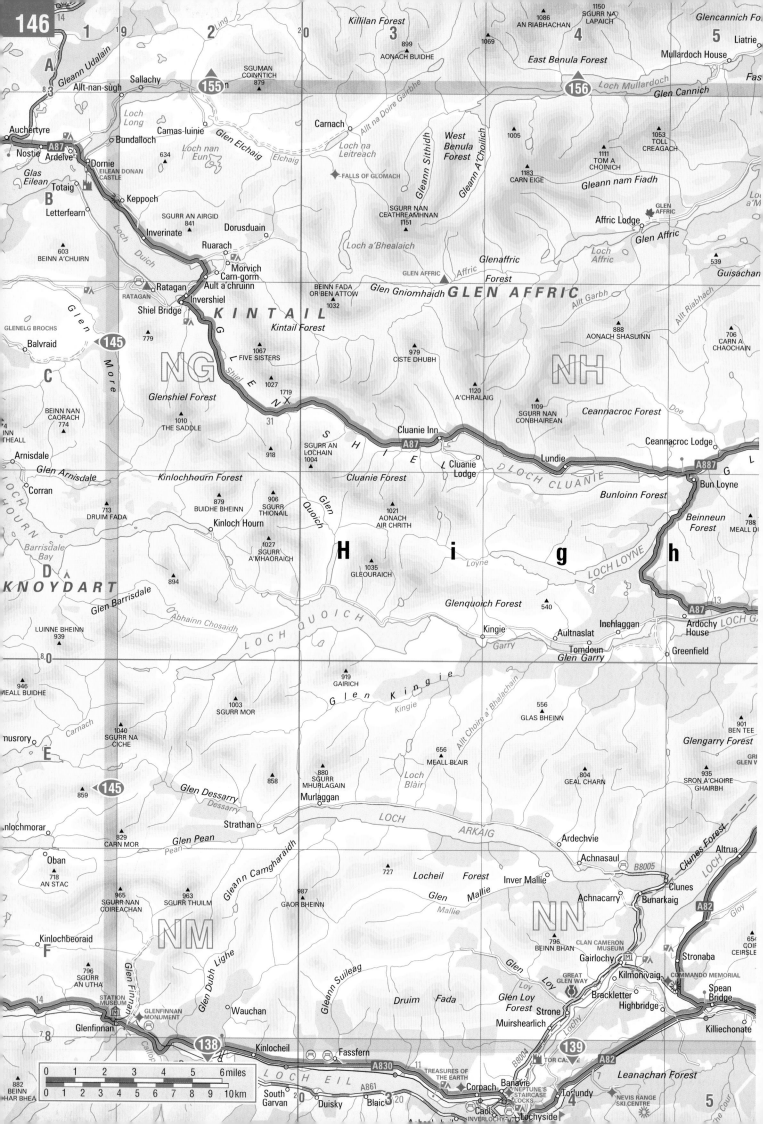

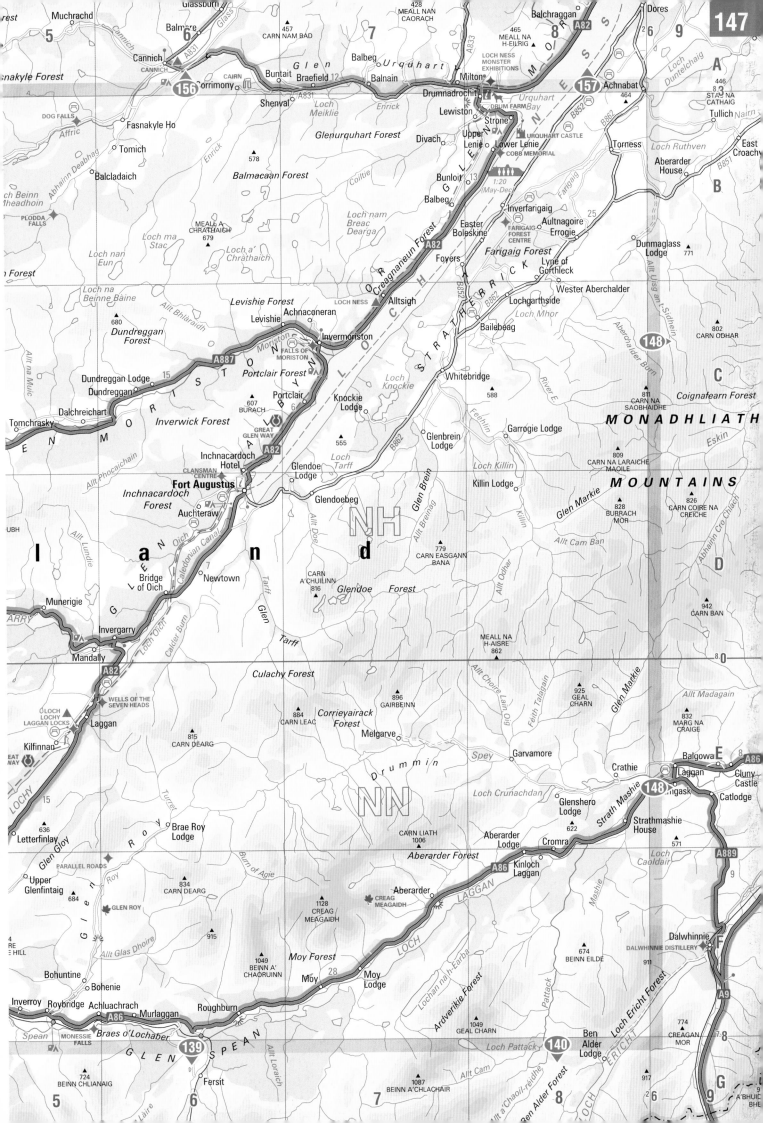

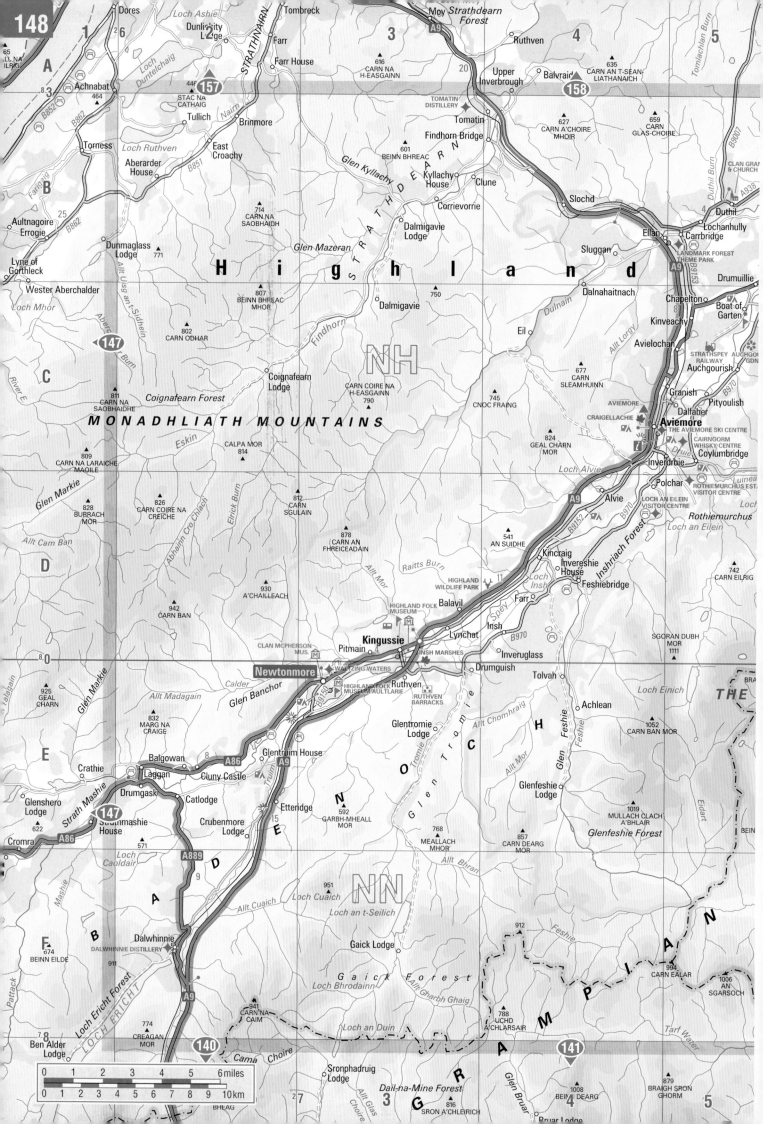

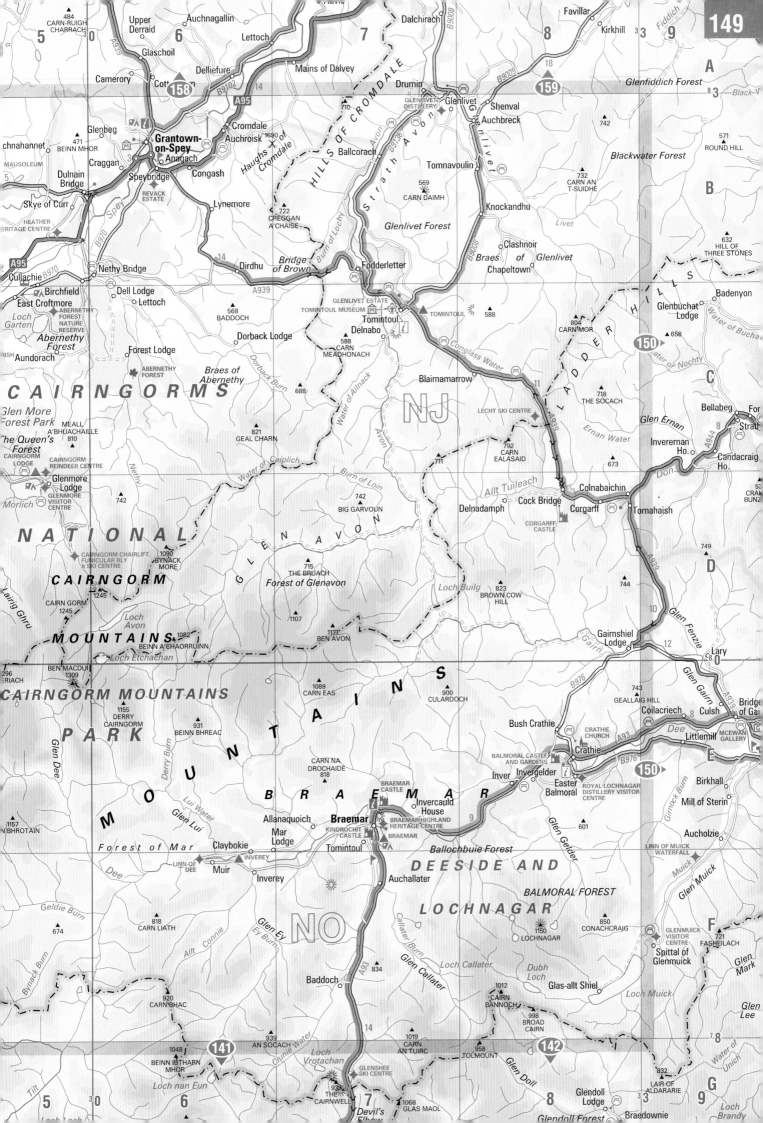

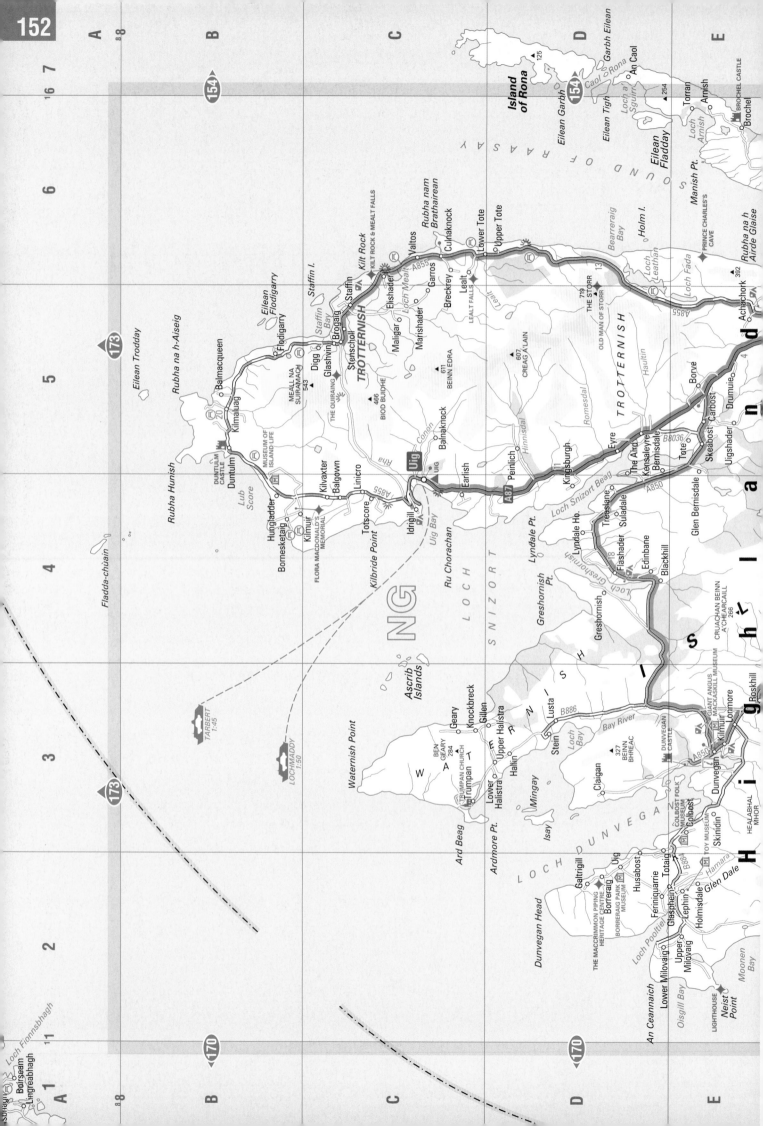

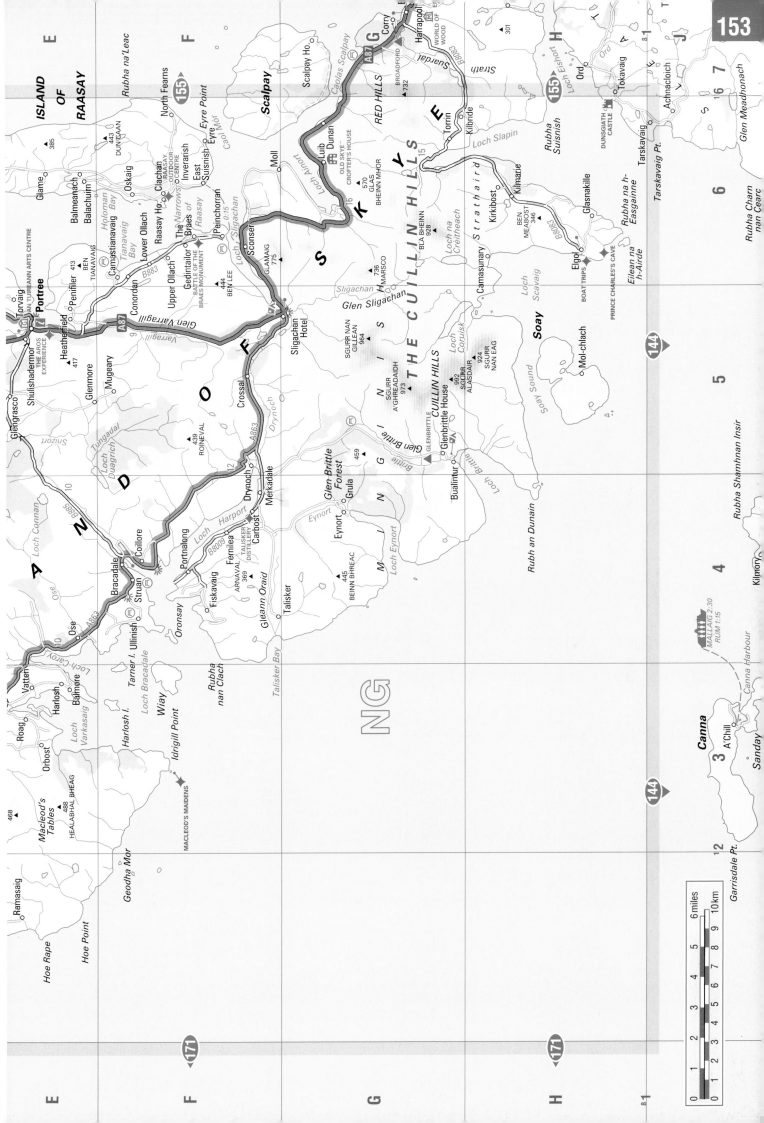

ISLAND

OF

RAASAY

Rubha na'Leac

Glame

Balmeanach
Balachuirn

385

443
DUNCAAN

North Fearns

Eyre Point

Caol Mór

Eyre

East
Suisnish

Holoman Bay

Oskaig

Clachan
Inverarish
RAASAY
OUTDOOR
CENTRE

Tianavaig
Bay

Lower Ollach

Raasay Ho.

The Narrows
Braes of
Raasay

Peinchorran

Camastianavaig

413
BEN
TIANAVAIG

Penifiler

Upper Ollach

Conordan

GEDINTAILOR
BATTLE OF THE
BRAES MONUMENT

444
BEN LEE

Loch
Sligachan

0:15

Scalpay Ho.

Moll

Scalpay

Scalpay

RED HILLS

Caolas Scalpay

Scuardal

BROADFORD

Harrapool
Corry

WORLD OF
WOOD

301

A87

B8065

Strath

G

E

Torrin

Kilbride

Loch Slapin

Rubha Suisnish

Loch Ainort

Dunan

Luib

570
GLAS
BHEINN MHOR

OLD SKYE
CROFTER'S HOUSE

732

DUNSGIATH
CASTLE

Tokavaig

Achnacloich

Ord

Rubha na h-
Easgainne

Tarskavaig Pt.

Rubha Charn
nan Cearc

Glen Meadhonach

S   K   Y   E

BLA BHEINN
928

Loch na
Crèitheach

Tarskavaig

Glasnakille

Kilmarie

Kirkibost

BEN
MEABOST
346

Elgol

PRINCE CHARLES'S CAVE

BOAT TRIPS

Eilean na
h-Airde

B8083

Kilmore

Glasnakille

Strathaird

Camasunary

THE CUILLIN HILLS

736
MARSCO

Sligachan

Glen Sligachan

SGURR NAN
GILLEAN
964

Glamaig
775

Sconser

GLAMAIG

Loch

Varragill

Glen Varragill

A87

Sligachan
Hotel

SGURR
A'GHREADAIDH
973

Loch
Coruisk

CUILLIN HILLS

992
SGURR
ALASDAIR

924
SGURR
NAN EAG

Soay

Soay Sound

Mol-chlach

Loch
Scavaig

Rubha Shamhnan Insir

Portree

Torvaig

THE AROS
EXPERIENCE

AN TUIREANN ARTS CENTRE

Heatherfield

417

Shulishadermor

Glengrasco

Glenmore

Mugeary

439
ROINEVAL

Crossal

A863

Drynoch

Merkadale

12

Glen Brittle
Forest

459

Grula

Eynort

GLENBRITTLE

Glen Brittle

Brittle

Glenbrittle House

Bualintur

Loch Brittle

Rubh an Dunain

Snizort

Loch
Duagrich

Tungadal

10

A

N

D

O

F

Coillore

Bracadale

Struan

Ose

A863

Ullinish

Tarner I.

Portnalong

Fiskavaig

Fernilea

B8009

ARNAVAL
369

Carbost

TALISKER
DISTILLERY

Oronsay

Gleann Oraid

Talisker

445
BEINN BHREAC

Loch Eynort

Eynort

Loch Harport

Loch Bracadale

Wiay

Harlosh I.

Idrigill Point

Rubha
nan Clach

Talisker Bay

NG

Roag

Orbost

Balmore

Harlosh

Vatten

Loch Caroy

Loch
Varkasaig

Ramasaig

Hoe Rape

Hoe Point

468

Macleod's
Tables

488
HEALABHAL BHEAG

Geodha Mor

MACLEOD'S MAIDENS

Garrisdale Pt.

Canna

A'Chill

Sanday

Canna Harbour

MALLAIG 2:30
RUM 1:15

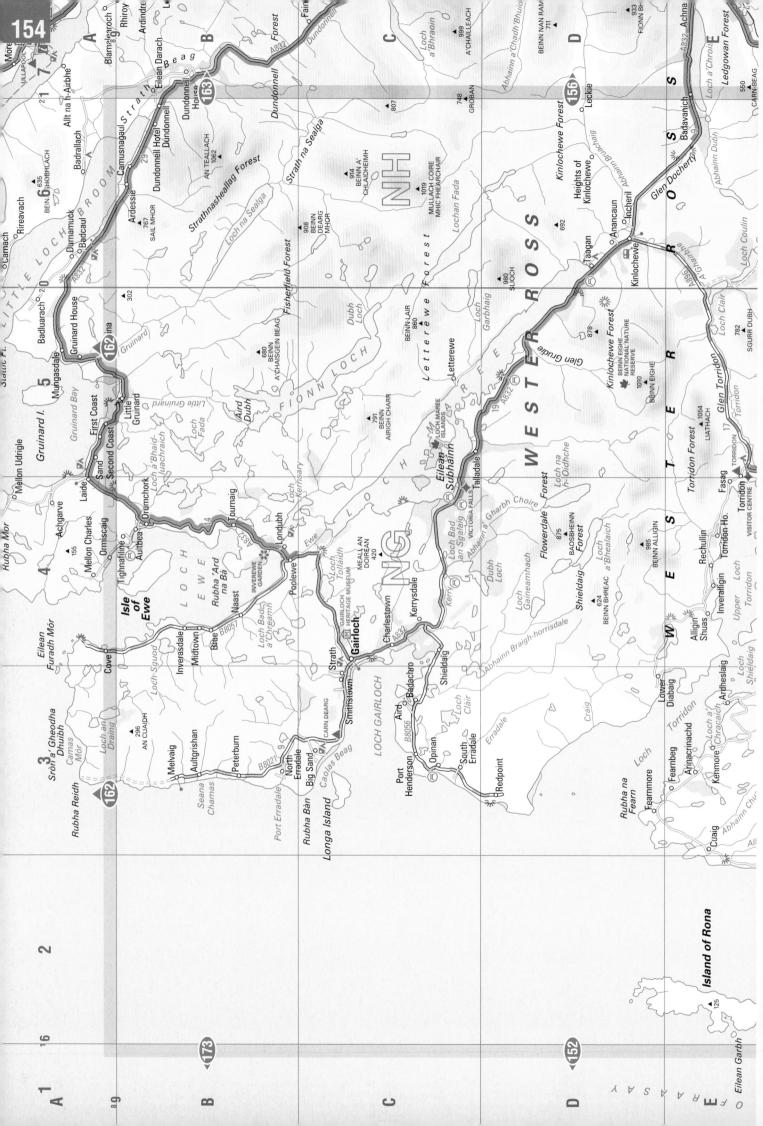

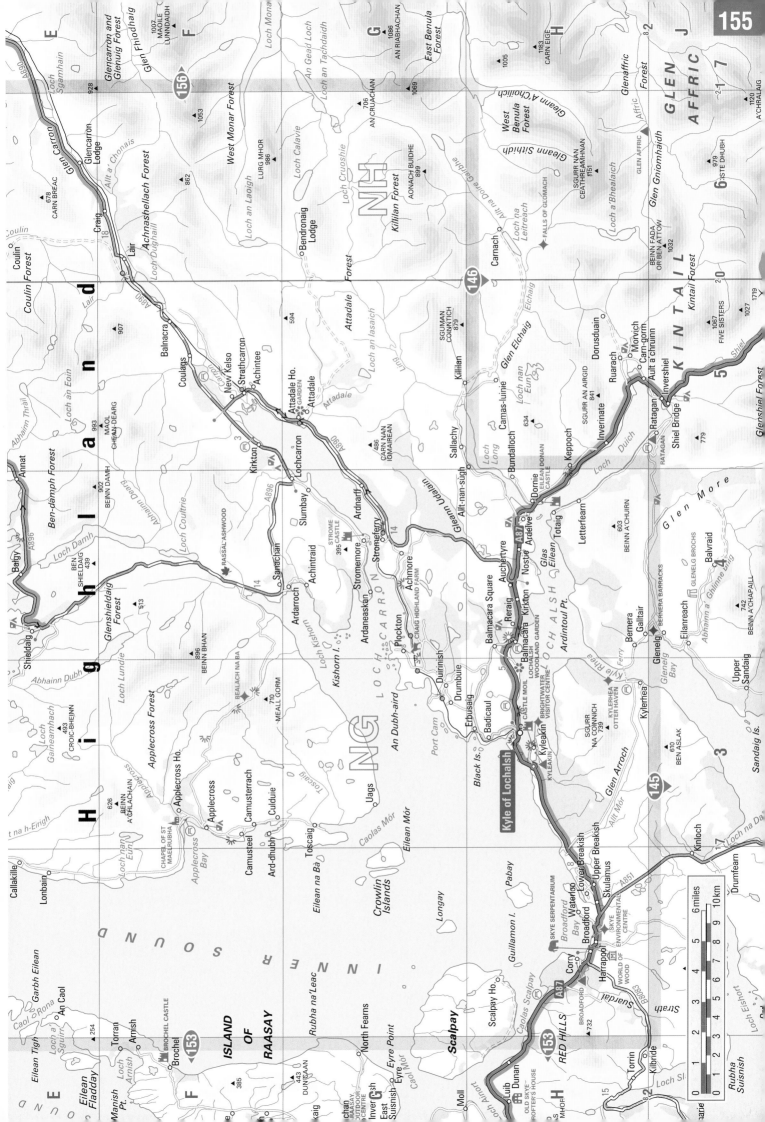

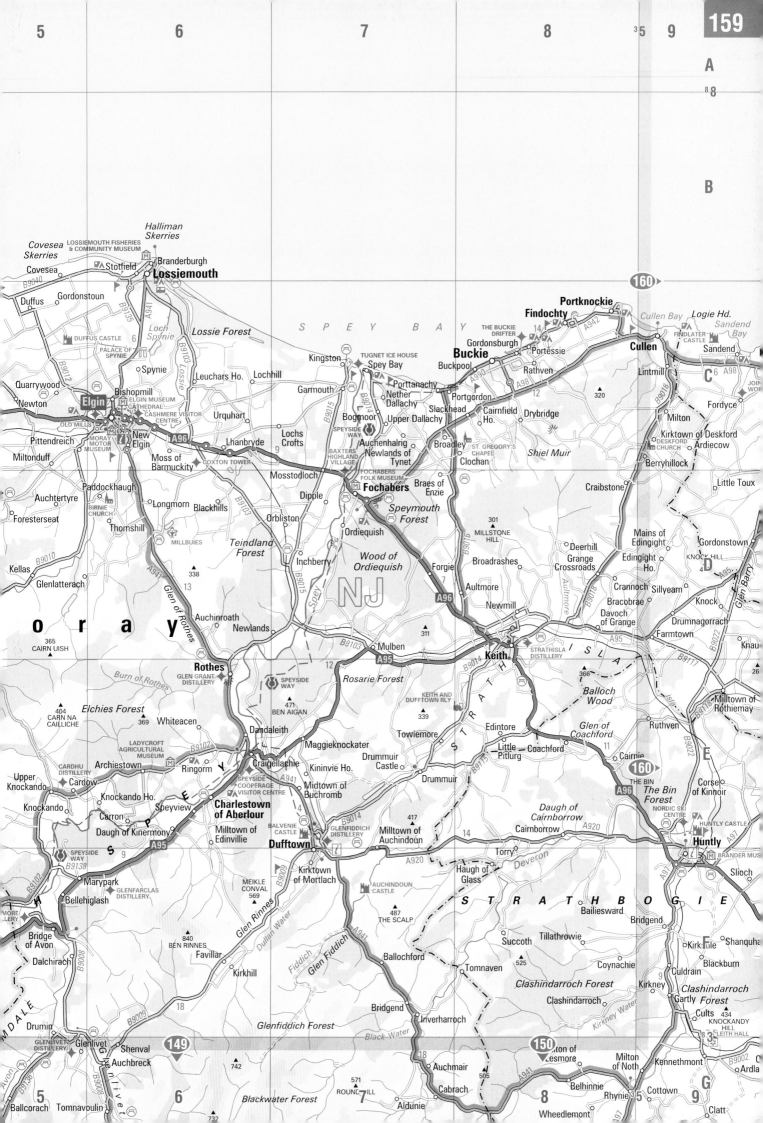

5   6   7   8   9

A

B

C

NK

D

E

F

G

Rosehearty
SANDHAVEN MEAL MILL
B9031
Pittulie
FRASERBURGH HERITAGE MUSEUM
Fraserburgh
Broadsea
Kinnaird Head
KINNAIRD CASTLE LIGHTHOUSE & SCOTLAND'S LIGHTHOUSE MUSEUM
PITSLIGO CASTLE
Sandhaven
Peathill
Quarry Hd.
Percyhorner
Pitblae
Fraserburgh Bay
Cairnbulg Pt.
Inverallochy
Coburty
A981
A90
B9033
Cairnbulg Castle
MAGGIE'S HOOSIE
Towie
Upper Boyndlie
Mid Ardlaw
Memsie
Gowanhill
St Combs
Inzie Head
New Aberdour
Tyrie
Whitewell
MEMSIE BURIAL CAIRN
Rathen
Strathellie
Cairness
Loch of Strathbeg
Ladysford
10
Hillhead of Auchentumb
Newburgh
230 MORMOND HILL
Lonmay
Crimonmogate
LOCH OF STRATHBEG NATURE RESERVE VISITOR CENTRE
Rattray Head
Nether Glasslaw
16
Craigmaud
Crimond
Old Rattray
New Pitsligo
Knowhead
Strichen
New Leeds
Nether Park
Blackhill
A90
Bonnykelly
B9093
Adziel
Longhill
Balearn
St Fergus Moss
Ironside
NJ
Little Skillymarno
Denhead
Leys
Backfolds
Kirktown
St Fergus
Scotstown Hd.
Oldwhat
11
Fetterangus
Hythie
Rora Moss
Rora
North Kirkton
Kirkton Hd.
Mains of Fedderate
Forest of Deer
DEER ABBEY
Toux
Dunshillock
Woodside
Lunderton
Culsh
B
U
C
H
A
N
Water
Newseat
Inverugie
INVERUGIE CASTLE
UGIE SALMON FISH HOUSE
Maud
MAUD RAILWAY MUSEUM
Old Deer
Mintlaw
Longside
Torterston
Buchanhaven
New Deer
B9029
Backhill of Clackriach
ABERDEENSHIRE FARMING MUSEUM
Flushing
Peterhead
S h i r e
Stuartfield
Millbreck
Inverquhomery
A950
ARBUTHNOT MUSEUM & ART GALLERY
Drymuir
Bulwark
Mains of Crichie
Nether Kinmundy
Hillhead of Cocklaw
PETERHEAD MARITIME
Keith Inch
Knaven
Crichie
Clola
Little Dens
Invernettie
Sandford Bay
Crofts of Meikle Ardo
Nethermuir
Kinnadie Skelmuir
Blackhill
Millbank
Boddam
Buchan Ness
Cairnorrie
Barrack
Auchnagatt
Mains of Annochie
Backhill of Fortree
Kinknockie Smallburn
Sandfordhill
Stirling
Brownhill
Mains of Inkhorn
Moss of Cruden
Coldwells
14
Skelmonae
Milton Coldwells
Backhill
Stoneygate
Teuchan
Longhaven
Quilquox
13
North Haven
BULLERS OF BUCHAN
Methlick
Drumwhindle
Muirtack
Arthrath
Hatton
Auchiries
Twa Havens
Ythan
Toll of Birness
Eastertown of Auchleuchries
Cruden Bay
HADDO HOUSE AND GARDENS
Ythanbank
Hilton
Mains of Birness
Bogbrae
Chapel Hill
Port Erroll
HADDO
Inverebrie
Broomfield
Nether Leask
Bay of Cruden
Wedderlairs
A90
Artrochie
Whinnyfold
Raxton
MEDIEVAL TOMB
West Kinharrachie
P&R
Auchmacoy
15
Tarves
Ythsie
Esslemont
Ellon
151
Kirkton of Logie Buchan
SLAINS CASTLE
Kirktown of Slains
A
R
T
I
N
E
TOLQUHON CASTLE
A920
Meikle Tarty
VISITOR CENTRE
Collieston
St Catherine's Dub
11
PITMEDDEN GARDENS
Pitmedden
Tipperty
Waterside
FORVIE
Sands of Forvie
Cairnbrogie
B9000
Tarty Burn
B9000
Hackley Hd. or Forvie Ness
Udny Green
Culterullen
Foveran
Newburgh
Pettymuick
Udny Station
Minnes Rashiereive
Drums
Newburgh Bar
Affleck
Whiterashes
Tillygreig
Tillycorthie
186
Straloch
14
Ardo Ho.
Delfrigs
Middlemuir
Newmachar
Craigie
Causeyend
Kinmundy
Whitecairns
Belhelvie
B9170
B979
BALMEDIE
Drumligair
Cothall
Balmedie
A90

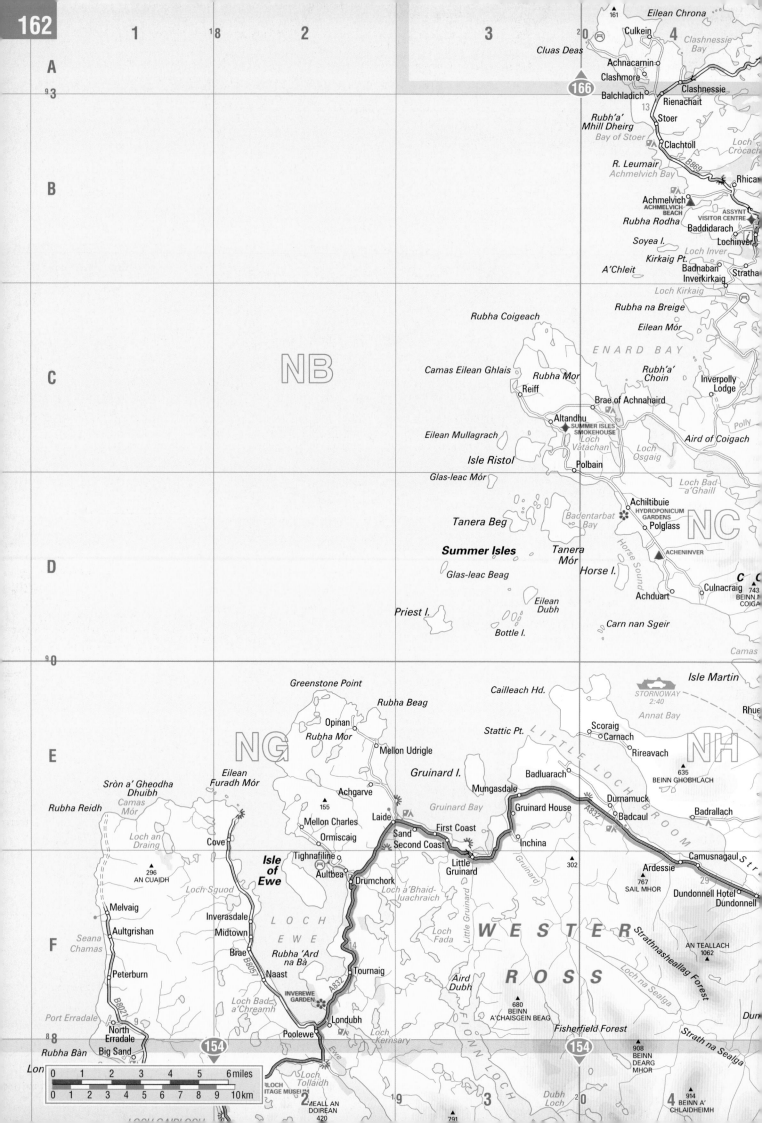

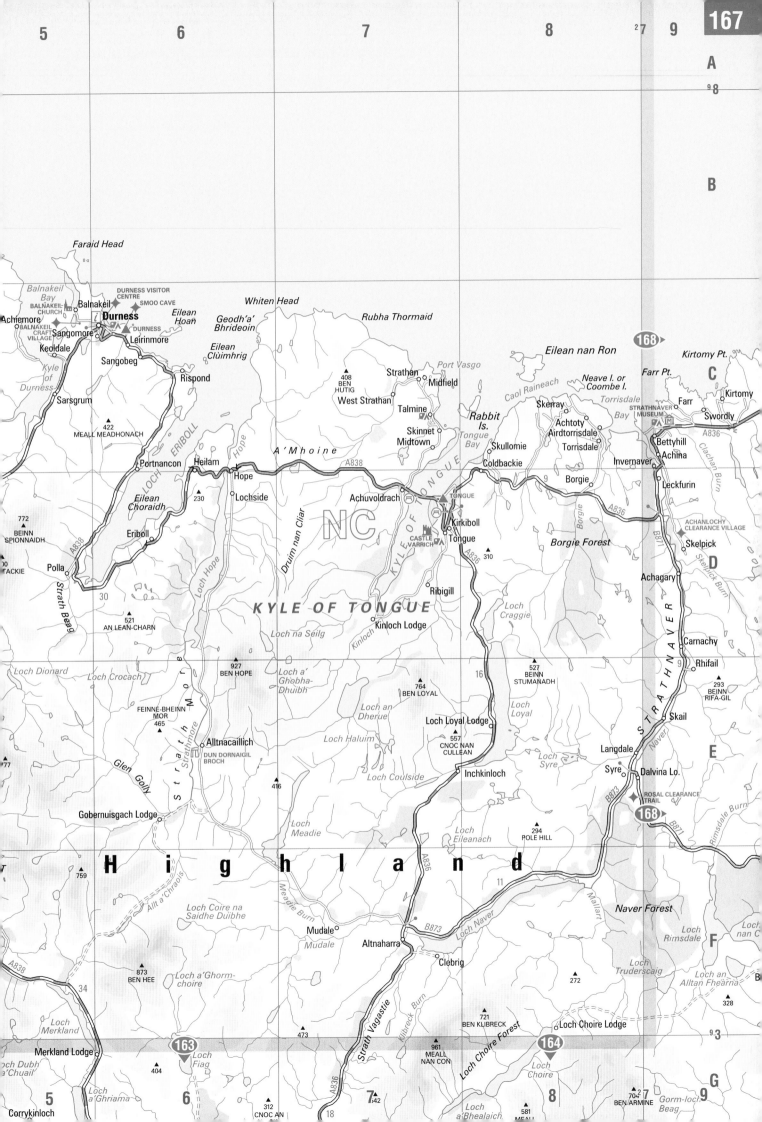

A

B

C

D

E

F

G

5 6 7 8 9

Faraid Head

Balnakeil
Bay
BALNAKEIL
CHURCH
Achiemore
BALNAKEIL
CRAFT
VILLAGE
Keoldale
Sarsgrum
Balnakeil
Durness
Sangomore
Leirinmore
Sangobeg
Rispond

DURNESS VISITOR
CENTRE
SMOO CAVE
DURNESS

Eilean
Hoan

Whiten Head

Geodh'a'
Bhrideoin

Eilean
Clùimhrig

Rubha Thormaid

408
BEN
HUTIG
West Strathan

Strathan
Midfield

Port Vasgo

Talmine

Skinnet
Midtown

Eilean nan Ron

Skerray

Neave I. or
Coombe I.

Kirtomy Pt.

Farr Pt.

STRATHNAVER
MUSEUM

Kirtomy

Farr
Swordly
A836

422
MEALL MEADHONACH

Rabbit
Is.

Tongue
Bay

Achtoty
Airdtorrisdale
Torrisdale

Torrisdale
Bay

Bettyhill
Invernaver
Achina

Clachan Burn

Kyle
of
Durness

Portnancon
Heilam
Hope

Skullomie

Coldbackie

Leckfurin

LOCH ERIBOLL

A'Mhoine

A838

Borgie

ACHANLOCHY
CLEARANCE VILLAGE

772
BEINN
SPIONNAIDH

TACKIE

Eilean
Choraidh

Eriboll

230
Lochside

Hope

Achuvoldrach

NC

Tongue

Kirkiboll
CASTLE
VARRICH
Tongue

Borgie Forest

Skelpick

Achagary

Polla

Strath Beag

A838

521
AN LEAN-CHARN

Druim nan Cliar

KYLE OF TONGUE

KYLE OF TONGUE

Ribigill

310

A836

Loch
Craggie

Loch
Craggie

STRATHNAVER

Carnachy

Rhifail

293
BEINN
RIFA-GIL

Loch Dionard

Loch Crocach

Loch na Seilg

Kinloch Lodge

Kinloch

30

927
BEN HOPE

Loch a'
Ghobha-
Dhuibh

527
BEINN
STUMANADH

16

764
BEN LOYAL

Loch
Loyal

Skail

FEINNE-BHEINN
MOR
465

Strath More

Loch an
Dherue

Loch Haluim

Loch Loyal Lodge

557
CNOC NAN
CULLEAN

Loch
Syre

Langdale
Syre
Dalvina Lo.

Naver

77

Alltnacaillich

DUN DORNAIGIL
BROCH

416

Loch Coulside

Inchkinloch

ROSAL CLEARANCE
TRAIL

B871

168

B871

Gobernuisgach Lodge

Glen Golly

Strathmore

Loch
Meadie

Loch
Eileanach

294
POLE HILL

Rimsdale Burn

Highland

759

Allt a'Chraois

Meadie Burn

Mudale

Mudale

Altnaharra

B873

Loch Naver

Mallart

Naver Forest

Loch
Rimsdale

Loch
nan C

A838

873
BEN HEE

Loch a'Ghorm-
choire

Clebrig

Strath Vagastie

Klibreck Burn

272

Loch
Truderscaig

Loch an
Alltan Fhearna

328

34

Loch
Merkland

473

Merkland Lodge

163

Loch
Fiag

404

721
BEN KLIBRECK

961
MEALL
NAN CON

Loch Choire Forest

164

Loch
Choire

Loch Choire Lodge

93

Loch Dubh
a'Chuail'

Corrykinloch

5

Loch
a'Ghriama

6

312
CNOC AN

7

42

18

8

581
MEALL

704
BEN ARMINE

Gorm-loch
Beag

9

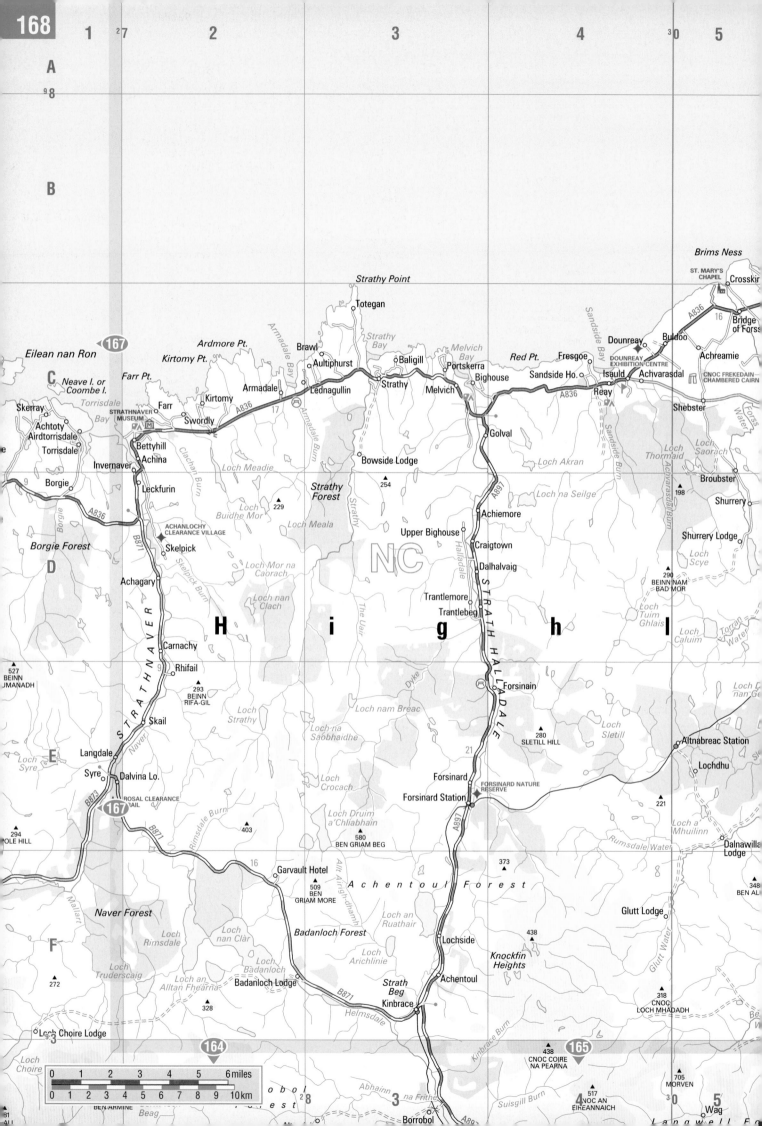

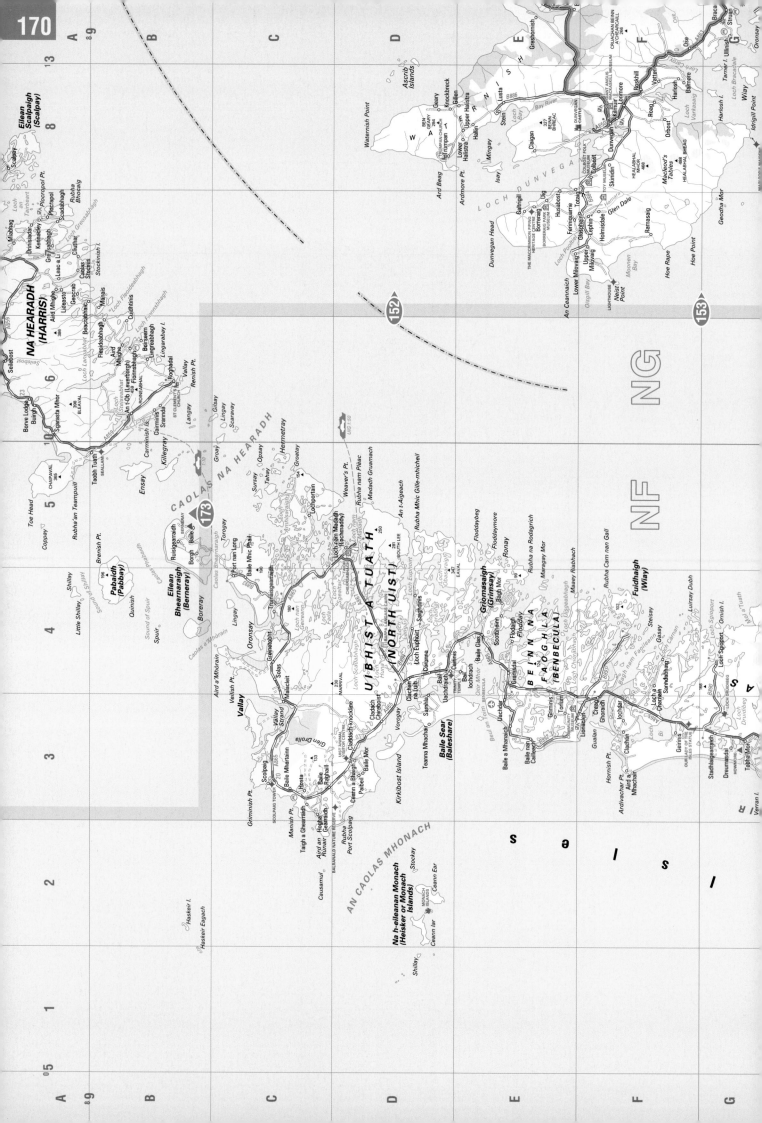

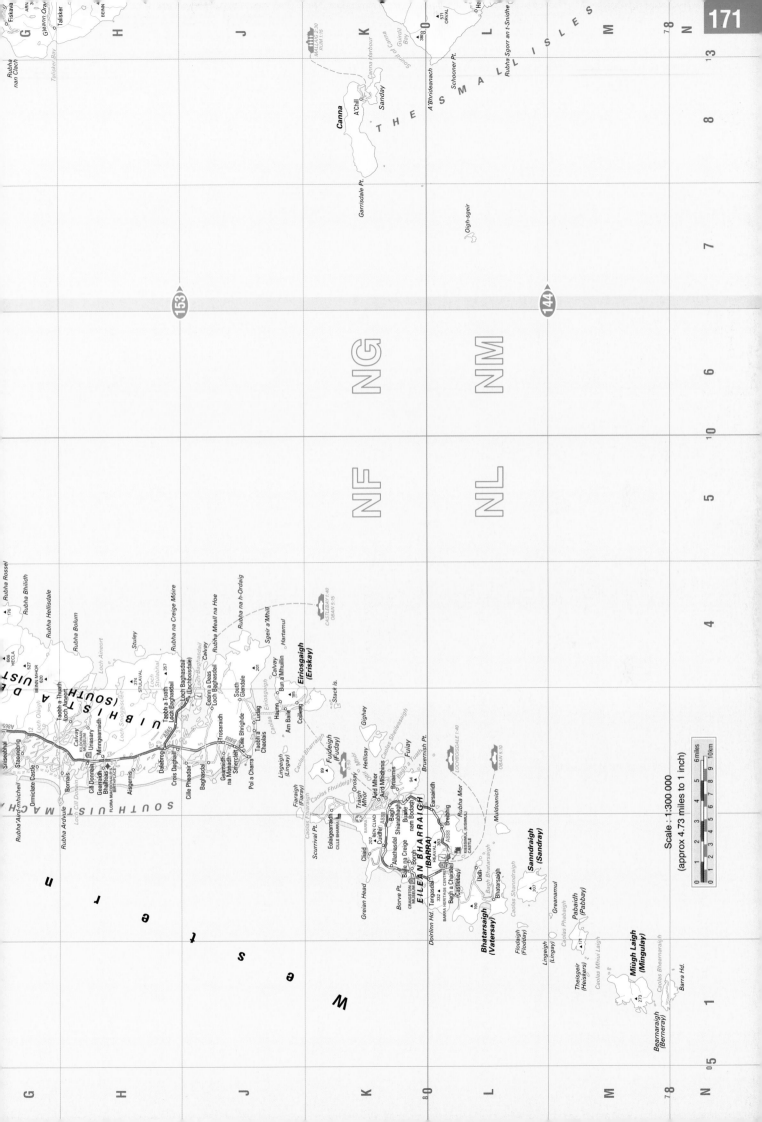

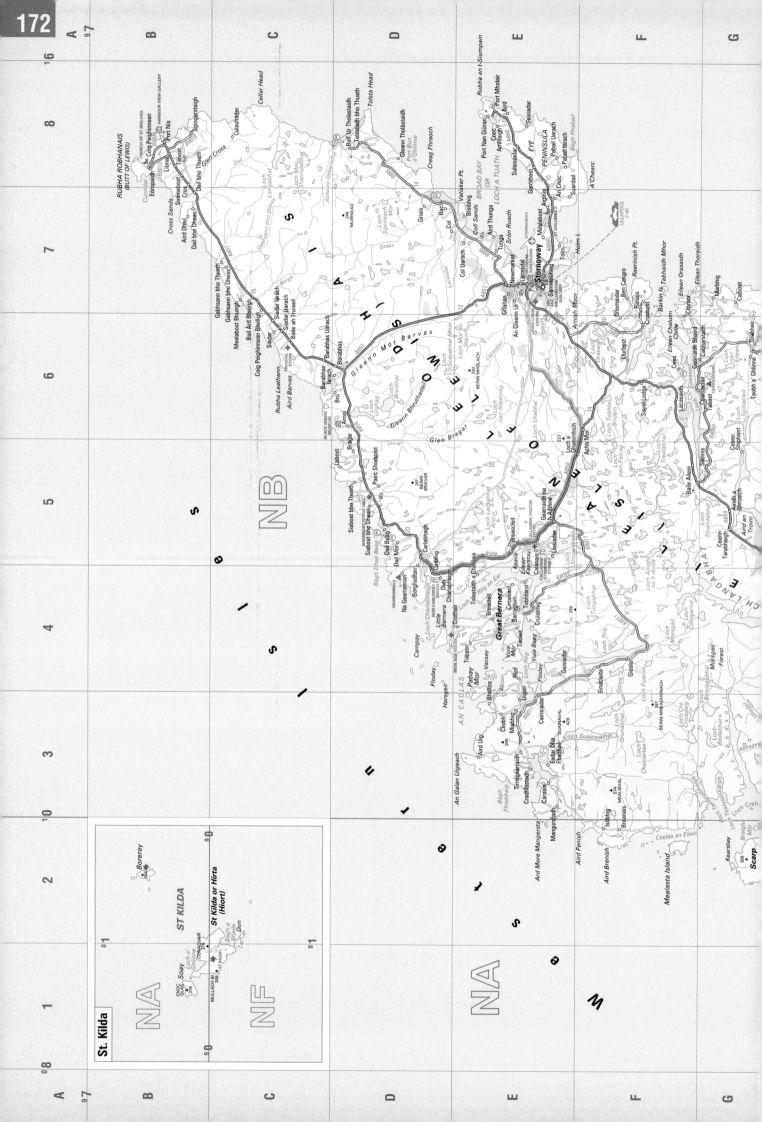

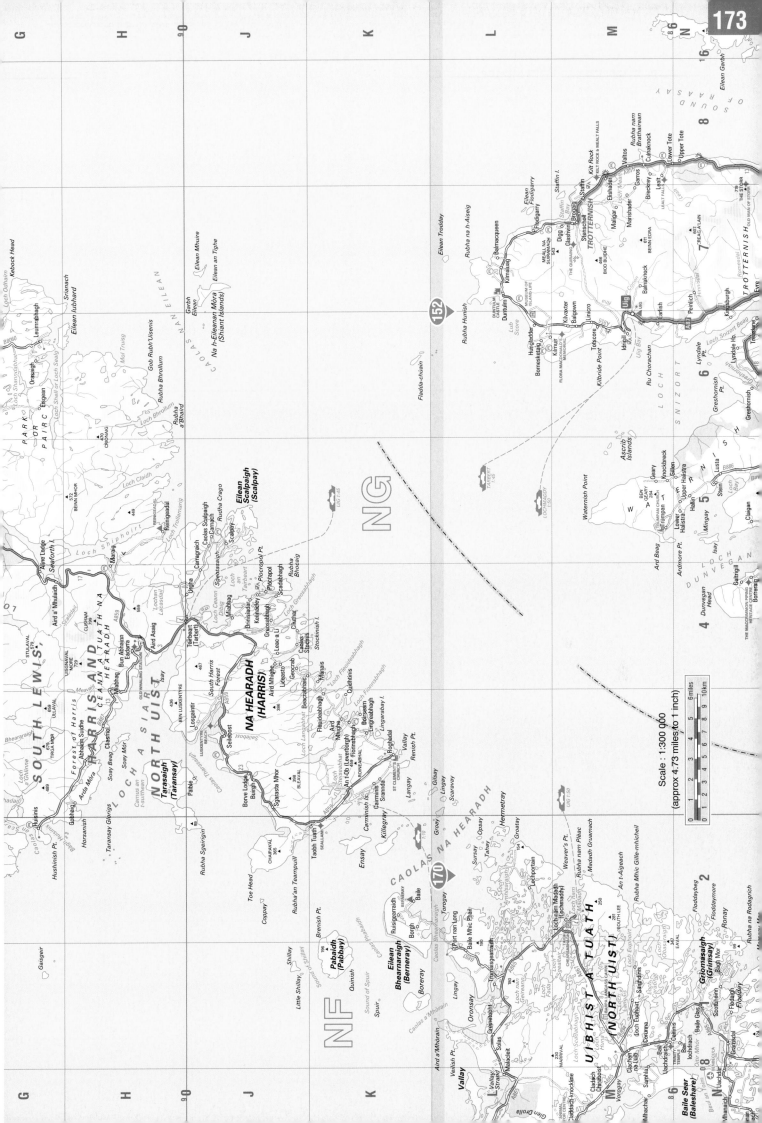

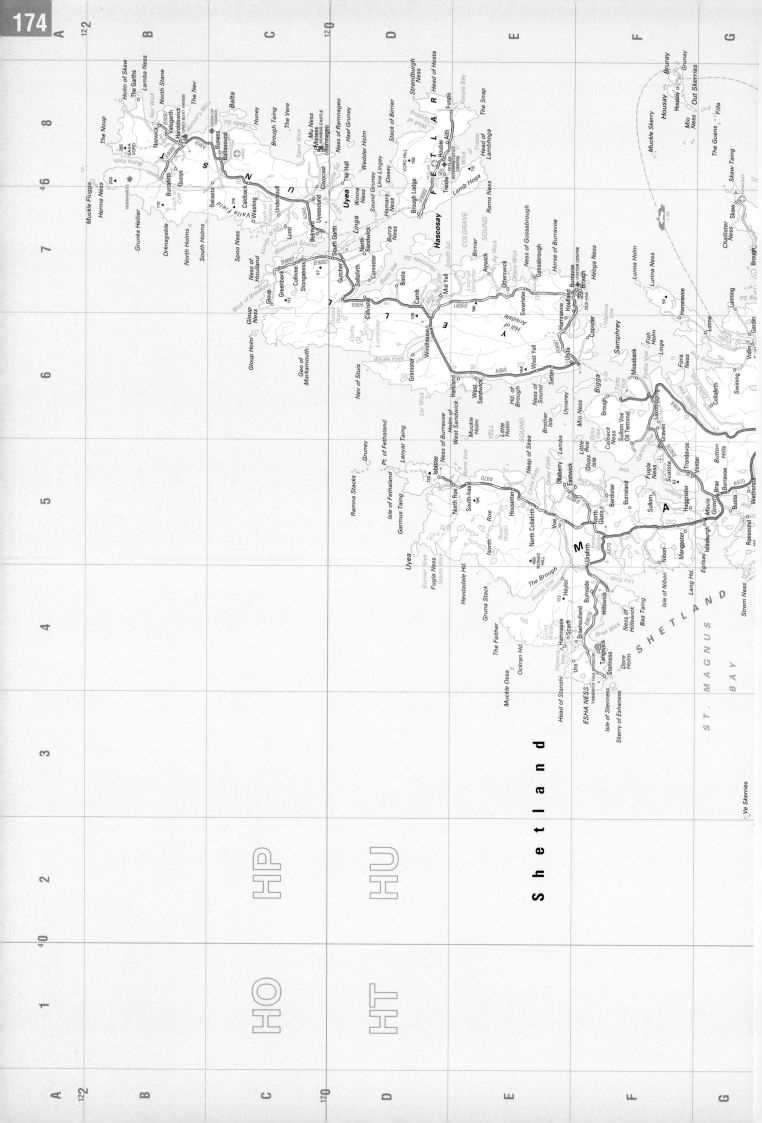

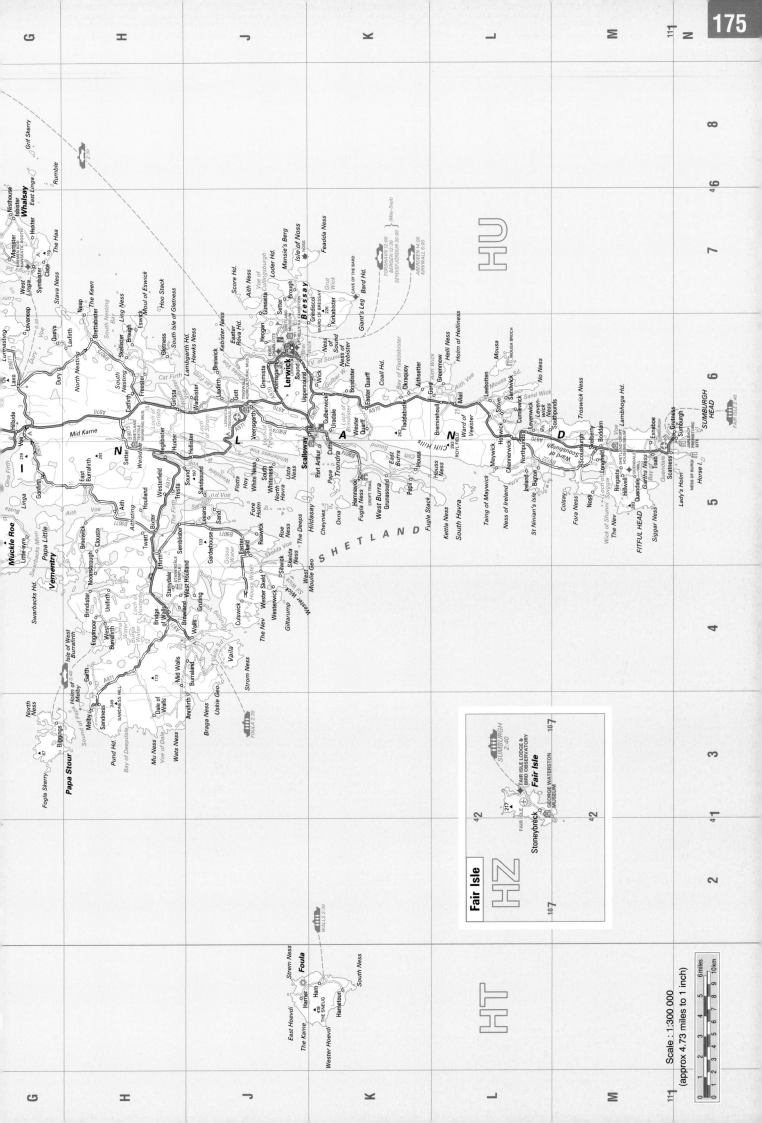

Scale : 1:300 000
(approx 4.73 miles to 1 inch)

Fair Isle

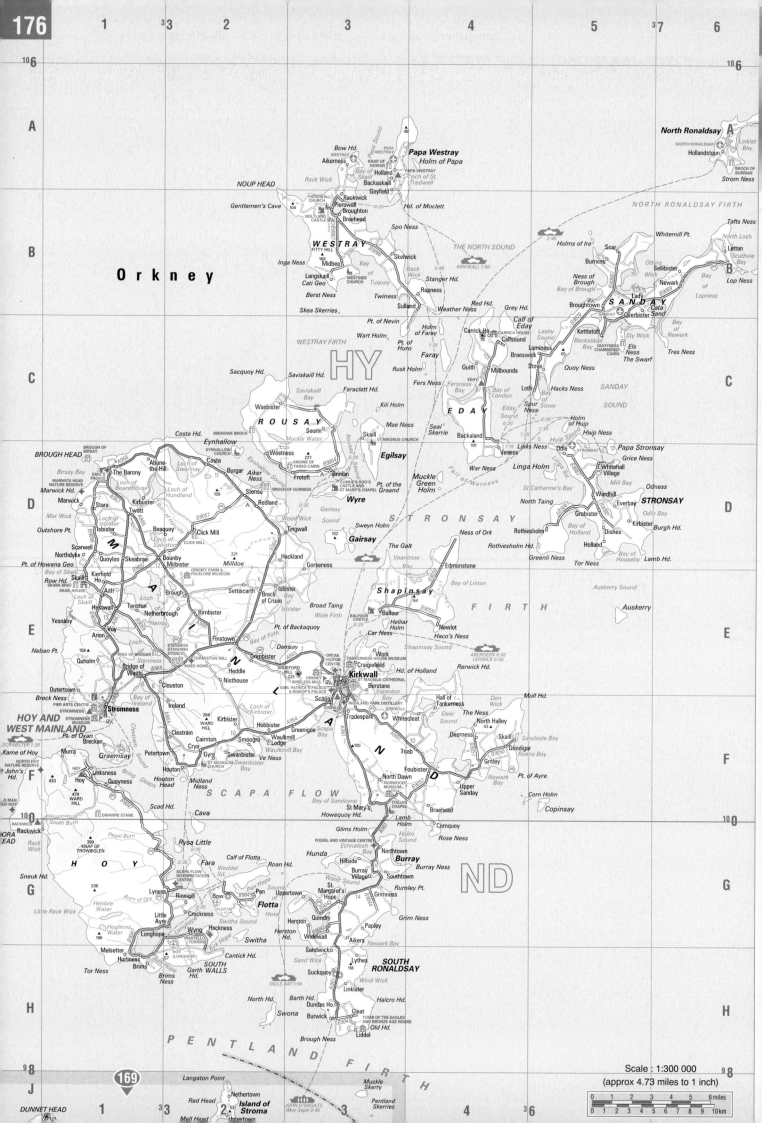

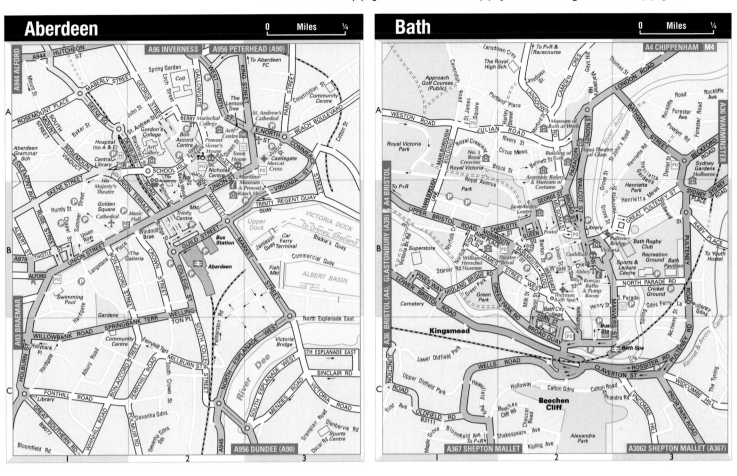

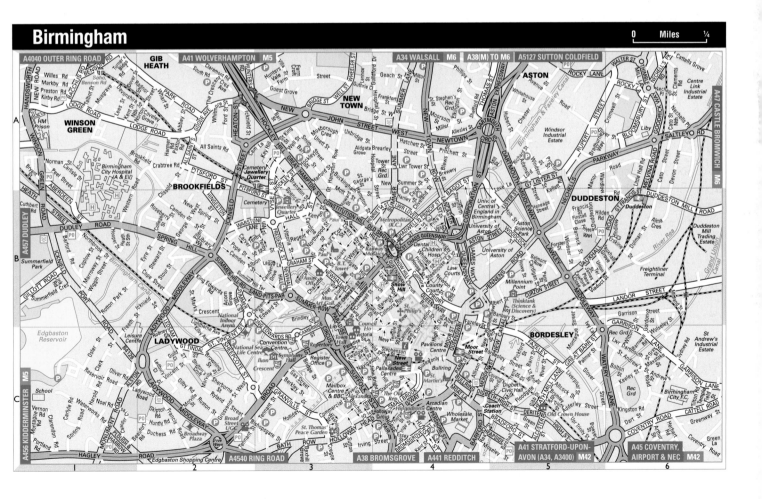

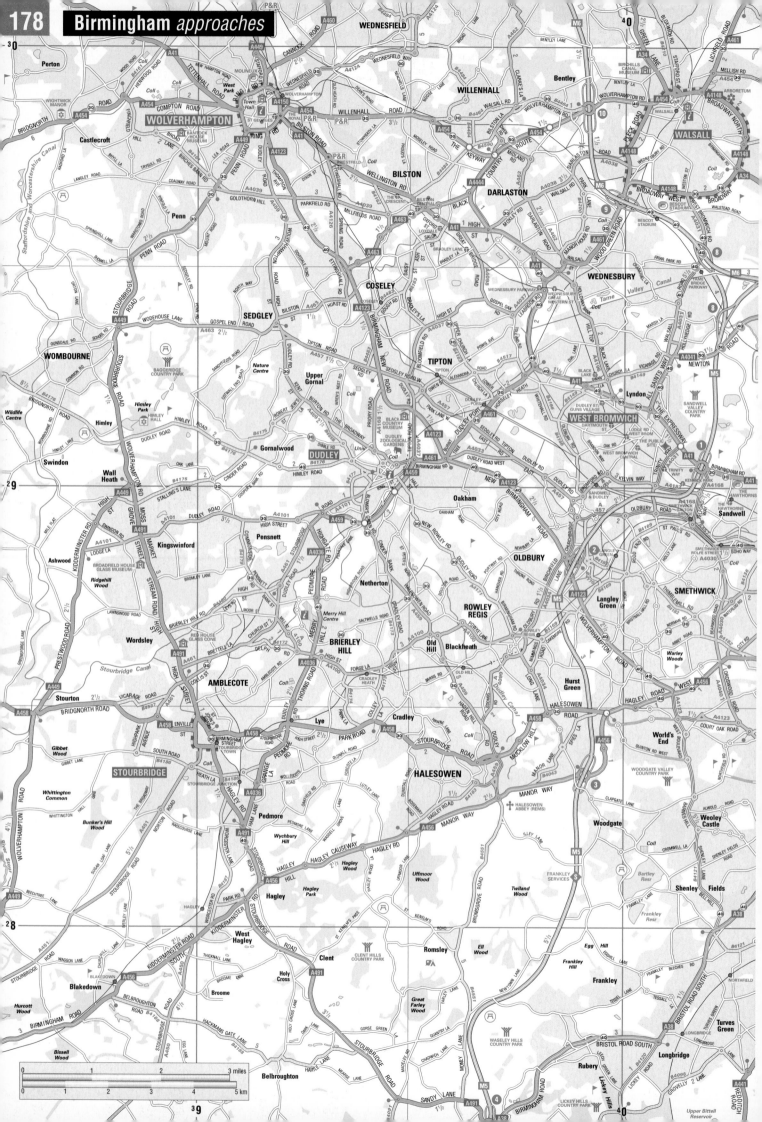

180

Blackpool road map page 92 • **Bournemouth** road map page 13 • **Bradford** road map page 94 • **Brighton** road map page 17

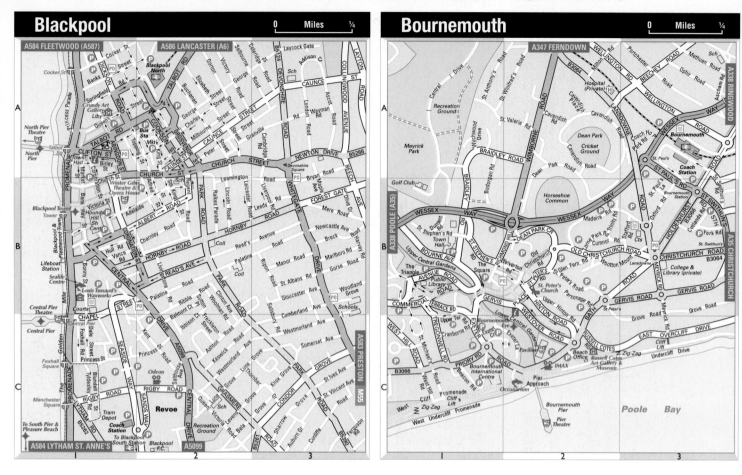

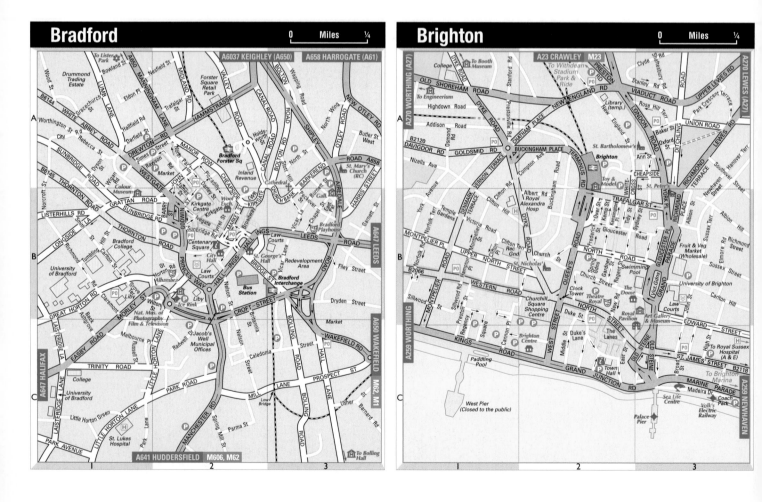

Bristol

0 — Miles — ¼

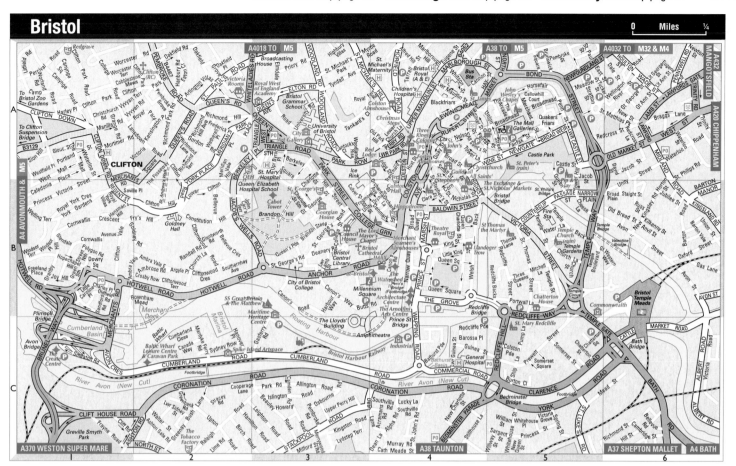

Cambridge

0 — Miles — ¼

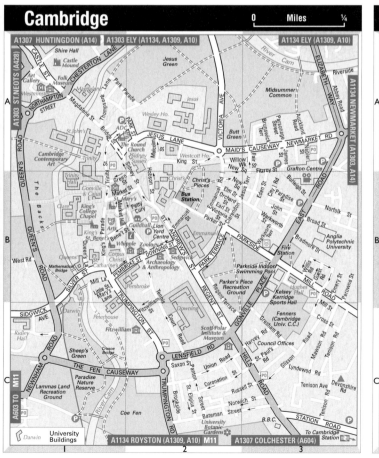

Canterbury

0 — Miles — ¼

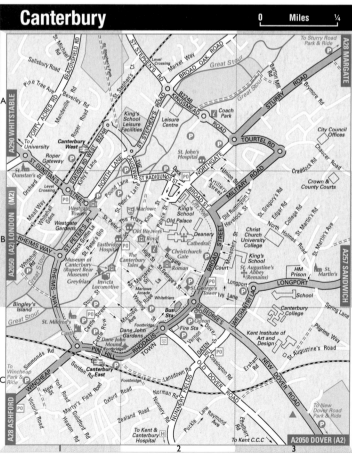

Cardiff / Caerdydd

0   Miles   ¼

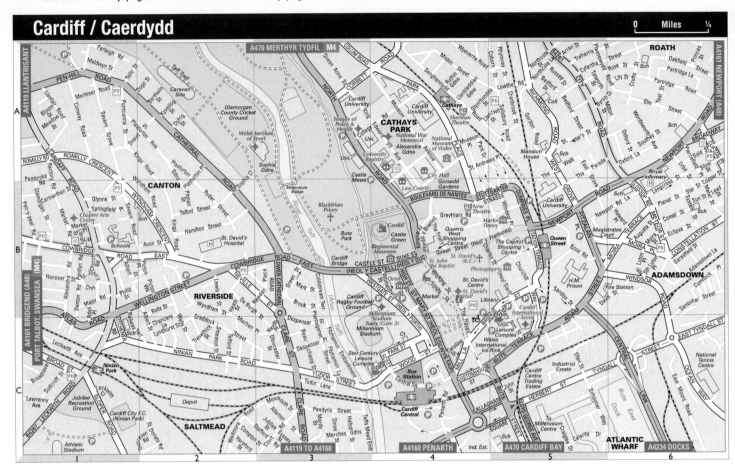

Cheltenham

0   Miles   ¼

Chester

0   Miles   ¼

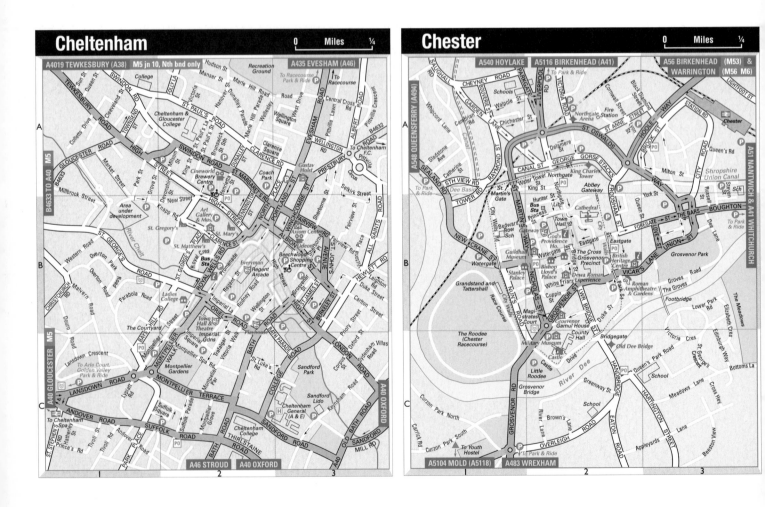

Colchester road map page 43 • **Coventry** road map page 51 • **Derby** road map page 76 • **Durham** road map page 111

185

Colchester

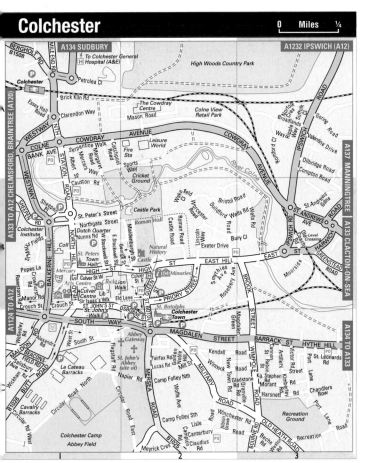

Coventry

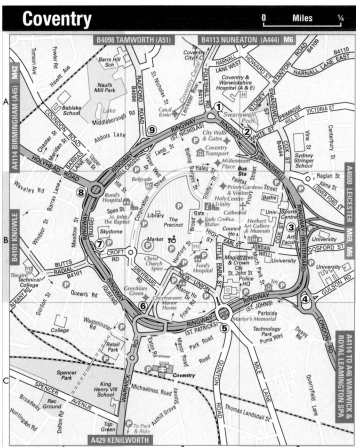

Derby

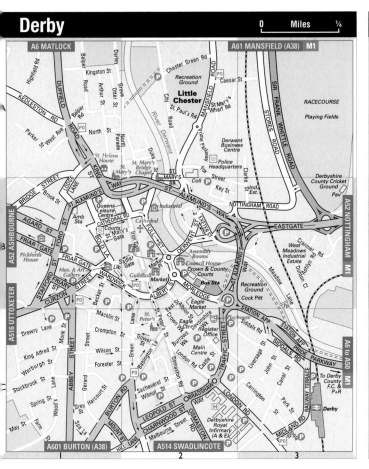

Durham

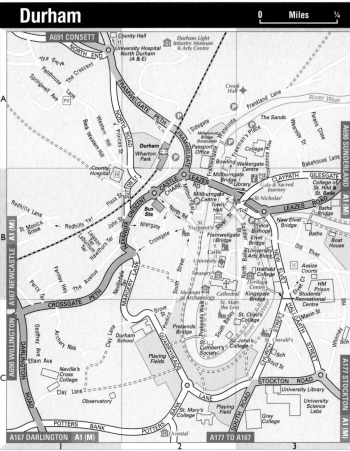

Edinburgh

0 Miles ¼

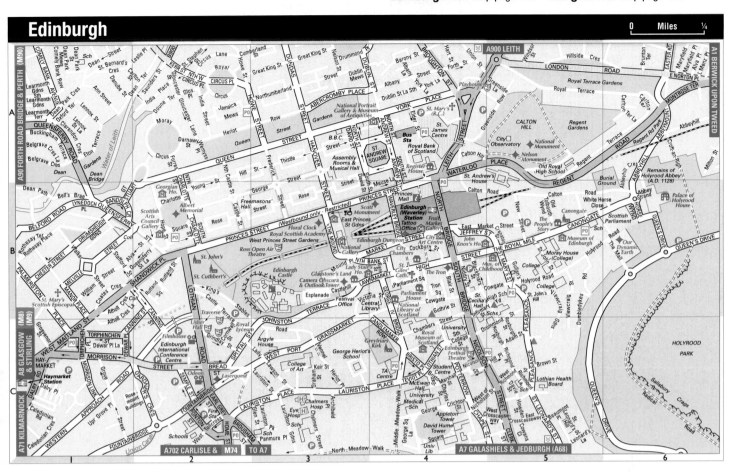

Glasgow

0 Miles ¼

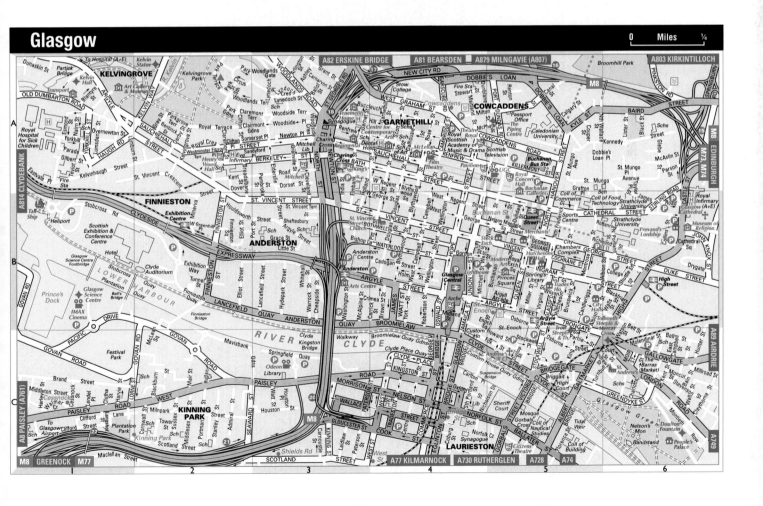

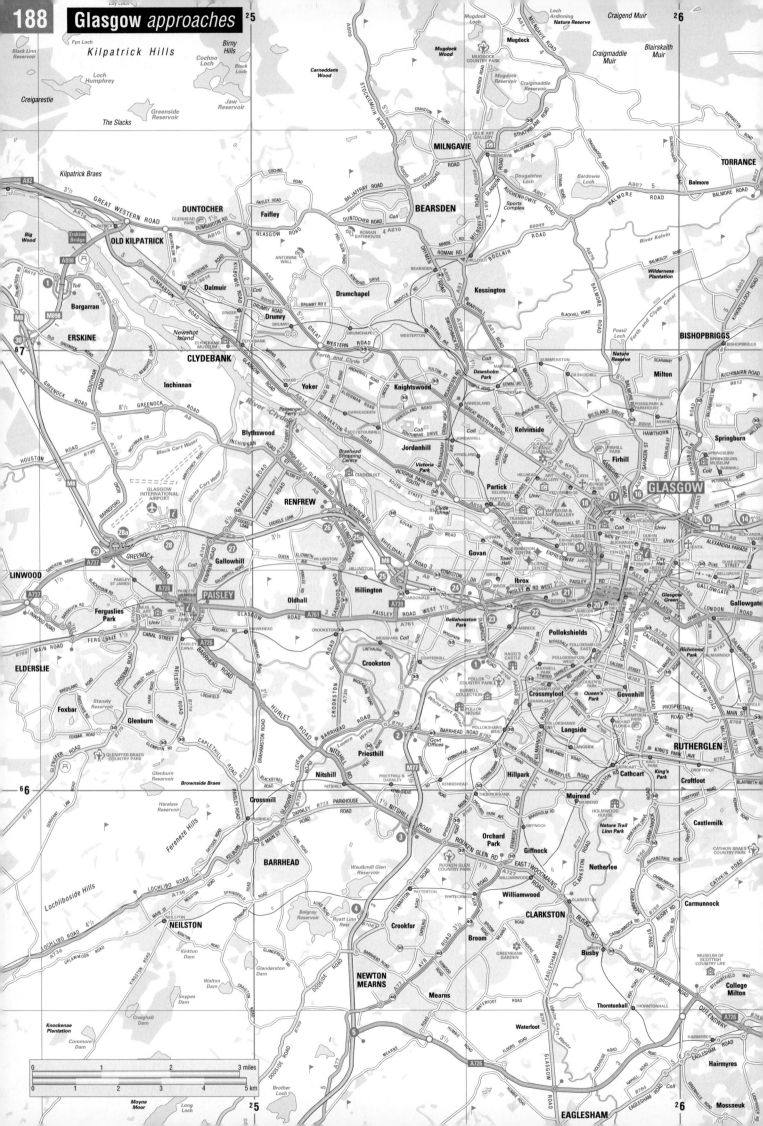

190

Exeter road map page 10 • **Gloucester** road map page 37 • **Hull** road map page 90 • **Ipswich** road map page 57

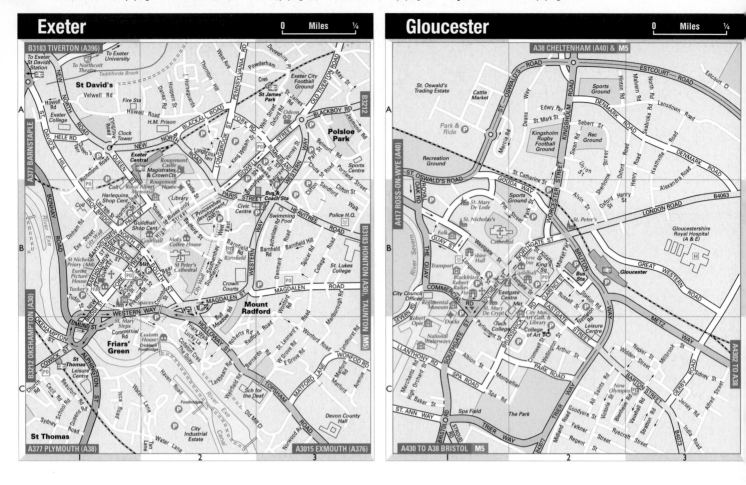

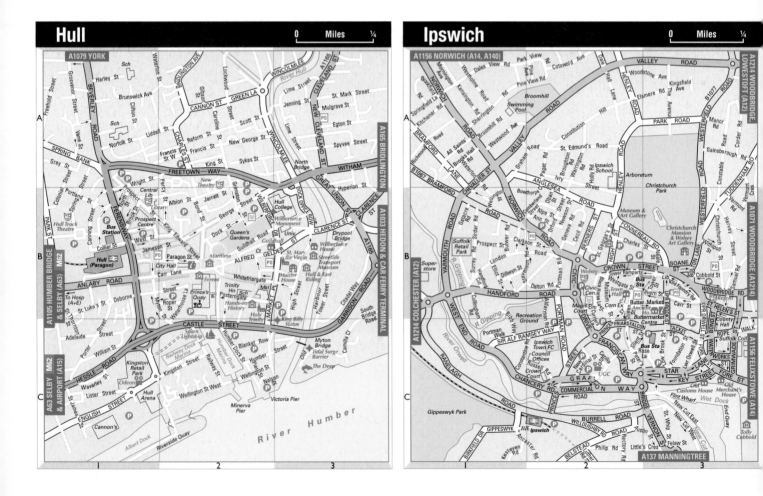

Leeds

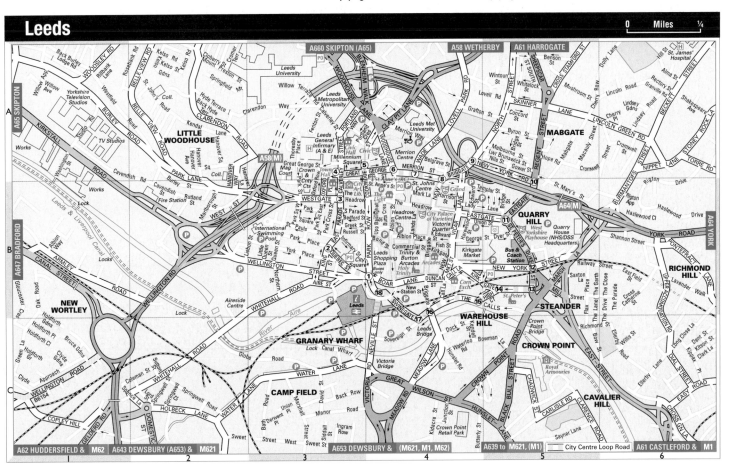

Lancaster

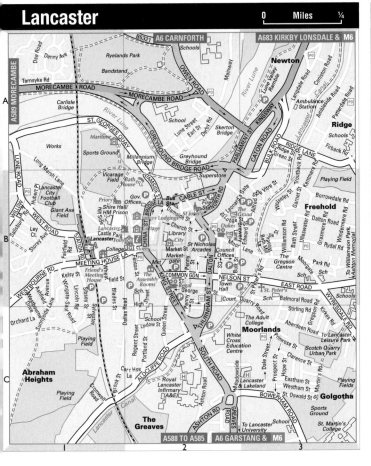

Leicester

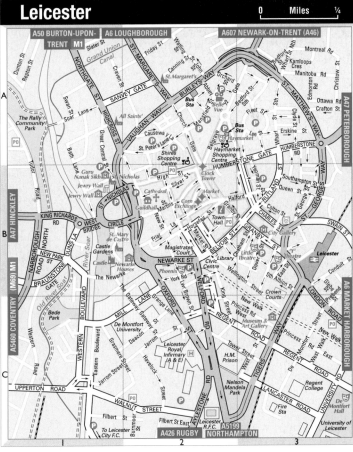

Liverpool

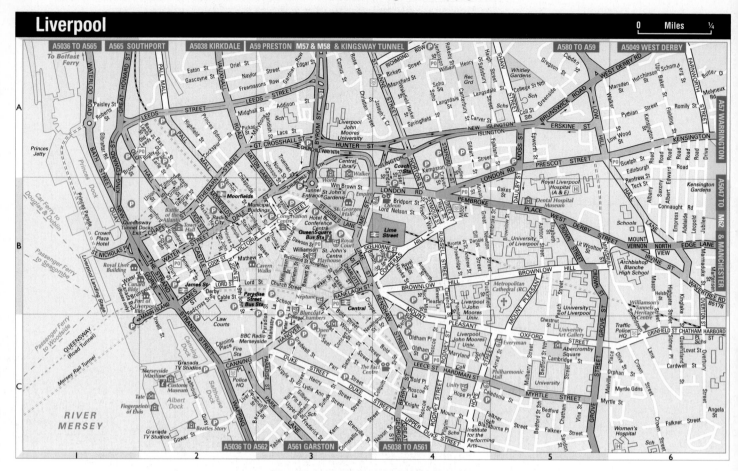

Lincoln

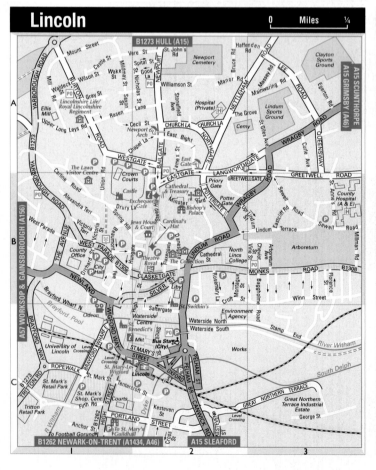

Middlesbrough

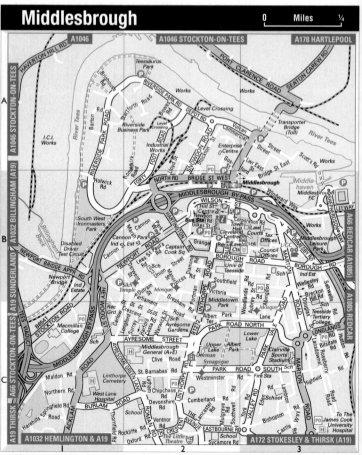

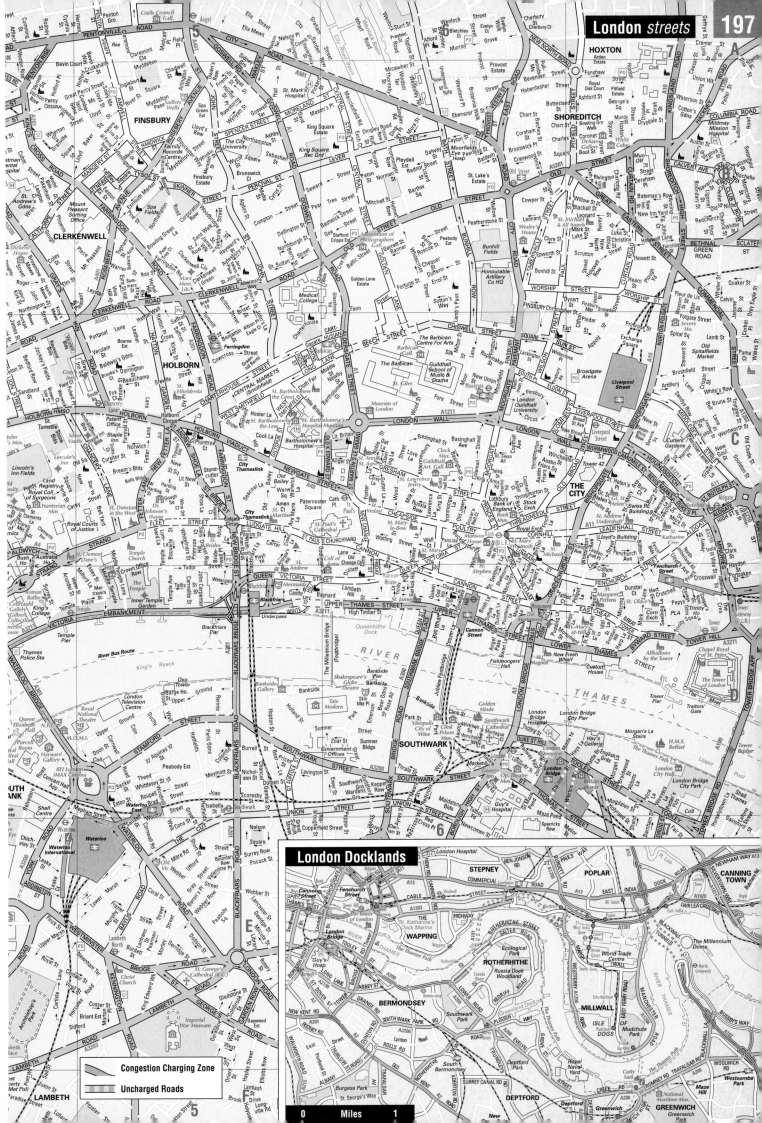

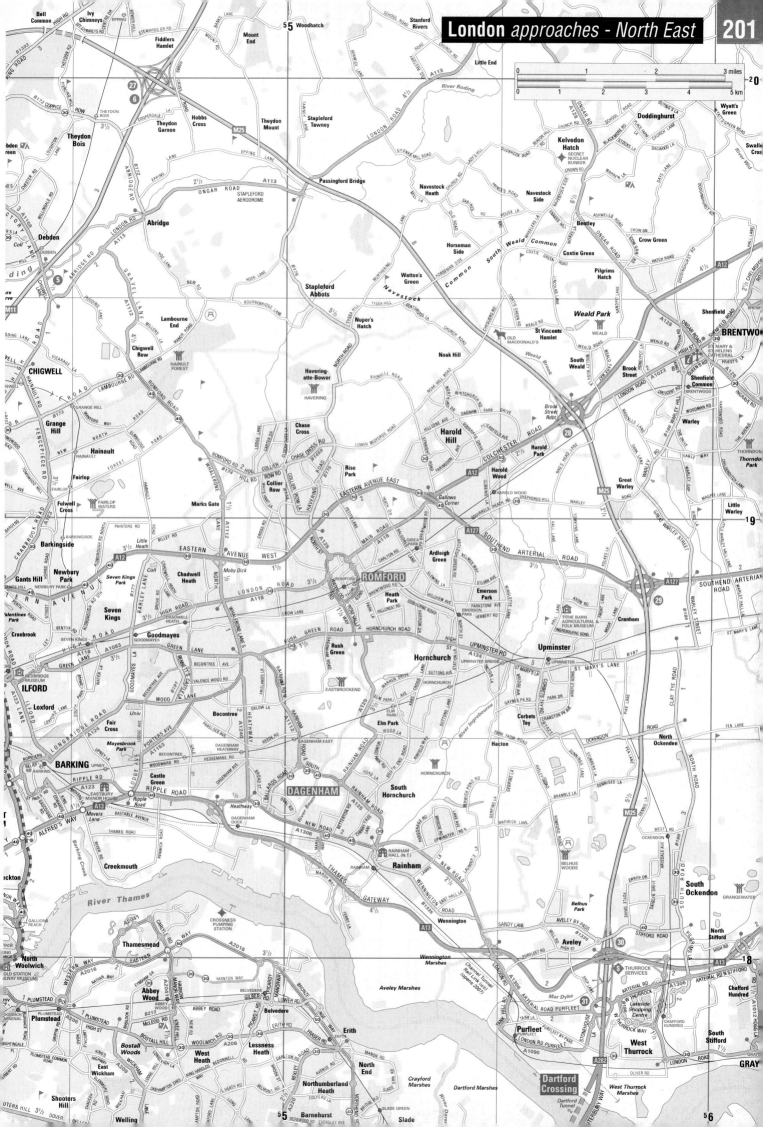

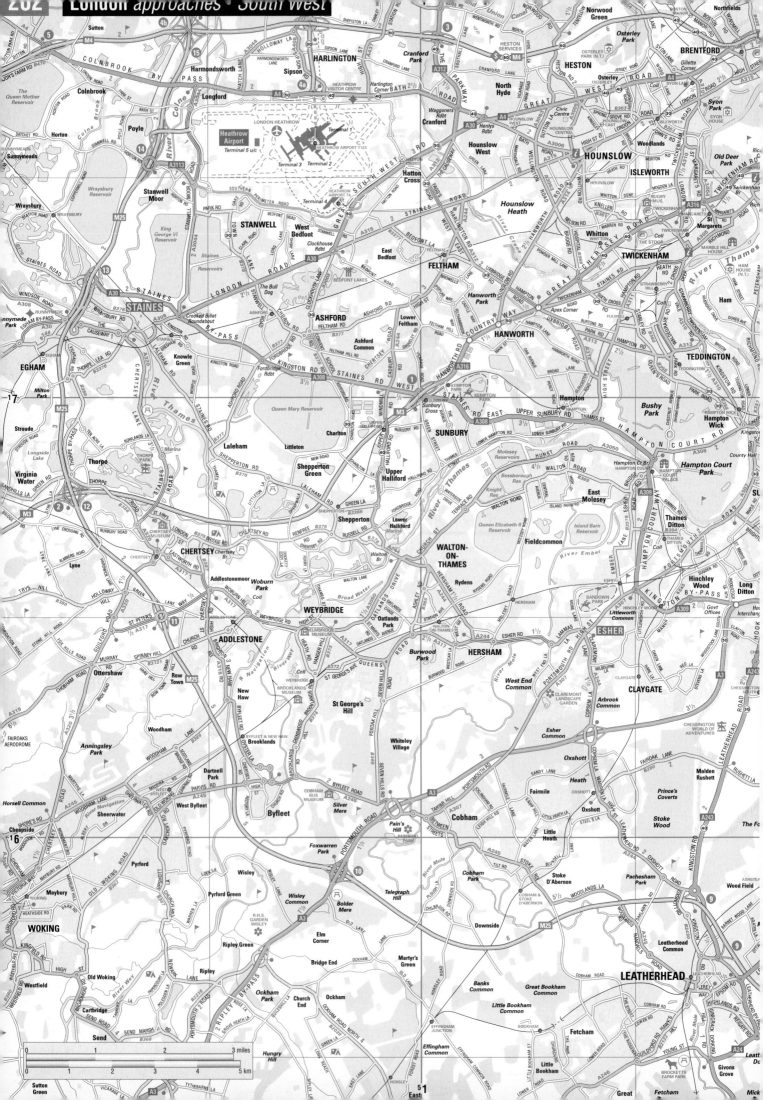

Manchester

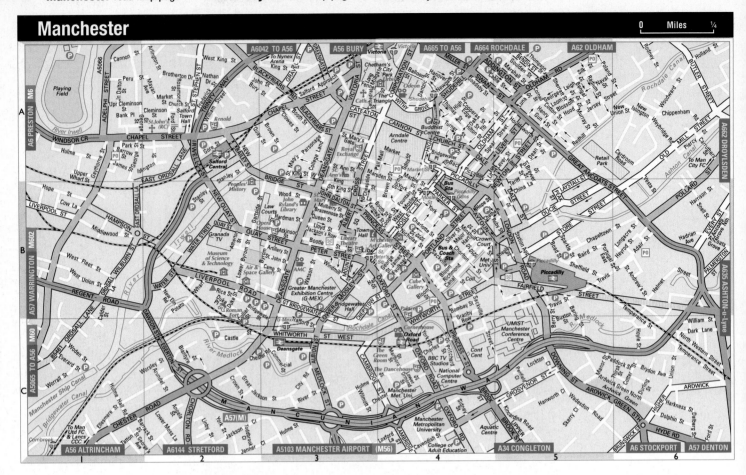

Milton Keynes

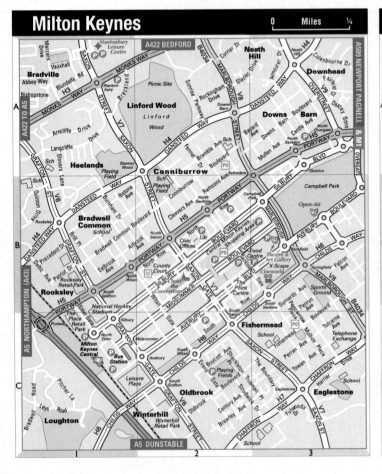

Northampton

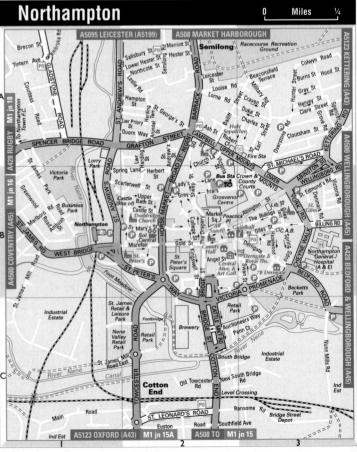

Newcastle upon Tyne

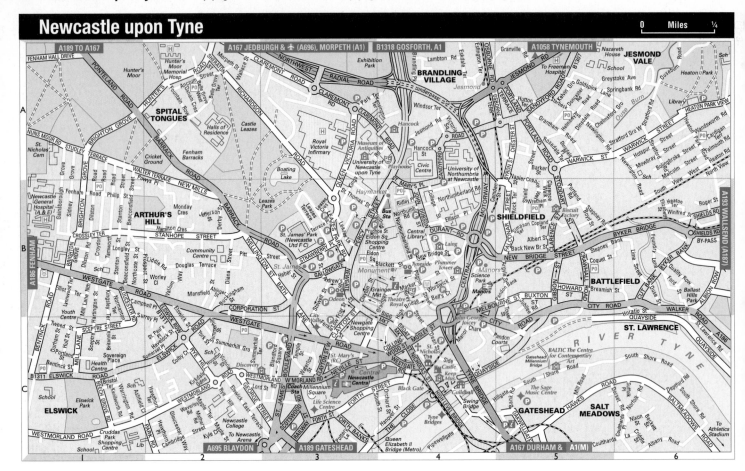

Norwich

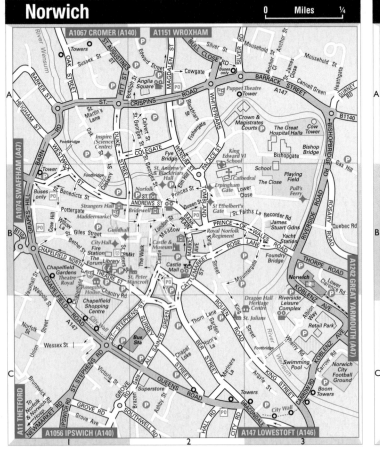

Oxford

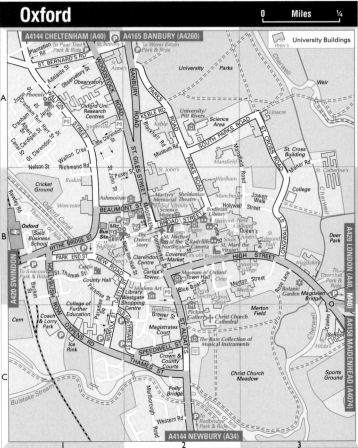

210

Nottingham road map page 77 • **Plymouth** road map page 6 • **Portsmouth** road map page 15 • **Preston** road map page 86

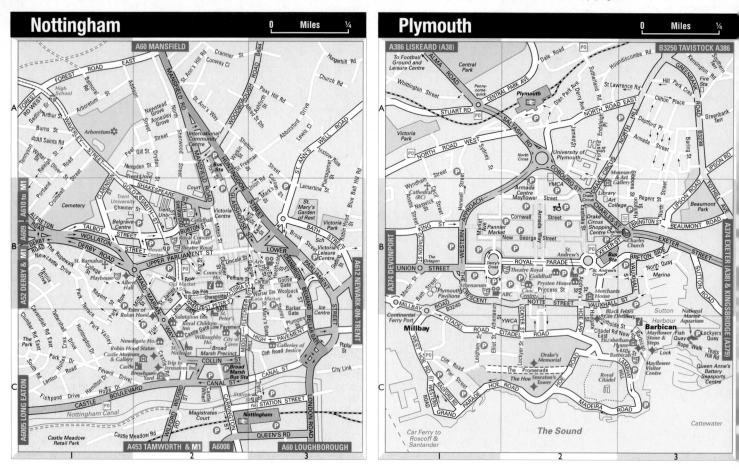

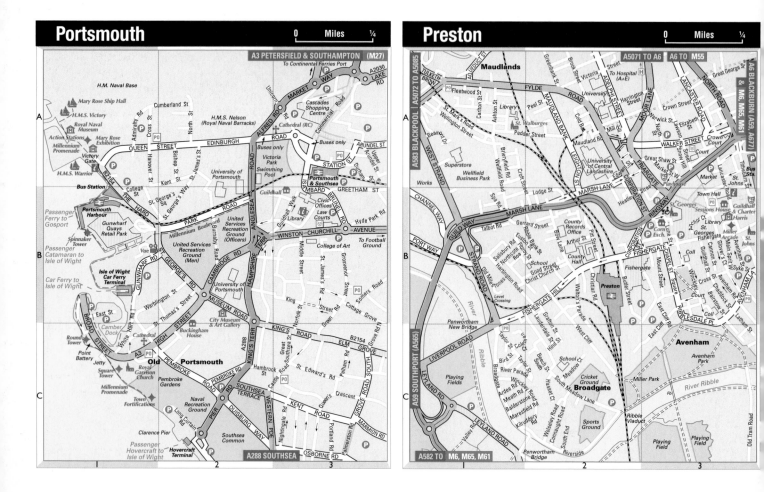

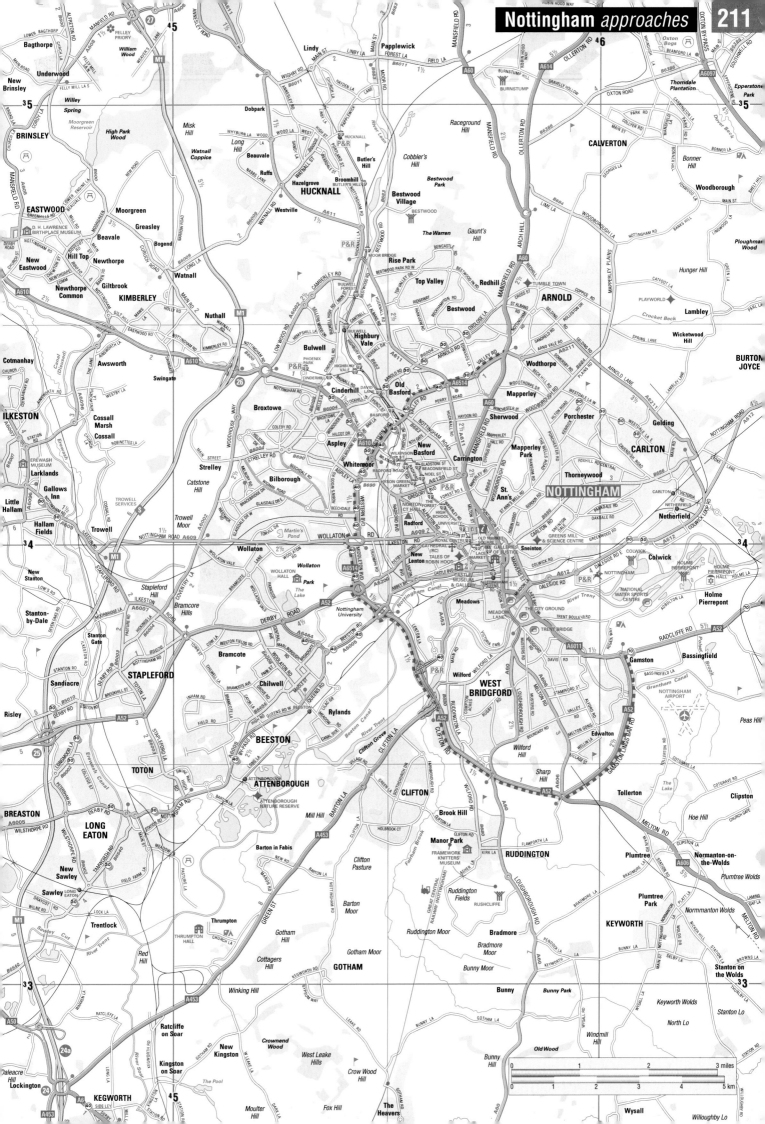

Reading

0 Miles ¼

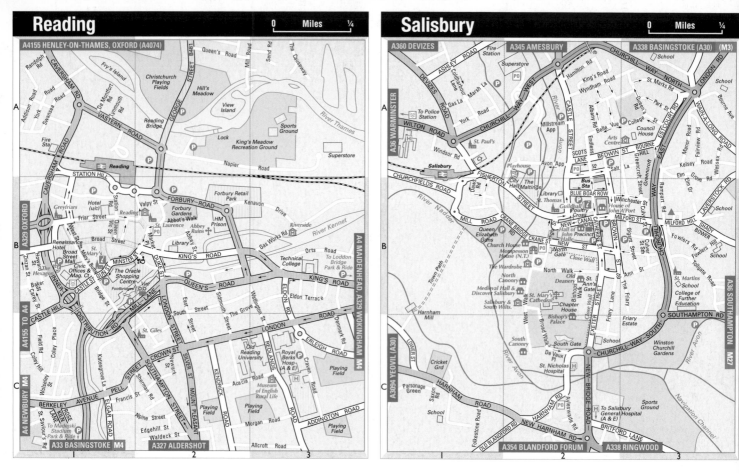

Salisbury

0 Miles ¼

Sheffield

0 Miles ¼

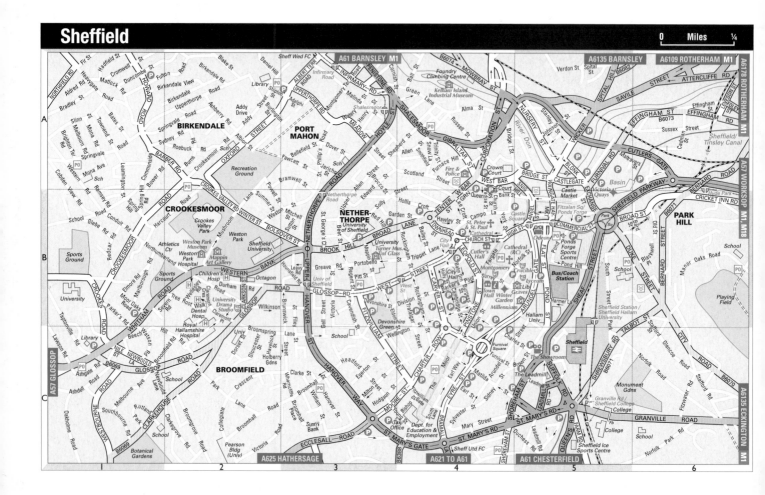

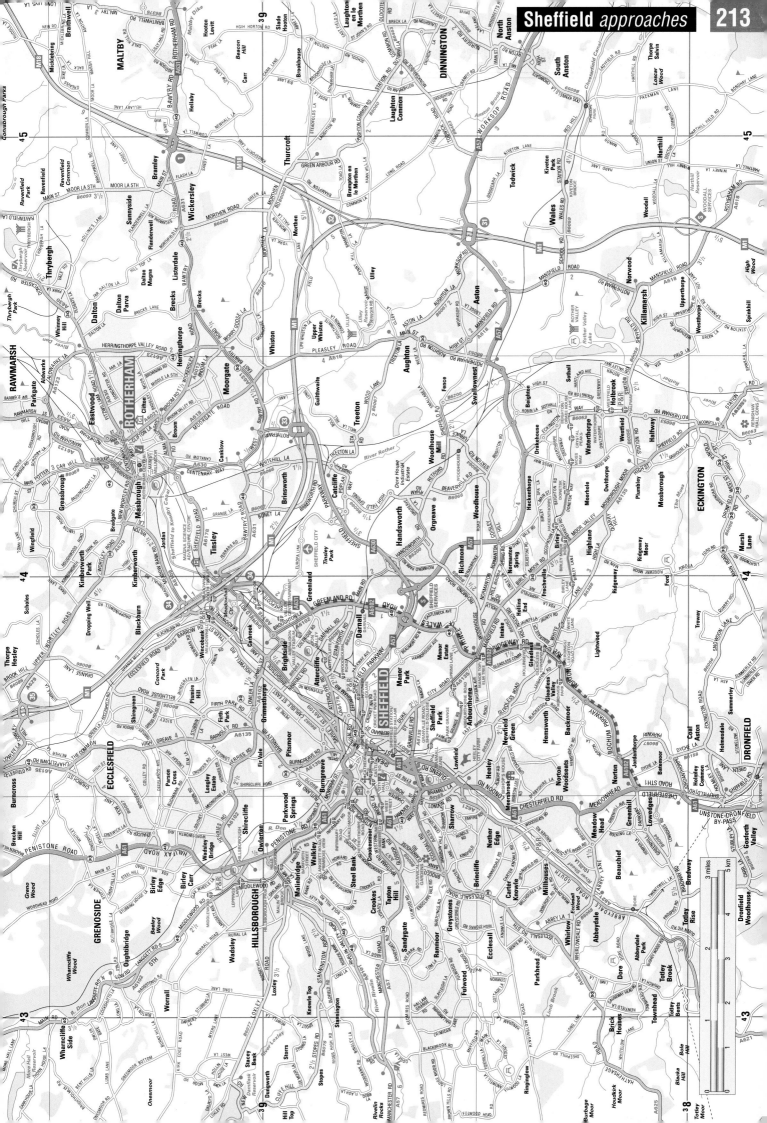

Scarborough

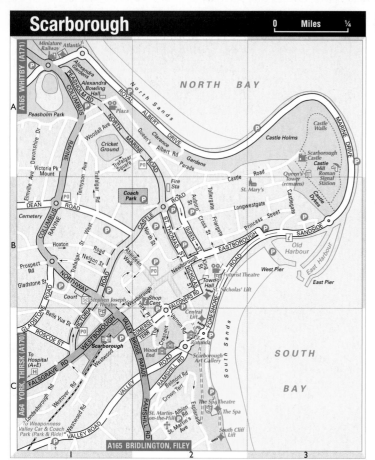

Southampton

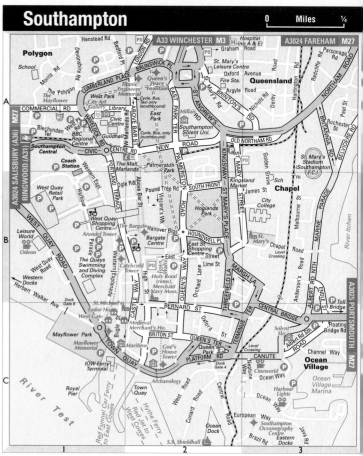

Stoke-on-Trent (Hanley)

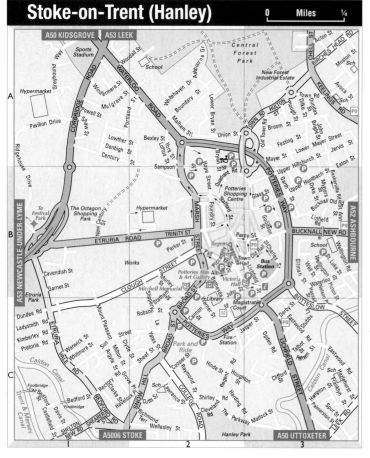

Stratford-upon-Avon

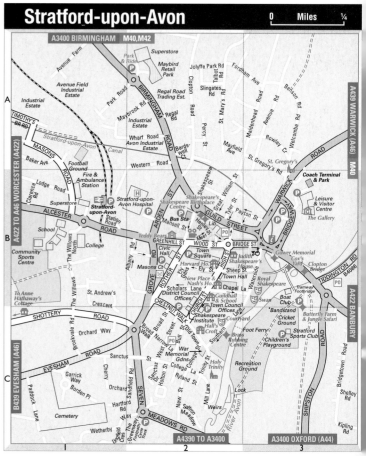

Sunderland road map page 111 • **Swansea** road map page 33 • **Telford** road map page 61 • **Torquay** road map page 7

215

Sunderland

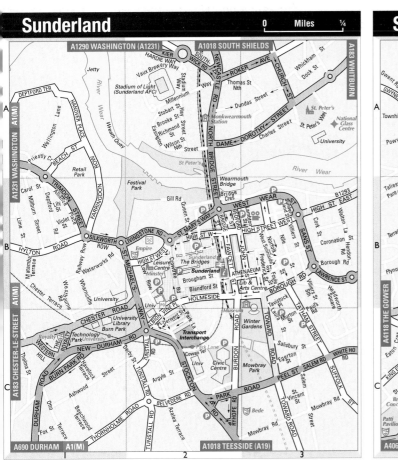

Swansea / Abertawe

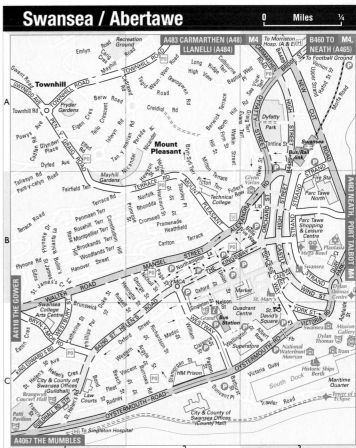

Telford

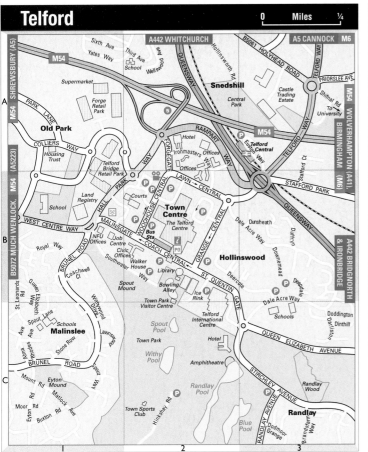

Torquay

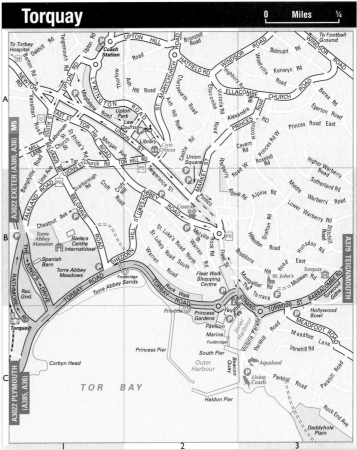

216

Winchester road map page 15 • **Windsor** road map page 27 • **Worcester** road map page 50 • **York** road map page 95

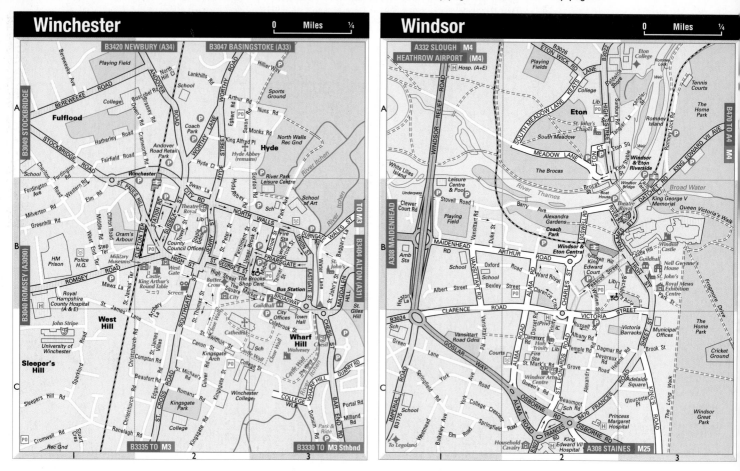

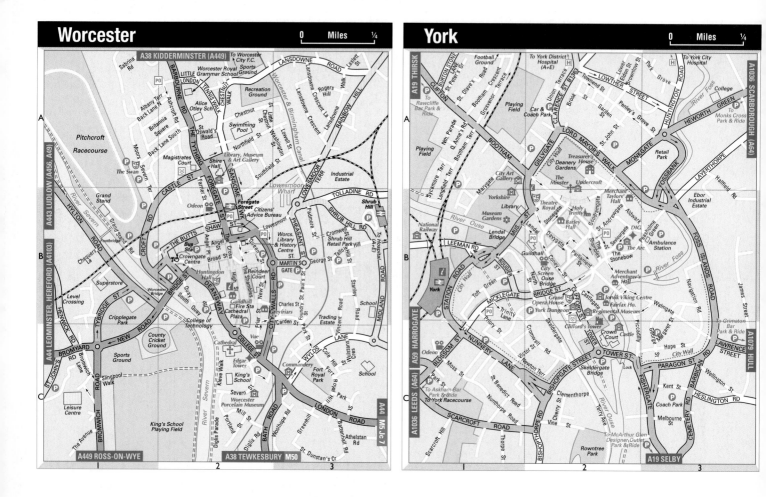

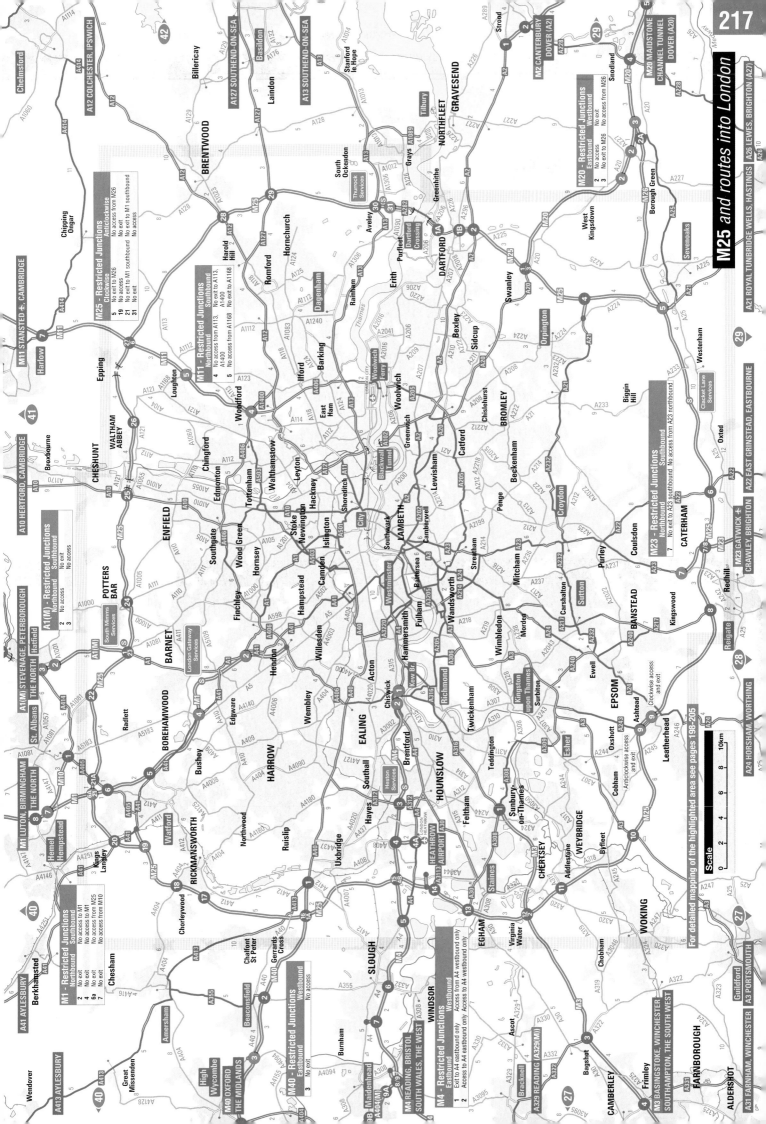

M25 *and routes into London*

A21 ROYAL TUNBRIDGE WELLS, HASTINGS | A26 LEWES, BRIGHTON (A27)
A22 EAST GRINSTEAD, EASTBOURNE
A23 CRAWLEY, BRIGHTON
A24 HORSHAM, WORTHING
A31 FARNHAM, WINCHESTER | A3 PORTSMOUTH | Guildford

M25 - Restricted Junctions

Clockwise	Anticlockwise
5 No exit to M26	No access from M26
19 No exit	No exit
21 No exit to M1 southbound	No exit to M1 southbound
31 No exit	No access

M11 - Restricted Junctions

Northbound	Southbound
4 No access from A113, A1400	No exit to A113, A1400
5 No access from A1168	No exit to A1168

A1(M) - Restricted Junctions

Northbound	Southbound
2 No access	No exit
3	No access

M1 - Restricted Junctions

Northbound	Southbound
2 No exit	No access to M1
4 No exit	No access to M1
6a No exit	No access from M25
7 No exit	No access from M10

M40 - Restricted Junctions

Eastbound	Westbound
3 No exit	No access

M4 - Restricted Junctions

Eastbound	Westbound
1 Exit to A4 eastbound only	Access from A4 westbound only
2 Access to A4 eastbound only	Access to A4 westbound only

M20 - Restricted Junctions

Eastbound	Westbound
2 No access	No exit
	No access from M26
	No exit to M26

M23 - Restricted Junctions

Northbound	Southbound
7 No exit to A23 southbound	No access from A23 northbound

For detailed mapping of the highlighted area see pages 198–205

Scale
0 2 4 6 8 10km

M3 BASINGSTOKE, WINCHESTER
SOUTHAMPTON, THE SOUTH WEST

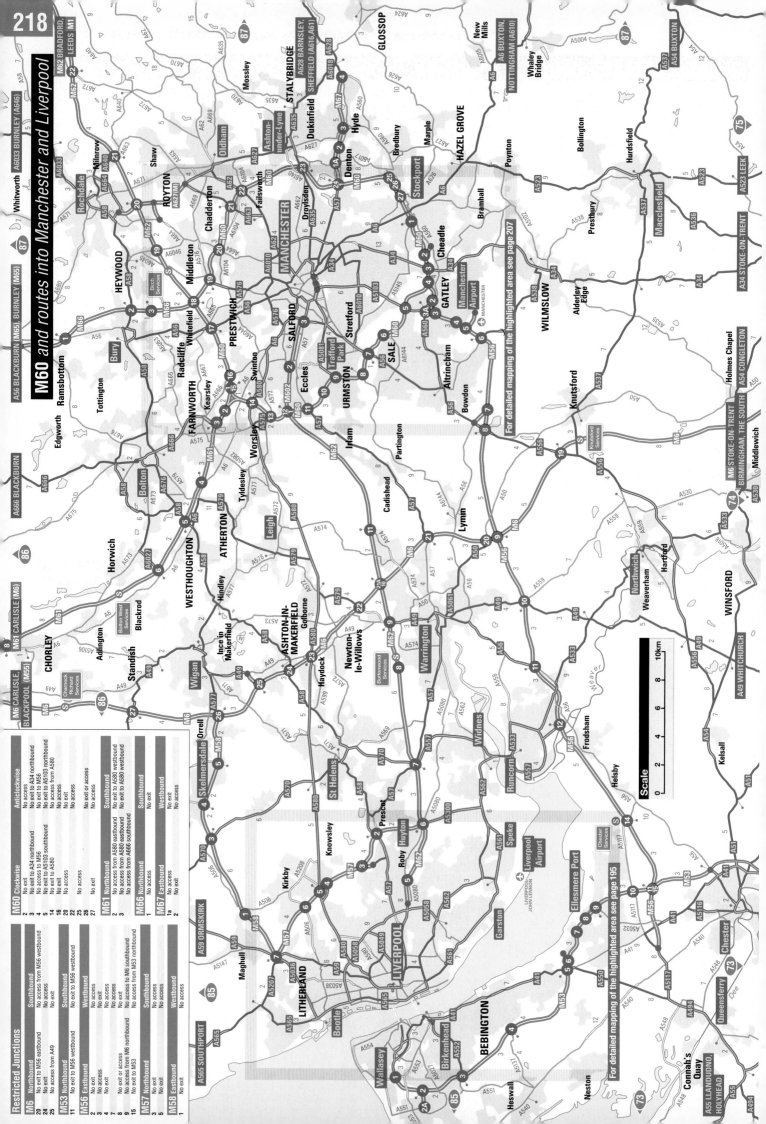

M60 and routes into Manchester and Liverpool

Restricted Junctions

M6
	Northbound	Southbound
20	No exit to M56 eastbound	No access from M56 westbound
24	No access	No exit
25	Northbound	No access

M53
	Northbound	Southbound
11	No exit to M56 westbound	No access from A5117 eastbound

M56
	Eastbound	Westbound
2	No access	No exit
3	No access	No exit
4	No access	No exit
7	No exit	No access
8	No exit or access	No access
9	No access from M6 southbound	No access to M6 northbound
15	No exit to M53	No access from M53 northbound

M57
	Northbound	Southbound
3	No exit	No access
5	No exit	No access

M58
	Eastbound	Westbound
1		No access

M60 Clockwise
		Anticlockwise
2	No exit	No exit to A34 northbound
3	No access from M56 westbound	No exit to A34 northbound
4	No access to M56	No exit to M56
5	No exit to A5103 southbound	No exit to A5103 northbound
14	No exit	No access from A580
16	No access	No access
20	No access	No exit
22		No access
25	No access	
26		No exit
27	No exit	No access

M61 Northbound
		Southbound
2	No access from A580 eastbound	No exit to A580 westbound
3	No access from A580 eastbound	No exit to A580 westbound

M66 Northbound
		Southbound
1	No access from A66 southbound	

M67 Eastbound
		Westbound
1	No access	No exit
2	No exit	No access

Scale
0 2 4 6 8 10km

For detailed mapping of the highlighted area see page 207

For detailed mapping of the highlighted area see page 195

Heathrow Airport (London)

0   Miles   ¼

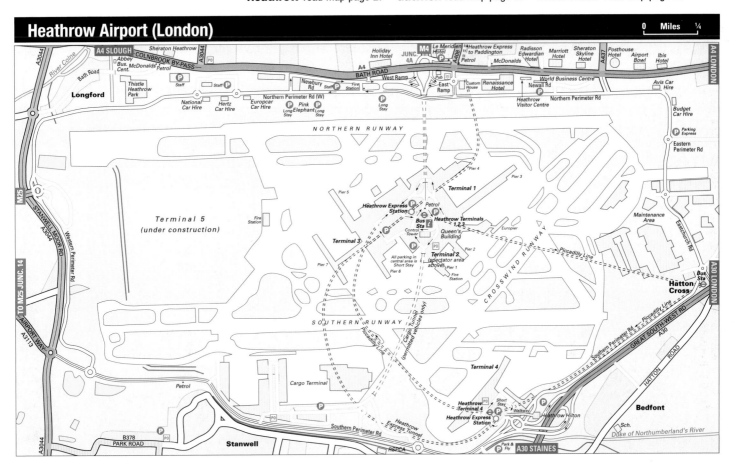

Gatwick Airport (London)

0   Miles   ¼

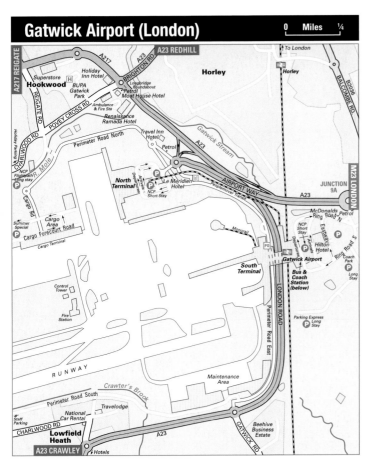

Manchester Airport

0   Miles   ¼

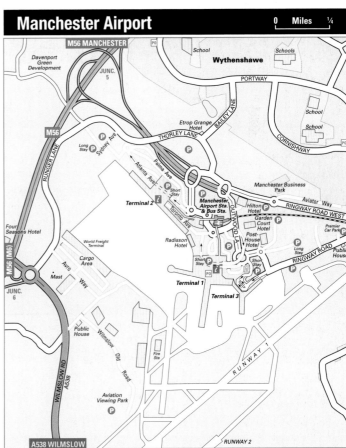

220

Dover road map page 31 • **Felixstowe** road map page 57 • **Portsmouth** road map page 15 • **Southampton** road map page 14

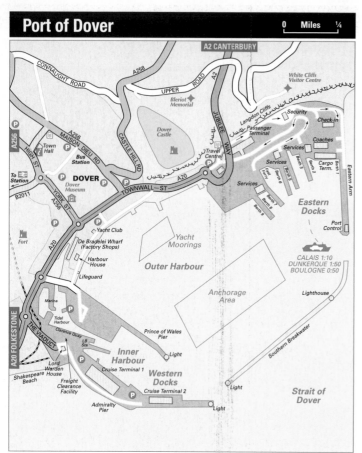

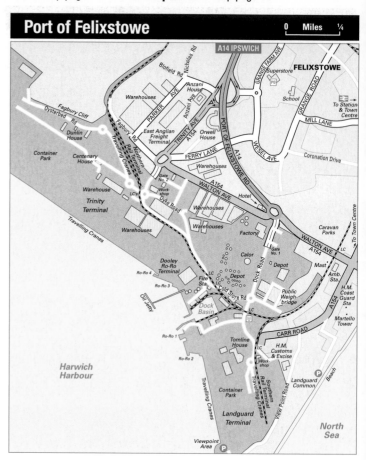

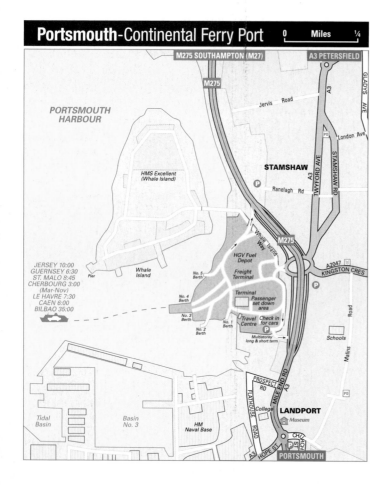

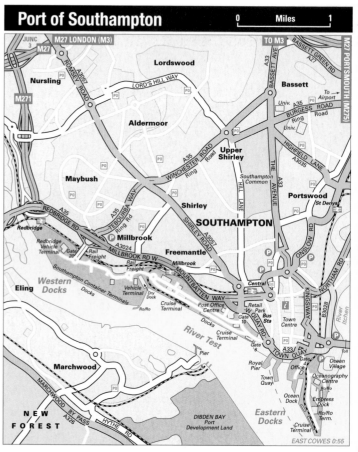

Boulogne

0 Miles ¼

D940 CALAIS & A16
EUROTUNNEL, CALAIS, DUNKERQUE

A16 EUROTUNNEL, CALAIS, DUNKERQUE

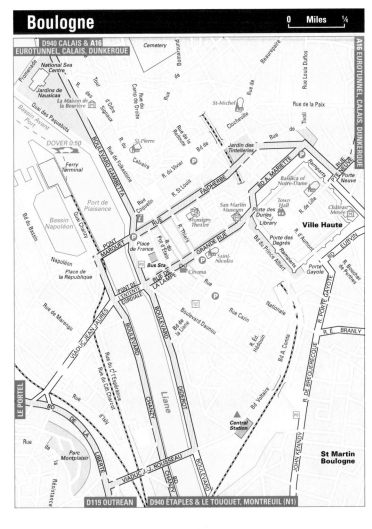

D119 OUTREAN D940 ÉTAPLES & LE TOUQUET, MONTREUIL (N1)

Calais

0 Miles ¼

A26 BOULOGNE, DUNKERQUE (A16) PARIS (A1)

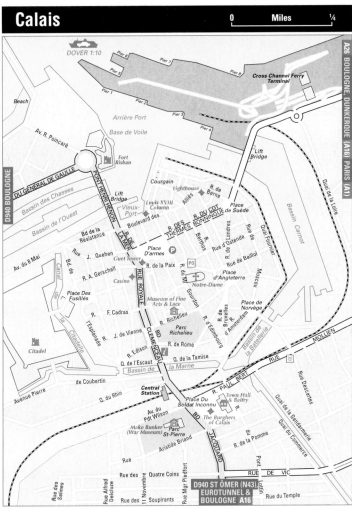

D940 ST ÔMER (N43),
EUROTUNNEL &
BOULOGNE A16

Boulogne and Calais *approaches*

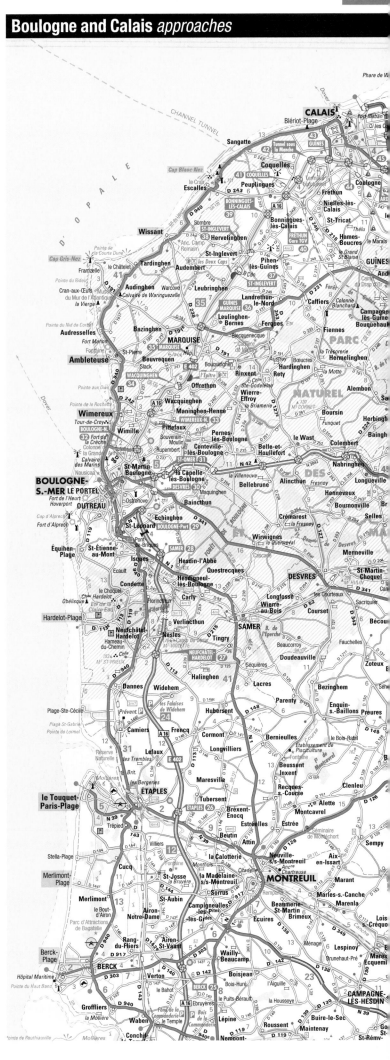

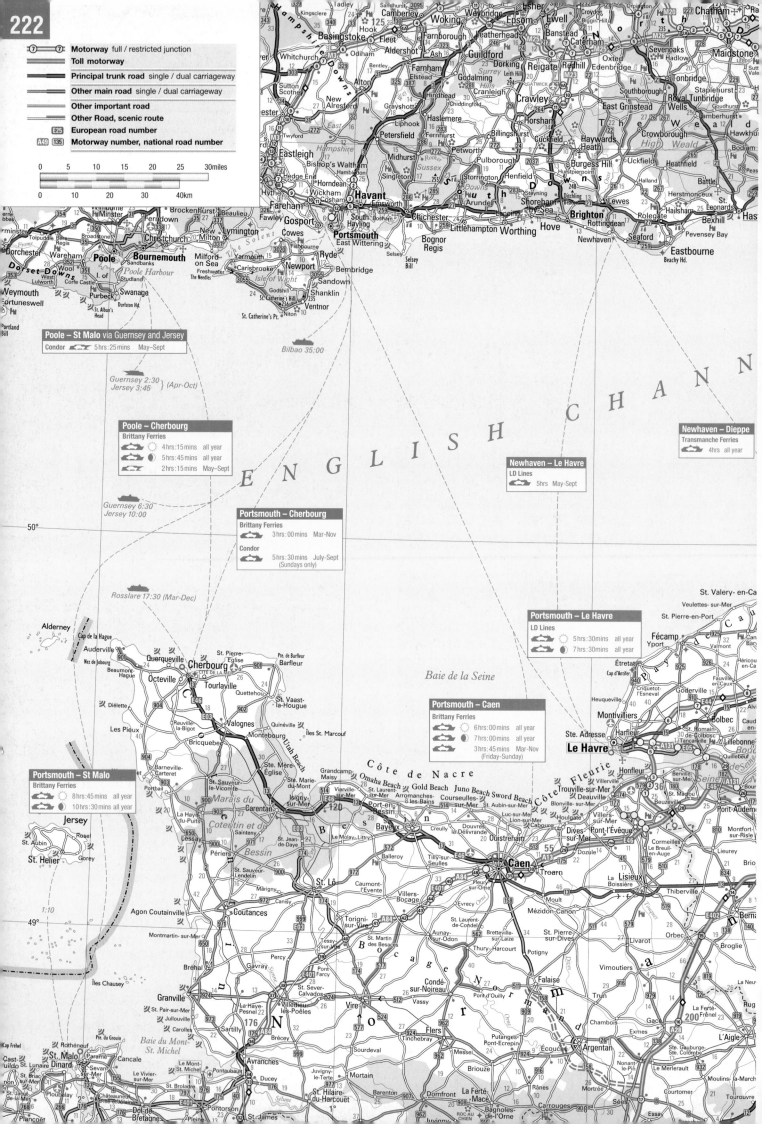

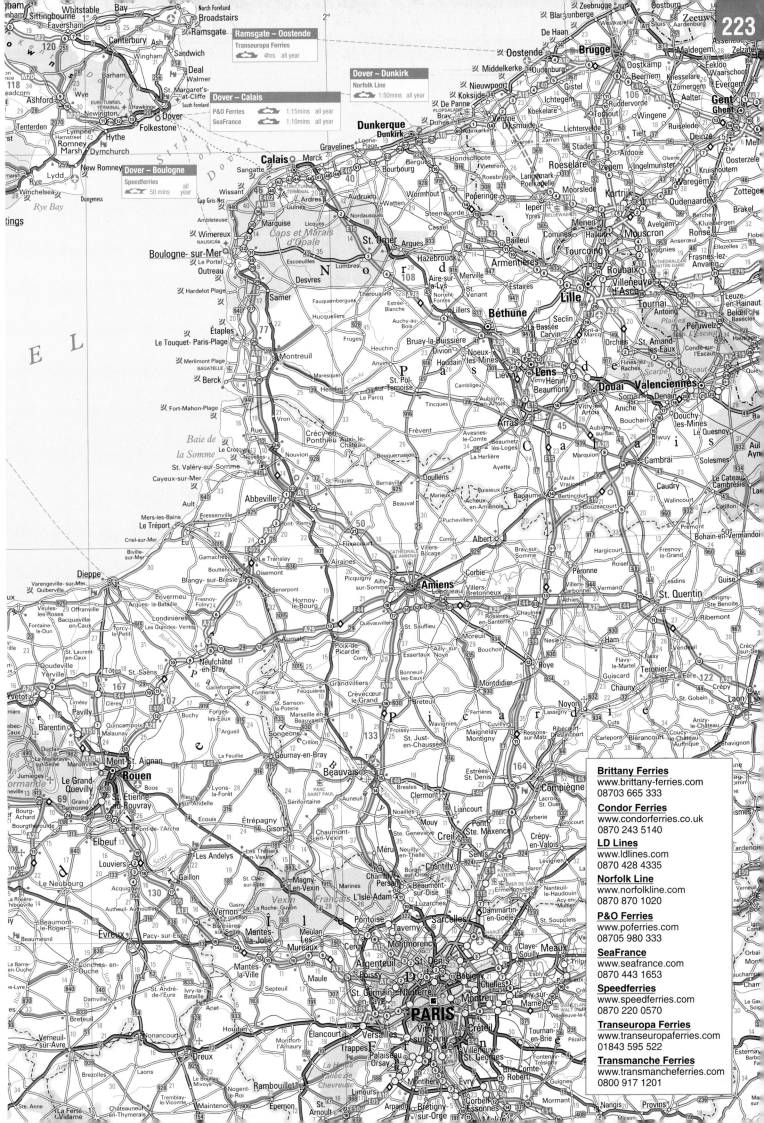

Ferry information panel

Brittany Ferries
www.brittany-ferries.com
08703 665 333

Condor Ferries
www.condorferries.co.uk
0870 243 5140

LD Lines
www.ldlines.com
0870 428 4335

Norfolk Line
www.norfolkline.com
0870 870 1020

P&O Ferries
www.poferries.com
08705 980 333

SeaFrance
www.seafrance.com
0870 443 1653

Speedferries
www.speedferries.com
0870 220 0570

Transeuropa Ferries
www.transeuropaferries.com
01843 595 522

Transmanche Ferries
www.transmancheferries.com
0800 917 1201

Ferry route boxes

Ramsgate – Oostende
Transeuropa Ferries
4hrs all year

Dover – Dunkirk
Norfolk Line
1:50mins all year

Dover – Calais
P&O Ferries 1:15mins all year
SeaFrance 1:10mins all year

Dover – Boulogne
Speedferries 50 mins all year

Index to road maps of Britain

How to use the index

Example

Trudoxhill Som **24** E2

- grid square
- page number
- county or unitary authority

Places of special interest are highlighted in magenta

Abbreviations used in the index

Aberdeen **Aberdeen City**
Aberds **Aberdeenshire**
Ald **Alderney**
Anglesey **Isle of Anglesey**
Angus **Angus**
Argyll **Argyll and Bute**
Bath **Bath and North East Somerset**
Beds **Bedfordshire**
Bl Gwent **Blaenau Gwent**
Blkburn **Blackburn with Darwen**
Blkpool **Blackpool**
Bmouth **Bournemouth**
Borders **Scottish Borders**
Brack **Bracknell**
Bridgend **Bridgend**
Brighton **City of Brighton and Hove**
Bristol **City and County of Bristol**
Bucks **Buckinghamshire**
Caerph **Caerphilly**
Cambs **Cambridgeshire**
Cardiff **Cardiff**
Carms **Carmarthenshire**
Ceredig **Ceredigion**
Ches **Cheshire**
Clack **Clackmannanshire**
Conwy **Conwy**
Corn **Cornwall**
Cumb **Cumbria**
Darl **Darlington**
Denb **Denbighshire**
Derby **City of Derby**
Derbys **Derbyshire**
Devon **Devon**
Dorset **Dorset**
Dumfries **Dumfries and Galloway**
Dundee **Dundee City**
Durham **Durham**
E Ayrs **East Ayrshire**
E Dunb **East Dunbartonshire**
E Loth **East Lothian**
E Renf **East Renfrewshire**
E Sus **East Sussex**
E Yorks **East Riding of Yorkshire**
Edin **City of Edinburgh**
Essex **Essex**
Falk **Falkirk**
Fife **Fife**
Flint **Flintshire**
Glasgow **City of Glasgow**
Glos **Gloucesterhire**
Gtr Man **Greater Manchester**
Guern **Guernsey**
Gwyn **Gwynedd**
Halton **Halton**
Hants **Hampshire**
Hereford **Herefordshire**
Herts **Hertfordshire**
Highld **Highland**
Hrtlpl **Hartlepool**
Hull **Hull**
I o M **Isle of Man**
I o W **Isle of Wight**
Invclyd **Inverclyde**
Jersey **Jersey**
Kent **Kent**
Lancs **Lancashire**
Leicester **City of Leicester**
Leics **Leicestershire**
Lincs **Lincolnshire**
London **Greater London**
Luton **Luton**
M Keynes **Milton Keynes**
M Tydf **Merthyr Tydfil**
M'bro **Middlesbrough**
Medway **Medway**
Mers **Merseyside**
Midloth **Midlothian**
Mon **Monmouthshire**
Moray **Moray**
N Ayrs **North Ayrshire**
N Lincs **North Lincolnshire**
N Lnrk **North Lanarkshire**
N Som **North Somerset**
N Yorks **North Yorkshire**
NE Lincs **North East Lincolnshire**
Neath **Neath Port Talbot**
Newport **City and County of Newport**
Norf **Norfolk**
Northants **Northamptonshire**
Northumb **Northumberland**
Nottingham **City of Nottingham**
Notts **Nottinghamshire**
Orkney **Orkney**
Oxon **Oxfordshire**
P'boro **Peterborough**
Pembs **Pembrokeshire**
Perth **Perth and Kinross**
Plym **Plymouth**
Poole **Poole**
Powys **Powys**
Ptsmth **Portsmouth**
Reading **Reading**
Redcar **Redcar and Cleveland**
Renfs **Renfrewshire**
Rhondda **Rhondda Cynon Taff**
Rutland **Rutland**
S Ayrs **South Ayrshire**
S Glos **South Gloucestershire**
S Lnrk **South Lanarkshire**
S Yorks **South Yorkshire**
Scilly **Scilly**
Shetland **Shetland**
Shrops **Shropshire**
Slough **Slough**
Som **Somerset**
Soton **Southampton**
Staffs **Staffordshire**
Sthend **Southend-on-Sea**
Stirl **Stirling**
Stockton **Stockton-on-Tees**
Stoke **Stoke-on-Trent**
Suff **Suffolk**
Sur **Surrey**
Swansea **Swansea**
Swindon **Swindon**
T & W **Tyne and Wear**
Telford **Telford and Wrekin**
Thurrock **Thurrock**
Torbay **Torbay**
Torf **Torfaen**
V Glam **The Vale of Glamorgan**
W Berks **West Berkshire**
W Dunb **West Dunbartonshire**
W Isles **Western Isles**
W Loth **West Lothian**
W Mid **West Midlands**
W Sus **West Sussex**
W Yorks **West Yorkshire**
Warks **Warwickshire**
Warr **Warrington**
Wilts **Wiltshire**
Windsor **Windsor and Maidenhead**
Wokingham **Wokingham**
Worcs **Worcestershire**
Wrex **Wrexham**
York **City of York**

A

Ab Kettleby Leics 64 B4
Ab Lench Worcs 50 D5
Abbas Combe Som 12 B5
Abberley Worcs 50 C2
Abberton Essex 43 C6
Abberton Worcs 50 D4
Abberwick Northumb 117 C7
Abbess Roding Essex 42 C1
Abbey Devon 11 C6
Abbey-cwm-hir Powys 48 B2
Abbey Dore Hereford 49 F5
Abbey Field Essex 43 B5
Abbey Hulton Stoke 75 E6
Abbey St Bathans Borders 124 C3
Abbey Town Cumb 107 D8
Abbey Village Lancs 86 B4
Abbey Wood London 29 B5
Abbeydale S Yorks 88 F4
Abbeystead Lancs 93 D5
Abbots Bickington Devon 9 C5
Abbots Bromley Staffs 62 B4
Abbots Langley Herts 40 D3
Abbots Leigh N Som 23 B7
Abbots Morton Worcs 50 D5
Abbots Ripton Cambs 54 B3
Abbots Salford Warks 51 D5
Abbotsbury Dorset 12 F3
Abbotsbury Sub Tropical Gardens Dorset 12 F3
Abbotsford House Borders 123 F8
Abbotsham Devon 9 B6
Abbotskerswell Devon 7 C6
Abbotsley Cambs 54 D3
Abbotswood Hants 14 B4
Abbotts Ann Hants 25 E8
Abcott Shrops 49 B5
Abdon Shrops 61 F5
Aber Ceredig 46 E3
Aber-Arad Carms 46 F2
Aber-banc Ceredig 46 E2
Aber Cowarch Gwyn 59 C5
Aber-Giâr Carms 46 E4
Aber-gwynfi Neath 34 E2
Aber-Hirnant Gwyn 72 F3
Aber-nant Rhondda 34 D4
Aber-Rhiwlech Gwyn 59 B6
Aber-Village Powys 35 B5
Aberaeron Ceredig 46 C3
Aberaman Rhondda 34 D4
Aberangell Gwyn 58 C5
Aberarder Highld 147 F7
Aberarder House Highld 148 B2
Aberarder Lodge Highld 147 F8
Aberargie Perth 134 C3
Aberarth Ceredig 46 C3
Aberavon Neath 33 E8
Aberbeeg Bl Gwent 35 D6
Abercanaid M Tydf 34 D4
Abercarn Caerph 35 E6
Abercastle Pembs 44 B3
Abercegir Powys 58 D5
Aberchirder Aberds 160 C3
Aberconwy House, Conwy Conwy 83 D7
Abercraf Powys 34 C2
Abercrombie Fife 135 D7
Abercych Pembs 45 E4
Abercynafon Powys 34 C4
Abercynon Rhondda 34 E4
Aberdalgie Perth 134 B2
Aberdâr = Aberdare Rhondda 34 D3
Aberdare = Aberdâr Rhondda 34 D3
Aberdaron Gwyn 70 E2
Aberdaugleddau = Milford Haven Pembs 44 E4
Aberdeen Aberdeen 151 D8
Aberdeen Airport Aberdeen 151 C7
Aberdesach Gwyn 82 F4
Aberdour Fife 134 F3
Aberdovey Gwyn 58 E3
Aberdulais Neath 34 D1
Aberedw Powys 48 E2
Abereiddy Pembs 44 B2
Abererch Gwyn 70 D4
Aberfan M Tydf 34 D4
Aberfeldy Perth 141 E5
Aberffraw Anglesey 82 E3
Aberffrwd Ceredig 47 B5
Aberford W Yorks 95 F7
Aberfoyle Stirl 132 D4
Abergavenny = Y Fenni Mon 35 C6
Abergele Conwy 72 B3
Abergorlech Carms 46 F4
Abergwaun = Fishguard Pembs 44 B4
Abergwesyn Powys 47 D7
Abergwili Carms 33 B5
Abergwynant Gwyn 58 C3
Abergwyngregyn Gwyn 83 D6
Abergynolwyn Gwyn 58 D3
Aberhonddu = Brecon Powys 34 B4
Aberhosan Powys 58 E5
Aberkenfig Bridgend 34 F2
Aberlady E Loth 135 F6
Aberlemno Angus 143 D5
Aberllefenni Gwyn 58 D4
Abermagwr Ceredig 47 B5
Abermaw = Barmouth Gwyn 58 C3
Abermeurig Ceredig 46 D4
Abermule Powys 59 E8
Abernaint Powys 59 B8
Abernant Carms 32 B4
Abernethy Perth 134 C3
Abernyte Perth 142 F2
Aberpennar = Mountain Ash Rhondda 34 E4
Aberporth Ceredig 45 D4
Abersoch Gwyn 70 E4
Abersychan Torf 35 D6
Abertawe = Swansea Swansea 33 E7
Aberteifi = Cardigan Ceredig 45 E3
Aberthin V Glam 22 B2
Abertillery = Abertyleri Bl Gwent 35 D6
Abertridwr Caerph 35 F5
Abertridwr Powys 59 C7
Abertyleri = Abertillery Bl Gwent 35 D6
Abertysswg Caerph 35 D5
Aberuthven Perth 133 C8
Aberyscir Powys 34 B3
Aberystwyth Ceredig 58 F2
Abhainn Suidhe W Isles 173 H3
Abingdon Oxon 38 E4
Abinger Common Sur 28 E2
Abinger Hammer Sur 27 E8
Abington S Lnrk 114 B2
Abington Pigotts Cambs 54 E4
Ablington Glos 37 D8
Ablington Wilts 25 E6
Abney Derbys 75 B8
Aboyne Aberds 150 E4
Abram Gtr Man 86 D4
Abriachan Highld 157 F6
Abridge Essex 41 E7
Abronhill N Lnrk 121 B7
Abson S Glos 24 B2
Abthorpe Northants 52 E4
Abune-the-Hill Orkney 176 D1
Aby Lincs 79 B7
Acaster Malbis York 95 E8
Acaster Selby N Yorks 95 E8
Accrington Lancs 87 B5
Acha Argyll 136 C2
Acha Mor W Isles 172 F6
Achabraid Argyll 128 B3
Achachork Highld 152 E5
Achafolla Argyll 130 D3
Achagary Highld 168 D2
Achahoish Argyll 128 C2
Achalader Perth 141 E8
Achallader Argyll 139 E7
Ach'an Todhair Highld 138 B4
Achanalt Highld 156 C3
Achanamara Argyll 128 B2
Achandunie Highld 157 B7
Achany Highld 164 D2
Achaphubuil Highld 138 B4
Acharacle Highld 137 B7
Acharn Highld 137 C8
Acharn Perth 140 E4
Acharole Highld 169 D7
Achath Aberds 151 C6
Achavanich Highld 169 E6
Achavraat Highld 158 E3
Achddu Carms 33 D5
Achduart Highld 162 D4
Achentoul Highld 168 F3
Achfary Highld 166 F4
Achgarve Highld 162 E2
Achiemore Highld 167 C5
Achiemore Highld 168 D3
A'Chill Highld 144 C2
Achiltibuie Highld 162 D4
Achina Highld 168 C2
Achinduich Highld 164 D2
Achinduin Argyll 130 B4
Achingills Highld 169 C6
Achintee Highld 139 B5
Achintee Highld 155 F5
Achintraid Highld 155 G4
Achlean Highld 148 E4
Achleck Argyll 137 D5
Achluachrach Highld 147 F5
Achlyness Highld 166 D4
Achmelvich Highld 162 B4
Achmore Highld 155 G4
Achmore Stirl 140 F2
Achnaba Argyll 130 B5
Achnaba Argyll 128 B4
Achnabat Highld 157 F6
Achnacarnin Highld 166 F2
Achnacarry Highld 146 F4
Achnacloich Argyll 131 B5
Achnacloich Highld 145 C5
Achnaconeran Highld 147 C7
Achnacraig Argyll 137 D5
Achnacroish Argyll 138 E2
Achnadrish Argyll 137 C5
Achnafalnich Argyll 131 C8
Achnagarron Highld 157 C7
Achnaha Highld 137 B5
Achnahanat Highld 164 E2
Achnahannet Highld 149 B5
Achnairn Highld 164 C2
Achnaluachrach Highld 164 D3
Achnasaul Highld 146 F4
Achnasheen Highld 156 D2
Achosnich Highld 137 B5
Achranich Highld 137 D8
Achreamie Highld 168 C5
Achriabhach Highld 139 C5
Achriesgill Highld 166 D4
Achrimsdale Highld 165 D6
Achtoty Highld 167 C8
Achurch Northants 65 F7
Achuvoldrach Highld 167 D7
Achvaich Highld 164 E4
Achvarasdal Highld 168 C4
Ackergill Highld 169 D8
Acklam M'bro 102 C2
Acklam N Yorks 96 C3
Ackleton Shrops 61 E7
Acklington Northumb 117 D8
Ackton W Yorks 88 B5
Ackworth Moor Top W Yorks 88 C5
Acle Norf 69 C7
Acock's Green W Mid 62 F5
Acol Kent 31 C7
Acomb Northumb 110 C2
Acomb York 95 D8
Aconbury Hereford 49 F7
Acre Lancs 87 B5
Acre Street W Sus 15 E8
Acrefair Wrex 73 E6
Acton Ches 74 D3
Acton Dorset 13 G7
Acton London 41 F5
Acton Shrops 60 F3
Acton Suff 56 E2
Acton Wrex 73 D7
Acton Beauchamp Hereford 49 D8
Acton Bridge Ches 74 B2
Acton Burnell Shrops 60 D5
Acton Green Hereford 49 D8
Acton Pigott Shrops 60 D5
Acton Round Shrops 61 E6
Acton Scott Shrops 60 F4
Acton Trussell Staffs 62 C3
Acton Turville S Glos 37 F5
Adbaston Staffs 61 B7
Adber Dorset 12 B3
Adderley Shrops 74 E3
Adderstone Northumb 125 F7
Addiewell W Loth 122 C2
Addingham W Yorks 94 E3
Addington Bucks 39 B7
Addington London 28 C4
Addington Kent 29 D7
Addinston Borders 123 D8
Addiscombe London 28 C4
Addlestone Sur 27 C8
Addlethorpe Lincs 79 C8
Adel W Yorks 95 F5
Adeney Telford 61 C7
Adfa Powys 59 D7
Adforton Hereford 49 B6
Adisham Kent 31 D6
Adlestrop Glos 38 B2
Adlingfleet E Yorks 90 B2
Adlington Lancs 86 C4
Admaston Staffs 62 B4
Admaston Telford 61 C6
Admington Warks 51 E7
Adstock Bucks 52 F5
Adstone Northants 52 D3
Adversane W Sus 16 B4
Advie Highld 158 F5
Adwalton W Yorks 88 B3
Adwell Oxon 39 E6
Adwick le Street S Yorks 89 D6
Adwick upon Dearne S Yorks 89 D5
Adziel Aberds 161 C6
Ae Village Dumfries 114 F2
Affleck Aberds 151 B7
Affpuddle Dorset 13 E6
Affric Lodge Highld 146 B4
Afon-wen Flint 72 B5
Afton I o W 14 F4
Agglethorpe N Yorks 101 F5
Agneash I o M 84 D4
Aigburth Mers 85 F4
Aiginis W Isles 172 E7
Aike E Yorks 97 E6
Aikerness Orkney 176 A3
Aikers Orkney 176 G3
Aiketgate Cumb 108 E4
Aikton Cumb 108 D2
Ailey Hereford 48 E5
Ailstone Warks 51 D7
Ailsworth P'boro 65 E8
Ainderby Quernhow N Yorks 102 F1
Ainderby Steeple N Yorks 101 E8
Aingers Green Essex 43 B7
Ainsdale Mers 85 C4
Ainsdale-on-Sea Mers 85 C4
Ainstable Cumb 108 E5
Ainsworth Gtr Man 87 C5
Ainthorpe N Yorks 103 D5
Aintree Mers 85 E4
Aintree Racecourse Mers 85 E4
Aird Argyll 130 E3
Aird Dumfries 104 C4
Aird Highld 154 C3
Aird W Isles 172 E8
Aird a Mhachair W Isles 170 F3
Aird a'Mhulaidh W Isles 173 G4
Aird Asaig W Isles 173 H4
Aird Dhail W Isles 172 B7
Aird Mhidhinis W Isles 171 K3
Aird Mhighe W Isles 173 J4
Aird Mhighe W Isles 173 K3
Aird Mhor W Isles 171 K3
Aird of Sleat Highld 145 C5
Aird Thunga W Isles 172 E7
Aird Uig W Isles 172 E3
Airdens Highld 164 E3
Airdrie N Lnrk 121 C7
Airdtorrisdale Highld 167 C8
Airidh a Bhruaich W Isles 172 G5
Airieland Dumfries 106 D4
Airmyn E Yorks 89 B8
Airntully Perth 141 F7
Airor Highld 145 C7
Airth Falk 133 F7
Airton N Yorks 94 D2
Airyhassen Dumfries 105 E7
Aisby Lincs 90 E2
Aisby Lincs 78 F3
Aisgernis W Isles 171 H3
Aiskew N Yorks 101 F7
Aislaby N Yorks 103 F5
Aislaby N Yorks 103 D6
Aislaby Stockton 102 C2
Aisthorpe Lincs 78 A2
Aith Orkney 176 E1
Aith Shetland 175 H5
Aith Shetland 174 D8
Aithsetter Shetland 175 K6
Aitkenhead S Ayrs 112 D3
Aitnoch Highld 158 F3
Akeld Northumb 117 B5
Akeley Bucks 52 F5
Akenham Suff 56 E5
Albaston Corn 6 B2
Alberbury Shrops 60 C3
Albert Dock, Liverpool Mers 85 F4
Albourne W Sus 17 C6
Albrighton Shrops 60 C4
Albrighton Shrops 62 D2
Alburgh Norf 69 F5
Albury Herts 41 B7
Albury Sur 27 E8
Albury End Herts 41 B7
Alby Hill Norf 81 D7
Alcaig Highld 157 D6
Alcaston Shrops 60 F4
Alcester Warks 51 D5
Alciston E Sus 18 E2
Alcombe Som 21 E8
Alcombe Wilts 24 C3
Alconbury Cambs 54 B2
Alconbury Weston Cambs 54 B2
Aldbar Castle Angus 143 D5
Aldborough Norf 81 D7
Aldborough N Yorks 95 C7
Aldbourne Wilts 25 B7
Aldbrough E Yorks 97 F8
Aldbrough St John N Yorks 101 C7
Aldbury Herts 40 C2
Aldcliffe Lancs 92 C4
Aldclune Perth 141 C6
Aldeburgh Suff 57 D8
Aldeby Norf 69 E7
Aldenham Herts 40 E4
Alderbury Wilts 14 B2
Aldercar Derbys 76 E4
Alderford Norf 68 C4
Alderholt Dorset 14 C2
Alderley Glos 36 E4
Alderley Edge Ches 74 B5
Aldermaston W Berks 26 C3
Aldermaston Wharf W Berks 26 C4
Alderminster Warks 51 E7
Alderney Airport Ald 16
Alder's End Hereford 49 E8
Aldersey Green Ches 73 D8
Aldershot Hants 27 D6
Alderton Glos 50 F5
Alderton Northants 52 E5
Alderton Shrops 60 B4
Alderton Suff 57 E7
Alderton Wilts 37 F5
Alderwasley Derbys 76 D3
Aldfield N Yorks 95 C5
Aldford Ches 73 D8
Aldham Essex 43 B5
Aldham Suff 56 E4
Aldie Highld 164 F4
Aldingbourne W Sus 16 D3
Aldingham Cumb 92 B2
Aldington Kent 19 B7
Aldington Worcs 51 E5
Aldington Frith Kent 19 B7
Aldochlay Argyll 132 E2
Aldreth Cambs 54 B5
Aldridge W Mid 62 D4
Aldringham Suff 57 C8
Aldsworth Glos 38 C1
Aldunie Moray 150 B2
Aldwark Derbys 76 D2
Aldwark N Yorks 95 C7
Aldwick W Sus 16 E3
Aldwincle Northants 65 F7
Aldworth W Berks 26 B3
Alexandria W Dunb 120 B3
Alfardisworthy Devon 8 C4
Alfington Devon 11 E6
Alfold Sur 27 F8
Alfold Bars W Sus 27 F8
Alfold Crossways Sur 27 E8
Alford Aberds 150 C4
Alford Lincs 79 B7
Alford Som 23 F8
Alfreton Derbys 76 D4
Alfrick Worcs 50 D2
Alfrick Pound Worcs 50 D2
Alfriston E Sus 18 E2
Algaltraig Argyll 129 C5
Algarkirk Lincs 79 F5
Alhampton Som 23 F8
Aline Lodge W Isles 173 G4
Alisary Highld 145 F7
Alkborough N Lincs 90 B2
Alkerton Oxon 51 E8
Alkham Kent 31 E6
Alkington Shrops 74 F2
Alkmonton Derbys 75 F8
All Cannings Wilts 25 C5
All Saints Church, Godshill I o W 15 F6
All Saints South Elmham Suff 69 F6
All Stretton Shrops 60 E4
Alladale Lodge Highld 163 F8
Allaleigh Devon 7 D6
Allanaquoich Aberds 149 E7
Allangrange Mains Highld 157 D7
Allanton Borders 124 D4
Allanton N Lnrk 121 D8
Allathasdal W Isles 171 K2
Allendale Town Northumb 109 D8
Allenheads Northumb 109 E8
Allens Green Herts 41 C7
Allensford Durham 110 D3
Allensmore Hereford 49 F6
Allenton Derby 76 F3
Aller Som 12 B2
Allerby Cumb 107 F7
Allerford Som 21 E8
Allerston N Yorks 103 F6
Allerthorpe E Yorks 96 E3
Allerton Mers 86 F2
Allerton W Yorks 94 F4
Allerton Bywater W Yorks 88 B5
Allerton Mauleverer N Yorks 95 D7
Allesley W Mid 63 F7
Allestree Derby 76 F3
Allet Corn 3 B6
Allexton Leics 64 D5
Allgreave Ches 75 C6
Allhallows Medway 30 B2
Allhallows-on-Sea Medway 30 B2
Alligin Shuas Highld 154 E4
Allimore Green Staffs 62 C2
Allington Lincs 77 E8
Allington Wilts 25 F7
Allington Wilts 25 C5
Allithwaite Cumb 92 B3
Alloa Clack 133 E7
Allonby Cumb 107 E7
Alloway S Ayrs 112 C3
Allt Carms 33 D6
Allt na h-Airbhe Highld 163 E5
Allt-nan-sùgh Highld 146 B2
Alltchaorunn Highld 139 D5
Alltforgan Powys 59 B6
Alltmawr Powys 48 E2
Alltnacaillich Highld 167 E6
Alltsigh Highld 147 C7
Alltwalis Carms 46 F3
Alltwen Neath 33 D8
Alltyblaca Ceredig 46 E4
Allwood Green Suff 56 B4
Almeley Hereford 48 D5
Almer Dorset 13 E7
Almholme S Yorks 89 D6
Almington Staffs 74 F4
Alminstone Cross Devon 8 B5
Almondbank Perth 134 B2
Almondbury W Yorks 88 C2
Almondsbury S Glos 36 F3

Alne N Yorks 95 C7
Alness Highld 157 C7
Alnham Northumb 117 C5
Alnmouth Northumb 117 C8
Alnwick Northumb 117 C7
Alperton London 40 F4
Alphamstone Essex 56 F2
Alpheton Suff 56 D2
Alphington Devon 10 E4
Alport Derbys 76 C2
Alpraham Ches 74 D2
Alresford Essex 43 B6
Alrewas Staffs 63 C5
Alsager Ches 74 D4
Alsagers Bank Staffs 74 E5
Alsop en le Dale Derbys 75 D8
Alston Cumb 109 E7
Alston Devon 11 D8
Alstone Glos 50 F4
Alstonefield Staffs 75 D8
Alswear Devon 10 B2
Altandhu Highld 162 C3
Altanduin Highld 165 B5
Altarnun Corn 8 F4
Altass Highld 164 D1
Alterwall Highld 169 C7
Altham Lancs 93 F7
Althorne Essex 43 E5
Althorp House, Great Brington Northants 52 C4
Althorpe N Lincs 90 D2
Alticry Dumfries 105 D6
Altnabreac Station Highld 168 E5
Altnacealgach Hotel Highld 163 C6
Altnacraig Argyll 130 C4
Altnafeadh Highld 139 D6
Altnaharra Highld 167 F7
Altofts W Yorks 88 B4
Alton Derbys 76 C3
Alton Hants 26 F5
Alton Staffs 75 E7
Alton Pancras Dorset 12 D5
Alton Priors Wilts 25 C6
Alton Towers Staffs 75 E7
Altrincham Gtr Man 87 F5
Altrua Highld 146 F5
Altskeith Stirl 132 D3
Altyre Ho. Moray 158 D4
Alva Clack 133 E7
Alvanley Ches 73 B8
Alvaston Derby 76 F3
Alvechurch Worcs 50 B5
Alvecote Warks 63 D6
Alvediston Wilts 13 B7
Alveley Shrops 61 F7
Alverdiscott Devon 9 B7
Alverstoke Hants 15 E7
Alverstone I o W 15 F6
Alverton Notts 77 E7
Alves Moray 158 C5
Alvescot Oxon 38 D2
Alveston S Glos 36 F3
Alveston Warks 51 D7
Alvie Highld 148 D4
Alvingham Lincs 91 E7
Alvington Glos 36 D3
Alwalton Cambs 65 E8
Alweston Dorset 12 C4
Alwinton Northumb 116 D5
Alwoodley W Yorks 95 F5
Alyth Perth 142 E2
Am Baile W Isles 171 J3
Am Buth Argyll 130 C4
Amatnatua Highld 164 E1
Amber Hill Lincs 78 E5
Ambergate Derbys 76 D3
Amberley Glos 37 D5
Amberley W Sus 16 C4
Amble Northumb 117 D8
Amblecote W Mid 62 F2
Ambler Thorn W Yorks 87 B8
Ambleside Cumb 99 D5
Ambleston Pembs 44 C5
Ambrosden Oxon 39 C6
Amcotts N Lincs 90 C2
American Air Museum, Duxford Cambs 55 E5
Amersham Bucks 40 E2
Amerton Working Farm, Stowe-by-Chartley Staffs 62 B3
Amesbury Wilts 25 E6
Amington Staffs 63 D6
Amisfield Dumfries 114 F2
Amlwch Anglesey 82 B4
Amlwch Port Anglesey 82 B4
Ammanford = Rhydaman Carms 33 C7
Amod Argyll 118 C4
Amotherby N Yorks 96 B3
Ampfield Hants 14 B5
Ampleforth N Yorks 95 B8
Ampney Crucis Glos 37 D7
Ampney St Mary Glos 37 D7
Ampney St Peter Glos 37 D7
Amport Hants 25 E7
Ampthill Beds 53 F8
Ampton Suff 56 B2
Amroth Pembs 32 D2
Amulree Perth 141 F5
An Caol Highld 155 E2
An Cnoc W Isles 172 E7
An Gleann Ur W Isles 172 E7
An t-Ob = Leverburgh W Isles 173 K3
Anagach Highld 149 B6
Anaheilt Highld 138 C2
Anancaun Highld 154 D6
Ancaster Lincs 78 E2
Anchor Shrops 59 F8
Anchorsholme Blkpool 92 E3
Ancroft Northumb 125 E5
Ancrum Borders 116 B2
Anderby Lincs 79 B8
Anderson Dorset 13 E6
Anderton Ches 74 B3
Andover Hants 25 E8
Andover Down Hants 25 E8
Andoversford Glos 37 C7
Andreas I o M 84 C4
Anfield Mers 85 E4
Angersleigh Som 11 C6
Angle Pembs 44 E3
Angmering W Sus 16 D4
Angram N Yorks 95 E8
Angram N Yorks 100 E3
Anie Stirl 132 C4
Ankerville Highld 158 B2
Anlaby E Yorks 90 B4
Anmer Norf 80 E3
Anna Valley Hants 25 E8
Annan Dumfries 107 C8
Annat Argyll 131 C6
Annat Highld 155 E4
Annbank S Ayrs 112 B4
Anne Hathaway's Cottage, Stratford-upon-Avon Warks 51 D6
Annesley Notts 76 D5
Annesley Woodhouse Notts 76 D4
Annfield Plain Durham 110 D4
Annifirth Shetland 175 J3
Annitsford T & W 111 B5
Annscroft Shrops 60 D4
Ansdell Lancs 85 B4
Ansford Som 23 F8
Ansley Warks 63 E6
Anslow Staffs 63 B6
Anslow Gate Staffs 63 B5
Anstey Herts 54 F5
Anstey Leics 64 D2
Anstruther Easter Fife 135 D7
Anstruther Wester Fife 135 D7
Ansty Hants 26 E5
Ansty Warks 63 F7
Ansty Wilts 13 B7
Ansty W Sus 17 B6
Anthill Common Hants 15 C7
Anthorn Cumb 107 D8
Antingham Norf 81 D8
Anton's Gowt Lincs 79 E5
Antonshill Falk 133 F7
Antony Corn 5 D8
Anwick Lincs 78 D4
Anwoth Dumfries 106 D2
Aoradh Argyll 126 C2
Apes Hall Cambs 67 E5
Apethorpe Northants 65 E7
Apeton Staffs 62 C2
Apley Lincs 78 B4
Apperknowle Derbys 76 B3
Apperley Glos 37 B5
Apperley Bridge W Yorks 94 F4
Appersett N Yorks 100 E3
Appin Argyll 138 E3
Appin House Argyll 138 E3
Appleby N Lincs 90 C3
Appleby-in-Westmorland Cumb 100 B1
Appleby Magna Leics 63 D7
Appleby Parva Leics 63 D7
Applecross Highld 155 F3
Applecross Ho. Highld 155 F3
Appledore Devon 20 F3
Appledore Devon 11 C5
Appledore Kent 19 C6
Appledore Heath Kent 19 B6
Appleford Oxon 39 E5
Applegarthtown Dumfries 114 F4
Appleshaw Hants 25 E8
Applethwaite Cumb 98 B4
Appleton Halton 86 F3
Appleton Oxon 38 D4
Appleton-le-Moors N Yorks 103 F5
Appleton-le-Street N Yorks 96 B3
Appleton Roebuck N Yorks 95 E8
Appleton Thorn Warr 86 F4
Appleton Wiske N Yorks 102 D1
Appletreehall Borders 115 C8
Appletreewick N Yorks 94 C3
Appley Som 11 B5
Appley Bridge Lancs 86 D3
Apse Heath I o W 15 F6
Apsley End Beds 54 F2
Apuldram W Sus 16 D2
Aquhythie Aberds 151 C6
Arabella Highld 158 B2
Arbeadie Aberds 151 E5
Arbeia Roman Fort and Museum T & W 111 C6
Arberth = Narberth Pembs 32 C2
Arbirlot Angus 143 E6
Arboll Highld 165 F5
Arborfield Wokingham 27 C5
Arborfield Cross Wokingham 27 C5
Arborfield Garrison Wokingham 27 C5
Arbour-thorne S Yorks 88 F4
Arbroath Angus 143 E6
Arbuthnott Aberds 143 B7
Archiestown Moray 159 E6
Arclid Ches 74 C4
Ard-dhubh Highld 155 F3
Ardachu Highld 164 D3
Ardalanish Argyll 136 G4
Ardanaiseig Argyll 131 C6
Ardaneaskan Highld 155 G4
Ardanstur Argyll 130 D4
Ardargie House Hotel Perth 134 C2
Ardarroch Highld 155 G4
Ardbeg Argyll 126 E4
Ardbeg Argyll 129 B6
Ardbeg Distillery, Port Ellen Argyll 126 E4
Ardcharnich Highld 163 F5
Ardchiavaig Argyll 136 G4
Ardchullarie More Stirl 132 C4
Ardchyle Stirl 132 B4
Arddleen Powys 60 C2
Ardechvie Highld 146 E4
Ardeley Herts 41 B6
Ardelve Highld 155 H4
Arden Argyll 132 F2
Ardens Grafton Warks 51 D6
Ardentinny Argyll 129 B6
Ardentraive Argyll 129 C5
Ardeonaig Stirl 140 F3
Ardersier Highld 157 D8
Ardessie Highld 162 F4
Ardfern Argyll 130 E4
Ardgartan Argyll 131 E8
Ardgay Highld 164 E2
Ardgour Highld 138 C4
Ardheslaig Highld 154 E3
Ardiecow Moray 160 B2
Ardindrean Highld 163 F5
Ardingly W Sus 17 B7
Ardington Oxon 38 F4
Ardlair Aberds 150 B4
Ardlamont Ho. Argyll 128 D4
Ardleigh Essex 43 B6
Ardler Perth 142 E2
Ardley Oxon 39 B5
Ardlui Argyll 132 C2
Ardlussa Argyll 127 D4
Ardmair Highld 163 E5
Ardmay Argyll 131 E8
Ardminish Argyll 118 B3
Ardmolich Highld 145 F7
Ardmore Argyll 130 C3
Ardmore Highld 166 D4
Ardmore Highld 164 F4
Ardnacross Argyll 137 D6
Ardnadam Argyll 129 C6
Ardnagrask Highld 157 E6
Ardnarff Highld 155 G4
Ardnastang Highld 138 C2
Ardnave Argyll 126 B2
Ardno Argyll 131 E7
Ardo Aberds 160 E5
Ardo Ho. Aberds 151 B8
Ardoch Perth 141 F7
Ardochy House Highld 146 D5
Ardoyne Aberds 151 B5
Ardpatrick Argyll 128 D2
Ardpatrick Ho. Argyll 128 E2
Ardpeaton Argyll 129 B7
Ardrishaig Argyll 128 B3
Ardross Fife 135 D7
Ardross Highld 157 B7
Ardross Castle Highld 157 B7
Ardrossan N Ayrs 120 E2
Ardshealach Highld 137 B7
Ardsley S Yorks 88 D4
Ardslignish Highld 137 B6
Ardtalla Argyll 126 D4
Ardtalnaig Perth 140 F4
Ardtoe Highld 145 F6
Ardtrostan Perth 133 B5
Arduaine Argyll 130 D3
Ardullie Highld 157 C6
Ardvasar Highld 145 C6
Ardvorlich Perth 132 B5
Ardwell Dumfries 104 E5
Ardwell Mains Dumfries 104 E5
Ardwick Gtr Man 87 E6
Areley Kings Worcs 50 B3
Arford Hants 27 F6
Argoed Caerph 35 E5
Argoed Mill Powys 47 C8
Argyll & Sutherland Highlanders Museum (See Stirling Castle) Stirl 133 E6
Arichamish Argyll 130 E5
Arichastlich Argyll 131 B8
Aridhglas Argyll 136 F4
Arileod Argyll 136 C2
Arinacrinachd Highld 154 E3
Arinagour Argyll 136 C3
Arion Orkney 176 E1
Arisaig Highld 145 E6
Ariundle Highld 138 C2
Arkendale N Yorks 95 C6
Arkesden Essex 55 F5
Arkholme Lancs 93 B5
Arkle Town N Yorks 101 D5
Arkley London 41 E5
Arksey S Yorks 89 D6
Arkwright Town Derbys 76 B4
Arle Glos 37 B6
Arlecdon Cumb 98 C2
Arlesey Beds 54 F2
Arleston Telford 61 C6
Arley Ches 86 F4
Arlingham Glos 36 C4
Arlington Devon 20 E5
Arlington E Sus 18 E2
Arlington Glos 37 D8
Arlington Court Devon 20 E5
Armadale Highld 168 C2
Armadale W Loth 120 C2
Armadale Castle Highld 145 C6
Armathwaite Cumb 108 E5
Arminghall Norf 69 D5
Armitage Staffs 62 C4
Armley W Yorks 95 F5
Armscote Warks 51 E7
Armthorpe S Yorks 89 D7
Arnabost Argyll 136 C3
Arncliffe N Yorks 94 B2
Arncroach Fife 135 D7
Arne Dorset 13 F7
Arnesby Leics 64 E3
Arngask Perth 134 C3
Arnisdale Highld 145 B8
Arnish Highld 152 E6
Arniston Engine Midloth 123 C6
Arnol W Isles 172 D6
Arnold E Yorks 97 E7
Arnold Notts 77 E5
Arnolfini Gallery Bristol 23 B7
Arnprior Stirl 132 E5
Arnside Cumb 92 B4
Aros Mains Argyll 137 D6
Arowry Wrex 73 F8
Arpafeelie Highld 157 D7
Arrad Foot Cumb 99 F5
Arram E Yorks 97 E6
Arrathorne N Yorks 101 E7
Arreton I o W 15 F6
Arrington Cambs 54 D4
Arrivain Argyll 131 B8
Arrochar Argyll 131 E8
Arrow Warks 51 D5
Arthington W Yorks 95 E5
Arthingworth Northants 64 F4
Arthog Gwyn 58 C3
Arthrath Aberds 161 E6
Arthurstone Perth 142 E2
Artrochie Aberds 161 E7
Arundel W Sus 16 D4
Arundel Castle W Sus 16 D4
Aryhoulan Highld 138 C4
Asby Cumb 98 B2
Ascog Argyll 129 D6
Ascot Windsor 27 C7
Ascot Racecourse Windsor 27 C7
Ascott Warks 51 F8
Ascott-under-Wychwood Oxon 38 C3
Asenby N Yorks 95 B6
Asfordby Leics 64 C4
Asfordby Hill Leics 64 C4
Asgarby Lincs 78 E4
Asgarby Lincs 79 C6
Ash Kent 29 C6
Ash Kent 31 D6
Ash Som 12 B2
Ash Sur 27 D6
Ash Bullayne Devon 10 D2
Ash Green Warks 63 F7
Ash Magna Shrops 74 F2
Ash Mill Devon 10 B2
Ash Priors Som 11 B6
Ash Street Suff 56 E4
Ash Thomas Devon 10 C5
Ash Vale Sur 27 D6
Ashampstead W Berks 26 B3
Ashbocking Suff 57 D5
Ashbourne Derbys 75 E8
Ashbrittle Som 11 B5
Ashburton Devon 7 C5
Ashbury Devon 9 E7
Ashbury Oxon 38 F2
Ashby N Lincs 90 D3
Ashby by Partney Lincs 79 C7
Ashby cum Fenby NE Lincs 91 D6
Ashby de la Launde Lincs 78 D3
Ashby-de-la-Zouch Leics 63 C7
Ashby Folville Leics 64 C4
Ashby Magna Leics 64 E2
Ashby Parva Leics 64 F2
Ashby Puerorum Lincs 79 B6
Ashby St Ledgers Northants 52 C3
Ashby St Mary Norf 69 D6
Ashchurch Glos 50 F4
Ashcombe Devon 7 B7
Ashcott Som 23 F6
Ashdon Essex 55 E6
Ashe Hants 26 E3
Asheldham Essex 43 D5
Ashen Essex 55 E8
Ashendon Bucks 39 C7
Ashfield Carms 33 B7
Ashfield Stirl 133 D6
Ashfield Suff 57 C6
Ashfield Green Suff 57 B6
Ashfold Crossways W Sus 17 B6
Ashford Devon 20 F4
Ashford Hants 14 C2
Ashford Kent 30 E4
Ashford Sur 27 B8
Ashford Bowdler Shrops 49 B7
Ashford Carbonell Shrops 49 B7
Ashford Hill Hants 26 C3
Ashford in the Water Derbys 75 C8
Ashgill S Lnrk 121 E7
Ashill Devon 11 C5
Ashill Norf 67 D8
Ashill Som 11 C8
Ashingdon Essex 42 E4
Ashington Northumb 117 F8
Ashington Som 12 B3
Ashington W Sus 16 C5
Ashintully Castle Perth 141 C8
Ashkirk Borders 115 B7
Ashlett Hants 15 D5
Ashleworth Glos 37 B5
Ashley Cambs 55 C7
Ashley Ches 87 F5
Ashley Devon 9 C8
Ashley Dorset 14 D2
Ashley Glos 37 E6
Ashley Hants 14 E3
Ashley Hants 25 F8
Ashley Northants 64 E4
Ashley Staffs 74 F4
Ashley Green Bucks 40 D2
Ashley Heath Dorset 14 D2
Ashley Heath Staffs 74 F4
Ashmanhaugh Norf 69 B6
Ashmansworth Hants 26 D2
Ashmansworthy Devon 8 C5
Ashmore Dorset 13 C7
Ashorne Warks 51 D8
Ashover Derbys 76 C3
Ashow Warks 51 B8
Ashprington Devon 7 D6
Ashreigney Devon 9 C8
Ashtead Sur 28 D2
Ashton Ches 74 C2
Ashton Corn 2 D5
Ashton Hants 15 C6
Ashton Hereford 49 C7
Ashton Invclyd 129 C7
Ashton Northants 53 E5
Ashton Northants 65 F7
Ashton Common Wilts 24 D3
Ashton-In-Makerfield Gtr Man 86 E3
Ashton Keynes Wilts 37 E7
Ashton under Hill Worcs 50 F4
Ashton-under-Lyne Gtr Man 87 E7
Ashton upon Mersey Gtr Man 87 E5
Ashurst Hants 14 C4
Ashurst Kent 18 B2
Ashurst W Sus 17 C5
Ashurstwood W Sus 28 F5
Ashwater Devon 9 E5
Ashwell Herts 54 F3
Ashwell Rutland 65 C5
Ashwell Som 11 C8
Ashwellthorpe Norf 68 E4
Ashwick Som 23 E8
Ashwicken Norf 67 C7
Ashybank Borders 115 C8
Askam in Furness Cumb 92 B2
Askern S Yorks 89 C6
Askerswell Dorset 12 E3
Askett Bucks 39 D8
Askham Cumb 99 B7
Askham Notts 77 B7
Askham Bryan York 95 E8
Askham Richard York 95 E8
Asknish Argyll 128 A4
Askrigg N Yorks 100 E4
Askwith N Yorks 94 E4
Aslackby Lincs 78 F3
Aslacton Norf 68 E4
Aslockton Notts 77 F7
Asloun Aberds 150 C4
Aspatria Cumb 107 E8
Aspenden Herts 41 B6
Asperton Lincs 79 F5
Aspley Guise Beds 53 F7
Aspley Heath Beds 53 F7
Aspull Gtr Man 86 D4
Asselby E Yorks 89 B8
Asserby Lincs 79 B7
Assington Suff 56 F3
Assynt Ho. Highld 157 C6
Astbury Ches 74 C5
Astcote Northants 52 D4
Asterley Shrops 60 D3
Asterton Shrops 60 E3
Asthall Oxon 38 C2
Asthall Leigh Oxon 38 C3
Astley Shrops 60 C5
Astley Warks 63 F7
Astley Worcs 50 C2
Astley Abbotts Shrops 61 E7
Astley Bridge Gtr Man 86 C5
Astley Cross Worcs 50 C3
Astley Green Gtr Man 86 E5
Aston Ches 74 E3
Aston Ches 74 B2
Aston Derbys 88 F2
Aston Hereford 49 B6
Aston Herts 41 B5
Aston Oxon 38 D3
Aston Shrops 60 B5
Aston Staffs 74 E4
Aston S Yorks 89 F5
Aston Telford 61 D6
Aston W Mid 62 F4
Aston Wokingham 39 F7
Aston Abbotts Bucks 39 B8
Aston Botterell Shrops 61 F6
Aston-By-Stone Staffs 75 F6
Aston Cantlow Warks 51 D6
Aston Clinton Bucks 40 C1
Aston Crews Hereford 36 B3
Aston Cross Glos 50 F4
Aston End Herts 41 B5
Aston Eyre Shrops 61 E6
Aston Fields Worcs 50 C4
Aston Flamville Leics 63 E8
Aston Ingham Hereford 36 B3
Aston juxta Mondrum Ches 74 D3
Aston le Walls Northants 52 D2
Aston Magna Glos 51 F6
Aston Munslow Shrops 60 F5
Aston on Clun Shrops 60 F3
Aston-on-Trent Derbys 63 B8
Aston Rogers Shrops 60 D3
Aston Rowant Oxon 39 E7
Aston Sandford Bucks 39 D7
Aston Somerville Worcs 50 F5
Aston Subedge Glos 51 E6
Aston Tirrold Oxon 39 F5
Aston Upthorpe Oxon 39 F5
Astrop Northants 52 F3
Astwick Beds 54 F3
Astwood M Keynes 53 E7
Astwood Worcs 50 D3
Astwood Bank Worcs 50 C5
Aswarby Lincs 78 F3
Aswardby Lincs 79 B6
Atch Lench Worcs 50 D5
Atcham Shrops 60 D5
Athelhampton Dorset 13 E5
Athelington Suff 57 B6
Athelney Som 11 B8
Athelstaneford E Loth 123 B8
Atherington Devon 9 B7
Atherstone Warks 63 E7
Atherstone on Stour Warks 51 D7
Atherton Gtr Man 86 D4
Atley Hill N Yorks 101 D7
Atlow Derbys 76 E2
Attadale Highld 155 G5
Attadale Ho. Highld 155 G5
Attenborough Notts 76 F5
Atterby Lincs 90 E3
Attercliffe S Yorks 88 F4
Attleborough Norf 68 E3
Attleborough Warks 63 E7
Attlebridge Norf 68 C4
Atwick E Yorks 97 D7
Atworth Wilts 24 C3
Aubourn Lincs 78 C2
Auchagallon N Ayrs 119 C5
Auchallater Aberds 149 F7
Aucharnie Aberds 160 D3
Auchattie Aberds 151 E5
Auchavan Angus 142 C1
Auchbreck Moray 149 B8
Auchenback E Renf 120 D5
Auchenbainzie Dumfries 113 E8
Auchenblae Aberds 143 B7
Auchenbrack Dumfries 113 E7
Auchenbreck Argyll 129 B5
Auchencairn Dumfries 106 D4
Auchencairn Dumfries 114 F2
Auchencairn N Ayrs 119 D7
Auchencrosh S Ayrs 104 B5
Auchencrow Borders 124 C4
Auchendinny Midloth 123 C5
Auchengray S Lnrk 122 D2
Auchenhalrig Moray 159 C7
Auchenheath S Lnrk 121 E8
Auchenlochan Argyll 128 C4
Auchenmalg Dumfries 105 D6
Auchensoul S Ayrs 112 E2
Auchentiber N Ayrs 120 E3
Auchertyre Highld 155 H4
Auchgourish Highld 148 C5
Auchincarroch W Dunb 132 F3
Auchindrain Argyll 131 E6
Auchindrean Highld 163 F5
Auchininna Aberds 160 D3
Auchinleck E Ayrs 113 B5
Auchinloch N Lnrk 121 B6
Auchinroath Moray 159 D6
Auchintoul Aberds 150 C4
Auchiries Aberds 161 E7
Auchlee Aberds 151 E7
Auchleven Aberds 150 B5
Auchlochan S Lnrk 121 F8
Auchlossan Aberds 150 D4
Auchlunies Aberds 151 E7
Auchlyne Stirl 132 B4
Auchmacoy Aberds 161 E6
Auchmair Moray 150 B2
Auchmantle Dumfries 105 C5
Auchmillan E Ayrs 112 B5
Auchmithie Angus 143 E6
Auchmuirbridge Fife 134 D4
Auchmull Angus 143 B5
Auchnacree Angus 142 C4
Auchnagallin Highld 158 F4
Auchnagatt Aberds 161 D6
Auchnaha Argyll 128 B4
Auchnashelloch Perth 133 C6
Aucholzie Aberds 150 E2
Auchrannie Angus 142 D2
Auchroisk Highld 149 B6
Auchronie Angus 150 F3
Auchterarder Perth 133 C8
Auchteraw Highld 147 D6
Auchterderran Fife 134 E4
Auchterhouse Angus 142 F3
Auchtermuchty Fife 134 C4
Auchterneed Highld 157 D5
Auchtertool Fife 134 E4
Auchtertyre Moray 159 D5
Auchtubh Stirl 132 B4
Auckengill Highld 169 C8
Auckley S Yorks 89 D7
Audenshaw Gtr Man 87 E7
Audlem Ches 74 E3
Audley Staffs 74 D4
Audley End Essex 56 F2
Audley End House Essex 55 F6
Auds Aberds 160 B3
Aughton E Yorks 96 F3
Aughton Lancs 85 D4
Aughton Lancs 93 C5
Aughton S Yorks 89 F5
Aughton Wilts 25 D7
Aughton Park Lancs 86 D2
Auldearn Highld 158 D3
Aulden Hereford 49 D6
Auldgirth Dumfries 114 F2
Auldhame E Loth 135 F7
Auldhouse S Lnrk 121 D6
Ault a'chruinn Highld 146 B2
Aultanrynie Highld 166 F5
Aultbea Highld 162 F2
Aultdearg Highld 156 C3
Aultgrishan Highld 154 B3
Aultguish Inn Highld 156 B4
Aultibea Highld 165 B7
Aultiphurst Highld 168 C3
Aultmore Moray 159 D8
Aultnagoire Highld 147 B8
Aultnamain Inn Highld 164 F3
Aultnaslat Highld 146 D4
Aulton Aberds 150 B5
Aundorach Highld 149 C5
Aunsby Lincs 78 F3
Auquhorthies Aberds 151 B7
Aust S Glos 36 F2
Austendike Lincs 66 B2
Austerfield S Yorks 89 E7
Austrey Warks 63 D6
Austwick N Yorks 93 C7
Authorpe Lincs 91 F8
Authorpe Row Lincs 79 B8
Avebury Wilts 25 C6
Aveley Thurrock 42 F1
Avening Glos 37 E5
Averham Notts 77 D7
Aveton Gifford Devon 6 E4
Avielochan Highld 148 C5
Aviemore Highld 148 C4
Avington Hants 26 F3
Avington W Berks 25 C8
Avoch Highld 157 D8
Avon Hants 14 E2
Avon Dassett Warks 52 E2
Avonbridge Falk 122 B2
Avonmouth Bristol 23 B7
Avonwick Devon 6 D5
Awbridge Hants 14 B4
Awhirk Dumfries 104 D4
Awkley S Glos 36 F2
Awliscombe Devon 11 D6
Awre Glos 36 D4
Awsworth Notts 76 E4
Axbridge Som 23 D6
Axford Hants 26 E4
Axford Wilts 25 B7
Axminster Devon 11 E7
Axmouth Devon 11 E7
Axton Flint 85 F2
Aycliff Kent 31 E7
Aycliffe Durham 101 B7
Aydon Northumb 110 C3
Aylburton Glos 36 D3
Ayle Northumb 109 E7
Aylesbeare Devon 10 E5
Aylesbury Bucks 39 C8
Aylesby NE Lincs 91 D6
Aylesford Kent 29 D8
Aylesham Kent 31 D6
Aylestone Leicester 64 D2
Aylmerton Norf 81 D7
Aylsham Norf 81 E7
Aylton Hereford 49 F8
Aymestrey Hereford 49 C6
Aynho Northants 52 F3
Ayot St Lawrence Herts 40 C4
Ayot St Peter Herts 41 C5
Ayr S Ayrs 112 B3
Ayr Racecourse S Ayrs 112 B3
Aysgarth N Yorks 101 F5
Ayside Cumb 99 F5
Ayston Rutland 65 D5
Aythorpe Roding Essex 42 C1
Ayton Borders 124 C5
Aywick Shetland 174 E7
Azerley N Yorks 95 B5

B

Babbacombe Torbay 7 C7
Babbinswood Shrops 73 F7
Babcary Som 12 B3
Babel Carms 47 F7
Babell Flint 73 B5
Babraham Cambs 55 D6
Babworth Notts 89 F7
Bac W Isles 172 D7
Bachau Anglesey 82 C4
Back of Keppoch Highld 145 E6
Back Rogerton E Ayrs 113 B5
Backaland Orkney 176 C4
Backaskaill Orkney 176 A3
Backbarrow Cumb 99 F5
Backe Carms 32 C3
Backfolds Aberds 161 C7
Backford Ches 73 B8
Backford Cross Ches 73 B7
Backhill Aberds 160 E4
Backhill Aberds 161 E7
Backhill of Clackriach Aberds 161 D6
Backhill of Fortree Aberds 161 D6
Backhill of Trustach Aberds 150 E5
Backies Highld 165 D5
Backlass Highld 169 D7
Backwell N Som 23 C6
Backworth T & W 111 B6
Bacon End Essex 42 C2
Baconsthorpe Norf 81 D7
Bacton Hereford 49 F5
Bacton Norf 81 D9
Bacton Suff 56 C4
Bacton Green Suff 56 C4
Bacup Lancs 87 B6
Badachro Highld 154 C3
Badanloch Lodge Highld 168 F2
Badavanich Highld 156 D2
Badbury Swindon 38 F1
Badby Northants 52 D3
Badcall Highld 166 D4
Badcaul Highld 162 E4
Baddeley Green Stoke 75 D6
Baddesley Clinton Warks 51 B7
Baddesley Clinton Hall Warks 51 B7
Baddesley Ensor Warks 63 E6
Baddidarach Highld 162 B4
Baddoch Aberds 149 F7
Baddock Highld 157 D8
Badenscoth Aberds 160 E4
Badenyon Aberds 150 C2
Badger Shrops 61 E7
Badger's Mount Kent 29 C5
Badgeworth Glos 37 C6
Badgworth Som 23 D5
Badicaul Highld 155 H3
Badingham Suff 57 C7
Badlesmere Kent 30 D4
Badlipster Highld 169 E7
Badluarach Highld 162 E3
Badminton S Glos 37 F5
Badnaban Highld 162 B4
Badninish Highld 164 E4
Badrallach Highld 162 E4
Badsey Worcs 51 E5
Badshot Lea Sur 27 E6
Badsworth W Yorks 89 C5
Badwell Ash Suff 56 C3
Bae Colwyn = Colwyn Bay Conwy 83 D8
Bag Enderby Lincs 79 B6
Bagby N Yorks 102 F2
Bagendon Glos 37 D7
Bagh a Chaisteil = Castlebay W Isles 171 L2
Bagh Mor W Isles 170 E4
Bagh Shiarabhagh W Isles 171 K3
Baghasdal W Isles 171 J3
Bagillt Flint 73 B6
Baginton Warks 51 B8
Baglan Neath 33 E8
Bagley Shrops 60 B4
Bagnall Staffs 75 D6
Bagnor W Berks 26 C2
Bagshot Sur 27 C7
Bagshot Wilts 25 C8
Bagthorpe Norf 80 D3
Bagthorpe Notts 76 D4
Bagworth Leics 63 D8
Bagwy Llydiart Hereford 35 B8
Bail Àrd Bhuirgh W Isles 172 C7
Bail Uachdraich W Isles 170 D4
Baildon W Yorks 94 F4
Baile W Isles 173 K2
Baile a Mhanaich W Isles 170 E3
Baile Ailein W Isles 172 F5
Baile an Truiseil W Isles 172 C6
Baile Boidheach Argyll 128 C2
Baile Glas W Isles 170 E4
Baile Mhartainn W Isles 170 C3
Baile Mhic Phail W Isles 170 C4
Baile Mor Argyll 136 F3
Baile Mor W Isles 170 D3
Baile na Creige W Isles 171 K2
Baile nan Cailleach W Isles 170 E3
Baile Raghaill W Isles 170 C3
Bailebeag Highld 147 C8
Baileyhead Cumb 108 B5
Bailiesward Aberds 159 F8
Baillieston Glasgow 121 C6
Bail'lochdrach W Isles 170 E4
Bail'Ur Tholastaidh W Isles 172 D8
Bainbridge N Yorks 100 E4
Bainsford Falk 133 F7
Bainshole Aberds 160 E3
Bainton E Yorks 97 D5
Bainton P'boro 65 D7
Bairnkine Borders 116 C2
Baker Street Thurrock 42 F2
Baker's End Herts 41 C6
Bakewell Derbys 76 C2
Bala = Y Bala Gwyn 72 F3
Balachuirn Highld 153 E6
Balavil Highld 148 D3
Balbeg Highld 147 B7
Balbeg Highld 157 F5
Balbeggie Perth 134 B3
Balbithan Aberds 151 C6
Balbithan Ho. Aberds 151 C7
Balblair Highld 157 C8
Balblair Highld 164 E2
Balby S Yorks 89 D6
Balchladich Highld 166 F2
Balchraggan Highld 157 F6
Balchraggan Highld 157 E6
Balchrick Highld 166 D3
Balchrystie Fife 135 D6
Balcladaich Highld 147 B5
Balcombe W Sus 28 F4
Balcombe Lane W Sus 28 F4
Balcomie Fife 135 C8
Balcurvie Fife 134 D5
Baldersby N Yorks 95 B6
Baldersby St James N Yorks 95 B6
Balderstone Lancs 93 F6
Balderton Ches 73 C7
Balderton Notts 77 D8
Baldhu Corn 3 B6
Baldinnie Fife 135 C6
Baldock Herts 54 F3
Baldovie Dundee 142 F4
Baldrine I o M 84 D4
Baldslow E Sus 18 D4
Baldwin I o M 84 D3
Baldwinholme Cumb 108 D3
Baldwin's Gate Staffs 74 E4
Bale Norf 81 D6
Balearn Aberds 161 C7
Balemartine Argyll 136 F1
Balephuil Argyll 136 F1
Balerno Edin 122 C4
Balevullin Argyll 136 F1

Bilting Kent 30 E4
Bilton E Yorks 97 F7
Bilton Northumb 117 C8
Bilton Warks 52 B2
Bilton in Ainsty N Yorks 95 E7
Bimbister Orkney 176 E2
Binbrook Lincs 91 E6
Binchester Blocks Durham 110 F5
Bincombe Dorset 12 F4
Bindal Highld 165 F6
Binegar Som 23 E8
Binfield Brack 27 B6
Binfield Heath Oxon 26 B5
Bingfield Northumb 110 B2
Bingham Notts 77 F7
Bingley W Yorks 94 F4
Bings Heath Shrops 60 C5
Binham Norf 81 D5
Binley Hants 26 D2
Binley W Mid 51 B8
Binley Woods Warks 51 B8
Binniehill Falk 121 B8
Binsoe N Yorks 94 B5
Binstead I o W 15 E6
Binsted Hants 27 E5
Binton Warks 51 D6
Bintree Norf 81 E6
Binweston Shrops 60 D3
Birch Essex 43 C5
Birch Gtr Man 87 D6
Birch Green Essex 43 C5
Birch Heath Ches 74 C2
Birch Hill Ches 74 B2
Birch Vale Derbys 87 F8
Bircham Newton Norf 80 D3
Bircham Tofts Norf 80 D3
Birchanger Essex 41 B8
Birchencliffe W Yorks 88 C2
Bircher Hereford 49 C6
Birchfield Highld 149 B5
Birchgrove Cardiff 22 B3
Birchgrove Swansea 33 E8
Birchington Kent 31 C6
Birchmoor Warks 63 D6
Birchover Derbys 76 C2
Birchwood Lincs 78 C2
Birchwood Warr 86 E4
Bircotes Notts 89 E7
Birdbrook Essex 55 E8
Birdforth N Yorks 95 B7
Birdham W Sus 16 E2
Birdholme Derbys 76 C3
Birdingbury Warks 52 C2
Birdland Park, Bourton-on-the-Water Glos 38 B1
Birdlip Glos 37 C6
Birds Edge W Yorks 88 D3
Birdsall N Yorks 96 C4
Birdsgreen Shrops 61 F7
Birdsmoor Gate Dorset 11 D8
Birdston E Dunb 121 B6
Birdwell S Yorks 88 D4
Birdwood Glos 36 C4
Birgham Borders 124 F3
Birkby N Yorks 101 D8
Birkdale Mers 85 C4
Birkenhead Mers 85 F4
Birkenhills Aberds 160 D4
Birkenshaw N Lnrk 121 C6
Birkenshaw W Yorks 88 B3
Birkhall Aberds 150 E2
Birkhill Angus 142 F3
Birkhill Dumfries 114 C5
Birkholme Lincs 65 B6
Birkin N Yorks 89 B6
Birley Hereford 49 D6
Birling Kent 29 C7
Birling Northumb 117 D8
Birling Gap E Sus 18 F2
Birlingham Worcs 50 E4
Birmingham W Mid 62 F4
Birmingham Botanical Gardens W Mid 62 F4
Birmingham International Airport W Mid 63 F5
Birmingham Museum and Art Gallery W Mid 62 F4
Birmingham Museum of Science and Technology W Mid 62 F4
Birnam Perth 141 E7
Birse Aberds 150 E4
Birsemore Aberds 150 E4
Birstall Leics 64 D2
Birstall W Yorks 88 B3
Birstwith N Yorks 94 D5
Birthorpe Lincs 78 F4
Birtley Hereford 49 C5
Birtley Northumb 109 B8
Birtley T & W 111 D5
Birts Street Worcs 50 F2
Bisbrooke Rutland 65 E5
Biscathorpe Lincs 91 F6
Biscot Luton 40 B3
Bish Mill Devon 10 B2
Bisham Windsor 39 F8
Bishampton Worcs 50 D4
Bishop Auckland Durham 101 B7
Bishop Burton E Yorks 97 F5
Bishop Middleham Durham 111 F6
Bishop Monkton N Yorks 95 C6
Bishop Norton Lincs 90 E3
Bishop Sutton Bath 23 D7
Bishop Thornton N Yorks 95 C5
Bishop Wilton E Yorks 96 D3
Bishopbridge Lincs 90 E4
Bishopbriggs E Dunb 121 C6
Bishopmill Moray 159 C6
Bishops Cannings Wilts 24 C5
Bishop's Castle Shrops 60 F3
Bishop's Caundle Dorset 12 C4
Bishop's Cleeve Glos 37 B6
Bishops Frome Hereford 49 E8
Bishop's Green Essex 42 C2
Bishop's Hull Som 11 B7
Bishop's Itchington Warks 51 D8
Bishops Lydeard Som 11 B6
Bishops Nympton Devon 10 B2
Bishop's Offley Staffs 61 B7
Bishop's Stortford Herts 41 B7
Bishop's Sutton Hants 26 F4
Bishop's Tachbrook Warks 51 C8
Bishops Tawton Devon 20 F4
Bishop's Waltham Hants 15 C6
Bishop's Wood Staffs 62 D2
Bishopsbourne Kent 31 D5
Bishopsteignton Devon 7 B7
Bishopstoke Hants 15 C5
Bishopston Swansea 33 F6
Bishopstone Bucks 39 C8
Bishopstone E Sus 17 D8
Bishopstone Hereford 49 E6
Bishopstone Swindon 38 F2
Bishopstone Wilts 13 B8
Bishopstrow Wilts 24 E3
Bishopswood Som 11 C7
Bishopsworth Bristol 23 C7
Bishopthorpe York 95 E8
Bishopton Darl 102 B1
Bishopton Dumfries 105 E8
Bishopton N Yorks 95 B6
Bishopton Renfs 120 B4
Bishopton Warks 51 D6
Bishton Newport 35 F7
Bisley Glos 37 D6
Bisley Sur 27 D7
Bispham Blkpool 92 E3
Bispham Green Lancs 86 C2
Bissoe Corn 3 B6
Bisterne Close Hants 14 D3
Bitchfield Lincs 65 B6
Bittadon Devon 20 E4
Bittaford Devon 6 D4
Bittering Norf 68 C2
Bitterley Shrops 49 B7
Bitterne Soton 15 C5
Bitteswell Leics 64 F2
Bitton S Glos 23 C8
Bix Oxon 39 F7
Bixter Shetland 175 H5
Blaby Leics 64 E2
Black Bourton Oxon 38 D2
Black Callerton T & W 110 C4
Black Clauchrie S Ayrs 112 F2
Black Corries Lodge Highld 139 D6
Black Crofts Argyll 130 B5
Black Dog Devon 10 D3
Black Heddon Northumb 110 B3
Black Lane Gtr Man 87 D5
Black Marsh Shrops 60 E3
Black Mount Argyll 139 E6
Black Notley Essex 42 B3
Black Pill Swansea 33 E7
Black Tar Pembs 44 E4
Black Torrington Devon 9 D6
Blackacre Dumfries 114 E3
Blackadder West Borders 124 D4
Blackawton Devon 7 D6
Blackborough Devon 11 D5
Blackborough End Norf 67 C6
Blackboys E Sus 18 C2
Blackbrook Derbys 76 E3
Blackbrook Mers 86 E3
Blackbrook Staffs 74 F4
Blackburn Aberds 160 E2
Blackburn Aberds 151 C7
Blackburn Blkburn 86 B4
Blackburn W Loth 122 C2
Blackcraig Dumfries 113 F7
Blackden Heath Ches 74 B4
Blackdog Aberds 151 C8
Blackfell T & W 111 D5
Blackfield Hants 14 D5
Blackford Cumb 108 C3
Blackford Perth 133 D7
Blackford Som 23 E6
Blackford Som 12 B4
Blackfordby Leics 63 C7
Blackgang I o W 15 G5
Blackgang Chine Fantasy I o W 15 G5
Blackhall Colliery Durham 111 F7
Blackhall Mill T & W 110 D4
Blackhall Rocks Durham 111 F7
Blackham E Sus 29 F5
Blackhaugh Borders 123 F7
Blackheath Essex 43 B6
Blackheath Suff 57 B8
Blackheath Sur 27 E8
Blackheath W Mid 62 F3
Blackhill Aberds 161 D7
Blackhill Aberds 161 C7
Blackhill Highld 152 D4
Blackhills Highld 158 D3
Blackhills Moray 159 D6
Blackhorse S Glos 23 B8
Blackland Wilts 24 C5
Blacklaw Aberds 160 C3
Blackley Gtr Man 87 D6
Blacklunans Perth 142 C1
Blackmill Bridgend 34 F3
Blackmoor Hants 27 F5
Blackmoor Gate Devon 21 E5
Blackmore Essex 42 D2
Blackmore End Essex 55 F8
Blackmore End Herts 40 C4
Blackness Falk 122 B3
Blacknest Hants 27 E5
Blacko Lancs 93 E8
Blackpool Blkpool 92 F3
Blackpool Devon 7 E6
Blackpool Pembs 32 C1
Blackpool Airport Lancs 92 F3
Blackpool Gate Cumb 108 B5
Blackpool Pleasure Beach Blkpool 92 F3
Blackpool Sea Life Centre Blkpool 92 F3
Blackpool Tower Blkpool 92 F3
Blackpool Zoo Park Blkpool 92 F3
Blackridge W Loth 121 C8
Blackrock Argyll 126 C3
Blackrock Mon 35 C6
Blackrod Gtr Man 86 C4
Blackshaw Dumfries 107 C7
Blackshaw Head W Yorks 87 B7
Blacksmith's Green Suff 56 C5
Blackstone W Sus 17 C6
Blackthorn Oxon 39 C6
Blackthorpe Suff 56 C3
Blacktoft E Yorks 90 B2
Blacktop Aberdeen 151 D7
Blacktown Newport 35 F6
Blackwall Tunnel London 41 F6
Blackwater Corn 3 B6
Blackwater Hants 27 D6
Blackwater I o W 15 F6
Blackwaterfoot N Ayrs 119 D5
Blackwell Darl 101 C7
Blackwell Derbys 75 B8
Blackwell Derbys 76 D4
Blackwell Warks 51 E7
Blackwell Worcs 50 B4
Blackwell W Sus 28 F4
Blackwood S Lnrk 121 E7
Blackwood = Coed Duon Caerph 35 E5
Blackwood Hill Staffs 75 D6
Blacon Ches 73 C7
Bladnoch Dumfries 105 D8
Bladon Oxon 38 C4
Blaen-gwynfi Neath 34 E2
Blaen-waun Carms 32 B3
Blaen-y-coed Carms 32 B4
Blaen-y-Cwm Denb 72 F4
Blaen-y-cwm Gwyn 71 E8
Blaen-y-cwm Powys 59 B7
Blaenannerch Ceredig 45 E4
Blaenau Ffestiniog Gwyn 71 C8
Blaenavon Torf 35 D6
Blaencelyn Ceredig 46 D2
Blaendyryn Powys 47 F8
Blaenffos Pembs 45 F3
Blaengarw Bridgend 34 E3
Blaengwrach Neath 34 D2
Blaenpennal Ceredig 46 C5
Blaenplwyf Ceredig 46 B4
Blaenporth Ceredig 45 E4
Blaenrhondda Rhondda 34 D3
Blaenycwm Ceredig 47 B7
Blagdon N Som 23 D7
Blagdon Torbay 7 C6
Blagdon Hill Som 11 C7
Blagill Cumb 109 E7
Blaguegate Lancs 86 D2
Blaich Highld 138 B4
Blain Highld 137 B7
Blaina Bl Gwent 35 D6
Blair Atholl Perth 141 C5
Blair Castle, Blair Atholl Perth 141 C5
Blair Drummond Stirl 133 E6
Blair Drummond Safari Park, Dunblane Stirl 133 E6
Blairbeg N Ayrs 119 C7
Blairdaff Aberds 151 C5
Blairglas Argyll 129 B8
Blairgowrie Perth 142 E1
Blairhall Fife 134 F2
Blairingone Perth 133 E8
Blairland N Ayrs 120 E3
Blairlogie Stirl 133 E7
Blairlomond Argyll 131 F7
Blairmore Argyll 129 B6
Blairnamarrow Moray 149 C8
Blairquhosh Stirl 132 F4
Blair's Ferry Argyll 128 D4
Blairskaith E Dunb 121 B5
Blaisdon Glos 36 C4
Blakebrook Worcs 50 B3
Blakedown Worcs 50 B3
Blakelaw Borders 124 F3
Blakeley Staffs 62 E2
Blakeley Lane Staffs 75 E6
Blakemere Hereford 49 E5
Blakeney Glos 36 D3
Blakeney Norf 81 C6
Blakeney Point NNR Norf 81 C6
Blakenhall Ches 74 E4
Blakenhall W Mid 62 E3
Blakeshall Worcs 62 F2
Blakesley Northants 52 D4
Blanchland Northumb 110 D2
Bland Hill N Yorks 94 D5
Blandford Forum Dorset 13 D6
Blandford St Mary Dorset 13 D6
Blanefield Stirl 121 B5
Blankney Lincs 78 C3
Blantyre S Lnrk 121 D6
Blar a'Chaorainn Highld 139 C5
Blaran Argyll 130 D4
Blarghour Argyll 131 D5
Blarmachfoldach Highld 138 C4
Blarnalearoch Highld 163 E5
Blashford Hants 14 D2
Blaston Leics 64 E5
Blatherwycke Northants 65 E6
Blawith Cumb 98 F4
Blaxhall Suff 57 D7
Blaxton S Yorks 89 D7
Blaydon T & W 110 C4
Bleadon N Som 22 D5
Bleak Hey Nook Gtr Man 87 D8
Blean Kent 30 C5
Bleasby Lincs 90 F5
Bleasby Notts 77 E7
Bleasdale Lancs 93 E5
Bleatarn Cumb 100 C2
Blebocraigs Fife 135 C6
Bleddfa Powys 48 C4
Bledington Glos 38 B2
Bledlow Bucks 39 D7
Bledlow Ridge Bucks 39 E7
Blegbie E Loth 123 C7
Blencarn Cumb 109 F6
Blencogo Cumb 107 E8
Blendworth Hants 15 C8
Blenheim Palace, Woodstock Oxon 38 C4
Blenheim Park Norf 80 D4
Blennerhasset Cumb 107 E8
Blervie Castle Moray 158 D4
Bletchingdon Oxon 39 C5
Bletchingley Sur 28 D4
Bletchley M Keynes 53 F6
Bletchley Shrops 74 F3
Bletherston Pembs 32 B1
Bletsoe Beds 53 D8
Blewbury Oxon 39 F5
Blickling Norf 81 E7
Blickling Hall, Aylsham Norf 81 E7
Blidworth Notts 77 D5
Blindburn Northumb 116 C4
Blindcrake Cumb 107 F8
Blindley Heath Sur 28 E4
Blisland Corn 5 B6
Bliss Gate Worcs 50 B2
Blissford Hants 14 C2
Blisworth Northants 52 D5
Blithbury Staffs 62 B4
Blitterlees Cumb 107 D8
Blockley Glos 51 F6
Blofield Norf 69 D6
Blofield Heath Norf 69 C6
Blo'Norton Norf 56 B4
Bloomfield Borders 115 B8
Blore Staffs 75 E8
Blount's Green Staffs 75 F7
Blowick Mers 85 C4
Bloxham Oxon 52 F2
Bloxholm Lincs 78 D3
Bloxwich W Mid 62 D3
Bloxworth Dorset 13 E6
Blubberhouses N Yorks 94 D4
Blue Anchor Som 22 E2
Blue Anchor Swansea 33 E6
Blue Planet Aquarium Ches 73 B8
Blue Row Essex 43 C6
Blundeston Suff 69 E8
Blunham Beds 54 D2
Blunsdon St Andrew Swindon 37 F8
Bluntington Worcs 50 B3
Bluntisham Cambs 54 B4
Blunts Corn 5 C8
Blyborough Lincs 90 E3
Blyford Suff 57 B8
Blymhill Staffs 62 C2
Blyth Notts 89 F7
Blyth Northumb 117 F9
Blyth Bridge Borders 122 E4
Blythburgh Suff 57 B8
Blythe Borders 123 E8
Blythe Bridge Staffs 75 E6
Blyton Lincs 90 E2
Boarhills Fife 135 C7
Boarhunt Hants 15 D7
Boars Head Gtr Man 86 D3
Boars Hill Oxon 38 D4
Boarshead E Sus 18 B2
Boarstall Bucks 39 C6
Boasley Cross Devon 9 E6
Boat of Garten Highld 148 C5
Boath Highld 157 B6
Bobbing Kent 30 C2
Bobbington Staffs 62 E2
Bobbingworth Essex 41 D8
Bocaddon Corn 5 D6
Bochastle Stirl 132 D5
Bocking Essex 42 B3
Bocking Churchstreet Essex 42 B3
Boddam Aberds 161 D8
Boddam Shetland 175 M5
Boddington Glos 37 B5
Bodedern Anglesey 82 C3
Bodelwyddan Denb 72 B4
Bodenham Hereford 49 D7
Bodenham Wilts 14 B2
Bodenham Arboretum and Earth Centre Worcs 62 F2
Bodenham Moor Hereford 49 D7
Bodermid Gwyn 70 E2
Bodewryd Anglesey 82 B3
Bodfari Denb 72 B4
Bodffordd Anglesey 82 D4
Bodham Norf 81 C7
Bodiam E Sus 18 C4
Bodiam Castle E Sus 18 C4
Bodicote Oxon 52 F2
Bodieve Corn 4 B4
Bodinnick Corn 5 D6
Bodle Street Green E Sus 18 D3
Bodmin Corn 5 C5
Bodnant Garden, Colwyn Bay Conwy 83 D8
Bodney Norf 67 E8
Bodorgan Anglesey 82 E3
Bodsham Kent 30 E5
Boduan Gwyn 70 D4
Bodymoor Heath Warks 63 E5
Bogallan Highld 157 D7
Bogbrae Aberds 161 E7
Bogend Borders 124 E3
Bogend S Ayrs 120 F3
Boghall W Loth 122 C2
Boghead S Lnrk 121 E7
Bogmoor Moray 159 C7
Bogniebrae Aberds 160 D2
Bognor Regis W Sus 16 E3
Bograxie Aberds 151 C6
Bogside N Lnrk 121 D8
Bogton Aberds 160 C3
Bogue Dumfries 113 F6
Bohenie Highld 147 F5
Bohortha Corn 3 C7
Bohuntine Highld 147 F5
Boirseam W Isles 173 K3
Bojewyan Corn 2 C2
Bolam Durham 101 B6
Bolam Northumb 117 F6
Bolberry Devon 6 F4
Bold Heath Mers 86 F3
Boldon T & W 111 C6
Boldon Colliery T & W 111 C6
Boldre Hants 14 E4
Boldron Durham 101 C5
Bole Notts 89 F8
Bolehill Derbys 76 D2
Boleside Borders 123 F7
Bolham Devon 10 C4
Bolham Water Devon 11 C6
Bolingey Corn 4 D2
Bollington Ches 75 B6
Bollington Cross Ches 75 B6
Bolney W Sus 17 B6
Bolnhurst Beds 53 D8
Bolshan Angus 143 D6
Bolsover Derbys 76 B4
Bolsterstone S Yorks 88 E3
Bolstone Hereford 49 F7
Boltby N Yorks 102 F2
Bolter End Bucks 39 E7
Bolton Cumb 99 B8
Bolton E Loth 123 B8
Bolton E Yorks 96 D3
Bolton Gtr Man 86 D5
Bolton Northumb 117 C7
Bolton Abbey N Yorks 94 D3
Bolton Abbey, Skipton N Yorks 94 D3
Bolton Bridge N Yorks 94 D3
Bolton-by-Bowland Lancs 93 E7
Bolton Castle, Leyburn N Yorks 101 E5
Bolton le Sands Lancs 92 C4
Bolton Low Houses Cumb 108 E2
Bolton-on-Swale N Yorks 101 E7
Bolton Percy N Yorks 95 E8
Bolton Town End Lancs 92 C4
Bolton upon Dearne S Yorks 89 D5
Boltonfellend Cumb 108 C4
Boltongate Cumb 108 E2
Bolventor Corn 5 B6
Bomere Heath Shrops 60 C4
Bon-y-maen Swansea 33 E7
Bonar Bridge Highld 164 E3
Bonawe Argyll 131 B6
Bonby N Lincs 90 C4
Boncath Pembs 45 F4
Bonchester Bridge Borders 115 C8
Bonchurch I o W 15 G6
Bondleigh Devon 9 D8
Bonehill Devon 6 B5
Bonehill Staffs 63 D5
Bo'ness Falk 133 F8
Bonhill W Dunb 120 B3
Boningale Shrops 62 D2
Bonjedward Borders 116 B2
Bonkle N Lnrk 121 D8
Bonnavoulin Highld 137 C6
Bonnington Edin 122 C4
Bonnington Kent 19 B7
Bonnybank Fife 135 D6
Bonnybridge Falk 133 F7
Bonnykelly Aberds 161 C5
Bonnyrigg and Lasswade Midloth 123 C6
Bonnyton Aberds 160 E3
Bonnyton Angus 142 F3
Bonnyton Angus 143 D6
Bonsall Derbys 76 D2
Bonskeid House Perth 141 C5
Bont Mon 35 C7
Bont-Dolgadfan Powys 59 D5
Bont-goch Ceredig 58 F3
Bont-newydd Conwy 72 B4
Bont Newydd Gwyn 71 C8
Bont Newydd Gwyn 71 E8
Bontddu Gwyn 58 C3
Bonthorpe Lincs 79 B7
Bontnewydd Ceredig 46 C5
Bontnewydd Gwyn 82 F4
Bontuchel Denb 72 D4
Bonvilston V Glam 22 B2
Booker Bucks 39 E8
Boon Borders 123 E8
Boosbeck Redcar 102 C4
Boot Cumb 98 D3
Boot Street Suff 57 E6
Booth W Yorks 87 B8
Booth Wood W Yorks 87 C8
Boothby Graffoe Lincs 78 D2
Boothby Pagnell Lincs 78 F2
Boothen Stoke 75 E5
Boothferry E Yorks 89 B8
Boothville Northants 53 C5
Bootle Cumb 98 F3
Bootle Mers 85 E4
Booton Norf 81 E7
Boquhan Stirl 132 F4
Boraston Shrops 49 B8
Borden Kent 30 C2
Borden W Sus 16 B2
Bordley N Yorks 94 C2
Bordon Hants 27 F6
Bordon Camp Hants 27 F5
Boreham Essex 42 D3
Boreham Wilts 24 E3
Boreham Street E Sus 18 D3
Borehamwood Herts 40 E4
Boreland Dumfries 114 E4
Boreland Stirl 140 F2
Borgh W Isles 171 K2
Borgh W Isles 173 K2
Borghastan W Isles 172 D5
Borgie Highld 167 D8
Borgue Dumfries 106 E3
Borgue Highld 165 B8
Borley Essex 56 E2
Bornais W Isles 171 H3
Bornesketaig Highld 152 B4
Borness Dumfries 106 E3
Borough Green Kent 29 D7
Boroughbridge N Yorks 95 C6
Borras Head Wrex 73 D7
Borreraig Highld 152 D2
Borrobol Lodge Highld 165 B5
Borrowash Derbys 76 F4
Borrowby N Yorks 102 F2
Borrowdale Cumb 98 C4
Borrowfield Aberds 151 E7
Borth Ceredig 58 E3
Borth-y-Gest Gwyn 71 D6
Borthwickbrae Borders 115 C7
Borthwickshiels Borders 115 C7
Borve Highld 152 E5
Borve Lodge W Isles 173 J3
Borwick Lancs 92 B5
Bosavern Corn 2 C2
Bosbury Hereford 49 E8
Boscastle Corn 8 E3
Boscombe Bmouth 14 E2
Boscombe Wilts 25 F7
Boscoppa Corn 4 D5
Bosham W Sus 16 D2
Bosherston Pembs 44 F4
Boskenna Corn 2 D3
Bosley Ches 75 C6
Bossall N Yorks 96 C3
Bossiney Corn 8 F2
Bossingham Kent 31 E5
Bossington Som 21 E7
Bostock Green Ches 74 C3
Boston Lincs 79 E6
Boston Long Hedges Lincs 79 E6
Boston Spa W Yorks 95 E7
Boston West Lincs 79 E5
Boswinger Corn 3 B8
Botallack Corn 2 C2
Botany Bay London 41 E5
Botcherby Cumb 108 D4
Botcheston Leics 63 D8
Botesdale Suff 56 B4
Bothal Northumb 117 F8
Bothamsall Notts 77 B6
Bothel Cumb 107 F8
Bothenhampton Dorset 12 E2
Bothwell S Lnrk 121 D7
Botley Bucks 40 D2
Botley Hants 15 C6
Botley Oxon 38 D4
Botolph Claydon Bucks 39 B7
Botolphs W Sus 17 D5
Bottacks Highld 157 C5
Bottesford Leics 77 F8
Bottesford N Lincs 90 D2
Bottisham Cambs 55 C6
Bottlesford Wilts 25 D6
Bottom Boat W Yorks 88 B4
Bottom House Staffs 75 D7
Bottom of Hutton Lancs 86 B2
Bottom o'th'Moor Gtr Man 86 C4
Bottomcraig Fife 135 B5
Botusfleming Corn 6 C2
Botwnnog Gwyn 70 D3
Bough Beech Kent 29 E5
Boughrood Powys 48 F3
Boughspring Glos 36 E2
Boughton Norf 67 D6
Boughton Notts 77 C6
Boughton Northants 53 C5
Boughton Aluph Kent 30 E4
Boughton Lees Kent 30 E4
Boughton Malherbe Kent 30 E2
Boughton Monchelsea Kent 29 D8
Boughton Street Kent 30 D4
Boulby Redcar 103 C5
Boulden Shrops 60 F5
Boulmer Northumb 117 C8
Boulston Pembs 44 D4
Boultenstone Aberds 150 C3
Boultham Lincs 78 C2
Bourn Cambs 54 D4
Bourne Lincs 65 B7
Bourne End Beds 53 E7
Bourne End Bucks 40 F1
Bourne End Herts 40 D3
Bournemouth Bmouth 13 E8
Bournemouth International Airport Dorset 14 E2
Bournes Green Glos 37 D6
Bournes Green Sthend 43 F5
Bournheath Worcs 50 B4
Bournmoor Durham 111 D6
Bournville W Mid 62 F4
Bourton Dorset 24 F2
Bourton N Som 23 C5
Bourton Oxon 38 F2
Bourton Shrops 61 E5
Bourton on Dunsmore Warks 52 B2
Bourton on the Hill Glos 51 F6
Bourton-on-the-Water Glos 38 B1
Bousd Argyll 136 B3
Boustead Hill Cumb 108 D2
Bouth Cumb 99 F5
Bouthwaite N Yorks 94 B4
Boveney Bucks 27 B7
Boverton V Glam 21 C8
Bovey Tracey Devon 7 B6
Bovingdon Herts 40 D3
Bovingdon Green Bucks 39 F8
Bovingdon Green Herts 40 D3
Bovinger Essex 41 D8
Bovington Camp Dorset 13 F6
Bow Borders 123 E7
Bow Devon 10 D2
Bow Orkney 176 G2
Bow Brickhill M Keynes 53 F7
Bow of Fife Fife 134 C5
Bow Street Ceredig 58 F3
Bowbank Durham 100 B4
Bowburn Durham 111 F6
Bowcombe I o W 15 F5
Bowd Devon 11 E6
Bowden Borders 123 F8
Bowden Devon 7 E6
Bowden Hill Wilts 24 C4
Bowderdale Cumb 100 D1
Bowdon Gtr Man 87 F5
Bower Northumb 116 F3
Bower Hinton Som 12 C2
Bowerchalke Wilts 13 B8
Bowerhill Wilts 24 C4
Bowermadden Highld 169 C7
Bowers Gifford Essex 42 F3
Bowershall Fife 134 E2
Bowertower Highld 169 C7
Bowes Durham 100 C4
Bowgreave Lancs 92 E4
Bowgreen Gtr Man 87 F5
Bowhill Borders 115 B7
Bowhouse Dumfries 107 C7
Bowland Bridge Cumb 99 F6
Bowley Hereford 49 D7
Bowlhead Green Sur 27 F7
Bowling W Dunb 120 B4
Bowling W Yorks 94 F4
Bowling Bank Wrex 73 E7
Bowling Green Worcs 50 D3
Bowmanstead Cumb 99 E5
Bowmore Argyll 126 D3
Bowness-on-Solway Cumb 108 C2
Bowness-on-Windermere Cumb 99 E6
Bowood House and Gardens, Calne Wilts 24 C4
Bowsden Northumb 125 E5
Bowside Lodge Highld 168 C3
Bowston Cumb 99 E6
Bowthorpe Norf 68 D4
Box Glos 37 D5
Box Wilts 24 C3
Box End Beds 53 E8
Boxbush Glos 36 C4
Boxford Suff 56 E3
Boxford W Berks 26 B2
Boxgrove W Sus 16 D3
Boxley Kent 29 D8
Boxmoor Herts 40 D3
Boxted Essex 56 F4
Boxted Suff 56 D2
Boxted Cross Essex 56 F4
Boxted Heath Essex 56 F4
Boxworth Cambs 54 C4
Boxworth End Cambs 54 C4
Boyden Gate Kent 31 C6
Boylestone Derbys 75 F8
Boyndie Aberds 160 B3
Boynton E Yorks 97 C7
Boysack Angus 143 E6
Boyton Corn 8 E5
Boyton Suff 57 E7
Boyton Wilts 24 F4
Boyton Cross Essex 42 D2
Boyton End Suff 55 E8
Bozeat Northants 53 D7
Braaid I o M 84 E3
Braal Castle Highld 169 C6
Brabling Green Suff 57 C6
Brabourne Kent 30 E4
Brabourne Lees Kent 30 E4
Brabster Highld 169 C8
Bracadale Highld 153 F4
Bracara Highld 145 D7
Braceborough Lincs 65 C7
Bracebridge Lincs 78 C2
Bracebridge Heath Lincs 78 C2
Bracebridge Low Fields Lincs 78 C2
Braceby Lincs 78 F3
Bracewell Lancs 93 E8
Brackenfield Derbys 76 D3
Brackenthwaite Cumb 108 E2
Brackenthwaite N Yorks 95 D5
Bracklesham W Sus 16 E2
Brackletter Highld 146 F4
Brackley Argyll 118 B4
Brackley Northants 52 F3
Brackloch Highld 163 B5
Bracknell Brack 27 C6
Braco Perth 133 D7
Bracobrae Moray 160 C2
Bracon Ash Norf 68 E4
Bracorina Highld 145 D7
Bradbourne Derbys 76 D2
Bradbury Durham 101 B8
Bradda I o M 84 F1
Bradden Northants 52 E4
Braddock Corn 5 C6
Bradeley Stoke 75 D5
Bradenham Bucks 39 E8
Bradenham Norf 68 D2
Bradenstoke Wilts 24 B5
Bradfield Essex 56 F5
Bradfield Norf 81 D8
Bradfield W Berks 26 B4
Bradfield Combust Suff 56 D2
Bradfield Green Ches 74 D3
Bradfield Heath Essex 43 B7
Bradfield St Clare Suff 56 D3
Bradfield St George Suff 56 C3
Bradford Corn 5 B6
Bradford Derbys 76 C2
Bradford Devon 9 D6
Bradford Northumb 125 F7
Bradford W Yorks 94 F4
Bradford Abbas Dorset 12 C3
Bradford Cathedral W Yorks 94 F4
Bradford Industrial Museum W Yorks 94 F4
Bradford Leigh Wilts 24 C3
Bradford-on-Avon Wilts 24 C3
Bradford on Tone Som 11 B6
Bradford Peverell Dorset 12 E4
Brading I o W 15 F7
Bradley Derbys 76 E2
Bradley Hants 26 E4
Bradley NE Lincs 91 D6
Bradley Staffs 62 C2
Bradley W Mid 62 E3
Bradley W Yorks 88 B2
Bradley Green Worcs 50 C4
Bradley in the Moors Staffs 75 E7
Bradlow Hereford 50 F2
Bradmore Notts 77 F5
Bradmore W Mid 62 E2
Bradninch Devon 10 D5
Bradnop Staffs 75 D7
Bradpole Dorset 12 E2
Bradshaw Gtr Man 86 C5
Bradshaw W Yorks 87 C8
Bradstone Devon 9 F5
Bradwall Green Ches 74 C4
Bradway S Yorks 88 F4
Bradwell Derbys 88 F2
Bradwell Essex 42 B4
Bradwell M Keynes 53 F6
Bradwell Norf 69 D8
Bradwell Staffs 74 E5
Bradwell Grove Oxon 38 D2
Bradwell on Sea Essex 43 D6
Bradwell Waterside Essex 43 D5
Bradworthy Devon 8 C5
Bradworthy Cross Devon 8 C5
Brae Dumfries 107 B5
Brae Highld 154 B4
Brae Highld 163 D8
Brae Shetland 174 G5
Brae of Achnahaird Highld 162 C4
Brae Roy Lodge Highld 147 E6
Braeantra Highld 157 B6
Braedownie Angus 142 B2
Braefield Highld 156 F5
Braegrum Perth 134 B2
Braehead Dumfries 105 D8
Braehead Orkney 176 F4
Braehead Orkney 176 B3
Braehead S Lnrk 121 F8
Braehead S Lnrk 122 D2
Braehead of Lunan Angus 143 D6
Braehoulland Shetland 174 F4
Braehungie Highld 169 F6
Braelangwell Lodge Highld 164 E2
Braemar Aberds 149 E7
Braemore Highld 169 F5
Braemore Highld 156 B2
Braes of Enzie Moray 159 D7
Braeside Invclyd 129 C7
Braeswick Orkney 176 C5
Braewick Shetland 175 H5
Brafferton Darl 101 B7
Brafferton N Yorks 95 B7
Brafield-on-the-Green Northants 53 D6
Bragar W Isles 172 D5
Bragbury End Herts 41 B5
Bragleenmore Argyll 130 C5
Braichmelyn Gwyn 83 E6
Braid Edin 122 C5
Braides Lancs 92 D4
Braidley N Yorks 101 F5
Braidwood S Lnrk 121 E8

Braigo Argyll 126 C2
Brailsford Derbys 76 E2
Brainshaugh Northumb 117 D8
Braintree Essex 42 B3
Braiseworth Suff 56 B5
Braishfield Hants 14 B4
Braithwaite Cumb 98 B4
Braithwaite S Yorks 89 C7
Braithwaite W Yorks 94 E3
Braithwell S Yorks 89 E6
Bramber W Sus 17 C5
Bramcote Notts 76 F5
Bramcote Warks 63 F8
Bramdean Hants 15 B7
Bramerton Norf 69 D5
Bramfield Herts 41 C5
Bramfield Suff 57 B7
Bramford Suff 56 E5
Bramhall Gtr Man 87 F6
Bramham W Yorks 95 E7
Bramhope W Yorks 95 E5
Bramley Hants 26 D4
Bramley Sur 27 E8
Bramley S Yorks 89 E5
Bramley W Yorks 94 F5
Bramling Kent 31 D6
Brampford Speke Devon 10 E4
Brampton Cambs 54 B3
Brampton Cumb 100 B1
Brampton Cumb 108 C5
Brampton Derbys 76 B3
Brampton Hereford 49 F6
Brampton Lincs 77 B8
Brampton Norf 81 E8
Brampton Suff 69 F7
Brampton S Yorks 88 D5
Brampton Abbotts Hereford 36 B3
Brampton Ash Northants 64 F4
Brampton Bryan Hereford 49 B5
Brampton en le Morthen S Yorks 89 F5
Bramshall Staffs 75 F7
Bramshaw Hants 14 C3
Bramshill Hants 26 C5
Bramshott Hants 27 F6
Bran End Essex 42 B2
Branault Highld 137 B6
Brancaster Norf 80 C3
Brancaster Staithe Norf 80 C3
Brancepeth Durham 110 F5
Branch End Northumb 110 C3
Branchill Moray 158 D4
Brand Green Glos 36 B4
Branderburgh Moray 159 B6
Brandesburton E Yorks 97 E7
Brandeston Suff 57 C6
Brandhill Shrops 49 B6
Brandis Corner Devon 9 D6
Brandiston Norf 81 E7
Brandon Durham 110 F5
Brandon Lincs 78 E2
Brandon Northumb 117 C6
Brandon Suff 67 F7
Brandon Warks 52 B2
Brandon Bank Norf 67 F6
Brandon Creek Norf 67 E6
Brandon Parva Norf 68 D3
Brands Hatch Motor Racing Circuit Kent 29 C6
Brandsby N Yorks 95 B8
Brandy Wharf Lincs 90 E4
Brane Corn 2 D3
Branksome Poole 13 E8
Branksome Park Poole 13 E8
Bransby Lincs 77 B8
Branscombe Devon 11 F6
Bransford Worcs 50 D2
Bransgore Hants 14 E2
Branshill Clack 133 E7
Bransholme Hull 97 F7
Branson's Cross Worcs 51 B5
Branston Leics 64 B5
Branston Lincs 78 C3
Branston Staffs 63 B6
Branston Booths Lincs 78 C3
Branstone I o W 15 F6
Bransty Cumb 98 C1
Brant Broughton Lincs 78 D2
Brantham Suff 56 F5
Branthwaite Cumb 98 B2
Branthwaite Cumb 108 F2
Brantingham E Yorks 90 B3
Branton Northumb 117 C6
Branton S Yorks 89 D7
Branxholm Park Borders 115 C7
Branxholme Borders 115 C7
Branxton Northumb 124 F4
Brassey Green Ches 74 C2
Brassington Derbys 76 D2
Brasted Kent 29 D5
Brasted Chart Kent 29 D5
Brathens Aberds 151 E5
Bratoft Lincs 79 C7
Brattleby Lincs 90 F3
Bratton Telford 61 C6
Bratton Wilts 24 D4
Bratton Clovelly Devon 9 E6
Bratton Fleming Devon 20 F5
Bratton Seymour Som 12 B4
Braughing Herts 41 B6
Braunston Northants 52 C3
Braunston-in-Rutland Rutland 64 D5
Braunstone Town Leics 64 D2
Braunton Devon 20 F3
Brawby N Yorks 96 B3
Brawl Highld 168 C3
Brawlbin Highld 169 D5
Bray Windsor 27 B7
Bray Shop Corn 5 B8
Bray Wick Windsor 27 B6
Braybrooke Northants 64 F4
Braye Ald 16
Brayford Devon 21 F5
Braystones Cumb 98 D2
Braythorn N Yorks 94 E5
Brayton N Yorks 95 F9
Brazacott Corn 8 E4
Breach Kent 30 C2
Breachacha Castle Argyll 136 C2
Breachwood Green Herts 40 B4
Breacleit W Isles 172 E4
Breaden Heath Shrops 73 F8
Breadsall Derbys 76 F3
Breadstone Glos 36 D4
Breage Corn 2 D5
Breakachy Highld 157 E5
Bream Glos 36 D3
Breamore Hants 14 C2
Brean Som 22 D4
Breanais W Isles 172 F2
Brearton N Yorks 95 C6
Breascleit W Isles 172 E5
Breaston Derbys 76 F4
Brechfa Carms 46 F4
Brechin Angus 143 C5
Breck of Cruan Orkney 176 E2
Breckan Orkney 176 F1
Breckrey Highld 152 C6
Brecon = Aberhonddu Powys 34 B4
Brecon Beacons Mountain Centre Powys 34 B3
Bredbury Gtr Man 87 E7
Brede E Sus 18 D5
Bredenbury Hereford 49 D8
Bredfield Suff 57 D6
Bredgar Kent 30 C2
Bredhurst Kent 29 C8
Bredicot Worcs 50 D4
Bredon Worcs 50 F4
Bredon's Norton Worcs 50 F4
Bredwardine Hereford 48 E5
Breedon on the Hill Leics 63 B8
Breibhig W Isles 171 L2
Breibhig W Isles 172 E7
Breich W Loth 122 C2
Breightmet Gtr Man 86 D5
Breighton E Yorks 96 F3
Breinton Hereford 49 F6
Breinton Common Hereford 49 E6
Breiwick Shetland 175 J6
Bremhill Wilts 24 B4
Bremirehoull Shetland 175 L6
Brenchley Kent 29 E7
Brendon Devon 21 E6
Brenkley T & W 110 B5
Brent Eleigh Suff 56 E3
Brent Knoll Som 22 D5
Brent Pelham Herts 54 F5
Brentford London 28 B2
Brentingby Leics 64 C4
Brentwood Essex 42 E1
Brenzett Kent 19 C7
Brereton Staffs 62 C4
Brereton Green Ches 74 C4
Brereton Heath Ches 74 C5
Bressingham Norf 68 F3
Bretby Derbys 63 B6
Bretford Warks 52 B2
Bretforton Worcs 51 E5
Bretherdale Head Cumb 99 D7
Bretherton Lancs 86 B2
Brettabister Shetland 175 H6
Brettenham Norf 68 F2
Brettenham Suff 56 D3
Bretton Derbys 76 B2
Bretton Flint 73 C7
Brewer Street Sur 28 D4
Brewlands Bridge Angus 142 C1
Brewood Staffs 62 D2
Briach Moray 158 D4
Briants Puddle Dorset 13 E6
Brick End Essex 42 B1
Brickendon Herts 41 D6
Bricket Wood Herts 40 D4
Bricklehampton Worcs 50 E4
Bride I o M 84 B4
Bridekirk Cumb 107 F8
Bridell Pembs 45 E3
Bridestowe Devon 9 F7
Brideswell Aberds 160 E2
Bridford Devon 10 F3
Bridfordmills Devon 10 F3
Bridge Kent 31 D5
Bridge End Lincs 78 F4
Bridge Green Essex 55 F5
Bridge Hewick N Yorks 95 B6
Bridge of Alford Aberds 150 C4
Bridge of Allan Stirl 133 E6
Bridge of Avon Moray 159 F5
Bridge of Awe Argyll 131 C6
Bridge of Balgie Perth 140 E2
Bridge of Cally Perth 141 D8
Bridge of Canny Aberds 151 E5
Bridge of Craigisla Angus 142 D2
Bridge of Dee Dumfries 106 D4
Bridge of Don Aberdeen 151 C8
Bridge of Dun Angus 143 D6
Bridge of Dye Aberds 151 F5
Bridge of Earn Perth 134 C3
Bridge of Ericht Perth 140 D2
Bridge of Feugh Aberds 151 E6
Bridge of Forss Highld 168 C5
Bridge of Gairn Aberds 150 E2
Bridge of Gaur Perth 140 D2
Bridge of Muchalls Aberds 151 E7
Bridge of Oich Highld 147 D6
Bridge of Orchy Argyll 131 B8
Bridge of Waith Orkney 176 E1
Bridge of Walls Shetland 175 H4
Bridge of Weir Renfs 120 C3
Bridge Sollers Hereford 49 E6
Bridge Street Suff 56 E2
Bridge Trafford Ches 73 B8
Bridge Yate S Glos 23 B8
Bridgefoot Angus 142 F3
Bridgefoot Cumb 98 B2
Bridgehampton Som 12 B3
Bridgehill Durham 110 D3
Bridgemary Hants 15 D6
Bridgemont Derbys 87 F8
Bridgend Aberds 160 E2
Bridgend Aberds 150 C4
Bridgend Angus 143 C5
Bridgend Argyll 128 A3
Bridgend Argyll 126 C3
Bridgend Argyll 118 C4
Bridgend Cumb 99 C5
Bridgend Fife 135 C5
Bridgend Moray 159 F7
Bridgend N Lnrk 121 B6
Bridgend Pembs 45 E3
Bridgend W Loth 122 B3
Bridgend = Pen-y-bont ar Ogwr Bridgend 21 B8
Bridgend of Lintrathen Angus 142 D2
Bridgerule Devon 8 D4
Bridges Shrops 60 E3
Bridgeton Glasgow 121 C6
Bridgetown Corn 8 F5
Bridgetown Som 21 F8
Bridgham Norf 68 F2
Bridgnorth Shrops 61 E7
Bridgnorth Cliff Railway Shrops 61 E7
Bridgtown Staffs 62 D3
Bridgwater Som 22 F5
Bridlington E Yorks 97 C7
Bridport Dorset 12 E2
Bridstow Hereford 36 B2
Brierfield Lancs 93 F8
Brierley Glos 36 C3
Brierley Hereford 49 D6
Brierley S Yorks 88 C5
Brierley Hill W Mid 62 F3
Briery Hill Bl Gwent 35 D5
Brig o'Turk Stirl 132 D4
Brigg N Lincs 90 D4
Briggswath N Yorks 103 D6
Brigham Cumb 107 F7
Brigham E Yorks 97 D6
Brighouse W Yorks 88 B2
Brighstone I o W 14 F5
Brightgate Derbys 76 D2
Brighthampton Oxon 38 D3
Brightling E Sus 18 C3
Brightlingsea Essex 43 C6
Brighton Brighton 17 D7
Brighton Corn 4 D4
Brighton Hill Hants 26 E4
Brighton Museum and Art Gallery Brighton 17 D7
Brighton Racecourse Brighton 17 D7
Brighton Sea Life Centre Brighton 17 D7
Brightons Falk 122 B2
Brightwalton W Berks 26 B2
Brightwell Suff 57 E6
Brightwell Baldwin Oxon 39 E6
Brightwell cum Sotwell Oxon 39 E5
Brignall Durham 101 C5
Brigsley NE Lincs 91 D6
Brigsteer Cumb 99 F6
Brigstock Northants 65 F6
Brill Bucks 39 C6
Brilley Hereford 48 E4
Brimaston Pembs 44 C4
Brimfield Hereford 49 C7
Brimington Derbys 76 B4
Brimley Devon 7 B5
Brimpsfield Glos 37 C6
Brimpton W Berks 26 C3
Brims Orkney 176 H1
Brimscombe Glos 37 D5
Brimstage Mers 85 F4
Brinacory Highld 145 D7
Brind E Yorks 96 F3
Brindister Shetland 175 H4
Brindister Shetland 175 K6
Brindle Lancs 86 B4
Brindley Ford Staffs 75 D5
Brineton Staffs 62 C2
Bringhurst Leics 64 E5
Brington Cambs 53 B8
Brinian Orkney 176 D3
Briningham Norf 81 D6
Brinkhill Lincs 79 B6
Brinkley Cambs 55 D7
Brinklow Warks 52 B2
Brinkworth Wilts 37 F7
Brinmore Highld 148 B2
Brinscall Lancs 86 B4
Brinsea N Som 23 C6
Brinsley Notts 76 E4
Brinsop Hereford 49 E6
Brinsworth S Yorks 88 F5
Brinton Norf 81 D6
Brisco Cumb 108 D4
Brisley Norf 81 E5
Brislington Bristol 23 B8
Bristol Bristol 23 B7
Bristol City Museum and Art Gallery Bristol 23 B7
Bristol International Airport N Som 23 C7
Bristol Zoo Bristol 23 B7
Briston Norf 81 D6
Britannia Lancs 87 B6
Britford Wilts 14 B2
Brithdir Gwyn 58 C4
British Legion Village Kent 29 D8
British Museum London 41 F5
Briton Ferry Neath 33 E8
Britwell Salome Oxon 39 E6
Brixham Torbay 7 D7
Brixton Devon 6 D3
Brixton London 28 B4
Brixton Deverill Wilts 24 F3
Brixworth Northants 52 B5
Brize Norton Oxon 38 D3
Broad Blunsdon Swindon 38 E1
Broad Campden Glos 51 F6
Broad Chalke Wilts 13 B8
Broad Green Beds 53 E7
Broad Green Essex 42 B4
Broad Green Worcs 50 D2
Broad Haven Pembs 44 D3
Broad Heath Worcs 49 C8
Broad Hill Cambs 55 B6
Broad Hinton Wilts 25 B6
Broad Laying Hants 26 C2
Broad Marston Worcs 51 E6
Broad Oak Carms 33 B6
Broad Oak Cumb 98 E3
Broad Oak Dorset 12 E2
Broad Oak Dorset 13 C5
Broad Oak E Sus 18 D5
Broad Oak E Sus 18 C3
Broad Oak Hereford 36 B1
Broad Oak Mers 86 E3
Broad Street Kent 30 D2
Broad Street Green Essex 42 D4
Broad Town Wilts 25 B5
Broadbottom Gtr Man 87 E7
Broadbridge W Sus 16 D2
Broadbridge Heath W Sus 28 F2
Broadclyst Devon 10 E4
Broadfield Gtr Man 87 C6
Broadfield Lancs 86 B3
Broadfield Pembs 32 D2
Broadfield W Sus 28 F3
Broadford Highld 155 H2
Broadford Bridge W Sus 16 B4
Broadhaugh Borders 115 D7
Broadhaven Highld 169 D8
Broadheath Gtr Man 87 F5
Broadhembury Devon 11 D6
Broadhempston Devon 7 C6
Broadholme Derbys 76 E3
Broadholme Lincs 77 B8
Broadland Row E Sus 18 D5
Broadlay Carms 32 D4
Broadley Lancs 87 C6
Broadley Moray 159 C7
Broadley Common Essex 41 D7
Broadmayne Dorset 12 F5
Broadmeadows Borders 123 F7
Broadmere Hants 26 E4
Broadmoor Pembs 32 D1
Broadoak Kent 31 C5
Broadrashes Moray 159 D8
Broadsea Aberds 161 B6
Broadstairs Kent 31 C7
Broadstone Poole 13 E8
Broadstone Shrops 60 F5
Broadtown Lane Wilts 25 B5
Broadview Gardens, Hadlow Kent 29 E7
Broadwas Worcs 50 D2
Broadwater Herts 41 B5
Broadwater W Sus 17 D5
Broadway Carms 32 D3
Broadway Pembs 44 D3
Broadway Som 11 C8
Broadway Suff 57 B7
Broadway Worcs 51 F5
Broadwell Glos 38 B2
Broadwell Glos 36 C2
Broadwell Oxon 38 D2
Broadwell Warks 52 C2
Broadwell House Northumb 110 D2
Broadwey Dorset 12 F4
Broadwindsor Dorset 12 D2
Broadwood Kelly Devon 9 D8
Broadwoodwidger Devon 9 F6
Brobury Hereford 48 E5
Brochel Highld 152 E6
Brochloch Dumfries 113 E5
Brochroy Argyll 131 B6
Brockamin Worcs 50 D2
Brockbridge Hants 15 C7
Brockdam Northumb 117 B7
Brockdish Norf 57 B6
Brockenhurst Hants 14 D4
Brocketsbrae S Lnrk 121 F8
Brockford Street Suff 56 C5
Brockhall Northants 52 C4
Brockham Sur 28 E2
Brockhampton Glos 37 B7
Brockhampton Hereford 49 F7
Brockhole -National Park Visitor Centre, Windermere Cumb 99 D5
Brockholes W Yorks 88 C2
Brockhurst Derbys 76 C3
Brockhurst Hants 15 D7
Brocklebank Cumb 108 E3
Brocklesby Lincs 90 C5
Brockley N Som 23 C6
Brockley Green Suff 56 D2
Brockleymoor Cumb 108 F4
Brockton Shrops 60 F3
Brockton Shrops 61 E5
Brockton Shrops 60 D3
Brockton Shrops 61 D7
Brockton Telford 61 C7
Brockweir Glos 36 D2
Brockwood Hants 15 B7
Brockworth Glos 37 C5
Brocton Staffs 62 C3
Brodick N Ayrs 119 C7
Brodick Castle N Ayrs 119 C7
Brodsworth S Yorks 89 D6
Brogaig Highld 152 C5
Brogborough Beds 53 F7
Broken Cross Ches 74 B3
Broken Cross Ches 75 B5
Brokenborough Wilts 37 F6
Bromborough Mers 85 F4
Brome Suff 56 B5
Brome Street Suff 57 B5
Bromeswell Suff 57 D7
Bromfield Cumb 107 E8
Bromfield Shrops 49 B6
Bromham Beds 53 D8
Bromham Wilts 24 C4
Bromley London 28 C5
Bromley W Mid 62 F3
Bromley Common London 28 C5
Bromley Green Kent 19 B6
Brompton Medway 29 C8
Brompton N Yorks 102 E1
Brompton N Yorks 103 F7
Brompton-on-Swale N Yorks 101 E7
Brompton Ralph Som 22 F2
Brompton Regis Som 21 F8
Bromsash Hereford 36 B3
Bromsberrow Heath Glos 50 F2
Bromsgrove Worcs 50 B4
Bromyard Hereford 49 D8
Bromyard Downs Hereford 49 D8
Bronaber Gwyn 71 D8
Brongest Ceredig 46 E2
Bronington Wrex 73 F8
Bronllys Powys 48 F3
Bronnant Ceredig 46 C5
Bronte Parsonage Museum, Keighley W Yorks 94 F3
Bronwydd Arms Carms 33 B5
Bronydd Powys 48 E4
Bronygarth Shrops 73 F6
Brook Carms 32 D3
Brook Hants 14 C3
Brook Hants 14 B4
Brook I o W 14 F4
Brook Kent 30 E4
Brook Sur 27 F7
Brook Sur 27 E8
Brook End Beds 53 C8
Brook Hill Hants 14 C3
Brook Street Kent 29 E6
Brook Street Kent 19 B6
Brook Street W Sus 17 B7
Brooke Norf 69 E5
Brooke Rutland 64 D5
Brookenby Lincs 91 E6
Brookend Glos 36 E2
Brookfield Renfs 120 C4
Brookhouse Lancs 92 C5
Brookhouse Green Ches 74 C5
Brookland Kent 19 C6
Brooklands Dumfries 106 B5
Brooklands Gtr Man 87 E5
Brooklands Shrops 74 E2
Brookmans Park Herts 41 D5
Brooks Powys 59 E8
Brooks Green W Sus 16 B5
Brookthorpe Glos 37 C5
Brookville Norf 67 E7
Brookwood Sur 27 D7
Broom Beds 54 E2
Broom S Yorks 88 E5
Broom Warks 51 D5
Broom Worcs 50 B4
Broom Green Norf 81 E5
Broom Hill Dorset 13 D8
Broome Norf 69 E6
Broome Shrops 60 F4
Broome Park Northumb 117 C7
Broomedge Warr 86 F5
Broomer's Corner W Sus 16 B5
Broomfield Aberds 161 E6
Broomfield Essex 42 C3
Broomfield Kent 30 D2
Broomfield Kent 31 C5
Broomfield Som 22 F4
Broomfleet E Yorks 90 B2
Broomhall Ches 74 E3
Broomhall Windsor 27 C7
Broomhaugh Northumb 110 C3
Broomhill Norf 67 D6
Broomhill Northumb 117 D8
Broomhill S Yorks 88 D5
Broomholm Norf 81 D9
Broomley Northumb 110 C3
Broompark Durham 110 E5
Broom's Green Hereford 50 F2
Broomy Lodge Hants 14 C3
Brora Highld 165 D6
Broseley Shrops 61 D6
Brotherhouse Bar Lincs 66 C2
Brotherstone Borders 124 F2
Brothertoft Lincs 79 E5
Brotherton N Yorks 89 B5
Brotton Redcar 102 C4
Broubster Highld 168 C5
Brough Cumb 100 C2
Brough Derbys 88 F2
Brough E Yorks 90 B3
Brough Highld 169 B7
Brough Notts 77 D8
Brough Orkney 176 E2
Brough Shetland 174 F6
Brough Shetland 174 G7
Brough Shetland 174 F7
Brough Shetland 175 J7
Brough Shetland 175 H6
Brough Lodge Shetland 174 D7
Brough Sowerby Cumb 100 C2
Broughall Shrops 74 E2
Broughton Borders 122 F4
Broughton Cambs 54 B3
Broughton Flint 73 C7
Broughton Hants 25 F8
Broughton Lancs 92 F5
Broughton M Keynes 53 E6
Broughton N Lincs 90 D3
Broughton Northants 53 B6
Broughton N Yorks 94 D2
Broughton N Yorks 96 B3
Broughton Orkney 176 B3
Broughton Oxon 52 F2
Broughton V Glam 21 B8
Broughton Astley Leics 64 E2
Broughton Beck Cumb 98 F4
Broughton Common Wilts 24 C3
Broughton Gifford Wilts 24 C3
Broughton Hackett Worcs 50 D4
Broughton in Furness Cumb 98 F4
Broughton Mills Cumb 98 E4
Broughton Moor Cumb 107 F7
Broughton Park Gtr Man 87 D6
Broughton Poggs Oxon 38 D2
Broughtown Orkney 176 B5
Broughty Ferry Dundee 142 F4
Browhouses Dumfries 108 C2
Browland Shetland 175 H4
Brown Candover Hants 26 F3
Brown Edge Lancs 85 C4
Brown Edge Staffs 75 D6
Brown Heath Ches 73 C8
Brownhill Aberds 161 D5
Brownhill Aberds 160 D3
Brownhill Blkburn 93 F6
Brownhill Shrops 60 B4
Brownhills Fife 135 C7
Brownhills W Mid 62 D4
Brownlow Ches 74 C5
Brownlow Heath Ches 74 C5
Brownmuir Aberds 143 B7
Brown's End Glos 50 F2
Brownshill Glos 37 D5
Brownston Devon 6 D4
Brownyside Northumb 117 B7
Broxa N Yorks 103 E7
Broxbourne Herts 41 D6
Broxburn E Loth 124 B2
Broxburn W Loth 122 B3
Broxholme Lincs 78 B2
Broxted Essex 42 B1
Broxton Ches 73 D8
Broxwood Hereford 49 D5
Broyle Side E Sus 17 C8
Brù W Isles 172 D6
Bruairnis W Isles 171 K3
Bruan Highld 169 F8
Bruar Lodge Perth 141 B5
Brucehill W Dunb 120 B3
Bruera Ches 73 C8
Bruern Abbey Oxon 38 B2
Bruichladdich Argyll 126 C2
Bruisyard Suff 57 C7
Brumby N Lincs 90 D2
Brund Staffs 75 C8
Brundall Norf 69 D6
Brundish Suff 57 C6
Brundish Street Suff 57 B6
Brunery Highld 145 F7
Brunshaw Lancs 93 F8
Brunswick Village T & W 110 B5
Bruntcliffe W Yorks 88 B3
Bruntingthorpe Leics 64 E3
Brunton Fife 134 B5
Brunton Northumb 117 B8
Brunton Wilts 25 D7
Brushford Devon 9 D8
Brushford Som 10 B4
Bruton Som 23 F8
Bryanston Dorset 13 D6
Brydekirk Dumfries 107 B8
Bryher Scilly 2 E3
Brymbo Wrex 73 D6
Brympton Som 12 C3
Bryn Carms 33 D6
Bryn Gtr Man 86 D3
Bryn Neath 34 E2
Bryn Shrops 60 F2
Bryn-coch Neath 33 E8
Bryn Du Anglesey 82 D3
Bryn Gates Gtr Man 86 D3
Bryn-glas Conwy 83 E8
Bryn Golau Rhondda 34 F3
Bryn-Iwan Carms 46 F2
Bryn-mawr Gwyn 70 D3
Bryn-nantllech Conwy 72 C3
Bryn-penarth Powys 59 D8
Bryn Rhyd-yr-Arian Conwy 72 C3
Bryn Saith Marchog Denb 72 D4
Bryn Sion Gwyn 59 C5
Bryn-y-gwenin Mon 35 C7
Bryn-y-maen Conwy 83 D8
Bryn-yr-eryr Gwyn 70 C4
Brynamman Carms 33 C8
Brynberian Pembs 45 F3
Brynbryddan Neath 34 E1
Brynbuga = Usk Mon 35 D7
Bryncae Rhondda 34 F3
Bryncethin Bridgend 34 F3
Bryncir Gwyn 71 C5
Bryncroes Gwyn 70 D3
Bryncrug Gwyn 58 D3
Bryneglwys Denb 72 E5
Brynford Flint 73 B5
Bryngwran Anglesey 82 D3
Bryngwyn Ceredig 45 E4
Bryngwyn Mon 35 D7
Bryngwyn Powys 48 E3
Brynhenllan Pembs 45 F2
Brynhoffnant Ceredig 46 D2
Brynithel Bl Gwent 35 D6
Brynmawr Bl Gwent 35 C5
Brynmenyn Bridgend 34 F3
Brynmill Swansea 33 E7
Brynna Rhondda 34 F3
Brynrefail Anglesey 82 C4
Brynrefail Gwyn 83 E5
Brynsadler Rhondda 34 F4
Brynsiencyn Anglesey 82 E4
Brynteg Anglesey 82 C4
Brynteg Ceredig 46 E3
Buaile nam Bodach W Isles 171 K3
Bualintur Highld 153 G5
Buarthmeini Gwyn 72 F2
Bubbenhall Warks 51 B8
Bubwith E Yorks 96 F3
Buccleuch Borders 115 C6
Buchanhaven Aberds 161 D8
Buchanty Perth 133 B8
Buchlyvie Stirl 132 E4
Buckabank Cumb 108 E3
Buckden Cambs 54 C2
Buckden N Yorks 94 B2
Buckenham Norf 69 D6
Buckerell Devon 11 D6
Buckfast Devon 6 C5
Buckfast Abbey, Buckfastleigh Devon 6 C5
Buckfastleigh Devon 6 C5
Buckhaven Fife 135 E5
Buckholm Borders 123 F7
Buckholt Mon 36 C2
Buckhorn Weston Dorset 13 B5
Buckhurst Hill Essex 41 E7
Buckie Moray 159 C8
Buckies Highld 169 C6
Buckingham Bucks 52 F4
Buckingham Palace London 28 B3
Buckland Bucks 40 C1
Buckland Devon 6 E4
Buckland Glos 51 F5
Buckland Hants 14 E4
Buckland Herts 54 F4
Buckland Kent 31 E7
Buckland Oxon 38 E3
Buckland Sur 28 D3
Buckland Abbey Devon 6 C2
Buckland Brewer Devon 9 B6
Buckland Common Bucks 40 D2
Buckland Dinham Som 24 D2
Buckland Filleigh Devon 9 D6
Buckland in the Moor Devon 6 B5
Buckland Monachorum Devon 6 C2
Buckland Newton Dorset 12 D4
Buckland St Mary Som 11 C7
Bucklebury W Berks 26 B3
Bucklegate Lincs 79 F6
Bucklerheads Angus 142 F4
Bucklers Hard Hants 14 E5
Bucklesham Suff 57 E6
Buckley = Bwcle Flint 73 C6
Bucklow Hill Ches 86 F5
Buckminster Leics 65 B5
Bucknall Lincs 78 C4
Bucknall Stoke 75 E6
Bucknell Oxon 39 B5
Bucknell Shrops 49 B5
Buckpool Moray 159 C8
Buck's Cross Devon 8 B5
Bucks Green W Sus 27 F8
Bucks Horn Oak Hants 27 E6
Buck's Mills Devon 9 B5
Bucksburn Aberdeen 151 D7
Buckskin Hants 26 D4
Buckton E Yorks 97 B7
Buckton Hereford 49 B5
Buckton Northumb 125 F6
Buckworth Cambs 54 B2
Budbrooke Warks 51 C7
Budby Notts 77 C6
Budd's Titson Corn 8 D4
Bude Corn 8 D4
Budlake Devon 10 E4
Budle Northumb 125 F7
Budleigh Salterton Devon 11 F5
Budock Water Corn 3 C6
Buerton Ches 74 E3
Buffler's Holt Bucks 52 F4
Bugbrooke Northants 52 D4
Buglawton Ches 75 C5
Bugle Corn 4 D5
Bugley Wilts 24 E3
Bugthorpe E Yorks 96 D3
Buildwas Shrops 61 D6
Builth Road Powys 48 D2
Builth Wells = Llanfair-ym-Muallt Powys 48 D2
Buirgh W Isles 173 J3
Bulby Lincs 65 B7
Bulcote Notts 77 E6
Buldoo Highld 168 C4
Bulford Wilts 25 E6
Bulford Camp Wilts 25 E6
Bulkeley Ches 74 D2
Bulkington Warks 63 F7
Bulkington Wilts 24 D4
Bulkworthy Devon 9 C5
Bull Hill Hants 14 E4
Bullamoor N Yorks 102 E1
Bullbridge Derbys 76 D3
Bullbrook Brack 27 C6
Bulley Glos 36 C4
Bullgill Cumb 107 F7
Bullington Hants 26 E2
Bullington Lincs 78 B3
Bull's Green Herts 41 C5
Bullwood Argyll 129 C6
Bulmer Essex 56 E2
Bulmer N Yorks 96 C2
Bulmer Tye Essex 56 F2
Bulphan Thurrock 42 F2
Bulverhythe E Sus 18 E4
Bulwark Aberds 161 D6
Bulwell Nottingham 76 E5
Bulwick Northants 65 E6
Bumble's Green Essex 41 D7
Bun Abhainn Eadarra W Isles 173 H4
Bun a'Mhuillin W Isles 171 J3
Bun Loyne Highld 146 D5
Bunacaimb Highld 145 E6
Bunarkaig Highld 146 F4
Bunbury Ches 74 D2
Bunbury Heath Ches 74 D2
Bunchrew Highld 157 E7
Bundalloch Highld 155 H4
Buness Shetland 174 C8
Bunessan Argyll 136 F4
Bungay Suff 69 F6
Bunker's Hill Lincs 78 B2
Bunker's Hill Lincs 79 D5
Bunkers Hill Oxon 38 C4
Bunloit Highld 147 B8
Bunnahabhain Argyll 126 B4
Bunny Notts 64 B2
Buntait Highld 156 F4
Buntingford Herts 41 B6
Bunwell Norf 68 E4
Burbage Derbys 75 B7
Burbage Leics 63 E8
Burbage Wilts 25 C7
Burchett's Green Windsor 39 F8
Burcombe Wilts 25 F5
Burcot Oxon 39 E5
Burcott Bucks 40 B1
Burdon T & W 111 D6
Bures Suff 56 F3
Bures Green Suff 56 F3
Burford Ches 74 D3
Burford Oxon 38 C2
Burford Shrops 49 C7
Burg Argyll 136 D4
Burgar Orkney 176 D2
Burgate Hants 14 C2
Burgate Suff 56 B4
Burgess Hill W Sus 17 C7
Burgh Suff 57 D6
Burgh-by-Sands Cumb 108 D3
Burgh Castle Norf 69 D7
Burgh Heath Sur 28 D3
Burgh le Marsh Lincs 79 C8
Burgh Muir Aberds 151 B6
Burgh next Aylsham Norf 81 E8
Burgh on Bain Lincs 91 F6
Burgh St Margaret Norf 69 C7
Burgh St Peter Norf 69 E7
Burghclere Hants 26 C2
Burghead Moray 158 C5
Burghfield W Berks 26 C4
Burghfield Common W Berks 26 C4
Burghfield Hill W Berks 26 C4
Burghill Hereford 49 E6
Burghwallis S Yorks 89 C6
Burham Kent 29 C8
Buriton Hants 15 B8
Burland Ches 74 D3
Burlawn Corn 4 B4
Burleigh Brack 27 C6
Burlescombe Devon 11 C5
Burleston Dorset 13 E5
Burley Hants 14 D3
Burley Rutland 65 C5
Burley W Yorks 95 F5
Burley Gate Hereford 49 E7
Burley in Wharfedale W Yorks 94 E4
Burley Lodge Hants 14 D3
Burley Street Hants 14 D3
Burleydam Ches 74 E3
Burlingjobb Powys 48 D4
Burlow E Sus 18 D2
Burlton Shrops 60 B4
Burmarsh Kent 19 B7
Burmington Warks 51 F7
Burn N Yorks 89 B6
Burn of Cambus Stirl 133 D6
Burnaston Derbys 76 F2
Burnbank S Lnrk 121 D7
Burnby E Yorks 96 E4
Burncross S Yorks 88 E4
Burneside Cumb 99 E7
Burness Orkney 176 B5
Burneston N Yorks 101 F8
Burnett Bath 23 C8
Burnfoot Borders 115 C7
Burnfoot Borders 115 C8
Burnfoot E Ayrs 112 D4
Burnfoot Perth 133 D8

Chadwick End W Mid 51 B7
Chadwick Green Mers 86 E3
Chaffcombe Som 11 C8
Chagford Devon 10 F2
Chailey E Sus 17 C7
Chain Bridge Lincs 79 E6
Chainbridge Cambs 66 D4
Chainhurst Kent 29 E8
Chalbury Dorset 13 D8
Chalbury Common Dorset 13 D8
Chaldon Sur 28 D4
Chaldon Herring Dorset 13 F5
Chale I o W 15 G5
Chale Green I o W 15 G5
Chalfont Common Bucks 40 E3
Chalfont St Giles Bucks 40 E2
Chalfont St Peter Bucks 40 E3
Chalford Glos 37 D5
Chalgrove Oxon 39 E6
Chalk Kent 29 B7
Challacombe Devon 21 E5
Challoch Dumfries 105 C7
Challock Kent 30 D4
Chalton Beds 40 B3
Chalton Hants 15 C8
Chalvington E Sus 18 E2
Chancery Ceredig 46 B4
Chandler's Ford Hants 14 B5
Channel Tunnel Kent 19 B8
Channerwick Shetland 175 L6
Chantry Som 24 E2
Chantry Suff 56 E5
Chapel Fife 134 E4
Chapel Allerton Som 23 D6
Chapel Allerton W Yorks 95 F6
Chapel Amble Corn 4 B4
Chapel Brampton Northants 52 C5
Chapel Chorlton Staffs 74 F5
Chapel-en-le-Frith Derbys 87 F8
Chapel End Warks 63 E7
Chapel Green Warks 63 F6
Chapel Green Warks 52 C2
Chapel Haddlesey N Yorks 89 B6
Chapel Head Cambs 66 F3
Chapel Hill Aberds 161 E7
Chapel Hill Lincs 78 D5
Chapel Hill Mon 36 E2
Chapel Hill N Yorks 95 E6
Chapel Lawn Shrops 48 B5
Chapel-le-Dale N Yorks 93 B7
Chapel Milton Derbys 87 F8
Chapel of Garioch Aberds 151 B6
Chapel Row W Berks 26 C3
Chapel St Leonards Lincs 79 B8
Chapel Stile Cumb 99 D5
Chapelgate Lincs 66 B4
Chapelhall N Lnrk 121 C7
Chapelhill Dumfries 114 E3
Chapelhill Highld 158 B2
Chapelhill N Ayrs 120 E2
Chapelhill Perth 134 B4
Chapelhill Perth 141 F7
Chapelknowe Dumfries 108 B3
Chapelton Angus 143 E6
Chapelton Devon 9 B7
Chapelton Highld 148 C5
Chapelton S Lnrk 121 E6
Chapeltown Blkburn 86 C5
Chapeltown Moray 149 B8
Chapeltown S Yorks 88 E4
Chapmans Well Devon 9 E5
Chapmanslade Wilts 24 E3
Chapmore End Herts 41 C6
Chappel Essex 42 B4
Chard Som 11 D8
Chardstock Devon 11 D8
Charfield S Glos 36 E4
Charford Worcs 50 C4
Charing Kent 30 E3
Charing Cross Dorset 14 C2
Charing Heath Kent 30 E3
Charingworth Glos 51 F7
Charlbury Oxon 38 C3
Charlcombe Bath 24 C2
Charlecote Warks 51 D7
Charlecote Park, Wellesbourne Warks 51 D7
Charles Devon 21 F5
Charles Manning's Amusement Park, Felixstowe Suff 57 F6
Charles Tye Suff 56 D4
Charlesfield Dumfries 107 C8
Charleston Angus 142 E3
Charleston Renfs 120 C4
Charlestown Aberdeen 151 D8
Charlestown Corn 4 D5
Charlestown Derbys 87 E8
Charlestown Dorset 12 G4
Charlestown Fife 134 F2
Charlestown Gtr Man 87 D6
Charlestown Highld 157 E7
Charlestown Highld 154 C4
Charlestown W Yorks 87 B7
Charlestown of Aberlour Moray 159 E6
Charlesworth Derbys 87 E8
Charleton Devon 7 E5
Charlton London 28 B5
Charlton Hants 25 E8
Charlton Herts 40 B4
Charlton Northants 52 F3
Charlton Northumb 116 F4
Charlton Som 23 D8
Charlton Telford 61 C5
Charlton Wilts 13 B7
Charlton Wilts 25 D6
Charlton Wilts 37 F6
Charlton Worcs 50 E5
Charlton W Sus 16 C2
Charlton Abbots Glos 37 B7
Charlton Adam Som 12 B3
Charlton-All-Saints Wilts 14 B2
Charlton Down Dorset 12 E4
Charlton Horethorne Som 12 B4
Charlton Kings Glos 37 B6
Charlton Mackerell Som 12 B3
Charlton Marshall Dorset 13 D6
Charlton Musgrove Som 12 B5
Charlton on Otmoor Oxon 39 C5
Charltons Redcar 102 C4
Charlwood Sur 28 E3
Charlynch Som 22 F4
Charminster Dorset 12 E4
Charmouth Dorset 11 E8
Charndon Bucks 39 B6
Charney Bassett Oxon 38 E3
Charnock Richard Lancs 86 C3
Charsfield Suff 57 D6
Chart Corner Kent 29 D8
Chart Sutton Kent 30 E2
Charter Alley Hants 26 D3
Charterhouse Som 23 D6
Charterville Allotments Oxon 38 C3
Chartham Kent 30 D5
Chartham Hatch Kent 30 D5
Chartridge Bucks 40 D2
Chartwell, Westerham Kent 29 D5
Charvil Wokingham 27 B5
Charwelton Northants 52 D3
Chasetown Staffs 62 D4
Chastleton Oxon 38 B2
Chasty Devon 8 D5
Chatburn Lancs 93 E7
Chatcull Staffs 74 F4
Chatham Medway 29 C8
Chathill Northumb 117 B7
Chatsworth, Bakewell Derbys 76 B2
Chattenden Medway 29 B8
Chatteris Cambs 66 F3
Chattisham Suff 56 E4
Chatto Borders 116 C3
Chatton Northumb 117 B6
Chawleigh Devon 10 C2
Chawley Oxon 38 D4
Chawston Beds 54 D2
Chawton Hants 26 F5
Cheadle Gtr Man 87 F6
Cheadle Staffs 75 E7
Cheadle Heath Gtr Man 87 F6
Cheadle Hulme Gtr Man 87 F6
Cheam London 28 C3
Cheapside Sur 27 D8
Chearsley Bucks 39 C7
Chebsey Staffs 62 B2
Checkendon Oxon 39 F6
Checkley Ches 74 E4
Checkley Hereford 49 F7
Checkley Staffs 75 F7
Chedburgh Suff 55 D8
Cheddar Som 23 D6
Cheddar Showcaves and Gorge Som 23 D6
Cheddington Bucks 40 C2
Cheddleton Staffs 75 D6
Cheddon Fitzpaine Som 11 B7
Chedglow Wilts 37 E6
Chedgrave Norf 69 E6
Chedington Dorset 12 D2
Chediston Suff 57 B7
Chedworth Glos 37 C7
Chedworth Roman Villa Glos 37 C7
Chedzoy Som 22 F5
Cheeklaw Borders 124 D3
Cheeseman's Green Kent 19 B7
Cheglinch Devon 20 E4
Cheldon Devon 10 C2
Chelford Ches 74 B5
Chell Heath Stoke 75 D5
Chellaston Derby 76 F3
Chellington Beds 53 D7
Chelmarsh Shrops 61 F7
Chelmer Village Essex 42 D3
Chelmondiston Suff 57 F6
Chelmorton Derbys 75 C8
Chelmsford Essex 42 D3
Chelsea London 28 B3
Chelsfield London 29 C5
Chelsworth Suff 56 E3
Cheltenham Glos 37 B6
Cheltenham Racecourse Glos 37 B6
Chelveston Northants 53 C7
Chelvey N Som 23 C6
Chelwood Bath 23 C8
Chelwood Common E Sus 17 B8
Chelwood Gate E Sus 17 B8
Chelworth Wilts 37 E6
Chelworth Green Wilts 37 E7
Chemistry Shrops 74 E2
Chenies Bucks 40 E3
Cheny Longville Shrops 60 F4
Chepstow = Cas-gwent Mon 36 E2
Chepstow Racecourse Mon 36 E2
Chequerfield W Yorks 89 B5
Cherhill Wilts 24 B5
Cherington Glos 37 E6
Cherington Warks 51 F7
Cheriton Devon 21 E6
Cheriton Hants 15 B6
Cheriton Kent 19 B8
Cheriton Swansea 33 E5
Cheriton Bishop Devon 10 E2
Cheriton Fitzpaine Devon 10 D3
Cheriton or Stackpole Elidor Pembs 44 F4
Cherrington Telford 61 B6
Cherry Burton E Yorks 97 E5
Cherry Hinton Cambs 55 D5
Cherry Orchard Worcs 50 D3
Cherry Willingham Lincs 78 B3
Cherrybank Perth 134 B3
Chertsey Sur 27 C8
Cheselbourne Dorset 13 E5
Chesham Bucks 40 D2
Chesham Bois Bucks 40 E2
Cheshire Candle Workshops, Burwardsley Ches 74 D2
Cheshunt Herts 41 D6
Cheslyn Hay Staffs 62 D3
Chessington London 28 C2
Chessington World of Adventures London 28 C2
Chester Ches 73 C8
Chester Cathedral Ches 73 C7
Chester-Le-Street Durham 111 D5
Chester Moor Durham 111 E5
Chester Racecourse Ches 73 C7
Chester Zoo Ches 73 B8
Chesterblade Som 23 E8
Chesterfield Derbys 76 B3
Chesters Borders 116 C2
Chesters Borders 116 B2
Chesters Roman Fort Northumb 110 B2
Chesterton Cambs 65 E8
Chesterton Cambs 55 C5
Chesterton Glos 37 D7
Chesterton Oxon 39 B5
Chesterton Shrops 61 E7
Chesterton Staffs 74 E5
Chesterton Warks 51 D8
Chesterwood Northumb 109 C8
Chestfield Kent 30 C5
Cheston Devon 6 D4
Cheswardine Shrops 61 B7
Cheswick Northumb 125 E6
Chetnole Dorset 12 D4
Chettiscombe Devon 10 C4
Chettisham Cambs 66 F5
Chettle Dorset 13 C7
Chetton Shrops 61 E6
Chetwode Bucks 39 B6
Chetwynd Aston Telford 61 C7
Cheveley Cambs 55 C7
Chevening Kent 29 D5
Chevington Suff 55 D8
Chevithorne Devon 10 C4
Chew Magna Bath 23 C7
Chew Stoke Bath 23 C7
Chewton Keynsham Bath 23 C8
Chewton Mendip Som 23 D7
Chicheley M Keynes 53 E7
Chichester W Sus 16 D2
Chichester Cathedral W Sus 16 D2
Chickerell Dorset 12 F4
Chicklade Wilts 24 F4
Chicksgrove Wilts 24 F4
Chidden Hants 15 C7
Chiddingfold Sur 27 F7
Chiddingly E Sus 18 D2
Chiddingstone Kent 29 E5
Chiddingstone Causeway Kent 29 E6
Chiddingstone Hoath Kent 29 E5
Chideock Dorset 12 E2
Chidham W Sus 15 D8
Chidswell W Yorks 88 B3
Chieveley W Berks 26 B2
Chignall St James Essex 42 D2
Chignall Smealy Essex 42 C2
Chigwell Essex 41 E7
Chigwell Row Essex 41 E7
Chilbolton Hants 25 F8
Chilcomb Hants 15 B6
Chilcombe Dorset 12 E3
Chilcompton Som 23 D8
Chilcote Leics 63 C6
Child Okeford Dorset 13 C6
Childer Thornton Ches 73 B7
Childrey Oxon 38 F3
Child's Ercall Shrops 61 B6
Childswickham Worcs 51 F5
Childwall Mers 86 F2
Childwick Green Herts 40 C4
Chilfrome Dorset 12 E3
Chilgrove W Sus 16 C2
Chilham Kent 30 D4
Chilhampton Wilts 25 F5
Chilla Devon 9 D6
Chillaton Devon 9 F6
Chillenden Kent 31 D6
Chillerton I o W 15 F5
Chillesford Suff 57 D7
Chillingham Northumb 117 B6
Chillington Devon 7 E5
Chillington Som 11 C8
Chilmark Wilts 24 F4
Chilson Oxon 38 C3
Chilsworthy Corn 6 B2
Chilsworthy Devon 8 D5
Chilthorne Domer Som 12 C3
Chiltington E Sus 17 C7
Chilton Bucks 39 C6
Chilton Durham 101 B7
Chilton Oxon 38 F4
Chilton Cantelo Som 12 B3
Chilton Foliat Wilts 25 B8
Chilton Lane Durham 111 F6
Chilton Polden Som 23 F5
Chilton Street Suff 55 E8
Chilton Trinity Som 22 F4
Chilvers Coton Warks 63 E7
Chilwell Notts 76 F5
Chilworth Hants 14 C5
Chilworth Sur 27 E8
Chimney Oxon 38 D3
Chineham Hants 26 D4
Chingford London 41 E6
Chinley Derbys 87 F8
Chinley Head Derbys 87 F8
Chinnor Oxon 39 D7
Chipnall Shrops 74 F4
Chippenhall Green Suff 57 B6
Chippenham Cambs 55 C7
Chippenham Wilts 24 B4
Chipperfield Herts 40 D3
Chipping Herts 54 F4
Chipping Lancs 93 E6
Chipping Campden Glos 51 F6
Chipping Hill Essex 42 C4
Chipping Norton Oxon 38 B3
Chipping Ongar Essex 42 D1
Chipping Sodbury S Glos 36 F4
Chipping Warden Northants 52 E2
Chipstable Som 10 B5
Chipstead Kent 29 D5
Chipstead Sur 28 D3
Chirbury Shrops 60 E2
Chirk = Y Waun Wrex 73 F6
Chirk Bank Shrops 73 F6
Chirk Castle Wrex 73 F6
Chirmorrie S Ayrs 105 B6
Chirnside Borders 124 D4
Chirnsidebridge Borders 124 D4
Chirton Wilts 25 D5
Chisbury Wilts 25 C7
Chiselborough Som 12 C2
Chiseldon Swindon 25 B6
Chiserley W Yorks 87 B8
Chislehampton Oxon 39 E5
Chislehurst London 28 B5
Chislet Kent 31 C6
Chiswell Green Herts 40 D4
Chiswick London 28 B3
Chiswick End Cambs 54 E4
Chisworth Derbys 87 E7
Chithurst W Sus 16 B2
Chittering Cambs 55 B5
Chitterne Wilts 24 E4
Chittlehamholt Devon 9 B8
Chittlehampton Devon 9 B8
Chittoe Wilts 24 C4
Chivenor Devon 20 F4
Chobham Sur 27 C7
Choicelee Borders 124 D3
Cholderton Wilts 25 E7
Cholesbury Bucks 40 D2
Chollerford Northumb 110 B2
Chollerton Northumb 110 B2
Cholmondeston Ches 74 C3
Cholsey Oxon 39 F5
Cholstrey Hereford 49 D6
Chop Gate N Yorks 102 E3
Choppington Northumb 117 F8
Chopwell T & W 110 D4
Chorley Ches 74 D2
Chorley Lancs 86 C3
Chorley Shrops 61 F6
Chorley Staffs 62 C4
Chorleywood Herts 40 E3
Chorlton cum Hardy Gtr Man 87 E6
Chorlton Lane Ches 73 E8
Choulton Shrops 60 F3
Chowdene T & W 111 D5
Chowley Ches 73 D8
Chrishall Essex 54 F5
Christ Church Oxford Oxon 39 D5
Christchurch Cambs 66 E4
Christchurch Dorset 14 E2
Christchurch Glos 36 C2
Christchurch Newport 35 F7
Christchurch Priory Dorset 14 E2
Christian Malford Wilts 24 B4
Christleton Ches 73 C8
Christmas Common Oxon 39 E7
Christon N Som 23 D5
Christon Bank Northumb 117 B8
Christow Devon 10 F3
Chryston N Lnrk 121 B6
Chudleigh Devon 7 B6
Chudleigh Knighton Devon 7 B6
Chulmleigh Devon 9 C8
Chunal Derbys 87 E8
Church Lancs 86 B5
Church Aston Telford 61 C7
Church Brampton Northants 52 C5
Church Broughton Derbys 76 F2
Church Crookham Hants 27 D6
Church Eaton Staffs 62 C2
Church End Beds 40 B2
Church End Beds 54 F2
Church End Beds 53 F7
Church End Cambs 66 F2
Church End Cambs 66 D3
Church End E Yorks 97 D6
Church End Essex 55 E6
Church End Essex 42 B3
Church End Hants 26 D4
Church End Lincs 78 F5
Church End Warks 63 E6
Church End Warks 63 E6
Church End Wilts 24 B5
Church Enstone Oxon 38 B3
Church Fenton N Yorks 95 F8
Church Green Devon 11 E6
Church Green Norf 68 E3
Church Gresley Derbys 63 C6
Church Hanborough Oxon 38 C4
Church Hill Ches 74 C3
Church Houses N Yorks 102 E4
Church Knowle Dorset 13 F7
Church Laneham Notts 77 B8
Church Langton Leics 64 E4
Church Lawford Warks 52 B2
Church Lawton Ches 74 D5
Church Leigh Staffs 75 F7
Church Lench Worcs 50 D5
Church Mayfield Staffs 75 E8
Church Minshull Ches 74 C3
Church Norton W Sus 16 E2
Church Preen Shrops 60 E5
Church Pulverbatch Shrops 60 D4
Church Stoke Powys 60 E2
Church Stowe Northants 52 D4
Church Street Kent 29 B8
Church Stretton Shrops 60 E4
Church Town N Lincs 89 D8
Church Town Sur 28 D4
Church Village Rhondda 34 F4
Church Warsop Notts 77 C5
Churcham Glos 36 C4
Churchbank Shrops 48 B4
Churchbridge Staffs 62 D3
Churchdown Glos 37 C5
Churchend Essex 42 B2
Churchend Essex 43 E6
Churchend S Glos 36 E4
Churchfield W Mid 62 E4
Churchgate Street Essex 41 C7
Churchill Devon 20 E4
Churchill Devon 11 D8
Churchill N Som 23 D6
Churchill Oxon 38 B2
Churchill Worcs 50 B3
Churchill Worcs 50 D4
Churchinford Som 11 C7
Churchover Warks 64 F2
Churchstanton Som 11 C6
Churchstow Devon 6 E5
Churchtown Derbys 76 C2
Churchtown I o M 84 C4
Churchtown Lancs 92 E4
Churchtown Mers 85 C4
Churnsike Lodge Northumb 109 B6
Churston Ferrers Torbay 7 D7
Churt Sur 27 F6
Churton Ches 73 D8
Churwell W Yorks 88 B3
Chute Standen Wilts 25 D8
Chwilog Gwyn 70 D5
Chyandour Corn 2 C3
Cilan Uchaf Gwyn 70 E3
Cilcain Flint 73 C5
Cilcennin Ceredig 46 C4
Cilfor Gwyn 71 D7
Cilfrew Neath 34 D1
Cilfynydd Rhondda 34 E4
Cilgerran Pembs 45 E3
Cilgwyn Carms 33 B8
Cilgwyn Gwyn 82 F4
Cilgwyn Pembs 45 F2
Ciliau Aeron Ceredig 46 D3
Cill Donnain W Isles 171 H3
Cille Bhrighde W Isles 171 J3
Cille Pheadair W Isles 171 J3
Cilmery Powys 48 D2
Cilsan Carms 33 B6
Ciltalgarth Gwyn 72 E2
Cilwendeg Pembs 45 F4
Cilybebyll Neath 33 D8
Cilycwm Carms 47 F6
Cimla Neath 34 E1
Cinderford Glos 36 C3
Cippyn Pembs 45 E3
Circebost W Isles 172 E4
Cirencester Glos 37 D7
Ciribhig W Isles 172 D4
City Powys 60 F2
City Dulas Anglesey 82 C4
City of London = London, City of London 41 F6
Clachaig Argyll 129 B6
Clachan Argyll 128 E2
Clachan Argyll 130 D3
Clachan Argyll 138 E2
Clachan Argyll 131 D7
Clachan Highld 153 F6
Clachan W Isles 170 F3
Clachan na Luib W Isles 170 D4
Clachan of Campsie E Dunb 121 B6
Clachan of Glendaruel Argyll 128 B4
Clachan-Seil Argyll 130 D3
Clachan Strachur Argyll 131 E6
Clachaneasy Dumfries 105 B7
Clachanmore Dumfries 104 E4
Clachbreck Argyll 128 C2
Clachnabrain Angus 142 C3
Clachtoll Highld 162 B4
Clackmannan Clack 133 E8
Clacton-on-Sea Essex 43 C7
Cladach Chireboist W Isles 170 D3
Claddach-knockline W Isles 170 D3
Cladich Argyll 131 C6
Claggan Highld 137 D7
Claggan Highld 139 B5
Claigan Highld 152 D3
Claines Worcs 50 D3
Clandown Bath 23 D8
Clanfield Hants 15 C7
Clanfield Oxon 38 D2
Clanville Hants 25 E8
Claonaig Argyll 128 E3
Claonel Highld 164 D2
Clap Hill Kent 19 B7
Clapgate Dorset 13 D8
Clapgate Herts 41 B7
Clapham Beds 53 D8
Clapham London 28 B3
Clapham N Yorks 93 C7
Clapham W Sus 16 D4
Clappers Borders 124 D5
Clappersgate Cumb 99 D5
Clapton Som 12 D2
Clapton-in-Gordano N Som 23 B6
Clapton-on-the-Hill Glos 38 C1
Clapworthy Devon 9 B8
Clara Vale T & W 110 C4
Clarach Ceredig 58 F3
Clarbeston Pembs 32 B1
Clarbeston Road Pembs 32 B1
Clarborough Notts 89 F8
Clardon Highld 169 C6
Clare Suff 55 E8
Clarebrand Dumfries 106 C4
Claremont Landscape Garden, Esher Sur 28 C2
Clarencefield Dumfries 107 C7
Clarilaw Borders 115 C8
Clark's Green Sur 28 F2
Clarkston E Renf 121 D5
Clashandorran Highld 157 E6
Clashcoig Highld 164 E3
Clashindarroch Aberds 159 F8
Clashmore Highld 166 F2
Clashmore Highld 164 F4
Clashnessie Highld 166 F2
Clashnoir Moray 149 B8
Clate Shetland 175 G7
Clathy Perth 133 C8
Clatt Aberds 150 B4
Clatter Powys 59 E6
Clatterford I o W 15 F5
Clatterin Bridge Aberds 143 B6
Clatworthy Som 22 F2
Claughton Lancs 92 E5
Claughton Lancs 93 C5
Claughton Mers 85 F4
Claverdon Warks 51 C6
Claverham N Som 23 C6
Clavering Essex 55 F5
Claverley Shrops 61 E7
Claverton Bath 24 C2
Clawdd-newydd Denb 72 D4
Clawthorpe Cumb 92 B5
Clawton Devon 9 E5
Claxby Lincs 90 E5
Claxby Lincs 79 B7
Claxton Norf 69 D6
Claxton N Yorks 96 C2
Clay Common Suff 69 F7
Clay Coton Northants 52 B3
Clay Cross Derbys 76 C3
Clay Hill W Berks 26 B3
Clay Lake Lincs 66 B2
Claybokie Aberds 149 E6
Claybrooke Magna Leics 63 F8
Claybrooke Parva Leics 63 F8
Claydon Oxon 52 D2
Claydon Suff 56 D5
Claygate Dumfries 108 B3
Claygate Kent 29 E8
Claygate Sur 28 C2
Claygate Cross Kent 29 D7
Clayhanger Devon 10 B5
Clayhanger W Mid 62 D4
Clayhidon Devon 11 C6
Clayhill E Sus 18 C5
Clayhill Hants 14 D4
Clayock Highld 169 D6
Claypole Lincs 77 E8
Clayton Staffs 75 E5
Clayton S Yorks 89 D5
Clayton W Sus 17 C6
Clayton W Yorks 94 F4
Clayton Green Lancs 86 B3
Clayton-le-Moors Lancs 93 F7
Clayton-le-Woods Lancs 86 B3
Clayton West W Yorks 88 C3
Clayworth Notts 89 F8
Cleadale Highld 144 E4
Cleadon T & W 111 C6
Clearbrook Devon 6 C3
Clearwell Glos 36 D2
Cleasby N Yorks 101 C7
Cleat Orkney 176 H3
Cleatlam Durham 101 C6
Cleator Cumb 98 C2
Cleator Moor Cumb 98 C2
Clebrig Highld 167 F7
Cleckheaton W Yorks 88 B2
Clee St Margaret Shrops 61 F5
Cleedownton Shrops 61 F5
Cleehill Shrops 49 B7
Cleethorpes NE Lincs 91 D7
Cleeton St Mary Shrops 49 B8
Cleeve N Som 23 C6
Cleeve Hill Glos 37 B6
Cleeve Prior Worcs 51 E5
Clegyrnant Powys 59 D6
Clehonger Hereford 49 F6
Cleish Perth 134 E2
Cleland N Lnrk 121 D8
Clench Common Wilts 25 C6
Clenchwarton Norf 67 B5
Clent Worcs 50 B4
Cleobury Mortimer Shrops 49 B8
Cleobury North Shrops 61 F6
Cleongart Argyll 118 C3
Clephanton Highld 158 D2
Clerklands Borders 115 B8
Clestrain Orkney 176 F2
Cleuch Head Borders 115 C8
Cleughbrae Dumfries 107 B7
Clevancy Wilts 25 B5
Clevedon N Som 23 B6
Cleveley Oxon 38 B3
Cleveleys Lancs 92 E3
Cleverton Wilts 37 F6
Clevis Bridgend 21 B7
Clewer Som 23 D6
Cley next the Sea Norf 81 C6
Cliaid W Isles 171 K2
Cliasmol W Isles 173 H3
Cliburn Cumb 99 B7
Click Mill Orkney 176 D2
Cliddesden Hants 26 E4
Cliff End E Sus 19 D5
Cliffburn Angus 143 E6
Cliffe Medway 29 B8
Cliffe N Yorks 96 F2
Cliffe Woods Medway 29 B8
Clifford Hereford 48 E4
Clifford W Yorks 95 E7
Clifford Chambers Warks 51 D6
Clifford's Mesne Glos 36 B4
Cliffsend Kent 31 C7
Clifton Beds 54 F2
Clifton Bristol 23 B7
Clifton Cumb 99 B7
Clifton Derbys 75 E8
Clifton Lancs 92 F4
Clifton Nottingham 77 F5
Clifton Northumb 117 F8
Clifton N Yorks 94 E4
Clifton Oxon 52 F2
Clifton Stirl 139 F7
Clifton S Yorks 89 E6
Clifton Worcs 50 E3
Clifton York 95 D8
Clifton Campville Staffs 63 C6
Clifton Green Gtr Man 87 D5
Clifton Hampden Oxon 39 E5
Clifton Reynes M Keynes 53 D7
Clifton upon Dunsmore Warks 52 B3
Clifton upon Teme Worcs 50 C2
Cliftoncote Borders 116 B4
Cliftonville Kent 31 B7
Climaen gwyn Neath 33 D8
Climping W Sus 16 D4
Climpy S Lnrk 122 D2
Clink Som 24 E2
Clint N Yorks 95 D5
Clint Green Norf 68 C3
Clintmains Borders 124 F2
Cliobh W Isles 172 E3
Clippesby Norf 69 C7
Clipsham Rutland 65 C6
Clipston Northants 64 F4
Clipstone Notts 77 C5
Clitheroe Lancs 93 E7
Cliuthar W Isles 173 J4
Clive Shrops 60 B5
Clivocast Shetland 174 C8
Clixby Lincs 90 D5
Clocaenog Denb 72 D4
Clochan Moray 159 C8
Clock Face Mers 86 E3
Clockmill Borders 124 D3
Cloddiau Powys 60 D2
Clodock Hereford 35 B7
Clola Aberds 161 D7
Clophill Beds 53 F8
Clopton Northants 65 F7
Clopton Suff 57 D6
Clopton Corner Suff 57 D6
Clopton Green Suff 55 D8
Close Clark I o M 84 E2
Closeburn Dumfries 113 E8
Closworth Som 12 C3
Clothall Herts 54 F3
Clotton Ches 74 C2
Clough Foot W Yorks 87 B7
Cloughton N Yorks 103 E8
Cloughton Newlands N Yorks 103 E8
Clousta Shetland 175 H5
Clouston Orkney 176 E1
Clova Aberds 150 B3
Clova Angus 142 B3
Clove Lodge Durham 100 C4
Clovelly Devon 8 B5
Clovelly Village Devon 8 B5
Clovenfords Borders 123 F7
Clovenstone Aberds 151 C6
Clovullin Highld 138 C4
Clow Bridge Lancs 87 B6
Clowne Derbys 76 B4
Clows Top Worcs 50 B2
Cloy Wrex 73 E7
Cluanie Inn Highld 146 C3
Cluanie Lodge Highld 146 C3
Clun Shrops 60 F3
Clunbury Shrops 60 F3
Clunderwen Carms 32 C2
Clune Highld 148 B3
Clunes Highld 146 F5
Clungunford Shrops 49 B5
Clunie Aberds 160 C3
Clunie Perth 141 E8
Clunton Shrops 60 F3
Cluny Fife 134 E4
Cluny Castle Highld 148 E2
Clutton Bath 23 D8
Clutton Ches 73 D8
Clwt-grugoer Conwy 72 C3
Clwt-y-bont Gwyn 83 E5
Clydach Mon 35 C6
Clydach Swansea 33 D7
Clydach Vale Rhondda 34 E3
Clydebank W Dunb 120 B4
Clydey Pembs 45 F4
Clyffe Pypard Wilts 25 B5
Clynder Argyll 129 B7
Clyne Neath 34 D2
Clynelish Highld 165 D5
Clynnog-fawr Gwyn 82 F4
Clyro Powys 48 E4
Clyst Honiton Devon 10 E4
Clyst Hydon Devon 10 D5
Clyst St George Devon 10 F4
Clyst St Lawrence Devon 10 D5
Clyst St Mary Devon 10 E4
Cnoc Amhlaigh W Isles 172 E8
Cnwch-coch Ceredig 47 B5
Coachford Aberds 159 E8
Coad's Green Corn 5 B7
Coal Aston Derbys 76 B3
Coalbrookdale Telford 61 D6
Coalbrookvale Bl Gwent 35 D5
Coalburn S Lnrk 121 F8
Coalburns T & W 110 C4
Coalcleugh Northumb 109 E8
Coaley Glos 36 D4
Coalhall E Ayrs 112 C4
Coalhill Essex 42 E3
Coalpit Heath S Glos 36 F3
Coalport Telford 61 D6
Coalsnaughton Clack 133 E8
Coaltown of Balgonie Fife 134 E4
Coaltown of Wemyss Fife 134 E5
Coalville Leics 63 C8
Coalway Glos 36 C2
Coat Som 12 B2
Coatbridge N Lnrk 121 C7
Coatdyke N Lnrk 121 C7
Coate Swindon 38 F1
Coate Wilts 24 C5
Coates Cambs 66 E3
Coates Glos 37 D6
Coates Lancs 93 E8
Coates Notts 90 F2
Coates W Sus 16 C3
Coatham Redcar 102 B3
Coatham Mundeville Darl 101 B7
Coatsgate Dumfries 114 D3
Cobbaton Devon 9 B8
Cobbler's Green Norf 69 E5
Coberley Glos 37 C6
Cobham Kent 29 C7
Cobham Sur 28 C2
Cobholm Island Norf 69 D8
Cobleland Stirl 132 E4
Cobnash Hereford 49 C6
Coburty Aberds 161 B6
Cock Bank Wrex 73 E7
Cock Bridge Aberds 149 D8
Cock Clarks Essex 42 D4
Cockayne N Yorks 102 E4
Cockayne Hatley Cambs 54 E3
Cockburnspath Borders 124 B3
Cockenzie and Port Seton E Loth 123 B7
Cockerham Lancs 92 D4
Cockermouth Cumb 107 F8
Cockernhoe Green Herts 40 B4
Cockfield Durham 101 B6
Cockfield Suff 56 D3
Cockfosters London 41 E5
Cocking W Sus 16 C2
Cockington Torbay 7 C6
Cocklake Som 23 E6
Cockley Beck Cumb 98 D4
Cockley Cley Norf 67 D7
Cockshutt Shrops 60 B4
Cockthorpe Norf 81 C5
Cockwood Devon 10 F4
Cockyard Hereford 49 F6
Codda Corn 5 B6
Coddenham Suff 56 D5
Coddington Ches 73 D8
Coddington Hereford 50 E2
Coddington Notts 77 D8
Codford St Mary Wilts 24 F4
Codford St Peter Wilts 24 F4
Codicote Herts 41 C5
Codmore Hill W Sus 16 B4
Codnor Derbys 76 E4
Codrington S Glos 24 B2
Codsall Staffs 62 D2
Codsall Wood Staffs 62 D2
Coed Duon = Blackwood Caerph 35 E5
Coed Mawr Gwyn 83 D5
Coed Morgan Mon 35 C7
Coed-Talon Flint 73 D6
Coed-y-bryn Ceredig 46 E2
Coed-y-paen Mon 35 E7
Coed-yr-ynys Powys 35 B5

Forty Hill London 41 E6
Forward Green Suff 56 D4
Fosbury Wilts 25 D8
Fosdyke Lincs 79 F6
Foss Perth 140 D4
Foss Cross Glos 37 D7
Fossebridge Glos 37 C7
Foster Street Essex 41 D7
Fosterhouses S Yorks 89 C7
Foston Derbys 75 F8
Foston Lincs 77 E8
Foston N Yorks 96 C2
Foston on the Wolds E Yorks 97 D7
Fotherby Lincs 91 E7
Fotheringhay Northants 65 E7
Foubister Orkney 176 F4
Foul Mile E Sus 18 D3
Foulby W Yorks 88 C4
Foulden Borders 124 D5
Foulden Norf 67 E7
Foulis Castle Highld 157 C6
Foulridge Lancs 93 E8
Foulsham Norf 81 E6
Fountainhall Borders 123 E7
Fountains Abbey, Ripon N Yorks 95 C5
Four Ashes Staffs 62 F2
Four Ashes Suff 56 B4
Four Crosses Powys 59 D7
Four Crosses Powys 60 C2
Four Crosses Wrex 73 D6
Four Elms Kent 29 E5
Four Forks Som 22 F4
Four Gotes Cambs 66 C4
Four Lane Ends Ches 74 C2
Four Lanes Corn 3 C5
Four Marks Hants 26 F4
Four Mile Bridge Anglesey 82 D2
Four Oaks E Sus 19 C5
Four Oaks W Mid 63 F6
Four Oaks W Mid 62 E5
Four Roads Carms 33 D5
Four Roads I o M 84 F2
Four Throws Kent 18 C4
Fourlane Ends Derbys 76 D3
Fourlanes End Ches 74 D5
Fourpenny Highld 165 E5
Fourstones Northumb 109 C8
Fovant Wilts 13 B8
Foveran Aberds 151 B8
Fowey Corn 5 D6
Fowley Common Warr 86 E4
Fowlis Angus 142 F3
Fowlis Wester Perth 133 B8
Fowlmere Cambs 54 E5
Fownhope Hereford 49 F7
Fox Corner Sur 27 D7
Fox Lane Hants 27 D6
Fox Street Essex 43 B6
Foxbar Renfs 120 C4
Foxcombe Hill Oxon 38 D4
Foxdale I o M 84 E2
Foxearth Essex 56 E2
Foxfield Cumb 98 F4
Foxham Wilts 24 B4
Foxhole Corn 4 D4
Foxhole Swansea 33 E7
Foxholes N Yorks 97 B6
Foxhunt Green E Sus 18 D2
Foxley Norf 81 E6
Foxley Wilts 37 F5
Foxt Staffs 75 E7
Foxton Cambs 54 E5
Foxton Durham 102 B1
Foxton Leics 64 E4
Foxton Canal Locks Leics 64 F3
Foxup N Yorks 93 B8
Foxwist Green Ches 74 C3
Foxwood Shrops 49 B8
Foy Hereford 36 B2
Foyers Highld 147 B7
Fraddam Corn 2 C4
Fraddon Corn 4 D4
Fradley Staffs 63 C5
Fradswell Staffs 75 F6
Fraisthorpe E Yorks 97 C7
Framfield E Sus 17 B8
Framingham Earl Norf 69 D5
Framingham Pigot Norf 69 D5
Framlingham Suff 57 C6
Framlingham Castle Suff 57 C6
Frampton Dorset 12 E4
Frampton Lincs 79 F6
Frampton Cotterell S Glos 36 F3
Frampton Mansell Glos 37 D6
Frampton on Severn Glos 36 D4
Frampton West End Lincs 79 E5
Framsden Suff 57 D5
Framwellgate Moor Durham 111 E5
Franche Worcs 50 B3
Frankby Mers 85 F3
Frankley Worcs 62 F3
Frank's Bridge Powys 48 D3
Frankton Warks 52 B2
Frant E Sus 18 B2
Fraserburgh Aberds 161 B6
Frating Green Essex 43 B6
Fratton Ptsmth 15 E7
Freathy Corn 5 D8
Freckenham Suff 55 B7
Freckleton Lancs 86 B2
Freeby Leics 64 B5
Freehay Staffs 75 E7
Freeland Oxon 38 C4
Freeport Hornsea Outlet Village E Yorks 97 E7
Freester Shetland 175 H6
Freethorpe Norf 69 D7
Freiston Lincs 79 E6
Fremington Devon 20 F4
Fremington N Yorks 101 E5
Frenchay S Glos 23 B8
Frenchbeer Devon 9 F8
Frenich Stirl 132 D3
Frensham Sur 27 E6
Fresgoe Highld 168 C4
Freshfield Mers 85 D3
Freshford Bath 24 C2
Freshwater I o W 14 F4
Freshwater Bay I o W 14 F4
Freshwater East Pembs 32 E1
Fressingfield Suff 57 B6
Freston Suff 57 F5
Freswick Highld 169 C8
Fretherne Glos 36 D4
Frettenham Norf 68 C5
Freuchie Fife 134 D4
Freuchies Angus 142 C2
Freystrop Pembs 44 D4
Friar's Gate E Sus 29 F5
Friarton Perth 134 B3
Friday Bridge Cambs 66 D4
Friday Street E Sus 18 E3
Fridaythorpe E Yorks 96 D4
Friern Barnet London 41 E5
Friesland Argyll 136 C2
Friesthorpe Lincs 90 F4
Frieston Lincs 78 E2
Frieth Bucks 39 E7
Frilford Oxon 38 E4
Frilsham W Berks 26 B3
Frimley Sur 27 D6
Frimley Green Sur 27 D6
Frindsbury Medway 29 B8
Fring Norf 80 D3
Fringford Oxon 39 B6
Frinsted Kent 30 D2
Frinton-on-Sea Essex 43 B8
Friockheim Angus 143 E5
Friog Gwyn 58 C3
Frisby on the Wreake Leics 64 C3
Friskney Lincs 79 D7
Friskney Eaudike Lincs 79 D7
Friskney Tofts Lincs 79 D7
Friston E Sus 18 F2
Friston Suff 57 C8
Fritchley Derbys 76 D3
Frith Bank Lincs 79 E6
Frith Common Worcs 49 C8
Fritham Hants 14 C3
Frithelstock Devon 9 C6
Frithelstock Stone Devon 9 C6
Frithville Lincs 79 D6
Frittenden Kent 30 E2
Frittiscombe Devon 7 E6
Fritton Norf 68 E5
Fritton Norf 69 D7
Fritwell Oxon 39 B5
Frizinghall W Yorks 94 F4
Frizington Cumb 98 C2
Frocester Glos 36 D4
Frodesley Shrops 60 D5
Frodingham N Lincs 90 C2
Frodsham Ches 74 B2
Frogden Borders 116 B3
Froggatt Derbys 76 B2
Froghall Staffs 75 E7
Frogmore Devon 7 E5
Frogmore Hants 27 D6
Frognall Lincs 65 C8
Frogshail Norf 81 D8
Frolesworth Leics 64 E2
Frome Som 24 E2
Frome St Quintin Dorset 12 D3
Fromes Hill Hereford 49 E8
Fron Denb 72 C4
Fron Gwyn 82 F5
Fron Gwyn 70 D4
Fron Powys 48 C2
Fron Powys 60 D2
Fron Powys 59 E8
Froncysyllte Wrex 73 E6
Frongoch Gwyn 72 F3
Frostenden Suff 69 F7
Frosterley Durham 110 F3
Frotoft Orkney 176 D3
Froxfield Wilts 25 C7
Froxfield Green Hants 15 B8
Froyle Hants 27 E5
Fryerning Essex 42 D2
Fryton N Yorks 96 B2
Fulbeck Lincs 78 D2
Fulbourn Cambs 55 D6
Fulbrook Oxon 38 C2
Fulford Som 11 B7
Fulford Staffs 75 F6
Fulford York 96 E2
Fulham London 28 B3
Fulking W Sus 17 C6
Full Sutton E Yorks 96 D3
Fullarton Glasgow 121 C6
Fullarton N Ayrs 120 F3
Fuller Street Essex 42 C3
Fuller's Moor Ches 73 D8
Fullerton Hants 25 F8
Fulletby Lincs 79 B5
Fullwood E Ayrs 120 D4
Fulmer Bucks 40 F2
Fulmodestone Norf 81 D5
Fulnetby Lincs 78 B3
Fulstow Lincs 91 E7
Fulwell T & W 111 D6
Fulwood Lancs 92 F5
Fulwood S Yorks 88 F4
Fundenhall Norf 68 E4
Fundenhall Street Norf 68 E4
Funtington W Sus 15 D8
Funtley Hants 15 D6
Funtullich Perth 133 B6
Funzie Shetland 174 D8
Furley Devon 11 D7
Furnace Argyll 131 E6
Furnace Carms 33 D6
Furnace End Warks 63 E6
Furneaux Pelham Herts 41 B7
Furness Vale Derbys 87 F8
Furze Platt Windsor 40 F1
Furzehill Devon 21 E6
Fyfett Som 11 C7
Fyfield Essex 42 D1
Fyfield Glos 38 D2
Fyfield Hants 25 E7
Fyfield Oxon 38 E4
Fyfield Wilts 25 C6
Fylingthorpe N Yorks 103 D7
Fyvie Aberds 160 E4

G

Gabhsann bho Dheas W Isles 172 C7
Gabhsann bho Thuath W Isles 172 C7
Gablon Highld 164 E4
Gabroc Hill E Ayrs 120 D4
Gaddesby Leics 64 C3
Gadebridge Herts 40 D3
Gaer Powys 35 B5
Gaerllwyd Mon 35 E8
Gaerwen Anglesey 82 D4
Gagingwell Oxon 38 B4
Gaick Lodge Highld 148 F3
Gailey Staffs 62 C3
Gainford Durham 101 C6
Gainsborough Lincs 90 E2
Gainsborough Suff 57 E5
Gainsford End Essex 55 F8
Gairloch Highld 154 C4
Gairlochy Highld 146 F4
Gairney Bank Perth 134 E3
Gairnshiel Lodge Aberds 149 D8
Gaisgill Cumb 99 D8
Gaitsgill Cumb 108 E3
Galashiels Borders 123 F7
Galgate Lancs 92 D4
Galhampton Som 12 B4
Gallaberry Dumfries 114 F2
Gallachoille Argyll 128 B2
Gallanach Argyll 130 C4
Gallanach Argyll 136 B3
Gallantry Bank Ches 74 D2
Gallatown Fife 134 E4
Galley Common Warks 63 E7
Galley Hill Cambs 54 C4
Galleyend Essex 42 D3
Galleywood Essex 42 D3
Gallin Perth 140 E2
Gallowfauld Angus 142 E4
Gallows Green Staffs 75 E7
Galltair Highld 155 H4
Galmisdale Highld 144 E4
Galmpton Devon 6 E4
Galmpton Torbay 7 D6
Galphay N Yorks 95 B5
Galston E Ayrs 120 F5
Galtrigill Highld 152 D2
Gamblesby Cumb 109 F6
Gamesley Derbys 87 E8
Gamlingay Cambs 54 D3
Gammersgill N Yorks 101 F5
Gamston Notts 77 B7
Ganarew Hereford 36 C2
Ganavan Argyll 130 B4
Gang Corn 5 C8
Ganllwyd Gwyn 71 E8
Gannochy Angus 143 B5
Gannochy Perth 134 B3
Gansclet Highld 169 E8
Ganstead E Yorks 97 F7
Ganthorpe N Yorks 96 B2
Ganton N Yorks 97 B5
Garbat Highld 156 C5
Garbhallt Argyll 131 F6
Garboldisham Norf 68 F3
Garden City Flint 73 C7
Garden Village Wrex 73 D7
Garden Village W Yorks 95 F7
Gardenstown Aberds 160 B4
Garderhouse Shetland 175 J5
Gardham E Yorks 97 E5
Gardin Shetland 174 G6
Gare Hill Som 24 E2
Garelochhead Argyll 129 A7
Garford Oxon 38 E4
Garforth W Yorks 95 F7
Gargrave N Yorks 94 D2
Gargunnock Stirl 133 E6
Garlic Street Norf 68 F5
Garlieston Dumfries 105 E8
Garlinge Green Kent 30 D5
Garlogie Aberds 151 D6
Garmond Aberds 160 C5
Garmony Argyll 137 D7
Garmouth Moray 159 C7
Garn-yr-erw Torf 35 C6
Garnant Carms 33 C7
Garndiffaith Torf 35 D6
Garndolbenmaen Gwyn 71 C5
Garnedd Conwy 83 F7
Garnett Bridge Cumb 99 E7
Garnfadryn Gwyn 70 D3
Garnkirk N Lnrk 121 C6
Garnlydan Bl Gwent 35 C5
Garnswllt Swansea 33 D7
Garrabost W Isles 172 E8
Garraron Argyll 130 E4
Garras Corn 3 D6
Garreg Gwyn 71 C7
Garrick Perth 133 C7
Garrigill Cumb 109 E7
Garriston N Yorks 101 E6
Garroch Dumfries 113 F5
Garrogie Lodge Highld 147 C8
Garros Highld 152 C5
Garrow Perth 141 E5
Garryhorn Dumfries 113 E5
Garsdale Cumb 100 F2
Garsdale Head Cumb 100 E2
Garsdon Wilts 37 F6
Garshall Green Staffs 75 F6
Garsington Oxon 39 D5
Garstang Lancs 92 E4
Garston Mers 86 F2
Garswood Mers 86 E3
Gartcosh N Lnrk 121 C6
Garth Bridgend 34 E2
Garth Gwyn 83 D5
Garth Powys 47 E8
Garth Shetland 175 H4
Garth Wrex 73 E6
Garth Row Cumb 99 E7
Garthamlock Glasgow 121 C6
Garthbrengy Powys 48 F2
Garthdee Aberdeen 151 D8
Gartheli Ceredig 46 D4
Garthmyl Powys 59 E8
Garthorpe Leics 64 B5
Garthorpe N Lincs 90 C2
Gartly Aberds 160 E2
Gartmore Stirl 132 E4
Gartnagrenach Argyll 128 E2
Gartness N Lnrk 121 C7
Gartness Stirl 132 F4
Gartocharn W Dunb 132 F3
Garton E Yorks 97 F8
Garton-on-the-Wolds E Yorks 97 D5
Gartsherrie N Lnrk 121 C7
Gartymore Highld 165 C7
Garvald E Loth 123 B8
Garvamore Highld 147 E8
Garvard Argyll 127 C1
Garvault Hotel Highld 168 F2
Garve Highld 156 C4
Garvestone Norf 68 D3
Garvock Aberds 143 B7
Garvock Invclyd 129 C7
Garway Hereford 36 B1
Garway Hill Hereford 35 B8
Gaskan Highld 138 B1
Gastard Wilts 24 C3
Gasthorpe Norf 68 F2
Gatcombe I o W 15 F5
Gate Burton Lincs 90 F2
Gate Helmsley N Yorks 96 D2
Gateacre Mers 86 F2
Gatebeck Cumb 99 F7
Gateford Notts 89 F6
Gateforth N Yorks 89 B6
Gatehead E Ayrs 120 F3
Gatehouse Northumb 116 F3
Gatehouse of Fleet Dumfries 106 D3
Gatelawbridge Dumfries 114 E2
Gateley Norf 81 E5
Gatenby N Yorks 101 F8
Gateshead T & W 111 C5
Gateshead International Stadium T & W 111 C5
Gatesheath Ches 73 C8
Gateside Aberds 150 C5
Gateside Angus 142 E4
Gateside E Renf 120 D4
Gateside Fife 134 D3
Gateside N Ayrs 120 D3
Gathurst Gtr Man 86 D3
Gatley Gtr Man 87 F6
Gattonside Borders 123 F8
Gaufron Powys 47 C8
Gaulby Leics 64 D3
Gauldry Fife 135 B5
Gaunt's Common Dorset 13 D8
Gautby Lincs 78 B4
Gavinton Borders 124 D3
Gawber S Yorks 88 D4
Gawcott Bucks 52 F4
Gawsworth Ches 75 C5
Gawthorpe W Yorks 88 B3
Gawthrop Cumb 100 F1
Gawthwaite Cumb 98 F4
Gay Street W Sus 16 B4
Gaydon Warks 51 D8
Gayfield Orkney 176 A3
Gayhurst M Keynes 53 E6
Gayle N Yorks 100 F3
Gayles N Yorks 101 D6
Gayton Mers 85 F3
Gayton Norf 67 C7
Gayton Northants 52 D5
Gayton Staffs 62 B3
Gayton le Marsh Lincs 91 F8
Gayton le Wold Lincs 91 F6
Gayton Thorpe Norf 67 C7
Gaywood Norf 67 B6
Gazeley Suff 55 C8
Geanies House Highld 158 B2
Gearraidh Bhailteas W Isles 171 H3
Gearraidh Bhaird W Isles 172 F6
Gearraidh na h-Aibhne W Isles 172 E5
Gearraidh na Monadh W Isles 171 J3
Geary Highld 152 C3
Geddes House Highld 158 D2
Gedding Suff 56 D3
Geddington Northants 65 F5
Gedintailor Highld 153 F6
Gedling Notts 77 E6
Gedney Lincs 66 B4
Gedney Broadgate Lincs 66 B4
Gedney Drove End Lincs 66 B4
Gedney Dyke Lincs 66 B4
Gedney Hill Lincs 66 C3
Gee Cross Gtr Man 87 E7
Geilston Argyll 120 B3
Geirinis W Isles 170 F3
Geise Highld 169 C6
Geisiadar W Isles 172 E4
Geldeston Norf 69 E6
Gell Conwy 83 E8
Gelli Pembs 32 C1
Gelli Rhondda 34 E3
Gellideg M Tydf 34 D4
Gellifor Denb 72 C5
Gelligaer Caerph 35 E5
Gellilydan Gwyn 71 D7
Gellinudd Neath 33 D8
Gellyburn Perth 141 F7
Gellywen Carms 32 B3
Gelston Dumfries 106 D4
Gelston Lincs 78 E2
Gembling E Yorks 97 D7
Gentleshaw Staffs 62 C4
Geocrab W Isles 173 J4
George Green Bucks 40 F3
George Nympton Devon 10 B2
Georgefield Dumfries 115 E5
Georgeham Devon 20 F3
Georgetown Bl Gwent 35 D5
Gerlan Gwyn 83 E6
Germansweek Devon 9 E6
Germoe Corn 2 D4
Gerrans Corn 3 C7
Gerrards Cross Bucks 40 F3
Gestingthorpe Essex 56 F2
Geuffordd Powys 60 C2
Gib Hill Ches 74 B3
Gibbet Hill Warks 64 F2
Gibbshill Dumfries 106 B4
Gidea Park London 41 F8
Gidleigh Devon 9 F8
Giffnock E Renf 121 D5
Gifford E Loth 123 C8
Giffordland N Ayrs 120 E2
Giffordtown Fife 134 C4
Giggleswick N Yorks 93 C8
Gilberdyke E Yorks 90 B2
Gilchriston E Loth 123 C7
Gilcrux Cumb 107 F8
Gildersome W Yorks 88 B3
Gildingwells S Yorks 89 F6
Gileston V Glam 22 C2
Gilfach Caerph 35 E5
Gilfach Goch Rhondda 34 F3
Gilfachrheda Ceredig 46 D3
Gillamoor N Yorks 102 F4
Gillar's Green Mers 86 E2
Gillen Highld 152 D3
Gilling East N Yorks 96 B2
Gilling West N Yorks 101 D6
Gillingham Dorset 13 B6
Gillingham Medway 29 C8
Gillingham Norf 69 E7
Gillock Highld 169 D7
Gillow Heath Staffs 75 D5
Gills Highld 169 B8
Gill's Green Kent 18 B4
Gilmanscleuch Borders 115 B6
Gilmerton Edin 123 C5
Gilmerton Perth 133 B7
Gilmonby Durham 100 C4
Gilmorton Leics 64 F2
Gilmourton S Lnrk 121 E6
Gilsland Cumb 109 C6
Gilsland Spa Cumb 109 C6
Gilston Borders 123 D7
Gilston Herts 41 C7
Gilwern Mon 35 C6
Gimingham Norf 81 D8
Giosla W Isles 172 F4
Gipping Suff 56 C4
Gipsey Bridge Lincs 79 E5
Girdle Toll N Ayrs 120 E3
Girlsta Shetland 175 H6
Girsby N Yorks 102 D1
Girtford Beds 54 D2
Girthon Dumfries 106 D3
Girton Cambs 54 C5
Girton Notts 77 C8
Girvan S Ayrs 112 E1
Gisburn Lancs 93 E8
Gisleham Suff 69 F8
Gislingham Suff 56 B4
Gissing Norf 68 F4
Gittisham Devon 11 E6
Gladestry Powys 48 D4
Gladsmuir E Loth 123 B7
Glais Swansea 33 D8
Glaisdale N Yorks 103 D5
Glame Highld 153 E6
Glamis Angus 142 E3
Glamis Castle Angus 142 E3
Glan Adda Gwyn 83 D5
Glan-Conwy Conwy 83 F8
Glan Conwy Conwy 83 D8
Glan-Duar Carms 46 E4
Glan-Dwyfach Gwyn 71 C5
Glan Gors Anglesey 82 D4
Glan-rhyd Gwyn 82 F4
Glan-traeth Anglesey 82 D2
Glan-y-don Flint 73 B5
Glan-y-nant Powys 59 F6
Glan-y-wern Gwyn 71 D7
Glan-yr-afon Anglesey 83 C6
Glan-yr-afon Gwyn 72 E3
Glan-yr-afon Gwyn 72 E4
Glanaman Carms 33 C7
Glandford Norf 81 C6
Glandwr Pembs 32 B2
Glandy Cross Carms 32 B2
Glandyfi Ceredig 58 E3
Glangrwyney Powys 35 C6
Glanmule Powys 59 E8
Glanrafon Ceredig 58 F3
Glanrhyd Gwyn 70 D3
Glanrhyd Pembs 45 E3
Glanton Northumb 117 C6
Glanton Pike Northumb 117 C6
Glanvilles Wootton Dorset 12 D4
Glapthorn Northants 65 E7
Glapwell Derbys 76 C4
Glas-allt Shiel Aberds 149 F8
Glasbury Powys 48 F3
Glaschoil Highld 158 F4
Glascoed Denb 72 B3
Glascoed Mon 35 D7
Glascoed Powys 59 C8
Glascorrie Aberds 150 E2
Glascote Staffs 63 D6
Glascwm Powys 48 D3
Glasdrum Argyll 138 E4
Glasfryn Conwy 72 D3
Glasgow Glasgow 121 C5
Glasgow Airport Renfs 120 C4
Glasgow Art Gallery & Museum Glasgow 121 C5
Glasgow Botanic Gardens Glasgow 121 C5
Glasgow Cathedral Glasgow 121 C6
Glasgow Prestwick International Airport S Ayrs 112 B3
Glashvin Highld 152 C5
Glasinfryn Gwyn 83 E5
Glasnacardoch Highld 145 D6
Glasnakille Highld 153 H6
Glasphein Highld 152 E2
Glaspwll Powys 58 E4
Glassburn Highld 156 F4
Glasserton Dumfries 105 F8
Glassford S Lnrk 121 E7
Glasshouse Hill Glos 36 B4
Glasshouses N Yorks 94 C4
Glasslie Fife 134 D4
Glasson Cumb 108 C2
Glasson Lancs 92 D4
Glassonby Cumb 109 F5
Glasterlaw Angus 143 D5
Glaston Rutland 65 D5
Glastonbury Som 23 F7
Glastonbury Abbey Som 23 F6
Glatton Cambs 65 F8
Glazebrook Warr 86 E4
Glazebury Warr 86 E4
Glazeley Shrops 61 F7
Gleadless S Yorks 88 F4
Gleadsmoss Ches 74 C5
Gleann Tholàstaidh W Isles 172 D8
Gleaston Cumb 92 B2
Gleiniant Powys 59 E6
Glemsford Suff 56 E2
Glen Dumfries 106 D2
Glen Dumfries 106 B5
Glen Auldyn I o M 84 C4
Glen Bernisdale Highld 152 E5
Glen Ho. Borders 123 F5
Glen Mona I o M 84 D4
Glen Nevis House Highld 139 B5
Glen Parva Leics 64 E2
Glen Sluain Argyll 131 F6
Glen Tanar House Aberds 150 E3
Glen Trool Lodge Dumfries 112 F4
Glen Village Falk 121 B8
Glen Vine I o M 84 E3
Glenamachrie Argyll 130 C5
Glenbarr Argyll 118 C3
Glenbeg Highld 137 B6
Glenbeg Highld 149 B6
Glenbervie Aberds 151 F6
Glenboig N Lnrk 121 C7
Glenborrodale Highld 137 B7
Glenbranter Argyll 131 F7
Glenbreck Borders 114 B3
Glenbrein Lodge Highld 147 C7
Glenbrittle House Highld 153 G5
Glenbuchat Lodge Aberds 150 C2
Glenbuck E Ayrs 113 B7
Glenburn Renfs 120 C4
Glencalvie Lodge Highld 164 F1
Glencanisp Lodge Highld 163 B5
Glencaple Dumfries 107 C6
Glencarron Lodge Highld 155 E6
Glencarse Perth 134 B3
Glencassley Castle Highld 163 D8
Glenceitlein Highld 139 E5
Glencoe Highld 138 D4
Glencraig Fife 134 E3
Glencripesdale Highld 137 C7
Glencrosh Dumfries 113 F7
Glendavan Ho. Aberds 150 D3
Glendevon Perth 133 D8
Glendoe Lodge Highld 147 D7
Glendoebeg Highld 147 D7
Glendoick Perth 134 B4
Glendoll Lodge Angus 142 B2
Glendoune S Ayrs 112 E1
Glenduckie Fife 134 C4
Glendye Lodge Aberds 150 F5
Gleneagles Hotel Perth 133 C8
Gleneagles House Perth 133 D8
Glenegedale Argyll 126 D3
Glenelg Highld 145 B8
Glenernie Moray 158 E4
Glenfarg Perth 134 C3
Glenfarquhar Lodge Aberds 151 F6
Glenferness House Highld 158 E3
Glenfeshie Lodge Highld 148 E4
Glenfiddich Distillery, Dufftown Moray 159 E7
Glenfield Leics 64 D2
Glenfinnan Highld 145 E8
Glenfoot Perth 134 C3
Glenfyne Lodge Argyll 131 D8
Glengap Dumfries 106 D3
Glengarnock N Ayrs 120 D3
Glengorm Castle Argyll 137 C5
Glengrasco Highld 153 E5
Glenhead Farm Angus 142 C2
Glenhoul Dumfries 113 F6
Glenhurich Highld 138 C2
Glenkerry Borders 115 C5
Glenkiln Dumfries 106 B5
Glenkindie Aberds 150 C3
Glenlatterach Moray 159 D5
Glenlee Dumfries 113 F6
Glenlichorn Perth 133 C6
Glenlivet Moray 149 B7
Glenlochsie Perth 141 B7
Glenloig N Ayrs 119 C6
Glenluce Dumfries 105 D6
Glenmallan Argyll 131 F8
Glenmarksie Highld 156 D4
Glenmassan Argyll 129 B6
Glenmavis N Lnrk 121 C7
Glenmaye I o M 84 E2
Glenmidge Dumfries 113 F8
Glenmore Argyll 130 D4
Glenmore Highld 153 E5
Glenmore Lodge Highld 149 D5
Glenmoy Angus 142 C4
Glenogil Angus 142 C4
Glenprosen Lodge Angus 142 C2
Glenprosen Village Angus 142 C3
Glenquiech Angus 142 C4
Glenreasdell Mains Argyll 128 E3
Glenree N Ayrs 119 D6
Glenridding Cumb 99 C5
Glenrossal Highld 164 D1
Glenrothes Fife 134 D4
Glensanda Highld 138 E2
Glensaugh Aberds 143 B6
Glenshero Lodge Highld 147 E8
Glenstockadale Dumfries 104 C4
Glenstriven Argyll 129 C5
Glentaggart S Lnrk 113 B8
Glentham Lincs 90 E4
Glentirranmuir Stirl 133 E5
Glenton Aberds 150 B5
Glentress Borders 123 F5
Glentromie Lodge Highld 148 E3
Glentrool Village Dumfries 105 B7
Glentruan I o M 84 B4
Glentruim House Highld 148 E2
Glenturret Distillery, Crieff Perth 133 B7
Glentworth Lincs 90 F3
Glenuig Highld 145 F6
Glenurquhart Highld 157 C8
Glespin S Lnrk 113 B8
Gletness Shetland 175 H6
Glewstone Hereford 36 B2
Glinton P'boro 65 D8
Glooston Leics 64 E4
Glororum Northumb 125 F7
Glossop Derbys 87 E8
Gloster Hill Northumb 117 D8
Gloucester Glos 37 C5
Gloucester Cathedral Glos 37 C5
Gloucestershire Airport Glos 37 B5
Gloup Shetland 174 C7
Glusburn N Yorks 94 E3
Glutt Lodge Highld 168 F4
Glutton Bridge Derbys 75 C7
Glympton Oxon 38 B4
Glyn-Ceiriog Wrex 73 F6
Glyn-cywarch Gwyn 71 D7
Glyn Ebwy = Ebbw Vale Bl Gwent 35 D5
Glyn-neath = Glynedd Neath 34 D2
Glynarthen Ceredig 46 E2
Glynbrochan Powys 59 F6
Glyncoch Rhondda 34 E4
Glyncorrwg Neath 34 E2
Glynde E Sus 17 D8
Glyndebourne E Sus 17 C8
Glyndyfrdwy Denb 72 E5
Glynedd = Glyn-neath Neath 34 D2
Glynogwr Bridgend 34 F3
Glyntaff Rhondda 34 F4
Glyntawe Powys 34 C2
Gnosall Staffs 62 B2
Gnosall Heath Staffs 62 B2
Goadby Leics 64 E4
Goadby Marwood Leics 64 B4
Goat Lees Kent 30 E4
Goatacre Wilts 24 B5
Goathill Dorset 12 C4
Goathland N Yorks 103 D6
Goathurst Som 22 F4
Gobernuisgach Lodge Highld 167 E6
Gobhaig W Isles 173 H3
Gobowen Shrops 73 F7
Godalming Sur 27 E7
Godley Gtr Man 87 E7
Godmanchester Cambs 54 B3
Godmanstone Dorset 12 E4
Godmersham Kent 30 D4
Godney Som 23 E6
Godolphin Cross Corn 2 C5
Godre'r-graig Neath 34 D1
Godshill Hants 14 C2
Godshill I o W 15 F6
Godstone Sur 28 D4
Godstone Farm Sur 28 D4
Godwinscroft Hants 14 E2
Goetre Mon 35 D7
Goferydd Anglesey 82 C2
Goff's Oak Herts 41 D6
Gogar Edin 122 B4
Goginan Ceredig 58 F3
Golan Gwyn 71 C6
Golant Corn 5 D6
Golberdon Corn 5 B8
Golborne Gtr Man 86 E4
Golcar W Yorks 88 C2
Gold Hill Norf 66 E5
Goldcliff Newport 35 F7
Golden Cross E Sus 18 D2
Golden Green Kent 29 E7
Golden Grove Carms 33 C6
Golden Hill Hants 14 E3
Golden Pot Hants 26 E5
Golden Valley Glos 37 B6
Goldenhill Stoke 75 D5
Golders Green London 41 F5
Goldhanger Essex 43 D5
Golding Shrops 60 D5
Goldington Beds 53 D8
Goldsborough N Yorks 95 D6
Goldsborough N Yorks 103 C6
Goldsithney Corn 2 C4
Goldsworthy Devon 9 B5
Goldthorpe S Yorks 89 D5
Gollanfield Highld 158 D2
Golspie Highld 165 D5
Golval Highld 168 C3
Gomeldon Wilts 25 F6
Gomersal W Yorks 88 B3
Gomshall Sur 27 E8
Gonalston Notts 77 E6
Gonfirth Shetland 175 G5
Good Easter Essex 42 C2
Gooderstone Norf 67 D7
Goodleigh Devon 20 F5
Goodmanham E Yorks 96 E4
Goodnestone Kent 30 C4
Goodnestone Kent 31 D6
Goodrich Hereford 36 C2
Goodrington Torbay 7 D6
Goodshaw Lancs 87 B6
Goodwick = Wdig Pembs 44 B4
Goodwood Racecourse W Sus 16 C2
Goodworth Clatford Hants 25 E8
Goole E Yorks 89 B8
Goonbell Corn 3 B6
Goonhavern Corn 4 D2
Goose Eye W Yorks 94 E3
Goose Green Gtr Man 86 D3
Goose Green Norf 68 F4
Goose Green W Sus 16 C5
Gooseham Corn 8 C4
Goosey Oxon 38 E3
Goosnargh Lancs 93 F5
Goostrey Ches 74 B4
Gorcott Hill Warks 51 C5
Gord Shetland 175 L6
Gordon Borders 124 E2
Gordonbush Highld 165 D5
Gordonsburgh Moray 159 C8
Gordonstoun Moray 159 C5
Gordonstown Aberds 160 C2
Gordonstown Aberds 160 E4
Gore Kent 31 D7
Gore Cross Wilts 24 D5
Gore Pit Essex 42 C4
Gorebridge Midloth 123 C6
Gorefield Cambs 66 C4
Gorey Jersey 17
Gorgie Edin 122 B5
Goring Oxon 39 F6
Goring-by-Sea W Sus 16 D5
Goring Heath Oxon 26 B4
Gorleston-on-Sea Norf 69 D8
Gornalwood W Mid 62 E3
Gorrachie Aberds 160 C4
Gorran Churchtown Corn 3 B8
Gorran Haven Corn 3 B9
Gorrenberry Borders 115 E7
Gors Ceredig 46 B5
Gorse Hill Swindon 38 F1
Gorsedd Flint 73 B5
Gorseinon Swansea 33 E6
Gorseness Orkney 176 E3
Gorsgoch Ceredig 46 D3
Gorslas Carms 33 C6
Gorsley Glos 36 B3
Gorstan Highld 156 C4
Gorstanvorran Highld 138 B2
Gorsteyhill Staffs 74 D4
Gorsty Hill Staffs 62 B5
Gortantaoid Argyll 126 B3
Gorton Gtr Man 87 E6
Gosbeck Suff 57 D5
Gosberton Lincs 78 F5
Gosberton Clough Lincs 65 B8
Gosfield Essex 42 B3
Gosford Hereford 49 C7
Gosforth Cumb 98 D2
Gosforth T & W 110 C5
Gosmore Herts 40 B4
Gosport Hants 15 E7
Gossabrough Shetland 174 E7
Gossington Glos 36 D4
Goswick Northumb 125 E6
Gotham Notts 76 F5
Gotherington Glos 37 B6
Gott Shetland 175 J6
Goudhurst Kent 18 B4
Goulceby Lincs 79 B5

Gourdas Aberds 160 D4
Gourdon Aberds 143 B8
Gourock Invclyd 129 C7
Govan Glasgow 121 C5
Govanhill Glasgow 121 C5
Goveton Devon 7 E5
Govilon Mon 35 C6
Gowanhill Aberds 161 B7
Gowdall E Yorks 89 B7
Gowerton Swansea 33 E6
Gowkhall Fife 134 F2
Gowthorpe E Yorks 96 D3
Goxhill E Yorks 97 E7
Goxhill N Lincs 90 B5
Goxhill Haven N Lincs 90 B5
Goybre Neath 34 F1
Grabhair W Isles 172 G6
Graby Lincs 65 B7
Grade Corn 3 E6
Graffham W Sus 16 C3
Grafham Cambs 54 C2
Grafham Sur 27 E8
Grafton Hereford 49 F6
Grafton N Yorks 95 C7
Grafton Oxon 38 D2
Grafton Shrops 60 C4
Grafton Worcs 49 C7
Grafton Flyford Worcs 50 D4
Grafton Regis Northants 53 E5
Grafton Underwood Northants 65 F6
Grafty Green Kent 30 E2
Graianrhyd Denb 73 D6
Graig Conwy 83 D8
Graig Denb 72 B4
Graig-fechan Denb 72 D5
Grain Medway 30 B2
Grainsby Lincs 91 E6
Grainthorpe Lincs 91 E7
Grampound Corn 3 B8
Grampound Road Corn 4 D4
Gramsdal W Isles 170 E4
Granborough Bucks 39 B7
Granby Notts 77 F7
Grandborough Warks 52 C2
Grandtully Perth 141 D6
Grange Cumb 98 C4
Grange E Ayrs 120 F4
Grange Medway 29 C8
Grange Mers 85 F3
Grange Perth 134 B4
Grange Crossroads Moray 159 D8
Grange Hall Moray 158 C4
Grange Hill Essex 41 E7
Grange Moor W Yorks 88 C3
Grange of Lindores Fife 134 C4
Grange-over-Sands Cumb 92 B4
Grange Villa Durham 110 D5
Grangemill Derbys 76 D2
Grangemouth Falk 133 F8
Grangepans Falk 134 F2
Grangetown Cardiff 22 B3
Grangetown Redcar 102 B3
Granish Highld 148 C5
Gransmoor E Yorks 97 D7
Granston Pembs 44 B3
Grantchester Cambs 54 D5
Grantham Lincs 78 F2
Grantley N Yorks 94 C5
Grantlodge Aberds 151 C6
Granton Dumfries 114 D3
Granton Edin 122 B5
Grantown-on-Spey Highld 149 B6
Grantshouse Borders 124 C4
Grappenhall Warr 86 F4
Grasby Lincs 90 D4
Grasmere Cumb 99 D5
Grasscroft Gtr Man 87 D7
Grassendale Mers 85 F4
Grassholme Durham 100 B4
Grassington N Yorks 94 C3
Grassmoor Derbys 76 C4
Grassthorpe Notts 77 C7
Grateley Hants 25 E7
Gratwich Staffs 75 F7
Graveley Cambs 54 C3
Graveley Herts 41 B5
Gravelly Hill W Mid 62 E5
Gravels Shrops 60 D3
Graven Shetland 174 F6
Graveney Kent 30 C4
Gravesend Herts 41 B7
Gravesend Kent 29 B7
Grayingham Lincs 90 E3
Grayrigg Cumb 99 E7
Grays Thurrock 29 B7
Grayshott Hants 27 F6
Grayswood Sur 27 F7
Graythorp Hrtlpl 102 B3
Grazeley Wokingham 26 C4
Greasbrough S Yorks 88 E5
Greasby Mers 85 F3
Great Abington Cambs 55 E6
Great Addington Northants 53 B7
Great Alne Warks 51 D6
Great Altcar Lancs 85 D4
Great Amwell Herts 41 C6
Great Asby Cumb 100 C1
Great Ashfield Suff 56 C3
Great Ayton N Yorks 102 C3
Great Baddow Essex 42 D3
Great Bardfield Essex 55 F7
Great Barford Beds 54 D2
Great Barr W Mid 62 E4
Great Barrington Glos 38 C2
Great Barrow Ches 73 C8
Great Barton Suff 56 C2
Great Barugh N Yorks 96 B3
Great Bavington Northumb 117 F5
Great Bealings Suff 57 E6
Great Bedwyn Wilts 25 C7
Great Bentley Essex 43 B7
Great Billing Northants 53 C6
Great Bircham Norf 80 D3
Great Blakenham Suff 56 D5
Great Blencow Cumb 108 F4
Great Bolas Telford 61 B6
Great Bookham Sur 28 D2
Great Bourton Oxon 52 E2
Great Bowden Leics 64 F4
Great Bradley Suff 55 D7
Great Braxted Essex 42 C4
Great Bricett Suff 56 D4
Great Brickhill Bucks 53 F7
Great Bridge W Mid 62 E3
Great Bridgeford Staffs 62 B2
Great Brington Northants 52 C4
Great Bromley Essex 43 B6
Great Broughton Cumb 107 F7
Great Broughton N Yorks 102 D3
Great Budworth Ches 74 B3
Great Burdon Darl 101 C8
Great Burgh Sur 28 D3
Great Burstead Essex 42 E2
Great Busby N Yorks 102 D3
Great Canfield Essex 42 C1
Great Carlton Lincs 91 F8
Great Casterton Rutland 65 D7
Great Chart Kent 30 E3
Great Chatwell Staffs 61 C7
Great Chesterford Essex 55 E6
Great Cheverell Wilts 24 D4
Great Chishill Cambs 54 F5
Great Clacton Essex 43 C7
Great Cliff W Yorks 88 C4
Great Clifton Cumb 98 B2
Great Coates NE Lincs 91 D6
Great Comberton Worcs 50 E4
Great Corby Cumb 108 D4
Great Cornard Suff 56 E2
Great Cowden E Yorks 97 E8
Great Coxwell Oxon 38 E2
Great Crakehall N Yorks 101 E7
Great Cransley Northants 53 B6
Great Cressingham Norf 67 D8
Great Crosby Mers 85 E4
Great Cubley Derbys 75 F8
Great Dalby Leics 64 C4
Great Denham Beds 53 E8
Great Doddington Northants 53 C6
Great Dunham Norf 67 C8
Great Dunmow Essex 42 B2
Great Durnford Wilts 25 F6
Great Easton Essex 42 B2
Great Easton Leics 64 E5
Great Eccleston Lancs 92 E4
Great Edstone N Yorks 103 F5
Great Ellingham Norf 68 E3
Great Elm Som 24 E2
Great Eversden Cambs 54 D4
Great Fencote N Yorks 101 E7
Great Finborough Suff 56 D4
Great Fransham Norf 67 C8
Great Gaddesden Herts 40 C3
Great Gidding Cambs 65 F8
Great Givendale E Yorks 96 D4
Great Glemham Suff 57 C7
Great Glen Leics 64 E3
Great Gonerby Lincs 77 F8
Great Gransden Cambs 54 D3
Great Green Norf 69 F5
Great Green Suff 56 D3
Great Habton N Yorks 96 B3
Great Hale Lincs 78 E4
Great Hallingbury Essex 41 C8
Great Hampden Bucks 39 D8
Great Harrowden Northants 53 B6
Great Harwood Lancs 93 F7
Great Haseley Oxon 39 D6
Great Hatfield E Yorks 97 E7
Great Haywood Staffs 62 B4
Great Heath W Mid 63 F7
Great Heck N Yorks 89 B6
Great Henny Essex 56 F2
Great Hinton Wilts 24 D4
Great Hockham Norf 68 E2
Great Holland Essex 43 C8
Great Horkesley Essex 56 F3
Great Hormead Herts 41 B6
Great Horton W Yorks 94 F4
Great Horwood Bucks 53 F5
Great Houghton Northants 53 D5
Great Houghton S Yorks 88 D5
Great Hucklow Derbys 75 B8
Great Kelk E Yorks 97 D7
Great Kimble Bucks 39 D8
Great Kingshill Bucks 40 E1
Great Langton N Yorks 101 E7
Great Leighs Essex 42 C3
Great Leighs Racecourse Essex 42 C3
Great Lever Gtr Man 86 D5
Great Limber Lincs 90 D5
Great Linford M Keynes 53 E6
Great Livermere Suff 56 B2
Great Longstone Derbys 76 B2
Great Lumley Durham 111 E5
Great Lyth Shrops 60 D4
Great Malvern Worcs 50 E2
Great Maplestead Essex 56 F2
Great Marton Blkpool 92 F3
Great Massingham Norf 80 E3
Great Melton Norf 68 D4
Great Milton Oxon 39 D6
Great Missenden Bucks 40 D1
Great Mitton Lancs 93 F7
Great Mongeham Kent 31 D7
Great Moulton Norf 68 E4
Great Munden Herts 41 B6
Great Musgrave Cumb 100 C2
Great Ness Shrops 60 C3
Great Notley Essex 42 B3
Great Oakley Essex 43 B7
Great Oakley Northants 65 F5
Great Offley Herts 40 B4
Great Orme Tramway, Llandudno Conwy 83 C7
Great Ormside Cumb 100 C2
Great Orton Cumb 108 D3
Great Ouseburn N Yorks 95 C7
Great Oxendon Northants 64 F4
Great Oxney Green Essex 42 D2
Great Palgrave Norf 67 C8
Great Parndon Essex 41 D7
Great Paxton Cambs 54 C3
Great Plumpton Lancs 92 F3
Great Plumstead Norf 69 C6
Great Ponton Lincs 78 F2
Great Preston W Yorks 88 B5
Great Raveley Cambs 66 F2
Great Rissington Glos 38 C1
Great Rollright Oxon 51 F8
Great Ryburgh Norf 81 E5
Great Ryle Northumb 117 C6
Great Ryton Shrops 60 D4
Great Saling Essex 42 B3
Great Salkeld Cumb 109 F5
Great Sampford Essex 55 F7
Great Sankey Warr 86 F3
Great Saxham Suff 55 C8
Great Shefford W Berks 25 B8
Great Shelford Cambs 55 D5
Great Smeaton N Yorks 101 D8
Great Snoring Norf 80 D5
Great Somerford Wilts 37 F6
Great Stainton Darl 101 B8
Great Stambridge Essex 42 E4
Great Staughton Cambs 54 C2
Great Steeping Lincs 79 C7
Great Stonar Kent 31 D7
Great Strickland Cumb 99 B7
Great Stukeley Cambs 54 B3
Great Sturton Lincs 78 B5
Great Sutton Ches 73 B7
Great Sutton Shrops 60 F5
Great Swinburne Northumb 110 B2
Great Tew Oxon 38 B3
Great Tey Essex 42 B4
Great Thurlkeby N Yorks 95 B7
Great Thurlow Suff 55 D7
Great Torrington Devon 9 C6
Great Tosson Northumb 117 D6
Great Totham Essex 42 C4
Great Totham Essex 42 C4
Great Tows Lincs 91 E6
Great Urswick Cumb 92 B2
Great Wakering Essex 43 F5
Great Waldingfield Suff 56 E3
Great Walsingham Norf 80 D5
Great Waltham Essex 42 C2
Great Warley Essex 42 E1
Great Washbourne Glos 50 F4
Great Weldon Northants 65 F6
Great Welnetham Suff 56 D2
Great Wenham Suff 56 F4
Great Whittington Northumb 110 B3
Great Wigborough Essex 43 C5
Great Wilbraham Cambs 55 D6
Great Wishford Wilts 25 F5
Great Witcombe Glos 37 C6
Great Witley Worcs 50 C2
Great Wolford Warks 51 F7
Great Wratting Suff 55 E7
Great Wymondley Herts 41 B5
Great Wyrley Staffs 62 D3
Great Wytheford Shrops 61 C5
Great Yarmouth Norf 69 D8
Great Yarmouth Sea Life Centre Norf 69 D8
Great Yeldham Essex 55 F8
Greater Doward Hereford 36 C2
Greatford Lincs 65 C7
Greatgate Staffs 75 E7
Greatham Hants 27 F5
Greatham Hrtlpl 102 B2
Greatham W Sus 16 C4
Greatstone on Sea Kent 19 C7
Greatworth Northants 52 E3
Greave Lancs 87 B6
Greeba I o M 84 D3
Green Denb 72 C4
Green End Beds 54 D2
Green Hammerton N Yorks 95 D7
Green Lane Powys 59 E8
Green Ore Som 23 D7
Green St Green London 29 C5
Green Street Herts 40 E4
Greenbank Shetland 174 C7
Greenburn W Loth 122 C2
Greendikes Northumb 117 B6
Greenfield Beds 53 F8
Greenfield Flint 73 B5
Greenfield Gtr Man 87 D7
Greenfield Highld 146 D5
Greenfield Oxon 39 E7
Greenford London 40 F4
Greengairs N Lnrk 121 B7
Greenham W Berks 26 C2
Greenhaugh Northumb 116 F3
Greenhead Northumb 109 C6
Greenhill Falk 121 B8
Greenhill London 40 F4
Greenhill Kent 31 C5
Greenhill Leics 63 C8
Greenhills N Ayrs 120 D3
Greenhithe Kent 29 B6
Greenholm E Ayrs 120 F5
Greenholme Cumb 99 D7
Greenhouse Borders 115 B8
Greenhow Hill N Yorks 94 C4
Greenigoe Orkney 176 F3
Greenland Highld 169 C7
Greenlands Bucks 39 F7
Greenlaw Aberds 160 C3
Greenlaw Borders 124 E3
Greenlea Dumfries 107 B7
Greenloaning Perth 133 D7
Greenmeadow Community Farm, Pontnewydd Torf 35 E6
Greenmount Gtr Man 87 C5
Greenmow Shetland 175 L6
Greenock Invclyd 129 C7
Greenock West Invclyd 129 C7
Greenodd Cumb 99 F5
Greenrow Cumb 107 D8
Greens Norton Northants 52 E4
Greenside T & W 110 C4
Greensidehill Northumb 117 C5
Greenstead Green Essex 42 B4
Greensted Essex 41 D8
Greensted Church, Chipping Ongar Essex 41 D8
Greenwich London 28 B4
Greet Glos 50 F5
Greete Shrops 49 B7
Greetham Lincs 79 B6
Greetham Rutland 65 C6
Greetland W Yorks 87 B8
Gregg Hall Cumb 99 E6
Gregson Lane Lancs 86 B3
Greinetobht W Isles 170 C4
Greinton Som 23 F6
Gremista Shetland 175 J6
Grenaby I o M 84 E2
Grendon Northants 53 C6
Grendon Warks 63 D6
Grendon Common Warks 63 E6
Grendon Green Hereford 49 D7
Grendon Underwood Bucks 39 B6
Grenofen Devon 6 B2
Grenoside S Yorks 88 E4
Greosabhagh W Isles 173 J4
Gresford Wrex 73 D7
Gresham Norf 81 D7
Greshornish Highld 152 D4
Gressenhall Norf 68 C2
Gressingham Lancs 93 C5
Gresty Green Ches 74 D4
Greta Bridge Durham 101 C5
Gretna Dumfries 108 C3
Gretna Green Dumfries 108 C3
Gretton Glos 50 F5
Gretton Northants 65 E5
Gretton Shrops 60 E5
Grewelthorpe N Yorks 94 B5
Grey Green N Lincs 89 D8
Greygarth N Yorks 94 B4
Greynor Carms 33 D6
Greysouthen Cumb 98 B2
Greystoke Cumb 108 F4
Greystone Angus 143 E5
Greystone Dumfries 107 B6
Greywell Hants 26 D5
Griais W Isles 172 D7
Grianan W Isles 172 E7
Gribthorpe E Yorks 96 F3
Gridley Corner Devon 9 E5
Griff Warks 63 F7
Griffithstown Torf 35 E6
Grimbister Orkney 176 E2
Grimblethorpe Lincs 91 F6
Grimeford Village Lancs 86 C4
Grimethorpe S Yorks 88 D5
Griminis W Isles 170 E3
Grimister Shetland 174 D6
Grimley Worcs 50 C3
Grimness Orkney 176 G3
Grimoldby Lincs 91 F7
Grimpo Shrops 60 B3
Grimsargh Lancs 93 F5
Grimsbury Oxon 52 E2
Grimsby NE Lincs 91 C6
Grimscote Northants 52 D4
Grimscott Corn 8 D4
Grimsthorpe Lincs 65 B7
Grimston E Yorks 97 F8
Grimston Leics 64 B3
Grimston Norf 80 E3
Grimston York 96 D2
Grimstone Dorset 12 E4
Grinacombe Moor Devon 9 E6
Grindale E Yorks 97 B7
Grindigar Orkney 176 F4
Grindiscol Shetland 175 K6
Grindle Shrops 61 D7
Grindleford Derbys 76 B2
Grindleton Lancs 93 E7
Grindley Staffs 62 B4
Grindley Brook Shrops 74 E2
Grindlow Derbys 75 B8
Grindon Northumb 124 E5
Grindon Staffs 75 D7
Grindonmoor Gate Staffs 75 D7
Gringley on the Hill Notts 89 E8
Grinsdale Cumb 108 D3
Grinshill Shrops 60 B5
Grinton N Yorks 101 E5
Griomsidar W Isles 172 F6
Grishipoll Argyll 136 C2
Grisling Common E Sus 17 B8
Gristhorpe N Yorks 103 F8
Griston Norf 68 E2
Gritley Orkney 176 F4
Grittenham Wilts 37 F7
Grittleton Wilts 37 F5
Grizebeck Cumb 98 F4
Grizedale Cumb 99 E5
Grobister Orkney 176 D5
Groby Leics 64 D2
Groes Conwy 72 C4
Groes Neath 34 F1
Groes-faen Rhondda 34 F4
Groes-lwyd Powys 60 C2
Groesffordd Marli Denb 72 B4
Groeslon Gwyn 82 E5
Groeslon Gwyn 82 F4
Grogport Argyll 118 B5
Gromford Suff 57 D7
Gronant Flint 72 A4
Groombridge E Sus 18 B2
Grosmont Mon 35 B8
Grosmont N Yorks 103 D6
Grosvenor Museum, Chester Ches 73 C8
Groton Suff 56 E3
Groudle Glen Railway I o M 84 E4
Grougfoot Falk 122 B3
Grouville Jersey 17
Grove Dorset 12 G5
Grove Kent 31 C6
Grove Notts 77 B7
Grove Oxon 38 E4
Grove Park London 28 B5
Grove Vale W Mid 62 E4
Grovesend Swansea 33 D6
Grudie Highld 156 C4
Gruids Highld 164 D2
Gruinard House Highld 162 E3
Grula Highld 153 G4
Gruline Argyll 137 D6
Grunasound Shetland 175 K5
Grundisburgh Suff 57 D6
Grunsagill Lancs 93 D7
Gruting Shetland 175 J4
Grutness Shetland 175 N6
Gualachulain Highld 139 E5
Gualin Ho. Highld 166 D5
Guardbridge Fife 135 C6
Guarlford Worcs 50 E3
Guay Perth 141 E7
Guernsey Airport Guern 16
Guestling Green E Sus 19 D5
Guestling Thorn E Sus 18 D5
Guestwick Norf 81 E6
Guestwick Green Norf 81 E6
Guide Blkburn 86 B5
Guide Post Northumb 117 F8
Guilden Morden Cambs 54 E3
Guilden Sutton Ches 73 C8
Guildford Sur 27 E7
Guildtown Perth 141 F8
Guilsborough Northants 52 B4
Guilsfield Powys 60 C2
Guilton Kent 31 D6
Guineaford Devon 20 F4
Guisborough Redcar 102 C4
Guiseley W Yorks 94 E4
Guist Norf 81 E5
Guith Orkney 176 C4
Guiting Power Glos 37 B7
Gulberwick Shetland 175 K6
Gullane E Loth 135 F6
Gulval Corn 2 C3
Gulworthy Devon 6 B2
Gumfreston Pembs 32 D2
Gumley Leics 64 E3
Gummow's Shop Corn 4 D3
Gun Hill E Sus 18 D2
Gunby E Yorks 96 F3
Gunby Lincs 65 B6
Gundleton Hants 26 F4
Gunn Devon 20 F5
Gunnerside N Yorks 100 E4
Gunnerton Northumb 110 B2
Gunness N Lincs 90 C2
Gunnislake Corn 6 B2
Gunnista Shetland 175 J7
Gunthorpe Norf 81 D6
Gunthorpe Notts 77 E6
Gunthorpe P'boro 65 D8
Gunville I o W 15 F5
Gunwalloe Corn 3 D5
Gurnard I o W 15 E5
Gurnett Ches 75 B6
Gurney Slade Som 23 E8
Gurnos Powys 34 D1
Gussage All Saints Dorset 13 C8
Gussage St Michael Dorset 13 C7
Guston Kent 31 E7
Gutcher Shetland 174 D7
Guthrie Angus 143 D5
Guyhirn Cambs 66 D3
Guyhirn Gull Cambs 66 D3
Guy's Head Lincs 66 B4
Guy's Marsh Dorset 13 B6
Guyzance Northumb 117 D8
Gwaenysgor Flint 72 A4
Gwalchmai Anglesey 82 D3
Gwaun-Cae-Gurwen Neath 33 C8
Gwaun-Leision Neath 33 C8
Gwbert Ceredig 45 E3
Gweek Corn 3 D6
Gwehelog Mon 35 D7
Gwenddwr Powys 48 E2
Gwennap Corn 3 C6
Gwenter Corn 3 E6
Gwernaffield Flint 73 C6
Gwernesney Mon 35 D8
Gwernogle Carms 46 F4
Gwernymynydd Flint 73 C6
Gwersyllt Wrex 73 D7
Gwespyr Flint 85 F2
Gwithian Corn 2 B4
Gwredog Anglesey 82 C4
Gwyddelwern Denb 72 E4
Gwyddgrug Carms 46 F3
Gwydyr Uchaf Conwy 83 E7
Gwynfryn Wrex 73 D6
Gwystre Powys 48 C2
Gwytherin Conwy 83 E8
Gyfelia Wrex 73 E7
Gyffin Conwy 83 D7
Gyre Orkney 176 F2
Gyrn-goch Gwyn 70 C5

H

Habberley Shrops 60 D3
Habergham Lancs 93 F8
Habrough NE Lincs 90 C5
Haceby Lincs 78 F3
Hacheston Suff 57 D7
Hackbridge London 28 C3
Hackenthorpe S Yorks 88 F5
Hackford Norf 68 D3
Hackforth N Yorks 101 E7
Hackland Orkney 176 D2
Hackleton Northants 53 D6
Hackness N Yorks 103 E7
Hackness Orkney 176 G2
Hackney London 41 F6
Hackthorn Lincs 90 F3
Hackthorpe Cumb 99 B7
Haconby Lincs 65 B8
Hacton London 41 F8
Hadden Borders 124 F3
Haddenham Bucks 39 D7
Haddenham Cambs 55 B5
Haddington E Loth 123 B8
Haddington Lincs 78 C2
Haddiscoe Norf 69 E7
Haddon Cambs 65 E8
Haddon Ches 75 C6
Haddon Hall Derbys 76 C2
Hade Edge W Yorks 88 D2
Hademore Staffs 63 D5
Hadfield Derbys 87 E8
Hadham Cross Herts 41 C7
Hadham Ford Herts 41 B7
Hadleigh Essex 42 F4
Hadleigh Suff 56 E4
Hadley Telford 61 C6
Hadley End Staffs 62 B5
Hadlow Kent 29 E7
Hadlow Down E Sus 18 C2
Hadnall Shrops 60 C5
Hadstock Essex 55 E6
Hady Derbys 76 B3
Hadzor Worcs 50 C4
Haffenden Quarter Kent 30 E2
Hafod-Dinbych Conwy 83 F8
Hafod-Iom Conwy 83 D8
Haggate Lancs 93 F8
Haggbeck Cumb 108 B4
Haggerston Northumb 125 E6
Haggrister Shetland 174 F5
Hagley Hereford 49 E7
Hagley Worcs 62 F3
Hagworthingham Lincs 79 C6
Haigh Gtr Man 86 D4
Haigh S Yorks 88 C3
Haigh Moor W Yorks 88 B3
Haighton Green Lancs 93 F5
Hail Weston Cambs 54 C2
Haile Cumb 98 D2
Hailes Glos 50 F5
Hailey Herts 41 C6
Hailey Oxon 38 C3
Hailsham E Sus 18 E2
Haimer Highld 169 C6
Hainault London 41 E7
Hainford Norf 68 C5
Hainton Lincs 91 F5
Hairmyres S Lnrk 121 D6
Haisthorpe E Yorks 97 C7
Hakin Pembs 44 E3
Halam Notts 77 D6
Halbeath Fife 134 F3
Halberton Devon 10 C5
Halcro Highld 169 C7
Hale Gtr Man 87 F5
Hale Halton 86 F2
Hale Hants 14 C2
Hale Bank Halton 86 F2
Hale Street Kent 29 E7
Halebarns Gtr Man 87 F5
Hales Norf 69 E6
Hales Staffs 74 F4
Hales Place Kent 30 D5
Halesfield Telford 61 D7
Halesgate Lincs 66 B3
Halesowen W Mid 62 F3
Halesworth Suff 57 B7
Halewood Mers 86 F2
Halford Shrops 60 F4
Halford Warks 51 E7
Halfpenny Furze Carms 32 C3
Halfpenny Green Staffs 62 E2
Halfway Carms 46 F5
Halfway Carms 47 F7
Halfway W Berks 26 C2
Halfway Bridge W Sus 16 B3
Halfway House Shrops 60 C3
Halfway Houses Kent 30 B3
Halifax W Yorks 87 B8
Halket E Ayrs 120 D4
Halkirk Highld 169 D6
Halkyn Flint 73 B6
Hall Dunnerdale Cumb 98 E4
Hall Green W Mid 62 F5
Hall Green W Yorks 88 C4
Hall Grove Herts 41 C5
Hall of Tankerness Orkney 176 F4
Hall of the Forest Shrops 60 F2
Halland E Sus 18 D2
Hallaton Leics 64 E4
Hallatrow Bath 23 D8
Hallbankgate Cumb 109 D5
Hallen S Glos 36 F2
Halliburton Borders 124 E2
Hallin Highld 152 D3
Halling Medway 29 C8
Hallington Lincs 91 F7
Hallington Northumb 110 B2
Halliwell Gtr Man 86 C5
Halloughton Notts 77 D6
Hallow Worcs 50 D3
Hallrule Borders 115 C8
Halls E Loth 124 B2
Hall's Green Herts 41 B5
Hallsands Devon 7 F6
Hallthwaites Cumb 98 F3
Hallworthy Corn 8 F3
Hallyburton House Perth 142 F2
Hallyne Borders 122 E4
Halmer End Staffs 74 E4
Halmore Glos 36 D3
Halmyre Mains Borders 122 E4
Halnaker W Sus 16 D3
Halsall Lancs 85 C4
Halse Northants 52 E3
Halse Som 11 B6
Halsetown Corn 2 C4
Halsham E Yorks 91 B6
Halsinger Devon 20 F4
Halstead Essex 56 F2
Halstead Kent 29 C5
Halstead Leics 64 D4
Halstock Dorset 12 D3
Haltham Lincs 78 C5
Haltoft End Lincs 79 E6
Halton Bucks 40 C1
Halton Halton 86 F3
Halton Lancs 92 C5
Halton Northumb 110 C2
Halton Wrex 73 F7
Halton W Yorks 95 F6
Halton East N Yorks 94 D3
Halton Gill N Yorks 93 B8
Halton Holegate Lincs 79 C7
Halton Lea Gate Northumb 109 D6
Halton West N Yorks 93 D8
Haltwhistle Northumb 109 C7
Halvergate Norf 69 D7
Halwell Devon 7 D5
Halwill Devon 9 E6
Halwill Junction Devon 9 D6
Ham Devon 11 D7
Ham Glos 36 E3
Ham London 28 B2
Ham Highld 169 B7
Ham Kent 31 D7
Ham Shetland 175 K1
Ham Wilts 25 C8
Ham Common Dorset 13 B6
Ham Green Hereford 50 E2
Ham Green Kent 19 C5
Ham Green Kent 30 C2
Ham Green N Som 23 B7
Ham Green Worcs 50 C5
Ham Street Som 23 F7
Hamble-le-Rice Hants 15 D5
Hambleden Bucks 39 F7
Hambledon Hants 15 C7
Hambledon Sur 27 F7
Hambleton Lancs 92 E3
Hambleton N Yorks 95 F8
Hambridge Som 11 B8
Hambrook S Glos 23 B8
Hambrook W Sus 15 D8
Hameringham Lincs 79 C6
Hamerton Cambs 54 B2
Hametoun Shetland 175 K1
Hamilton S Lnrk 121 D7
Hamilton Park Racecourse S Lnrk 121 D7
Hammer W Sus 27 F6
Hammerpot W Sus 16 D4
Hammersmith London 28 B3
Hammerwich Staffs 62 D4
Hammerwood E Sus 28 F5
Hammond Street Herts 41 D6
Hammoon Dorset 13 C6
Hamnavoe Shetland 174 E4
Hamnavoe Shetland 175 K5
Hamnavoe Shetland 174 E6
Hamnavoe Shetland 174 F6
Hampden National Stadium Glasgow 121 C5
Hampden Park E Sus 18 E3
Hamperden End Essex 55 F6
Hampnett Glos 37 C7
Hampole S Yorks 89 C6
Hampreston Dorset 13 E8
Hampstead London 41 F5
Hampstead Norreys W Berks 26 B3
Hampsthwaite N Yorks 95 D5
Hampton London 28 C2
Hampton Shrops 61 F7
Hampton Worcs 50 E5
Hampton Bishop Hereford 49 F7
Hampton Court Palace, Teddington London 28 C2
Hampton Heath Ches 73 E8
Hampton in Arden W Mid 63 F6
Hampton Loade Shrops 61 F7
Hampton Lovett Worcs 50 C3
Hampton Lucy Warks 51 D7
Hampton on the Hill Warks 51 C7
Hampton Poyle Oxon 39 C5
Hamrow Norf 80 E5
Hamsey E Sus 17 C8
Hamsey Green Sur 28 D4
Hamstall Ridware Staffs 62 C5
Hamstead I o W 14 E5
Hamstead W Mid 62 E4
Hamstead Marshall W Berks 26 C2
Hamsterley Durham 110 F4
Hamsterley Durham 110 D4
Hamstreet Kent 19 B7
Hamworthy Poole 13 E7
Hanbury Staffs 63 B5
Hanbury Worcs 50 C4
Hanbury Woodend Staffs 63 B5
Hanby Lincs 78 F3
Hanchurch Staffs 74 E5
Handbridge Ches 73 C8
Handcross W Sus 17 B6
Handforth Ches 87 F6
Handley Ches 73 D8
Handsacre Staffs 62 C4
Handsworth S Yorks 88 F5
Handsworth W Mid 62 E4
Handy Cross Devon 9 B6
Hanford Stoke 75 E5
Hanging Langford Wilts 24 F5
Hangleton W Sus 16 D4
Hanham S Glos 23 B8
Hankelow Ches 74 E3
Hankerton Wilts 37 E6
Hankham E Sus 18 E3
Hanley Stoke 75 E5
Hanley Castle Worcs 50 E3
Hanley Child Worcs 49 C8
Hanley Swan Worcs 50 E3
Hanley William Worcs 49 C8
Hanlith N Yorks 94 C2
Hanmer Wrex 73 F8
Hannah Lincs 79 B8
Hannington Hants 26 D3
Hannington Northants 53 B6
Hannington Swindon 38 E1
Hannington Wick Swindon 38 E1
Hansel Village S Ayrs 120 F3
Hanslope M Keynes 53 E6
Hanthorpe Lincs 65 B7
Hanwell London 40 F4
Hanwell Oxon 52 E2
Hanwood Shrops 60 D4
Hanworth London 28 B2
Hanworth Norf 81 D7
Happendon S Lnrk 121 F8
Happisburgh Norf 69 A6
Happisburgh Common Norf 69 B6
Hapsford Ches 73 B8
Hapton Lancs 93 F7
Hapton Norf 68 E4
Harberton Devon 7 D5
Harbertonford Devon 7 D5
Harbledown Kent 30 D5
Harborne W Mid 62 F4
Harborough Magna Warks 52 B2
Harbottle Northumb 117 D5
Harbour Park, Littlehampton W Sus 16 D4
Harbury Warks 51 D8
Harby Leics 77 F7
Harby Notts 77 B8
Harcombe Devon 11 E6
Harden W Mid 62 D4
Harden W Yorks 94 F3
Hardenhuish Wilts 24 B4
Hardgate Aberds 151 D6
Hardham W Sus 16 C4
Hardingham Norf 68 D3
Hardingstone Northants 53 D5
Hardington Som 24 D2
Hardington Mandeville Som 12 C3
Hardington Marsh Som 12 D3
Hardley Hants 14 D5
Hardley Street Norf 69 D6
Hardmead M Keynes 53 E7
Hardrow N Yorks 100 E3
Hardstoft Derbys 76 C4
Hardway Hants 15 D7
Hardway Som 24 F2
Hardwick Bucks 39 C8
Hardwick Cambs 54 D4
Hardwick Norf 67 C6
Hardwick Norf 68 F5
Hardwick Notts 77 B6
Hardwick Northants 53 C6
Hardwick Oxon 38 D3
Hardwick Oxon 39 B5
Hardwick W Mid 62 E4
Hardwick Hall Derbys 76 C4
Hardwicke Glos 36 C4
Hardwicke Glos 37 B6

Hardwicke Hereford 48 E4
Hardy's Green Essex 43 B5
Hare Green Essex 43 B6
Hare Hatch Wokingham 27 B6
Hare Street Herts 41 B6
Hareby Lincs 79 C6
Hareden Lancs 93 D6
Harefield London 40 E3
Harehills W Yorks 95 F6
Harehope Northumb 117 B6
Haresceugh Cumb 109 E6
Harescombe Glos 37 C5
Haresfield Glos 37 C5
Hareshaw N Lnrk 121 C8
Hareshaw Head Northumb 116 F4
Harewood W Yorks 95 E6
Harewood End Hereford 36 B2
Harewood House, Wetherby W Yorks 95 E6
Harford Carms 46 E5
Harford Devon 6 D4
Hargate Norf 68 E4
Hargatewall Derbys 75 B8
Hargrave Ches 73 C8
Hargrave Northants 53 B8
Hargrave Suff 55 D8
Harker Cumb 108 C3
Harkland Shetland 174 E6
Harkstead Suff 57 F5
Harlaston Staffs 63 C6
Harlaw Ho. Aberds 151 B6
Harlaxton Lincs 77 F8
Harle Syke Lancs 93 F8
Harlech Gwyn 71 D6
Harlech Castle Gwyn 71 D6
Harlequin Notts 77 F6
Harlescott Shrops 60 C5
Harlesden London 41 F5
Harleston Devon 7 E5
Harleston Norf 68 F5
Harleston Suff 56 D4
Harlestone Northants 52 C5
Harley Shrops 61 D5
Harley S Yorks 88 E4
Harleyholm S Lnrk 122 F2
Harlington Beds 53 F8
Harlington London 27 B8
Harlington S Yorks 89 D5
Harlosh Highld 153 E3
Harlow Essex 41 C7
Harlow Carr RHS Garden, Harrogate N Yorks 95 D5
Harlow Hill Northumb 110 C3
Harlow Hill N Yorks 95 D5
Harlthorpe E Yorks 96 F3
Harlton Cambs 54 D4
Harman's Cross Dorset 13 F7
Harmby N Yorks 101 F6
Harmer Green Herts 41 C5
Harmer Hill Shrops 60 B4
Harmondsworth London 27 B8
Harmston Lincs 78 C2
Harnham Northumb 110 B3
Harnhill Glos 37 D7
Harold Hill London 41 E8
Harold Wood London 41 E8
Haroldston West Pembs 44 D3
Haroldswick Shetland 174 B8
Harome N Yorks 102 F4
Harpenden Herts 40 C4
Harpford Devon 11 E5
Harpham E Yorks 97 C6
Harpley Norf 80 E3
Harpley Worcs 49 C8
Harpole Northants 52 C4
Harpsdale Highld 169 D6
Harpsden Oxon 39 F7
Harpswell Lincs 90 F3
Harpur Hill Derbys 75 B7
Harpurhey Gtr Man 87 D6
Harraby Cumb 108 D4
Harrapool Highld 155 H2
Harrier Shetland 175 J1
Harrietfield Perth 133 B8
Harrietsham Kent 30 D2
Harrington Cumb 98 B1
Harrington Lincs 79 B6
Harrington Northants 64 F4
Harringworth Northants 65 E6
Harris Highld 144 D3
Harris Museum, Preston Lancs 86 B3
Harrogate N Yorks 95 D6
Harrold Beds 53 D7
Harrow London 40 F4
Harrow on the Hill London 40 F4
Harrow Street Suff 56 F3
Harrow Weald London 40 E4
Harrowbarrow Corn 5 C8
Harrowden Beds 53 E8
Harrowgate Hill Darl 101 C7
Harston Cambs 54 D5
Harston Leics 77 F8
Harswell E Yorks 96 E4
Hart Hrtlpl 111 F7
Hart Common Gtr Man 86 D4
Hart Hill Luton 40 B4
Hart Station Hrtlpl 111 F7
Hartburn Northumb 117 F6
Hartburn Stockton 102 C2
Hartest Suff 56 D2
Hartfield E Sus 29 F5
Hartford Cambs 54 B3
Hartford Ches 74 B3
Hartford End Essex 42 C2
Hartfordbridge Hants 27 D5
Hartforth N Yorks 101 D6
Harthill Ches 74 D2
Harthill N Lnrk 122 C2
Harthill S Yorks 89 F5
Hartington Derbys 75 C8
Hartland Devon 8 B4
Hartlebury Worcs 50 B3
Hartlepool Hrtlpl 111 F8
Hartlepool's Maritime Experience Hrtlpl 111 F8
Hartley Cumb 100 D2
Hartley Kent 29 C7
Hartley Kent 18 B4
Hartley Northumb 111 B6
Hartley Westpall Hants 26 D4
Hartley Wintney Hants 27 D5
Hartlip Kent 30 C2
Hartoft End N Yorks 103 E5
Harton N Yorks 96 C3
Harton Shrops 60 F4
Harton T & W 111 C6
Hartpury Glos 36 B4
Hartshead W Yorks 88 B2
Hartshill Warks 63 E7
Hartshorne Derbys 63 B7
Hartsop Cumb 99 C6
Hartwell Northants 53 D5
Hartwood N Lnrk 121 D8
Harvieston Stirl 132 F4
Harvington Worcs 51 E5
Harvington Cross Worcs 51 E5
Harwell Oxon 38 F4
Harwich Essex 57 F6
Harwood Durham 109 F8
Harwood Gtr Man 86 C5
Harwood Dale N Yorks 103 E7
Harworth Notts 89 E7
Hasbury W Mid 62 F3
Hascombe Sur 27 E7
Haselbech Northants 52 B5
Haselbury Plucknett Som 12 C2
Haseley Warks 51 C7
Haselor Warks 51 D6
Hasfield Glos 37 B5
Hasguard Pembs 44 E3
Haskayne Lancs 85 D4
Hasketon Suff 57 D6
Hasland Derbys 76 C3
Haslemere Sur 27 F7
Haslingden Lancs 87 B5
Haslingfield Cambs 54 D5
Haslington Ches 74 D4
Hassall Ches 74 D4
Hassall Green Ches 74 D4
Hassell Street Kent 30 E4
Hassendean Borders 115 B8
Hassingham Norf 69 D6
Hassocks W Sus 17 C6
Hassop Derbys 76 B2
Hastigrow Highld 169 C7
Hastingleigh Kent 30 E4
Hastings E Sus 18 E5
Hastings Castle E Sus 18 D5
Hastings Sea Life Centre E Sus 18 E5
Hastingwood Essex 41 D7
Hastoe Herts 40 D2
Haswell Durham 111 E6
Haswell Plough Durham 111 E6
Hatch Beds 54 E2
Hatch Hants 26 D4
Hatch Wilts 13 B7
Hatch Beauchamp Som 11 B8
Hatch End London 40 E4
Hatch Green Som 11 C8
Hatchet Gate Hants 14 D4
Hatching Green Herts 40 C4
Hatchmere Ches 74 B2
Hatcliffe NE Lincs 91 D6
Hatfield Hereford 49 D7
Hatfield Herts 41 D5
Hatfield S Yorks 89 D7
Hatfield Worcs 50 D3
Hatfield Broad Oak Essex 41 C8
Hatfield Garden Village Herts 41 D5
Hatfield Heath Essex 41 C8
Hatfield House Herts 41 D5
Hatfield Hyde Herts 41 C5
Hatfield Peverel Essex 42 C3
Hatfield Woodhouse S Yorks 89 D7
Hatford Oxon 38 E3
Hatherden Hants 25 D8
Hatherleigh Devon 9 D7
Hathern Leics 63 B8
Hatherop Glos 38 D1
Hathersage Derbys 88 F3
Hathershaw Gtr Man 87 D7
Hatherton Ches 74 E3
Hatherton Staffs 62 C3
Hatley St George Cambs 54 D3
Hatt Corn 5 C8
Hattingley Hants 26 F4
Hatton Aberds 161 E7
Hatton Derbys 63 B6
Hatton Lincs 78 B4
Hatton Shrops 60 E4
Hatton Warks 51 C7
Hatton Warr 86 F3
Hatton Castle Aberds 160 D4
Hatton Country World Warks 51 C7
Hatton Heath Ches 73 C8
Hatton of Fintray Aberds 151 C7
Hattoncrook Aberds 151 B7
Haugh E Ayrs 112 B4
Haugh Gtr Man 87 C7
Haugh Lincs 79 B7
Haugh Head Northumb 117 B6
Haugh of Glass Moray 159 F8
Haugh of Urr Dumfries 106 C5
Haugham Lincs 91 F7
Haughley Suff 56 C4
Haughley Green Suff 56 C4
Haughs of Clinterty Aberdeen 151 C7
Haughton Notts 77 B6
Haughton Shrops 61 E6
Haughton Shrops 60 B3
Haughton Shrops 61 C5
Haughton Shrops 61 D7
Haughton Staffs 62 B2
Haughton Castle Northumb 110 B2
Haughton Green Gtr Man 87 E7
Haughton Le Skerne Darl 101 C8
Haughton Moss Ches 74 D2
Haultwick Herts 41 B6
Haunn Argyll 136 D4
Haunn W Isles 171 J3
Haunton Staffs 63 C6
Hauxley Northumb 117 D8
Hauxton Cambs 54 D5
Havant Hants 15 D8
Haven Hereford 49 D6
Haven Bank Lincs 78 D5
Haven Side E Yorks 91 B5
Havenstreet I o W 15 E6
Havercroft W Yorks 88 C4
Haverfordwest = Hwlffordd Pembs 44 D4
Haverhill Suff 55 E7
Haverigg Cumb 92 B1
Havering-atte-Bower London 41 E8
Haveringland Norf 81 E7
Haversham M Keynes 53 E6
Haverthwaite Cumb 99 F5
Haverton Hill Stockton 102 B2
Hawarden = Penarlâg Flint 73 C7
Hawcoat Cumb 92 B2
Hawen Ceredig 46 E2
Hawes N Yorks 100 F3
Hawes Side Blkpool 92 F3
Hawes'Green Norf 68 E5
Hawford Worcs 50 C3
Hawick Borders 115 C8
Hawk Green Gtr Man 87 F7
Hawkchurch Devon 11 D8
Hawkedon Suff 55 D8
Hawkenbury Kent 30 E2
Hawkenbury Kent 18 B2
Hawkeridge Wilts 24 D3
Hawkerland Devon 11 F5
Hawkes End W Mid 63 F7
Hawkesbury S Glos 36 F4
Hawkesbury Warks 63 F7
Hawkesbury Upton S Glos 36 F4
Hawkhill Northumb 117 C8
Hawkhurst Kent 18 B4
Hawkinge Kent 31 F6
Hawkley Hants 15 B8
Hawkridge Som 21 F7
Hawkshead Cumb 99 E5
Hawkshead Hill Cumb 99 E5
Hawksland S Lnrk 121 F8
Hawkswick N Yorks 94 B2
Hawksworth Notts 77 E7
Hawksworth W Yorks 94 E4
Hawksworth W Yorks 95 F5
Hawkwell Essex 42 E4
Hawley Hants 27 D6
Hawley Kent 29 B6
Hawling Glos 37 B7
Hawnby N Yorks 102 F3
Haworth W Yorks 94 F3
Hawstead Suff 56 D2
Hawthorn Durham 111 E7
Hawthorn Rhondda 35 F5
Hawthorn Wilts 24 C3
Hawthorn Hill Brack 27 B6
Hawthorn Hill Lincs 78 D5
Hawthorpe Lincs 65 B7
Hawton Notts 77 D7
Haxby York 96 D2
Haxey N Lincs 89 D8
Hay Green Norf 66 C5
Hay-on-Wye = Y Gelli Gandryll Powys 48 E4
Hay Street Herts 41 B6
Haydock Mers 86 E3
Haydock Park Racecourse Mers 86 E3
Haydon Dorset 12 C4
Haydon Bridge Northumb 109 C8
Haydon Wick Swindon 37 F8
Haye Corn 5 C8
Hayes London 28 C5
Hayes London 40 F4
Hayfield Derbys 87 F8
Hayfield Fife 134 E4
Hayhill E Ayrs 112 C4
Hayhillock Angus 143 E5
Hayle Corn 2 C4
Haynes Beds 53 E8
Haynes Church End Beds 53 E8
Hayscastle Pembs 44 C3
Hayscastle Cross Pembs 44 C4
Hayshead Angus 143 E6
Hayton Aberdeen 151 D8
Hayton Cumb 107 E8
Hayton Cumb 108 D5
Hayton E Yorks 96 E4
Hayton Notts 89 F8
Hayton's Bent Shrops 60 F5
Haytor Vale Devon 7 B5
Haywards Heath W Sus 17 B7
Haywood S Yorks 89 C6
Haywood Oaks Notts 77 D6
Hazel Grove Gtr Man 87 F7
Hazel Street Kent 18 B3
Hazelbank S Lnrk 121 E8
Hazelbury Bryan Dorset 12 D5
Hazeley Hants 26 D5
Hazelhurst Gtr Man 87 D7
Hazelslade Staffs 62 C4
Hazelton Glos 37 C7
Hazelton Walls Fife 134 B5
Hazelwood Derbys 76 E3
Hazlemere Bucks 40 E1
Hazlerigg T & W 110 B5
Hazlewood N Yorks 94 D3
Hazon Northumb 117 D7
Heacham Norf 80 D2
Head of Muir Falk 133 F7
Headbourne Worthy Hants 26 F2
Headbrook Hereford 48 D5
Headcorn Kent 30 E2
Headingley W Yorks 95 F5
Headington Oxon 39 D5
Headlam Durham 101 C6
Headless Cross Worcs 50 C5
Headley Hants 26 C3
Headley Hants 27 F6
Headley Sur 28 D3
Headon Notts 77 B7
Heads S Lnrk 121 E7
Heads Nook Cumb 108 D4
Heage Derbys 76 D3
Healaugh N Yorks 95 E7
Healaugh N Yorks 101 E5
Heald Green Gtr Man 87 F6
Heale Devon 20 E5
Heale Som 23 E8
Healey Gtr Man 87 C6
Healey Northumb 110 D3
Healey N Yorks 101 F6
Healing NE Lincs 91 C6
Heamoor Corn 2 C3
Heanish Argyll 136 F2
Heanor Derbys 76 E4
Heanton Punchardon Devon 20 F4
Heapham Lincs 90 F2
Heart of the National Forest Leics 63 C7
Hearthstane Borders 114 B4
Heasley Mill Devon 21 F6
Heast Highld 145 B6
Heath Cardiff 22 B3
Heath Derbys 76 C4
Heath and Reach Beds 40 B2
Heath End Hants 26 C3
Heath End Sur 27 E6
Heath End Warks 51 C7
Heath Hayes Staffs 62 C4
Heath Hill Shrops 61 C7
Heath House Som 23 E6
Heath Town W Mid 62 E3
Heathcote Derbys 75 C8
Heather Leics 63 C7
Heatherfield Highld 153 E5
Heathfield Devon 7 B6
Heathfield E Sus 18 C2
Heathfield Som 11 B6
Heathhall Dumfries 107 B6
Heathstock Devon 11 D7
Heathton Shrops 62 E2
Heatley Warr 86 F5
Heaton Lancs 92 C4
Heaton Staffs 75 C6
Heaton T & W 111 C5
Heaton W Yorks 94 F4
Heaton Moor Gtr Man 87 E6
Heaverham Kent 29 D6
Heaviley Gtr Man 87 F7
Heavitree Devon 10 E4
Hebburn T & W 111 C6
Hebden N Yorks 94 C3
Hebden Bridge W Yorks 87 B7
Hebron Anglesey 82 C4
Hebron Carms 32 B2
Hebron Northumb 117 F7
Heck Dumfries 114 F3
Heckfield Hants 26 C5
Heckfield Green Suff 57 B5
Heckfordbridge Essex 43 B5
Heckington Lincs 78 E4
Heckmondwike W Yorks 88 B3
Heddington Wilts 24 C4
Heddle Orkney 176 E2
Heddon-on-the-Wall Northumb 110 C4
Hedenham Norf 69 E6
Hedge End Hants 15 C5
Hedgerley Bucks 40 F2
Hedging Som 11 B8
Hedley on the Hill Northumb 110 D3
Hednesford Staffs 62 C4
Hedon E Yorks 91 B5
Hedsor Bucks 40 F2
Hedworth T & W 111 C6
Heeley City Farm, Sheffield S Yorks 88 F4
Hegdon Hill Hereford 49 D7
Heggerscales Cumb 100 C3
Heglibister Shetland 175 H5
Heighington Darl 101 B7
Heighington Lincs 78 C3
Heights of Brae Highld 157 C6
Heights of Kinlochewe Highld 154 D6
Heilam Highld 167 C6
Heiton Borders 124 F3
Hele Devon 20 E4
Hele Devon 10 D4
Helensburgh Argyll 129 B7
Helford Corn 3 D6
Helford Passage Corn 3 D6
Helhoughton Norf 80 E4
Helions Bumpstead Essex 55 E7
Hellaby S Yorks 89 E6
Helland Corn 5 B5
Hellesdon Norf 68 C5
Hellidon Northants 52 D3
Hellifield N Yorks 93 D8
Hellingly E Sus 18 D2
Hellington Norf 69 D6
Hellister Shetland 175 J5
Helm Northumb 117 E7
Helmdon Northants 52 E3
Helmingham Suff 57 D5
Helmington Row Durham 110 F4
Helmsdale Highld 165 C7
Helmshore Lancs 87 B5
Helmsley N Yorks 102 F4
Helperby N Yorks 95 C7
Helperthorpe N Yorks 97 B5
Helpringham Lincs 78 E4
Helpston P'boro 65 D8
Helsby Ches 73 B8
Helsey Lincs 79 B8
Helston Corn 3 D5
Helstone Corn 8 F2
Helton Cumb 99 B7
Helwith Bridge N Yorks 93 C8
Hemblington Norf 69 C6
Hemel Hempstead Herts 40 D3
Hemingbrough N Yorks 96 F2
Hemingby Lincs 78 B5
Hemingford Abbots Cambs 54 B3
Hemingford Grey Cambs 54 B3
Hemingstone Suff 57 D5
Hemington Leics 63 B8
Hemington Northants 65 F7
Hemington Som 24 D2
Hemley Suff 57 E6
Hemlington M'bro 102 C3
Hemp Green Suff 57 C7
Hempholme E Yorks 97 D6
Hempnall Norf 68 E5
Hempnall Green Norf 68 E5
Hempriggs House Highld 169 E8
Hempstead Essex 55 F7
Hempstead Medway 29 C8
Hempstead Norf 81 D7
Hempstead Norf 69 B7
Hempsted Glos 37 C5
Hempton Norf 80 E5
Hempton Oxon 52 F2
Hemsby Norf 69 C7
Hemswell Lincs 90 E3
Hemswell Cliff Lincs 90 F3
Hemsworth W Yorks 88 C5
Hemyock Devon 11 C6
Hen-feddau fawr Pembs 45 F4
Henbury Bristol 23 B7
Henbury Ches 75 B5
Hendon London 41 F5
Hendon T & W 111 D7
Hendre Flint 73 C5
Hendre-ddu Conwy 83 E8
Hendreforgan Rhondda 34 F3
Hendy Carms 33 D6
Heneglwys Anglesey 82 D4
Henfield W Sus 17 C6
Henford Devon 9 E5
Henghurst Kent 19 B6
Hengoed Caerph 35 E5
Hengoed Powys 48 D4
Hengoed Shrops 73 F6
Hengrave Suff 56 C2
Henham Essex 41 B8
Heniarth Powys 59 D8
Henlade Som 11 B7
Henley Shrops 49 B7
Henley Som 23 F6
Henley Suff 57 D5
Henley W Sus 16 B2
Henley-in-Arden Warks 51 C6
Henley-on-Thames Oxon 39 F7
Henley's Down E Sus 18 D4
Henllan Ceredig 46 E2
Henllan Denb 72 C4
Henllan Amgoed Carms 32 B2
Henllys Torf 35 E6
Henlow Beds 54 F2
Hennock Devon 10 F3
Henny Street Essex 56 F2
Henryd Conwy 83 D7
Henry's Moat Pembs 32 B1
Hensall N Yorks 89 B6
Henshaw Northumb 109 C7
Hensingham Cumb 98 C1
Henstead Suff 69 F7
Henstridge Som 12 C5
Henstridge Ash Som 12 B5
Henstridge Marsh Som 12 B5
Henton Oxon 39 D7
Henton Som 23 E6
Henwood Corn 5 B7
Heogan Shetland 175 J6
Heol-las Swansea 33 E7
Heol Senni Powys 34 B3
Heol-y-Cyw Bridgend 34 F3
Hepburn Northumb 117 B6
Hepple Northumb 117 D5
Hepscott Northumb 117 F8
Heptonstall W Yorks 87 B7
Hepworth Suff 56 B3
Hepworth W Yorks 88 D2
Herbrandston Pembs 44 E3
Hereford Hereford 49 E7
Hereford Cathedral Hereford 49 F7
Hereford Racecourse Hereford 49 E7
Heritage Motor Centre, Gaydon Warks 51 D8
Hermiston Edin 122 B4
Hermitage Borders 115 E8
Hermitage Dorset 12 D4
Hermitage W Berks 26 B3
Hermitage W Sus 15 D8
Hermon Anglesey 82 E3
Hermon Carms 46 F2
Hermon Carms 33 B7
Hermon Pembs 45 F4
Herne Kent 31 C5
Herne Bay Kent 31 C5
Herner Devon 9 B7
Hernhill Kent 30 C4
Herodsfoot Corn 5 C7
Herongate Essex 42 E2
Heronsford S Ayrs 104 A5
Herriard Hants 26 E4
Herringfleet Suff 69 E7
Herringswell Suff 55 B8
Hersden Kent 31 C6
Hersham Corn 8 D4
Hersham Sur 28 C2
Herstmonceux E Sus 18 D3
Herston Orkney 176 G3
Hertford Herts 41 C6
Hertford Heath Herts 41 C6
Hertingfordbury Herts 41 C6
Hesket Newmarket Cumb 108 F3
Hesketh Bank Lancs 86 B2
Hesketh Lane Lancs 93 E6
Heskin Green Lancs 86 C3
Hesleden Durham 111 F7
Hesleyside Northumb 116 F4
Heslington York 96 D2
Hessay York 95 D8
Hessenford Corn 5 D8
Hessett Suff 56 C3
Hessle E Yorks 90 B4
Hest Bank Lancs 92 C4
Heston London 28 B2
Hestwall Orkney 176 E1
Heswall Mers 85 F3
Hethe Oxon 39 B5
Hethersett Norf 68 D4
Hethersgill Cumb 108 C4
Hethpool Northumb 116 B4
Hett Durham 111 F5
Hetton N Yorks 94 D2
Hetton-le-Hole T & W 111 E6
Hetton Steads Northumb 125 F6
Heugh Northumb 110 B3
Heugh-head Aberds 150 C2
Heveningham Suff 57 B7
Hever Kent 29 E5
Hever Castle and Gardens Kent 29 E5
Heversham Cumb 99 F6
Hevingham Norf 81 E7
Hewas Water Corn 3 B8
Hewelsfield Glos 36 D2
Hewish N Som 23 C6
Hewish Som 12 D2
Heworth York 96 D2
Hexham Northumb 110 C2
Hexham Abbey Northumb 110 C2
Hexham Racecourse Northumb 110 C2
Hextable Kent 29 B6
Hexton Herts 54 F2
Hexworthy Devon 6 B4
Hey Lancs 93 E8
Heybridge Essex 42 D4
Heybridge Essex 42 E2
Heybridge Basin Essex 42 D4
Heybrook Bay Devon 6 E3
Heydon Cambs 54 E5
Heydon Norf 81 E7
Heydour Lincs 78 F3
Heylipol Argyll 136 F1
Heylor Shetland 174 E4
Heysham Lancs 92 C4
Heyshott W Sus 16 C2
Heyside Gtr Man 87 D7
Heytesbury Wilts 24 E4
Heythrop Oxon 38 B3
Heywood Gtr Man 87 C6
Heywood Wilts 24 D3
Hibaldstow N Lincs 90 D3
Hickleton S Yorks 89 D5
Hickling Norf 69 B7
Hickling Notts 64 B3
Hickling Green Norf 69 B7
Hickling Heath Norf 69 B7
Hickstead W Sus 17 B6
Hidcote Boyce Glos 51 E6
Hidcote Manor Garden, Moreton-in-Marsh Glos 51 E6
High Ackworth W Yorks 88 C5
High Angerton Northumb 117 F6
High Bankhill Cumb 109 E5
High Barnes T & W 111 D6
High Beach Essex 41 E7
High Bentham N Yorks 93 C6
High Bickington Devon 9 B8
High Birkwith N Yorks 93 B7
High Blantyre S Lnrk 121 D6
High Bonnybridge Falk 121 B8
High Bradfield S Yorks 88 E3
High Bray Devon 21 F5
High Brooms Kent 29 E6
High Bullen Devon 9 B7
High Buston Northumb 117 D8
High Callerton Northumb 110 B4
High Catton E Yorks 96 D3
High Cogges Oxon 38 D3
High Coniscliffe Darl 101 C7
High Cross Hants 15 B8
High Cross Herts 41 C6
High Easter Essex 42 C2
High Eggborough N Yorks 89 B6
High Ellington N Yorks 101 F6
High Ercall Telford 61 C5
High Etherley Durham 101 B6
High Garrett Essex 42 B3
High Grange Durham 110 F4
High Green Norf 68 D4
High Green S Yorks 88 E4
High Green Worcs 50 E3
High Halden Kent 19 B5
High Halstow Medway 29 B8
High Ham Som 23 F6
High Harrington Cumb 98 B2
High Hatton Shrops 61 B6
High Hawsker N Yorks 103 D7
High Hesket Cumb 108 E4
High Hesleden Durham 111 F7
High Hoyland S Yorks 88 C3
High Hunsley E Yorks 97 F5
High Hurstwood E Sus 17 B8
High Hutton N Yorks 96 C3
High Ireby Cumb 108 F2
High Kelling Norf 81 C7
High Kilburn N Yorks 95 B8
High Lands Durham 101 B6
High Lane Gtr Man 87 F7
High Lane Hereford 49 C8
High Laver Essex 41 D8
High Legh Ches 86 F5
High Leven Stockton 102 C2
High Littleton Bath 23 D8
High Lorton Cumb 98 B3
High Marishes N Yorks 96 B4
High Marnham Notts 77 B8
High Melton S Yorks 89 D6
High Mickley Northumb 110 C3
High Mindork Dumfries 105 D7
High Moorland Visitor Centre, Princetown Devon 6 B3
High Newton Cumb 99 F6
High Newton-by-the-Sea Northumb 117 B8
High Nibthwaite Cumb 98 F4
High Offley Staffs 61 B7
High Ongar Essex 42 D1
High Onn Staffs 62 C2
High Roding Essex 42 C2
High Row Cumb 108 F3
High Salvington W Sus 16 D5
High Sellafield Cumb 98 D2
High Shaw N Yorks 100 E3
High Spen T & W 110 D4
High Stoop Durham 110 E4
High Street Corn 4 D4
High Street Kent 18 B4
High Street Suff 57 D8
High Street Suff 57 B8
High Street Suff 56 E2
High Street Green Suff 56 D4
High Throston Hrtlpl 111 F7
High Toynton Lincs 79 C5
High Trewhitt Northumb 117 D6
High Valleyfield Fife 134 F2
High Westwood Durham 110 D4
High Wray Cumb 99 E5
High Wych Herts 41 C7
High Wycombe Bucks 40 E1
Higham Derbys 76 D3
Higham Kent 29 B8
Higham Lancs 93 F8
Higham Suff 56 F4
Higham Suff 55 C8
Higham Dykes Northumb 110 B4
Higham Ferrers Northants 53 C7
Higham Gobion Beds 54 F2
Higham on the Hill Leics 63 E7
Higham Wood Kent 29 E6
Highampton Devon 9 D6
Highbridge Highld 146 F4
Highbridge Som 22 E5
Highbrook W Sus 28 F4
Highburton W Yorks 88 C2
Highbury Som 23 E8
Highclere Hants 26 C2
Highcliffe Dorset 14 E3
Higher Ansty Dorset 13 D5
Higher Ashton Devon 10 F3
Higher Ballam Lancs 92 F3
Higher Bartle Lancs 92 F5
Higher Boscaswell Corn 2 C2
Higher Burwardsley Ches 74 D2
Higher Clovelly Devon 8 B5
Higher End Gtr Man 86 D3
Higher Kinnerton Flint 73 C7
Higher Penwortham Lancs 86 B3
Higher Town Scilly 2 E4
Higher Walreddon Devon 6 B2
Higher Walton Lancs 86 B3
Higher Walton Warr 86 F3
Higher Wheelton Lancs 86 B4
Higher Whitley Ches 86 F4
Higher Wincham Ches 74 B3
Higher Wych Ches 73 E8
Highfield E Yorks 96 F3
Highfield Gtr Man 86 D5
Highfield N Ayrs 120 D3
Highfield Oxon 39 B5
Highfield S Yorks 88 F4
Highfield T & W 110 D4
Highfields Cambs 54 D4
Highfields Northumb 125 D5
Highgate London 41 F5
Highland Folk Museum, Aultlairie Highld 148 E3
Highland Folk Museum, Kingussie Highld 148 D3
Highlane Ches 75 C5
Highlane Derbys 88 F5
Highlaws Cumb 107 E8
Highleadon Glos 36 B4
Highleigh W Sus 16 E2
Highley Shrops 61 F7
Highmoor Cross Oxon 39 F7
Highmoor Hill Mon 36 F1
Highnam Glos 36 C4
Highnam Green Glos 36 B4
Highsted Kent 30 C3
Highstreet Green Essex 55 F8
Hightae Dumfries 107 B7
Hightown Ches 75 C5
Hightown Mers 85 D4
Hightown Green Suff 56 D3
Highway Wilts 24 B5
Highweek Devon 7 B6
Highworth Swindon 38 E2
Hilborough Norf 67 D8
Hilcote Derbys 76 D4
Hilcott Wilts 25 D6
Hilden Park Kent 29 E6
Hildenborough Kent 29 E6
Hildersham Cambs 55 E6
Hilderstone Staffs 75 F6
Hilderthorpe E Yorks 97 C7
Hilfield Dorset 12 D4
Hilgay Norf 67 E6
Hill Pembs 32 D2
Hill S Glos 36 E3
Hill W Mid 62 E5
Hill Brow W Sus 15 B8
Hill Dale Lancs 86 C2
Hill Dyke Lincs 79 E6
Hill End Durham 110 F3
Hill End Fife 134 E2
Hill End N Yorks 94 D3
Hill Head Hants 15 D6
Hill Head Northumb 110 C2
Hill Mountain Pembs 44 E4
Hill of Beath Fife 134 E3
Hill of Fearn Highld 158 B2
Hill of Mountblairy Aberds 160 C3
Hill Ridware Staffs 62 C4
Hill Top Durham 100 B4
Hill Top Hants 14 D5
Hill Top W Mid 62 E3
Hill Top W Yorks 88 C4
Hill Top, Sawrey Cumb 99 E5
Hill View Dorset 13 E7
Hillam N Yorks 89 B6
Hillbeck Cumb 100 C2
Hillborough Kent 31 C6
Hillbrae Aberds 151 B6
Hillbrae Aberds 160 D3
Hillbutts Dorset 13 D7
Hillclifflane Derbys 76 E2
Hillcommon Som 11 B6
Hillend Fife 134 F3
Hillerton Devon 10 E2
Hillesden Bucks 39 B6
Hillesley Glos 36 F4
Hillfarance Som 11 B6
Hillhead Aberds 160 E2
Hillhead Devon 7 D7
Hillhead S Ayrs 112 C4
Hillhead of Auchentumb Aberds 161 C6
Hillhead of Cocklaw Aberds 161 D7
Hillhouse Borders 123 D8
Hilliclay Highld 169 C6
Hillier Gardens and Arboretum Hants 14 B4
Hillingdon London 40 F3
Hillington Glasgow 120 C5
Hillington Norf 80 E3
Hillmorton Warks 52 B3
Hillockhead Aberds 150 C3
Hillockhead Aberds 150 D2
Hillside Aberds 151 E8
Hillside Angus 143 C7
Hillside Mers 85 C4
Hillside Orkney 176 G3
Hillside Shetland 175 G6
Hillswick Shetland 174 F4
Hillway I o W 15 F7
Hillwell Shetland 175 M5
Hilmarton Wilts 24 B5
Hilperton Wilts 24 D3
Hilsea Ptsmth 15 D7
Hilston E Yorks 97 F8
Hilton Aberds 161 E6
Hilton Cambs 54 C3
Hilton Cumb 100 B2
Hilton Derbys 76 F2
Hilton Dorset 13 D5
Hilton Durham 101 B6
Hilton Highld 164 F4
Hilton Shrops 61 E7
Hilton Stockton 102 C2
Hilton of Cadboll Highld 158 B2
Himbleton Worcs 50 D4
Himley Staffs 62 E2
Hincaster Cumb 99 F7
Hinckley Leics 63 E8
Hinderclay Suff 56 B4
Hinderton Ches 73 B7
Hinderwell N Yorks 103 C5
Hindford Shrops 73 F7
Hindhead Sur 27 F6
Hindley Gtr Man 86 D4
Hindley Green Gtr Man 86 D4
Hindlip Worcs 50 D3
Hindolveston Norf 81 E6
Hindon Wilts 24 F4
Hindringham Norf 81 D5
Hingham Norf 68 D3
Hinstock Shrops 61 B6
Hintlesham Suff 56 E4
Hinton Hants 14 E3
Hinton Hereford 48 F5
Hinton Northants 52 D3

Hinton Shrops 60 D4
Hinton S Glos 24 B2
Hinton Ampner Hants 15 B6
Hinton Blewett Bath 23 D7
Hinton Charterhouse Bath 24 D2
Hinton-in-the-Hedges Northants 52 F3
Hinton Martell Dorset 13 D8
Hinton on the Green Worcs 50 E5
Hinton Parva Swindon 38 F2
Hinton St George Som 12 C2
Hinton St Mary Dorset 13 C5
Hinton Waldrist Oxon 38 E3
Hints Shrops 49 B8
Hints Staffs 63 D5
Hinwick Beds 53 C7
Hinxhill Kent 30 E4
Hinxton Cambs 55 E5
Hinxworth Herts 54 E3
Hipperholme W Yorks 88 B2
Hipswell N Yorks 101 E6
Hirael Gwyn 83 D5
Hiraeth Carms 32 B2
Hirn Aberds 151 D6
Hirnant Powys 59 B7
Hirst N Lnrk 121 C8
Hirst Northumb 117 F8
Hirst Courtney N Yorks 89 B7
Hirwaen Denb 72 C5
Hirwaun Rhondda 34 D3
Hiscott Devon 9 B7
Histon Cambs 54 C5
Historic Royal Dockyard Ptsmth 15 D7
Hitcham Suff 56 D3
Hitchin Herts 40 B4
Hither Green London 28 B4
Hittisleigh Devon 10 E2
Hive E Yorks 96 F4
Hixon Staffs 62 B4
HMS Victory Ptsmth 15 D7
HMY Britannia Edin 123 B5
Hoaden Kent 31 D6
Hoaldalbert Mon 35 B7
Hoar Cross Staffs 62 B5
Hoarwithy Hereford 36 B2
Hoath Kent 31 C6
Hobarris Shrops 48 B5
Hobbister Orkney 176 F2
Hobkirk Borders 115 C8
Hobson Durham 110 D4
Hoby Leics 64 C3
Hockering Norf 68 C3
Hockerton Notts 77 D7
Hockley Essex 42 E4
Hockley Heath W Mid 51 B6
Hockliffe Beds 40 B2
Hockwold cum Wilton Norf 67 F7
Hockworthy Devon 10 C5
Hoddesdon Herts 41 D6
Hoddlesden Blkburn 86 B5
Hoddom Mains Dumfries 107 B8
Hoddomcross Dumfries 107 B8
Hodgeston Pembs 32 E1
Hodley Powys 59 E8
Hodnet Shrops 61 B6
Hodthorpe Derbys 76 B5
Hoe Hants 15 C6
Hoe Norf 68 C2
Hoe Gate Hants 15 C7
Hoff Cumb 100 C1
Hog Patch Sur 27 E6
Hoggard's Green Suff 56 D2
Hoggeston Bucks 39 B8
Hogha Gearraidh W Isles 170 C3
Hoghton Lancs 86 B4
Hognaston Derbys 76 D2
Hogsthorpe Lincs 79 B8
Holbeach Lincs 66 B3
Holbeach Bank Lincs 66 B3
Holbeach Clough Lincs 66 B3
Holbeach Drove Lincs 66 C3
Holbeach Hurn Lincs 66 B3
Holbeach St Johns Lincs 66 C3
Holbeach St Marks Lincs 79 F6
Holbeach St Matthew Lincs 79 F7
Holbeck Notts 76 B5
Holbeck W Yorks 95 F5
Holbeck Woodhouse Notts 76 B5
Holberrow Green Worcs 50 D5
Holbeton Devon 6 D4
Holborn London 41 F6
Holbrook Derbys 76 E3
Holbrook Suff 57 F5
Holbrook S Yorks 88 F5
Holburn Northumb 125 F6
Holbury Hants 14 D5
Holcombe Devon 7 B7
Holcombe Som 23 E8
Holcombe Rogus Devon 11 C5
Holcot Northants 53 C5
Holden Lancs 93 E7
Holdenby Northants 52 C4
Holdenhurst Bmouth 14 E2
Holdgate Shrops 61 F5
Holdingham Lincs 78 E3
Holditch Dorset 11 D8
Hole-in-the-Wall Hereford 36 B3
Holefield Borders 124 F4
Holehouses Ches 74 B4
Holemoor Devon 9 D6
Holestane Dumfries 113 E8
Holford Som 22 E3
Holgate York 95 D8
Holker Cumb 92 B3
Holkham Norf 80 C4
Hollacombe Devon 9 D5
Holland Orkney 176 A3
Holland Orkney 176 D5
Holland Fen Lincs 78 E5
Holland-on-Sea Essex 43 C8
Hollandstoun Orkney 176 A6
Hollee Dumfries 108 C2
Hollesley Suff 57 E7
Hollicombe Torbay 7 C6
Hollingbourne Kent 30 D2
Hollington Derbys 76 F2
Hollington E Sus 18 D4
Hollington Staffs 75 F7
Hollington Grove Derbys 76 F2
Hollingworth Gtr Man 87 E8
Hollins Gtr Man 87 D6
Hollins Green Warr 86 E4
Hollins Lane Lancs 92 D4
Hollinsclough Staffs 75 C7
Hollinwood Gtr Man 87 D7
Hollinwood Shrops 74 F2
Hollocombe Devon 9 C8
Hollow Meadows S Yorks 88 F3
Holloway Derbys 76 D3
Hollowell Northants 52 B4
Holly End Norf 66 D4
Holly Green Worcs 50 E3
Hollybush Caerph 35 D5
Hollybush E Ayrs 112 C3
Hollybush Worcs 50 F2
Hollym E Yorks 91 B7
Hollywood Worcs 51 B5
Holmbridge W Yorks 88 D2
Holmbury St Mary Sur 28 E2
Holmbush Corn 4 D5
Holmcroft Staffs 62 B3
Holme Cambs 65 F8
Holme Cumb 92 B5
Holme Notts 77 D8
Holme N Yorks 102 F1
Holme W Yorks 88 D2
Holme Chapel Lancs 87 B6
Holme Green N Yorks 95 E8
Holme Hale Norf 67 D8
Holme Lacy Hereford 49 F7
Holme Marsh Hereford 48 D5
Holme next the Sea Norf 80 C3
Holme-on-Spalding-Moor E Yorks 96 F4
Holme on the Wolds E Yorks 97 E5
Holme Pierrepont Notts 77 F6
Holme St Cuthbert Cumb 107 E8
Holme Wood W Yorks 94 F4
Holmer Hereford 49 E7
Holmer Green Bucks 40 E2
Holmes Chapel Ches 74 C4
Holmesfield Derbys 76 B3
Holmeswood Lancs 86 C2
Holmewood Derbys 76 C4
Holmfirth W Yorks 88 D2
Holmhead Dumfries 113 F7
Holmhead E Ayrs 113 B5
Holmisdale Highld 152 E2
Holmpton E Yorks 91 B7
Holmrook Cumb 98 E2
Holmsgarth Shetland 175 J6
Holmwrangle Cumb 108 E5
Holne Devon 6 C5
Holnest Dorset 12 D4
Holsworthy Devon 8 D5
Holsworthy Beacon Devon 9 D5
Holt Dorset 13 D8
Holt Norf 81 D6
Holt Wilts 24 C3
Holt Worcs 50 C3
Holt Wrex 73 D8
Holt End Hants 26 F4
Holt End Worcs 51 C5
Holt Fleet Worcs 50 C3
Holt Heath Worcs 50 C3
Holt Park W Yorks 95 E5
Holtby York 96 D2
Holton Oxon 39 D6
Holton Som 12 B4
Holton Suff 57 B7
Holton cum Beckering Lincs 90 F5
Holton Heath Dorset 13 E7
Holton le Clay Lincs 91 D6
Holton le Moor Lincs 90 E4
Holton St Mary Suff 56 F4
Holwell Dorset 12 C5
Holwell Herts 54 F2
Holwell Leics 64 B4
Holwell Oxon 38 D2
Holwick Durham 100 B4
Holworth Dorset 13 F5
Holy Cross Worcs 50 B4
Holy Island Northumb 125 E7
Holybourne Hants 26 E5
Holyhead = Caergybi Anglesey 82 C2
Holymoorside Derbys 76 C3
Holyport Windsor 27 B6
Holystone Northumb 117 D5
Holytown N Lnrk 121 C7
Holywell Cambs 54 B4
Holywell Corn 4 D2
Holywell Dorset 12 D3
Holywell E Sus 18 F2
Holywell Northumb 111 B6
Holywell = Treffynnon Flint 73 B5
Holywell Bay Fun Park, Newquay Corn 4 D2
Holywell Green W Yorks 87 C8
Holywell Lake Som 11 B6
Holywell Row Suff 55 B8
Holywood Dumfries 114 F2
Hom Green Hereford 36 B2
Homer Shrops 61 D6
Homersfield Suff 69 F5
Homington Wilts 14 B2
Honey Hill Kent 30 C5
Honey Street Wilts 25 C6
Honey Tye Suff 56 F3
Honeyborough Pembs 44 E4
Honeybourne Worcs 51 E6
Honeychurch Devon 9 D8
Honiley Warks 51 B7
Honing Norf 69 B6
Honingham Norf 68 C4
Honington Lincs 78 E2
Honington Suff 56 B3
Honington Warks 51 E7
Honiton Devon 11 D6
Honley W Yorks 88 C2
Hoo Green Ches 86 F5
Hoo St Werburgh Medway 29 B8
Hood Green S Yorks 88 D4
Hooe E Sus 18 E3
Hooe Plym 6 D3
Hooe Common E Sus 18 D3
Hook E Yorks 89 B8
Hook London 28 C2
Hook Hants 26 D5
Hook Pembs 44 D4
Hook Wilts 37 F7
Hook Green Kent 18 B3
Hook Green Kent 29 C7
Hook Norton Oxon 51 F8
Hooke Dorset 12 E3
Hookgate Staffs 74 F4
Hookway Devon 10 E3
Hookwood Sur 28 E3
Hoole Ches 73 C8
Hooley Sur 28 D3
Hoop Mon 36 D2
Hooton Ches 73 B7
Hooton Levitt S Yorks 89 E6
Hooton Pagnell S Yorks 89 D5
Hooton Roberts S Yorks 89 E5
Hop Pole Lincs 65 C8
Hope Derbys 88 F2
Hope Devon 6 F4
Hope Highld 167 D6
Hope Powys 60 D2
Hope Shrops 60 D3
Hope Staffs 75 D8
Hope = Yr Hôb Flint 73 D7
Hope Bagot Shrops 49 B7
Hope Bowdler Shrops 60 E4
Hope End Green Essex 42 B1
Hope Green Ches 87 F7
Hope Mansell Hereford 36 C3
Hope under Dinmore Hereford 49 D7
Hopeman Moray 158 C5
Hope's Green Essex 42 F3
Hopesay Shrops 60 F3
Hopley's Green Hereford 48 D5
Hopperton N Yorks 95 D7
Hopstone Shrops 61 E7
Hopton Shrops 60 B3
Hopton Shrops 61 B5
Hopton Staffs 62 B3
Hopton Suff 56 B3
Hopton Cangeford Shrops 60 F5
Hopton Castle Shrops 49 B5
Hopton on Sea Norf 69 D8
Hopton Wafers Shrops 49 B8
Hoptonheath Shrops 49 B5
Hopwas Staffs 63 D5
Hopwood Gtr Man 87 D6
Hopwood Worcs 50 B5
Horam E Sus 18 D2
Horbling Lincs 78 F4
Horbury W Yorks 88 C3
Horcott Glos 38 D1
Horden Durham 111 E7
Horderley Shrops 60 F4
Hordle Hants 14 E3
Hordley Shrops 73 F7
Horeb Ceredig 46 E2
Horeb Carms 33 D5
Horeb Carms 33 B6
Horfield Bristol 23 B8
Horham Suff 57 B6
Horkesley Heath Essex 43 B5
Horkstow N Lincs 90 C3
Horley Oxon 52 E2
Horley Sur 28 E3
Hornblotton Green Som 23 F7
Hornby Lancs 93 C5
Hornby N Yorks 101 E7
Hornby N Yorks 102 D1
Horncastle Lincs 79 C5
Hornchurch London 41 F8
Horncliffe Northumb 124 E5
Horndean Borders 124 E4
Horndean Hants 15 C8
Horndon Devon 6 B3
Horndon on the Hill Thurrock 42 F2
Horne Sur 28 E4
Horniehaugh Angus 142 C4
Horning Norf 69 C6
Horninghold Leics 64 E5
Horninglow Staffs 63 B6
Horningsea Cambs 55 C5
Horningsham Wilts 24 E3
Horningtoft Norf 80 E5
Horns Corner Kent 18 C4
Horns Cross Devon 9 B5
Horns Cross E Sus 18 C5
Hornsby Cumb 108 D5
Hornsea E Yorks 97 E8
Hornsea Bridge E Yorks 97 E8
Hornsey London 41 F6
Hornton Oxon 51 E8
Horrabridge Devon 6 C3
Horringer Suff 56 C2
Horringford I o W 15 F6
Horse Bridge Staffs 75 D6
Horsebridge Devon 6 B2
Horsebridge Hants 25 F8
Horsebrook Staffs 62 C2
Horsehay Telford 61 D6
Horseheath Cambs 55 E7
Horsehouse N Yorks 101 F5
Horsell Sur 27 D7
Horseman's Green Wrex 73 E8
Horseway Cambs 66 F4
Horsey Norf 69 B7
Horsford Norf 68 C4
Horsforth W Yorks 94 F5
Horsham Worcs 50 D2
Horsham W Sus 28 F2
Horsham St Faith Norf 68 C5
Horsington Lincs 78 C4
Horsington Som 12 B5
Horsley Derbys 76 E3
Horsley Glos 37 E5
Horsley Northumb 110 C3
Horsley Northumb 116 E4
Horsley Cross Essex 43 B7
Horsley Woodhouse Derbys 76 E3
Horsleycross Street Essex 43 B7
Horsleyhill Borders 115 C8
Horsleyhope Durham 110 E3
Horsmonden Kent 29 E7
Horspath Oxon 39 D5
Horstead Norf 69 C5
Horsted Keynes W Sus 17 B7
Horton Bucks 40 C2
Horton Dorset 13 D8
Horton Lancs 93 D8
Horton Northants 53 D6
Horton Shrops 60 B4
Horton S Glos 36 F4
Horton Som 11 C8
Horton Staffs 75 D6
Horton Swansea 33 F5
Horton Wilts 25 C5
Horton Windsor 27 B8
Horton-cum-Studley Oxon 39 C5
Horton Green Ches 73 E8
Horton Heath Hants 15 C5
Horton in Ribblesdale N Yorks 93 B8
Horton Kirby Kent 29 C6
Hortonlane Shrops 60 C4
Horwich Gtr Man 86 C4
Horwich End Derbys 87 F8
Horwood Devon 9 B7
Hose Leics 64 B4
Hoselaw Borders 124 F4
Hoses Cumb 98 E4
Hosh Perth 133 B7
Hosta W Isles 170 C3
Hoswick Shetland 175 L6
Hotham E Yorks 96 F4
Hothfield Kent 30 E3
Hoton Leics 64 B2
Houbie Shetland 174 D8
Houdston S Ayrs 112 E1
Hough Ches 74 D4
Hough Ches 75 B5
Hough Green Halton 86 F2
Hough-on-the-Hill Lincs 78 E2
Hougham Lincs 77 E8
Houghton Cambs 54 B3
Houghton Cumb 108 D4
Houghton Hants 25 F8
Houghton Pembs 44 E4
Houghton W Sus 16 C4
Houghton Conquest Beds 53 E8
Houghton Green E Sus 19 C6
Houghton Green Warr 86 E4
Houghton-le-Side Darl 101 B7
Houghton-Le-Spring T & W 111 E6
Houghton on the Hill Leics 64 D3
Houghton Regis Beds 40 B3
Houghton St Giles Norf 80 D5
Houlland Shetland 175 H5
Houlland Shetland 174 F7
Houlsyke N Yorks 103 D5
Hound Hants 15 D5
Hound Green Hants 26 D5
Houndslow Borders 124 E2
Houndwood Borders 124 C4
Hounslow London 28 B2
Hounslow Green Essex 42 C2
Housay Shetland 174 F8
House of Daviot Highld 157 E8
House of Glenmuick Aberds 150 E2
Housesteads Roman Fort Northumb 109 C7
Housetter Shetland 174 E5
Houss Shetland 175 K5
Houston Renfs 120 C4
Houstry Highld 169 F6
Houton Orkney 176 F2
Hove Brighton 17 D6
Hoveringham Notts 77 E6
Hoveton Norf 69 C6
Hovingham N Yorks 96 B2
How Cumb 108 D5
How Caple Hereford 49 F8
How End Beds 53 E8
How Green Kent 29 E5
Howbrook S Yorks 88 E4
Howden Borders 116 B2
Howden E Yorks 89 B8
Howden-le-Wear Durham 110 F4
Howe Highld 169 C8
Howe Norf 69 D5
Howe N Yorks 101 F8
Howe Bridge Gtr Man 86 D4
Howe Green Essex 42 D3
Howe of Teuchar Aberds 160 D4
Howe Street Essex 42 C2
Howe Street Essex 55 F7
Howell Lincs 78 E4
Howey Powys 48 D2
Howgate Midloth 122 D5
Howick Northumb 117 C8
Howle Durham 101 B5
Howle Telford 61 B6
Howlett End Essex 55 F6
Howley Som 11 D7
Hownam Borders 116 C3
Hownam Mains Borders 116 B3
Howpasley Borders 115 D6
Howsham N Lincs 90 D4
Howsham N Yorks 96 C3
Howslack Dumfries 114 D3
Howtel Northumb 124 F4
Howton Hereford 35 B8
Howtown Cumb 99 C6
Howwood Renfs 120 C3
Hoxne Suff 57 B5
Hoy Orkney 176 F1
Hoylake Mers 85 F3
Hoyland S Yorks 88 D4
Hoylandswaine S Yorks 88 D3
Hubberholme N Yorks 94 B2
Hubbert's Bridge Lincs 79 E5
Huby N Yorks 95 E5
Huby N Yorks 95 C8
Hucclecote Glos 37 C5
Hucking Kent 30 D2
Hucknall Notts 76 E5
Huddersfield W Yorks 88 C2
Huddington Worcs 50 D4
Hudswell N Yorks 101 D6
Huggate E Yorks 96 D4
Hugglescote Leics 63 C8
Hugh Town Scilly 2 E4
Hughenden Valley Bucks 40 E1
Hughley Shrops 61 E5
Huish Devon 9 C7
Huish Wilts 25 C6
Huish Champflower Som 11 B5
Huish Episcopi Som 12 B2
Huisinis W Isles 173 G2
Hulcott Bucks 40 C1
Hulland Derbys 76 E2
Hulland Ward Derbys 76 E2
Hullavington Wilts 37 F5
Hullbridge Essex 42 E4
Hulme Gtr Man 87 E6
Hulme End Staffs 75 D8
Hulme Walfield Ches 74 C5
Hulver Street Suff 69 F7
Hulverstone I o W 14 F4
Humber Hereford 49 D7
Humber Bridge E Yorks 90 B4
Humberside International Airport N Lincs 90 C4
Humberston NE Lincs 91 D7
Humbie E Loth 123 C7
Humbleton E Yorks 97 F8
Humbleton Northumb 117 B5
Humby Lincs 78 F3
Hume Borders 124 E3
Humshaugh Northumb 110 B2
Huna Highld 169 B8
Huncoat Lancs 93 F7
Huncote Leics 64 E2
Hundalee Borders 116 C2
Hunderthwaite Durham 100 B4
Hundle Houses Lincs 79 D5
Hundleby Lincs 79 C6
Hundleton Pembs 44 E4
Hundon Suff 55 E8
Hundred Acres Hants 15 C6
Hundred End Lancs 86 B2
Hundred House Powys 48 D3
Hungarton Leics 64 D3
Hungerford Hants 14 C2
Hungerford W Berks 25 C8
Hungerford Newtown W Berks 25 B8
Hungerton Lincs 65 B5
Hungladder Highld 152 B4
Hunmanby N Yorks 97 B6
Hunmanby Moor N Yorks 97 B7
Hunningham Warks 51 C8
Hunny Hill I o W 15 F5
Hunsdon Herts 41 C7
Hunsingore N Yorks 95 D7
Hunslet W Yorks 95 F6
Hunsonby Cumb 109 F5
Hunspow Highld 169 B7
Hunstanton Norf 80 C2
Hunstanworth Durham 110 E2
Hunsterson Ches 74 E3
Hunston Suff 56 C3
Hunston W Sus 16 D2
Hunstrete Bath 23 C8
Hunt End Worcs 50 C5
Hunter's Quay Argyll 129 C6
Hunthill Lodge Angus 142 B4
Hunting-tower Perth 134 B2
Huntingdon Cambs 54 B3
Huntingdon Racecourse Cambs 54 B3
Huntingfield Suff 57 B7
Huntingford Dorset 24 F3
Huntington E Loth 123 B7
Huntington Hereford 48 D4
Huntington Staffs 62 C3
Huntington York 96 D2
Huntley Glos 36 C4
Huntly Aberds 160 E2
Huntlywood Borders 124 E2
Hunton Kent 29 E8
Hunton N Yorks 101 E6
Hunt's Corner Norf 68 F3
Hunt's Cross Mers 86 F2
Huntsham Devon 10 B5
Huntspill Som 22 E5
Huntworth Som 22 F5
Hunwick Durham 110 F4
Hunworth Norf 81 D6
Hurdsfield Ches 75 B6
Hurley Warks 63 E6
Hurley Windsor 39 F8
Hurlford E Ayrs 120 F4
Hurliness Orkney 176 H1
Hurn Dorset 14 E2
Hurn's End Lincs 79 E7
Hursley Hants 14 B5
Hurst N Yorks 101 D5
Hurst Som 12 C2
Hurst Wokingham 27 B5
Hurst Green E Sus 18 C4
Hurst Green Lancs 93 F6
Hurst Wickham W Sus 17 C6
Hurstbourne Priors Hants 26 E2
Hurstbourne Tarrant Hants 25 D8
Hurstpierpoint W Sus 17 C6
Hurstwood Lancs 93 F8
Hurtmore Sur 27 E7
Hurworth Place Darl 101 D7
Hury Durham 100 C4
Husabost Highld 152 D3
Husbands Bosworth Leics 64 F3
Husborne Crawley Beds 53 F7
Husthwaite N Yorks 95 B8
Hutchwns Bridgend 21 B7
Huthwaite Notts 76 D4
Huttoft Lincs 79 B8
Hutton Borders 124 D5
Hutton Cumb 99 B6
Hutton E Yorks 97 D6
Hutton Essex 42 E2
Hutton Lancs 86 B2
Hutton N Som 22 D5
Hutton Buscel N Yorks 103 F7
Hutton Conyers N Yorks 95 B6
Hutton Cranswick E Yorks 97 D6
Hutton End Cumb 108 F4
Hutton Gate Redcar 102 C3
Hutton Henry Durham 111 F7
Hutton-le-Hole N Yorks 103 E5
Hutton Magna Durham 101 C6
Hutton Roof Cumb 108 F3
Hutton Roof Cumb 93 B5
Hutton Rudby N Yorks 102 D2
Hutton Sessay N Yorks 95 B7
Hutton Village Redcar 102 C3
Hutton Wandesley N Yorks 95 D8
Huxley Ches 74 C2
Huxter Shetland 175 H5
Huxter Shetland 175 G7
Huxton Borders 124 C4
Huyton Mers 86 E2
Hwlffordd = Haverfordwest Pembs 44 D4
Hycemoor Cumb 98 F2
Hyde Glos 37 D5
Hyde Gtr Man 87 E7
Hyde Hants 14 C2
Hyde Heath Bucks 40 D2
Hyde Park S Yorks 89 D6
Hydestile Sur 27 E7
Hylton Castle T & W 111 D6
Hyndford Bridge S Lnrk 122 E2
Hynish Argyll 136 G1
Hyssington Powys 60 E3
Hythe Hants 14 D5
Hythe Kent 19 B8
Hythe End Windsor 27 B8
Hythie Aberds 161 C7

I

Ibberton Dorset 13 D5
Ible Derbys 76 D2
Ibsley Hants 14 D2
Ibstock Leics 63 C8
Ibstone Bucks 39 E7
Ibthorpe Hants 25 D8
Ibworth Hants 26 D3
Ichrachan Argyll 131 B6
Ickburgh Norf 67 E8
Ickenham London 40 F3
Ickford Bucks 39 D6
Ickham Kent 31 D6
Ickleford Herts 54 F2
Icklesham E Sus 19 D5
Ickleton Cambs 55 E5
Icklingham Suff 55 B8
Ickwell Green Beds 54 E2
Ickworth House Suff 56 C2
Icomb Glos 38 B2
Idbury Oxon 38 C2
Iddesleigh Devon 9 D7
Ide Devon 10 E3
Ide Hill Kent 29 D5
Ideford Devon 7 B6
Iden E Sus 19 C6
Iden Green Kent 18 B4
Iden Green Kent 18 B5
Idle W Yorks 94 F4
Idlicote Warks 51 E7
Idmiston Wilts 25 F6
Idole Carms 33 C5
Idridgehay Derbys 76 E2
Idrigill Highld 152 C4
Idstone Oxon 38 F2
Idvies Angus 143 E5
Iffley Oxon 39 D5
Ifield W Sus 28 F3
Ifold W Sus 27 F8
Iford E Sus 17 D8
Ifton Heath Shrops 73 F7
Ightfield Shrops 74 F2
Ightham Kent 29 D6
Ightham Mote, Sevenoaks Kent 29 D6
Iken Suff 57 D8
Ilam Staffs 75 D8
Ilchester Som 12 B3
Ilderton Northumb 117 B6
Ilford London 41 F7
Ilfracombe Devon 20 E4
Ilkeston Derbys 76 E4
Ilketshall St Andrew Suff 69 F6
Ilketshall St Lawrence Suff 69 F6
Ilketshall St Margaret Suff 69 F6
Ilkley W Yorks 94 E4
Illey W Mid 62 F3
Illingworth W Yorks 87 B8
Illogan Corn 3 B5
Illston on the Hill Leics 64 E4
Ilmer Bucks 39 D7
Ilmington Warks 51 E7
Ilminster Som 11 C8
Ilsington Devon 7 B5
Ilston Swansea 33 E6
Ilton N Yorks 94 B4
Ilton Som 11 C8
Imachar N Ayrs 119 B5
Imeraval Argyll 126 E3
Immingham NE Lincs 91 C5
Imperial War Museum London 28 B4
Imperial War Museum North Gtr Man 87 E5
Impington Cambs 54 C5
Ince Ches 73 B8
Ince Blundell Mers 85 D4
Ince in Makerfield Gtr Man 86 D3
Inch of Arnhall Aberds 143 B6
Inchbare Angus 143 C6
Inchberry Moray 159 D7
Inchbraoch Angus 143 D7
Incheril Highld 154 D6
Inchgrundle Angus 142 B4
Inchina Highld 162 E3
Inchinnan Renfs 120 C4
Inchkinloch Highld 167 E7
Inchlaggan Highld 146 D4
Inchlumpie Highld 157 B6
Inchmore Highld 156 E4
Inchnacardoch Hotel Highld 147 C6
Inchnadamph Highld 163 B6
Inchree Highld 138 C4
Inchture Perth 134 B4
Inchyra Perth 134 B3
Indian Queens Corn 4 D4
Inerval Argyll 126 E3
Ingatestone Essex 42 E2
Ingbirchworth S Yorks 88 D3
Ingestre Staffs 62 B3
Ingham Lincs 90 F3
Ingham Norf 69 B6
Ingham Suff 56 B2
Ingham Corner Norf 69 B6
Ingleborough Norf 66 C4
Ingleby Derbys 63 B7
Ingleby Lincs 77 B8
Ingleby Arncliffe N Yorks 102 D2
Ingleby Barwick Stockton 102 C2
Ingleby Greenhow N Yorks 102 D3
Inglemire Hull 97 F6
Inglesbatch Bath 24 C2
Inglesham Swindon 38 E2
Ingleton Durham 101 B6
Ingleton N Yorks 93 B6
Inglewhite Lancs 92 E5
Ingliston Edin 122 B4
Ingoe Northumb 110 B3
Ingol Lancs 92 F5
Ingoldisthorpe Norf 80 D2
Ingoldmells Lincs 79 C8
Ingoldsby Lincs 78 F3
Ingon Warks 51 D7
Ingram Northumb 117 C6
Ingrave Essex 42 E2
Ingrow W Yorks 94 F3
Ings Cumb 99 E6
Ingst S Glos 36 F2
Ingworth Norf 81 E7
Inham's End Cambs 66 E2
Inkberrow Worcs 50 D5
Inkpen W Berks 25 C8
Inkstack Highld 169 B7
Inn Cumb 99 D6
Innellan Argyll 129 C6
Innerleithen Borders 123 F6
Innerleven Fife 135 D5
Innermessan Dumfries 104 C4
Innerwick E Loth 124 B3
Innerwick Perth 140 E2
Innis Chonain Argyll 131 C7
Insch Aberds 150 B5
Insh Highld 148 D4
Inshore Highld 166 C5
Inskip Lancs 92 F4
Instoneville S Yorks 89 C6
Instow Devon 20 F3
Intake S Yorks 89 D6
Inver Aberds 149 E8
Inver Highld 165 F5
Inver Perth 141 E7
Inver Mallie Highld 146 F4
Inverailort Highld 145 E7
Inveraldie Angus 142 F4
Inveralligin Highld 154 E4
Inverallochy Aberds 161 B7
Inveran Highld 164 E2
Inveraray Argyll 131 E6
Inveraray Jail Argyll 131 E6
Inverarish Highld 153 F6
Inverarity Angus 142 E4
Inverarnan Stirl 132 C2
Inverasdale Highld 154 B4
Inverbeg Argyll 132 E2
Inverbervie Aberds 143 B8
Inverboyndie Aberds 160 B3
Inverbroom Highld 163 F5
Invercassley Highld 164 D1
Invercauld House Aberds 149 E7
Inverchaolain Argyll 129 C5
Invercharnan Highld 139 E5
Inverchoran Highld 156 D3
Invercreran Argyll 138 E4
Inverdruie Highld 148 C5
Inverebrie Aberds 161 E6
Invereck Argyll 129 B6
Inverernan Ho. Aberds 150 C2
Invereshie House Highld 148 D4
Inveresk E Loth 123 B6
Inverewe Gardens, Gairloch Highld 154 B4
Inverey Aberds 149 F6
Inverfarigaig Highld 147 B8
Invergarry Highld 147 D6
Invergelder Aberds 149 E8
Invergeldie Perth 133 B6
Invergordon Highld 157 C8
Invergowrie Perth 142 F3
Inverguseran Highld 145 C7
Inverhadden Perth 140 D3
Inverharroch Moray 159 F7
Inverherive Stirl 132 B2
Inverie Highld 145 D7
Inverinan Argyll 131 D5
Inverinate Highld 146 B2
Inverkeilor Angus 143 E6
Inverkeithing Fife 134 F3
Inverkeithny Aberds 160 D3
Inverkip Inverclyd 129 C7
Inverkirkaig Highld 162 C4
Inverlael Highld 163 F5
Inverlochlarig Stirl 132 C3
Inverlochy Argyll 131 C7
Inverlochy Highld 139 B5
Inverlussa Argyll 127 D4
Invermark Lodge Angus 150 F3
Invermoidart Highld 145 F6
Invermoriston Highld 147 C7
Invernaver Highld 168 C2
Inverneill Argyll 128 B3
Inverness Highld 157 E7
Inverness Airport Highld 157 D8
Invernettie Aberds 161 D8
Invernoaden Argyll 131 F7
Inveroran Hotel Argyll 139 E6
Inverpolly Lodge Highld 162 C4
Inverquharity Angus 142 D4
Inverquhomery Aberds 161 D7
Inverroy Highld 147 F5
Inversanda Highld 138 D3
Invershiel Highld 146 C2
Invershin Highld 164 E2
Inversnaid Hotel Stirl 132 D2
Inverugie Aberds 161 D8
Inveruglas Argyll 132 D2
Inveruglass Highld 148 D4
Inverurie Aberds 151 B6
Invervar Perth 140 E3
Inverythan Aberds 160 D4
Inwardleigh Devon 9 E7
Inworth Essex 42 C4
Iochdar W Isles 170 F3
Iona Abbey and Cathedral Argyll 136 F3
Iping W Sus 16 B2
Ipplepen Devon 7 C6
Ipsden Oxon 39 F6
Ipsley Worcs 51 C5
Ipstones Staffs 75 D7
Ipswich Suff 57 E5
Irby Mers 85 F3
Irby in the Marsh Lincs 79 C7
Irby upon Humber NE Lincs 91 D5
Irchester Northants 53 C7
Ireby Cumb 108 F2
Ireby Lancs 93 B6
Ireland Orkney 176 F2
Ireland Shetland 175 L5
Ireland's Cross Shrops 74 E4
Ireleth Cumb 92 B2
Ireshopeburn Durham 109 F8
Irlam Gtr Man 86 E5
Irnham Lincs 65 B7
Iron Acton S Glos 36 F3
Iron Cross Warks 51 D5
Ironbridge Telford 61 D6
Ironbridge Gorge Museum, Telford Shrops 61 D6
Irongray Dumfries 107 B6
Ironmacannie Dumfries 106 B3
Ironside Aberds 161 C5
Ironville Derbys 76 D4
Irstead Norf 69 B6
Irthington Cumb 108 C4
Irthlingborough Northants 53 B7
Irton N Yorks 103 F8
Irvine N Ayrs 120 F3
Isauld Highld 168 C4
Isbister Orkney 176 D1
Isbister Orkney 176 E2
Isbister Shetland 174 D5
Isbister Shetland 175 G7
Isfield E Sus 17 C8

Isham Northants 53 B6
Islay Airport Argyll 126 D3
Isle Abbotts Som 11 B8
Isle Brewers Som 11 B8
Isle of Man Airport I o M 84 F2
Isle of Man Steam Railway I o M 84 F1
Isle of Whithorn Dumfries 105 F8
Isleham Cambs 55 B7
Isleornsay Highld 145 B7
Islesburgh Shetland 174 G5
Islesteps Dumfries 107 B6
Isleworth London 28 B2
Isley Walton Leics 63 B8
Islibhig W Isles 172 F2
Islington London 41 F6
Islip Northants 53 B7
Islip Oxon 39 C5
Istead Rise Kent 29 C7
Isycoed Wrex 73 D8
Itchen Soton 14 C5
Itchen Abbas Hants 26 F3
Itchen Stoke Hants 26 F3
Itchingfield W Sus 16 B5
Itchington S Glos 36 F3
Itteringham Norf 81 D7
Itton Devon 9 E8
Itton Common Mon 36 E1
Ivegill Cumb 108 E4
Iver Bucks 40 F3
Iver Heath Bucks 40 F3
Iveston Durham 110 D4
Ivinghoe Bucks 40 C2
Ivinghoe Aston Bucks 40 C2
Ivington Hereford 49 D6
Ivington Green Hereford 49 D6
Ivy Chimneys Essex 41 D7
Ivy Cross Dorset 13 B6
Ivy Hatch Kent 29 D6
Ivybridge Devon 6 D4
Ivychurch Kent 19 C7
Iwade Kent 30 C3
Iwerne Courtney or Shroton Dorset 13 C6
Iwerne Minster Dorset 13 C6
Ixworth Suff 56 B3
Ixworth Thorpe Suff 56 B3

J

Jack Hill N Yorks 94 D5
Jack in the Green Devon 10 E5
Jacksdale Notts 76 D4
Jackstown Aberds 160 E4
Jacobstow Corn 8 E3
Jacobstowe Devon 9 D7
Jameston Pembs 32 E1
Jamestown Dumfries 115 E6
Jamestown Highld 157 D5
Jamestown W Dunb 132 F2
Jarlshof Prehistoric Site Shetland 175 M5
Jarrow T & W 111 C6
Jarvis Brook E Sus 18 C2
Jasper's Green Essex 42 B3
Java Argyll 130 B3
Jawcraig Falk 121 B8
Jaywick Essex 43 C7
Jealott's Hill Brack 27 B6
Jedburgh Borders 116 B2
Jeffreyston Pembs 32 D1
Jellyhill E Dunb 121 B6
Jemimaville Highld 157 C8
Jersey Airport Jersey 17
Jersey Farm Herts 40 D4
Jersey Zoo & Wildlife Park Jersey 17
Jesmond T & W 111 C5
Jevington E Sus 18 E2
Jockey End Herts 40 C3
Jodrell Bank Visitor Centre, Holmes Chapel Ches 74 B4
John o'Groats Highld 169 B8
Johnby Cumb 108 F4
John's Cross E Sus 18 C4
Johnshaven Aberds 143 C7
Johnston Pembs 44 D4
Johnstone Renfs 120 C4
Johnstonebridge Dumfries 114 E3
Johnstown Carms 33 C5
Johnstown Wrex 73 E7
Joppa Edin 123 B6
Joppa S Ayrs 112 C4
Jordans Bucks 40 E2
Jordanthorpe S Yorks 88 F4
Jorvik Centre York 96 D2
Judges Lodging, Presteigne Powys 48 C5
Jump S Yorks 88 D4
Jumpers Green Dorset 14 E2
Juniper Green Edin 122 C4
Jurby East I o M 84 C3
Jurby South Motor Racing Circuit I o M 84 C3
Jurby West I o M 84 C3

K

Kaber Cumb 100 C2
Kaimend S Lnrk 122 E2
Kaimes Edin 123 C5
Kalemouth Borders 116 B3
Kames Argyll 128 C4
Kames Argyll 130 D4
Kames E Ayrs 113 B6
Kea Corn 3 B7
Keadby N Lincs 90 C2
Keal Cotes Lincs 79 C6
Kearsley Gtr Man 87 D5
Kearstwick Cumb 99 F8
Kearton N Yorks 100 E4
Kearvaig Highld 166 B4
Keasden N Yorks 93 C7
Keckwick Halton 86 F3
Keddington Lincs 91 F7
Kedington Suff 55 E8
Kedleston Derbys 76 E3
Kedleston Hall Derbys 76 E3
Keelby Lincs 91 C5
Keele Staffs 74 E5
Keeley Green Beds 53 E8
Keeston Pembs 44 D4
Keevil Wilts 24 D4
Kegworth Leics 63 B8
Kehelland Corn 2 B5
Keig Aberds 150 C5
Keighley W Yorks 94 E3
Keighley and Worth Valley Railway W Yorks 94 F3
Keil Highld 138 D3
Keilarsbrae Clack 133 E7
Keilhill Aberds 160 C4
Keillmore Argyll 128 B1
Keillor Perth 142 E2
Keillour Perth 133 B8
Keills Argyll 126 C4
Keils Argyll 127 F3
Keinton Mandeville Som 23 F7
Keir Mill Dumfries 113 E8
Keisby Lincs 65 B7
Keiss Highld 169 C8
Keith Moray 159 D8
Keith Inch Aberds 161 D8
Keithock Angus 143 C6
Kelbrook Lancs 94 E2
Kelby Lincs 78 E3
Keld Cumb 99 C7
Keld N Yorks 100 D3
Keldholme N Yorks 103 F5
Kelfield N Lincs 90 D2
Kelfield N Yorks 95 F8
Kelham Notts 77 D7
Kellan Argyll 137 D6
Kellas Angus 142 F4
Kellas Moray 159 D5
Kellaton Devon 7 F6
Kelleth Cumb 100 D1
Kelleythorpe E Yorks 97 D5
Kelling Norf 81 C6
Kellingley N Yorks 89 B6
Kellington N Yorks 89 B6
Kelloe Durham 111 F6
Kelloholm Dumfries 113 C7
Kelly Devon 9 F5
Kelly Bray Corn 5 B8
Kelmarsh Northants 52 B5
Kelmscot Oxon 38 E2
Kelsale Suff 57 C7
Kelsall Ches 74 C2
Kelsall Hill Ches 74 C2
Kelshall Herts 54 F4
Kelsick Cumb 107 D8
Kelso Borders 124 F3
Kelso Racecourse Borders 124 F3
Kelstedge Derbys 76 C3
Kelstern Lincs 91 E6
Kelston Bath 24 C2
Keltneyburn Perth 140 E4
Kelton Dumfries 107 B6
Kelty Fife 134 E3
Kelvedon Essex 42 C4
Kelvedon Hatch Essex 42 E1
Kelvin S Lnrk 121 D6
Kelvinside Glasgow 121 C5
Kelynack Corn 2 C2
Kemback Fife 135 C6
Kemberton Shrops 61 D7
Kemble Glos 37 E6
Kemerton Worcs 50 F4
Kemeys Commander Mon 35 D7
Kemnay Aberds 151 C6
Kemp Town Brighton 17 D7
Kempley Glos 36 B3
Kemps Green Warks 51 B6
Kempsey Worcs 50 E3
Kempsford Glos 38 E1
Kempshott Hants 26 D4
Kempston Beds 53 E8
Kempston Hardwick Beds 53 E8
Kempton Shrops 60 F3
Kempton Park Racecourse Sur 28 B2
Kemsing Kent 29 D6
Kemsley Kent 30 C3
Kenardington Kent 19 B6
Kenchester Hereford 49 E6
Kencot Oxon 38 D2
Kendal Cumb 99 E7
Kendoon Dumfries 113 F6
Kendray S Yorks 88 D4
Kenfig Bridgend 34 F2
Kenfig Hill Bridgend 34 F2
Kenilworth Warks 51 B7
Kenilworth Castle Warks 51 B7
Kenknock Stirl 140 F1
Kenley London 28 D4
Kenley Shrops 61 D5
Kenmore Highld 154 E3
Kenmore Perth 140 E4
Kenn Devon 10 F4
Kenn N Som 23 C6
Kennacley W Isles 173 J4
Kennacraig Argyll 128 D3
Kennerleigh Devon 10 D3
Kennet Clack 133 E8
Kennethmont Aberds 150 B4
Kennett Cambs 55 C7
Kennford Devon 10 F4
Kenninghall Norf 68 F3
Kenninghall Heath Norf 68 F3
Kennington Kent 30 E4
Kennington Oxon 39 D5
Kennoway Fife 135 D5
Kenny Hill Suff 55 B7
Kennythorpe N Yorks 96 C3
Kenovay Argyll 136 F1
Kensaleyre Highld 152 D5
Kensington London 28 B3
Kensworth Beds 40 C3
Kensworth Common Beds 40 C3
Kent International Airport Kent 31 C7
Kent Street E Sus 18 D4
Kent Street Kent 29 D7
Kent Street W Sus 17 B6
Kentallen Highld 138 D4
Kentchurch Hereford 35 B8
Kentford Suff 55 C8
Kentisbeare Devon 11 D5
Kentisbury Devon 20 E5
Kentisbury Ford Devon 20 E5
Kentmere Cumb 99 D6
Kenton Devon 10 F4
Kenton Suff 57 C5
Kenton T & W 110 C5
Kenton Bankfoot T & W 110 C5
Kentra Highld 137 B7
Kents Bank Cumb 92 B3
Kent's Green Glos 36 B4
Kent's Oak Hants 14 B4
Kenwick Shrops 73 F8
Kenwyn Corn 3 B7
Keoldale Highld 167 C5
Keppanach Highld 138 C4
Keppoch Highld 146 B2
Keprigan Argyll 118 E3
Kepwick N Yorks 102 E2
Kerchesters Borders 124 F3
Keresley W Mid 63 F7
Kernborough Devon 7 E5
Kerne Bridge Hereford 36 C2
Kerris Corn 2 D3
Kerry Powys 59 F8
Kerrycroy Argyll 129 D6
Kerry's Gate Hereford 49 F5
Kerrysdale Highld 154 C4
Kersall Notts 77 C7
Kersey Suff 56 E4
Kershopefoot Cumb 115 F7
Kersoe Worcs 50 F4
Kerswell Devon 11 D5
Kerswell Green Worcs 50 E3
Kesgrave Suff 57 E6
Kessingland Suff 69 F8
Kessingland Beach Suff 69 F8
Kessington E Dunb 121 B5
Kestle Corn 3 B8
Kestle Mill Corn 4 D3
Keston London 28 C5
Keswick Cumb 98 B4
Keswick Norf 68 D5
Keswick Norf 81 D9
Ketley Telford 61 C6
Ketley Bank Telford 61 C6
Ketsby Lincs 79 B6
Kettering Northants 53 B6
Ketteringham Norf 68 D4
Kettins Perth 142 F2
Kettlebaston Suff 56 D3
Kettlebridge Fife 134 D5
Kettleburgh Suff 57 C6
Kettlehill Fife 134 D5
Kettleholm Dumfries 107 B8
Kettleness N Yorks 103 C6
Kettleshume Ches 75 B6
Kettlesing Bottom N Yorks 94 D5
Kettlesing Head N Yorks 94 D5
Kettlestone Norf 81 D5
Kettlethorpe Lincs 77 B8
Kettletoft Orkney 176 C5
Kettlewell N Yorks 94 B2
Ketton Rutland 65 D6
Kew London 28 B2
Kew Br. London 28 B2
Kew Gardens London 28 B2
Kewstoke N Som 22 C5
Kexbrough S Yorks 88 D4
Kexby Lincs 90 F2
Kexby York 96 D3
Key Green Ches 75 C5
Keyham Leics 64 D3
Keyhaven Hants 14 E4
Keyingham E Yorks 91 B6
Keymer W Sus 17 C7
Keynsham Bath 23 C8
Keysoe Beds 53 C8
Keysoe Row Beds 53 C8
Keyston Cambs 53 B8
Keyworth Notts 77 F6
Kibblesworth T & W 110 D5
Kibworth Beauchamp Leics 64 E3
Kibworth Harcourt Leics 64 E3
Kidbrooke London 28 B5
Kiddemore Green Staffs 62 D2
Kidderminster Worcs 50 B3
Kiddington Oxon 38 B4
Kidlington Oxon 38 C4
Kidmore End Oxon 26 B4
Kidsgrove Staffs 74 D5
Kidstones N Yorks 100 F4
Kidwelly = Cydweli Carms 33 D5
Kiel Crofts Argyll 130 B5
Kielder Northumb 116 E2
Kielder Castle Visitor Centre Northumb 116 E2
Kierfiold Ho. Orkney 176 E1
Kilbagie Clack 133 F8
Kilbarchan Renfs 120 C4
Kilbeg Highld 145 C6
Kilberry Argyll 128 D2
Kilbirnie N Ayrs 120 D3
Kilbride Argyll 130 C4
Kilbride Argyll 130 C5
Kilbride Highld 153 G6
Kilburn Angus 142 C3
Kilburn Derbys 76 E3
Kilburn London 41 F5
Kilburn N Yorks 95 B8
Kilby Leics 64 E3
Kilchamaig Argyll 128 D3
Kilchattan Argyll 127 C1
Kilchattan Bay Argyll 129 E6
Kilchenzie Argyll 118 D3
Kilcheran Argyll 130 B4
Kilchiaran Argyll 126 C2
Kilchoan Argyll 130 D3
Kilchoan Highld 137 B5
Kilchoman Argyll 126 C2
Kilchrenan Argyll 131 C6
Kilconquhar Fife 135 D6
Kilcot Glos 36 B3
Kilcoy Highld 157 D6
Kilcreggan Argyll 129 B7
Kildale N Yorks 102 D4
Kildalloig Argyll 118 E4
Kildary Highld 157 B8
Kildermorie Lodge Highld 157 B6
Kildonan N Ayrs 119 D7
Kildonan Lodge Highld 165 B6
Kildonnan Highld 144 E4
Kildrummy Aberds 150 C3
Kildwick N Yorks 94 E3
Kilfinan Argyll 128 C4
Kilfinnan Highld 147 E5
Kilgetty Pembs 32 D2
Kilgwrrwg Common Mon 36 E1
Kilham E Yorks 97 C6
Kilham Northumb 124 F4
Kilkenneth Argyll 136 F1
Kilkerran Argyll 118 E4
Kilkhampton Corn 8 C4
Killamarsh Derbys 89 F5
Killay Swansea 33 E7
Killbeg Argyll 137 D7
Killean Argyll 118 B3
Killearn Stirl 132 F4
Killen Highld 157 D7
Killerby Darl 101 C6
Killerton House, Exeter Devon 10 D4
Killichonan Perth 140 D2
Killiechonate Highld 146 F5
Killiechronan Argyll 137 D6
Killiecrankie Perth 141 C6
Killiemor Argyll 137 E5
Killiemore House Argyll 137 F5
Killilan Highld 155 G5
Killimster Highld 169 D8
Killin Stirl 140 F2
Killin Lodge Highld 147 D8
Killinallan Argyll 126 B3
Killinghall N Yorks 95 D5
Killington Cumb 99 F8
Killingworth T & W 111 B5
Killmahumaig Argyll 128 A2
Killochyett Borders 123 E7
Killocraw Argyll 118 C3
Killundine Highld 137 D6
Kilmacolm Invclyd 120 C3
Kilmaha Argyll 130 E5
Kilmahog Stirl 132 D5
Kilmalieu Highld 138 D2
Kilmaluag Highld 152 B5
Kilmany Fife 135 B5
Kilmarie Highld 153 H6
Kilmarnock E Ayrs 120 F4
Kilmaron Castle Fife 135 C5
Kilmartin Argyll 130 F4
Kilmaurs E Ayrs 120 E4
Kilmelford Argyll 130 D4
Kilmeny Argyll 126 C3
Kilmersdon Som 23 D8
Kilmeston Hants 15 B6
Kilmichael Argyll 118 D3
Kilmichael Glassary Argyll 128 A3
Kilmichael of Inverlussa Argyll 128 B2
Kilmington Devon 11 E7
Kilmington Wilts 24 F2
Kilmonivaig Highld 146 F4
Kilmorack Highld 157 E5
Kilmore Argyll 130 C4
Kilmore Highld 145 C6
Kilmory Argyll 128 C2
Kilmory Highld 137 A6
Kilmory Highld 144 C3
Kilmory N Ayrs 119 D6
Kilmuir Highld 152 E3
Kilmuir Highld 157 E7
Kilmuir Highld 157 B8
Kilmuir Highld 152 B4
Kilmun Argyll 129 B6
Kilmun Argyll 130 D5
Kiln Pit Hill Northumb 110 D3
Kilncadzow S Lnrk 121 E8
Kilndown Kent 18 B4
Kilnhurst S Yorks 89 E5
Kilninian Argyll 136 D4
Kilninver Argyll 130 C4
Kilnsea E Yorks 91 C8
Kilnsey N Yorks 94 C2
Kilnwick E Yorks 97 E5
Kilnwick Percy E Yorks 96 D4
Kiloran Argyll 127 C1
Kilpatrick N Ayrs 119 D6
Kilpeck Hereford 49 F6
Kilphedir Highld 165 C6
Kilpin E Yorks 89 B8
Kilpin Pike E Yorks 89 B8
Kilrenny Fife 135 D7
Kilsby Northants 52 B3
Kilspindie Perth 134 B4
Kilsyth N Lnrk 121 B7
Kiltarlity Highld 157 E6
Kilton Notts 77 B5
Kilton Som 22 E3
Kilton Thorpe Redcar 102 C4
Kilvaxter Highld 152 C4
Kilve Som 22 E3
Kilvington Notts 77 E7
Kilwinning N Ayrs 120 E3
Kimber worth S Yorks 88 E5
Kimberley Norf 68 D3
Kimberley Notts 76 E5
Kimble Wick Bucks 39 D8
Kimblesworth Durham 111 E5
Kimbolton Cambs 53 C8
Kimbolton Hereford 49 C7
Kimcote Leics 64 F2
Kimmeridge Dorset 13 G7
Kimmerston Northumb 125 F5
Kimpton Hants 25 E7
Kimpton Herts 40 C4
Kinbrace Highld 168 F3
Kinbuck Stirl 133 D6
Kincaple Fife 135 C6
Kincardine Fife 133 F8
Kincardine Highld 164 F3
Kincardine Bridge Fife 133 F8
Kincardine O'Neil Aberds 150 E4
Kinclaven Perth 142 F1
Kincorth Aberdeen 151 D8
Kincorth Ho. Moray 158 C4
Kincraig Highld 148 D4
Kincraigie Perth 141 E6
Kindallachan Perth 141 E6
Kinderland, Scarborough N Yorks 103 E8
Kineton Glos 37 B7
Kineton Warks 51 D8
Kinfauns Perth 134 B3
King Edward Aberds 160 C4
King Sterndale Derbys 75 B7
Kingairloch Highld 138 D2
Kingarth Argyll 129 E5
Kingcoed Mon 35 D8
Kingerby Lincs 90 E4
Kingham Oxon 38 B2
Kingholm Quay Dumfries 107 B6
Kinghorn Fife 134 F4
Kingie Highld 146 D4
Kinglassie Fife 134 E4
Kingoodie Perth 134 B5
King's Acre Hereford 49 E6
King's Bromley Staffs 62 C5
King's Caple Hereford 36 B2
King's Cliffe Northants 65 E7
Kings College Chapel, Cambridge Cambs 54 D5
King's Coughton Warks 51 D5
King's Heath W Mid 62 F4
Kings Hedges Cambs 55 C5
Kings Langley Herts 40 D3
King's Lynn Norf 67 B6
King's Meaburn Cumb 99 B8
King's Mills Wrex 73 E7
Kings Muir Borders 123 F5
King's Newnham Warks 52 B2
King's Newton Derbys 63 B7
King's Norton Leics 64 D3
King's Norton W Mid 51 B5
King's Nympton Devon 9 C8
King's Pyon Hereford 49 D6
King's Ripton Cambs 54 B3
King's Somborne Hants 25 F8
King's Stag Dorset 12 C5
King's Stanley Glos 37 D5
King's Sutton Northants 52 F2
King's Thorn Hereford 49 F7
King's Walden Herts 40 B4
Kings Worthy Hants 26 F2
Kingsand Corn 6 D2
Kingsbarns Fife 135 C7
Kingsbridge Devon 6 E5
Kingsbridge Som 21 F8
Kingsburgh Highld 152 D4
Kingsbury London 41 F5
Kingsbury Warks 63 E6
Kingsbury Episcopi Som 12 B2
Kingsclere Hants 26 D3
Kingscote Glos 37 E5
Kingscott Devon 9 C7
Kingscross N Ayrs 119 D7
Kingsdon Som 12 B3
Kingsdown Kent 31 E7
Kingseat Fife 134 E3
Kingsey Bucks 39 D7
Kingsfold W Sus 28 F2
Kingsford E Ayrs 120 E4
Kingsford Worcs 62 F2
Kingsforth N Lincs 90 C4
Kingsgate Kent 31 B7
Kingsheanton Devon 20 F4
Kingshouse Hotel Highld 139 D6
Kingside Hill Cumb 107 D8
Kingskerswell Devon 7 C6
Kingskettle Fife 134 D5
Kingsland Anglesey 82 C2
Kingsland Hereford 49 C6
Kingsley Ches 74 B2
Kingsley Hants 27 F5
Kingsley Staffs 75 E7
Kingsley Green W Sus 27 F6
Kingsley Holt Staffs 75 E7
Kingsley Park Northants 53 C5
Kingsmuir Angus 142 E4
Kingsmuir Fife 135 D7
Kingsnorth Kent 19 B7
Kingstanding W Mid 62 E4
Kingsteignton Devon 7 B6
Kingsthorpe Northants 53 C5
Kingston Cambs 54 D4
Kingston Devon 6 E4
Kingston Dorset 13 D5
Kingston Dorset 13 G7
Kingston E Loth 135 F7
Kingston Hants 14 D2
Kingston I o W 15 F5
Kingston Kent 31 D5
Kingston Moray 159 C7
Kingston Bagpuize Oxon 38 E4
Kingston Blount Oxon 39 E7
Kingston by Sea W Sus 17 D6
Kingston Deverill Wilts 24 F3
Kingston Gorse W Sus 16 D4
Kingston Lacy, Wimborne Minster Dorset 13 D7
Kingston Lisle Oxon 38 F3
Kingston Maurward Dorset 12 E5
Kingston near Lewes E Sus 17 D7
Kingston on Soar Notts 64 B2
Kingston Russell Dorset 12 E3
Kingston St Mary Som 11 B7
Kingston Seymour N Som 23 C6
Kingston Upon Hull Hull 90 B4
Kingston upon Thames London 28 C2
Kingston Vale London 28 B3
Kingstone Hereford 49 F6
Kingstone Som 11 C8
Kingstone Staffs 62 B4
Kingstown Cumb 108 D3
Kingswear Devon 7 D6
Kingswells Aberdeen 151 D7
Kingswinford W Mid 62 F2
Kingswood Bucks 39 C6
Kingswood Glos 36 E4
Kingswood Hereford 48 D4
Kingswood Kent 30 D2
Kingswood Powys 60 D2
Kingswood S Glos 23 B8
Kingswood Sur 28 D3
Kingswood Warks 51 B6
Kingthorpe Lincs 78 B4
Kington Hereford 48 D4
Kington Worcs 50 D4
Kington Langley Wilts 24 B4
Kington Magna Dorset 13 B5
Kington St Michael Wilts 24 B4
Kingussie Highld 148 D3
Kingweston Som 23 F7
Kininvie Ho. Moray 159 E7
Kinkell Bridge Perth 133 C8
Kinknockie Aberds 161 D7
Kinlet Shrops 61 F7
Kinloch Fife 134 C4
Kinloch Highld 144 D3
Kinloch Highld 166 F5
Kinloch Highld 145 B6
Kinloch Perth 141 E8
Kinloch Perth 142 E2
Kinloch Hourn Highld 146 D2
Kinloch Laggan Highld 147 F8
Kinloch Lodge Highld 167 D7
Kinloch Rannoch Perth 140 D3
Kinlochan Highld 138 C2
Kinlochard Stirl 132 D3
Kinlochbeoraid Highld 145 E8
Kinlochbervie Highld 166 D4
Kinlocheil Highld 138 B3
Kinlochewe Highld 154 D6
Kinlochleven Highld 139 C5
Kinlochmoidart Highld 145 F7
Kinlochmorar Highld 145 D8
Kinlochmore Highld 139 C5
Kinlochspelve Argyll 130 C2
Kinloid Highld 145 E6
Kinloss Moray 158 C4
Kinmel Bay Conwy 72 A3
Kinmuck Aberds 151 C7
Kinmundy Aberds 151 C7
Kinnadie Aberds 161 D6
Kinnaird Perth 134 B4
Kinnaird Castle Angus 143 D6
Kinneff Aberds 143 B8
Kinnelhead Dumfries 114 D3
Kinnell Angus 143 D6
Kinnerley Shrops 60 B3
Kinnersley Hereford 48 E5
Kinnersley Worcs 50 E3
Kinnerton Powys 48 C4
Kinnesswood Perth 134 D3
Kinninvie Durham 101 B5
Kinnordy Angus 142 D3
Kinoulton Notts 77 F6
Kinross Perth 134 D3
Kinrossie Perth 142 F1
Kinsbourne Green Herts 40 C4
Kinsey Heath Ches 74 E3
Kinsham Hereford 49 C5
Kinsham Worcs 50 F4
Kinsley W Yorks 88 C5
Kinson Bmouth 13 E8
Kintbury W Berks 25 C8
Kintessack Moray 158 C3
Kintillo Perth 134 C3
Kintocher Aberds 150 D4
Kinton Hereford 49 B6
Kinton Shrops 60 C3
Kintore Aberds 151 C6
Kintour Argyll 126 D4
Kintra Argyll 136 F4
Kintra Argyll 126 E3
Kintraw Argyll 130 E4
Kinuachdrachd Argyll 130 F3
Kinveachy Highld 148 C5
Kinver Staffs 62 F2
Kippax W Yorks 95 F7
Kippen Stirl 133 E5
Kippford or Scaur Dumfries 106 D5
Kirbister Orkney 176 F2
Kirbister Orkney 176 D5
Kirbuster Orkney 176 D1
Kirby Bedon Norf 69 D5
Kirby Bellars Leics 64 C4
Kirby Cane Norf 69 E6
Kirby Cross Essex 43 B8
Kirby Grindalythe N Yorks 96 C5
Kirby Hill N Yorks 95 C6
Kirby Hill N Yorks 101 D6
Kirby Knowle N Yorks 102 F2
Kirby-le-Soken Essex 43 B8
Kirby Misperton N Yorks 96 B3
Kirby Muxloe Leics 64 D2
Kirby Row Norf 69 E6
Kirby Sigston N Yorks 102 E2
Kirby Underdale E Yorks 96 D4
Kirby Wiske N Yorks 102 F1
Kirdford W Sus 16 B4
Kirk Highld 169 D7
Kirk Bramwith S Yorks 89 C7
Kirk Deighton N Yorks 95 D6
Kirk Ella E Yorks 90 B4
Kirk Hallam Derbys 76 E4
Kirk Hammerton N Yorks 95 D7
Kirk Ireton Derbys 76 D2
Kirk Langley Derbys 76 F2
Kirk Merrington Durham 111 F5
Kirk Michael I o M 84 C3
Kirk of Shotts N Lnrk 121 C8
Kirk Sandall S Yorks 89 D7
Kirk Smeaton N Yorks 89 C6
Kirk Yetholm Borders 116 B4
Kirkabister Shetland 175 K6
Kirkandrews Dumfries 106 E3
Kirkandrews upon Eden Cumb 108 D3
Kirkbampton Cumb 108 D3
Kirkbean Dumfries 107 D6
Kirkbride Cumb 108 D2
Kirkbuddo Angus 143 E5
Kirkburn Borders 123 F5
Kirkburn E Yorks 97 D5
Kirkburton W Yorks 88 C2
Kirkby Lincs 90 E4
Kirkby Mers 86 E2
Kirkby N Yorks 102 D3
Kirkby Fleetham N Yorks 101 E7
Kirkby Green Lincs 78 D3
Kirkby In Ashfield Notts 76 D5
Kirkby-in-Furness Cumb 98 F4
Kirkby la Thorpe Lincs 78 E4
Kirkby Lonsdale Cumb 93 B6
Kirkby Malham N Yorks 93 C8
Kirkby Mallory Leics 63 D8
Kirkby Malzeard N Yorks 94 B5
Kirkby Mills N Yorks 103 F5
Kirkby on Bain Lincs 78 C5
Kirkby Overblow N Yorks 95 E6
Kirkby Stephen Cumb 100 D2
Kirkby Thore Cumb 99 B8
Kirkby Underwood Lincs 65 B7
Kirkby Wharfe N Yorks 95 E8
Kirkbymoorside N Yorks 102 F4
Kirkcaldy Fife 134 E4
Kirkcambeck Cumb 108 C5
Kirkcarswell Dumfries 106 E4
Kirkcolm Dumfries 104 C4
Kirkconnel Dumfries 113 C7
Kirkconnell Dumfries 107 C6
Kirkcowan Dumfries 105 C7
Kirkcudbright Dumfries 106 D3
Kirkdale Mers 85 E4
Kirkfieldbank S Lnrk 121 E8
Kirkgunzeon Dumfries 107 C5
Kirkham Lancs 92 F4
Kirkham N Yorks 96 C3
Kirkhamgate W Yorks 88 B3
Kirkharle Northumb 117 F6
Kirkheaton Northumb 110 B3
Kirkheaton W Yorks 88 C2
Kirkhill Angus 143 C6
Kirkhill Highld 157 E6
Kirkhill Midloth 122 C5
Kirkhill Moray 159 F6
Kirkhope Borders 115 B6
Kirkhouse Borders 123 F6
Kirkiboll Highld 167 D7
Kirkibost Highld 153 H6
Kirkinch Angus 142 E3
Kirkinner Dumfries 105 D8
Kirkintilloch E Dunb 121 B6
Kirkland Cumb 98 C2
Kirkland Cumb 109 F6
Kirkland Dumfries 113 E8
Kirkland Dumfries 113 C7
Kirkleatham Redcar 102 B3
Kirklevington Stockton 102 D2
Kirkley Suff 69 E8
Kirklington Notts 77 D6
Kirklington N Yorks 101 F8
Kirklinton Cumb 108 C4
Kirkliston Edin 122 B4
Kirkmaiden Dumfries 104 F5
Kirkmichael Perth 141 D7
Kirkmichael S Ayrs 112 D3
Kirkmuirhill S Lnrk 121 E7
Kirknewton Northumb 124 F5
Kirknewton W Loth 122 C4
Kirkney Aberds 160 E2
Kirkoswald Cumb 109 E5
Kirkoswald S Ayrs 112 D2
Kirkpatrick Durham Dumfries 106 B4
Kirkpatrick-Fleming Dumfries 108 B2
Kirksanton Cumb 98 F3
Kirkstall W Yorks 95 F5
Kirkstead Lincs 78 C4
Kirkstile Aberds 160 E2
Kirkstyle Highld 169 B8
Kirkton Aberds 150 B5
Kirkton Aberds 160 D3
Kirkton Angus 142 E4
Kirkton Angus 142 F4
Kirkton Borders 115 C8
Kirkton Dumfries 114 F2
Kirkton Fife 135 B5
Kirkton Highld 155 H4
Kirkton Highld 155 F5
Kirkton Highld 164 E4
Kirkton Highld 157 D8
Kirkton Perth 133 C8
Kirkton S Lnrk 114 B2
Kirkton Stirl 132 D4
Kirkton Manor Borders 122 F5
Kirkton of Airlie Angus 142 D3
Kirkton of Auchterhouse Angus 142 F3
Kirkton of Auchterless Aberds 160 D4
Kirkton of Barevan Highld 158 E2
Kirkton of Bourtie Aberds 151 B7
Kirkton of Collace Perth 142 F1
Kirkton of Craig Angus 143 D7
Kirkton of Culsalmond Aberds 160 E3
Kirkton of Durris Aberds 151 E6
Kirkton of Glenbuchat Aberds 150 C2
Kirkton of Glenisla Angus 142 C2
Kirkton of Kingoldrum Angus 142 D3
Kirkton of Largo Fife 135 D6
Kirkton of Lethendy Perth 141 E8
Kirkton of Logie Buchan Aberds 151 B8
Kirkton of Maryculter Aberds 151 E7
Kirkton of Menmuir Angus 143 C5
Kirkton of Monikie Angus 142 F4
Kirkton of Oyne Aberds 151 B5
Kirkton of Rayne Aberds 160 F3
Kirkton of Skene Aberds 151 D7
Kirkton of Tough Aberds 150 C5
Kirktonhill Borders 123 D7
Kirktown Aberds 161 C7
Kirktown of Alvah Aberds 160 B3
Kirktown of Deskford Moray 160 B2
Kirktown of Fetteresso Aberds 151 F7
Kirktown of Mortlach Moray 159 F7
Kirktown of Slains Aberds 161 F7
Kirkurd Borders 122 E4
Kirkwall Orkney 176 E3
Kirkwall Airport Orkney 176 F3
Kirkwhelpington Northumb 117 F5
Kirmington N Lincs 90 C5
Kirmond le Mire Lincs 91 E5
Kirn Argyll 129 C6
Kirriemuir Angus 142 D3
Kirstead Green Norf 69 E5
Kirtlebridge Dumfries 108 B2
Kirtleton Dumfries 115 F5
Kirtling Cambs 55 D7
Kirtling Green Cambs 55 D7
Kirtlington Oxon 38 C4
Kirtomy Highld 168 C2
Kirton Lincs 79 F6
Kirton Notts 77 C6
Kirton Suff 57 F6
Kirton End Lincs 79 E5
Kirton Holme Lincs 79 E5
Kirton in Lindsey N Lincs 90 E3
Kislingbury Northants 52 D4
Kites Hardwick Warks 52 C2
Kittisford Som 11 B5
Kittle Swansea 33 F6
Kitt's Green W Mid 63 F5
Kitt's Moss Gtr Man 87 F6
Kittybrewster Aberdeen 151 D8
Kitwood Hants 26 F4
Kivernoll Hereford 49 F6
Kiveton Park S Yorks 89 F5
Knaith Lincs 90 F2
Knaith Park Lincs 90 F2
Knap Corner Dorset 13 B6
Knaphill Sur 27 D7
Knapp Perth 142 F2
Knapp Som 11 B8
Knapthorpe Notts 77 D7
Knapton Norf 81 D9
Knapton York 95 D8
Knapton Green Hereford 49 D6
Knapwell Cambs 54 C4

Little Harrowden Northants 53 B6
Little Haseley Oxon 39 D6
Little Hatfield E Yorks 97 E7
Little Hautbois Norf 81 E8
Little Haven Pembs 44 D3
Little Hay Staffs 62 D5
Little Hayfield Derbys 87 F8
Little Haywood Staffs 62 B4
Little Heath W Mid 63 F7
Little Hereford Hereford 49 C7
Little Horkesley Essex 56 F3
Little Horsted E Sus 17 C8
Little Horton W Yorks 94 F4
Little Horwood Bucks 53 F5
Little Houghton Northants 53 D6
Little Houghton S Yorks 88 D5
Little Hucklow Derbys 75 B8
Little Hulton Gtr Man 86 D5
Little Humber E Yorks 91 B5
Little Hungerford W Berks 26 B3
Little Irchester Northants 53 C7
Little Kimble Bucks 39 D8
Little Kineton Warks 51 D8
Little Kingshill Bucks 40 E1
Little Langdale Cumb 99 D5
Little Langford Wilts 25 F5
Little Laver Essex 41 D8
Little Leigh Ches 74 B3
Little Leighs Essex 42 C3
Little Lever Gtr Man 87 D5
Little London Bucks 39 C6
Little London E Sus 18 D2
Little London Hants 25 E8
Little London Hants 26 D4
Little London Lincs 66 B2
Little London Lincs 66 B4
Little London Norf 81 E7
Little London Powys 59 F7
Little Longstone Derbys 75 B8
Little Lynturk Aberds 150 C4
Little Malvern Worcs 50 E2
Little Maplestead Essex 56 F2
Little Marcle Hereford 49 F8
Little Marlow Bucks 40 F1
Little Marsden Lancs 93 F8
Little Massingham Norf 80 E3
Little Melton Norf 68 D4
Little Mill Mon 35 D7
Little Milton Oxon 39 D6
Little Missenden Bucks 40 E2
Little Musgrave Cumb 100 C2
Little Ness Shrops 60 C4
Little Neston Ches 73 B6
Little Newcastle Pembs 44 C4
Little Newsham Durham 101 C6
Little Oakley Essex 43 B8
Little Oakley Northants 65 F5
Little Orton Cumb 108 D3
Little Ouseburn N Yorks 95 C7
Little Paxton Cambs 54 C2
Little Petherick Corn 4 B4
Little Pitlurg Moray 159 E8
Little Plumpton Lancs 92 F3
Little Plumstead Norf 69 C6
Little Ponton Lincs 78 F2
Little Raveley Cambs 54 B3
Little Reedness E Yorks 90 B2
Little Ribston N Yorks 95 D6
Little Rissington Glos 38 C1
Little Ryburgh Norf 81 E5
Little Ryle Northumb 117 C6
Little Salkeld Cumb 109 F5
Little Sampford Essex 55 F7
Little Sandhurst Brack 27 C6
Little Saxham Suff 55 C8
Little Scatwell Highld 156 D4
Little Sessay N Yorks 95 B7
Little Shelford Cambs 54 D5
Little Singleton Lancs 92 F3
Little Skillymarno Aberds 161 C6
Little Smeaton N Yorks 89 C6
Little Snoring Norf 81 D5
Little Sodbury S Glos 36 F4
Little Somborne Hants 25 F8
Little Somerford Wilts 37 F6
Little Stainforth N Yorks 93 C8
Little Stainton Darl 101 B8
Little Stanney Ches 73 B8
Little Staughton Beds 54 C2
Little Steeping Lincs 79 C7
Little Stoke Staffs 75 F6
Little Stonham Suff 56 C5
Little Stretton Leics 64 D3
Little Stretton Shrops 60 E4
Little Strickland Cumb 99 C7
Little Stukeley Cambs 54 B3
Little Sutton Ches 73 B7
Little Tew Oxon 38 B3
Little Thetford Cambs 55 B6
Little Thirkleby N Yorks 95 B7
Little Thurlow Suff 55 D7
Little Thurrock Thurrock 29 B7
Little Torboll Highld 164 E4
Little Torrington Devon 9 C6
Little Totham Essex 42 C4
Little Toux Aberds 160 C2
Little Town Cumb 98 C4
Little Town Lancs 93 F6
Little Urswick Cumb 92 B2
Little Wakering Essex 43 F5
Little Walden Essex 55 E6
Little Waldingfield Suff 56 E3
Little Walsingham Norf 80 D5
Little Waltham Essex 42 C3
Little Warley Essex 42 E2
Little Weighton E Yorks 97 F5
Little Weldon Northants 65 F6
Little Welnetham Suff 56 C2
Little Wenlock Telford 61 D6
Little Whittingham Green Suff 57 B6
Little Wilbraham Cambs 55 D6
Little Wishford Wilts 25 F5
Little Witley Worcs 50 C2
Little Wittenham Oxon 39 E5
Little Wolford Warks 51 F7
Little Wratting Suff 55 E7
Little Wymington Beds 53 C7
Little Wymondley Herts 41 B5
Little Wyrley Staffs 62 D4
Little Yeldham Essex 55 F8
Littlebeck N Yorks 103 D6
Littleborough Gtr Man 87 C7
Littleborough Notts 90 F2
Littlebourne Kent 31 D6
Littlebredy Dorset 12 F3
Littlebury Essex 55 F6
Littlebury Green Essex 55 F5
Littledean Glos 36 C3
Littleferry Highld 165 E5
Littleham Devon 10 F5
Littleham Devon 9 B6
Littlehampton W Sus 16 D4
Littlehempston Devon 7 C6
Littlehoughton Northumb 117 C8
Littlemill Aberds 150 E2
Littlemill E Ayrs 112 C4
Littlemill Highld 158 D3
Littlemill Northumb 117 C8
Littlemoor Dorset 12 F4
Littlemore Oxon 39 D5
Littleover Derby 76 F3
Littleport Cambs 67 F5
Littlestone on Sea Kent 19 C7
Littlethorpe Leics 64 E2
Littlethorpe N Yorks 95 C6
Littleton Ches 73 C8
Littleton Hants 26 F2
Littleton Perth 142 F2
Littleton Som 23 F6
Littleton Sur 27 C8
Littleton Sur 27 E7
Littleton Drew Wilts 37 F5
Littleton-on-Severn S Glos 36 F2
Littleton Pannell Wilts 24 D5
Littletown Durham 111 E6
Littlewick Green Windsor 27 B6
Littleworth Beds 53 E8
Littleworth Glos 37 D5
Littleworth Oxon 38 E3
Littleworth Staffs 62 C4
Littleworth Worcs 50 D3
Litton Derbys 75 B8
Litton N Yorks 94 B2
Litton Som 23 D7
Litton Cheney Dorset 12 E3
Liurbost W Isles 172 F6
Liverpool Mers 85 E4
Liverpool Cathedral (C of E) Mers 85 F4
Liverpool Cathedral (RC) Mers 85 E4
Liverpool John Lennon Airport Mers 86 F2
Liversedge W Yorks 88 B3
Liverton Devon 7 B6
Liverton Redcar 103 C5
Livingston W Loth 122 C3
Livingston Village W Loth 122 C3
Lixwm Flint 73 B5
Lizard Corn 3 E6
Llaingoch Anglesey 82 C2
Llaithddu Powys 59 F7
Llan Powys 59 D5
Llan Ffestiniog Gwyn 71 C8
Llan-y-pwll Wrex 73 D7
Llanaber Gwyn 58 C3
Llanaelhaearn Gwyn 70 C4
Llanafan Ceredig 47 B5
Llanafan-fawr Powys 47 D8
Llanallgo Anglesey 82 C4
Llanandras = Presteigne Powys 48 C5
Llanarmon Gwyn 70 D5
Llanarmon Dyffryn Ceiriog Wrex 73 F5
Llanarmon-yn-Ial Denb 73 D5
Llanarth Ceredig 46 D3
Llanarth Mon 35 C7
Llanarthne Carms 33 B6
Llanasa Flint 85 F2
Llanbabo Anglesey 82 C3
Llanbadarn Fawr Ceredig 58 F3
Llanbadarn Fynydd Powys 48 B3
Llanbadarn-y-Garreg Powys 48 E3
Llanbadoc Mon 35 E7
Llanbadrig Anglesey 82 B3
Llanbeder Newport 35 E7
Llanbedr Gwyn 71 E6
Llanbedr Powys 48 E3
Llanbedr Powys 35 B6
Llanbedr-Dyffryn-Clwyd Denb 72 D5
Llanbedr Pont Steffan = Lampeter Ceredig 46 E4
Llanbedr-y-cennin Conwy 83 E7
Llanbedrgoch Anglesey 82 C5
Llanbedrog Gwyn 70 D4
Llanberis Gwyn 83 E5
Llanbethêry V Glam 22 C2
Llanbister Powys 48 B3
Llanblethian V Glam 21 B8
Llanboidy Carms 32 B3
Llanbradach Caerph 35 E5
Llanbrynmair Powys 59 D5
Llancarfan V Glam 22 B2
Llancayo Mon 35 D7
Llancloudy Hereford 36 B1
Llancynfelyn Ceredig 58 E3
Llandaff Cardiff 22 B3
Llandanwg Gwyn 71 E6
Llandarcy Neath 33 E8
Llandawke Carms 32 C3
Llanddaniel Fab Anglesey 82 D4
Llanddarog Carms 33 C6
Llanddeiniol Ceredig 46 B4
Llanddeiniolen Gwyn 82 E5
Llandderfel Gwyn 72 F3
Llanddeusant Anglesey 82 C3
Llanddeusant Carms 34 B1
Llanddew Powys 48 F2
Llanddewi Swansea 33 F5
Llanddewi-Brefi Ceredig 47 D5
Llanddewi Rhydderch Mon 35 C7
Llanddewi Velfrey Pembs 32 C2
Llanddewi'r Cwm Powys 48 E2
Llanddoged Conwy 83 E8
Llanddona Anglesey 83 D5
Llanddowror Carms 32 C3
Llanddulas Conwy 72 B3
Llanddwywe Gwyn 71 E6
Llanddyfynan Anglesey 82 D5
Llandefaelog Fach Powys 48 F2
Llandefaelog-tre'r-graig Powys 35 B5
Llandefalle Powys 48 F3
Llandegai Gwyn 83 D5
Llandegfan Anglesey 83 D5
Llandegla Denb 73 D5
Llandegley Powys 48 C3
Llandegveth Mon 35 E7
Llandegwning Gwyn 70 D3
Llandeilo Carms 33 B7
Llandeilo Graban Powys 48 E2
Llandeilo'r Fan Powys 47 F7
Llandeloy Pembs 44 C3
Llandenny Mon 35 D8
Llandevenny Mon 35 F8
Llandewednock Corn 3 E6
Llandewi Ystradenny Powys 48 C3
Llandinabo Hereford 36 B2
Llandinam Powys 59 F7
Llandissilio Pembs 32 B2
Llandogo Mon 36 D2
Llandough V Glam 21 B8
Llandough V Glam 22 B3
Llandovery = Llanymddyfri Carms 47 F6
Llandow V Glam 21 B8
Llandre Ceredig 58 F3
Llandre Carms 47 E5
Llandrillo Denb 72 F4
Llandrillo-yn-Rhos Conwy 83 C8
Llandrindod = Llandrindod Wells Powys 48 C2
Llandrindod Wells = Llandrindod Powys 48 C2
Llandrinio Powys 60 C2
Llandudno Conwy 83 C7
Llandudno Junction = Cyffordd Llandudno Conwy 83 D7
Llandwrog Gwyn 82 F4
Llandybie Carms 33 C7
Llandyfaelog Carms 33 C5
Llandyfan Carms 33 C7
Llandyfriog Ceredig 46 E2
Llandyfrydog Anglesey 82 C4
Llandygwydd Ceredig 45 E4
Llandynan Denb 73 E5
Llandyrnog Denb 72 C5
Llandysilio Powys 60 C2
Llandyssil Powys 59 E8
Llandysul Ceredig 46 E3
Llanedeyrn Cardiff 35 F6
Llanedi Carms 33 D6
Llaneglwys Powys 48 F2
Llanegryn Gwyn 58 D2
Llanegwad Carms 33 B6
Llaneilian Anglesey 82 B4
Llanelian-yn-Rhos Conwy 83 D8
Llanelidan Denb 72 D5
Llanelieu Powys 48 F3
Llanellen Mon 35 C7
Llanelli Carms 33 E6
Llanelltyd Gwyn 58 C4
Llanelly Mon 35 C6
Llanelly Hill Mon 35 C6
Llanelwedd Powys 48 D2
Llanelwy = St Asaph Denb 72 B4
Llanenddwyn Gwyn 71 E6
Llanengan Gwyn 70 E3
Llanerchymedd Anglesey 82 C4
Llanerfyl Powys 59 D7
Llanfachraeth Anglesey 82 C3
Llanfachreth Gwyn 71 E8
Llanfaelog Anglesey 82 D3
Llanfaelrhys Gwyn 70 E3
Llanfaenor Mon 35 C8
Llanfaes Anglesey 83 D6
Llanfaes Powys 34 B4
Llanfaethlu Anglesey 82 C3
Llanfaglan Gwyn 82 E4
Llanfair Gwyn 71 E6
Llanfair-ar-y-bryn Carms 47 F7
Llanfair Caereinion Powys 59 D8
Llanfair Clydogau Ceredig 46 D5
Llanfair-Dyffryn-Clwyd Denb 72 D5
Llanfair Kilgheddin Mon 35 D7
Llanfair-Nant-Gwyn Pembs 45 F3
Llanfair Talhaiarn Conwy 72 B3
Llanfair Waterdine Shrops 48 B4
Llanfair-ym-Muallt = Builth Wells Powys 48 D2
Llanfairfechan Conwy 83 D6
Llanfairpwll-gwyngyll Anglesey 82 D5
Llanfairyneubwll Anglesey 82 D3
Llanfairynghornwy Anglesey 82 B3
Llanfallteg Carms 32 C2
Llanfaredd Powys 48 D2
Llanfarian Ceredig 46 B4
Llanfechain Powys 59 B8
Llanfechan Powys 47 D8
Llanfechell Anglesey 82 B3
Llanfendigaid Gwyn 58 D2
Llanferres Denb 73 C5
Llanfflewyn Anglesey 82 C3
Llanfihangel-ar-arth Carms 46 F3
Llanfihangel-Crucorney Mon 35 B7
Llanfihangel Glyn Myfyr Conwy 72 E3
Llanfihangel Nant Bran Powys 47 F8
Llanfihangel-nant-Melan Powys 48 D3
Llanfihangel Rhydithon Powys 48 C3
Llanfihangel Rogiet Mon 35 F8
Llanfihangel Tal-y-llyn Powys 35 B5
Llanfihangel-uwch-Gwili Carms 33 B5
Llanfihangel-y-Creuddyn Ceredig 47 B5
Llanfihangel-y-pennant Gwyn 71 C6
Llanfihangel-y-pennant Gwyn 58 D3
Llanfihangel-y-traethau Gwyn 71 D6
Llanfihangel-yn-Ngwynfa Powys 59 C7
Llanfihangel yn Nhowyn Anglesey 82 D3
Llanfilo Powys 48 F3
Llanfoist Mon 35 C6
Llanfor Gwyn 72 F3
Llanfrechfa Torf 35 E7
Llanfrothen Gwyn 71 C7
Llanfrynach Powys 34 B4
Llanfwrog Anglesey 82 C3
Llanfwrog Denb 72 D5
Llanfyllin Powys 59 C8
Llanfynydd Carms 33 B6
Llanfynydd Flint 73 D6
Llanfyrnach Pembs 45 F4
Llangadfan Powys 59 C7
Llangadog Carms 33 B8
Llangadwaladr Anglesey 82 E3
Llangadwaladr Powys 73 F5
Llangaffo Anglesey 82 E4
Llangain Carms 32 C4
Llangammarch Wells Powys 47 E8
Llangan V Glam 21 B8
Llangarron Hereford 36 B2
Llangasty Talyllyn Powys 35 B5
Llangathen Carms 33 B6
Llangattock Powys 35 C6
Llangattock Lingoed Mon 35 B7
Llangattock nigh Usk Mon 35 D7
Llangattock-Vibon-Avel Mon 36 C1
Llangedwyn Powys 59 B8
Llangefni Anglesey 82 D4
Llangeinor Bridgend 34 F3
Llangeitho Ceredig 46 D5
Llangeler Carms 46 F2
Llangelynin Gwyn 58 D2
Llangendeirne Carms 33 C5
Llangennech Carms 33 D6
Llangennith Swansea 33 E5
Llangenny Powys 35 C6
Llangernyw Conwy 83 E8
Llangian Gwyn 70 E3
Llanglydwen Carms 32 B2
Llangoed Anglesey 83 D6
Llangoedmor Ceredig 45 E3
Llangollen Denb 73 E6
Llangolman Pembs 32 B2
Llangors Powys 35 B5
Llangovan Mon 36 D1
Llangower Gwyn 72 F3
Llangrannog Ceredig 46 D2
Llangristiolus Anglesey 82 D4
Llangrove Hereford 36 C2
Llangua Mon 35 B7
Llangunllo Powys 48 B4
Llangunnor Carms 33 C5
Llangurig Powys 47 B8
Llangwm Conwy 72 E3
Llangwm Mon 35 D8
Llangwm Pembs 44 E4
Llangwnnadl Gwyn 70 D3
Llangwyfan Denb 72 C5
Llangwyfan-isaf Anglesey 82 E3
Llangwyllog Anglesey 82 D4
Llangwyryfon Ceredig 46 B4
Llangybi Ceredig 46 D5
Llangybi Gwyn 70 C5
Llangybi Mon 35 E7
Llangyfelach Swansea 33 E7
Llangynhafal Denb 72 C5
Llangynidr Powys 35 C5
Llangynin Carms 32 C3
Llangynog Carms 32 C4
Llangynog Powys 59 B7
Llangynwyd Bridgend 34 F2
Llanhamlach Powys 34 B4
Llanharan Rhondda 34 F4
Llanharry Rhondda 34 F4
Llanhennock Mon 35 E7
Llanhiledd = Llanhilleth Bl Gwent 35 D6
Llanhilleth = Llanhiledd Bl Gwent 35 D6
Llanidloes Powys 59 F6
Llaniestyn Gwyn 70 D3
Llanifyny Powys 59 F5
Llanigon Powys 48 F4
Llanilar Ceredig 46 B5
Llanilid Rhondda 34 F3
Llanilltud Fawr = Llantwit Major V Glam 21 C8
Llanishen Cardiff 35 F5
Llanishen Mon 36 D1
Llanllawddog Carms 33 B5
Llanllechid Gwyn 83 E6
Llanllowell Mon 35 E7
Llanllugan Powys 59 D7
Llanllwch Carms 32 C4
Llanllwchaiarn Powys 59 E8
Llanllwni Carms 46 F3
Llanllyfni Gwyn 82 F4
Llanmadoc Swansea 33 E5
Llanmaes V Glam 21 C8
Llanmartin Newport 35 F7
Llanmihangel V Glam 21 B8
Llanmorlais Swansea 33 E6
Llannefydd Conwy 72 B3
Llannon Carms 33 D6
Llannor Gwyn 70 D4
Llanon Ceredig 46 C4
Llanover Mon 35 D7
Llanpumsaint Carms 33 B5
Llanreithan Pembs 44 C3
Llanrhaeadr Denb 72 C4
Llanrhaeadr-ym-Mochnant Powys 59 B8
Llanrhian Pembs 44 B3
Llanrhidian Swansea 33 E5
Llanrhos Conwy 83 C7
Llanrhyddlad Anglesey 82 C3
Llanrhystud Ceredig 46 C4
Llanrosser Hereford 48 F4
Llanrothal Hereford 36 C1
Llanrug Gwyn 82 E5
Llanrumney Cardiff 35 F6
Llanrwst Conwy 83 E8
Llansadurnen Carms 32 C3
Llansadwrn Anglesey 83 D5
Llansadwrn Carms 47 F5
Llansaint Carms 32 D4
Llansamlet Swansea 33 E7
Llansannan Conwy 72 C3
Llansannor V Glam 21 B8
Llansantffraed Ceredig 46 C4
Llansantffraed Powys 35 B5
Llansantffraed Cwmdeuddwr Powys 47 C8
Llansantffraed-in-Elvel Powys 48 D2
Llansantffraid-ym-Mechain Powys 60 B2
Llansawel Carms 46 F5
Llansilin Powys 60 B2
Llansoy Mon 35 D8
Llanspyddid Powys 34 B4
Llanstadwell Pembs 44 E4
Llansteffan Carms 32 C4
Llanstephan Powys 48 E3
Llantarnam Torf 35 E7
Llanteg Pembs 32 C2
Llanthony Mon 35 B6
Llantilio Crossenny Mon 35 C7
Llantilio Pertholey Mon 35 C7
Llantood Pembs 45 E3
Llantrisant Anglesey 82 C3
Llantrisant Mon 35 E7
Llantrisant Rhondda 34 F4
Llantrithyd V Glam 22 B2
Llantwit Fardre Rhondda 34 F4
Llantwit Major = Llanilltud Fawr V Glam 21 C8
Llanuwchllyn Gwyn 72 F2
Llanvaches Newport 35 E8
Llanvair Discoed Mon 35 E8
Llanvapley Mon 35 C7
Llanvetherine Mon 35 C7
Llanveynoe Hereford 48 F5
Llanvihangel Gobion Mon 35 D7
Llanvihangel-Ystern-Llewern Mon 35 C8
Llanwarne Hereford 36 B2
Llanwddyn Powys 59 C7
Llanwenog Ceredig 46 E3
Llanwern Newport 35 F7
Llanwinio Carms 32 B3
Llanwnda Gwyn 82 F4
Llanwnda Pembs 44 B4
Llanwnnen Ceredig 46 E4
Llanwnog Powys 59 E7
Llanwrda Carms 47 F6
Llanwrin Powys 58 D4
Llanwrthwl Powys 47 C8
Llanwrtud = Llanwrtyd Wells Powys 47 E7
Llanwrtyd Powys 47 E7
Llanwrtyd Wells = Llanwrtud Powys 47 E7
Llanwyddelan Powys 59 D7
Llanyblodwel Shrops 60 B2
Llanybri Carms 32 C4
Llanybydder Carms 46 E4
Llanycefn Pembs 32 B1
Llanychaer Pembs 44 B4
Llanycil Gwyn 72 F3
Llanycrwys Carms 46 E5
Llanymawddwy Gwyn 59 C6
Llanymddyfri = Llandovery Carms 47 F6
Llanymynech Powys 60 B2
Llanynghenedl Anglesey 82 C3
Llanynys Denb 72 C5
Llanyre Powys 48 C2
Llanystumdwy Gwyn 71 D5
Llanywern Powys 35 B5
Llawhaden Pembs 32 C1
Llawnt Shrops 73 F6
Llawr Dref Gwyn 70 E3
Llawryglyn Powys 59 E6
Llay Wrex 73 D7
Llechcynfarwy Anglesey 82 C3
Llecheiddior Gwyn 71 C5
Llechfaen Powys 34 B4
Llechryd Caerph 35 D5
Llechryd Ceredig 45 E4
Llechrydau Powys 73 F6
Llechwedd Slate Caverns, Blaenau Ffestiniog Gwyn 71 C8
Lledrod Ceredig 46 B5
Llenmerewig Powys 59 E8
Llethrid Swansea 33 E6
Llidiad Nenog Carms 46 F4
Llidiardau Gwyn 72 F2
Llidiart-y-parc Denb 72 E5
Llithfaen Gwyn 70 C4
Llong Flint 73 C6
Llowes Powys 48 E3
Llundain-fach Ceredig 46 D4
Llwydcoed Rhondda 34 D3
Llwyn Shrops 60 F2
Llwyn-du Mon 35 C6
Llwyn-hendy Carms 33 E6
Llwyn-têg Carms 33 D6
Llwyn-y-brain Carms 32 C2
Llwyn-y-groes Ceredig 46 D4
Llwyncelyn Ceredig 46 D3
Llwyndafydd Ceredig 46 D2
Llwynderw Powys 60 D2
Llwyndyrys Gwyn 70 C4
Llwyngwril Gwyn 58 D2
Llwynmawr Wrex 73 F6
Llwynypia Rhondda 34 E3
Llynclys Shrops 60 B2
Llynfaes Anglesey 82 D4
Llys-y-frân Pembs 32 B1
Llysfaen Conwy 83 D8
Llyswen Powys 48 F3
Llysworney V Glam 21 B8
Llywel Powys 47 F7
Loan Falk 122 B2
Loanend Northumb 124 D5
Loanhead Midloth 123 C5
Loans S Ayrs 120 F3
Loans of Tullich Highld 158 B2
Lobb Devon 20 F3
Loch a Charnain W Isles 170 F4
Loch a'Ghainmhich W Isles 172 F5
Loch Baghasdail = Lochboisdale W Isles 171 J3
Loch Choire Lodge Highld 167 F8
Loch Euphoirt W Isles 170 D4
Loch Head Dumfries 105 E7
Loch Loyal Lodge Highld 167 E8
Loch nam Madadh = Lochmaddy W Isles 170 D5
Loch Ness Monster Exhibition, Drumnadrochit Highld 157 F6
Loch Sgioport W Isles 170 G4
Lochailort Highld 145 E7
Lochaline Highld 137 D7
Lochanhully Highld 148 B5
Lochans Dumfries 104 D4
Locharbriggs Dumfries 114 F2
Lochassynt Lodge Highld 163 B5
Lochavich Ho. Argyll 130 D5
Lochawe Argyll 131 C7
Lochboisdale = Loch Baghasdail W Isles 171 J3
Lochbuie Argyll 137 F7
Lochcarron Highld 155 G4
Lochdhu Highld 168 E5
Lochdochart House Stirl 132 B3
Lochdon Argyll 130 B3
Lochdrum Highld 156 B3
Lochead Argyll 128 C2
Lochearnhead Stirl 132 B4
Lochee Dundee 142 F3
Lochend Highld 157 F6
Lochend Highld 169 C7
Locherben Dumfries 114 E2
Lochfoot Dumfries 107 B5
Lochgair Argyll 128 A4
Lochgarthside Highld 147 C8
Lochgelly Fife 134 E3
Lochgilphead Argyll 128 B3
Lochgoilhead Argyll 131 E8
Lochhill Moray 159 C6
Lochindorb Lodge Highld 158 F3
Lochinver Highld 162 B4
Lochlane Perth 133 B7
Lochluichart Highld 156 C4
Lochmaben Dumfries 114 F3
Lochmaddy = Loch nam Madadh W Isles 170 D5
Lochmore Cottage Highld 169 E5
Lochmore Lodge Highld 166 F4
Lochore Fife 134 E3
Lochportain W Isles 170 C5
Lochranza N Ayrs 119 A6
Lochs Crofts Moray 159 C7
Lochside Aberds 143 C7
Lochside Highld 167 D6
Lochside Highld 168 F3
Lochside Highld 158 D2
Lochslin Highld 165 F5
Lochstack Lodge Highld 166 E4
Lochton Aberds 151 E6
Lochty Angus 143 C5
Lochty Fife 135 D7
Lochty Perth 134 B2
Lochuisge Highld 138 D1
Lochurr Dumfries 113 F7
Lochwinnoch Renfs 120 D3
Lochwood Dumfries 114 E3
Lochyside Highld 139 B5
Lockengate Corn 4 C5
Lockerbie Dumfries 114 F4
Lockeridge Wilts 25 C6
Lockerley Hants 14 B3
Locking N Som 23 D5
Lockinge Oxon 38 F4
Lockington E Yorks 97 E5
Lockington Leics 63 B8
Lockleywood Shrops 61 B6
Locks Heath Hants 15 D6
Lockton N Yorks 103 E6
Lockwood W Yorks 88 C2
Locomotion Museum, Shildon Durham 101 B7
Loddington Leics 64 D4
Loddington Northants 53 B6
Loddiswell Devon 6 E5
Loddon Norf 69 E6
Lode Cambs 55 C6
Loders Dorset 12 E2
Lodsworth W Sus 16 B3
Lofthouse N Yorks 94 B4
Lofthouse W Yorks 88 B4
Loftus Redcar 103 C5
Logan E Ayrs 113 B5
Logan Mains Dumfries 104 E4
Loganlea W Loth 122 C2
Loggerheads Staffs 74 F4
Logie Angus 143 C6
Logie Fife 135 B6
Logie Moray 158 D4
Logie Coldstone Aberds 150 D3
Logie Hill Highld 157 B8
Logie Newton Aberds 160 E3
Logie Pert Angus 143 C6
Logiealmond Lodge Perth 141 F6
Logierait Perth 141 D6
Login Carms 32 B2
Lolworth Cambs 54 C4
Lonbain Highld 155 E2
Londesborough E Yorks 96 E4
London, City of = City of London London 41 F6
London City Airport London 41 F7
London Colney Herts 40 D4
London Gatwick Airport W Sus 28 E3
London Heathrow Airport London 27 B8
London Luton Airport Luton 40 B4
London Stansted Airport Essex 41 B8
London Zoo London 41 F5
Londonderry N Yorks 101 F8
Londonthorpe Lincs 78 F2
Londubh Highld 154 B4
Lonemore Highld 164 F4
Long Ashton N Som 23 B7
Long Bredy Dorset 12 E3
Long Buckby Northants 52 C4
Long Clawson Leics 64 B4
Long Common Hants 15 C6
Long Compton Staffs 62 B2
Long Compton Warks 51 F7
Long Crendon Bucks 39 D6
Long Crichel Dorset 13 C7
Long Ditton Sur 28 C2
Long Drax N Yorks 89 B7
Long Duckmanton Derbys 76 B4
Long Eaton Derbys 76 F4
Long Green Worcs 50 F3
Long Hanborough Oxon 38 C4
Long Itchington Warks 52 C2
Long Lawford Warks 52 B2
Long Load Som 12 B2
Long Marston Herts 40 C1
Long Marston N Yorks 95 D8
Long Marston Warks 51 E6
Long Marton Cumb 100 B1
Long Melford Suff 56 E2
Long Newnton Glos 37 E6
Long Newton E Loth 123 C8
Long Preston N Yorks 93 D8
Long Riston E Yorks 97 E7
Long Sight Gtr Man 87 D7
Long Stratton Norf 68 E4
Long Street M Keynes 53 E5
Long Sutton Hants 26 E5
Long Sutton Lincs 66 B4
Long Sutton Som 12 B2
Long Thurlow Suff 56 C4
Long Whatton Leics 63 B8
Long Wittenham Oxon 39 E5
Longbar N Ayrs 120 D3
Longbenton T & W 111 C5
Longborough Glos 38 B1
Longbridge Warks 51 C7
Longbridge W Mid 50 B5
Longbridge Deverill Wilts 24 E3
Longburton Dorset 12 C4
Longcliffe Derbys 76 D2
Longcot Oxon 38 E2
Longcroft Falk 121 B7
Longden Shrops 60 D4
Longdon Staffs 62 C4
Longdon Worcs 50 F3
Longdon Green Staffs 62 C4
Longdon on Tern Telford 61 C6
Longdown Devon 10 E3
Longdowns Corn 3 C6
Longfield Kent 29 C7
Longfield Shetland 175 M5
Longford Derbys 76 F2
Longford Glos 37 B5
Longford London 27 B8
Longford Shrops 74 F3
Longford Telford 61 C7
Longford W Mid 63 F7
Longfordlane Derbys 76 F2
Longforgan Perth 134 B5
Longformacus Borders 124 D2
Longframlington Northumb 117 D7
Longham Dorset 13 E8
Longham Norf 68 C2
Longhaven Aberds 161 E8
Longhill Aberds 161 C6
Longhirst Northumb 117 F8
Longhope Glos 36 C3
Longhope Orkney 176 G2
Longhorsley Northumb 117 E7
Longhoughton Northumb 117 C8
Longlane Derbys 76 F2
Longlane W Berks 26 B2
Longleat, Warminster Wilts 24 E3
Longlevens Glos 37 B5
Longley W Yorks 88 D2
Longley Green Worcs 50 D2
Longmanhill Aberds 160 B4
Longmoor Camp Hants 27 F5
Longmorn Moray 159 D6
Longnewton Borders 115 B8
Longnewton Stockton 102 C1
Longney Glos 36 C4
Longniddry E Loth 123 B7
Longnor Shrops 60 D4
Longnor Staffs 75 C7
Longparish Hants 26 E2
Longport Stoke 75 E5
Longridge Lancs 93 F6
Longridge Staffs 62 C3
Longridge W Loth 122 C2
Longriggend N Lnrk 121 B8
Longsdon Staffs 75 D6
Longshaw Gtr Man 86 D3
Longside Aberds 161 D7
Longstanton Cambs 54 C4
Longstock Hants 25 F8
Longstone Pembs 32 D2
Longstowe Cambs 54 D4
Longthorpe P'boro 65 E8
Longthwaite Cumb 99 B6
Longton Lancs 86 B2
Longton Stoke 75 E6
Longtown Cumb 108 C3
Longtown Hereford 35 B7
Longview Mers 86 E2
Longville in the Dale Shrops 60 E5
Longwick Bucks 39 D7
Longwitton Northumb 117 F6
Longwood Shrops 61 D6
Longworth Oxon 38 E3
Longyester E Loth 123 C8
Lonmay Aberds 161 C7
Lonmore Highld 152 E3
Looe Corn 5 D7
Loose Kent 29 D8
Loosley Row Bucks 39 D8
Lopcombe Corner Wilts 25 F7
Lopen Som 12 C2
Loppington Shrops 60 B4
Lopwell Devon 6 C2
Lorbottle Northumb 117 D6
Lorbottle Hall Northumb 117 D6
Lord's Cricket Ground London 41 F5
Lornty Perth 142 E1
Loscoe Derbys 76 E4
Losgaintir W Isles 173 J3
Lossiemouth Moray 159 B6
Lossit Argyll 126 D1
Lostford Shrops 74 F3
Lostock Gralam Ches 74 B3
Lostock Green Ches 74 B3
Lostock Hall Lancs 86 B3
Lostock Junction Gtr Man 86 D4
Lostwithiel Corn 5 D6
Loth Orkney 176 C5
Lothbeg Highld 165 C6
Lothersdale N Yorks 94 E2
Lothmore Highld 165 C6
Loudwater Bucks 40 E2

Loughborough Leics 64 C2
Loughor Swansea 33 E6
Loughton Essex 41 E7
Loughton M Keynes 53 F6
Loughton Shrops 61 F6
Louis Tussaud's Waxworks Blkpool 92 F3
Lound Lincs 65 C7
Lound Notts 89 F7
Lound Suff 69 E8
Lount Leics 63 C7
Louth Lincs 91 F7
Love Clough Lancs 87 B6
Lovedean Hants 15 C7
Lover Wilts 14 B3
Loversall S Yorks 89 E6
Loves Green Essex 42 D2
Lovesome Hill N Yorks 102 E1
Loveston Pembs 32 D1
Lovington Som 23 F7
Low Ackworth W Yorks 89 C5
Low Barlings Lincs 78 B3
Low Bentham N Yorks 93 C6
Low Bradfield S Yorks 88 E3
Low Bradley N Yorks 94 E3
Low Braithwaite Cumb 108 E4
Low Brunton Northumb 110 B2
Low Burnham N Lincs 89 D8
Low Burton N Yorks 101 F7
Low Buston Northumb 117 D8
Low Catton E Yorks 96 D3
Low Clanyard Dumfries 104 F5
Low Coniscliffe Darl 101 C7
Low Crosby Cumb 108 D4
Low Dalby N Yorks 103 F6
Low Dinsdale Darl 101 C8
Low Ellington N Yorks 101 F7
Low Etherley Durham 101 B6
Low Fell T & W 111 D5
Low Fulney Lincs 66 B2
Low Garth N Yorks 103 D5
Low Gate Northumb 110 C2
Low Grantley N Yorks 94 B5
Low Habberley Worcs 50 B3
Low Ham Som 12 B2
Low Hesket Cumb 108 E4
Low Hesleyhurst Northumb 117 E6
Low Hutton N Yorks 96 C3
Low Laithe N Yorks 94 C4
Low Leighton Derbys 87 F8
Low Lorton Cumb 98 B3
Low Marishes N Yorks 96 B4
Low Marnham Notts 77 C8
Low Mill N Yorks 102 E4
Low Moor Lancs 93 E7
Low Moor W Yorks 88 B2
Low Moorsley T & W 111 E6
Low Newton Cumb 99 F6
Low Newton-by-the-Sea Northumb 117 B8
Low Row Cumb 108 F3
Low Row Cumb 109 C5
Low Row N Yorks 100 E4
Low Salchrie Dumfries 104 C4
Low Smerby Argyll 118 D4
Low Torry Fife 134 F2
Low Worsall N Yorks 102 D1
Low Wray Cumb 99 D5
Lowbridge House Cumb 99 D7
Lowca Cumb 98 B1
Lowdham Notts 77 E6
Lowe Shrops 74 F2
Lowe Hill Staffs 75 D6
Lower Aisholt Som 22 F4
Lower Arncott Oxon 39 C6
Lower Ashton Devon 10 F3
Lower Assendon Oxon 39 F7
Lower Badcall Highld 166 E3
Lower Bartle Lancs 92 F4
Lower Basildon W Berks 26 B4
Lower Beeding W Sus 17 B6
Lower Benefield Northants 65 F6
Lower Boddington Northants 52 D2
Lower Brailes Warks 51 F8
Lower Breakish Highld 155 H2
Lower Broadheath Worcs 50 D3
Lower Bullingham Hereford 49 F7
Lower Cam Glos 36 D4
Lower Chapel Powys 48 F2
Lower Chute Wilts 25 D8
Lower Cragabus Argyll 126 E3
Lower Crossings Derbys 87 F8
Lower Cumberworth W Yorks 88 D3
Lower Cwm-twrch Powys 34 C1
Lower Darwen Blkburn 86 B4
Lower Dean Beds 53 C8
Lower Diabaig Highld 154 D3
Lower Dicker E Sus 18 D2
Lower Dinchope Shrops 60 F4
Lower Down Shrops 60 F3
Lower Drift Corn 2 D3
Lower Dunsforth N Yorks 95 C7
Lower Egleton Hereford 49 E8
Lower Elkstone Staffs 75 D7
Lower End Beds 40 B2
Lower Everleigh Wilts 25 D6
Lower Farringdon Hants 26 F5
Lower Foxdale I o M 84 E2
Lower Frankton Shrops 73 F7
Lower Froyle Hants 27 E5
Lower Gledfield Highld 164 E2
Lower Green Norf 81 D5
Lower Hacheston Suff 57 D7
Lower Halistra Highld 152 D3
Lower Halstow Kent 30 C2
Lower Hardres Kent 31 D5
Lower Hawthwaite Cumb 98 F4
Lower Heath Ches 75 C5
Lower Hempriggs Moray 158 C5
Lower Hergest Hereford 48 D4
Lower Heyford Oxon 38 B4
Lower Higham Kent 29 B8
Lower Holbrook Suff 57 F5
Lower Hordley Shrops 60 B3
Lower Horsebridge E Sus 18 D2
Lower Killeyan Argyll 126 E2
Lower Kingswood Sur 28 D3
Lower Kinnerton Ches 73 C7
Lower Langford N Som 23 C6
Lower Largo Fife 135 D6
Lower Leigh Staffs 75 F7
Lower Lemington Glos 51 F7
Lower Lenie Highld 147 B8
Lower Lydbrook Glos 36 C2
Lower Lye Hereford 49 C6
Lower Machen Newport 35 F6
Lower Maes-coed Hereford 48 F5
Lower Mayland Essex 43 D5
Lower Midway Derbys 63 B7
Lower Milovaig Highld 152 D2
Lower Moor Worcs 50 E4
Lower Nazeing Essex 41 D6
Lower Netchwood Shrops 61 E6
Lower Ollach Highld 153 F6
Lower Penarth V Glam 22 B3
Lower Penn Staffs 62 E2
Lower Pennington Hants 14 E4
Lower Peover Ches 74 B4
Lower Pexhill Ches 75 B5
Lower Place Gtr Man 87 C7
Lower Quinton Warks 51 E6
Lower Rochford Worcs 49 C8
Lower Seagry Wilts 37 F6
Lower Shelton Beds 53 E7
Lower Shiplake Oxon 27 B5
Lower Shuckburgh Warks 52 C2
Lower Slaughter Glos 38 B1
Lower Stanton St Quintin Wilts 37 F6
Lower Stoke Medway 30 B2
Lower Stondon Beds 54 F2
Lower Stow Bedon Norf 68 E2
Lower Street Norf 81 D8
Lower Street Norf 69 C6
Lower Strensham Worcs 50 E4
Lower Stretton Warr 86 F4
Lower Sundon Beds 40 B3
Lower Swanwick Hants 15 D5
Lower Swell Glos 38 B1
Lower Tean Staffs 75 F7
Lower Thurlton Norf 69 E7
Lower Tote Highld 152 C6
Lower Town Pembs 44 B4
Lower Tysoe Warks 51 E8
Lower Upham Hants 15 C6
Lower Vexford Som 22 F3
Lower Weare Som 23 D6
Lower Welson Hereford 48 D4
Lower Whitley Ches 74 B3
Lower Wield Hants 26 E4
Lower Winchendon Bucks 39 C7
Lower Withington Ches 74 C5
Lower Woodend Bucks 39 F8
Lower Woodford Wilts 25 F6
Lower Wyche Worcs 50 E2
Lowesby Leics 64 D4
Lowestoft Suff 69 E8
Loweswater Cumb 98 B3
Lowford Hants 15 C5
Lowgill Cumb 99 E8
Lowgill Lancs 93 C6
Lowick Northants 65 F6
Lowick Northumb 125 F6
Lowick Bridge Cumb 98 F4
Lowick Green Cumb 98 F4
Lowlands Torf 35 E6
Lowmoor Row Cumb 99 B8
Lownie Moor Angus 142 E4
Lowsonford Warks 51 C6
Lowther Cumb 99 B7
Lowthorpe E Yorks 97 C6
Lowton Gtr Man 86 E4
Lowton Common Gtr Man 86 E4
Loxbeare Devon 10 C4
Loxhill Sur 27 F8
Loxhore Devon 20 F5
Loxley Warks 51 D7
Loxton N Som 23 D5
Loxwood W Sus 27 F8
Lubcroy Highld 163 D7
Lubenham Leics 64 F4
Luccombe Som 21 E8
Luccombe Village I o W 15 G6
Lucker Northumb 125 F7
Luckett Corn 5 B8
Luckington Wilts 37 F5
Lucklawhill Fife 135 B6
Luckwell Bridge Som 21 F8
Lucton Hereford 49 C6
Ludag W Isles 171 J3
Ludborough Lincs 91 E6
Ludchurch Pembs 32 C2
Luddenden W Yorks 87 B8
Luddenden Foot W Yorks 87 B8
Luddesdown Kent 29 C7
Luddington N Lincs 90 C2
Luddington Warks 51 D6
Luddington in the Brook Northants 65 F8
Lude House Perth 141 C5
Ludford Lincs 91 F6
Ludford Shrops 49 B7
Ludgershall Bucks 39 C6
Ludgershall Wilts 25 D7
Ludgvan Corn 2 C4
Ludham Norf 69 C6
Ludlow Shrops 49 B7
Ludlow Racecourse Shrops 49 B6
Ludwell Wilts 13 B7
Ludworth Durham 111 E6
Luffincott Devon 8 E5
Lugar E Ayrs 113 B5
Lugg Green Hereford 49 C6
Luggate Burn E Loth 124 B2
Luggiebank N Lnrk 121 B7
Lugton E Ayrs 120 D4
Lugwardine Hereford 49 E7
Luib Highld 153 G6
Lulham Hereford 49 E6
Lullenden Sur 28 E5
Lullington Derbys 63 C6
Lullington Som 24 D2
Lulsgate Bottom N Som 23 C7
Lulsley Worcs 50 D2
Lulworth Castle Dorset 13 F6
Lumb W Yorks 87 B8
Lumby N Yorks 95 F7
Lumloch E Dunb 121 C6
Lumphanan Aberds 150 D4
Lumphinnans Fife 134 E3
Lumsdaine Borders 124 C4
Lumsden Aberds 150 B3
Lunan Angus 143 D6
Lunanhead Angus 142 D4
Luncarty Perth 134 B2
Lund E Yorks 97 E5
Lund N Yorks 96 F2
Lund Shetland 174 C7
Lunderton Aberds 161 D8
Lundie Angus 142 F2
Lundie Highld 146 C4
Lundin Links Fife 135 D6
Lunga Argyll 130 E3
Lunna Shetland 174 G6
Lunning Shetland 174 G7
Lunnon Swansea 33 F6
Lunsford's Cross E Sus 18 D4
Lunt Mers 85 D4
Luntley Hereford 49 D5
Luppitt Devon 11 D6
Lupset W Yorks 88 C4
Lupton Cumb 99 F7
Lurgashall W Sus 16 B3
Lusby Lincs 79 C6
Luson Devon 6 E4
Luss Argyll 132 E2
Lussagiven Argyll 127 D4
Lusta Highld 152 D3
Lustleigh Devon 10 F2
Luston Hereford 49 C6
Luthermuir Aberds 143 C6
Luthrie Fife 134 C5
Luton Devon 7 B7
Luton Luton 40 B3
Luton Medway 29 C8
Lutterworth Leics 64 F2
Lutton Devon 6 D3
Lutton Lincs 66 B4
Lutton Northants 65 F8
Lutworthy Devon 10 C2
Luxborough Som 21 F8
Luxulyan Corn 5 D5
Lybster Highld 169 F7
Lydbury North Shrops 60 F3
Lydcott Devon 21 F5
Lydd Kent 19 C7
Lydd on Sea Kent 19 C7
Lydden Kent 31 E6
Lydden Motor Racing Circuit Kent 31 E6
Lyddington Rutland 65 E5
Lyde Green Hants 26 D5
Lydeard St Lawrence Som 22 F3
Lydford Devon 9 F7
Lydford-on-Fosse Som 23 F7
Lydgate W Yorks 87 B7
Lydham Shrops 60 E3
Lydiard Green Wilts 37 F7
Lydiard Millicent Wilts 37 F7
Lydiate Mers 85 D4
Lydlinch Dorset 12 C5
Lydney Glos 36 D3
Lydstep Pembs 32 E1
Lye W Mid 62 F3
Lye Green Bucks 40 D2
Lye Green E Sus 18 B2
Lyford Oxon 38 E3
Lymbridge Green Kent 30 E5
Lyme Park, Disley Ches 87 F7
Lyme Regis Dorset 11 E8
Lyminge Kent 31 E5
Lymington Hants 14 E4
Lyminster W Sus 16 D4
Lymm Warr 86 F4
Lymore Hants 14 E3
Lympne Kent 19 B8
Lympsham Som 22 D5
Lympstone Devon 10 F4
Lynchat Highld 148 D3
Lyndale Ho. Highld 152 D4
Lyndhurst Hants 14 D4
Lyndon Rutland 65 D6
Lyne Sur 27 C8
Lyne Down Hereford 49 F8
Lyne of Gorthleck Highld 147 B8
Lyne of Skene Aberds 151 C6
Lyneal Shrops 73 F8
Lyneham Oxon 38 B2
Lyneham Wilts 24 B5
Lynemore Highld 149 B6
Lynemouth Northumb 117 E8
Lyness Orkney 176 G2
Lyng Norf 68 C3
Lyng Som 11 B8
Lynmouth Devon 21 E6
Lynsted Kent 30 C3
Lynton Devon 21 E6
Lynton & Lynmouth Cliff Railway Devon 21 E6
Lyon's Gate Dorset 12 D4
Lyonshall Hereford 48 D5
Lytchett Matravers Dorset 13 E7
Lytchett Minster Dorset 13 E7
Lyth Highld 169 C7
Lytham Lancs 85 B4
Lytham St Anne's Lancs 85 B4
Lythe N Yorks 103 C6
Lythes Orkney 176 H3

M

Mabe Burnthouse Corn 3 C6
Mabie Dumfries 107 B6
Mablethorpe Lincs 91 F9
Macclesfield Ches 75 B6
Macclesfield Forest Ches 75 B6
Macduff Aberds 160 B4
Mace Green Suff 56 E5
Macharioch Argyll 118 F4
Machen Caerph 35 F6
Machrihanish Argyll 118 D3
Machynlleth Powys 58 D4
Machynys Carms 33 E6
Mackerel's Common W Sus 16 B4
Mackworth Derbys 76 F3
Macmerry E Loth 123 B7
Madame Tussaud's London 41 F5
Madderty Perth 133 B8
Maddiston Falk 122 B2
Madehurst W Sus 16 C3
Madeley Staffs 74 E4
Madeley Telford 61 D6
Madeley Heath Staffs 74 E4
Madeley Park Staffs 74 E4
Madingley Cambs 54 C4
Madley Hereford 49 F6
Madresfield Worcs 50 E3
Madron Corn 2 C3
Maen-y-groes Ceredig 46 D2
Maenaddwyn Anglesey 82 C4
Maenclochog Pembs 32 B1
Maendy V Glam 22 B2
Maentwrog Gwyn 71 C7
Maer Staffs 74 F4
Maerdy Conwy 72 E4
Maerdy Rhondda 34 E3
Maes-Treylow Powys 48 C4
Maesbrook Shrops 60 B2
Maesbury Shrops 60 B3
Maesbury Marsh Shrops 60 B3
Maesgwyn-Isaf Powys 59 C8
Maesgwynne Carms 32 B3
Maeshafn Denb 73 C6
Maesllyn Ceredig 46 E2
Maesmynis Powys 48 E2
Maesteg Bridgend 34 E2
Maestir Ceredig 46 E4
Maesy cwmmer Caerph 35 E5
Maesybont Carms 33 C6
Maesycrugiau Carms 46 E3
Maesymeillion Ceredig 46 E3
Magdalen Laver Essex 41 D8
Maggieknockater Moray 159 E7
Magham Down E Sus 18 D3
Maghull Mers 85 D4
Magna Science Adventure Centre, Rotherham S Yorks 88 E5
Magor Mon 35 F8
Magpie Green Suff 56 B4
Maiden Bradley Wilts 24 F3
Maiden Law Durham 110 E4
Maiden Newton Dorset 12 E3
Maiden Wells Pembs 44 F4
Maidencombe Torbay 7 C7
Maidenhall Suff 57 E5
Maidenhead Windsor 40 F1
Maidens S Ayrs 112 D2
Maiden's Green Brack 27 B6
Maidensgrave Suff 57 E6
Maidenwell Corn 5 B6
Maidenwell Lincs 79 B6
Maidford Northants 52 D4
Maids Moreton Bucks 52 F5
Maidstone Kent 29 D8
Maidwell Northants 52 B5
Mail Shetland 175 L6
Main Powys 59 C8
Maindee Newport 35 F7
Mains of Airies Dumfries 104 C3
Mains of Allardice Aberds 143 B8
Mains of Annochie Aberds 161 D6
Mains of Ardestie Angus 143 F5
Mains of Balhall Angus 143 C5
Mains of Ballindarg Angus 142 D4
Mains of Balnakettle Aberds 143 B6
Mains of Birness Aberds 161 E6
Mains of Burgie Moray 158 D4
Mains of Clunas Highld 158 E2
Mains of Crichie Aberds 161 D6
Mains of Dalvey Highld 158 F5
Mains of Dellavaird Aberds 151 F6
Mains of Drum Aberds 151 E7
Mains of Edingight Moray 160 C2
Mains of Fedderate Aberds 161 D5
Mains of Inkhorn Aberds 161 E6
Mains of Mayen Moray 160 D2
Mains of Melgund Angus 143 D5
Mains of Thornton Aberds 143 B6
Mains of Watten Highld 169 D7
Mainsforth Durham 111 F6
Mainsriddle Dumfries 107 D6
Mainstone Shrops 60 F2
Maisemore Glos 37 B5
Malacleit W Isles 170 C3
Malborough Devon 6 F5
Malcoff Derbys 87 F8
Maldon Essex 42 D4
Malham N Yorks 94 C2
Maligar Highld 152 C5
Mallaig Highld 145 D6
Malleny Mills Edin 122 C4
Malling Stirl 132 D4
Mallory Park Motor Racing Circuit Leics 63 D8
Malltraeth Anglesey 82 E4
Mallwyd Gwyn 59 C5
Malmesbury Wilts 37 F6
Malmsmead Devon 21 E6
Malpas Ches 73 E8
Malpas Corn 3 B7
Malpas Newport 35 E7
Malswick Glos 36 B4
Maltby Stockton 102 C2
Maltby S Yorks 89 E6
Maltby le Marsh Lincs 91 F8
Malting Green Essex 43 B5
Maltman's Hill Kent 30 E3
Malton N Yorks 96 B3
Malvern Link Worcs 50 E2
Malvern Wells Worcs 50 E2
Mamble Worcs 49 B8
Man-moel Caerph 35 D5
Manaccan Corn 3 D6
Manafon Powys 59 D8
Manais W Isles 173 K4
Manar Ho. Aberds 151 B6
Manaton Devon 10 F2
Manby Lincs 91 F7
Mancetter Warks 63 E7
Manchester Gtr Man 87 E6
Manchester Airport Gtr Man 87 F6
Manchester National Velodrome Gtr Man 87 E6
Mancot Flint 73 C7
Mandally Highld 147 D5
Manea Cambs 66 F4
Manfield N Yorks 101 C7
Mangaster Shetland 174 F5
Mangotsfield S Glos 23 B8
Mangurstadh W Isles 172 E3
Mankinholes W Yorks 87 B7
Manley Ches 74 B2
Mannal Argyll 136 F1
Mannerston W Loth 122 B3
Manningford Bohune Wilts 25 D6
Manningford Bruce Wilts 25 D6
Manningham W Yorks 94 F4
Mannings Heath W Sus 17 B6
Mannington Dorset 13 D8
Manningtree Essex 56 F4
Mannofield Aberdeen 151 D8
Manor Estate S Yorks 88 F4
Manor Park London 41 F7
Manorbier Pembs 32 E1
Manordeilo Carms 33 B7
Manorhill Borders 124 F2
Manorowen Pembs 44 B4
Mansel Lacy Hereford 49 E6
Manselfield Swansea 33 F6
Mansell Gamage Hereford 49 E5
Mansergh Cumb 99 F8
Mansfield E Ayrs 113 C6
Mansfield Notts 76 C5
Mansfield Woodhouse Notts 76 C5
Mansriggs Cumb 98 F4
Manston Dorset 13 C6
Manston Kent 31 C7
Manston W Yorks 95 F6
Manswood Dorset 13 D7
Manthorpe Lincs 65 C7
Manthorpe Lincs 78 F2
Manton N Lincs 90 D3
Manton Notts 77 B5
Manton Rutland 65 D5
Manton Wilts 25 C6
Manuden Essex 41 B7
Manx Electric Railway I o M 84 C4
Maperton Som 12 B4
Maple Cross Herts 40 E3
Maplebeck Notts 77 C7
Mapledurham Oxon 26 B4
Mapledurwell Hants 26 D4
Maplehurst W Sus 17 B5
Maplescombe Kent 29 C6
Mapleton Derbys 75 E8
Mapleton E Yorks 97 E8
Mapperley Derbys 76 E4
Mapperley Park Nottingham 77 E5
Mapperton Dorset 12 E3
Mappleborough Green Warks 51 C5
Mappowder Dorset 12 D5
Mar Lodge Aberds 149 E6
Maraig W Isles 173 H4
Marazanvose Corn 4 D3
Marazion Corn 2 C4
Marbhig W Isles 172 G7
Marbury Ches 74 E2
March Cambs 66 E4
March S Lnrk 114 C2
Marcham Oxon 38 E4
Marchamley Shrops 61 B5
Marchington Staffs 75 F8
Marchington Woodlands Staffs 62 B5
Marchroes Gwyn 70 E4
Marchwiel Wrex 73 E7
Marchwood Hants 14 C4
Marcross V Glam 21 C8
Marden Hereford 49 E7
Marden Kent 29 E8
Marden T & W 111 B6
Marden Wilts 25 D5
Marden Beech Kent 29 E8
Marden Thorn Kent 29 E8
Mardy Mon 35 C7
Marefield Leics 64 D4
Mareham le Fen Lincs 79 C5
Mareham on the Hill Lincs 79 C5
Marehay Derbys 76 E3
Marehill W Sus 16 C4
Maresfield E Sus 17 B8
Marfleet Hull 90 B5
Marford Wrex 73 D7
Margam Neath 34 F1
Margaret Marsh Dorset 13 C6
Margaret Roding Essex 42 C1
Margaretting Essex 42 D2
Margate Kent 31 B7
Margnaheglish N Ayrs 119 C7
Margrove Park Redcar 102 C4
Marham Norf 67 C7
Marhamchurch Corn 8 D4
Marholm P'boro 65 D8
Mariandyrys Anglesey 83 C6
Marianglas Anglesey 82 C5
Mariansleigh Devon 10 B2
Marionburgh Aberds 151 D6
Marishader Highld 152 C5
Maritime and Industrial Museum Swansea 33 E7
Marjoriebanks Dumfries 114 F3
Mark Dumfries 104 D5
Mark S Ayrs 104 B4
Mark Som 23 E5
Mark Causeway Som 23 E5
Mark Cross E Sus 17 C8
Mark Cross E Sus 18 B2
Markbeech Kent 29 E5
Markby Lincs 79 B7
Market Bosworth Leics 63 D8
Market Deeping Lincs 65 D8
Market Drayton Shrops 74 F3
Market Harborough Leics 64 F4
Market Lavington Wilts 24 D5
Market Overton Rutland 65 C5
Market Rasen Lincs 90 F5
Market Rasen Racecourse Lincs 90 F5
Market Stainton Lincs 78 B5
Market Warsop Notts 77 C5
Market Weighton E Yorks 96 E4
Market Weston Suff 56 B3
Markethill Perth 142 F2
Markfield Leics 63 C8
Markham Caerph 35 D5
Markham Moor Notts 77 B7
Markinch Fife 134 D4
Markington N Yorks 95 C5
Marks Tey Essex 43 B5
Marksbury Bath 23 C8
Markyate Herts 40 C3
Marland Gtr Man 87 C6
Marlborough Wilts 25 C6
Marlbrook Hereford 49 D7
Marlbrook Worcs 50 B4
Marlcliff Warks 51 D5
Marldon Devon 7 C6
Marlesford Suff 57 D7
Marley Green Ches 74 E2
Marley Hill T & W 110 D5
Marley Mount Hants 14 E3
Marlingford Norf 68 D4
Marloes Pembs 44 E2
Marlow Bucks 39 F8
Marlow Hereford 49 B6
Marlow Bottom Bucks 40 F1
Marlpit Hill Kent 28 E5
Marlpool Derbys 76 E4
Marnhull Dorset 13 C5
Marnoch Aberds 160 C2
Marnock N Lnrk 121 C7
Marple Gtr Man 87 F7
Marple Bridge Gtr Man 87 F7
Marr S Yorks 89 D6
Marrel Highld 165 C7
Marrick N Yorks 101 E5
Marrister Shetland 175 G7
Marros Carms 32 D3
Marsden T & W 111 C6
Marsden W Yorks 87 C8
Marsett N Yorks 100 F4
Marsh Devon 11 C7
Marsh W Yorks 94 F3
Marsh Baldon Oxon 39 E5
Marsh Gibbon Bucks 39 B6
Marsh Green Devon 10 E5
Marsh Green Kent 28 E5
Marsh Green Staffs 75 D5
Marsh Lane Derbys 76 B4
Marsh Street Som 21 E8
Marshall's Heath Herts 40 C4
Marshalsea Dorset 11 D8
Marshalswick Herts 40 D4
Marsham Norf 81 E7
Marshaw Lancs 93 D5
Marshborough Kent 31 D7
Marshbrook Shrops 60 F4
Marshchapel Lincs 91 E7
Marshfield Newport 35 F6
Marshfield S Glos 24 B2
Marshgate Corn 8 E3
Marshland St James Norf 66 D5
Marshside Mers 85 C4
Marshwood Dorset 11 E8
Marske N Yorks 101 D6
Marske-by-the-Sea Redcar 102 B4
Marston Ches 74 B3
Marston Hereford 49 D5
Marston Lincs 77 E8
Marston Oxon 39 D5
Marston Staffs 62 C2
Marston Staffs 62 B3
Marston Warks 63 E6
Marston Wilts 24 D4
Marston Doles Warks 52 D2
Marston Green W Mid 63 F5
Marston Magna Som 12 B3
Marston Meysey Wilts 37 E8
Marston Montgomery Derbys 75 F8
Marston Moretaine Beds 53 E7
Marston on Dove Derbys 63 B6
Marston St Lawrence Northants 52 E3
Marston Stannett Hereford 49 D7
Marston Trussell Northants 64 F3
Marstow Hereford 36 C2
Marsworth Bucks 40 C2
Marten Wilts 25 D7
Marthall Ches 74 B5
Martham Norf 69 C7
Martin Hants 13 C8
Martin Kent 31 E7
Martin Lincs 78 D4
Martin Lincs 78 C5
Martin Dales Lincs 78 C4
Martin Drove End Hants 13 B8
Martin Hussingtree Worcs 50 C3
Martin Mill Kent 31 E7
Martinhoe Devon 21 E5
Martinhoe Cross Devon 21 E5
Martinscroft Warr 86 F4
Martinstown Dorset 12 F4
Martlesham Suff 57 E6
Martlesham Heath Suff 57 E6
Martletwy Pembs 32 C1
Martley Worcs 50 D2
Martock Som 12 C2
Marton Ches 75 C5
Marton E Yorks 97 F7
Marton Lincs 90 F2
Marton M'bro 102 C3
Marton N Yorks 95 C7
Marton N Yorks 103 F5
Marton Shrops 60 D2
Marton Shrops 60 B4
Marton Warks 52 C2
Marton-le-Moor N Yorks 95 B6
Martyr Worthy Hants 26 F3
Martyr's Green Sur 27 D8
Marwell Zoo, Bishop's Waltham Hants 15 B6
Marwick Orkney 176 D1
Marwood Devon 20 F4
Mary Arden's House, Stratford-upon-Avon Warks 51 D6
Mary Rose Ptsmth 15 D7
Mary Tavy Devon 6 B3
Marybank Highld 157 D5
Maryburgh Highld 157 D6
Maryhill Glasgow 121 C5
Marykirk Aberds 143 C6
Marylebone Gtr Man 86 D3
Marypark Moray 159 F5
Maryport Cumb 107 F7
Maryport Dumfries 104 F5
Maryton Angus 143 D6
Marywell Aberds 150 E4
Marywell Aberds 151 E8
Marywell Angus 143 E6
Masham N Yorks 101 F7
Mashbury Essex 42 C2
Masongill N Yorks 93 B6
Masonhill S Ayrs 112 B3
Mastin Moor Derbys 76 B4
Mastrick Aberdeen 151 D7
Matching Essex 41 C8
Matching Green Essex 41 C8
Matching Tye Essex 41 C8
Matfen Northumb 110 B3
Matfield Kent 29 E7
Mathern Mon 36 E2
Mathon Hereford 50 E2
Mathry Pembs 44 B3
Matlaske Norf 81 D7
Matlock Derbys 76 C2
Matlock Bath Derbys 76 D2
Matson Glos 37 C5
Matterdale End Cumb 99 B5
Mattersey Notts 89 F7
Mattersey Thorpe Notts 89 F7
Mattingley Hants 26 D5
Mattishall Norf 68 C3
Mattishall Burgh Norf 68 C3
Mauchline E Ayrs 112 B4
Maud Aberds 161 D6
Maugersbury Glos 38 B2
Maughold I o M 84 C4
Mauld Highld 156 F5
Maulden Beds 53 F8
Maulds Meaburn Cumb 99 C8
Maunby N Yorks 102 F1
Maund Bryan Hereford 49 D7
Maundown Som 11 B5
Mautby Norf 69 C7
Mavis Enderby Lincs 79 C6
Maw Green Ches 74 D4
Mawbray Cumb 107 E7
Mawdesley Lancs 86 C2
Mawdlam Bridgend 34 F2
Mawgan Corn 3 D6
Mawla Corn 3 B6
Mawnan Corn 3 D6
Mawnan Smith Corn 3 D6
Mawsley Northants 53 B6
Maxey P'boro 65 D8
Maxstoke Warks 63 F6
Maxton Borders 124 F2
Maxton Kent 31 E7
Maxwellheugh Borders 124 F3
Maxwelltown Dumfries 107 B6
Maxworthy Corn 8 E4
May Bank Staffs 75 E5
Mayals Swansea 33 E7
Maybole S Ayrs 112 D3
Mayfield E Sus 18 C2
Mayfield Midloth 123 C6
Mayfield Staffs 75 E8
Mayfield W Loth 122 C2
Mayford Sur 27 D7
Mayland Essex 43 D5
Maynard's Green E Sus 18 D2
Maypole Mon 36 C1
Maypole Scilly 2 E4
Maypole Green Essex 43 B5
Maypole Green Norf 69 E7
Maypole Green Suff 57 C6
Maywick Shetland 175 L5
Meadle Bucks 39 D8
Meadowtown Shrops 60 D3
Meaford Staffs 75 F5
Meal Bank Cumb 99 E7
Mealabost W Isles 172 E7
Mealabost Bhuirgh W Isles 172 C7
Mealsgate Cumb 108 E2
Meanwood W Yorks 95 F5
Mearbeck N Yorks 93 C8
Meare Som 23 E6
Meare Green Som 11 B8
Mears Ashby Northants 53 C6
Measham Leics 63 C7
Meath Green Sur 28 E3
Meathop Cumb 99 F6
Meaux E Yorks 97 F6
Meavy Devon 6 C3
Medbourne Leics 64 E4
Medburn Northumb 110 B4
Meddon Devon 8 C4
Meden Vale Notts 77 C5
Medlam Lincs 79 D6
Medmenham Bucks 39 F8
Medomsley Durham 110 D4
Medstead Hants 26 F4
Meer End W Mid 51 B7
Meerbrook Staffs 75 C6
Meers Bridge Lincs 91 F8
Meesden Herts 54 F5
Meeth Devon 9 D7
Meggethead Borders 114 B4
Meidrim Carms 32 B3
Meifod Denb 72 D4
Meifod Powys 59 C8
Meigle N Ayrs 129 D6
Meigle Perth 142 E2
Meikle Earnock S Lnrk 121 D7
Meikle Ferry Highld 164 F4
Meikle Forter Angus 142 C1
Meikle Gluich Highld 164 F3
Meikle Pinkerton E Loth 124 B3
Meikle Strath Aberds 143 B6
Meikle Tarty Aberds 151 B8
Meikle Wartle Aberds 160 E4
Meikleour Perth 142 F1
Meinciau Carms 33 C5
Meir Stoke 75 E6
Meir Heath Staffs 75 E6
Melbourn Cambs 54 E4
Melbourne Derbys 63 B7
Melbourne E Yorks 96 E3
Melbourne S Lnrk 122 E3
Melbury Abbas Dorset 13 B6
Melbury Bubb Dorset 12 D3
Melbury Osmond Dorset 12 D3
Melbury Sampford Dorset 12 D3
Melby Shetland 175 H3
Melchbourne Beds 53 C8
Melcombe Bingham Dorset 13 D5
Melcombe Regis Dorset 12 F4
Meldon Devon 9 E7
Meldon Northumb 117 F7
Meldreth Cambs 54 E4

Meldrum Ho. Aberds 151 B7
Melfort Argyll 130 D4
Melgarve Highld 147 E7
Meliden Denb 72 A4
Melin-y-coed Conwy 83 E8
Melin-y-ddôl Powys 59 D7
Melin-y-grug Powys 59 D7
Melin-y-Wig Denb 72 E4
Melinbyrhedyn Powys 58 E5
Melincourt Neath 34 D2
Melkinthorpe Cumb 99 B7
Melkridge Northumb 109 C7
Melksham Wilts 24 C4
Melldalloch Argyll 128 C4
Melling Lancs 93 B5
Melling Mers 85 D4
Melling Mount Mers 86 D2
Mellis Suff 56 B5
Mellon Charles Highld 162 E2
Mellon Udrigle Highld 162 E2
Mellor Gtr Man 87 F7
Mellor Lancs 93 F6
Mellor Brook Lancs 93 F6
Mells Som 24 E2
Melmerby Cumb 109 F6
Melmerby N Yorks 95 B6
Melmerby N Yorks 101 F5
Melplash Dorset 12 E2
Melrose Borders 123 F8
Melsetter Orkney 176 H1
Melsonby N Yorks 101 D6
Meltham W Yorks 88 C2
Melton Suff 57 D6
Melton Constable Norf 81 D6
Melton Mowbray Leics 64 C4
Melton Ross N Lincs 90 C4
Meltonby E Yorks 96 D3
Melvaig Highld 154 B3
Melverley Shrops 60 C3
Melverley Green Shrops 60 C3
Melvich Highld 168 C3
Membury Devon 11 D7
Memsie Aberds 161 B6
Memus Angus 142 D4
Menabilly Corn 5 D5
Menai Bridge = Porthaethwy Anglesey 83 D5
Mendham Suff 69 F5
Mendlesham Suff 56 C5
Mendlesham Green Suff 56 C4
Menheniot Corn 5 C7
Mennock Dumfries 113 D8
Menston W Yorks 94 E4
Menstrie Clack 133 E7
Menthorpe N Yorks 96 F2
Mentmore Bucks 40 C2
Meoble Highld 145 E7
Meole Brace Shrops 60 C4
Meols Mers 85 E3
Meonstoke Hants 15 C7
Meopham Kent 29 C7
Meopham Station Kent 29 C7
Mepal Cambs 66 F4
Meppershall Beds 54 F2
Merbach Hereford 48 E5
Mere Ches 86 F5
Mere Wilts 24 F3
Mere Brow Lancs 86 C2
Mere Green W Mid 62 E5
Mereclough Lancs 93 F8
Mereside Blkpool 92 F3
Mereworth Kent 29 D7
Mergie Aberds 151 F6
Meriden W Mid 63 F6
Merkadale Highld 153 F4
Merkland Dumfries 106 B4
Merkland S Ayrs 112 E2
Merkland Lodge Highld 163 B8
Merley Poole 13 E8
Merlin's Bridge Pembs 44 D4
Merrington Shrops 60 B4
Merrion Pembs 44 F4
Merriott Som 12 C2
Merrivale Devon 6 B3
Merrow Sur 27 D8
Merrymeet Corn 5 C7
Merseyside Maritime Museum Mers 85 F4
Mersham Kent 19 B7
Merstham Sur 28 D3
Merston W Sus 16 D2
Merstone I o W 15 F6
Merther Corn 3 B7
Merthyr Carms 32 B4
Merthyr Cynog Powys 47 F8
Merthyr-Dyfan V Glam 22 C3
Merthyr Mawr Bridgend 21 B7
Merthyr Tudful = Merthyr Tydfil M Tydf 34 D4
Merthyr Tydfil = Merthyr Tudful M Tydf 34 D4
Merthyr Vale M Tydf 34 E4
Merton Devon 9 C7
Merton London 28 B3
Merton Norf 68 E2
Merton Oxon 39 C5
Mervinslaw Borders 116 C2
Meshaw Devon 10 C2
Messing Essex 42 C4
Messingham N Lincs 90 D2
Metfield Suff 69 F5
Metheringham Lincs 78 C3
Methil Fife 135 E5
Methlem Gwyn 70 D2
Methley W Yorks 88 B4
Methlick Aberds 161 E5
Methven Perth 134 B2
Methwold Norf 67 E7
Methwold Hythe Norf 67 E7
Metroland, Gateshead T & W 110 C5
Mettingham Suff 69 F6
Mevagissey Corn 3 B9
Mewith Head N Yorks 93 C7
Mexborough S Yorks 89 D5
Mey Highld 169 B7
Meysey Hampton Glos 37 E8
Miabhag W Isles 173 J4
Miabhag W Isles 173 H3
Miabhig W Isles 172 E3
Michaelchurch Hereford 36 B2
Michaelchurch Escley Hereford 48 F5
Michaelchurch on Arrow Powys 48 D4
Michaelston-le-Pit V Glam 22 B3
Michaelston-y-Fedw Newport 35 F6
Michaelstow Corn 5 B5
Michealston-super-Ely Cardiff 22 B3
Micheldever Hants 26 F3
Michelmersh Hants 14 B4
Mickfield Suff 56 C5
Mickle Trafford Ches 73 C8
Micklebring S Yorks 89 E6
Mickleby N Yorks 103 C6
Mickleham Sur 28 D2
Mickleover Derby 76 F3
Micklethwaite W Yorks 94 E4
Mickleton Durham 100 B4
Mickleton Glos 51 E6
Mickletown W Yorks 88 B4
Mickley N Yorks 95 B5
Mickley Square Northumb 110 C3
Mid Ardlaw Aberds 161 B6
Mid Auchinlech Invclyd 120 B3
Mid Beltie Aberds 150 D5
Mid Calder W Loth 122 C3
Mid Cloch Forbie Aberds 160 C4
Mid Clyth Highld 169 F7
Mid-Hants Railway (Watercress Line), New Alresford Hants 26 F3
Mid Lavant W Sus 16 D2
Mid Main Highld 156 F5
Mid Urchany Highld 158 E2
Mid Walls Shetland 175 H4
Mid Yell Shetland 174 D7
Midbea Orkney 176 B3
Middle Assendon Oxon 39 F7
Middle Aston Oxon 38 B4
Middle Barton Oxon 38 B4
Middle Cairncake Aberds 160 D5
Middle Claydon Bucks 39 B7
Middle Drums Angus 143 D5
Middle Handley Derbys 76 B4
Middle Littleton Worcs 51 E5
Middle Maes-coed Hereford 48 F5
Middle Mill Pembs 44 C3
Middle Rasen Lincs 90 F4
Middle Rigg Perth 134 D2
Middle Tysoe Warks 51 E8
Middle Wallop Hants 25 F7
Middle Winterslow Wilts 25 F7
Middle Woodford Wilts 25 F6
Middlebie Dumfries 108 B2
Middleforth Green Lancs 86 B3
Middleham N Yorks 101 F6
Middlehope Shrops 60 F4
Middlemarsh Dorset 12 D4
Middlemuir Aberds 151 B8
Middlesbrough M'bro 102 B2
Middleshaw Cumb 99 F7
Middleshaw Dumfries 107 B8
Middlesmoor N Yorks 94 B3
Middlestone Durham 111 F5
Middlestone Moor Durham 110 F5
Middlestown W Yorks 88 C3
Middlethird Borders 124 E2
Middleton Aberds 151 C7
Middleton Argyll 136 F1
Middleton Cumb 99 F8
Middleton Derbys 76 D2
Middleton Derbys 75 C8
Middleton Essex 56 F2
Middleton Gtr Man 87 D6
Middleton Hants 26 E2
Middleton Hereford 49 C7
Middleton Lancs 92 D4
Middleton Midloth 123 D6
Middleton Norf 67 C6
Middleton Northants 64 F5
Middleton Northumb 117 F6
Middleton Northumb 125 F7
Middleton N Yorks 103 F5
Middleton Perth 134 D3
Middleton Perth 141 E8
Middleton Shrops 49 B7
Middleton Shrops 60 E2
Middleton Shrops 60 B3
Middleton Suff 57 C8
Middleton Swansea 33 F5
Middleton Warks 63 E5
Middleton W Yorks 88 B3
Middleton W Yorks 94 E4
Middleton Cheney Northants 52 E2
Middleton Green Staffs 75 F6
Middleton Hall Northumb 117 B5
Middleton-in-Teesdale Durham 100 B4
Middleton Moor Suff 57 C8
Middleton-on-Leven N Yorks 102 D2
Middleton-on-Sea W Sus 16 D3
Middleton on the Hill Hereford 49 C7
Middleton-on-the-Wolds E Yorks 96 E5
Middleton One Row Darl 102 C1
Middleton Priors Shrops 61 E6
Middleton Quernham N Yorks 95 B6
Middleton Railway, Hunslet W Yorks 88 B4
Middleton St George Darl 101 C8
Middleton Scriven Shrops 61 F6
Middleton Stoney Oxon 39 B5
Middleton Tyas N Yorks 101 D7
Middletown Cumb 98 D1
Middletown Powys 60 C3
Middlewich Ches 74 C3
Middlewood Green Suff 56 C4
Middlezoy Som 23 F5
Middridge Durham 101 B7
Midfield Highld 167 C7
Midge Hall Lancs 86 B3
Midgeholme Cumb 109 D6
Midgham W Berks 26 C3
Midgley W Yorks 87 B8
Midgley W Yorks 88 C3
Midhopestones S Yorks 88 E3
Midhurst W Sus 16 B2
Midlem Borders 115 B8
Midmar Aberds 151 D5
Midsomer Norton Bath 23 D8
Midton Invclyd 129 C7
Midtown Highld 167 C7
Midtown Highld 154 B4
Midtown of Buchromb Moray 159 E7
Midville Lincs 79 D6
Midway Ches 87 F7
Migdale Highld 164 E3
Migvie Aberds 150 D3
Milarrochy Stirl 132 E3
Milborne Port Som 12 C4
Milborne St Andrew Dorset 13 E6
Milborne Wick Som 12 B4
Milbourne Northumb 110 B4
Milburn Cumb 100 B1
Milbury Heath S Glos 36 E3
Milcombe Oxon 52 F2
Milden Suff 56 E3
Mildenhall Suff 55 B8
Mildenhall Wilts 25 C7
Mile Cross Norf 68 C5
Mile Elm Wilts 24 C4
Mile End Essex 43 B5
Mile End Glos 36 C2
Mile Oak Brighton 17 D6
Milebrook Powys 48 B5
Milebush Kent 29 E8
Mileham Norf 68 C2
Milesmark Fife 134 F2
Milestones, Basingstoke Hants 26 D4
Milfield Northumb 124 F5
Milford Derbys 76 E3
Milford Devon 8 B4
Milford Powys 59 E7
Milford Staffs 62 B3
Milford Sur 27 E7
Milford Wilts 14 B2
Milford Haven = Aberdaugleddau Pembs 44 E4
Milford on Sea Hants 14 E3
Milkwall Glos 36 D2
Milkwell Wilts 13 B7
Mill Bank W Yorks 87 B8
Mill Common Suff 69 F7
Mill End Bucks 39 F7
Mill End Herts 54 F4
Mill Green Essex 42 D2
Mill Green Norf 68 F4
Mill Green Suff 56 E3
Mill Hill London 41 E5
Mill Lane Hants 27 D5
Mill of Kingoodie Aberds 151 B7
Mill of Muiresk Aberds 160 D3
Mill of Sterin Aberds 150 E2
Mill of Uras Aberds 151 F7
Mill Place N Lincs 90 D3
Mill Side Cumb 99 F6
Mill Street Norf 68 C3
Milland W Sus 16 B2
Millarston Renfs 120 C4
Millbank Aberds 161 D8
Millbank Highld 169 C6
Millbeck Cumb 98 B4
Millbounds Orkney 176 C4
Millbreck Aberds 161 D7
Millbridge Sur 27 E6
Millbrook Beds 53 F8
Millbrook Corn 6 D2
Millbrook Soton 14 C4
Millburn S Ayrs 112 B4
Millcombe Devon 7 E6
Millcorner E Sus 18 C5
Milldale Staffs 75 D8
Millden Lodge Angus 143 B5
Milldens Angus 143 D5
Millennium Stadium Cardiff 22 B3
Millerhill Midloth 123 C6
Miller's Dale Derbys 75 B8
Miller's Green Derbys 76 D2
Millgreen Shrops 61 B6
Millhalf Hereford 48 E4
Millhayes Devon 11 D7
Millhead Lancs 92 B4
Millheugh S Lnrk 121 D7
Millholme Cumb 99 E7
Millhouse Argyll 128 C4
Millhouse Cumb 108 F3
Millhouse Green S Yorks 88 D3
Millhousebridge Dumfries 114 F4
Millhouses S Yorks 88 F4
Millikenpark Renfs 120 C4
Millin Cross Pembs 44 D4
Millington E Yorks 96 D4
Millmeece Staffs 74 F5
Millom Cumb 98 F3
Millook Corn 8 E3
Millpool Corn 5 B6
Millport N Ayrs 129 E6
Millquarter Dumfries 113 F6
Millthorpe Lincs 78 F4
Millthrop Cumb 100 E1
Milltimber Aberdeen 151 D7
Milltown Corn 5 D6
Milltown Derbys 76 C3
Milltown Devon 20 F4
Milltown Dumfries 108 B3
Milltown of Aberdalgie Perth 134 B2
Milltown of Auchindoun Moray 159 E7
Milltown of Craigston Aberds 160 C4
Milltown of Edinvillie Moray 159 E6
Milltown of Kildrummy Aberds 150 C3
Milltown of Rothiemay Moray 160 D2
Milltown of Towie Aberds 150 C3
Milnathort Perth 134 D3
Milner's Heath Ches 73 C8
Milngavie E Dunb 121 B5
Milnrow Gtr Man 87 C7
Milnshaw Lancs 87 B5
Milnthorpe Cumb 99 F6
Milo Carms 33 C6
Milson Shrops 49 B8
Milstead Kent 30 D3
Milston Wilts 25 E6
Milton Angus 142 E3
Milton Cambs 55 C5
Milton Cumb 109 C5
Milton Derbys 63 B7
Milton Dumfries 105 D6
Milton Dumfries 106 B5
Milton Dumfries 113 F8
Milton Highld 156 D4
Milton Highld 157 F5
Milton Highld 157 E6
Milton Highld 169 D8
Milton Highld 157 B8
Milton Moray 160 B2
Milton Notts 77 B7
Milton N Som 22 C5
Milton Oxon 52 F2
Milton Oxon 38 E4
Milton Pembs 32 D1
Milton Perth 133 C8
Milton Ptsmth 15 E7
Milton Stirl 132 D4
Milton Stoke 75 D6
Milton W Dunb 120 B4
Milton Abbas Dorset 13 D6
Milton Abbot Devon 6 B2
Milton Bridge Midloth 122 C5
Milton Bryan Beds 53 F7
Milton Clevedon Som 23 F8
Milton Coldwells Aberds 161 E6
Milton Combe Devon 6 C2
Milton Damerel Devon 9 C5
Milton End Glos 37 D8
Milton Ernest Beds 53 D8
Milton Green Ches 73 D8
Milton Hill Oxon 38 E4
Milton Keynes M Keynes 53 F6
Milton Keynes Village M Keynes 53 F6
Milton Lilbourne Wilts 25 C6
Milton Malsor Northants 52 D5
Milton Morenish Perth 140 F3
Milton of Auchinhove Aberds 150 D4
Milton of Balgonie Fife 134 D5
Milton of Buchanan Stirl 132 E3
Milton of Campfield Aberds 150 D5
Milton of Campsie E Dunb 121 B6
Milton of Corsindae Aberds 151 D5
Milton of Cushnie Aberds 150 C4
Milton of Dalcapon Perth 141 D6
Milton of Edradour Perth 141 D6
Milton of Gollanfield Highld 157 D8
Milton of Lesmore Aberds 150 B3
Milton of Logie Aberds 150 D3
Milton of Murtle Aberdeen 151 D7
Milton of Noth Aberds 150 B4
Milton of Tullich Aberds 150 E2
Milton on Stour Dorset 13 B5
Milton Regis Kent 30 C3
Milton under Wychwood Oxon 38 C2
Miltonduff Moray 159 C5
Miltonhill Moray 158 C4
Miltonise Dumfries 105 B5
Milverton Som 11 B6
Milverton Warks 51 C8
Milwich Staffs 75 F6
Minard Argyll 131 F5
Minchinhampton Glos 37 D5
Mindrum Northumb 124 F4
Minehead Som 21 E8
Minera Wrex 73 D6
Minesmere RSPB Nature Reserve Suff 57 C8
Minety Wilts 37 E7
Minffordd Gwyn 71 D6
Minffordd Gwyn 58 C4
Minffordd Gwyn 83 D5
Miningsby Lincs 79 C6
Minions Corn 5 B7
Minishant S Ayrs 112 C3
Minllyn Gwyn 59 C5
Minnes Aberds 151 B8
Minngearraidh W Isles 171 H3
Minnigaff Dumfries 105 C8
Minnonie Aberds 160 B4
Minskip N Yorks 95 C6
Minstead Hants 14 C3
Minsted W Sus 16 B2
Minster Kent 30 B3
Minster Kent 31 C7
Minster Lovell Oxon 38 C3
Minsterley Shrops 60 D3
Minsterworth Glos 36 C4
Minterne Magna Dorset 12 D4
Minting Lincs 78 B4
Mintlaw Aberds 161 D7
Minto Borders 115 B8
Minton Shrops 60 E4
Minwear Pembs 32 C1
Minworth W Mid 63 E5
Mirbister Orkney 176 D2
Mirehouse Cumb 98 C1
Mireland Highld 169 C8
Mirfield W Yorks 88 C3
Miserden Glos 37 D6
Miskin Rhondda 34 F4
Misson Notts 89 E7
Misterton Leics 64 F2
Misterton Notts 89 E8
Misterton Som 12 D2
Mistley Essex 56 F5
Mitcham London 28 C3
Mitchel Troy Mon 36 C1
Mitcheldean Glos 36 C3
Mitchell Corn 4 D3
Mitcheltroy Common Mon 36 D1
Mitford Northumb 117 F7
Mithian Corn 4 D2
Mitton Staffs 62 C2
Mixbury Oxon 52 F4
Moat Cumb 108 B4
Moats Tye Suff 56 D4
Mobberley Ches 74 B4
Mobberley Staffs 75 E7
Moccas Hereford 49 E5
Mochdre Conwy 83 D8
Mochdre Powys 59 F7
Mochrum Dumfries 105 E7
Mockbeggar Hants 14 D2
Mockerkin Cumb 98 B2
Modbury Devon 6 D4
Moddershall Staffs 75 F6
Model Village, Babbacombe Devon 7 C7
Moelfre Anglesey 82 C5
Moelfre Powys 59 B8
Moffat Dumfries 114 D3
Moggerhanger Beds 54 E2
Moira Leics 63 C7
Mol-chlach Highld 153 H5
Molash Kent 30 D4
Mold = Yr Wyddgrug Flint 73 C6
Moldgreen W Yorks 88 C2
Molehill Green Essex 42 B1
Molescroft E Yorks 97 E6
Molesden Northumb 117 F7
Molesworth Cambs 53 B8
Moll Highld 153 F6
Molland Devon 10 B3
Mollington Ches 73 B7
Mollington Oxon 52 E2
Mollinsburn N Lnrk 121 B7
Monachty Ceredig 46 C4
Monachylemore Stirl 132 C3
Monar Lodge Highld 156 E3
Monaughty Powys 48 C4
Monboddo House Aberds 143 B7
Mondynes Aberds 143 B7
Monevechadan Argyll 131 E7
Monewden Suff 57 D6
Moneydie Perth 134 B2
Moniaive Dumfries 113 E7
Monifieth Angus 142 F4
Monikie Angus 142 F4
Monimail Fife 134 C4
Monington Pembs 45 E3
Monk Bretton S Yorks 88 D4
Monk Fryston N Yorks 89 B6
Monk Sherborne Hants 26 D4
Monk Soham Suff 57 C6
Monk Street Essex 42 B2
Monken Hadley London 41 E5
Monkhopton Shrops 61 E6
Monkland Hereford 49 D6
Monkleigh Devon 9 B6
Monknash V Glam 21 B8
Monkokehampton Devon 9 D7
Monks Eleigh Suff 56 E3
Monk's Gate W Sus 17 B6
Monks Heath Ches 74 B5
Monks Kirby Warks 63 F8
Monks Risborough Bucks 39 D8
Monkseaton T & W 111 B6
Monkshill Aberds 160 D4
Monksilver Som 22 F2
Monkspath W Mid 51 B6
Monkswood Mon 35 D7
Monkton Devon 11 D6
Monkton Kent 31 C6
Monkton Pembs 44 E4
Monkton S Ayrs 112 B3
Monkton Combe Bath 24 C2
Monkton Deverill Wilts 24 F3
Monkton Farleigh Wilts 24 C3
Monkton Heathfield Som 11 B7
Monkton Up Wimborne Dorset 13 C8
Monkwearmouth T & W 111 D6
Monkwood Hants 26 F4
Monmouth = Trefynwy Mon 36 C2
Monmouth Cap Mon 35 B7
Monnington on Wye Hereford 49 E5
Monreith Dumfries 105 E7
Monreith Mains Dumfries 105 E7
Mont Saint Guern 16
Montacute Som 12 C2
Montacute House Som 12 C3
Montcoffer Ho. Aberds 160 B3
Montford Argyll 129 D6
Montford Shrops 60 C4
Montford Bridge Shrops 60 C4
Montgarrie Aberds 150 C4
Montgomery = Trefaldwyn Powys 60 E2
Montrave Fife 135 D5
Montrose Angus 143 D7
Montsale Essex 43 E6
Monxton Hants 25 E8
Monyash Derbys 75 C8
Monymusk Aberds 151 C5
Monzie Perth 133 B7
Monzie Castle Perth 133 B7
Moodiesburn N Lnrk 121 B6
Moonzie Fife 134 C5
Moor Allerton W Yorks 95 F5
Moor Crichel Dorset 13 D7
Moor End E Yorks 96 F4
Moor End York 96 D2
Moor Monkton N Yorks 95 D8
Moor of Granary Moray 158 D4
Moor of Ravenstone Dumfries 105 E7
Moor Row Cumb 98 C2
Moor Street Kent 30 C2
Moorby Lincs 79 C5
Moordown Bmouth 13 E8
Moore Halton 86 F3
Moorend Glos 36 D4
Moorends S Yorks 89 C7
Moorgate S Yorks 88 E5
Moorgreen Notts 76 E4
Moorhall Derbys 76 B3
Moorhampton Hereford 49 E5
Moorhead W Yorks 94 F4
Moorhouse Cumb 108 D3
Moorhouse Notts 77 C7
Moorlinch Som 23 F5
Moorsholm Redcar 102 C4
Moorside Gtr Man 87 D7
Moorthorpe W Yorks 89 C5
Moortown Hants 14 D2
Moortown I o W 14 F5
Moortown Lincs 90 E4
Morangie Highld 164 F4
Morar Highld 145 D6
Morborne Cambs 65 E8
Morchard Bishop Devon 10 D2
Morcombelake Dorset 12 E2
Morcott Rutland 65 D6
Morda Shrops 60 B2
Morden Dorset 13 E7
Morden London 28 C3
Mordiford Hereford 49 F7
Mordon Durham 101 B8
More Shrops 60 E3
Morebath Devon 10 B4
Morebattle Borders 116 B3
Morecambe Lancs 92 C4
Morefield Highld 163 E5
Moreleigh Devon 7 D5
Morenish Perth 140 F2
Moresby Cumb 98 B1
Moresby Parks Cumb 98 C1
Morestead Hants 15 B6
Moreton Dorset 13 F6
Moreton Essex 41 D8
Moreton Mers 85 E3
Moreton Oxon 39 D6
Moreton Staffs 61 C7
Moreton Corbet Shrops 61 B5
Moreton-in-Marsh Glos 51 F7
Moreton Jeffries Hereford 49 E8
Moreton Morrell Warks 51 D8
Moreton on Lugg Hereford 49 E7
Moreton Pinkney Northants 52 E3
Moreton Say Shrops 74 F3
Moreton Valence Glos 36 D4
Moretonhampstead Devon 10 F2
Morfa Carms 33 C6
Morfa Carms 33 E6
Morfa Bach Carms 32 C4
Morfa Bychan Gwyn 71 D6
Morfa Dinlle Gwyn 82 F4
Morfa Glas Neath 34 D2
Morfa Nefyn Gwyn 70 C3
Morfydd Denb 72 E5
Morgan's Vale Wilts 14 B2
Moriah Ceredig 46 B5
Morland Cumb 99 B7
Morley Derbys 76 E3
Morley Durham 101 B6
Morley W Yorks 88 B3
Morley Green Ches 87 F6
Morley St Botolph Norf 68 E3
Morningside Edin 122 B5
Morningside N Lnrk 121 D8
Morningthorpe Norf 68 E5
Morpeth Northumb 117 F8
Morphie Aberds 143 C7
Morrey Staffs 62 C5
Morris Green Essex 55 F8
Morriston Swansea 33 E7
Morston Norf 81 C6
Mortehoe Devon 20 E3
Mortimer W Berks 26 C4
Mortimer West End Hants 26 C4
Mortimer's Cross Hereford 49 C6
Mortlake London 28 B3
Morton Cumb 108 D3
Morton Derbys 76 C4
Morton Lincs 65 B7
Morton Lincs 90 E2
Morton Lincs 77 C8
Morton Norf 68 C4
Morton Notts 77 D7
Morton Shrops 60 B2
Morton S Glos 36 E3
Morton Bagot Warks 51 C6
Morton-on-Swale N Yorks 101 E8
Morvah Corn 2 C3
Morval Corn 5 D7
Morvich Highld 146 B2
Morvich Highld 164 D4
Morville Shrops 61 E6
Morville Heath Shrops 61 E6
Morwenstow Corn 8 C4
Mosborough S Yorks 88 F5
Moscow E Ayrs 120 E4
Mosedale Cumb 108 F3
Moseley W Mid 62 F4
Moseley W Mid 62 E3
Moseley Worcs 50 D3
Mosquito Aircraft Museum, London Colney Herts 40 D4
Moss Argyll 136 F1
Moss Highld 137 B7
Moss S Yorks 89 C6
Moss Wrex 73 D7
Moss Bank Mers 86 E3
Moss Edge Lancs 92 E4
Moss End Brack 27 B6
Moss of Barmuckity Moray 159 C6
Moss Pit Staffs 62 B3
Moss-side Highld 158 D2
Moss Side Lancs 92 F3
Mossat Aberds 150 C3
Mossbank Shetland 174 F6
Mossbay Cumb 98 B1
Mossblown S Ayrs 112 B4
Mossbrow Gtr Man 86 F5
Mossburnford Borders 116 C2
Mossdale Dumfries 106 B3
Mossend N Lnrk 121 C7
Mosser Cumb 98 B3
Mossfield Highld 157 B7
Mossgiel E Ayrs 112 B4
Mosside Angus 142 D4
Mossley Ches 75 C5
Mossley Gtr Man 87 D7
Mossley Hill Mers 85 F4
Mosstodloch Moray 159 D7
Mosston Angus 143 E5
Mossy Lea Lancs 86 C3
Mosterton Dorset 12 D2
Moston Gtr Man 87 D6
Moston Shrops 61 B5
Moston Green Ches 74 C4
Mostyn Flint 85 F2
Mostyn Quay Flint 85 F2
Motcombe Dorset 13 B6
Mothecombe Devon 6 E4
Motherby Cumb 99 B6
Motherwell N Lnrk 121 D7
Mottingham London 28 B5
Mottisfont Hants 14 B4
Mottisfont Abbey Garden Hants 14 B4
Mottistone I o W 14 F5
Mottram in Longdendale Gtr Man 87 E7
Mottram St Andrew Ches 75 B5
Mouilpied Guern 16
Mouldsworth Ches 74 B2
Moulin Perth 141 D6
Moulsecoomb Brighton 17 D7
Moulsford Oxon 39 F5
Moulsoe M Keynes 53 E7
Moulton Ches 74 C3
Moulton Lincs 66 B3
Moulton Northants 53 C5
Moulton N Yorks 101 D7
Moulton Suff 55 C7
Moulton V Glam 22 B2
Moulton Chapel Lincs 66 C2
Moulton Eaugate Lincs 66 C3
Moulton St Mary Norf 69 D6
Moulton Seas End Lincs 66 B3
Mounie Castle Aberds 151 B6
Mount Corn 4 D2
Mount Corn 5 C6
Mount Highld 158 E3
Mount Bures Essex 56 F3
Mount Canisp Highld 157 B8
Mount Hawke Corn 3 B6
Mount Pleasant Ches 74 D5
Mount Pleasant Derbys 76 E3
Mount Pleasant Derbys 63 C6
Mount Pleasant Flint 73 B6
Mount Pleasant Hants 14 E3
Mount Pleasant W Yorks 88 B3
Mount Sorrel Wilts 13 B8
Mount Tabor W Yorks 87 B8
Mountain W Yorks 94 F3
Mountain Ash = Aberpennar Rhondda 34 E4
Mountain Cross Borders 122 E4
Mountain Water Pembs 44 C4
Mountbenger Borders 115 B6
Mountfield E Sus 18 C4
Mountgerald Highld 157 C6
Mountjoy Corn 4 C3
Mountnessing Essex 42 E2
Mounton Mon 36 E2
Mountsorrel Leics 64 C2
Mousehole Corn 2 D3
Mousen Northumb 125 F7
Mouswald Dumfries 107 B7
Mow Cop Ches 75 D5
Mowhaugh Borders 116 B4
Mowsley Leics 64 F3
Moxley W Mid 62 E3
Moy Highld 147 F7
Moy Highld 157 F8
Moy Hall Highld 157 F8
Moy Ho. Moray 158 C4
Moy Lodge Highld 147 F7
Moyles Court Hants 14 D2
Moylgrove Pembs 45 E3
Muasdale Argyll 118 B3
Much Birch Hereford 49 F7
Much Cowarne Hereford 49 E8
Much Dewchurch Hereford 49 F6
Much Hadham Herts 41 C7
Much Hoole Lancs 86 B2
Much Marcle Hereford 49 F8
Much Wenlock Shrops 61 D6
Muchalls Aberds 151 E8
Muchelney Som 12 B2
Muchlarnick Corn 5 D7
Muchrachd Highld 156 F3
Muckernich Highld 157 D6
Mucking Thurrock 42 F2
Muckleford Dorset 12 E4
Mucklestone Staffs 74 F4
Muckleton Shrops 61 B5
Muckletown Aberds 150 B4
Muckley Corner Staffs 62 D4
Muckton Lincs 91 F7
Mudale Highld 167 F7
Muddiford Devon 20 F4
Mudeford Dorset 14 E2
Mudford Som 12 C3
Mudgley Som 23 E6
Mugdock Stirl 121 B5
Mugeary Highld 153 F5
Mugginton Derbys 76 E2
Muggleswick Durham 110 E3
Muie Highld 164 D3
Muir Aberds 149 F6
Muir of Fairburn Highld 157 D5
Muir of Fowlis Aberds 150 C4
Muir of Ord Highld 157 D6
Muir of Pert Angus 142 F4
Muirden Aberds 160 C4
Muirdrum Angus 143 F5
Muirhead Angus 142 F3
Muirhead Fife 134 D4
Muirhead N Lnrk 121 C6
Muirhead S Ayrs 120 F3
Muirhouselaw Borders 116 B2
Muirhouses Falk 134 F2
Muirkirk E Ayrs 113 B6
Muirmill Stirl 133 F6
Muirshearlich Highld 146 F4
Muirskie Aberds 151 E7
Muirtack Aberds 161 E6
Muirton Highld 157 C8
Muirton Perth 134 B3
Muirton Perth 133 C8
Muirton Mains Highld 157 D5
Muirton of Ardblair Perth 142 E1
Muirton of Ballochy Angus 143 C6
Muiryfold Aberds 160 C4
Muker N Yorks 100 E4
Mulbarton Norf 68 D4
Mulben Moray 159 D7
Mulindry Argyll 126 D3
Mullardoch House Highld 156 F3
Mullion Corn 3 E5
Mullion Cove Corn 3 E5
Mumby Lincs 79 B8
Muncaster Owl Trust World HQ Cumb 98 E3
Munderfield Row Hereford 49 D8
Munderfield Stocks Hereford 49 D8
Mundesley Norf 81 D9
Mundford Norf 67 E8
Mundham Norf 69 E6
Mundon Essex 42 D4
Mundurno Aberdeen 151 C8
Munerigie Highld 147 D5
Muness Shetland 174 C8
Mungasdale Highld 162 E3
Mungrisdale Cumb 108 F3
Munlochy Highld 157 D7
Munsley Hereford 49 E8
Munslow Shrops 60 F5
Murchington Devon 9 F8
Murcott Oxon 39 C5
Murkle Highld 169 C6
Murlaggan Highld 146 E3
Murlaggan Highld 147 F6

Parkstone Poole 13 E8
Parley Cross Dorset 13 E8
Parracombe Devon 21 E5
Parrog Pembs 45 F2
Parsley Hay Derbys 75 C8
Parson Cross S Yorks 88 E4
Parson Drove Cambs 66 D3
Parsonage Green Essex 42 D3
Parsonby Cumb 107 F8
Parson's Heath Essex 43 B6
Partick Glasgow 121 C5
Partington Gtr Man 86 E5
Partney Lincs 79 C7
Parton Cumb 98 B1
Parton Dumfries 106 B3
Parton Glos 37 B5
Partridge Green W Sus 17 C5
Parwich Derbys 75 D8
Passenham Northants 53 F5
Paston Norf 81 D9
Patchacott Devon 9 E6
Patcham Brighton 17 D7
Patching W Sus 16 D4
Patchole Devon 20 E5
Patchway S Glos 36 F3
Pateley Bridge N Yorks 94 C4
Paternoster Heath Essex 43 C5
Path of Condie Perth 134 C2
Pathe Som 23 F5
Pathhead Aberds 143 C7
Pathhead E Ayrs 113 C6
Pathhead Fife 134 E4
Pathhead Midloth 123 C6
Pathstruie Perth 134 C2
Patna E Ayrs 112 C4
Patney Wilts 25 D5
Patrick I o M 84 D2
Patrick Brompton N Yorks 101 E7
Patrington E Yorks 91 B7
Patrixbourne Kent 31 D5
Patterdale Cumb 99 C5
Pattingham Staffs 62 E2
Pattishall Northants 52 D4
Pattiswick Green Essex 42 B4
Patton Bridge Cumb 99 E7
Paul Corn 2 D3
Paulerspury Northants 52 E5
Paull E Yorks 91 B5
Paulton Bath 23 D8
Paultons Park, Totton Hants 14 C4
Pavenham Beds 53 D7
Pawlett Som 22 E5
Pawston Northumb 124 F4
Paxford Glos 51 F6
Paxton Borders 124 D5
Payhembury Devon 11 D5
Paythorne Lancs 93 D8
Peacehaven E Sus 17 D8
Peak Dale Derbys 75 B7
Peak Forest Derbys 75 B8
Peakirk P'boro 65 D8
Pearsie Angus 142 D3
Pease Pottage W Sus 28 F3
Peasedown St John Bath 24 D2
Peasemore W Berks 26 B2
Peasenhall Suff 57 C7
Peaslake Sur 27 E8
Peasley Cross Mers 86 E3
Peasmarsh E Sus 19 C5
Peaston E Loth 123 C7
Peastonbank E Loth 123 C7
Peat Inn Fife 135 D6
Peathill Aberds 161 B6
Peatling Magna Leics 64 E2
Peatling Parva Leics 64 F2
Peaton Shrops 60 F5
Peats Corner Suff 57 C5
Pebmarsh Essex 56 F2
Pebworth Worcs 51 E6
Pecket Well W Yorks 87 B7
Peckforton Ches 74 D2
Peckham London 28 B4
Peckleton Leics 63 D8
Pedlinge Kent 19 B8
Pedmore W Mid 62 F3
Pedwell Som 23 F6
Peebles Borders 123 E5
Peel I o M 84 D2
Peel Common Hants 15 D6
Peel Park S Lnrk 121 D6
Peening Quarter Kent 19 C5
Pegsdon Beds 54 F2
Pegswood Northumb 117 F8
Pegwell Kent 31 C7
Peinchorran Highld 153 F6
Peinlich Highld 152 D5
Pelaw T & W 111 C5
Pelcomb Bridge Pembs 44 D4
Pelcomb Cross Pembs 44 D4
Peldon Essex 43 C5
Pellon W Yorks 87 B8
Pelsall W Mid 62 D4
Pelton Durham 111 D5
Pelutho Cumb 107 E8
Pelynt Corn 5 D7
Pemberton Gtr Man 86 D3
Pembrey Carms 33 D5
Pembrey Motor Racing Circuit Carms 33 D5
Pembridge Hereford 49 D5
Pembroke = Penfro Pembs 44 E4
Pembroke Castle Pembs 44 E4
Pembroke Dock = Doc Penfro Pembs 44 E4
Pembury Kent 29 E7
Pen-bont Rhydybeddau Ceredig 58 F3
Pen-clawdd Swansea 33 E6
Pen-ffordd Pembs 32 B1
Pen-groes-oped Mon 35 D7
Pen-llyn Anglesey 82 C3
Pen-lon Anglesey 82 E4
Pen-sarn Gwyn 70 C5
Pen-sarn Gwyn 71 E6
Pen-twyn Mon 36 D2
Pen-y-banc Carms 33 B7
Pen-y-bont Carms 32 B4
Pen-y-bont Gwyn 58 D4
Pen-y-bont Gwyn 71 E7
Pen-y-bont Powys 60 B2
Pen-y-bont ar Ogwr = Bridgend Bridgend 21 B8
Pen-y-bryn Gwyn 58 C3
Pen-y-bryn Pembs 45 E3
Pen-y-cae Powys 34 C2
Pen-y-cae-mawr Mon 35 E8
Pen-y-cefn Flint 72 B5
Pen-y-clawdd Mon 36 D1
Pen-y-coedcae Rhondda 34 F4
Pen-y-fai Bridgend 34 F2
Pen-y-garn Ceredig 58 F3
Pen-y-garn Carms 46 F4
Pen-y-garnedd Anglesey 82 D5
Pen-y-gop Conwy 72 E3
Pen-y-graig Gwyn 70 D2
Pen-y-groes Carms 33 C6
Pen-y-groeslon Gwyn 70 D3
Pen-y-Gwryd Hotel Gwyn 83 F6
Pen-y-stryt Denb 73 D5
Pen-yr-heol Mon 35 C8
Pen-yr-Heolgerrig M Tydf 34 D4
Penallt Mon 36 C2
Penally Pembs 32 E2
Penalt Hereford 36 B2
Penare Corn 3 B8
Penarlâg = Hawarden Flint 73 C7
Penarth V Glam 22 B3
Penbryn Ceredig 45 D4
Pencader Carms 46 F3
Pencaenewydd Gwyn 70 C5
Pencaitland E Loth 123 C7
Pencarnisiog Anglesey 82 D3
Pencarreg Carms 46 E4
Pencelli Powys 34 B4
Pencoed Bridgend 34 F3
Pencombe Hereford 49 D7
Pencoyd Hereford 36 B2
Pencraig Hereford 36 B2
Pencraig Powys 59 B7
Pendeen Corn 2 C2
Pendennis Castle Corn 4 F3
Penderyn Rhondda 34 D3
Pendine Carms 32 D3
Pendlebury Gtr Man 87 D5
Pendleton Lancs 93 F7
Pendock Worcs 50 F2
Pendoggett Corn 4 B5
Pendomer Som 12 C3
Pendoylan V Glam 22 B2
Pendre Bridgend 34 F3
Penegoes Powys 58 D4
Penfro = Pembroke Pembs 44 E4
Pengam Caerph 35 E5
Penge London 28 B4
Pengenffordd Powys 48 F3
Pengorffwysfa Anglesey 82 B4
Pengover Green Corn 5 C7
Penhale Corn 3 E5
Penhale Corn 4 D4
Penhalvaen Corn 3 C6
Penhill Swindon 38 F1
Penhow Newport 35 E8
Penhurst E Sus 18 D3
Peniarth Gwyn 58 D3
Penicuik Midloth 122 C5
Peniel Carms 33 B5
Peniel Denb 72 C4
Penifiler Highld 153 E5
Peninver Argyll 118 D4
Penisarwaun Gwyn 83 E5
Penistone S Yorks 88 D3
Penjerrick Corn 3 C6
Penketh Warr 86 F3
Penkill S Ayrs 112 E2
Penkridge Staffs 62 C3
Penley Wrex 73 F8
Penllergaer Swansea 33 E7
Penllyn V Glam 21 B8
Penmachno Conwy 83 F7
Penmaen Swansea 33 F6
Penmaenan Conwy 83 D7
Penmaenmawr Conwy 83 D7
Penmaenpool Gwyn 58 C3
Penmark V Glam 22 C2
Penmarth Corn 3 C6
Penmon Anglesey 83 C6
Penmore Mill Argyll 137 C5
Penmorfa Ceredig 46 D2
Penmorfa Gwyn 71 C6
Penmynydd Anglesey 82 D5
Penn Bucks 40 E2
Penn W Mid 62 E2
Penn Street Bucks 40 E2
Pennal Gwyn 58 D4
Pennan Aberds 160 B5
Pennant Ceredig 46 C4
Pennant Denb 72 F4
Pennant Denb 72 D4
Pennant Powys 59 E5
Pennant Melangell Powys 59 B7
Pennar Pembs 44 E4
Pennard Swansea 33 F6
Pennerley Shrops 60 E3
Pennington Cumb 92 B2
Pennington Gtr Man 86 E4
Pennington Hants 14 E4
Penny Bridge Cumb 99 F5
Pennycross Argyll 137 F6
Pennygate Norf 69 B6
Pennygown Argyll 137 D6
Pennymoor Devon 10 C3
Pennywell T & W 111 D6
Penparc Ceredig 45 E4
Penparc Pembs 44 B3
Penparcau Ceredig 58 F2
Penperlleni Mon 35 D7
Penpillick Corn 5 D5
Penpol Corn 3 C7
Penpoll Corn 5 D6
Penpont Dumfries 113 E8
Penpont Powys 34 B3
Penrherber Carms 45 F4
Penrhiw goch Carms 33 C6
Penrhiw-llan Ceredig 46 E2
Penrhiw-pâl Ceredig 46 E2
Penrhiwceiber Rhondda 34 E4
Penrhos Gwyn 70 D4
Penrhôs Mon 35 C8
Penrhos Powys 34 C1
Penrhosfeilw Anglesey 82 C2
Penrhyn Bay Conwy 83 C8
Penrhyn Castle Gwyn 83 D6
Penrhyn-coch Ceredig 58 F3
Penrhyndeudraeth Gwyn 71 D7
Penrhynside Conwy 83 C8
Penrice Swansea 33 F5
Penrith Cumb 108 F5
Penrose Corn 4 B3
Penruddock Cumb 99 B6
Penryn Corn 3 C6
Pensarn Carms 33 C5
Pensarn Conwy 72 B3
Pensax Worcs 50 C2
Pensby Mers 85 F3
Penselwood Som 24 F2
Pensford Bath 23 C8
Penshaw T & W 111 D6
Penshurst Kent 29 E6
Pensilva Corn 5 C7
Penston E Loth 123 B7
Pentewan Corn 3 B9
Pentir Gwyn 83 E5
Pentire Corn 4 C2
Pentlow Essex 56 E2
Pentney Norf 67 C7
Penton Mewsey Hants 25 E8
Pentraeth Anglesey 82 D5
Pentre Carms 33 C6
Pentre Powys 59 F7
Pentre Powys 60 E2
Pentre Rhondda 34 E3
Pentre Shrops 60 C3
Pentre Wrex 73 E6
Pentre Wrex 72 F5
Pentre-bâch Ceredig 46 E4
Pentre-bach Powys 47 F8
Pentre Berw Anglesey 82 D4
Pentre-bont Conwy 83 F7
Pentre-celyn Denb 72 D5
Pentre-Celyn Powys 59 D5
Pentre-chwyth Swansea 33 E7
Pentre-cwrt Carms 46 F2
Pentre Dolau-Honddu Powys 47 E8
Pentre-dwr Swansea 33 E7
Pentre-galar Pembs 45 F3
Pentre-Gwenlais Carms 33 C7
Pentre Gwynfryn Gwyn 71 E6
Pentre Halkyn Flint 73 B6
Pentre-Isaf Conwy 83 E8
Pentre Llanrhaeadr Denb 72 C4
Pentre-llwyn-llŵyd Powys 47 D8
Pentre-llyn Ceredig 46 B5
Pentre-llyn cymmer Conwy 72 D3
Pentre Meyrick V Glam 21 B8
Pentre-poeth Newport 35 F6
Pentre-rhew Ceredig 47 D5
Pentre-tafarn-y-fedw Conwy 83 E8
Pentre-ty-gwyn Carms 47 F7
Pentrebach M Tydf 34 D4
Pentrebach Swansea 33 D7
Pentrebeirdd Powys 59 C8
Pentrecagal Carms 46 E2
Pentredwr Denb 73 E5
Pentrefelin Ceredig 46 E5
Pentrefelin Carms 33 B6
Pentrefelin Conwy 83 D8
Pentrefelin Gwyn 71 D6
Pentrefoelas Conwy 83 F8
Pentregat Ceredig 46 D2
Pentreheyling Shrops 60 E2
Pentre'r Felin Conwy 83 E8
Pentre'r-felin Powys 47 F8
Pentrich Derbys 76 D3
Pentridge Dorset 13 C8
Pentyrch Cardiff 35 F5
Penuchadre V Glam 21 B7
Penuwch Ceredig 46 C4
Penwithick Corn 4 D5
Penwyllt Powys 34 C2
Penybanc Carms 33 C7
Penybont Powys 48 C3
Penybontfawr Powys 59 B7
Penycae Wrex 73 E6
Penycwm Pembs 44 C3
Penyffordd Flint 73 C7
Penyffridd Gwyn 82 F5
Penygarnedd Powys 59 B8
Penygraig Rhondda 34 E3
Penygroes Gwyn 82 F4
Penygroes Pembs 45 F3
Penyrheol Caerph 35 F5
Penysarn Anglesey 82 B4
Penywaun Rhondda 34 D3
Penzance Corn 2 C3
Penzance Heliport Corn 2 C3
People's Palace Glasgow 121 C6
Peopleton Worcs 50 D4
Peover Heath Ches 74 B4
Peper Harow Sur 27 E7
Perceton N Ayrs 120 E3
Percie Aberds 150 E4
Percyhorner Aberds 161 B6
Periton Som 21 E8
Perivale London 40 F4
Perkinsville Durham 111 D5
Perlethorpe Notts 77 B6
Perranarworthal Corn 3 C6
Perranporth Corn 4 D2
Perranuthnoe Corn 2 D4
Perranzabuloe Corn 4 D2
Perry Barr W Mid 62 E4
Perry Green Herts 41 C7
Perry Green Wilts 37 F6
Perry Street Kent 29 B7
Perryfoot Derbys 88 F2
Pershall Staffs 74 F5
Pershore Worcs 50 E4
Pert Angus 143 C6
Pertenhall Beds 53 C8
Perth Perth 134 B3
Perth Racecourse Perth 134 B3
Perthy Shrops 73 F7
Perton Staffs 62 E2
Pertwood Wilts 24 F3
Peter Tavy Devon 6 B3
Peterborough P'boro 65 E8
Peterborough Cathedral P'boro 65 E8
Peterburn Highld 154 B3
Peterchurch Hereford 48 F5
Peterculter Aberdeen 151 D7
Peterhead Aberds 161 D8
Peterlee Durham 111 E7
Peter's Green Herts 40 C4
Peters Marland Devon 9 C6
Petersfield Hants 15 B8
Peterston super-Ely V Glam 22 B2
Peterstone Wentlooge Newport 35 F6
Peterstow Hereford 36 B2
Petertown Orkney 176 F2
Petham Kent 30 D5
Petrockstow Devon 9 D7
Pett E Sus 19 D5
Pettaugh Suff 57 D5
Petteridge Kent 29 E7
Pettinain S Lnrk 122 E2
Pettistree Suff 57 D6
Petton Devon 10 B5
Petton Shrops 60 B4
Petts Wood London 28 C5
Petty Aberds 160 E4
Pettycur Fife 134 F4
Pettymuick Aberds 151 B8
Petworth W Sus 16 B3
Petworth House W Sus 16 B3
Pevensey E Sus 18 E3
Pevensey Bay E Sus 18 E3
Pewsey Wilts 25 C6
Philham Devon 8 B4
Philiphaugh Borders 115 B7
Phillack Corn 2 C4
Philleigh Corn 3 C7
Philpstoun W Loth 122 B3
Phocle Green Hereford 36 B3
Phoenix Green Hants 27 D5
Pica Cumb 98 B2
Piccotts End Herts 40 D3
Pickering N Yorks 103 F5
Picket Piece Hants 25 E8
Picket Post Hants 14 D2
Pickhill N Yorks 101 F8
Picklescott Shrops 60 E4
Pickletillem Fife 135 B6
Pickmere Ches 74 B3
Pickney Som 11 B6
Pickstock Telford 61 B7
Pickwell Devon 20 E3
Pickwell Leics 64 C4
Pickworth Lincs 78 F3
Pickworth Rutland 65 C6
Picton Ches 73 B8
Picton Flint 85 F2
Picton N Yorks 102 D2
Piddinghoe E Sus 17 D8
Piddington Northants 53 D6
Piddington Oxon 39 C6
Piddlehinton Dorset 12 E5
Piddletrenthide Dorset 12 E5
Pidley Cambs 54 B4
Piece Hall Art Gallery, Halifax W Yorks 87 B8
Piercebridge Darl 101 C7
Pierowall Orkney 176 B3
Pigdon Northumb 117 F7
Pikehall Derbys 75 D8
Pilgrims Hatch Essex 42 E1
Pilham Lincs 90 E2
Pill N Som 23 B7
Pillaton Corn 5 C8
Pillerton Hersey Warks 51 E8
Pillerton Priors Warks 51 E7
Pilleth Powys 48 C4
Pilley Hants 14 E4
Pilley S Yorks 88 D4
Pilling Lancs 92 E4
Pilling Lane Lancs 92 E3
Pillowell Glos 36 D3
Pillwell Dorset 13 C5
Pilning S Glos 36 F2
Pilsbury Derbys 75 C8
Pilsdon Dorset 12 E2
Pilsgate P'boro 65 D7
Pilsley Derbys 76 B2
Pilsley Derbys 76 C4
Pilton Devon 20 F4
Pilton Northants 65 F7
Pilton Rutland 65 D6
Pilton Som 23 E7
Pilton Green Swansea 33 F5
Pimperne Dorset 13 D7
Pin Mill Suff 57 F6
Pinchbeck Lincs 66 B2
Pinchbeck Bars Lincs 65 B8
Pinchbeck West Lincs 66 B2
Pincheon Green S Yorks 89 C7
Pinehurst Swindon 38 F1
Pinfold Lancs 85 C4
Pinged Carms 33 D5
Pinhoe Devon 10 E4
Pinkneys Green Windsor 40 F1
Pinley W Mid 51 B8
Pinminnoch S Ayrs 112 E1
Pinmore S Ayrs 112 E2
Pinmore Mains S Ayrs 112 E2
Pinner London 40 F4
Pinvin Worcs 50 E4
Pinwherry S Ayrs 112 F1
Pinxton Derbys 76 D4
Pipe and Lyde Hereford 49 E7
Pipe Gate Shrops 74 E4
Piperhill Highld 158 D2
Piper's Pool Corn 8 F4
Pipewell Northants 64 F5
Pippacott Devon 20 F4
Pipton Powys 48 F3
Pirbright Sur 27 D7
Pirnmill N Ayrs 119 B5
Pirton Herts 54 F2
Pirton Worcs 50 E3
Pisgah Ceredig 47 B5
Pisgah Stirl 133 D6
Pishill Oxon 39 F7
Pistyll Gwyn 70 C4
Pitagowan Perth 141 C5
Pitblae Aberds 161 B6
Pitcairngreen Perth 134 B2
Pitcalnie Highld 158 B2
Pitcaple Aberds 151 B6
Pitch Green Bucks 39 D7
Pitch Place Sur 27 D7
Pitchcombe Glos 37 D5
Pitchcott Bucks 39 B7
Pitchford Shrops 60 D5
Pitcombe Som 23 F8
Pitcorthie Fife 135 D7
Pitcox E Loth 124 B2
Pitcur Perth 142 F2
Pitfichie Aberds 151 C5
Pitforthie Aberds 143 B8
Pitgrudy Highld 164 E4
Pitkennedy Angus 143 D5
Pitkevy Fife 134 D4
Pitkierie Fife 135 D7
Pitlessie Fife 134 D5
Pitlochry Perth 141 D6
Pitmachie Aberds 151 B5
Pitmain Highld 148 D3
Pitmedden Aberds 151 B7
Pitminster Som 11 C7
Pitmuies Angus 143 E5
Pitmunie Aberds 151 C5
Pitney Som 12 B2
Pitscottie Fife 135 C6
Pitsea Essex 42 F3
Pitsford Northants 53 C5
Pitsmoor S Yorks 88 F4
Pitstone Bucks 40 C2
Pitstone Green Bucks 40 C2
Pitt Rivers Museum (See University Museum) Oxon 39 D5
Pittendreich Moray 159 C5
Pittentrail Highld 164 D4
Pittenweem Fife 135 D7
Pittington Durham 111 E6
Pittodrie Aberds 151 B5
Pitton Wilts 25 F7
Pittswood Kent 29 E7
Pittulie Aberds 161 B6
Pity Me Durham 111 E5
Pityme Corn 4 B4
Pityoulish Highld 148 C5
Pixey Green Suff 57 B6
Pixham Sur 28 D2
Pixley Hereford 49 F8
Place Newton N Yorks 96 B4
Plaidy Aberds 160 C4
Plains N Lnrk 121 C7
Plaish Shrops 60 E5
Plaistow W Sus 27 F8
Plaitford Hants 14 C3
Plank Lane Gtr Man 86 E4
Plas-canol Gwyn 58 C2
Plas Gogerddan Ceredig 58 F3
Plas Llwyngwern Powys 58 D4
Plas Mawr, Conwy Conwy 83 D7
Plas Nantyr Wrex 73 F5
Plas-yn-Cefn Denb 72 B4
Plastow Green Hants 26 C3
Platt Kent 29 D7
Platt Bridge Gtr Man 86 D4
Platts Common S Yorks 88 D4
Plawsworth Durham 111 E5
Plaxtol Kent 29 D7
Play Hatch Oxon 26 B5
Playden E Sus 19 C6
Playford Suff 57 E6
Playing Place Corn 3 B7
Playley Green Glos 50 F2
Plealey Shrops 60 D4
Plean Stirl 133 F7
Pleasington Blkburn 86 B4
Pleasley Derbys 76 C5
Pleasure Island Theme Park NE Lincs 91 D7
Pleckgate Blkburn 93 F6
Plenmeller Northumb 109 C7
Pleshey Essex 42 C2
Plockton Highld 155 G4
Plocrapol W Isles 173 J4
Ploughfield Hereford 49 E5
Plowden Shrops 60 F3
Ploxgreen Shrops 60 D3
Pluckley Kent 30 E3
Pluckley Thorne Kent 30 E3
Plumbland Cumb 107 F8
Plumley Ches 74 B4
Plumpton Cumb 108 F4
Plumpton E Sus 17 C7
Plumpton Green E Sus 17 C7
Plumpton Head Cumb 108 F5
Plumpton Racecourse E Sus 17 C7
Plumstead London 29 B5
Plumstead Norf 81 D7
Plumtree Notts 77 F6
Plungar Leics 77 F7
Plush Dorset 12 D5
Plwmp Ceredig 46 D2
Plymouth Plym 6 D2
Plymouth City Airport Plym 6 C3
Plympton Plym 6 D3
Plymstock Plym 6 D3
Plymtree Devon 11 D5
Pockley N Yorks 102 F4
Pocklington E Yorks 96 E4
Pode Hole Lincs 66 B2
Podimore Som 12 B3
Podington Beds 53 C7
Podmore Staffs 74 F4
Point Clear Essex 43 C6
Pointon Lincs 78 F4
Pokesdown Bmouth 14 E2
Pol a Charra W Isles 171 J3
Polbae Dumfries 105 B6
Polbain Highld 162 C3
Polbathic Corn 5 D8
Polbeth W Loth 122 C3
Polchar Highld 148 D4
Pole Elm Worcs 50 E3
Polebrook Northants 65 F7
Polegate E Sus 18 E2
Poles Highld 164 E4
Polesden Lacey, Dorking Sur 28 D2
Polesworth Warks 63 D6
Polgigga Corn 2 D2
Polglass Highld 162 D4
Polgooth Corn 4 D4
Poling W Sus 16 D4
Polkerris Corn 5 D5
Polla Highld 167 D5
Pollington E Yorks 89 C7
Polloch Highld 138 C1
Pollok Glasgow 120 C5
Pollok House Glasgow 121 C5
Pollokshields Glasgow 121 C5
Polmassick Corn 3 B8
Polmont Falk 122 B2
Polnessan E Ayrs 112 C4
Polnish Highld 145 E7
Polperro Corn 5 D7
Polruan Corn 5 D6
Polsham Som 23 E7
Polstead Suff 56 F3
Poltalloch Argyll 130 F4
Poltimore Devon 10 E4
Polton Midloth 123 C5
Polwarth Borders 124 D3
Polyphant Corn 8 F4
Polzeath Corn 4 B4
Ponders End London 41 E6
Pondersbridge Cambs 66 E2
Pondtail Hants 27 D6
Ponsanooth Corn 3 C6
Ponsworthy Devon 6 B5
Pont Aber Carms 33 B8
Pont Aber-Geirw Gwyn 71 E8
Pont-ar-gothi Carms 33 B6
Pont ar Hydfer Powys 34 B2
Pont-ar-llechau Carms 33 B8
Pont Cwm Pydew Denb 72 F4
Pont Cyfyng Conwy 83 F7
Pont Cysyllte Wrex 73 E6
Pont Dolydd Prysor Gwyn 71 D8
Pont-faen Powys 47 F8
Pont Fronwydd Gwyn 58 B5
Pont-gareg Pembs 45 E3
Pont-Henri Carms 33 D5
Pont-Llogel Powys 59 C7
Pont Pen-y-benglog Gwyn 83 E6
Pont Rhyd-goch Conwy 83 E6
Pont-Rhyd-sarn Gwyn 59 B5
Pont Rhyd-y-cyff Bridgend 34 F2
Pont-rhyd-y-groes Ceredig 47 B6
Pont-rug Gwyn 82 E5
Pont Senni = Sennybridge Powys 34 B3
Pont-siân Ceredig 46 E3
Pont-y-gwaith Rhondda 34 E4
Pont-y-pant Conwy 83 F7
Pont y Pennant Gwyn 59 B6
Pont-y-Pŵl = Pontypool Torf 35 D6
Pont yclun Rhondda 34 F4
Pont yr Afon-Gam Gwyn 71 C8
Pont-yr-hafod Pembs 44 C4
Pontamman Carms 33 C7
Pontantwn Carms 33 C5
Pontardawe Neath 33 D8
Pontarddulais Swansea 33 D6
Pontarsais Carms 33 B5
Pontblyddyn Flint 73 C6
Pontbren Araeth Carms 33 B7
Pontbren Llwyd Rhondda 34 D3
Pontefract W Yorks 89 B5
Pontefract Racecourse W Yorks 88 B5
Ponteland Northumb 110 B4
Ponterwyd Ceredig 58 F4
Pontesbury Shrops 60 D3
Pontfadog Wrex 73 F6
Pontfaen Pembs 45 F2
Pontgarreg Ceredig 46 D2
Ponthir Torf 35 E7
Ponthirwaun Ceredig 45 E4
Pontllanfraith Caerph 35 E5
Pontlliw Swansea 33 D7
Pontllyfni Gwyn 82 F4
Pontlottyn Caerph 35 D5
Pontneddfechan Powys 34 D3
Pontnewydd Torf 35 E6
Pontrhydfendigaid Ceredig 47 C6
Pontrhydyfen Neath 34 E1
Pontrilas Hereford 35 B7
Pontrobert Powys 59 C8
Ponts Green E Sus 18 D3
Pontshill Hereford 36 B3
Pontsticill M Tydf 34 C4
Pontwgan Conwy 83 D7
Pontyates Carms 33 D5
Pontyberem Carms 33 C6
Pontycymer Bridgend 34 E3
Pontyglasier Pembs 45 F3
Pontypool = Pont-y-Pŵl Torf 35 D6
Pontypridd Rhondda 34 F4
Pontywaun Caerph 35 E6
Pooksgreen Hants 14 C4
Pool Corn 3 B5
Pool W Yorks 94 E5
Pool o'Muckhart Clack 134 D2
Pool Quay Powys 60 C2
Poole Poole 13 E8
Poole Keynes Glos 37 E6
Poolend Staffs 75 D6
Poolewe Highld 154 B4
Pooley Bridge Cumb 99 B6
Poolfold Staffs 75 D5
Poolhill Glos 36 B4
Poolsbrook Derbys 76 B4
Pootings Kent 29 E5
Pope Hill Pembs 44 D4
Popeswood Brack 27 C6
Popham Hants 26 E3
Poplar London 41 F6
Popley Hants 26 D4
Porchester Notts 77 E5
Porchfield I o W 14 E5
Porin Highld 156 D4
Poringland Norf 69 D5
Porkellis Corn 3 C5
Porlock Som 21 E7
Porlock Weir Som 21 E7
Port Ann Argyll 128 B4
Port Appin Argyll 138 E3
Port Arthur Shetland 175 K5
Port Askaig Argyll 126 C4
Port Bannatyne Argyll 129 D5
Port Carlisle Cumb 108 C2
Port Charlotte Argyll 126 D2
Port Clarence Stockton 102 B2
Port Driseach Argyll 128 C4
Port e Vullen I o M 84 C4
Port Ellen Argyll 126 E3
Port Elphinstone Aberds 151 C6
Port Erin I o M 84 F1
Port Erroll Aberds 161 E7
Port-Eynon Swansea 33 F5
Port Gaverne Corn 8 F2
Port Glasgow Invclyd 120 B3
Port Henderson Highld 154 C3
Port Isaac Corn 4 A4
Port Lamont Argyll 129 C5
Port Lion Pembs 44 E4
Port Logan Dumfries 104 E4
Port Mholair W Isles 172 E8
Port Mor Highld 144 F4
Port Mulgrave N Yorks 103 C5
Port Nan Giùran W Isles 172 E8
Port nan Long W Isles 170 C4
Port Nis W Isles 172 B8
Port of Menteith Stirl 132 D4
Port Quin Corn 4 A4
Port Ramsay Argyll 138 E2
Port St Mary I o M 84 F2
Port Sunlight Mers 85 F4
Port Talbot Neath 34 E1
Port Tennant Swansea 33 E7
Port Wemyss Argyll 126 D1
Port William Dumfries 105 E7
Portachoillan Argyll 128 E2
Portavadie Argyll 128 D4
Portbury N Som 23 B7
Portchester Hants 15 D7
Portclair Highld 147 C7
Portencalzie Dumfries 104 B4
Portencross N Ayrs 119 B8
Portesham Dorset 12 F4
Portessie Moray 159 C8
Portfield Gate Pembs 44 D4
Portgate Devon 9 F6
Portgordon Moray 159 C7
Portgower Highld 165 C7
Porth Corn 4 C3
Porth Rhondda 34 E4
Porth Navas Corn 3 D6
Porth Tywyn = Burry Port Carms 33 D5
Porth-y-waen Shrops 60 B2
Porthaethwy = Menai Bridge Anglesey 83 D5
Porthallow Corn 3 D6
Porthallow Corn 5 D7
Porthcawl Bridgend 21 B7
Porthcothan Corn 4 B3
Porthcurno Corn 2 D2
Porthgain Pembs 44 B3
Porthill Shrops 60 C4
Porthkerry V Glam 22 C2
Porthleven Corn 2 D5
Porthllechog Anglesey 82 B4
Porthmadog Gwyn 71 D6
Porthmeor Corn 2 C3
Portholland Corn 3 B8
Porthoustock Corn 3 D7
Porthpean Corn 4 D5
Porthtowan Corn 3 B5
Porthyrhyd Carms 33 C6
Porthyrhyd Carms 47 F6
Portincaple Argyll 129 A7
Portington E Yorks 96 F3
Portinnisherrich Argyll 131 D5
Portinscale Cumb 98 B4
Portishead N Som 23 B6
Portkil Argyll 129 B7
Portknockie Moray 159 C8
Portlethen Aberds 151 E8
Portling Dumfries 107 D5
Portloe Corn 3 C8
Portmahomack Highld 165 F6
Portmeirion Gwyn 71 D6
Portmeirion Village Gwyn 71 D6
Portmellon Corn 3 B9
Portmore Hants 14 E4
Portnacroish Argyll 138 E3
Portnahaven Argyll 126 D1
Portnalong Highld 153 F4
Portnaluchaig Highld 145 E6
Portnancon Highld 167 C6
Portnellan Stirl 132 B3
Portobello Edin 123 B6
Porton Wilts 25 F6
Portpatrick Dumfries 104 D4
Portreath Corn 3 B5
Portree Highld 153 E5
Portscatho Corn 3 C7
Portsea Ptsmth 15 D7
Portskerra Highld 168 C3
Portskewett Mon 36 F2
Portslade Brighton 17 D6
Portslade-by-Sea Brighton 17 D6
Portsmouth Ptsmth 15 D7
Portsmouth W Yorks 87 B7
Portsmouth Sea Life Centre Ptsmth 15 E7
Portsonachan Argyll 131 C6
Portsoy Aberds 160 B2
Portswood Soton 14 C5
Porttanachy Moray 159 C7
Portuairk Highld 137 B5
Portway Hereford 49 F6
Portway Worcs 51 B5
Portwrinkle Corn 5 D8
Poslingford Suff 55 E8
Postbridge Devon 6 B4
Postcombe Oxon 39 E7
Postling Kent 19 B8
Postwick Norf 69 D5
Potholm Dumfries 115 F6
Potsgrove Beds 40 B2
Pott Row Norf 80 E3
Pott Shrigley Ches 75 B6
Potten End Herts 40 D3
Potter Brompton N Yorks 97 B5
Potter Heigham Norf 69 C7
Potter Street Essex 41 D7
Potterhanworth Lincs 78 C3
Potterhanworth Booths Lincs 78 C3
Potteries Museum & Art Gallery, Stoke-on-Trent Stoke 75 E5
Potterne Wilts 24 D4
Potterne Wick Wilts 24 D5
Potternewton W Yorks 95 F6
Potters Bar Herts 41 D5
Potter's Cross Staffs 62 F2
Potterspury Northants 53 E5
Potterton Aberds 151 C8
Potterton W Yorks 95 F7
Potto N Yorks 102 D2
Potton Beds 54 E3
Poughill Corn 8 D4
Poughill Devon 10 D3
Poulshot Wilts 24 D4
Poulton Glos 37 D8
Poulton Mers 85 E4
Poulton-le-Fylde Lancs 92 F3
Pound Bank Worcs 50 B2
Pound Green E Sus 18 C2
Pound Green I o W 14 F4
Pound Green Worcs 50 B2
Pound Hill W Sus 28 F3
Poundfield E Sus 18 B2
Poundland S Ayrs 112 F1
Poundon Bucks 39 B6
Poundsgate Devon 6 B5
Poundstock Corn 8 E4
Powburn Northumb 117 C6
Powderham Devon 10 F4
Powderham Castle Devon 10 F4
Powerstock Dorset 12 E3
Powfoot Dumfries 107 C8
Powick Worcs 50 D3
Powis Castle, Welshpool Powys 60 D2
Powmill Perth 134 E2
Poxwell Dorset 12 F5
Poyle Slough 27 B8
Poynings W Sus 17 C6
Poyntington Dorset 12 C4
Poynton Ches 87 F7
Poynton Green Telford 61 C5
Poystreet Green Suff 56 D3
Praa Sands Corn 2 D4
Pratt's Bottom London 29 C5
Praze Corn 2 C4
Praze-an-Beeble Corn 2 C5

Predannack Wollas Corn 3 E5
Prees Shrops 74 F2
Prees Green Shrops 74 F2
Prees Heath Shrops 74 F2
Prees Higher Heath Shrops 74 F2
Prees Lower Heath Shrops 74 F2
Preesall Lancs 92 E3
Preesgweene Shrops 73 F6
Prenderguest Borders 124 D5
Prendwick Northumb 117 C6
Prengwyn Ceredig 46 E3
Prenteg Gwyn 71 C6
Prenton Mers 85 F4
Prescot Mers 86 E2
Prescott Shrops 60 B4
Pressen Northumb 124 F4
Prestatyn Denb 72 A4
Prestbury Ches 75 B6
Prestbury Glos 37 B6
Presteigne = Llanandras Powys 48 C5
Presthope Shrops 61 E5
Prestleigh Som 23 E8
Preston Borders 124 D3
Preston Brighton 17 D7
Preston Devon 7 B6
Preston Dorset 12 F5
Preston E Loth 123 B8
Preston E Yorks 97 F7
Preston Glos 37 D7
Preston Glos 49 F8
Preston Herts 40 B4
Preston Kent 30 C4
Preston Kent 31 C6
Preston Lancs 86 B3
Preston Northumb 117 B7
Preston Rutland 65 D5
Preston Shrops 60 C5
Preston Wilts 24 B5
Preston Wilts 25 B7
Preston Bagot Warks 51 C6
Preston Bissett Bucks 39 B6
Preston Bowyer Som 11 B6
Preston Brockhurst Shrops 60 B5
Preston Brook Halton 86 F3
Preston Candover Hants 26 E4
Preston Capes Northants 52 D3
Preston Crowmarsh Oxon 39 E6
Preston Gubbals Shrops 60 C4
Preston Hall Museum, Stockton-on-Tees Stockton 102 C2
Preston on Stour Warks 51 E7
Preston on the Hill Halton 86 F3
Preston on Wye Hereford 49 E5
Preston Plucknett Som 12 C3
Preston St Mary Suff 56 D3
Preston-under-Scar N Yorks 101 E5
Preston upon the Weald Moors Telford 61 C6
Preston Wynne Hereford 49 E7
Prestonmill Dumfries 107 D6
Prestonpans E Loth 123 B6
Prestwich Gtr Man 87 D6
Prestwick Northumb 110 B4
Prestwick S Ayrs 112 B3
Prestwood Bucks 40 D1
Price Town Bridgend 34 E3
Prickwillow Cambs 67 F5
Priddy Som 23 D7
Priest Hutton Lancs 92 B5
Priest Weston Shrops 60 E2
Priesthaugh Borders 115 D7
Primethorpe Leics 64 E2
Primrose Green Norf 68 C3
Primrose Valley N Yorks 97 B7
Primrosehill Herts 40 D3
Princes Gate Pembs 32 C2
Princes Risborough Bucks 39 D8
Princethorpe Warks 52 B2
Princetown Caerph 35 C5
Princetown Devon 6 B3
Prinknash Abbey, Gloucester Glos 37 C5
Prion Denb 72 C4
Prior Muir Fife 135 C7
Prior Park Northumb 125 D5
Priors Frome Hereford 49 F7
Priors Hardwick Warks 52 D2
Priors Marston Warks 52 D2
Priorslee Telford 61 C7
Priory Church, Lancaster Lancs 92 C4
Priory Wood Hereford 48 E4
Priston Bath 23 C8
Pristow Green Norf 68 F4
Prittlewell Sthend 42 F4
Privett Hants 15 B7
Prixford Devon 20 F4
Probus Corn 3 B7
Proncy Highld 164 E4
Prospect Cumb 107 E8
Prudhoe Northumb 110 C3
Ptarmigan Lodge Stirl 132 D2
Pubil Perth 140 E1
Puckeridge Herts 41 B6
Puckington Som 11 C8
Pucklechurch S Glos 23 B8
Pucknall Hants 14 B4
Puckrup Glos 50 F3
Puddinglake Ches 74 C4
Puddington Ches 73 B7
Puddington Devon 10 C3
Puddledock Norf 68 E3
Puddletown Dorset 13 E5
Pudleston Hereford 49 D7
Pudsey W Yorks 94 F5
Pulborough W Sus 16 C4
Puleston Telford 61 B7
Pulford Ches 73 D7
Pulham Dorset 12 D5
Pulham Market Norf 68 F4
Pulham St Mary Norf 68 F5
Pulloxhill Beds 53 F8
Pumpherston W Loth 122 C3
Pumsaint Carms 47 E5
Puncheston Pembs 32 B1
Puncknowle Dorset 12 F3
Punnett's Town E Sus 18 C3
Purbrook Hants 15 D7
Purewell Dorset 14 E2
Purfleet Thurrock 29 B6
Puriton Som 22 E5
Purleigh Essex 42 D4
Purley London 28 C4
Purley W Berks 26 B4
Purlogue Shrops 48 B4
Purls Bridge Cambs 66 F4
Purse Caundle Dorset 12 C4
Purslow Shrops 60 F3
Purston Jaglin W Yorks 88 C5
Purton Glos 36 D3
Purton Glos 36 D3
Purton Wilts 37 F7
Purton Stoke Wilts 37 E7
Pury End Northants 52 E5
Pusey Oxon 38 E3
Putley Hereford 49 F8
Putney London 28 B3
Putsborough Devon 20 E3
Puttenham Herts 40 C1
Puttenham Sur 27 E7
Puxton N Som 23 C6
Pwll Carms 33 D5
Pwll-glas Denb 72 D5
Pwll-trap Carms 32 C3
Pwll-y-glaw Neath 34 E1
Pwllcrochan Pembs 44 E4
Pwllgloyw Powys 48 F2
Pwllheli Gwyn 70 D4
Pwllmeyric Mon 36 E2
Pye Corner Newport 35 F7
Pye Green Staffs 62 C3
Pyecombe W Sus 17 C6
Pyewipe NE Lincs 91 C6
Pyle I o W 15 G5
Pyle = Y Pîl Bridgend 34 F2
Pylle Som 23 F8
Pymoor Cambs 66 F4
Pyrford Sur 27 D8
Pyrton Oxon 39 E6
Pytchley Northants 53 B6
Pyworthy Devon 8 D5

Q

Quabbs Shrops 60 F2
Quadring Lincs 78 F5
Quainton Bucks 39 C7
Quarley Hants 25 E7
Quarndon Derbys 76 E3
Quarrier's Homes Invclyd 120 C3
Quarrington Lincs 78 E3
Quarrington Hill Durham 111 F6
Quarry Bank W Mid 62 F3
Quarry Bank Mill, Wilmslow Ches 87 F6
Quarryford E Loth 123 C8
Quarryhill Highld 164 F4
Quarrywood Moray 159 C5
Quarter S Lnrk 121 D7
Quatford Shrops 61 E7
Quatt Shrops 61 F7
Quebec Durham 110 E4
Quedgeley Glos 37 C5
Queen Adelaide Cambs 67 F5
Queen Camel Som 12 B3
Queen Charlton Bath 23 C8
Queen Dart Devon 10 C3
Queen Oak Dorset 24 F2
Queen Street Kent 29 E7
Queen Street Wilts 37 F7
Queenborough Kent 30 B3
Queenhill Worcs 50 F3
Queen's Head Shrops 60 B3
Queen's Park Beds 53 E8
Queen's Park Northants 53 C5
Queen's View Centre, Loch Tummel Perth 141 D5
Queensbury W Yorks 94 F4
Queensferry Edin 122 B4
Queensferry Flint 73 C7
Queenstown Blkpool 92 F3
Queenzieburn N Lnrk 121 B6
Quemerford Wilts 24 C5
Quendale Shetland 175 M5
Quendon Essex 55 F6
Queniborough Leics 64 C3
Quenington Glos 37 D8
Quernmore Lancs 92 D5
Quethiock Corn 5 C8
Quholm Orkney 176 E1
Quicks Green W Berks 26 B3
Quidenham Norf 68 F3
Quidhampton Hants 26 D3
Quidhampton Wilts 25 F6
Quilquox Aberds 161 E6
Quina Brook Shrops 74 F2
Quindry Orkney 176 G3
Quinton Northants 53 D5
Quinton W Mid 62 F3
Quintrell Downs Corn 4 C3
Quixhill Staffs 75 E8
Quoditch Devon 9 E6
Quoig Perth 133 B7
Quorndon Leics 64 C2
Quothquan S Lnrk 122 F2
Quoyloo Orkney 176 D1
Quoyness Orkney 176 F1
Quoys Shetland 174 B8
Quoys Shetland 175 G6

R

Raasay Ho. Highld 153 F6
Rabbit's Cross Kent 29 E8
Raby Mers 73 B7
Rachan Mill Borders 122 F4
Rachub Gwyn 83 E6
Rackenford Devon 10 C3
Rackham W Sus 16 C4
Rackheath Norf 69 C5
Racks Dumfries 107 B7
Rackwick Orkney 176 G1
Rackwick Orkney 176 B3
Radbourne Derbys 76 F2
Radcliffe Gtr Man 87 D5
Radcliffe Northumb 117 D8
Radcliffe on Trent Notts 77 F6
Radclive Bucks 52 F4
Radcot Oxon 38 E2
Raddery Highld 157 D8
Radernie Fife 135 D6
Radford Semele Warks 51 C8
Radipole Dorset 12 F4
Radlett Herts 40 E4
Radley Oxon 39 E5
Radmanthwaite Notts 76 C5
Radmoor Shrops 61 B6
Radmore Green Ches 74 D2
Radnage Bucks 39 E7
Radstock Bath 23 D8
Radstone Northants 52 E3
Radway Warks 51 E8
Radway Green Ches 74 D4
Radwell Beds 53 D8
Radwell Herts 54 F3
Radwinter Essex 55 F7
Radyr Cardiff 35 F5
RAF Museum, Cosford Shrops 61 D7
RAF Museum, Hendon London 41 F5
Rafford Moray 158 D4
Ragdale Leics 64 C3
Raglan Mon 35 D8
Ragley Hall Warks 51 D5
Ragnall Notts 77 B8
Rahane Argyll 129 B7
Rainford Mers 86 D2
Rainford Junction Mers 86 D2
Rainham London 41 F8
Rainham Medway 30 C2
Rainhill Mers 86 E2
Rainhill Stoops Mers 86 E3
Rainow Ches 75 B6
Rainton N Yorks 95 B6
Rainworth Notts 77 D5
Raisbeck Cumb 99 D8
Raise Cumb 109 E7
Rait Perth 134 B4
Raithby Lincs 91 F7
Raithby Lincs 79 C6
Rake W Sus 16 B2
Rakewood Gtr Man 87 C7
Ram Carms 46 E4
Ram Lane Kent 30 E3
Ramasaig Highld 153 E2
Rame Corn 3 C6
Rame Corn 6 E2
Rameldry Mill Bank Fife 134 D5
Ramnageo Shetland 174 C8
Rampisham Dorset 12 D3
Rampside Cumb 92 C2
Rampton Cambs 54 C5
Rampton Notts 77 B7
Ramsbottom Gtr Man 87 C5
Ramsbury Wilts 25 B7
Ramscraigs Highld 165 B8
Ramsdean Hants 15 B8
Ramsdell Hants 26 D3
Ramsden Oxon 38 C3
Ramsden Bellhouse Essex 42 E3
Ramsden Heath Essex 42 E3
Ramsey Cambs 66 F2
Ramsey Essex 57 F6
Ramsey I o M 84 C4
Ramsey Forty Foot Cambs 66 F3
Ramsey Heights Cambs 66 F2
Ramsey Island Essex 43 D5
Ramsey Mereside Cambs 66 F2
Ramsey St Mary's Cambs 66 F2
Ramseycleuch Borders 115 C5
Ramsgate Kent 31 C7
Ramsgill N Yorks 94 B4
Ramshorn Staffs 75 E7
Ramsnest Common Sur 27 F7
Ranais W Isles 172 F7
Ranby Lincs 78 B5
Ranby Notts 89 F7
Rand Lincs 78 B4
Randwick Glos 37 D5
Ranfurly Renfs 120 C3
Rangag Highld 169 E6
Rangemore Staffs 63 B5
Rangeworthy S Glos 36 F3
Rankinston E Ayrs 112 C4
Ranmoor S Yorks 88 F4
Ranmore Common Sur 28 D2
Rannerdale Cumb 98 C3
Rannoch Station Perth 139 D8
Ranochan Highld 145 E8
Ranskill Notts 89 F7
Ranton Staffs 62 B2
Ranworth Norf 69 C6
Raploch Stirl 133 E6
Rapness Orkney 176 B4
Rascal Moor E Yorks 96 F4
Rascarrel Dumfries 106 E4
Rashiereive Aberds 151 B8
Raskelf N Yorks 95 B7
Rassau Bl Gwent 35 C5
Rastrick W Yorks 88 B2
Ratagan Highld 146 C2
Ratby Leics 64 D2
Ratcliffe Culey Leics 63 E7
Ratcliffe on Soar Leics 63 B8
Ratcliffe on the Wreake Leics 64 C3
Rathen Aberds 161 B7
Rathillet Fife 135 B5
Rathmell N Yorks 93 D8
Ratho Edin 122 B4
Ratho Station Edin 122 B4
Rathven Moray 159 C8
Ratley Warks 51 E8
Ratlinghope Shrops 60 E4
Rattar Highld 169 B7
Ratten Row Lancs 92 E4
Rattery Devon 6 C5
Rattlesden Suff 56 D3
Rattray Perth 142 E1
Raughton Head Cumb 108 E3
Raunds Northants 53 B7
Ravenfield S Yorks 89 E5
Ravenglass Cumb 98 E2
Ravenglass and Eskdale Railway & Museum Cumb 98 E2
Raveningham Norf 69 E6
Ravenscar N Yorks 103 D7
Ravenscraig Invclyd 129 C7
Ravensdale I o M 84 C3
Ravensden Beds 53 D8
Ravenseat N Yorks 100 D3
Ravenshead Notts 77 D5
Ravensmoor Ches 74 D3
Ravensthorpe Northants 52 B4
Ravensthorpe W Yorks 88 B3
Ravenstone Leics 63 C8
Ravenstone M Keynes 53 D6
Ravenstonedale Cumb 100 D2
Ravenstown Cumb 92 B3
Ravenstruther S Lnrk 122 E2
Ravensworth N Yorks 101 D6
Raw N Yorks 103 D7
Rawcliffe E Yorks 89 B7
Rawcliffe York 95 D8
Rawcliffe Bridge E Yorks 89 B7
Rawdon W Yorks 94 F5
Rawmarsh S Yorks 88 E5
Rawreth Essex 42 E3
Rawridge Devon 11 D7
Rawtenstall Lancs 87 B6
Raxton Aberds 161 E5
Raydon Suff 56 F4
Raylees Northumb 117 E5
Rayleigh Essex 42 E4
Rayne Essex 42 B3
Rayners Lane London 40 F4
Raynes Park London 28 C3
Reach Cambs 55 C6
Read Lancs 93 F7
Reading Reading 26 B5
Reading Street Kent 19 B6
Reagill Cumb 99 C8
Rearquhar Highld 164 E4
Rearsby Leics 64 C3
Reaster Highld 169 C7
Reawick Shetland 175 J5
Reay Highld 168 C4
Rechullin Highld 154 E4
Reculver Kent 31 C6
Red Dial Cumb 108 E2
Red Hill Worcs 50 D3
Red House Glass Cone, Wordsley W Mid 62 F2
Red Houses Jersey 17
Red Lodge Suff 55 B7
Red Rail Hereford 36 B2
Red Rock Gtr Man 86 D3
Red Roses Carms 32 C3
Red Row Northumb 117 E8
Red Street Staffs 74 D5
Red Wharf Bay Anglesey 82 C5
Redberth Pembs 32 D1
Redbourn Herts 40 C4
Redbourne N Lincs 90 E3
Redbrook Glos 36 C2
Redbrook Wrex 74 E2
Redburn Highld 157 C6
Redburn Highld 158 E3
Redburn Northumb 109 C7
Redcar Redcar 102 B4
Redcar Racecourse Redcar 102 B4
Redcastle Angus 143 D6
Redcastle Highld 157 E6
Redcliff Bay N Som 23 B6
Redding Falk 122 B2
Reddingmuirhead Falk 122 B2
Reddish Gtr Man 87 E6
Redditch Worcs 50 C5
Rede Suff 56 D2
Redenhall Norf 69 F5
Redesdale Camp Northumb 116 E4
Redesmouth Northumb 116 F4
Redford Aberds 143 B7
Redford Angus 143 E5
Redford Durham 110 F3
Redfordgreen Borders 115 C6
Redgorton Perth 134 B2
Redgrave Suff 56 B4
Redhill Aberds 160 E3
Redhill Aberds 151 D6
Redhill N Som 23 C7
Redhill Sur 28 D3
Redhouse Argyll 128 D3
Redhouses Argyll 126 C3
Redisham Suff 69 F7
Redland Bristol 23 B7
Redland Orkney 176 D2
Redlingfield Suff 57 B5
Redlynch Som 23 F9
Redlynch Wilts 14 B3
Redmarley D'Abitot Glos 50 F2
Redmarshall Stockton 102 B1
Redmile Leics 77 F7
Redmire N Yorks 101 E5
Redmoor Corn 5 C5
Rednal Shrops 60 B3
Redpath Borders 123 F8
Redpoint Highld 154 D3
Redruth Corn 3 B5
Redvales Gtr Man 87 D6
Redwick Newport 35 F8
Redwick S Glos 36 F2
Redworth Darl 101 B7
Reed Herts 54 F4
Reedham Norf 69 D7
Reedness E Yorks 89 B8
Reeds Beck Lincs 78 C5
Reepham Lincs 78 B3
Reepham Norf 81 E6
Reeth N Yorks 101 E5
Regaby I o M 84 C4
Regoul Highld 158 D2
Reiff Highld 162 C3
Reigate Sur 28 D3
Reighton N Yorks 97 B7
Reighton Gap N Yorks 97 B7
Reinigeadal W Isles 173 H5
Reiss Highld 169 D8
Rejerrah Corn 4 D2
Releath Corn 3 C5
Relubbus Corn 2 C4
Relugas Moray 158 E3
Remenham Wokingham 39 F7
Remenham Hill Wokingham 39 F7
Remony Perth 140 E4
Rempstone Notts 64 B2
Rendcomb Glos 37 D7
Rendham Suff 57 C7
Rendlesham Suff 57 D7
Renfrew Renfs 120 C5
Renhold Beds 53 D8
Renishaw Derbys 76 B4
Rennington Northumb 117 C8
Renton W Dunb 120 B3
Renwick Cumb 109 E5
Repps Norf 69 C7
Repton Derbys 63 B7
Reraig Highld 155 H4
Rescobie Angus 143 D5
Resipole Highld 137 B8
Resolis Highld 157 C7
Resolven Neath 34 D2
Reston Borders 124 C4
Reswallie Angus 143 D5
Retew Corn 4 D4
Retford Notts 89 F8
Rettendon Essex 42 E3
Rettendon Place Essex 42 E3
Revesby Lincs 79 C5
Revesby Bridge Lincs 79 C6
Rew Street I o W 15 E5
Rewe Devon 10 E4
Reydon Suff 57 B8
Reydon Smear Suff 57 B8
Reymerston Norf 68 D3
Reynalton Pembs 32 D1
Reynoldston Swansea 33 E5
Rezare Corn 5 B8
Rhaeadr Gwy = Rhayader Powys 47 C8
Rhandirmwyn Carms 47 E6
Rhayader = Rhaeadr Gwy Powys 47 C8
Rhedyn Gwyn 70 D3
Rhemore Highld 147 F8
Rhencullen I o M 84 C3
Rhes-y-cae Flint 73 B5
Rhewl Denb 72 C5
Rhewl Denb 73 E5
Rhian Highld 164 C2
Rhicarn Highld 162 B4
Rhiconich Highld 166 D4
Rhicullen Highld 157 B7
Rhidorroch Ho. Highld 163 E5
Rhifail Highld 168 E2
Rhigos Rhondda 34 D3
Rhilochan Highld 164 D4
Rhiroy Highld 163 F5
Rhisga = Risca Caerph 35 E6
Rhiw Gwyn 70 E3
Rhiwabon = Ruabon Wrex 73 E7
Rhiwbina Cardiff 35 F5
Rhiwbryfdir Gwyn 71 C7
Rhiwderin Newport 35 F6
Rhiwlas Gwyn 83 E5
Rhiwlas Gwyn 72 F3
Rhiwlas Powys 73 F5
Rhodes Gtr Man 87 D6
Rhodes Minnis Kent 31 E5
Rhodesia Notts 77 B5
Rhodiad Pembs 44 C2
Rhondda Rhondda 34 E3
Rhonehouse or Kelton Hill Dumfries 106 D4
Rhoose = Y Rhws V Glam 22 C2
Rhôs Carms 46 F2
Rhôs Neath 33 D8
Rhos-fawr Gwyn 70 D4
Rhos-goch Powys 48 E3
Rhos-hill Pembs 45 E3
Rhos-on-Sea Conwy 83 C8
Rhos-y-brithdir Powys 59 B8
Rhos-y-garth Ceredig 46 B5
Rhos-y-gwaliau Gwyn 72 F3
Rhos-y-llan Gwyn 70 D3
Rhos-y-Madoc Wrex 73 E7
Rhos-y-meirch Powys 48 C4
Rhosaman Carms 33 C8
Rhosbeirio Anglesey 82 B3
Rhoscefnhir Anglesey 82 D5
Rhoscolyn Anglesey 82 D2
Rhoscrowther Pembs 44 E4
Rhosesmor Flint 73 C6
Rhosgadfan Gwyn 82 F5
Rhosgoch Anglesey 82 C4
Rhoshirwaun Gwyn 70 E2
Rhoslan Gwyn 71 C5
Rhoslefain Gwyn 58 D2
Rhosllanerchrugog Wrex 73 E6
Rhosmaen Carms 33 B7
Rhosmeirch Anglesey 82 D4
Rhosneigr Anglesey 82 D3
Rhosnesni Wrex 73 D7
Rhosrobin Wrex 73 D7
Rhossili Swansea 33 F5
Rhosson Pembs 44 C2
Rhostryfan Gwyn 82 F4
Rhostyllen Wrex 73 E7
Rhosybol Anglesey 82 C4
RHS Garden, Wisley Sur 27 D8
Rhu Argyll 128 D3
Rhu Argyll 129 B7
Rhuallt Denb 72 B4
Rhuddall Heath Ches 74 C2
Rhuddlan Ceredig 46 E3
Rhuddlan Denb 72 B4
Rhue Highld 162 E4
Rhulen Powys 48 E3
Rhunahaorine Argyll 118 B4
Rhuthun = Ruthin Denb 72 D5
Rhyd Gwyn 71 C7
Rhyd Powys 59 D6
Rhyd-Ddu Gwyn 83 F5
Rhyd-moel-ddu Powys 48 B2
Rhyd-Rosser Ceredig 46 C4
Rhyd-uchaf Gwyn 72 F3
Rhyd-wen Gwyn 58 C4
Rhyd-y-clafdy Gwyn 70 D4
Rhŷd-y-foel Conwy 72 B3
Rhyd-y-fro Neath 33 D8
Rhyd-y-gwin Swansea 33 D7
Rhyd-y-meirch Mon 35 D7
Rhyd-y-meudwy Denb 72 D5
Rhyd-y-pandy Swansea 33 D7
Rhyd-y-sarn Gwyn 71 C7
Rhyd-yr-onen Gwyn 58 D3
Rhydaman = Ammanford Carms 33 C7
Rhydargaeau Carms 33 B5
Rhydcymerau Carms 46 F4
Rhydd Worcs 50 E3
Rhydding Neath 33 E8
Rhydfudr Ceredig 46 C4
Rhydlewis Ceredig 46 E2
Rhydlios Gwyn 70 D2
Rhydlydan Conwy 83 F8
Rhydness Powys 48 E3
Rhydowen Ceredig 46 E3
Rhydspence Hereford 48 E4
Rhydtalog Flint 73 D6
Rhydwyn Anglesey 82 C3
Rhydycroesau Shrops 73 F6
Rhydyfelin Ceredig 46 B4
Rhydyfelin Rhondda 34 F4
Rhydymain Gwyn 58 B5
Rhydymwyn Flint 73 C6
Rhyl = Y Rhyl Denb 72 A4
Rhymney = Rhymni Caerph 35 D5
Rhymni = Rhymney Caerph 35 D5
Rhynd Fife 135 B6
Rhynd Perth 134 B3
Rhynie Aberds 150 B3
Rhynie Highld 158 B2
Ribbesford Worcs 50 B2
Ribblehead N Yorks 93 B7
Ribbleton Lancs 93 F5
Ribchester Lancs 93 F6
Ribigill Highld 167 D7
Riby Lincs 91 D5
Riby Cross Roads Lincs 91 D5
Riccall N Yorks 96 F2
Riccarton E Ayrs 120 F4
Richards Castle Hereford 49 C6
Richings Park Bucks 27 B8
Richmond London 28 B2
Richmond N Yorks 101 D6
Rickarton Aberds 151 F7
Rickinghall Suff 56 B4
Rickleton T & W 111 D5
Rickling Essex 55 F5
Rickmansworth Herts 40 E3
Riddings Cumb 108 B4
Riddings Derbys 76 D4
Riddlecombe Devon 9 C8
Riddlesden W Yorks 94 E3
Riddrie Glasgow 121 C6
Ridge Dorset 13 F7
Ridge Hants 14 C4
Ridge Wilts 24 F4
Ridge Green Sur 28 E4
Ridge Lane Warks 63 E6
Ridgebourne Powys 48 C2
Ridgehill N Som 23 C7
Ridgeway Cross Hereford 50 E2
Ridgewell Essex 55 E8
Ridgewood E Sus 17 C8
Ridgmont Beds 53 F7
Riding Mill Northumb 110 C3
Ridleywood Wrex 73 D8
Ridlington Norf 69 A6
Ridlington Rutland 64 D5
Ridsdale Northumb 116 F5
Riechip Perth 141 E7
Riemore Perth 141 E7
Rienachait Highld 166 F2
Rievaulx N Yorks 102 F3
Rievaulx Abbey N Yorks 102 F3
Rift House Hrtlpl 111 F7
Rigg Dumfries 108 C2
Riggend N Lnrk 121 B7
Rigsby Lincs 79 B7
Rigside S Lnrk 121 F8
Riley Green Lancs 86 B4
Rileyhill Staffs 62 C5
Rilla Mill Corn 5 B7
Rillington N Yorks 96 B4
Rimington Lancs 93 E8
Rimpton Som 12 B4
Rimswell E Yorks 91 B7
Rinaston Pembs 44 C4
Ringasta Shetland 175 M5
Ringford Dumfries 106 D3
Ringinglow S Yorks 88 F3
Ringland Norf 68 C4
Ringles Cross E Sus 17 B8
Ringmer E Sus 17 C8
Ringmore Devon 6 E4
Ringorm Moray 159 E6
Ring's End Cambs 66 D3
Ringsfield Suff 69 F7
Ringsfield Corner Suff 69 F7
Ringshall Herts 40 C2
Ringshall Suff 56 D4
Ringshall Stocks Suff 56 D4
Ringstead Norf 80 C3
Ringstead Northants 53 B7
Ringwood Hants 14 D2
Ringwould Kent 31 E7
Rinmore Aberds 150 C3
Rinnigill Orkney 176 G2
Rinsey Corn 2 D4
Riof W Isles 172 E4
Ripe E Sus 18 D2
Ripley Derbys 76 D3
Ripley Hants 14 E2
Ripley N Yorks 95 C5
Ripley Sur 27 D8
Riplingham E Yorks 97 F5
Ripon N Yorks 95 B6
Ripon Cathedral N Yorks 95 B6
Ripon Racecourse N Yorks 95 C6
Rippingale Lincs 65 B7
Ripple Kent 31 E7
Ripple Worcs 50 F3
Ripponden W Yorks 87 C8
Rireavach Highld 162 E4
Risabus Argyll 126 E3
Risbury Hereford 49 D7
Risby Suff 55 C8
Risca = Rhisga Caerph 35 E6
Rise E Yorks 97 E7
Riseden E Sus 18 B3
Risegate Lincs 66 B2
Riseholme Lincs 78 B2
Riseley Beds 53 C8
Riseley Wokingham 26 C5
Rishangles Suff 57 C5
Rishton Lancs 93 F7
Rishworth W Yorks 87 C8
Rising Bridge Lancs 87 B5
Risley Derbys 76 F4
Risley Warr 86 E4
Risplith N Yorks 94 C5
Rispond Highld 167 C6
Rivar Wilts 25 C8
Rivenhall End Essex 42 C4
River Bank Cambs 55 C6
Riverhead Kent 29 D6
Rivington Lancs 86 C4
Roa Island Cumb 92 C2
Roachill Devon 10 B3
Road Green Norf 69 E5
Roade Northants 53 D5
Roadhead Cumb 108 B5
Roadmeetings S Lnrk 121 E8
Roadside Highld 169 C6
Roadside of Catterline Aberds 143 B8
Roadside of Kinneff Aberds 143 B8
Roadwater Som 22 F2
Roag Highld 153 E3
Roath Cardiff 22 B3
Rob Roy and Trossachs Visitor Centre, Callander Stirl 132 D5
Robert Burns Centre, Dumfries Dumfries 107 B6
Roberton Borders 115 C7
Roberton S Lnrk 114 B2
Robertsbridge E Sus 18 C4
Roberttown W Yorks 88 B2
Robeston Cross Pembs 44 E3
Robeston Wathen Pembs 32 C1
Robin Hood W Yorks 88 B4
Robin Hood Doncaster Sheffield International Airport S Yorks 89 E7
Robin Hood's Bay N Yorks 103 D7
Roborough Devon 9 C7
Roborough Devon 6 C3
Roby Mers 86 E2
Roby Mill Lancs 86 D3
Rocester Staffs 75 F8
Roch Pembs 44 C3
Roch Gate Pembs 44 C3
Rochdale Gtr Man 87 C6
Roche Corn 4 C4
Rochester Medway 29 C8
Rochester Northumb 116 E4
Rochester Castle Medway 29 C8
Rochester Cathedral Medway 29 C8
Rochford Essex 42 E4
Rock Corn 4 B4
Rock Northumb 117 B8
Rock Worcs 50 B2
Rock W Sus 16 C5
Rock Ferry Mers 85 F4
Rockbeare Devon 10 E5
Rockbourne Hants 14 C2
Rockcliffe Cumb 108 C3
Rockcliffe Dumfries 107 D5
Rockfield Highld 165 F6
Rockfield Mon 36 C1
Rockford Hants 14 D2
Rockhampton S Glos 36 E3
Rockingham Northants 65 E5
Rockingham Motor Speedway Northants 65 E6
Rockland All Saints Norf 68 E2
Rockland St Mary Norf 69 D6
Rockland St Peter Norf 68 E2
Rockley Wilts 25 B6
Rockwell End Bucks 39 F7
Rockwell Green Som 11 B6
Rodborough Glos 37 D5
Rodbourne Swindon 37 F8
Rodbourne Wilts 37 F6
Rodbourne Cheney Swindon 37 F8
Rodd Hereford 48 C5
Roddam Northumb 117 B6
Rodden Dorset 12 F4
Rode Som 24 D3
Rode Heath Ches 74 D5
Rodeheath Ches 75 C5
Roden Telford 61 C5
Rodhuish Som 22 F2
Rodington Telford 61 C5
Rodley Glos 36 C4
Rodley W Yorks 94 F5
Rodmarton Glos 37 E6
Rodmell E Sus 17 D8
Rodmersham Kent 30 C3
Rodney Stoke Som 23 D6
Rodsley Derbys 76 E2
Rodway Som 22 F4
Rodwell Dorset 12 G4
Roe Green Herts 54 F4
Roecliffe N Yorks 95 C6
Roehampton London 28 B3
Roesound Shetland 174 G5
Roffey W Sus 28 F2
Rogart Highld 164 D4
Rogart Station Highld 164 D4
Rogate W Sus 16 B2
Rogerstone Newport 35 F6
Roghadal W Isles 173 K3
Rogiet Mon 36 F1
Rogue's Alley Cambs 66 D3
Roke Oxon 39 E6
Roker T & W 111 D7
Rollesby Norf 69 C7
Rolleston Leics 64 D4
Rolleston Notts 77 D7
Rolleston-on-Dove Staffs 63 B6
Rolston E Yorks 97 E8
Rolvenden Kent 18 B5
Rolvenden Layne Kent 19 B5
Romaldkirk Durham 100 B4
Roman Baths & Pump Room, Bath Bath 24 C2
Romanby N Yorks 102 E1
Romannobridge Borders 122 E4
Romansleigh Devon 10 B2
Romford London 41 F8
Romiley Gtr Man 87 E7
Romney, Hythe and Dymchurch Light Railway Kent 19 B8
Romsey Hants 14 B4
Romsey Town Cambs 55 D5
Romsley Shrops 61 F7
Romsley Worcs 50 B4
Ronague I o M 84 E2
Rookhope Durham 110 E2
Rookley I o W 15 F6
Rooks Bridge Som 23 D5
Roos E Yorks 97 F8
Roosebeck Cumb 92 C2
Rootham's Green Beds 54 D2
Rootpark S Lnrk 122 D2
Ropley Hants 26 F4
Ropley Dean Hants 26 F4
Ropsley Lincs 78 F2
Rora Aberds 161 C7
Rorandle Aberds 151 C5
Rorrington Shrops 60 D3
Roscroggan Corn 3 B5
Rose Corn 4 D2
Rose Ash Devon 10 B2
Rose Green W Sus 16 E3
Rose Grove Lancs 93 F8
Rose Hill E Sus 17 C8
Rose Hill Lancs 93 F8
Rose Hill Suff 57 E5
Roseacre Kent 29 D8
Roseacre Lancs 92 F4
Rosebank S Lnrk 121 E8
Rosebrough Northumb 117 B7
Rosebush Pembs 32 B1
Rosecare Corn 8 E3
Rosedale Abbey N Yorks 103 E5
Roseden Northumb 117 B6
Rosefield Highld 158 D2
Rosehall Highld 164 D1
Rosehaugh Mains Highld 157 D7
Rosehearty Aberds 161 B6
Rosehill Shrops 74 F3
Roseisle Moray 158 C5
Roselands E Sus 18 E3
Rosemarket Pembs 44 E4

South Wheatley Corn 8 E4
South Wheatley Notts 89 F8
South Whiteness Shetland 175 J5
South Widcombe Bath 23 D7
South Wigston Leics 64 E2
South Willingham Lincs 91 F5
South Wingfield Derbys 76 D3
South Witham Lincs 65 C6
South Wonston Hants 26 F2
South Woodham Ferrers Essex 42 E4
South Wootton Norf 67 B6
South Wraxall Wilts 24 C3
South Zeal Devon 9 E8
Southall London 40 F4
Southam Glos 37 B6
Southam Warks 52 C2
Southampton Soton 14 C5
Southampton International Airport Hants 15 C5
Southborough Kent 29 E6
Southbourne Bmouth 14 E2
Southbourne W Sus 15 D8
Southburgh Norf 68 D2
Southburn E Yorks 97 D5
Southchurch Sthend 43 F5
Southcott Wilts 25 D6
Southcourt Bucks 39 C8
Southdean Borders 116 D2
Southdene Mers 86 E2
Southease E Sus 17 D8
Southend Argyll 118 F3
Southend W Berks 26 B3
Southend Wilts 25 B6
Southend Airport Essex 42 F4
Southend-on-Sea Sthend 42 F4
Southend Sea Life Centre Essex 42 E4
Southernden Kent 30 E2
Southerndown V Glam 21 B7
Southerness Dumfries 107 D6
Southery Norf 67 E6
Southfield Northumb 111 B5
Southfleet Kent 29 B7
Southgate Ceredig 46 B4
Southgate London 41 E5
Southgate Norf 81 E7
Southgate Swansea 33 F6
Southill Beds 54 E2
Southleigh Devon 11 E7
Southminster Essex 43 E5
Southmoor Oxon 38 E3
Southoe Cambs 54 C2
Southolt Suff 57 C5
Southorpe P'boro 65 D7
Southowram W Yorks 88 B2
Southport Mers 85 C4
Southpunds Shetland 175 L6
Southrepps Norf 81 D8
Southrey Lincs 78 C4
Southrop Glos 38 D1
Southrope Hants 26 E4
Southsea Ptsmth 15 E7
Southstoke Bath 24 C2
Southtown Norf 69 D8
Southtown Orkney 176 G3
Southwaite Cumb 108 E4
Southwark London 28 B4
Southwater W Sus 17 B5
Southwater Street W Sus 17 B5
Southway Som 23 E7
Southwell Dorset 12 G4
Southwell Notts 77 D6
Southwell Minster Notts 77 D7
Southwell Racecourse Notts 77 D7
Southwick Hants 15 D7
Southwick Northants 65 E7
Southwick T & W 111 D6
Southwick Wilts 24 D3
Southwick W Sus 17 D6
Southwold Suff 57 B9
Southwood Norf 69 D6
Southwood Som 23 F7
Soval Lodge W Isles 172 F6
Sowber Gate N Yorks 102 F1
Sowerby N Yorks 102 F2
Sowerby W Yorks 87 B8
Sowerby Bridge W Yorks 87 B8
Sowerby Row Cumb 108 F3
Sowood W Yorks 87 C8
Sowton Devon 10 E4
Soyal Highld 164 E2
Spa Common Norf 81 D8
Spacey Houses N Yorks 95 D6
Spadeadam Farm Cumb 109 B5
Spalding Lincs 66 B2
Spaldington E Yorks 96 F3
Spaldwick Cambs 54 B2
Spalford Notts 77 C8
Spanby Lincs 78 F3
Sparham Norf 68 C3
Spark Bridge Cumb 99 F5
Sparkford Som 12 B4
Sparkhill W Mid 62 F4
Sparkwell Devon 6 D3
Sparrow Green Norf 68 C2
Sparrowpit Derbys 87 F8
Sparsholt Hants 26 F2
Sparsholt Oxon 38 F3
Spartylea Northumb 109 E8
Spaunton N Yorks 103 F5
Spaxton Som 22 F4
Spean Bridge Highld 146 F5
Spear Hill W Sus 16 C5
Speen Bucks 39 E8
Speen W Berks 26 C2
Speeton N Yorks 97 B7
Speke Mers 86 F2
Speke Hall Mers 86 F2
Speldhurst Kent 29 E6
Spellbrook Herts 41 C7
Spelsbury Oxon 38 B3
Spelter Bridgend 34 E2
Spencers Wood Wokingham 26 C5
Spennithorne N Yorks 101 F6
Spennymoor Durham 111 F5
Spetchley Worcs 50 D3
Spetisbury Dorset 13 D7
Spexhall Suff 69 F6
Spey Bay Moray 159 C7
Speybridge Highld 149 B6
Speyview Moray 159 E6
Spilsby Lincs 79 C7
Spindlestone Northumb 125 F7
Spinkhill Derbys 76 B4
Spinningdale Highld 164 F3
Spirit of the West, St Columb Major Corn 4 C4
Spirthill Wilts 24 B4
Spital Hill S Yorks 89 E7
Spital in the Street Lincs 90 F3
Spitfire and Hurricane Memorial, Manston Kent 31 C7
Spithurst E Sus 17 C8
Spittal Dumfries 105 D7
Spittal E Loth 123 B7
Spittal Highld 169 D6
Spittal Northumb 125 D6
Spittal Pembs 44 C4
Spittal Stirl 132 F4
Spittal of Glenmuick Aberds 150 F2
Spittal of Glenshee Perth 141 B8
Spittalfield Perth 141 E8
Spixworth Norf 68 C5
Splayne's Green E Sus 17 B8
Spofforth N Yorks 95 D6
Spon End W Mid 51 B8
Spon Green Flint 73 C6
Spondon Derby 76 F4
Spooner Row Norf 68 E3
Sporle Norf 67 C8
Spott E Loth 124 B2
Spratton Northants 52 B5
Spreakley Sur 27 E6
Spreyton Devon 9 E8
Spridlington Lincs 90 F4
Spring Vale S Yorks 88 D3
Spring Valley I o M 84 E3
Springburn Glasgow 121 C6
Springfield Dumfries 108 C3
Springfield Essex 42 D3
Springfield Fife 134 C5
Springfield Moray 158 D4
Springfield W Mid 62 F4
Springhill Staffs 62 D3
Springholm Dumfries 106 C5
Springkell Dumfries 108 B2
Springside N Ayrs 120 F3
Springthorpe Lincs 90 F2
Springwell T & W 111 D5
Sproatley E Yorks 97 F7
Sproston Green Ches 74 C4
Sprotbrough S Yorks 89 D6
Sproughton Suff 56 E5
Sprouston Borders 124 F3
Sprowston Norf 68 C5
Sproxton Leics 65 B5
Sproxton N Yorks 102 F4
Spurstow Ches 74 D2
Spynie Moray 159 C6
Squires Gate Blkpool 92 F3
Srannda W Isles 173 K3
Sronphadruig Lodge Perth 140 B4
SS Great Britain Bristol 23 B7
Stableford Shrops 61 E7
Stableford Staffs 74 F5
Stacey Bank S Yorks 88 E3
Stackhouse N Yorks 93 C8
Stackpole Pembs 44 F4
Staddiscombe Devon 6 D3
Staddlethorpe E Yorks 90 B2
Stadhampton Oxon 39 E6
Stadhlaigearraidh W Isles 170 G3
Staffield Cumb 108 E5
Staffin Highld 152 C5
Stafford Staffs 62 B3
Stagsden Beds 53 E7
Stainburn Cumb 98 B2
Stainburn N Yorks 94 E5
Stainby Lincs 65 B6
Staincross S Yorks 88 C4
Staindrop Durham 101 B6
Staines Sur 27 B8
Stainfield Lincs 65 B7
Stainfield Lincs 78 B4
Stainforth N Yorks 93 C8
Stainforth S Yorks 89 C7
Staining Lancs 92 F3
Stainland W Yorks 87 C8
Stainsacre N Yorks 103 D7
Stainsby Derbys 76 C4
Stainton Cumb 99 F7
Stainton Cumb 99 B6
Stainton Durham 101 C5
Stainton M'bro 102 C2
Stainton N Yorks 101 E6
Stainton S Yorks 89 E6
Stainton by Langworth Lincs 78 B3
Stainton le Vale Lincs 91 E5
Stainton with Adgarley Cumb 92 B2
Staintondale N Yorks 103 E7
Stair Cumb 98 B4
Stair E Ayrs 112 B4
Stairhaven Dumfries 105 D6
Staithes N Yorks 103 C5
Stake Pool Lancs 92 E4
Stakeford Northumb 117 F8
Stalbridge Dorset 12 C5
Stalbridge Weston Dorset 12 C5
Stalham Norf 69 B6
Stalham Green Norf 69 B6
Stalisfield Green Kent 30 D3
Stalling Busk N Yorks 100 F4
Stallingborough NE Lincs 91 C5
Stalmine Lancs 92 E3
Stalybridge Gtr Man 87 E7
Stambourne Essex 55 F8
Stambourne Green Essex 55 F8
Stamford Lincs 65 D7
Stamford Bridge Ches 73 C8
Stamford Bridge E Yorks 96 D3
Stamfordham Northumb 110 B3
Stanah Cumb 99 C5
Stanborough Herts 41 C5
Stanbridge Beds 40 B2
Stanbridge Dorset 13 D8
Stanbrook Worcs 50 E3
Stanbury W Yorks 94 F3
Stand Gtr Man 87 D5
Stand N Lnrk 121 C7
Standburn Falk 122 B2
Standeford Staffs 62 D3
Standen Kent 30 E2
Standen, East Grinstead W Sus 28 F4
Standford Hants 27 F6
Standingstone Cumb 107 F7
Standish Gtr Man 86 C3
Standlake Oxon 38 D3
Standon Hants 14 B5
Standon Herts 41 B6
Standon Staffs 74 F5
Stane N Lnrk 121 D8
Stanfield Norf 80 E5
Stanford Beds 54 E2
Stanford Kent 19 B8
Stanford Bishop Hereford 49 D8
Stanford Bridge Worcs 50 C2
Stanford Dingley W Berks 26 B3
Stanford in the Vale Oxon 38 E3
Stanford-le-Hope Thurrock 42 F2
Stanford on Avon Northants 52 B3
Stanford on Soar Notts 64 B2
Stanford on Teme Worcs 50 C2
Stanford Rivers Essex 41 D8
Stanfree Derbys 76 B4
Stanghow Redcar 102 C4
Stanground P'boro 66 E2
Stanhoe Norf 80 D4
Stanhope Borders 114 B4
Stanhope Durham 110 F2
Stanion Northants 65 F6
Stanley Derbys 76 E4
Stanley Durham 110 D4
Stanley Lancs 86 D2
Stanley Perth 141 F8
Stanley Staffs 75 D6
Stanley W Yorks 88 B4
Stanley Common Derbys 76 E4
Stanley Gate Lancs 86 D2
Stanley Hill Hereford 49 E8
Stanlow Ches 73 B8
Stanmer Brighton 17 D7
Stanmore London 40 E4
Stanmore Hants 15 B5
Stanmore W Berks 26 B2
Stannergate Dundee 142 F4
Stanningley W Yorks 94 F5
Stannington Northumb 110 B5
Stannington S Yorks 88 F4
Stansbatch Hereford 48 C5
Stansfield Suff 55 D8
Stanstead Suff 56 E2
Stanstead Abbotts Herts 41 C6
Stansted Kent 29 C7
Stansted Mountfitchet Essex 41 B8
Stanton Glos 51 F5
Stanton Mon 35 B7
Stanton Northumb 117 F7
Stanton Staffs 75 E8
Stanton Suff 56 B3
Stanton by Bridge Derbys 63 B7
Stanton-by-Dale Derbys 76 F4
Stanton Drew Bath 23 C7
Stanton Fitzwarren Swindon 38 E1
Stanton Harcourt Oxon 38 D4
Stanton Hill Notts 76 C4
Stanton in Peak Derbys 76 C2
Stanton Lacy Shrops 49 B6
Stanton Long Shrops 61 E5
Stanton-on-the-Wolds Notts 77 F6
Stanton Prior Bath 23 C8
Stanton St Bernard Wilts 25 C5
Stanton St John Oxon 39 D5
Stanton St Quintin Wilts 24 B4
Stanton Street Suff 56 C3
Stanton under Bardon Leics 63 C8
Stanton upon Hine Heath Shrops 61 B5
Stanton Wick Bath 23 C8
Stanwardine in the Fields Shrops 60 B4
Stanwardine in the Wood Shrops 60 B4
Stanway Essex 43 B5
Stanway Glos 51 F5
Stanway Green Suff 57 B6
Stanwell Sur 27 B8
Stanwell Moor Sur 27 B8
Stanwick Northants 53 B7
Stanwick-St-John N Yorks 101 C6
Stanwix Cumb 108 D4
Stanydale Shetland 175 H4
Staoinebrig W Isles 171 G3
Stape N Yorks 103 E5
Stapehill Dorset 13 D8
Stapeley Ches 74 E3
Stapeley Water Gardens, Nantwich Ches 74 D3
Stapenhill Staffs 63 B6
Staple Kent 31 D6
Staple Som 22 E3
Staple Cross E Sus 18 C4
Staple Fitzpaine Som 11 C7
Staplefield W Sus 17 B6
Stapleford Cambs 55 D5
Stapleford Herts 41 C6
Stapleford Leics 64 C5
Stapleford Lincs 77 D8
Stapleford Notts 76 F4
Stapleford Wilts 25 F5
Stapleford Abbotts Essex 41 E8
Stapleford Tawney Essex 41 E8
Staplegrove Som 11 B7
Staplehay Som 11 B7
Staplehurst Kent 29 E8
Staplers I o W 15 F6
Stapleton Bristol 23 B8
Stapleton Cumb 108 B5
Stapleton Hereford 48 C5
Stapleton Leics 63 E8
Stapleton N Yorks 101 C7
Stapleton Shrops 60 D4
Stapleton Som 12 B2
Stapley Som 11 C6
Staploe Beds 54 C2
Staplow Hereford 49 E8
Star Fife 134 D5
Star Pembs 45 F4
Star Som 23 D6
Stara Orkney 176 D1
Starbeck N Yorks 95 D6
Starbotton N Yorks 94 B2
Starcross Devon 10 F4
Stareton Warks 51 B8
Starkholmes Derbys 76 D3
Starlings Green Essex 55 F5
Starston Norf 68 F5
Startforth Durham 101 C5
Startley Wilts 37 F6
Stathe Som 11 B8
Stathern Leics 77 F7
Station Town Durham 111 F7
Staughton Green Cambs 54 C2
Staughton Highway Cambs 54 C2
Staunton Glos 36 C2
Staunton Glos 36 B4
Staunton in the Vale Notts 77 E8
Staunton on Arrow Hereford 49 C5
Staunton on Wye Hereford 49 E5
Staveley Cumb 99 F5
Staveley Cumb 99 E6
Staveley Derbys 76 B4
Staveley N Yorks 95 C6
Staverton Devon 7 C5
Staverton Glos 37 B5
Staverton Northants 52 C3
Staverton Wilts 24 C3
Staverton Bridge Glos 37 B5
Stawell Som 23 F5
Staxigoe Highld 169 D8
Staxton N Yorks 97 B6
Staylittle Powys 59 E5
Staynall Lancs 92 E3
Staythorpe Notts 77 D7
Stean N Yorks 94 B3
Stearsby N Yorks 96 B2
Steart Som 22 E4
Stebbing Essex 42 B2
Stebbing Green Essex 42 B2
Stedham W Sus 16 B2
Steele Road Borders 115 E8
Steen's Bridge Hereford 49 D7
Steep Hants 15 B8
Steep Marsh Hants 15 B8
Steeple Dorset 13 F7
Steeple Essex 43 D5
Steeple Ashton Wilts 24 D4
Steeple Aston Oxon 38 B4
Steeple Barton Oxon 38 B4
Steeple Bumpstead Essex 55 E7
Steeple Claydon Bucks 39 B6
Steeple Gidding Cambs 65 F8
Steeple Langford Wilts 24 F5
Steeple Morden Cambs 54 E3
Steeton W Yorks 94 E3
Stein Highld 152 D3
Steinmanhill Aberds 160 D4
Stelling Minnis Kent 30 E5
Stemster Highld 169 C6
Stemster Ho. Highld 169 C6
Stenalees Corn 4 D5
Stenhousemuir Falk 133 F7
Stenigot Lincs 91 F6
Stenness Shetland 174 F4
Stenscholl Highld 152 C5
Stenso Orkney 176 D2
Stenson Derbys 63 B7
Stenton E Loth 124 B2
Stenton Fife 134 E4
Stenwith Lincs 77 F8
Stepaside Pembs 32 D2
Stepping Hill Gtr Man 87 F7
Steppingley Beds 53 F8
Stepps N Lnrk 121 C6
Sterndale Moor Derbys 75 C8
Sternfield Suff 57 C7
Sterridge Devon 20 E4
Stert Wilts 24 D5
Stetchworth Cambs 55 D7
Stevenage Herts 41 B5
Stevenston N Ayrs 120 E2
Steventon Hants 26 E3
Steventon Oxon 38 E4
Stevington Beds 53 D7
Stewartby Beds 53 E8
Stewarton Argyll 118 E3
Stewarton E Ayrs 120 E4
Stewkley Bucks 40 B1
Stewton Lincs 91 F7
Steyne Cross I o W 15 F7
Steyning W Sus 17 C5
Steynton Pembs 44 E4
Stibb Corn 8 C4
Stibb Cross Devon 9 C6
Stibb Green Wilts 25 C7
Stibbard Norf 81 E5
Stibbington Cambs 65 E7
Stichill Borders 124 F3
Sticker Corn 4 D4
Stickford Lincs 79 D6
Sticklepath Devon 9 E8
Stickney Lincs 79 D6
Stiffkey Norf 81 C5
Stifford's Bridge Hereford 50 E2
Stillingfleet N Yorks 95 E8
Stillington N Yorks 95 C8
Stillington Stockton 102 B1
Stilton Cambs 65 F8
Stinchcombe Glos 36 E4
Stinsford Dorset 12 E5
Stirchley Telford 61 D7
Stirkoke Ho. Highld 169 D8
Stirling Aberds 161 D8
Stirling Stirl 133 E6
Stirling Castle Stirl 133 E6
Stisted Essex 42 B3
Stithians Corn 3 C6
Stittenham Highld 157 B7
Stivichall W Mid 51 B8
Stixwould Lincs 78 C4
Stoak Ches 73 B8
Stobieside S Lnrk 121 F6
Stobo Borders 122 F4
Stoborough Dorset 13 F7
Stoborough Green Dorset 13 F7
Stobshiel E Loth 123 C7
Stobswood Northumb 117 E8
Stock Essex 42 E2
Stock Green Worcs 50 D4
Stock Wood Worcs 50 D5
Stockbridge Hants 25 F8
Stockbury Kent 30 C2
Stockcross W Berks 26 C2
Stockdalewath Cumb 108 E3
Stockerston Leics 64 E5
Stockheath Hants 15 D8
Stockiemuir Stirl 132 F4
Stocking Pelham Herts 41 B7
Stockingford Warks 63 E7
Stockland Devon 11 D7
Stockland Bristol Som 22 E4
Stockleigh English Devon 10 D3
Stockleigh Pomeroy Devon 10 D3
Stockley Wilts 24 C5
Stocklinch Som 11 C8
Stockport Gtr Man 87 E6
Stocksbridge S Yorks 88 E3
Stocksfield Northumb 110 C3
Stockton Hereford 49 C7
Stockton Norf 69 E6
Stockton Shrops 60 D2
Stockton Shrops 61 E7
Stockton Warks 52 C2
Stockton Wilts 24 F4
Stockton Heath Warr 86 F4
Stockton-on-Tees Stockton 102 C2
Stockton on Teme Worcs 50 C2
Stockton on the Forest York 96 D2
Stockwood Park Museum, Luton Luton 40 C3
Stodmarsh Kent 31 C6
Stody Norf 81 D6
Stoer Highld 162 B4
Stoford Som 12 C3
Stoford Wilts 25 F5
Stogumber Som 22 F2
Stogursey Som 22 E4
Stoke Devon 8 B4
Stoke Hants 26 D2
Stoke Hants 15 D8
Stoke Medway 30 B2
Stoke Suff 57 E5
Stoke Abbott Dorset 12 D2
Stoke Albany Northants 64 F5
Stoke Ash Suff 56 B5
Stoke Bardolph Notts 77 E6
Stoke Bliss Worcs 49 C8
Stoke Bruerne Northants 52 E5
Stoke by Clare Suff 55 E8
Stoke-by-Nayland Suff 56 F3
Stoke Canon Devon 10 E4
Stoke Charity Hants 26 F2
Stoke Climsland Corn 5 B8
Stoke D'Abernon Sur 28 D2
Stoke Doyle Northants 65 F7
Stoke Dry Rutland 65 E5
Stoke Farthing Wilts 13 B8
Stoke Ferry Norf 67 E7
Stoke Fleming Devon 7 E6
Stoke Gabriel Devon 7 D6
Stoke Gifford S Glos 23 B8
Stoke Golding Leics 63 E7
Stoke Goldington M Keynes 53 E6
Stoke Green Bucks 40 F2
Stoke Hammond Bucks 40 B1
Stoke Heath Shrops 61 B6
Stoke Holy Cross Norf 68 D5
Stoke Lacy Hereford 49 E8
Stoke Lyne Oxon 39 B5
Stoke Mandeville Bucks 39 C8
Stoke Newington London 41 F6
Stoke on Tern Shrops 61 B6
Stoke-on-Trent Stoke 75 E5
Stoke Orchard Glos 37 B6
Stoke Poges Bucks 40 F2
Stoke Prior Hereford 49 D7
Stoke Prior Worcs 50 C4
Stoke Rivers Devon 20 F5
Stoke Rochford Lincs 65 B6
Stoke Row Oxon 39 F6
Stoke St Gregory Som 11 B8
Stoke St Mary Som 11 B7
Stoke St Michael Som 23 E8
Stoke St Milborough Shrops 61 F5
Stoke sub Hamdon Som 12 C2
Stoke Talmage Oxon 39 E6
Stoke Trister Som 12 B5
Stoke Wake Dorset 13 D5
Stokeford Dorset 13 F6
Stokeham Notts 77 B7
Stokeinteignhead Devon 7 B7
Stokenchurch Bucks 39 E7
Stokenham Devon 7 E6
Stokesay Shrops 60 F4
Stokesby Norf 69 C7
Stokesley N Yorks 102 D3
Stolford Som 22 E4
Ston Easton Som 23 D8
Stondon Massey Essex 42 D1
Stone Bucks 39 C7
Stone Glos 36 E3
Stone Kent 19 C6
Stone Kent 29 B6
Stone Staffs 75 F6
Stone S Yorks 89 F6
Stone Worcs 50 B3
Stone Allerton Som 23 D6
Stone Bridge Corner P'boro 66 D2
Stone Chair W Yorks 88 B2
Stone Cross E Sus 18 E3
Stone Cross Kent 31 D7
Stone-edge Batch N Som 23 B6
Stone House Cumb 100 F2
Stone Street Kent 29 D6
Stone Street Suff 56 F3
Stone Street Suff 69 F6
Stonebroom Derbys 76 D4
Stoneferry Hull 97 F7
Stonefield S Lnrk 121 D6
Stonegate E Sus 18 C3
Stonegate N Yorks 103 D5
Stonegrave N Yorks 96 B2
Stonehaugh Northumb 109 B7
Stonehaven Aberds 151 F7
Stonehenge, Amesbury Wilts 25 E6
Stonehouse Glos 37 D5
Stonehouse Northumb 109 D6
Stonehouse S Lnrk 121 E7
Stoneleigh Warks 51 B8
Stonely Cambs 54 C2
Stoner Hill Hants 15 B8
Stone's Green Essex 43 B7
Stonesby Leics 64 B5
Stonesfield Oxon 38 C3
Stonethwaite Cumb 98 C4
Stoney Cross Hants 14 C3
Stoney Middleton Derbys 76 B2
Stoney Stanton Leics 63 E8
Stoney Stoke Som 24 F2
Stoney Stratton Som 23 F8
Stoney Stretton Shrops 60 D3
Stoneybreck Shetland 175 L3
Stoneyburn W Loth 122 C2
Stoneygate Aberds 161 E7
Stoneygate Leicester 64 D3
Stoneyhills Essex 43 E5
Stoneykirk Dumfries 104 D4
Stoneywood Aberdeen 151 C7
Stoneywood Falk 133 F6
Stonganess Shetland 174 C7
Stonham Aspal Suff 56 D5
Stonnall Staffs 62 D4
Stonor Oxon 39 F7
Stonton Wyville Leics 64 E4
Stony Cross Hereford 50 E2
Stony Stratford M Keynes 53 E5
Stonyfield Highld 157 B7
Stoodleigh Devon 10 C4
Stopes S Yorks 88 F3
Stopham W Sus 16 C4
Stopsley Luton 40 B4
Stores Corner Suff 57 E7
Storeton Mers 85 F4
Stornoway W Isles 172 E7
Stornoway Airport W Isles 172 E7
Storridge Hereford 50 E2
Storrington W Sus 16 C4
Storrs Cumb 99 E5
Storth Cumb 99 F6
Storwood E Yorks 96 E3
Stotfield Moray 159 B6
Stotfold Beds 54 F3
Stottesdon Shrops 61 F6
Stoughton Leics 64 D3
Stoughton Sur 27 D7
Stoughton W Sus 16 C2
Stoul Highld 145 D7
Stoulton Worcs 50 E4
Stour Provost Dorset 13 B5
Stour Row Dorset 13 B6
Stourbridge W Mid 62 F3
Stourhead Garden Wilts 24 F2
Stourpaine Dorset 13 D6
Stourport on Severn Worcs 50 B3
Stourton Staffs 62 F2
Stourton Warks 51 F7
Stourton Wilts 24 F2
Stourton Caundle Dorset 12 C5
Stove Orkney 176 C5
Stove Shetland 175 L6
Stoven Suff 69 F7
Stow Borders 123 E7
Stow Lincs 90 F2
Stow Lincs 78 F3
Stow Bardolph Norf 67 D6
Stow Bedon Norf 68 E2
Stow cum Quy Cambs 55 C6
Stow Longa Cambs 54 B2
Stow Maries Essex 42 E4
Stow-on-the-Wold Glos 38 B1
Stowbridge Norf 67 D6
Stowe Shrops 48 B5
Stowe-by-Chartley Staffs 62 B4
Stowe Green Glos 36 D2
Stowe House and Gardens, Buckingham Bucks 52 F4
Stowell Som 12 B4
Stowford Devon 9 F6
Stowlangtoft Suff 56 C3
Stowmarket Suff 56 D4
Stowting Kent 30 E5
Stowupland Suff 56 D4
Straad Argyll 129 D5
Strachan Aberds 151 E5
Stradbroke Suff 57 B6
Stradishall Suff 55 D8
Stradsett Norf 67 D6
Stragglethorpe Lincs 78 D2
Straid S Ayrs 112 E1
Straith Dumfries 113 F8
Straiton Edin 123 C5
Straiton S Ayrs 112 D3
Straloch Aberds 151 B7
Straloch Perth 141 C7
Stramshall Staffs 75 F7
Strang I o M 84 E3
Stranraer Dumfries 104 C4
Stratfield Mortimer W Berks 26 C4
Stratfield Saye Hants 26 C4
Stratfield Turgis Hants 26 D4
Stratford London 41 F6
Stratford Racecourse Warks 51 D6
Stratford St Andrew Suff 57 C7
Stratford St Mary Suff 56 F4
Stratford Sub Castle Wilts 25 F6
Stratford Tony Wilts 13 B8
Stratford-upon-Avon Warks 51 D6
Strath Highld 169 D7
Strath Highld 154 C3
Strathan Highld 146 E2
Strathan Highld 167 C7
Strathan Highld 162 B4
Strathaven S Lnrk 121 E7
Strathblane Stirl 121 B5
Strathcanaird Highld 163 D5
Strathcarron Highld 155 F5
Strathcoil Argyll 130 B2
Strathdon Aberds 150 C2
Strathellie Aberds 161 B7
Strathkinness Fife 135 C6
Strathmashie House Highld 147 E8
Strathmiglo Fife 134 C4
Strathmore Lodge Highld 169 E6
Strathpeffer Highld 157 D5
Strathrannoch Highld 156 B4
Strathtay Perth 141 D6
Strathvaich Lodge Highld 156 B4
Strathwhillan N Ayrs 119 C7
Strathy Highld 168 C3
Strathyre Stirl 132 C4
Stratton Corn 8 D4
Stratton Dorset 12 E4
Stratton Glos 37 D7
Stratton Audley Oxon 39 B6
Stratton on the Fosse Som 23 D8
Stratton St Margaret Swindon 38 F1
Stratton St Michael Norf 68 E5
Stratton Strawless Norf 81 E8
Stravithie Fife 135 C7
Streat E Sus 17 C7
Streatham London 28 B4
Streatley Beds 40 B3
Streatley W Berks 39 F5
Street Lancs 92 D5
Street N Yorks 103 D5
Street Som 23 F6
Street Dinas Shrops 73 F7
Street End Kent 30 D5
Street End W Sus 16 E2
Street Gate T & W 110 D5
Street Lydan Wrex 73 F8
Streethay Staffs 62 C5
Streetlam N Yorks 101 E8
Streetly W Mid 62 E4
Streetly End Cambs 55 E7
Strefford Shrops 60 F4
Strelley Notts 76 E5
Strensall York 96 C2
Stretcholt Som 22 E4
Strete Devon 7 E6
Stretford Gtr Man 87 E6
Strethall Essex 55 F5
Stretham Cambs 55 B6
Strettington W Sus 16 D2
Stretton Ches 73 D8
Stretton Derbys 76 C3
Stretton Rutland 65 C6
Stretton Staffs 62 C2
Stretton Staffs 63 B6
Stretton Warr 86 F4
Stretton Grandison Hereford 49 E8
Stretton-on-Dunsmore Warks 52 B2
Stretton-on-Fosse Warks 51 F7
Stretton Sugwas Hereford 49 E6
Stretton under Fosse Warks 63 F8
Stretton Westwood Shrops 61 E5
Strichen Aberds 161 C6
Strines Gtr Man 87 F7
Stringston Som 22 E3
Strixton Northants 53 C7
Stroat Glos 36 E2
Stromeferry Highld 155 G4
Stromemore Highld 155 G4
Stromness Orkney 176 F1
Stronaba Highld 146 F5
Stronachlachar Stirl 132 C3
Stronchreggan Highld 138 B4
Stronchrubie Highld 163 C6
Strone Argyll 129 B6
Strone Highld 147 B8
Strone Highld 146 F4
Strone Invclyd 129 C7
Stronmilchan Argyll 131 C7
Stronsay Airport Orkney 176 D5
Strontian Highld 138 C2
Strood Medway 29 C8
Strood Green Sur 28 E3
Strood Green W Sus 16 B4
Strood Green W Sus 16 B3
Stroud Glos 37 D5
Stroud Hants 15 B8
Stroud Green Essex 42 E4
Stroxton Lincs 78 F2
Struan Highld 153 F4
Struan Perth 141 C5
Strubby Lincs 91 F8
Strumpshaw Norf 69 D6
Strutherhill S Lnrk 121 E7
Struy Highld 156 F4
Stryt-issa Wrex 73 E6
Stuartfield Aberds 161 D6
Stub Place Cumb 98 E2
Stubbington Hants 15 D6
Stubbins Lancs 87 C5
Stubbs Cross Kent 19 B6
Stubb's Green Norf 69 E5
Stubbs Green Norf 69 E6
Stubhampton Dorset 13 C7
Stubton Lincs 77 E8
Stuckgowan Argyll 132 D2
Stuckton Hants 14 C2
Stud Green Windsor 27 B6
Studham Beds 40 C3
Studland Dorset 13 F8
Studley Warks 51 C5
Studley Wilts 24 B4
Studley Roger N Yorks 95 B5
Stump Cross Essex 55 E6
Stuntney Cambs 55 B6
Sturbridge Staffs 74 F5
Sturmer Essex 55 E7
Sturminster Marshall Dorset 13 D7
Sturminster Newton Dorset 13 C5
Sturry Kent 31 C5
Sturton N Lincs 90 D3
Sturton by Stow Lincs 90 F2
Sturton le Steeple Notts 89 F8
Stuston Suff 56 B5
Stutton N Yorks 95 E7
Stutton Suff 57 F5
Styal Ches 87 F6
Styrrup Notts 89 E7
Suainebost W Isles 172 B8
Suardail W Isles 172 E7
Succoth Aberds 159 F8
Succoth Argyll 131 E8
Suckley Worcs 50 D2
Suckquoy Orkney 176 H3
Sudborough Northants 65 F6
Sudbourne Suff 57 D8
Sudbrook Lincs 78 E2
Sudbrook Mon 36 F2
Sudbrooke Lincs 78 B3
Sudbury Derbys 75 F8
Sudbury London 40 F4
Sudbury Suff 56 E2
Suddie Highld 157 D7
Sudeley Castle and Gardens Glos 37 B7
Sudgrove Glos 37 D6
Suffield Norf 81 D8
Suffield N Yorks 103 E7
Sugnall Staffs 74 F4
Suladale Highld 152 D4
Sulaisiadar W Isles 172 E8
Sulby I o M 84 C3
Sulgrave Northants 52 E3
Sulham W Berks 26 B4
Sulhamstead W Berks 26 C4
Sulland Orkney 176 B4
Sullington W Sus 16 C4
Sullom Shetland 174 F5
Sullom Voe Oil Terminal Shetland 174 F5

West Horndon Essex 42 F2
West Horrington Som 23 E7
West Horsley Sur 27 D8
West Horton Northumb 125 F6
West Hougham Kent 31 E6
West Houlland Shetland 175 H4
West-houses Derbys 76 D4
West Huntington York 96 D2
West Hythe Kent 19 B8
West Ilsley W Berks 38 F4
West Itchenor W Sus 15 D8
West Keal Lincs 79 C6
West Kennett Wilts 25 C6
West Kilbride N Ayrs 120 E2
West Kingsdown Kent 29 C6
West Kington Wilts 24 B3
West Kinharrachie Aberds 161 E6
West Kirby Mers 85 F3
West Knapton N Yorks 96 B4
West Knighton Dorset 12 F5
West Knoyle Wilts 24 F3
West Kyloe Northumb 125 E6
West Lambrook Som 12 C2
West Langdon Kent 31 E7
West Langwell Highld 164 D3
West Lavington Wilts 24 D5
West Lavington W Sus 16 B2
West Layton N Yorks 101 D6
West Lea Durham 111 E7
West Leake Notts 64 B2
West Learmouth Northumb 124 F4
West Leigh Devon 9 D8
West Lexham Norf 67 C8
West Lilling N Yorks 96 C2
West Linton Borders 122 D4
West Liss Hants 15 B8
West Littleton S Glos 24 B2
West Looe Corn 5 D7
West Luccombe Som 21 E7
West Lulworth Dorset 13 F6
West Lutton N Yorks 96 C5
West Lydford Som 23 F7
West Lyng Som 11 B8
West Lynn Norf 67 B6
West Malling Kent 29 D7
West Malvern Worcs 50 E2
West Marden W Sus 15 C8
West Marina E Sus 18 E4
West Markham Notts 77 B7
West Marsh NE Lincs 91 C6
West Marton N Yorks 93 D8
West Meon Hants 15 B7
West Mersea Essex 43 C6
West Midlands Safari Park, Kidderminster Worcs 50 B3
West Milton Dorset 12 E3
West Minster Kent 30 B3
West Molesey Sur 28 C2
West Monkton Som 11 B7
West Moors Dorset 13 D8
West Morriston Borders 124 E2
West Muir Angus 143 C5
West Ness N Yorks 96 B2
West Newham Northumb 110 B3
West Newton E Yorks 97 F7
West Newton Norf 67 B6
West Norwood London 28 B4
West Ogwell Devon 7 B6
West Orchard Dorset 13 C6
West Overton Wilts 25 C6
West Park Hrtlpl 111 F7
West Parley Dorset 13 E8
West Peckham Kent 29 D7
West Pelton Durham 110 D5
West Pennard Som 23 F7
West Pentire Corn 4 C2
West Perry Cambs 54 C2
West Putford Devon 9 C5
West Quantoxhead Som 22 E3
West Rainton Durham 111 E6
West Rasen Lincs 90 F4
West Raynham Norf 80 E4
West Retford Notts 89 F7
West Rounton N Yorks 102 D2
West Row Suff 55 B7
West Rudham Norf 80 E4
West Runton Norf 81 C7
West Saltoun E Loth 123 C7
West Sandwick Shetland 174 E6
West Scrafton N Yorks 101 F5
West Sleekburn Northumb 117 F8
West Somerset Railway, Minehead Som 21 E8
West Somerton Norf 69 C7
West Stafford Dorset 12 F5
West Stockwith Notts 89 E8
West Stoke W Sus 16 D2
West Stonesdale N Yorks 100 D3
West Stoughton Som 23 E6
West Stour Dorset 13 B5
West Stourmouth Kent 31 C6
West Stow Suff 56 B2
West Stowell Wilts 25 C6
West Strathan Highld 167 C7
West Stratton Hants 26 E3
West Street Kent 30 D3
West Tanfield N Yorks 95 B5
West Taphouse Corn 5 C6
West Tarbert Argyll 128 D3
West Thirston Northumb 117 E7
West Thorney W Sus 15 D8
West Thurrock Thurrock 29 B6
West Tilbury Thurrock 29 B7
West Tisted Hants 15 B7
West Tofts Norf 67 E8
West Tofts Perth 141 F8
West Torrington Lincs 90 F5
West Town Hants 15 E8
West Town N Som 23 C6
West Tytherley Hants 14 B3
West Tytherton Wilts 24 B4
West Walton Norf 66 C4
West Walton Highway Norf 66 C4
West Wellow Hants 14 C3
West Wemyss Fife 134 E5
West Wick N Som 23 C5
West Wickham Cambs 55 E7
West Wickham London 28 C4
West Williamston Pembs 32 D1
West Willoughby Lincs 78 E2
West Winch Norf 67 C6
West Winterslow Wilts 25 F7
West Wittering W Sus 15 E8
West Witton N Yorks 101 F5
West Woodburn Northumb 116 F4
West Woodhay W Berks 25 C8
West Woodlands Som 24 E2
West Worldham Hants 26 F5
West Worlington Devon 10 C2
West Worthing W Sus 16 D5
West Wratting Cambs 55 D7
West Wycombe Bucks 39 E8
West Wylam Northumb 110 C4
West Yell Shetland 174 E6
Westacott Devon 20 F4
Westbere Kent 31 C5
Westborough Lincs 77 E8
Westbourne Bmouth 13 E8
Westbourne Suff 56 E5
Westbourne W Sus 15 D8
Westbrook W Berks 26 B2
Westbury Bucks 52 F4
Westbury Shrops 60 D3
Westbury Wilts 24 D3
Westbury Leigh Wilts 24 D3
Westbury-on-Severn Glos 36 C4
Westbury on Trym Bristol 23 B7
Westbury-sub-Mendip Som 23 E7
Westby Lancs 92 F3
Westcliff-on-Sea Sthend 42 F4
Westcombe Som 23 F8
Westcote Glos 38 B2
Westcott Bucks 39 C7
Westcott Devon 10 D5
Westcott Sur 28 E2
Westcott Barton Oxon 38 B4
Westdean E Sus 18 F2
Westdene Brighton 17 D6
Wester Aberchalder Highld 147 B8
Wester Balgedie Perth 134 D3
Wester Culbeuchly Aberds 160 B3
Wester Dechmont W Loth 122 C3
Wester Denoon Angus 142 E3
Wester Fintray Aberds 151 C7
Wester Gruinards Highld 164 E2
Wester Lealty Highld 157 B7
Wester Milton Highld 158 D3
Wester Newburn Fife 135 D6
Wester Quarff Shetland 175 K6
Wester Skeld Shetland 175 J4
Westerdale Highld 169 D6
Westerdale N Yorks 102 D4
Westerfield Shetland 175 H5
Westerfield Suff 57 E5
Westergate W Sus 16 D3
Westerham Kent 28 D5
Westerhope T & W 110 C4
Westerleigh S Glos 23 B9
Westerton Angus 143 D6
Westerton Durham 110 F5
Westerton W Sus 16 D2
Westerwick Shetland 175 J4
Westfield Cumb 98 B1
Westfield E Sus 18 D5
Westfield Hereford 50 E2
Westfield Highld 169 C5
Westfield N Lnrk 121 B7
Westfield Norf 68 D2
Westfield W Loth 122 B2
Westfields Dorset 12 D5
Westfields of Rattray Perth 142 E1
Westgate Durham 110 F2
Westgate N Lincs 89 D8
Westgate Norf 80 C4
Westgate Norf 81 C5
Westgate on Sea Kent 31 B7
Westhall Aberds 151 B5
Westhall Suff 69 F7
Westham Dorset 12 G4
Westham E Sus 18 E3
Westham Som 23 E6
Westhampnett W Sus 16 D2
Westhay Som 23 E6
Westhead Lancs 86 D2
Westhide Hereford 49 E7
Westhill Aberds 151 D7
Westhill Highld 157 E8
Westhope Hereford 49 D6
Westhope Shrops 60 F4
Westhorpe Lincs 78 F5
Westhorpe Suff 56 C4
Westhoughton Gtr Man 86 D4
Westhouse N Yorks 93 B6
Westhumble Sur 28 D2
Westing Shetland 174 C7
Westlake Devon 6 D4
Westleigh Devon 9 B6
Westleigh Devon 11 C5
Westleigh Gtr Man 86 D4
Westleton Suff 57 C8
Westley Shrops 60 D3
Westley Suff 56 C2
Westley Waterless Cambs 55 D7
Westlington Bucks 39 C7
Westlinton Cumb 108 C3
Westmarsh Kent 31 C6
Westmeston E Sus 17 C7
Westmill Herts 41 B6
Westminster London 28 B4
Westminster Cathedral London 28 B3
Westmuir Angus 142 D3
Westness Orkney 176 D2
Westnewton Cumb 107 E8
Westnewton Northumb 124 F5
Westoe T & W 111 C6
Weston Bath 24 C2
Weston Ches 74 D4
Weston Devon 11 F6
Weston Dorset 12 G4
Weston Halton 86 F3
Weston Hants 15 B8
Weston Herts 54 F3
Weston Lincs 66 B2
Weston Notts 77 C7
Weston Northants 52 E3
Weston N Yorks 94 E4
Weston Shrops 61 E5
Weston Shrops 61 B5
Weston Staffs 62 B3
Weston W Berks 25 B8
Weston Beggard Hereford 49 E7
Weston by Welland Northants 64 E4
Weston Colville Cambs 55 D7
Weston Coyney Stoke 75 E6
Weston Favell Northants 53 C5
Weston Green Cambs 55 D7
Weston Green Norf 68 C4
Weston Heath Shrops 61 C7
Weston Hills Lincs 66 B2
Weston-in-Gordano N Som 23 B6
Weston Jones Staffs 61 B7
Weston Longville Norf 68 C4
Weston Lullingfields Shrops 60 B4
Weston-on-the-Green Oxon 39 C5
Weston-on-Trent Derbys 63 B8
Weston Park Staffs 62 C2
Weston Patrick Hants 26 E4
Weston Rhyn Shrops 73 F6
Weston-Sub-Edge Glos 51 E6
Weston-super-Mare N Som 22 C5
Weston Turville Bucks 40 C1
Weston under Lizard Staffs 62 C2
Weston under Penyard Hereford 36 B3
Weston under Wetherley Warks 51 C8
Weston Underwood Derbys 76 E2
Weston Underwood M Keynes 53 D6
Westonbirt Glos 37 F5
Westonbirt Arboretum, Tetbury Glos 37 F5
Westoncommon Shrops 60 B4
Westoning Beds 53 F8
Westonzoyland Som 23 F5
Westow N Yorks 96 C3
Westport Argyll 118 D3
Westport Som 11 C8
Westray Airport Orkney 176 A3
Westrigg W Loth 122 C2
Westruther Borders 124 E2
Westry Cambs 66 E3
Westville Notts 76 E5
Westward Cumb 108 E2
Westward Ho! Devon 9 B6
Westwell Kent 30 E3
Westwell Oxon 38 D2
Westwell Leacon Kent 30 E3
Westwick Cambs 54 C5
Westwick Durham 101 C5
Westwick Norf 81 E8
Westwood Devon 10 E5
Westwood Wilts 24 D3
Westwoodside N Lincs 89 E8
Wetheral Cumb 108 D4
Wetherby W Yorks 95 E7
Wetherby Racecourse W Yorks 95 E7
Wetherden Suff 56 C4
Wetheringsett Suff 56 C5
Wethersfield Essex 55 F8
Wethersta Shetland 174 G5
Wetherup Street Suff 56 C5
Wetley Rocks Staffs 75 E6
Wettenhall Ches 74 C3
Wetton Staffs 75 D8
Wetwang E Yorks 96 D5
Wetwood Staffs 74 F4
Wexcombe Wilts 25 D7
Wexham Street Bucks 40 F2
Weybourne Norf 81 C7
Weybread Suff 68 F5
Weybridge Sur 27 C8
Weycroft Devon 11 E8
Weydale Highld 169 C6
Weyhill Hants 25 E8
Weymouth Dorset 12 G4
Weymouth Sea Life Park Dorset 12 F4
Whaddon Bucks 53 F6
Whaddon Cambs 54 E4
Whaddon Glos 37 C5
Whaddon Wilts 14 B2
Whale Cumb 99 B7
Whaley Derbys 76 B5
Whaley Bridge Derbys 87 F8
Whaley Thorns Derbys 76 B5
Whaligoe Highld 169 E8
Whalley Lancs 93 F7
Whalsay Airport Shetland 174 G7
Whalton Northumb 117 F7
Wham N Yorks 93 C7
Whaplode Lincs 66 B3
Whaplode Drove Lincs 66 C3
Whaplode St Catherine Lincs 66 B3
Wharfe N Yorks 93 C7
Wharles Lancs 92 F4
Wharncliffe Side S Yorks 88 E3
Wharram le Street N Yorks 96 C4
Wharton Ches 74 C3
Wharton Green Ches 74 C3
Whashton N Yorks 101 D6
Whatcombe Dorset 13 D6
Whatcote Warks 51 E8
Whatfield Suff 56 E4
Whatley Som 11 D8
Whatley Som 24 E2
Whatlington E Sus 18 D4
Whatstandwell Derbys 76 D3
Whatton Notts 77 F7
Whauphill Dumfries 105 E8
Whaw N Yorks 100 D4
Wheatacre Norf 69 E7
Wheatcroft Derbys 76 D3
Wheathampstead Herts 40 C4
Wheathill Shrops 61 F6
Wheatley Devon 10 E4
Wheatley Hants 27 E5
Wheatley Oxon 39 D5
Wheatley S Yorks 89 D6
Wheatley W Yorks 87 B8
Wheatley Hill Durham 111 F6
Wheaton Aston Staffs 62 C2
Wheddon Cross Som 21 F8
Wheedlemont Aberds 150 B3
Wheelerstreet Sur 27 E7
Wheelock Ches 74 D4
Wheelock Heath Ches 74 D4
Wheelton Lancs 86 B4
Wheen Angus 142 B3
Wheldrake York 96 E2
Whelford Glos 38 E1
Whelpley Hill Bucks 40 D2
Whempstead Herts 41 B6
Whenby N Yorks 96 C2
Whepstead Suff 56 D2
Wherstead Suff 57 E5
Wherwell Hants 25 E8
Wheston Derbys 75 B8
Whetsted Kent 29 E7
Whetstone Leics 64 E2
Whicham Cumb 98 F3
Whichford Warks 51 F8
Whickham T & W 110 C5
Whiddon Down Devon 9 E8
Whigstreet Angus 142 E4
Whilton Northants 52 C4
Whim Farm Borders 122 D5
Whimble Devon 9 D5
Whimple Devon 10 E5
Whimpwell Green Norf 69 B6
Whinburgh Norf 68 D3
Whinnieliggate Dumfries 106 D4
Whinnyfold Aberds 161 E7
Whippingham I o W 15 E6
Whipsnade Beds 40 C3
Whipsnade Wild Animal Park, Dunstable Beds 40 C3
Whipton Devon 10 E4
Whirlow S Yorks 88 F4
Whisby Lincs 78 C2
Whissendine Rutland 64 C5
Whissonsett Norf 80 E5
Whistlefield Argyll 129 A6
Whistlefield Argyll 129 A7
Whistley Green Wokingham 27 B5
Whiston Mers 86 E2
Whiston Northants 53 C6
Whiston Staffs 62 C2
Whiston Staffs 75 E7
Whiston S Yorks 88 F5
Whitbeck Cumb 98 F3
Whitbourne Hereford 50 D2
Whitbread Hop Farm, Beltring Kent 29 E7
Whitburn T & W 111 C7
Whitburn W Loth 122 C2
Whitburn Colliery T & W 111 C7
Whitby Ches 73 B7
Whitby N Yorks 103 C6
Whitby Abbey N Yorks 103 C7
Whitbyheath Ches 73 B7
Whitchurch Bath 23 C8
Whitchurch Bucks 39 B7
Whitchurch Cardiff 35 F5
Whitchurch Devon 6 B2
Whitchurch Hants 26 E2
Whitchurch Hereford 36 C2
Whitchurch Oxon 26 B4
Whitchurch Pembs 44 C2
Whitchurch Shrops 74 E2
Whitchurch Canonicorum Dorset 11 E8
Whitchurch Hill Oxon 26 B4
Whitcombe Dorset 12 F5
Whitcott Keysett Shrops 60 F2
White Coppice Lancs 86 C4
White Lackington Dorset 12 E5
White Ladies Aston Worcs 50 D4
White Lund Lancs 92 C4
White Mill Carms 33 B5
White Ness Shetland 175 J5
White Notley Essex 42 C3
White Pit Lincs 79 B6
White Post Notts 77 D6
White Post Farm Centre, Farnsfield Notts 77 D6
White Rocks Hereford 35 B8
White Roding Essex 42 C1
White Waltham Windsor 27 B6
Whiteacen Moray 159 E6
Whiteacre Heath Warks 63 E6
Whitebridge Highld 147 C7
Whitebrook Mon 36 D2
Whiteburn Borders 123 E8
Whitecairn Dumfries 105 D6
Whitecairns Aberds 151 C8
Whitecastle S Lnrk 122 E3
Whitechapel Lancs 93 E5
Whitecleat Orkney 176 F4
Whitecraig E Loth 123 B6
Whitecroft Glos 36 D3
Whitecross Corn 4 B4
Whitecross Falk 122 B2
Whitecross Staffs 62 B2
Whiteface Highld 164 F4
Whitefarland N Ayrs 119 B5
Whitefaulds S Ayrs 112 D2
Whitefield Gtr Man 87 D6
Whitefield Perth 142 F1
Whiteford Aberds 151 B6
Whitegate Ches 74 C3
Whitehall Blkburn 86 B4
Whitehall W Sus 16 B5
Whitehall Village Orkney 176 D5
Whitehaven Cumb 98 C1
Whitehill Hants 27 F5
Whitehills Aberds 160 B3
Whitehills S Lnrk 121 D6
Whitehough Derbys 87 F8
Whitehouse Aberds 150 C5
Whitehouse Argyll 128 D3
Whiteinch Glasgow 120 C5
Whitekirk E Loth 135 F7
Whitelaw S Lnrk 121 E6
Whiteleas T & W 111 C6
Whiteley Bank I o W 15 F6
Whiteley Green Ches 75 B6
Whiteley Village Sur 27 C8
Whitemans Green W Sus 17 B7
Whitemire Moray 158 D3
Whitemoor Corn 4 D4
Whitemore Staffs 75 C5
Whitenap Hants 14 B4
Whiteoak Green Oxon 38 C3
Whiteparish Wilts 14 B3
Whiterashes Aberds 151 B7
Whiterow Highld 169 E8
Whiteshill Glos 37 D5
Whiteside Northumb 109 C7
Whiteside W Loth 122 C2
Whitesmith E Sus 18 D2
Whitestaunton Som 11 C7
Whitestone Devon 10 E3
Whitestone Devon 20 E3
Whitestone Warks 63 F7
Whitestones Aberds 160 C5
Whitestreet Green Suff 56 F3
Whitewall Corner N Yorks 96 B3
Whiteway Glos 37 E5
Whiteway Glos 37 C6
Whitewell Aberds 161 B6
Whitewell Lancs 93 E6
Whitewell Bottom Lancs 87 B6
Whiteworks Devon 6 B4
Whitfield Kent 31 E7
Whitfield Northants 52 F4
Whitfield Northumb 109 D7
Whitfield S Glos 36 E3
Whitford Devon 11 E7
Whitford Flint 72 B5
Whitgift E Yorks 90 B2
Whitgreave Staffs 62 B2
Whithorn Dumfries 105 E8
Whiting Bay N Ayrs 119 D7
Whitkirk W Yorks 95 F6
Whitland Carms 32 C2
Whitletts S Ayrs 112 B3
Whitley N Yorks 89 B6
Whitley Reading 26 B5
Whitley Wilts 24 C3
Whitley Bay T & W 111 B6
Whitley Chapel Northumb 110 D2
Whitley Lower W Yorks 88 C3
Whitley Row Kent 29 D5
Whitlock's End W Mid 51 B6
Whitminster Glos 36 D4
Whitmore Staffs 74 E5
Whitnage Devon 10 C5
Whitnash Warks 51 C8
Whitney-on-Wye Hereford 48 E4
Whitrigg Cumb 108 F2
Whitrigg Cumb 108 D2
Whitsbury Hants 14 C2
Whitsome Borders 124 D4
Whitson Newport 35 F7
Whitstable Kent 30 C5
Whitstone Corn 8 E4
Whittingham Northumb 117 C6
Whittingslow Shrops 60 F4
Whittington Glos 37 B7
Whittington Lancs 93 B6
Whittington Norf 67 E7
Whittington Shrops 73 F7
Whittington Staffs 62 F2
Whittington Staffs 63 D5
Whittington Worcs 50 D3
Whittle-le-Woods Lancs 86 B3
Whittlebury Northants 52 E4
Whittlesey Cambs 66 E2
Whittlesford Cambs 55 E5
Whittlestone Head Blkburn 86 C5
Whitton Borders 116 B3
Whitton N Lincs 90 B3
Whitton Northumb 117 D6
Whitton Powys 48 C4
Whitton Shrops 49 B7
Whitton Stockton 102 B1
Whitton Suff 56 E5
Whittonditch Wilts 25 B7
Whittonstall Northumb 110 D3
Whitway Hants 26 D2
Whitwell Derbys 76 B5
Whitwell Herts 40 B4
Whitwell I o W 15 G6
Whitwell N Yorks 101 E7
Whitwell Rutland 65 D6
Whitwell-on-the-Hill N Yorks 96 C3
Whitwell Street Norf 81 E7
Whitwick Leics 63 C8
Whitwood W Yorks 88 B5
Whitworth Lancs 87 C6
Whixall Shrops 74 F2
Whixley N Yorks 95 D7
Whoberley W Mid 51 B8
Whorlton Durham 101 C6
Whorlton N Yorks 102 D2
Whygate Northumb 109 B7
Whyle Hereford 49 C7
Whyteleafe Sur 28 D4
Wibdon Glos 36 E2
Wibsey W Yorks 88 A2
Wibtoft Leics 63 F8
Wichenford Worcs 50 C2
Wichling Kent 30 D3
Wick Bmouth 14 E2
Wick Devon 11 D6
Wick Highld 169 D8
Wick S Glos 24 B2
Wick Shetland 175 K6
Wick V Glam 21 B8
Wick Wilts 14 B2
Wick Worcs 50 E4
Wick W Sus 16 D4
Wick Airport Highld 169 D8
Wick Hill Wokingham 27 C5
Wick St Lawrence N Som 23 C5
Wicken Cambs 55 B6
Wicken Northants 52 F5
Wicken Bonhunt Essex 55 F5
Wicken Green Village Norf 80 D4
Wickenby Lincs 90 F4
Wickersley S Yorks 89 E5
Wickford Essex 42 E3
Wickham Hants 15 C6
Wickham W Berks 25 B8
Wickham Bishops Essex 42 C4
Wickham Market Suff 57 D7
Wickham St Paul Essex 56 F2
Wickham Skeith Suff 56 C4
Wickham Street Suff 55 D8
Wickham Street Suff 56 C4
Wickhambreux Kent 31 D6
Wickhambrook Suff 55 D8
Wickhamford Worcs 51 E5
Wickhampton Norf 69 D7
Wicklewood Norf 68 D3
Wickmere Norf 81 D7
Wicksteed Park, Kettering Northants 53 B6
Wickwar S Glos 36 F4
Widdington Essex 55 F6
Widdrington Northumb 117 E8
Widdrington Station Northumb 117 E8
Wide Open T & W 110 B5
Widecombe in the Moor Devon 6 B5
Widegates Corn 5 D7
Widemouth Bay Corn 8 D4
Widewall Orkney 176 G3
Widford Essex 42 D2
Widford Herts 41 C7
Widham Wilts 37 F7
Widmer End Bucks 40 E1
Widmerpool Notts 64 B3
Widnes Halton 86 F3
Wigan Gtr Man 86 D3
Wigan Pier Gtr Man 86 D3
Wiggaton Devon 11 E6
Wiggenhall St Germans Norf 67 C5
Wiggenhall St Mary Magdalen Norf 67 C5
Wiggenhall St Mary the Virgin Norf 67 C5
Wigginton Herts 40 C2
Wigginton Oxon 51 F8
Wigginton Staffs 63 D6
Wigginton York 95 D8
Wigglesworth N Yorks 93 D8
Wiggonby Cumb 108 D2
Wiggonholt W Sus 16 C4
Wighill N Yorks 95 E7
Wighton Norf 80 D5
Wigley Hants 14 C4
Wigmore Hereford 49 C6
Wigmore Medway 30 C2
Wigsley Notts 77 B8
Wigsthorpe Northants 65 F7
Wigston Leics 64 E3
Wigthorpe Notts 89 F6
Wigtoft Lincs 79 F5
Wigton Cumb 108 E2
Wigtown Dumfries 105 D8
Wigtwizzle S Yorks 88 E3
Wike W Yorks 95 E6
Wike Well End S Yorks 89 C7
Wilbarston Northants 64 F5
Wilberfoss E Yorks 96 D3
Wilberlee W Yorks 87 C8
Wilburton Cambs 55 B5
Wilby Norf 68 F3
Wilby Northants 53 C6
Wilby Suff 57 B6
Wilcot Wilts 25 C6
Wilcott Shrops 60 C3
Wilcrick Newport 35 F8
Wilday Green Derbys 76 B3
Wildboarclough Ches 75 C6
Wilden Beds 53 D8
Wilden Worcs 50 B3
Wildfowl and Wetland Centre, Martin Mere Lancs 86 C2
Wildhern Hants 25 D8
Wildhill Herts 41 D5
Wildlife & Dinosaur Park, Combe Martin Devon 20 E4
Wildmoor Worcs 50 B4
Wildsworth Lincs 90 E2
Wilford Notts 77 F5
Wilkesley Ches 74 E3
Wilkhaven Highld 165 F6
Wilkieston W Loth 122 C4
Willand Devon 10 C5
Willaston Ches 73 B7
Willaston Ches 74 D3
Willen M Keynes 53 E6
Willenhall W Mid 51 B8
Willenhall W Mid 62 E3
Willerby E Yorks 97 F6
Willerby N Yorks 97 B6
Willersey Glos 51 F6
Willersley Hereford 48 E5
Willesborough Kent 30 E4
Willesborough Lees Kent 30 E4
Willesden London 41 F5
Willett Som 22 F3
Willey Shrops 61 E6
Willey Warks 63 F8
Willey Green Sur 27 D7
Williamscott Oxon 52 E2
Willian Herts 54 F3
Willingale Essex 42 D1
Willingdon E Sus 18 E2
Willingham Cambs 54 B5
Willingham by Stow Lincs 90 F2
Willington Beds 54 E2
Willington Derbys 63 B6
Willington Durham 110 F4
Willington T & W 111 C6
Willington Warks 51 F7
Willington Corner Ches 74 C2
Willisham Tye Suff 56 D4
Willitoft E Yorks 96 F3
Williton Som 22 E2
Willoughbridge Staffs 74 E4
Willoughby Lincs 79 B7
Willoughby Warks 52 C3
Willoughby-on-the-Wolds Notts 64 B3
Willoughby Waterleys Leics 64 E2
Willoughton Lincs 90 E3
Willows Green Essex 42 C3
Willsbridge S Glos 23 B8
Willsworthy Devon 9 F7
Wilmcote Warks 51 D6
Wilmington Devon 11 E7
Wilmington E Sus 18 E2
Wilmington Kent 29 B6
Wilminstone Devon 6 B2
Wilmslow Ches 87 F6
Wilnecote Staffs 63 D6
Wilpshire Lancs 93 F6
Wilsden W Yorks 94 F3
Wilsford Lincs 78 E3
Wilsford Wilts 25 D6
Wilsford Wilts 25 F6
Wilsill N Yorks 94 C4
Wilsley Pound Kent 18 B4
Wilsom Hants 26 F5
Wilson Leics 63 B8
Wilsontown S Lnrk 122 D2
Wilstead Beds 53 E8
Wilsthorpe Lincs 65 C7
Wilstone Herts 40 C2
Wilton Borders 115 C7
Wilton Cumb 98 C2
Wilton N Yorks 103 F6
Wilton Redcar 102 C3
Wilton Wilts 25 F5
Wilton Wilts 25 C7
Wilton House, Salisbury Wilts 25 F6
Wimbish Essex 55 F6
Wimbish Green Essex 55 F7
Wimblebury Staffs 62 C4
Wimbledon London 28 B3
Wimbledon All England Tennis Club London 28 B3
Wimblington Cambs 66 E4
Wimborne Minster Dorset 13 E8
Wimborne Minster Dorset 13 E8
Wimborne St Giles Dorset 13 C8
Wimbotsham Norf 67 D6
Wimpole Hall and Home Farm, Royston Cambs 54 D4
Wimpson Soton 14 C4
Wimpstone Warks 51 E7
Wincanton Som 12 B5
Wincanton Racecourse Som 12 B5
Wincham Ches 74 B3
Winchburgh W Loth 122 B3
Winchcombe Glos 37 B7
Winchelsea E Sus 19 D6
Winchelsea Beach E Sus 19 D6
Winchester Hants 15 B5
Winchester Cathedral Hants 15 B5
Winchet Hill Kent 29 E8
Winchfield Hants 27 D5
Winchmore Hill Bucks 40 E2
Winchmore Hill London 41 E6
Wincle Ches 75 C6
Wincobank S Yorks 88 E4
Windermere Cumb 99 E6
Winderton Warks 51 E8
Windhill Highld 157 E6
Windhouse Shetland 174 D6
Windlehurst Gtr Man 87 F7
Windlesham Sur 27 C7
Windley Derbys 76 E3
Windmill Hill E Sus 18 D3
Windmill Hill Som 11 C8
Windrush Glos 38 C1
Windsor N Lincs 89 C8
Windsor Windsor 27 B7
Windsor Castle Windsor 27 B7
Windsor Racecourse Windsor 27 B7
Windsoredge Glos 37 D5
Windygates Fife 134 D5
Windyknowe W Loth 122 C2
Windywalls Borders 124 F3
Wineham W Sus 17 B6
Winestead E Yorks 91 B6
Winewall Lancs 94 E2
Winfarthing Norf 68 F4
Winford I o W 15 F6
Winford N Som 23 C7
Winforton Hereford 48 E4
Winfrith Newburgh Dorset 13 F6
Wing Bucks 40 B1
Wing Rutland 65 D5
Wingate Durham 111 F7
Wingates Gtr Man 86 D4
Wingates Northumb 117 E7
Wingerworth Derbys 76 C3
Wingfield Beds 40 B2
Wingfield Suff 57 B6
Wingfield Wilts 24 D3
Wingham Kent 31 D6
Wingmore Kent 31 E5
Wingrave Bucks 40 C1
Winkburn Notts 77 D7
Winkfield Brack 27 B7
Winkfield Row Brack 27 B6
Winkhill Staffs 75 D7
Winklebury Hants 26 D4
Winkleigh Devon 9 D8
Winksley N Yorks 95 B5
Winkton Dorset 14 E2
Winlaton T & W 110 C4
Winless Highld 169 D8
Winmarleigh Lancs 92 E4
Winnal Hereford 49 F6
Winnall Hants 15 B5
Winnersh Wokingham 27 B5
Winscales Cumb 98 B2
Winscombe N Som 23 D6
Winsford Ches 74 C3
Winsford Som 21 F8
Winsham Som 11 D8
Winshill Staffs 63 B6
Winskill Cumb 109 F5
Winslade Hants 26 E4
Winsley Wilts 24 C3
Winslow Bucks 39 B7
Winson Glos 37 D7
Winson Green W Mid 62 F4
Winsor Hants 14 C4
Winster Cumb 99 E6
Winster Derbys 76 C2
Winston Durham 101 C6
Winston Suff 57 C5
Winston Green Suff 57 C5
Winstone Glos 37 D6
Winswell Devon 9 C6
Winter Gardens Essex 42 F3
Winterborne Bassett Wilts 25 B6
Winterborne Clenston Dorset 13 D6
Winterborne Herringston Dorset 12 F4
Winterborne Houghton Dorset 13 D6
Winterborne Kingston Dorset 13 E6
Winterborne Monkton Dorset 12 F4
Winterborne Monkton Wilts 25 B6
Winterborne Stickland Dorset 13 D6
Winterborne Whitechurch Dorset 13 D6
Winterborne Zelston Dorset 13 E6
Winterbourne S Glos 36 F3
Winterbourne W Berks 26 B2
Winterbourne Abbas Dorset 12 E4
Winterbourne Dauntsey Wilts 25 F6
Winterbourne Down S Glos 23 B8
Winterbourne Earls Wilts 25 F6

Winterbourne Gunner Wilts 25 F6
Winterbourne Steepleton Dorset 12 F4
Winterbourne Stoke Wilts 25 E5
Winterburn N Yorks 94 D2
Winteringham N Lincs 90 B3
Winterley Ches 74 D4
Wintersett W Yorks 88 C4
Wintershill Hants 15 C6
Winterton N Lincs 90 C3
Winterton-on-Sea Norf 69 C7
Winthorpe Lincs 79 C8
Winthorpe Notts 77 D8
Winton Bmouth 13 E8
Winton Cumb 100 C2
Winton N Yorks 102 E2
Wintringham N Yorks 96 B4
Winwick Cambs 65 F8
Winwick Northants 52 B4
Winwick Warr 86 E4
Wirksworth Derbys 76 D2
Wirksworth Moor Derbys 76 D3
Wirswall Ches 74 E2
Wisbech Cambs 66 D4
Wisbech St Mary Cambs 66 D4
Wisborough Green W Sus 16 B4
Wiseton Notts 89 F8
Wishaw N Lnrk 121 D7
Wishaw Warks 63 E5
Wisley Sur 27 D8
Wispington Lincs 78 B5
Wissenden Kent 30 E3
Wissett Suff 57 B7
Wistanstow Shrops 60 F4
Wistanswick Shrops 61 B6
Wistaston Ches 74 D3
Wistaston Green Ches 74 D3
Wiston Pembs 32 C1
Wiston S Lnrk 122 F2
Wiston W Sus 16 C5
Wistow Cambs 66 F2
Wistow N Yorks 95 F8
Wiswell Lancs 93 F7
Witcham Cambs 66 F4
Witchampton Dorset 13 D7
Witchford Cambs 55 B6
Witham Essex 42 C4
Witham Friary Som 24 E2
Witham on the Hill Lincs 65 C7
Withcall Lincs 91 F6
Withdean Brighton 17 D7
Witherenden Hill E Sus 18 C3
Witheridge Devon 10 C3
Witherley Leics 63 E7
Withern Lincs 91 F8
Withernsea E Yorks 91 B7
Withernwick E Yorks 97 E7
Withersdale Street Suff 69 F5
Withersfield Suff 55 E7
Witherslack Cumb 99 F6
Withiel Corn 4 C4
Withiel Florey Som 21 F8
Withington Glos 37 C7
Withington Gtr Man 87 E6
Withington Hereford 49 E7
Withington Shrops 61 C5
Withington Staffs 75 F7
Withington Green Ches 74 B5
Withleigh Devon 10 C4
Withnell Lancs 86 B4
Withybrook Warks 63 F8
Withycombe Som 22 E2
Withycombe Raleigh Devon 10 F5
Withyham E Sus 29 F5
Withypool Som 21 F7
Witley Sur 27 F7
Witnesham Suff 57 D5
Witney Oxon 38 C3
Wittering P'boro 65 D7
Wittersham Kent 19 C5
Witton Angus 143 B5
Witton Worcs 50 C3
Witton Bridge Norf 69 A6
Witton Gilbert Durham 110 E5
Witton-le-Wear Durham 110 F4
Witton Park Durham 110 F4
Wiveliscombe Som 11 B5
Wivelrod Hants 26 F4
Wivelsfield E Sus 17 B7
Wivelsfield Green E Sus 17 B7
Wivenhoe Essex 43 B6
Wivenhoe Cross Essex 43 B6
Wiveton Norf 81 C6
Wix Essex 43 B7
Wixford Warks 51 D5
Wixhill Shrops 61 B5
Wixoe Suff 55 E8
Woburn Beds 53 F7
Woburn Abbey, Woburn Beds 53 F7
Woburn Sands M Keynes 53 F7
Woburn Wild Animal Kingdom Beds 53 F7
Wokefield Park W Berks 26 C4
Woking Sur 27 D8
Wokingham Wokingham 27 C6
Wolborough Devon 7 B6
Wold Newton E Yorks 97 B6
Wold Newton NE Lincs 91 E6
Woldingham Sur 28 D4
Wolfclyde S Lnrk 122 F3
Wolferton Norf 67 B6
Wolfhill Perth 142 F1
Wolf's Castle Pembs 44 C4
Wolfsdale Pembs 44 C4
Woll Borders 115 B7
Wollaston Northants 53 C7
Wollaston Shrops 60 C3
Wollaton Nottingham 76 F5
Wollaton Hall Nottingham 76 F5
Wollerton Shrops 74 F3
Wollescote W Mid 62 F3
Wolsingham Durham 110 F3
Wolstanton Staffs 75 E5
Wolston Warks 52 B2
Wolvercote Oxon 38 D4
Wolverhampton W Mid 62 E3
Wolverhampton Racecourse W Mid 62 D3
Wolverley Shrops 73 F8
Wolverley Worcs 50 B3
Wolverton Hants 26 D3
Wolverton M Keynes 53 E6
Wolverton Warks 51 C7
Wolverton Common Hants 26 D3
Wolvesnewton Mon 36 E1
Wolvey Warks 63 F8
Wolviston Stockton 102 B2
Wombleton N Yorks 102 F4
Wombourne Staffs 62 E2
Wombwell S Yorks 88 D4
Womenswold Kent 31 D6
Womersley N Yorks 89 C6
Wonastow Mon 36 C1
Wonersh Sur 27 E8
Wonson Devon 9 F8
Wonston Hants 26 F2
Wooburn Bucks 40 F2
Wooburn Green Bucks 40 F2
Wood Dalling Norf 81 E6
Wood End Herts 41 B6
Wood End Warks 51 B6
Wood End Warks 63 E6
Wood Enderby Lincs 79 C5
Wood Field Sur 28 D2
Wood Green London 41 E6
Wood Green Animal Shelter, Godmanchester Cambs 54 C3
Wood Hayes W Mid 62 D3
Wood Lanes Ches 87 F7
Wood Norton Norf 81 E6
Wood Street Norf 69 B6
Wood Street Sur 27 D7
Wood Walton Cambs 66 F2
Woodacott Devon 9 D5
Woodale N Yorks 94 B3
Woodbank Argyll 118 E3
Woodbastwick Norf 69 C6
Woodbeck Notts 77 B7
Woodborough Notts 77 E6
Woodborough Wilts 25 D6
Woodbridge Dorset 12 C5
Woodbridge Suff 57 E6
Woodbury Devon 10 F5
Woodbury Salterton Devon 10 F5
Woodchester Glos 37 D5
Woodchurch Kent 19 B6
Woodchurch Mers 85 F3
Woodcombe Som 21 E8
Woodcote Oxon 39 F6
Woodcott Hants 26 D2
Woodcroft Glos 36 E2
Woodcutts Dorset 13 C7
Woodditton Cambs 55 D7
Woodeaton Oxon 39 C5
Woodend Cumb 98 E3
Woodend Northants 52 E4
Woodend W Sus 16 D2
Woodend Green Northants 52 E4
Woodfalls Wilts 14 B2
Woodfield Oxon 39 B5
Woodfield S Ayrs 112 B3
Woodford Corn 8 C4
Woodford Devon 7 D5
Woodford Glos 36 E3
Woodford London 41 E7
Woodford Gtr Man 87 F6
Woodford Northants 53 B7
Woodford Bridge London 41 E7
Woodford Halse Northants 52 D3
Woodgate Norf 68 C3
Woodgate W Mid 62 F3
Woodgate Worcs 50 C4
Woodgate W Sus 16 D3
Woodgreen Hants 14 C2
Woodhall Herts 41 C5
Woodhall Invclyd 120 B3
Woodhall N Yorks 100 E4
Woodhall Spa Lincs 78 C4
Woodham Sur 27 C8
Woodham Ferrers Essex 42 E3
Woodham Mortimer Essex 42 D4
Woodham Walter Essex 42 D4
Woodhaven Fife 135 B6
Woodhead Aberds 160 E4
Woodhey Gtr Man 87 C5
Woodhill Shrops 61 F7
Woodhorn Northumb 117 F8
Woodhouse Leics 64 C2
Woodhouse N Lincs 89 D8
Woodhouse S Yorks 88 F5
Woodhouse W Yorks 95 F5
Woodhouse W Yorks 88 B4
Woodhouse Eaves Leics 64 C2
Woodhouse Park Gtr Man 87 F6
Woodhouselee Midloth 122 C5
Woodhouselees Dumfries 108 B3
Woodhouses Staffs 63 C5
Woodhurst Cambs 54 B4
Woodingdean Brighton 17 D7
Woodkirk W Yorks 88 B3
Woodland Devon 7 C5
Woodland Durham 101 B5
Woodland Leisure Park, Dartmouth Devon 7 D6
Woodlands Aberds 151 E6
Woodlands Dorset 13 D8
Woodlands Hants 14 C4
Woodlands Highld 157 C6
Woodlands N Yorks 95 D6
Woodlands S Yorks 89 D6
Woodlands Park Windsor 27 B6
Woodlands St Mary W Berks 25 B8
Woodlane Staffs 62 B5
Woodleigh Devon 6 E5
Woodlesford W Yorks 88 B4
Woodley Gtr Man 87 E7
Woodley Wokingham 27 B5
Woodmancote Glos 36 E4
Woodmancote Glos 37 D7
Woodmancote Glos 37 B6
Woodmancote W Sus 15 D8
Woodmancote W Sus 17 C6
Woodmancott Hants 26 E3
Woodmansey E Yorks 97 F6
Woodmansterne Sur 28 D3
Woodminton Wilts 13 B8
Woodnesborough Kent 31 D7
Woodnewton Northants 65 E7
Woodplumpton Lancs 92 F5
Woodrising Norf 68 D2
Wood's Green E Sus 18 B3
Woodseaves Shrops 74 F3
Woodseaves Staffs 61 B7
Woodsend Wilts 25 B7
Woodsetts S Yorks 89 F6
Woodsford Dorset 13 E5
Woodside Aberdeen 151 D8
Woodside Aberds 161 D7
Woodside Brack 27 B7
Woodside Fife 135 D6
Woodside Hants 14 E4
Woodside Herts 41 D5
Woodside Perth 142 F2
Woodside Farm and Wildfowl Park, Luton Beds 40 C3
Woodside of Arbeadie Aberds 151 E6
Woodstock Oxon 38 C4
Woodstock Pembs 32 B1
Woodthorpe Derbys 76 B4
Woodthorpe Leics 64 C2
Woodthorpe Lincs 91 F8
Woodthorpe York 95 E8
Woodton Norf 69 E5
Woodtown Devon 9 B6
Woodtown Devon 9 B6
Woodvale Mers 85 C4
Woodville Derbys 63 C7
Woodyates Dorset 13 C8
Woofferton Shrops 49 C7
Wookey Som 23 E7
Wookey Hole Som 23 E7
Wookey Hole Caves & Papermill, Wells Som 23 E7
Wool Dorset 13 F6
Woolacombe Devon 20 E3
Woolage Green Kent 31 E6
Woolaston Glos 36 E2
Woolavington Som 22 E5
Woolbeding W Sus 16 B2
Wooldale W Yorks 88 D2
Wooler Northumb 117 B5
Woolfardisworthy Devon 8 B5
Woolfardisworthy Devon 10 D3
Woolfords Cottages S Lnrk 122 D3
Woolhampton W Berks 26 C3
Woolhope Hereford 49 F8
Woolhope Cockshoot Hereford 49 F8
Woolland Dorset 13 D5
Woollaton Devon 9 C6
Woolley Bath 24 C2
Woolley Cambs 54 B2
Woolley Corn 8 C4
Woolley Derbys 76 C3
Woolley W Yorks 88 C4
Woolmer Green Herts 41 C5
Woolmere Green Worcs 50 C4
Woolpit Suff 56 C3
Woolscott Warks 52 C2
Woolsington T & W 110 C4
Woolstanwood Ches 74 D3
Woolstaston Shrops 60 E4
Woolsthorpe Lincs 77 F8
Woolsthorpe Lincs 65 B6
Woolston Devon 6 E5
Woolston Shrops 60 F4
Woolston Shrops 60 B3
Woolston Soton 14 C5
Woolston Warr 86 F4
Woolstone M Keynes 53 F6
Woolstone Oxon 38 F2
Woolton Mers 86 F2
Woolton Hill Hants 26 C2
Woolverstone Suff 57 F5
Woolverton Som 24 D2
Woolwich London 28 B5
Woolwich Ferry London 28 B5
Woonton Hereford 49 D5
Wooperton Northumb 117 B6
Woore Shrops 74 E4
Wootten Green Suff 57 B6
Wootton Beds 53 E8
Wootton Hants 14 E3
Wootton Hereford 48 D5
Wootton Kent 31 E6
Wootton N Lincs 90 C4
Wootton Northants 53 D5
Wootton Oxon 38 C4
Wootton Oxon 38 D4
Wootton Shrops 49 B6
Wootton Shrops 60 B3
Wootton Staffs 62 B2
Wootton Staffs 75 E8
Wootton Bassett Wilts 37 F7
Wootton Bridge I o W 15 E6
Wootton Common I o W 15 E6
Wootton Courtenay Som 21 E8
Wootton Fitzpaine Dorset 11 E8
Wootton Rivers Wilts 25 C6
Wootton St Lawrence Hants 26 D3
Wootton Wawen Warks 51 C6
Worcester Worcs 50 D3
Worcester Cathedral Worcs 50 D3
Worcester Park London 28 C3
Worcester Racecourse Worcs 50 D3
Wordsley W Mid 62 F2
Worfield Shrops 61 E7
Work Orkney 176 E3
Workington Cumb 98 B1
Worksop Notts 77 B5
Worlaby N Lincs 90 C4
World of James Herriot N Yorks 102 F2
World's End W Berks 26 B2
Worle N Som 23 C5
Worleston Ches 74 D3
Worlingham Suff 69 F7
Worlington Suff 55 B7
Worlingworth Suff 57 C6
Wormald Green N Yorks 95 C6
Wormbridge Hereford 49 F6
Wormegay Norf 67 C6
Wormelow Tump Hereford 49 F6
Wormhill Derbys 75 B8
Wormingford Essex 56 F3
Worminghall Bucks 39 D6
Wormington Glos 50 F5
Worminster Som 23 E7
Wormit Fife 135 B5
Wormleighton Warks 52 D2
Wormley Herts 41 D6
Wormley Sur 27 F7
Wormley West End Herts 41 D6
Wormshill Kent 30 D2
Wormsley Hereford 49 E6
Worplesdon Sur 27 D7
Worrall S Yorks 88 E4
Worsbrough S Yorks 88 D4
Worsbrough Common S Yorks 88 D4
Worsley Gtr Man 86 D5
Worstead Norf 69 B6
Worsthorne Lancs 93 F8
Worston Lancs 93 E7
Worswell Devon 6 E3
Worth Kent 31 D7
Worth W Sus 28 F4
Worth Matravers Dorset 13 G7
Wortham Suff 56 B4
Worthen Shrops 60 D3
Worthenbury Wrex 73 E8
Worthing Norf 68 C2
Worthing W Sus 16 D5
Worthington Leics 63 B8
Worting Hants 26 D4
Wortley S Yorks 88 E4
Wortley W Yorks 95 F5
Worton N Yorks 100 E4
Worton Wilts 24 D4
Wortwell Norf 69 F5
Wotherton Shrops 60 D2
Wotter Devon 6 C3
Wotton Sur 28 E2
Wotton-under-Edge Glos 36 E4
Wotton Underwood Bucks 39 C6
Woughton on the Green M Keynes 53 F6
Wouldham Kent 29 C8
Wrabness Essex 57 F5
Wrafton Devon 20 F3
Wragby Lincs 78 B4
Wragby W Yorks 88 C5
Wragholme Lincs 91 E7
Wramplingham Norf 68 D4
Wrangbrook W Yorks 89 C5
Wrangham Aberds 160 E3
Wrangle Lincs 79 D7
Wrangle Bank Lincs 79 D7
Wrangle Lowgate Lincs 79 D7
Wrangway Som 11 C6
Wrantage Som 11 B8
Wrawby N Lincs 90 D4
Wraxall Dorset 12 D3
Wraxall N Som 23 B6
Wraxall Som 23 F8
Wray Lancs 93 C6
Wraysbury Windsor 27 B8
Wrayton Lancs 93 B6
Wrea Green Lancs 92 F3
Wreay Cumb 99 B6
Wreay Cumb 108 E4
Wrecclesham Sur 27 E6
Wrecsam = Wrexham Wrex 73 D7
Wrekenton T & W 111 D5
Wrelton N Yorks 103 F5
Wrenbury Ches 74 E2
Wrench Green N Yorks 103 F7
Wreningham Norf 68 E4
Wrentham Suff 69 F7
Wrenthorpe W Yorks 88 B4
Wrentnall Shrops 60 D4
Wressle E Yorks 96 F3
Wressle N Lincs 90 D3
Wrestlingworth Beds 54 E3
Wretham Norf 68 F2
Wretton Norf 67 E6
Wrexham = Wrecsam Wrex 73 D7
Wrexham Industrial Estate Wrex 73 E7
Wribbenhall Worcs 50 B2
Wrightington Bar Lancs 86 C3
Wrinehill Staffs 74 E4
Wrington N Som 23 C6
Writhlington Bath 24 D2
Writtle Essex 42 D2
Wrockwardine Telford 61 C6
Wroot N Lincs 89 D8
Wrotham Kent 29 D7
Wrotham Heath Kent 29 D7
Wroughton Swindon 37 F8
Wroxall I o W 15 G6
Wroxall Warks 51 B7
Wroxeter Shrops 61 D5
Wroxham Norf 69 C6
Wroxham Barns, Hoveton Norf 69 B6
Wroxton Oxon 52 E2
Wyaston Derbys 75 E8
Wyberton Lincs 79 E6
Wyboston Beds 54 D2
Wybunbury Ches 74 E4
Wych Cross E Sus 28 F5
Wychbold Worcs 50 C4
Wyck Hants 27 F5
Wyck Rissington Glos 38 B1
Wycoller Lancs 94 F2
Wycomb Leics 64 B4
Wycombe Marsh Bucks 40 E1
Wyddial Herts 54 F4
Wye Kent 30 E4
Wyesham Mon 36 C2
Wyfordby Leics 64 C4
Wyke Dorset 13 B5
Wyke Shrops 61 D6
Wyke Sur 27 D7
Wyke W Yorks 88 B2
Wyke Regis Dorset 12 G4
Wykeham N Yorks 103 F7
Wykeham N Yorks 96 B4
Wyken W Mid 63 F7
Wykey Shrops 60 B3
Wylam Northumb 110 C4
Wylde Green W Mid 62 E5
Wyllie Caerph 35 E5
Wylye Wilts 24 F5
Wymering Ptsmth 15 D7
Wymeswold Leics 64 B3
Wymington Beds 53 C7
Wymondham Leics 65 C5
Wymondham Norf 68 D4
Wyndham Bridgend 34 E3
Wynford Eagle Dorset 12 E3
Wyng Orkney 176 G2
Wynyard Village Stockton 102 B2
Wyre Piddle Worcs 50 E4
Wysall Notts 64 B3
Wythall Worcs 51 B5
Wytham Oxon 38 D4
Wythburn Cumb 99 C5
Wythenshawe Gtr Man 87 F6
Wythop Mill Cumb 98 B3
Wyton Cambs 54 B3
Wyverstone Suff 56 C4
Wyverstone Street Suff 56 C4
Wyville Lincs 65 B5
Wyvis Lodge Highld 157 B5

Y

Y Bala = Bala Gwyn 72 F3
Y Barri = Barry V Glam 22 C3
Y Bont-Faen = Cowbridge V Glam 21 B8
Y Drenewydd = Newtown Powys 59 E8
Y Felinheli Gwyn 82 E5
Y Fenni = Abergavenny Mon 35 C6
Y Fflint = Flint Flint 73 B6
Y Ffôr Gwyn 70 D4
Y-Ffrith Denb 72 A4
Y Gelli Gandryll = Hay-on-Wye Powys 48 E4
Y Mwmbwls = The Mumbles Swansea 33 F7
Y Pîl = Pyle Bridgend 34 F2
Y Rhws = Rhoose V Glam 22 C2
Y Rhyl = Rhyl Denb 72 A4
Y Trallwng = Welshpool Powys 60 D2
Y Waun = Chirk Wrex 73 F6
Yaddlethorpe N Lincs 90 D2
Yafford I o W 14 F5
Yafforth N Yorks 101 E8
Yalding Kent 29 D7
Yanworth Glos 37 C7
Yapham E Yorks 96 D3
Yapton W Sus 16 D3
Yarburgh Lincs 91 E7
Yarcombe Devon 11 D7
Yard Som 22 F2
Yardley W Mid 62 F5
Yardley Gobion Northants 53 E5
Yardley Hastings Northants 53 D6
Yardro Powys 48 D4
Yarkhill Hereford 49 E8
Yarlet Staffs 62 B3
Yarlington Som 12 B4
Yarlside Cumb 92 C2
Yarm Stockton 102 C2
Yarmouth I o W 14 F4
Yarmouth Racecourse Norf 69 C8
Yarnbrook Wilts 24 D3
Yarnfield Staffs 75 F5
Yarnscombe Devon 9 B7
Yarnton Oxon 38 C4
Yarpole Hereford 49 C6
Yarrow Borders 115 B6
Yarrow Feus Borders 115 B6
Yarsop Hereford 49 E6
Yarwell Northants 65 E7
Yate S Glos 36 F4
Yateley Hants 27 C6
Yatesbury Wilts 25 B5
Yattendon W Berks 26 B3
Yatton Hereford 49 C6
Yatton N Som 23 C6
Yatton Keynell Wilts 24 B3
Yaverland I o W 15 F7
Yaxham Norf 68 C3
Yaxley Cambs 65 E8
Yaxley Suff 56 B5
Yazor Hereford 49 E6
Yeading London 40 F4
Yeadon W Yorks 94 E5
Yealand Conyers Lancs 92 B5
Yealand Redmayne Lancs 92 B5
Yealmpton Devon 6 D3
Yearby Redcar 102 B4
Yearsley N Yorks 95 B8
Yeaton Shrops 60 C4
Yeaveley Derbys 75 E8
Yedingham N Yorks 96 B4
Yeldon Beds 53 C8
Yelford Oxon 38 D3
Yelland Devon 20 F3
Yelling Cambs 54 C3
Yelvertoft Northants 52 B3
Yelverton Devon 6 C3
Yelverton Norf 69 D5
Yenston Som 12 B5
Yeo Mill Devon 10 B3
Yeoford Devon 10 E2
Yeolmbridge Corn 8 F5
Yeovil Som 12 C3
Yeovil Marsh Som 12 C3
Yeovilton Som 12 B3
Yerbeston Pembs 32 D1
Yesnaby Orkney 176 E1
Yetlington Northumb 117 D6
Yetminster Dorset 12 C3
Yettington Devon 11 F5
Yetts o'Muckhart Clack 134 D2
Yieldshields S Lnrk 121 D8
Yiewsley London 40 F3
Ynys-meudwy Neath 33 D8
Ynysboeth Rhondda 34 E4
Ynysddu Caerph 35 E5
Ynysgyfflog Gwyn 58 C3
Ynyshir Rhondda 34 E4
Ynyslas Ceredig 58 E3
Ynystawe Swansea 33 D7
Ynysybwl Rhondda 34 E4
Yockenthwaite N Yorks 94 B2
Yockleton Shrops 60 C3
Yokefleet E Yorks 90 B2
Yoker Glasgow 120 C5
Yonder Bognie Aberds 160 D2
York York 95 D8
York Castle Museum York 96 D2
York Minster York 96 D2
York Racecourse York 95 E8
York Town Sur 27 C6
Yorkletts Kent 30 C4
Yorkley Glos 36 D3
Yorkshire Museum York 95 D8
Yorkshire Sculpture Park, Wakefield W Yorks 88 C3
Yorton Shrops 60 B5
Youlgreave Derbys 76 C2
Youlstone Devon 8 C4
Youlthorpe E Yorks 96 D3
Youlton N Yorks 95 C7
Young Wood Lincs 78 B4
Young's End Essex 42 C3
Yoxall Staffs 62 C5
Yoxford Suff 57 C7
Yr Hôb = Hope Flint 73 D7
Yr Wyddgrug = Mold Flint 73 C6
Ysbyty-Cynfyn Ceredig 47 B6
Ysbyty Ifan Conwy 72 E2
Ysbyty Ystwyth Ceredig 47 B6
Ysceifiog Flint 73 B5
Yspitty Carms 33 E6
Ystalyfera Neath 34 D1
Ystrad Rhondda 34 E3
Ystrad Aeron Ceredig 46 D4
Ystrad-mynach Caerph 35 E5
Ystradfellte Powys 34 C3
Ystradffin Carms 47 E6
Ystradgynlais Powys 34 C1
Ystradmeurig Ceredig 47 C6
Ystradowen Carms 33 C8
Ystradowen V Glam 22 B2
Ystumtuen Ceredig 47 B6
Ythanbank Aberds 161 E6
Ythanwells Aberds 160 E3
Ythsie Aberds 161 E5

Z

Zeal Monachorum Devon 10 D2
Zeals Wilts 24 F2
Zelah Corn 4 D3
Zennor Corn 2 C3

First published in 2006 by Philip's
a division of Octopus Publishing Group Ltd
2–4 Heron Quays
London E14 4JP
An Hachette Livre UK Company
www.philips-maps.co.uk

Second edition 2007
First impression 2007

Cartography by Philip's

Copyright © 2007 Philip's

Ordnance Survey®

This product includes mapping data licensed from Ordnance Survey®, with the permission of the Controller of Her Majesty's Stationery Office. © Crown copyright 2007. All rights reserved. Licence number 100011710

All rights reserved. Apart from any fair dealing for the purpose of private study, research, criticism or review, as permitted under the Copyright Designs and Patents Act, 1988, no part of this publication may be reproduced, stored in a retrieval system, or transmitted in any form or by any means, electronic, electrical, chemical, mechanical, optical, photocopying, recording, or otherwise, without prior written permission. All enquiries should be addressed to the Publisher.

To the best of the Publisher's knowledge, the information in this atlas was correct at the time of going to press. No responsibility can be accepted for any errors or their consequences.

The representation in this atlas of any road, drive or track is no evidence of the existence of a right of way.

Data for the speed cameras provided by PocketGPSWorld.com Ltd.

Information for Tourist Attractions shown on the mapping supplied by VisitBritain

Information for National Parks, Areas of Outstanding Natural Beauty, National Trails and Country Parks in Wales supplied by the Countryside Council for Wales.

Information for National Parks, Areas of Outstanding Natural Beauty, National Trails and Country Parks in England supplied by the Countryside Agency. Data for Regional Parks, Long Distance Footpaths and Country Parks in Scotland provided by Scottish Natural Heritage.

Gaelic name forms used in the Western Isles provided by Comhairle nan Eilean.

Data for the National Nature Reserves in England provided by English Nature. Data for the National Nature Reserves in Wales provided by Countryside Council for Wales. Darparwyd data'n ymwneud â Gwarchodfeydd Natur Cenedlaethol Cymru gan Gyngor Cefn Gwlad Cymru.

Information on the location of National Nature Reserves in Scotland was provided by Scottish Natural Heritage.

Data for National Scenic Areas in Scotland provided by the Scottish Executive Office. Crown copyright material is reproduced with the permission of the Controller of HMSO and the Queen's Printer for Scotland. Licence number C02W0003960.

Printed in Italy by Rotolito

Photographic acknowledgments

Cover: *Peter Adams Photography / Alamy*
Page II top *Mark Sykes / Alamy* • Page II bottom *South West Images Scotland / Alamy* • Page III, clockwise from top right: *Andy Hallam / Alamy; Iain Cooper / Alamy; Simon Holdcroft / Alamy; Mike Harrington / Alamy*

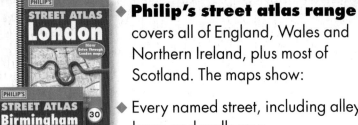
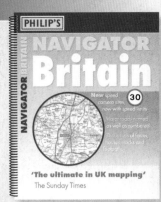
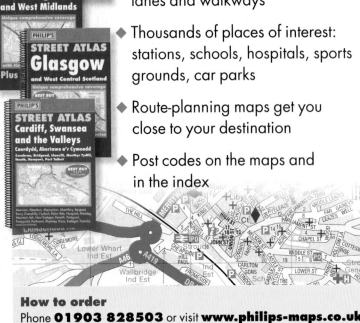